REPEATED-MEASURES ANOVA

$$SS_{\text{between}} = \Sigma \frac{T^2}{n} - \frac{G^2}{N} \qquad df_{\text{between}} = k - 1$$

$$SS_{\text{error}} = SS_{\text{within}} - SS_{\text{subjects}} \qquad df_{\text{error}} = (N - k) - (n - 1)$$

where $SS_{\text{within}} = \Sigma SS_{\text{inside each treatment}}$

and $SS_{\text{subjects}} = \Sigma \frac{P^2}{k} - \frac{G^2}{N}$

$$F = \frac{MS_{\text{between}}}{MS_{\text{error}}} \qquad \text{where each } MS = \frac{SS}{df}$$

TWO-FACTOR ANOVA

$$SS_{\text{between}} = \Sigma \frac{AB^2}{n} - \frac{G^2}{N} \qquad df_{\text{between}} = ab - 1$$

$$SS_{\text{factor A}} = \Sigma \frac{A^2}{bn} - \frac{G^2}{N} \qquad df_{\text{factor A}} = a - 1$$

$$SS_{\text{factor B}} = \Sigma \frac{B^2}{an} - \frac{G^2}{N} \qquad df_{\text{factor B}} = b - 1$$

$$SS_{A \times B} = SS_{\text{between}} - SS_A - SS_B \qquad df_{A \times B} = (a - 1)(b - 1)$$

$$SS_{\text{within}} = \Sigma SS_{\text{inside each treatment}} \qquad df_{\text{within}} = N - ab$$

$$F_A = \frac{MS_A}{MS_{\text{within}}} \qquad F_B = \frac{MS_B}{MS_{\text{within}}} \qquad F_{A \times B} = \frac{MS_{A \times B}}{MS_{\text{within}}}$$

where each $MS = \frac{SS}{df}$

PEARSON CORRELATION

$$r = \frac{SP}{\sqrt{SS_X SS_Y}}$$

where $SP = \Sigma(X - \overline{X})(Y - \overline{Y}) = \Sigma XY - \frac{(\Sigma X)(\Sigma Y)}{n}$

REGRESSION

$$\hat{Y} = bX + a \qquad \text{where } b = \frac{SP}{SS_X} \quad \text{and} \quad a = \overline{Y} - b\overline{X}$$

$$\text{Standard error of estimate} = \sqrt{\frac{\Sigma(Y - \hat{Y})^2}{n - 2}} = \sqrt{\frac{(1 - r^2)SS_Y}{n - 2}}$$

CHI-SQUARE STATISTIC

$$\chi^2 = \Sigma \frac{(f_o - f_e)}{f_e}$$

MANN-WHITNEY *U*

$$U_A = n_A n_B + \frac{n_A(n_A + 1)}{2} - \Sigma R_A$$

$$U_B = n_A n_B + \frac{n_B(n_B + 1)}{2} - \Sigma R_B$$

SPEARMAN CORRELATION

$$r_s = 1 - \frac{6\Sigma D^2}{n(n^2 - 1)}$$

TO THE STUDENT:

A complete study guide has been prepared by the authors to assist you in mastering concepts presented in this text. The study guide is available from your local bookstore under the title *Study Guide to Accompany Statistics for the Behavioral Sciences fourth edition.* If you cannot locate it in the bookstore, ask your bookstore manager to order it for you.

Chi-Square

$$\sum \frac{(O-E)^2}{E} + \frac{(O-E)^2}{}$$ df = # of cells - one   Goodness of fit

$$E = \frac{\text{\# of cells}}{n}$$

$$\sum \frac{(O-E)^2}{E}$$ df = (rows-1)(columns-1) Test of independence

$$E = \frac{(\text{row total})(\text{column total})}{N}$$

Summary Table

Source	SS	÷ df	= MS	E
Between				
within				
total				

$$SS_T = \sum x^2 - \frac{(\sum x)^2}{N}$$

$$SS_B = \frac{(\sum x)^2}{n} + \frac{(\sum x)^2}{n} + \text{etc.} \ldots - \frac{G^2}{N}$$

$$SS_W = \text{add up all SS}$$

$$F = \frac{\text{between groups ms}}{\text{within groups ms}}$$

STATISTICS for the
BEHAVIORAL SCIENCES
A First Course for Students
of Psychology and Education

FOURTH EDITION

✓ Z-test: compares sample mean w/ population. Interval level. Know μ & σ

single sample t: compare sample mean w/ pop. interval. μ known σ must be estimated by standard dev.

✓ repeated measures t: matched sample. Test/retest. Estimate denominator

✓ independent groups t: 2 sample means to compare. Pooled variance is denominator

ANOVA: one IV w/ 2 levels

Factorial ANOVA: Multiple IV w/ 2 levels

✓ correlation: magnitude of association

Regression: Predict one variables score from another

χ^2 goodness of fit: accross categories

✓ χ^2 test of indep: is row related to column

STATISTICS for the BEHAVIORAL SCIENCES

A First Course for Students of Psychology and Education

FOURTH EDITION

FREDERICK J GRAVETTER

State University of New York
College at Brockport

LARRY B. WALLNAU

State University of New York
College at Brockport

WEST PUBLISHING COMPANY

Minneapolis / St. Paul / New York / Los Angeles / San Francisco

COPYEDITING	Sheralyn S. Goldbecker
PROBLEM CHECKING	Roxy Peck
ART	B. Suter Graphics & Design, Inc.
COMPOSITION	The Clarinda Company
INDEXING	Lois Oster
COVER ART	"Small Pictures" by Vasily Kandinsky. Wolfgang Wittrock, Kunsthandel, Dusseldorf
COVER DESIGN	Roslyn Stendahl, Dapper Design

WEST'S COMMITMENT TO THE ENVIRONMENT

In 1906, West Publishing Company began recycling materials left over from the production of books. This began a tradition of efficient and responsible use of resources. Today, 100% of our legal bound volumes are printed on acid-free, recycled paper consisting of 50% new paper pulp and 50% paper that has undergone a de-inking process. We also use vegetable-based inks to print all of our books. West recycles nearly 22,650,000 pounds of scrap paper annually—the equivalent of 187,500 trees. Since the 1960s, West have devised ways to capture and recycle waste inks, solvents, oils, and vapors created in the printing process. We also recycle plastics of all kinds, wood, glass, corrugated cardboard, and batteries, and have eliminated the use of polystyrene book packaging. We at West are proud of the longevity and the scope of our commitment to the environment.

West pocket parts and advance sheets are printed on recyclable paper and can be collected and recycled with newspapers. Staples do not have to be removed. Bound volumes can be recycled after removing the cover.

BRITISH LIBRARY CATALOGING-IN-PUBLICATION DATA

A catalogue record for this book is available from the British Library.

COPYRIGHT ©1985, 1988, 1992
COPYRIGHT ©1996

By WEST PUBLISHING COMPANY
By WEST PUBLISHING COMPANY
610 Opperman Drive
P.O. Box 64526
St. Paul, MN 55164-0526

LIBRARY OF CONGRESS CATALOGING-IN-PUBLICATION DATA

Gravetter, Frederick J
    Statistics for the behavioral sciences   /   Frederick J Gravetter, Larry B. Wallnau.—4th ed.
      p.   cm.
    Includes bibliographical references and index.
     ISBN 0-314-06806-6 (alk. paper)
      1. Psychology—Statistical methods.   2. Educational statistics.
    I. Wallnau, Larry B.   II. Title.
    BF39.G72   1996
    518.5'0243—dc20

95-44462
CIP

 TEXT IS PRINTED ON 10% POST CONSUMER RECYCLED PAPER

CONTENTS

PREFACE

There are three kinds of lies: Lies, damned lies, and statistics.

This quote, attributed by Mark Twain to Benjamin Disraeli, reflects a commonly held belief that statistics (or perhaps even statisticians) should not be trusted. Unfortunately, this mistrust is sometimes justified. In this book, we shall see that statistical techniques are tools that are used to organize information and to make inferences from our data. Like any other tool, statistics can be misused, which may result in misleading, distorted, or incorrect conclusions. It is no small wonder that we are sometimes skeptical when a statistician presents findings. However, if we understand the correct uses of statistical techniques, then we will recognize those situations in which statistical procedures have been incorrectly applied. We can decide which statistics are more believable. Therefore, the goal of this book is to teach not only the methods of statistics, but also how to apply these methods appropriately. Finally, a certain amount of mistrust is healthy. That is, we should critically examine information and data before we accept their implications. As you will see, statistical techniques help us look at data with a critical eye.

For those of you who are familiar with previous editions of *Statistics for the Behavioral Sciences,* you will notice that some changes have been made. Our students are foremost in our minds when we revise the text. Over the years, they have provided honest and useful feedback. Their hard work and perseverance have made our writing and teaching most rewarding. We sincerely thank them.

Our friends at West Publishing once again have made an enormous contribution. We thank our editor Clark Baxter, developmental editor Patricia MacDonald, and production editor Emily Autumn. They are very capable people who possess many professional and technical skills. Just as important, they are very warm individuals who have worked with us in an atmosphere of friendship. We are most grateful to them for their contributions to this project and for their guidance and enthusiasm. We also give special thanks to Roxy Peck of California Polytechnic State University for carefully reviewing the manuscript in its final stages.

We were very fortunate to have many good people provide thoughtful reviews, helpful comments, and constructive criticism at various stages in the development of the manuscript. We thank the following colleagues for their earnest efforts:

Thomas Billimek
San Antonio College

Steven Brown
Rockhurst College (MO)

George Domino
University of Arizona

Lee Friedman
George Mason University

Dianne Haffly
St. Joseph's University (PA)

Lynda Harkins
Southwest Texas State University

Michael Hein
Middle Tennessee State University

Arnold Hyman
University of New Haven

James Johnson
University of North Carolina

Donald Lassiter
Methodist College (NC)

Kenneth Lichstein
Memphis State University

Daniel Moriarty
University of San Diego

David Mostofsky
Boston University

Raenel Neitz
Pima Community College (AZ)

Daniel Phillips
Trenton State College

Kerri Pickel
Ball State University (IN)

Robert Schneider
Metropolitan State College (CO)

Philip Tolin
Central Washington University

Richard Wielkiewicz
College of St. Benedict (MN)

Hilda Williams
Drake University

John Williams
University of North Carolina

Leonard Williams
Rowan College of New Jersey

Finally, the authors thank their spouses, Debbie and JoAnn, for their assistance, encouragement, leeway, and, above all, patience.

TO THE INSTRUCTOR   We have made a number of revisions to *Statistics for the Behavioral Sciences,* while at the same time retaining the features that help students. You will recognize its organization, for example, We continue to use intuitive explanations of formulas, analogies, and many opportunities for review. We still try to anticipate the problems students have with statistics. Some of the noteworthy revisions are as follows.

Chapter 3 (Central Tendency) has a revised section on the weighted mean. We return to this topic in Chapter 10 to show how the formula for pooled variance is like a weighted mean (that is, a weighted mean-square). Also, there is discussion of the difficulties of identifying the "center" of the distribution.

Chapter 4 (Variability) includes more discussion of topics such as degrees of freedom and rough estimates of standard deviation.

Chapter 6 (Probability) has been a troublesome chapter. We have revised the sections concerning probability and the normal distribution. This change simplifies the use of the unit normal table, which has been reformatted.

Chapter 7 (Probability and Samples: The Distribution of Sample Means) provides a more thorough treatment of standard error. We also introduce an alternate formula for standard error based on variance. This formula carries over to standard error measures in Chapters 9, 10, and 11. Chapter 7 has a new section on standard error and statistical inference, which serves as a bridge to hypothesis testing (Chapter 8).

Chapter 11 (Hypothesis Tests with Related Samples) contains more coverage of the problems posed by repeated-measures studies. There is a detailed look at the role of individual differences by comparing the independent-measures and repeated-measures t statistics. There is also a new discussion of carry-over effects and progressive error.

A more conceptual approach has been added to the presentation of analysis of variance (Chapter 13) with the new section "A Conceptual View of ANOVA."

Chapter 15 (Two-Factor ANOVA) has revisions on the topic of interactions. We have added a section covering simple main effects for two-factor analysis of variance.

In Chapter 16, the section on hypothesis tests with the Pearson correlation has been revised in its form so that it is easier to follow. We have revised and expanded the discussion of r^2 for clarification.

The text now contains "In the Literature" sections in nearly every chapter. These sections demonstrate how statistical results are reported in APA style and the jargon we use.

A "Time Out" section appears after each series of related chapters. These sections summarize and integrate the concepts from the preceding set of chapters and prepare the students for the next series.

The math review appendix has been revised with new items for the self-tests and a new section on the order of operations.

Finally, we have revised or replaced many of the older end-of-chapter problems, and computer coverage now is contained in separate manuals (for SPSS, Minitab, and Mystat).

TO THE STUDENT   At the beginning of every semester, we watch our new students walking into the classroom as though they were about to have their teeth extracted. The expressions on their faces do not lie. They might look stone-cold (as if in shock), or extremely serious, or even distraught. Clearly, the tension of fear and dread fills the air. Despite the fears and anxieties you may have about this course (the majority of students do have some fear or dread), we think it is important to become literate in basic statistics. This is evident when one considers that our world has become information-laden and information-dependent. The media inform us of the latest findings on oat bran and your health, global warming, economic trends, aging and memory, the effects of educational programs, and so on. Information and data flow through the Internet in unfathomable volumes. Pollsters give us weekly findings. All these data-gathering efforts provide an enormous and unmanageable amount of information. Enter the statisticians, who use statistical procedures to analyze, organize, and interpret vast amounts of data. Having a basic understanding of a variety of statistical procedures will help you understand these findings and, perhaps more important, to examine them critically.

What about the fear of taking a course in statistics? One way to deal with the fear is to get plenty of practice. You will notice that this book provides you with a number of opportunities to repeat the techniques you will be learning in the form of Learning Checks, Examples, Demonstrations, and end-of-chapter Problems. We encourage you to take advantage of these opportunities. Also, we encourage you to read the text, rather than just memorizing the formulas. We have taken great pains to present each statistical procedure in a conceptual context that explains why the procedure was developed and when it should be used. If you read this material and gain an understanding of the basic concepts underlying each statistical formula, you will find that learning the formulas and how to use them will be much easier.

Over the years, the students in our classes have given us many helpful suggestions. We learn from them. If you have any suggestions or comments about this book, you can send a note to us at the Department of Psychology, 350 New Campus Drive, SUNY College at Brockport, Brockport, NY 14420. We may not be able to answer every letter, but we always appreciate the feedback. (LBW also receives e-mail at the following Internet address: lwallnau@acspr1.acs.brockport.edu)

Frederick J Gravetter
Larry B. Wallnau

SUPPLEMENTS   *Instructor's Manual* with Problem Solutions and Test Bank to Accompany *Statistics for the Behavioral Sciences,* 4/e, offers

- Approximately 35 test questions per chapter consisting of true/false, multiple choice, and computational problems
- Complete solutions to all end of chapter problems.

Westest 3.1

- A computerized test generating software system intended to help instructors create, edit, and print tests with the personal computer.

Study Guide to Accompany *Statistics for the Behavioral Sciences,* 4/e, includes:

- Learning Objectives
- Chapter Summaries
- List of New Terms and Concepts
- List of New Formulas
- Hints and Cautions
- Self Test
- Reviews consisting of 10 to 15 questions and their answers.

MYSTAT Software:

- *MYSTAT™ Software* by SYSTAT™ Inc. is available for IBM® PCs and Macintosh® computers. This software provides a full screen data editor, algebraic variable transformations, sorting, ranking and weighting, descriptive statistics, multi-way tabulations, chi-square, correlation, regression, ANOVA, ANOCOVA, nonparametric tests, scatterplots, box plots, histograms, stem-and-leaf diagrams and time series plots. Available to adoptors upon their request.

New . . . MYSTAT and *Minitab Manuals:*

- Contains information in how the programs are used in behavioral statistics. The Minitab Manual contains examples from the text.

New . . . SPSS Manual by Zandra Gratz and Gloria Volpe of Kean College of New Jersey:

- Introduces students to the Statistics Package for Social Sciences followed by analyzed examples from the text.

New . . . Color Transparency Acetates

- Over 100 figures and tables from the book.

STATISTICS for the BEHAVIORAL SCIENCES

A First Course for Students of Psychology and Education

FOURTH EDITION

CHAPTER 1

INTRODUCTION TO STATISTICS

CONTENTS

PREVIEW

Before we begin our discussion of statistics, we ask you to take a few moments to read the following paragraph, which has been adapted from a psychology experiment reported by Bransford and Johnson (1972).

> The procedure is actually quite simple. First you arrange things into different groups depending on their makeup. Of course, one pile may be sufficient, depending on how much there is to do. If you have to go somewhere else due to lack of facilities, that is the next step; otherwise you are pretty well set. It is important not to overdo any particular endeavor. That is, it is better to do too few things at once than too many. In the short run this may not seem important, but complications from doing too many can easily arise. A mistake can be expensive as well. The manipulation of the appropriate mechanisms should be self-explanatory, and we need not dwell on it here. At first the whole procedure will seem complicated. Soon, however, it will become just another facet of life. It is difficult to foresee any end to the necessity for this task in the immediate future, but then one never can tell.*

You probably find the paragraph a little confusing, and most of you probably think it is describing some obscure statistical procedure. Actually, this paragraph describes the everyday task of doing laundry. Now that you know the topic of the paragraph, try reading it again—it should make sense now.

Why did we begin a statistics textbook with a paragraph about washing clothes? Our goal is to demonstrate the importance of context—when not in the proper context, even the simplest material can appear difficult and confusing. In the Bransford and Johnson experiment, people who knew the topic before reading the paragraph were able to recall 73% more than people who did not know that it was about doing laundry. When you have the appropriate background, it is much easier to fit new material into your memory and to recall it later. In this book, we begin each chapter with a preview. The purpose of the preview is to provide the back

ground or context for the new material in the chapter. As you read each preview section, you should gain a general overview of the chapter content. Remember, all statistical methods were developed to serve a purpose. If you understand why a new procedure is needed, you will find it much easier to learn the procedure.

The objectives for this first chapter are to provide an introduction to the topic of statistics and to give you some background for the rest of the book. We will discuss the role of statistics within the general field of scientific inquiry, and we will introduce some of the vocabulary and notation that are necessary for the statistical methods that follow. In some respects, this chapter serves as a preview section for the rest of the book.

As you read through the following chapters, keep in mind that the general topic of statistics follows a well-organized, logically developed progression that leads from basic concepts and definitions to increasingly sophisticated techniques. Thus, the material presented in the early chapters of this book will serve as a foundation for the material that follows. The content of the first nine chapters, for example, provides an essential background and context for the statistical methods presented in Chapter 10. If you turn directly to the Chapter 10 without reading the first nine chapters, you will find the material confusing and incomprehensible. However, if you learn and use the background material, you will have a good frame of reference for understanding and incorporating new concepts as they are presented. To help you take advantage of the logical, step-by-step development of statistics, we have included two specific elements in this book. First, the opening page of each chapter includes a section titled "Tools You Will Need." This section lists topics from earlier parts of the book that we have identified as essential background for the new material that will be introduced in the chapter. Second, we have included special "Time Out" sections that appear after a series of related chapters. The "Time Out" sections summarize and integrate concepts from the series of preceding chapters in order to help prepare you for the next series of chapters.

Finally, we cannot promise that learning statistics will be as easy as washing clothes. But if you begin each new topic with the proper context, you should eliminate some unnecessary confusion.

---

*Bransford, J. D., and Johnson, M. K. (1972), Contextual prerequisites for understanding: Some investigations of comprehension and recall. *Journal of Verbal Learning and Verbal Behavior, 11,* 717–726. Copyright by Academic Press. Reprinted by permission of the publisher and M. K. Johnson.

1.1 STATISTICS, SCIENCE, AND OBSERVATIONS

DEFINITIONS OF STATISTICS

Why study statistics? is a question countless students ask. One simple answer is that statistics have become a common part of everyday life and, therefore, deserve some attention. A quick glance at the newspaper yields statistics that deal with crime rates, birth rates, average income, average snowfall, and so on. By a common definition, therefore, statistics consist of facts and figures.

These statistics generally are informative and time saving because they condense large quantities of information into a few simple figures or statements. For example, the average snowfall in Chicago during the month of January is based on many observations made over many years. Few people would be interested in seeing a complete list of day-by-day snowfall amounts for the past 50 years. Even fewer people would be able to make much sense of all those numbers at a quick glance. But nearly everyone can understand and appreciate the meaning of an average.

In this book, however, we will use another definition of the term *statistics*. When researchers use the word *statistics,* they are referring to a set of mathematical procedures that are used to organize, summarize, and interpret information.

DEFINITION   The term *statistics* refers to a set of methods and rules for organizing, summarizing, and interpreting information.

Statistical procedures help ensure that the information or observations are presented and interpreted in an accurate and informative way. In somewhat grandiose terms, statistics help researchers bring order out of chaos. In addition, statistics provide researchers with a set of standardized techniques that are recognized and understood throughout the scientific community. Thus, the statistical methods used by one researcher will be familiar to other researchers, who can accurately interpret the statistical analyses with a full understanding of how the analysis was done and what the results signify. Although facts and figures can be important, this book will focus on the methods and procedures of statistics (see Box 1.1).

STATISTICS AND SCIENCE

These observations should be public, in the sense that others are able to repeat the observations using the same methods to see if the same findings will be obtained.

It is frequently said that science is *empirical.* That is, scientific investigation is based on making observations. Statistical methods enable researchers to describe and analyze the observations they have made. Thus, statistical methods are tools for science. We might think of science as consisting of methods for making observations and of statistics as consisting of methods for analyzing them.

On one mission of the space shuttle Columbia, so much scientific data were relayed to computers on earth that scientists were hard pressed to convey, in terms the public could grasp, how much information had been gathered. One individual made a few quick computations on a pocket calculator and determined that if all the data from the mission were printed on pages, they would pile up as high as the Washington Monument. Such an enormous amount of information is unmanageable in this crude form. To interpret the data, many months of work have to be done by many people to statistically analyze them. Statistical methods serve scientific investigation by organizing and interpreting data.

1.1 STATISTICS IN EVERYDAY LIFE

THE FOLLOWING article appeared in the *New York Times* January, 4, 1991, and provides a good example of why a basic understanding of statistics is important for everyday tasks such as reading (and understanding) a newspaper article. This article presents a variety of statistics, using both definitions of the term. First, the report includes numerous facts and figures. In addition, the article reports the results of statistical methods that were used to help organize and interpret the figures.

Although you probably can make some sense of this report, there are a few statistical terms, such as median income, that you may not understand. After you finish Chapter 3, come back and read this newspaper article again. It should be perfectly clear by then.

Purchase index up for homes:

WASHINGTON, Jan. 3 (AP)—Falling home prices and rising incomes combined to raise the typical American family's ability to buy a home to its highest level in 13 years, a real estate trade group said today.

The National Association of Realtors said its Housing Affordability Index reached 115.6 in November, up from 113.3 in October. This was the highest level since the index hit 116 in December 1977.

The 115.6 reading means a family earning the national median income of $35,467 had 115.6 percent of the income needed to qualify for conventional financing covering 80 percent of a median-priced home costing $91,300.

The median price of an existing home dropped $1,600, from $92,900 in October, while median income rose $114, from $32,353.

Improvement in housing affordability conditions were posted in all of the regions between October and November. But the typical family still fell short of having the funds to buy a median-priced home in the Northeast and the West, areas with the highest median prices.

In the northeast, a family earning the median income of $41,565 had 91.9 percent of the income needed to buy a median-priced home costing $133,600. A western family with the median income of $37,825 had 82.2 percent of the income needed to buy a $138,700 home.

1.2 POPULATIONS AND SAMPLES

WHAT ARE THEY? Scientific research typically begins with a general question about a specific group (or groups) of individuals. For example, a researcher may be interested in the effect of divorce on the self-esteem of preteen children. Or a researcher may want to examine the attitudes toward abortion for men versus women. In the first example, the researcher is interested in the group of *preteen children*. In the second example, the researcher wants to compare the group of *men* with the group of *women*. In statistical terminology, the entire group that a researcher wishes to study is called a *population*. By entire group, we literally mean every single individual.

DEFINITION　　A *population* is the set of all individuals of interest in a particular study.

As you can well imagine, a population can be quite large—for example, the entire set of women on the planet earth. A researcher might be more specific, limiting the population for study to women who are registered voters in the United States. Perhaps the investigator would like to study the population consisting of women who are heads of state. Populations can obviously vary in size from extremely large to very small, depending on how the investigator defines the population. The population being studied should always be identified by the researcher. In addition, the population need not consist of people—it could be a population of rats, corporations, parts produced in a factory, or anything else an investigator wants to study. In practice, populations are typically very large, such as the population of fourth-grade children in the United States or the population of small businesses.

Because populations are typically very large, it usually is impossible for a researcher to examine every single individual in the population of interest. Therefore, researchers typically select a smaller, more manageable group from the population and limit their studies to the individuals in the selected group. In statistical terms, a set of individuals selected from a population is called a *sample*. A sample is intended to be representative of its population, and a sample should always be identified in terms of the population from which it was selected.

DEFINITION
A *sample* is a set of individuals selected from a population, usually intended to represent the population in a study.

Just as we saw with populations, samples can vary greatly in size. Imagine that you are about to conduct an opinion poll in a large city. You are going to ask people if they believe the mayor is doing a good job. Since the poll will be conducted by telephone, you define your population as people who live in the city and are listed in the telephone directory. Realizing that it would take more time than you can spend to call everyone in the phone book (the entire population), you call 100 people. Notice that it is often necessary to study a sample because the population is so large that it would be impractical to study every member of the population. If you are more ambitious, you could use a larger sample—for example, 1000 people. Later in this book, we will examine the benefits of using large samples.

Before we move on, there are two final points that should be made about samples and populations.

1. Thus far we have defined populations and samples in terms of *individuals*. For example, we have discussed a population (or a sample) of preteen children. You should be forewarned, however, that we will also refer to populations or samples of *scores*. The change from individuals to scores is usually very straightforward because research typically involves measuring each individual and recording a score (measurement) for that individual. Thus, each sample (or population) of individuals produces a corresponding sample (or population) of scores. In fact, it is useful to make a distinction between a population of individuals and a statistical population. A population of individuals consists the entire set of individuals or items under study, and a statistical population is the set of measurements (usually numbers) obtained from the entire set of individuals. Accordingly, one can make similar a distinction between a sample of individuals and a statistical sample. The sample of individuals consists of the individuals that were selected from the population of individuals for study. Likewise, the statistical sample is comprised of the numbers (measurements) obtained from the sample of individuals. An especially noteworthy report of these distinctions was done by Hyman (1993).

2. In most research situations, a sample will be smaller (have fewer individuals) than the population from which it is selected. However, it is not neces-

sary that a sample be smaller than its population. When you are tossing a coin, for example, the entire set of possible outcomes consists of only two "individuals": Heads and Tails. Although this population consists of only two individuals, you can easily obtain a sample of 10 or more individuals by simply tossing the coin 10 or more times.

PARAMETERS AND STATISTICS

When describing data, it is necessary to distinguish whether the data come from a population or a sample. Any characteristic of a population, for example, its average, is called a population *parameter.* On the other hand, a characteristic of a sample is called a *statistic.* The average of the scores for a sample is a statistic. The range of scores for a sample is another type of statistic. As we will see later, statisticians frequently use different symbols for a parameter and a statistic. By using different symbols, we can readily tell if a characteristic, such as an average, is describing a population or a sample.

DEFINITIONS

A *parameter* is a value, usually a numerical value, that describes a population. A parameter may be obtained from a single measurement, or it may be derived from a set of measurements from the population.

A *statistic* is a value, usually a numerical value, that describes a sample. A statistic may be obtained from a single measurement, or it may be derived from a set of measurements from the sample.

Typically, every population parameter has a corresponding sample statistic, and much of this book is concerned with the relationship between sample statistics and the corresponding population parameters. In Chapter 7, for example, we examine the relationship between the mean obtained for a sample and the mean for the population from which the sample was obtained.

DESCRIPTIVE AND INFERENTIAL STATISTICAL METHODS

The task of answering a research question begins with gathering information. In science, information is gathered by making observations and recording measurements for the individuals to be studied. The measurement or observation obtained for each individual is called a *datum* or, more commonly, a *score* or *raw score.* The complete set of scores or measurements is called the *data set* or simply the *data.* After data are obtained, statistical methods are used to organize and interpret the data.

DEFINITIONS

Data (plural) are measurements or observations. A *data set* is a collection of measurements or observations. A *datum* (singular) is a single measurement or observation and is commonly called a *score* or *raw score.*

Although researchers have developed a variety of different statistical procedures to organize and interpret data, these different procedures can be classified into two general categories. The first category, *descriptive statistics,* consists of statistical procedures that are used to simplify and summarize data.

DEFINITION

Descriptive statistics are statistical procedures used to summarize, organize, and simplify data.

1.2 SAMPLING ERROR: A FIRST IMPRESSION

ALTHOUGH THE concept of sampling error has been presented in the context of inferential statistics, you should realize that the basic notion is something you confront every time you make an inference. For example, whenever you meet someone for the first time, you begin to form general attitudes and opinions based on your initial encounter. After talking with someone for only 5 minutes, you walk away with a general impression. You may leave the conversation thinking that the new person is intelligent or stupid, sophisticated or crude, nice or nasty. In statistical terms, you have used a sample (information obtained during 5 minutes of conversation) as the basis for a general conclusion about the individual's whole personality (the population). However, you should realize that your first impression may not be completely accurate—your opinion may change with further experience. This is the concept of sampling error: Any inference or conclusion based on limited information may not be accurate.

Descriptive statistics are techniques that take raw scores and summarize them in a form that is more manageable. There are many descriptive procedures, but a common technique is to compute an average. Note that even if the data set has hundreds of scores, the average of those scores provides a single descriptive value for the entire set. Other descriptive techniques, including tables and graphs, will be covered in the next several chapters.

The second general category of statistical techniques is called *inferential statistics*. Inferential statistics are methods that use sample data to make general statements about a population.

DEFINITION   *Inferential statistics* consist of techniques that allow us to study samples and then make generalizations about the populations from which they were selected.

As we saw with the telephone survey, it is usually not practical to make observations of every member of the population of interest. Because the population is much too large to telephone every individual, a sample is selected. By analyzing the results for the sample, we hope to make general statements about the population. In this example, results from the telephone survey (a sample) can be used to draw inferences about the opinions of the general population.

One problem with using samples, however, is that a sample provides only limited information about the population. Although samples are generally *representative* of their populations, a sample is not expected to give a perfectly accurate picture of the whole population. There usually is some discrepancy between a sample statistic and the corresponding population parameter. This discrepancy is called *sampling error,* and it creates another problem to be addressed by inferential statistics (see Box 1.2).

DEFINITION   *Sampling error* is the discrepancy, or amount of error, that exists between a sample statistic and the corresponding population parameter.

The concept of sampling error will be discussed in more detail in Chapter 7, but, for now, you should realize that a statistic obtained from a sample generally will not be identical to the corresponding population parameter. One common example of sampling error is the error associated with a sample proportion. For example, in newspaper articles reporting results from political polls, you frequently find statements such as

> Candidate Brown leads the poll with 51% of the vote. Candidate Jones has 42% approval, and the remaining 7% are undecided. This poll was taken from a sample of registered voters and has a margin of error of plus-or-minus 4 percentage points.

The "margin of error" is the sampling error. A sample of voters was selected, and 51% of the individuals in the sample expressed a preference for Candidate B. Thus, the 51% is a sample statistic. Because the sample is only a small part of the total population of voters, you should not expect the sample value to be equal to the population parameter. A statistic always has some "margin of error," which is defined as sampling error.

The following example shows the general stages of a research study and demonstrates how descriptive statistics and inferential statistics are used to organize and interpret the data. At the end of the example, notice how sampling error can affect the interpretation of experimental results, and consider why inferential statistical methods are needed to deal with this problem.

EXAMPLE 1.1

Figure 1.1 shows an overview of a general research situation and the role that descriptive and inferential statistics play. In this example, a researcher is examining the relative effectiveness of two teaching methods: method A and method B. One sample of students is taught by method A, and a second sample is taught by method B. Then all the students are given a standard achievement test. At the end of the experiment, the researcher has two sets of data: the scores for sample A and the scores for sample B (see Figure 1.1). Now is the time to begin using statistics.

First, descriptive statistics are used to simplify the pages of data. For example, the researcher could draw a graph showing the scores for each sample or compute the average score for each sample. Note that descriptive methods provide a simplified, organized description of the scores. In this example, the students taught by method A averaged 76 on the standardized test, and the students taught by method B averaged only 71.

Once the researcher has described the results, the next step is to interpret the outcome. This is the role of inferential statistics. In this example, the researcher must decide whether the 5-point difference between the two sample means reflects a real difference between the two teaching methods. Remember, sample A represents the population of students taught by method A, and sample B represents the population of students taught by method B. However, neither sample provides a perfectly accurate picture of its population. Thus, the 5-point difference between the two sample means does not necessarily mean there is a corresponding 5-point difference between the two population means. In fact, it is possible that there is actually no difference between the two teaching methods and the sample difference is simply the result of sampling error. One goal of inferential statistics is to help the researcher interpret sample data: Does the difference between samples represent a real difference between populations, or is the sample mean difference merely the result of sampling error? (See Figure 1.1.)

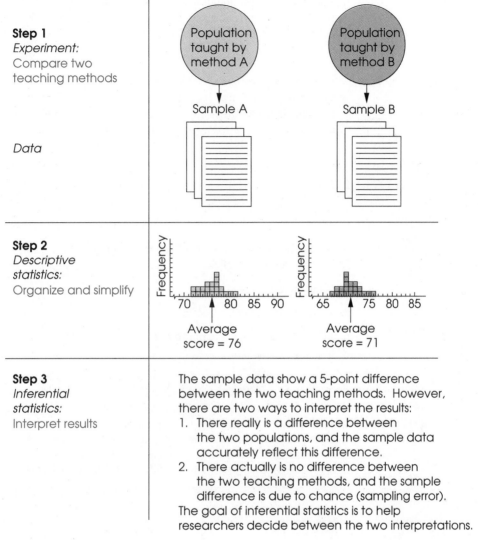

Step 1
Experiment:
Compare two
teaching methods

Data

Step 2
*Descriptive
statistics:*
Organize and simplify

Step 3
*Inferential
statistics:*
Interpret results

The sample data show a 5-point difference
between the two teaching methods. However,
there are two ways to interpret the results:
1. There really is a difference between
   the two populations, and the sample data
   accurately reflect this difference.
2. There actually is no difference between
   the two teaching methods, and the sample
   difference is due to chance (sampling error).
The goal of inferential statistics is to help
researchers decide between the two interpretations.

FIGURE 1.1

The role of statistics in experimental research.

Inferential statistics are a necessary part of conducting experiments. Suppose
that a researcher would like to test the effectiveness of a new therapy program for
depression. It would be too costly and time consuming to test the program on all
depressed individuals. Therefore, the treatment is tested on a sample of depressed
patients. Of course, the researcher would like to see these people overcome their
misery, but keep in mind that one is not just interested in this sample of individuals. The investigator would like to generalize the findings to the entire population.
If the treatment program is effective for the sample of depressed people, it would
be great to be able to state with confidence that it will also work for others. It is
important to note that inferential statistical methods will allow meaningful generalizations only if the individuals in the sample are representative of the population.
One way to ensure that the sample is representative is to use *random sampling,* or

random selection. Although there are several formally defined techniques for random sampling, one basic requirement is that all individuals in the population have the same chance of being selected. There will be more to say about this topic in later chapters.

DEFINITION   *Random selection,* or *random sampling,* is a process for obtaining a sample from a population that requires that every individual in the population have the same chance of being selected for the sample. A sample obtained by random selection is called a *random sample.*

LEARNING CHECK   1. Science is empirical. This means that science is based on _____.

2. Science consists of methods for making observations, and statistics are methods for _____ them.

3. A descriptive characteristic of a population is a _____. A characteristic of a sample is called a _____.

4. What are statistics?

5. What is the purpose of descriptive statistics?

6. Inferential statistics attempt to use _____ to make general statements about _____.

7. One way to ensure that a sample is representative of a population is to use _____ selection of the sample.

ANSWERS   1. observation   2. analyzing   3. parameter; statistic
4. By one definition, statistics are facts and figures. In this book, the term *statistics* refers to a set of methods for analyzing and interpreting data.
5. to simplify and summarize data   6. sample data; a population   7. random

1.3 THE SCIENTIFIC METHOD AND THE DESIGN OF EXPERIMENTS

OBJECTIVITY   As noted earlier, science is empirical in that knowledge is acquired by observation. Another important aspect of scientific inquiry is that it should be *objective.* That is, theoretical biases of the researcher should not be allowed to influence the findings. Usually when a study is conducted, the investigator has a hunch about how it will turn out. This hunch, actually a prediction about the outcome of the study, is typically based on a theory that the researcher has. It is important that scientists conduct their studies in a way that will prevent these hunches or biases from influencing the outcome of the research. Experimenter bias can operate very subtly. Rosenthal and Fode (1963) had student volunteers act as experimenters in a learning study. The students were given rats to train in a maze. Half of the students were led to believe that their rats were "maze-bright," and the remainder were told their rats were "maze-dull." In reality, they all received the same kind of rat. Nevertheless, the data showed real differences in the rats' performance for the two groups of experimenters. Somehow the students' expectations influenced the outcome of the experiment. Apparently there were differences between the groups in how the students handled the rats, and the differences accounted for the effect. For a detailed look at experimenter bias, you might read the review by Rosenthal (1963).

RELATIONSHIPS BETWEEN VARIABLES

Science attempts to discover orderliness in the universe. Even people of ancient civilizations noted regularity in the world around them—the change of seasons, changes in the moon's phases, changes in the tides—and they were able to make many observations to document these orderly changes. Something that can change or have different values is called a *variable*.

DEFINITION

A *variable* is a characteristic or condition that changes or has different values for different individuals.

Variables are often identified by letters (usually *X* or *Y*). For example, the variable *height* could be identified by the letter *X,* and *shoe size* could be identified by *Y*. It is reasonable to expect a consistent, orderly relationship between these two variables: As *X* changes, *Y* also changes in a predictable way.

A value that does not change or vary is called a *constant*. For example, an instructor may adjust the exam scores for a class by adding 4 points to each student's score. Because every individual gets the same 4 points, this value is a constant.

DEFINITION

A *constant* is a characteristic or condition that does not vary, but is the same for every individual.

A constant is often identified by its numerical value, such as 4, or by the letter *C*. Adding a constant to each score, for example, could be represented by the expression $X + C$.

Science involves a search for relationships between variables. For example, there is a relationship between the amount of rainfall and crop growth. Rainfall is one of the variables. It varies from year to year and season to season. Crop growth is the other variable. Some years the corn stalks seem short and stunted; other years they are tall and full. When there is very little rainfall, the crops are short and shriveled. When rain is ample, the crops show vigorous growth. Note that in order to document the relationship, one must make observations—that is, measurements of the amount of rainfall and size of the crops.

There are a variety of methods for obtaining observations and investigating relationships between variables. Most of these methods can be classified into three basic categories, *correlational, experimental,* and *quasi-experimental,* each of which is discussed in the following sections.

THE CORRELATIONAL METHOD

The simplest way to look for relationships between variables is to make observations of the two variables as they exist naturally. This is called the *observational* or *correlational* method.

DEFINITION   With the *correlational method*, two variables are observed to see if there is a relationship.

Suppose that a researcher wants to examine whether or not a relationship exists between length of time in an executive position and assertiveness. A large sample of executives takes a personality test designed to measure assertiveness. Also, the investigator determines how long each person has served in an executive-level job. Suppose that the investigator found that there is a relationship between the two variables—that the longer a person had an executive position, the more assertive that person tended to be. Naturally, one might jump to the conclusion that being an executive for a long time makes a person more assertive. The problem with the correlational method is that it provides no information about cause-and-effect relationships. An equally plausible explanation for the relationship is that assertive people choose to stay or survive longer in executive positions than less-assertive individuals. To determine the cause and the effect in a relationship, it is necessary to *manipulate and control* one of the variables being studied. This is accomplished by the experimental method.

THE EXPERIMENTAL METHOD

The goal of the experimental method is to establish a cause-and-effect relationship between two variables. That is, the method of observing variables is intended to show that changes in one variable are *caused* by changes in the other variable. To accomplish this goal, the experimental method has two distinguishing characteristics:

1. The researcher *manipulates* one of the variables and observes the second variable to determine whether or not the manipulation causes changes to occur.

2. The researcher must exercise some *control* over the research situation to ensure that other, extraneous variables do not influence the relationship being examined.

To demonstrate these two characteristics, consider an experiment where a researcher is examining the effects of room temperature on memory performance. The purpose of the experiment is to determine whether changes in room temperature *cause* changes in memory performance.

In more complex experiments, a researcher may systematically manipulate more than one variable and may observe more than one variable. Here we are considering the simplest case, where only one variable is manipulated and only one variable is observed.

The researcher manipulates temperature by creating two or more different treatment conditions. For example, our researcher could set the temperature at 70° for one condition and then change the temperature to 90° for a second condition. The experiment would consist of observing the memory performance for a group of individuals (often called *subjects*) in the 70° room and comparing their scores with another group that is tested in the 90° room. The structure of this experiment is shown in Figure 1.2.

To be able to say that differences in memory performance are caused by temperature, the researcher must rule out any other possible explanations for the difference. That is, any other variables that might affect memory performance must be controlled. Researchers typically use two basic techniques to control variables. First, the researcher could use *random assignment* so that each subject has an equal chance of being assigned to each of the treatment conditions. Random assignment helps assure that the subjects in one treatment condition are not substantially different from the subjects in another treatment condition. For example, a researcher should not assign all the young subjects to one condition and all the old subjects to

FIGURE 1.2 *good ex*

Volunteers are randomly assigned to one of two treatment groups: 70° room or 90° room. After memorizing a list of words, subjects are tested by having them write down as many words as possible from the list. A difference between the groups in performance is attributed to the treatment—the temperature of the room.

*remember
variable Temp.
control situation
random assign*

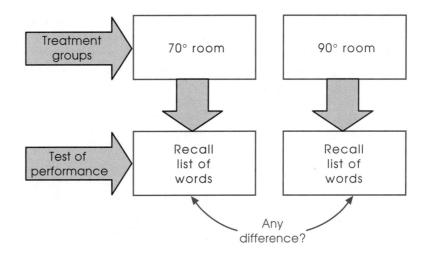

another. If this were done, the researcher could not be sure that the difference in memory performance was caused by temperature; instead, it could be caused by age differences. Second, the experimental method requires that the treatment conditions be identical except for the one variable that is being manipulated. This is accomplished by *controlling* or *holding constant* any other variables that might influence performance. For example, the researcher should test both groups of subjects at the same time of day, in the same room, with the same instructions, and so on. Again, the goal is to eliminate the contribution of all other variables, except for temperature, that might account for the difference in memory performance.

DEFINITION

In the *experimental method,* one variable is manipulated while changes are observed in another variable. To establish a cause-and-effect relationship between the two variables, an experiment attempts to eliminate or minimize the effect of all other variables by using *random assignment* and by *controlling* or *holding constant* other variables that might influence the results.

THE INDEPENDENT AND DEPENDENT VARIABLES

Specific names are used for the two variables that are studied by the experimental method. The variable that is manipulated by the experimenter is called the *independent variable*. It can be identified as the treatment conditions to which subjects are assigned. For the example in Figure 1.2, temperature is the independent variable. The variable that is observed to assess a possible effect of the manipulation is the *dependent variable*.

DEFINITIONS

The *independent variable* is the variable that is manipulated by the researcher. In behavioral research, the independent variable usually consists of the two (or more) treatment conditions to which subjects are exposed. The independent variable consists of the *antecedent* conditions that were manipulated *prior* to observing the dependent variable.

The *dependent variable* is the one that is observed for changes in order to assess the effect of the treatment.

In psychological research, the dependent variable is typically a measurement or score obtained for each subject. For the temperature experiment (Figure 1.2), the dependent variable is the number of words recalled on the memory test. Differences between groups in performance on the dependent variable suggest that the manipulation had an effect. That is, changes in the dependent variable *depend* on the independent variable.

Often we can identify one condition of the independent variable that receives no treatment. It is used for comparison purposes and is called the *control group*. The group that does receive the treatment is the *experimental group*.

DEFINITIONS

A *control group* is a condition of the independent variable that does not receive the experimental treatment. Typically, a control group either receives no treatment or receives a neutral, placebo treatment. The purpose of a control group is to provide a baseline for comparison with the experimental group.

An *experimental group* does receive an experimental treatment.

Note that the independent variable always consists of at least two values. (Something must have at least two different values before you can say that it is "variable.") For the temperature experiment (Figure 1.2), the independent variable is the 90° room versus the 70° room. For an experiment with an experimental group and a control group, the independent variable would be treatment versus no treatment.

PROBLEMS THAT CAN ARISE IN EXPERIMENTS

In general, the purpose of an experiment is to show that the manipulated variable, and *only* that variable, is responsible for the changes in the second variable. As noted earlier, this may be accomplished by controlling other variables. However, sometimes an uncontrolled variable can vary along with the independent variable. Any difference that exists between the treatment conditions other than the manipulated variable is called a *confounding variable*. When a researcher allows the treatment conditions to differ with respect to some variable other than the ones being manipulated or controlled, the experiment is flawed, and the researcher cannot interpret the results as demonstrating a cause-and-effect relationship.

DEFINITION

A *confounding variable* is an uncontrolled variable that is unintentionally allowed to vary systematically with the independent variable.

For example, an instructor would like to assess the effectiveness of computer laboratory exercises in assisting students to grasp the fundamentals of statistics. There are two treatment conditions. One section of statistics is taught three times a week as a lecture course. A second section of students also meets three times a week, but one of these meetings is devoted to computer exercises in statistics. Professor Smith teaches the lecture, and Professor Jones teaches the second group of students. At the end of the semester, both groups receive the same final exam, and their performances are compared. The experiment is summarized in Figure 1.3.

Let's assume that a statistical analysis determined that the lecture/lab students performed better on the final exam. Can the instructors conclude that the method of instruction had an effect on learning? The answer is emphatically *no*. The inde-

FIGURE 1.3

In this experiment, the effect of instructional method (the independent variable) on test performance (the dependent variable) is examined. However, any difference between groups in performance cannot be attributed to the method of instruction. In this experiment, there is a confounding variable. The instructor teaching the course varies with the independent variable, so that the treatment of the groups differs in more ways than one (instructional method and instructor vary).

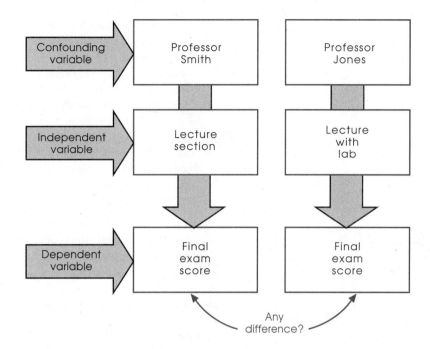

pendent variable, method of instruction, is not the only way the groups differ in terms of how they are treated. The instructor was allowed to vary along with the method of instruction. It is possible that the lecture/lab group performed better because Professor Jones is a better instructor, one who motivates students and can explain concepts in understandable terms. That is, the difference between groups in performance might be due to the different instructors rather than the different treatments. One cannot be sure which interpretation is correct. When a study is confounded, it is impossible to make meaningful conclusions about the results. The lesson in this example is that as many variables as possible must be controlled.

THE QUASI-EXPERIMENTAL METHOD

In many research situations, the rigorous control required by the experimental method is difficult or impossible to achieve. In these situations, researchers will often abandon some of the requirements of an experiment and conduct what is called a *quasi-experimental* research study. As the name implies, the quasi-experimental method is "almost but not quite" a true experiment. Specifically, the quasi-experimental method is always missing at least one basic element that would be necessary for the experimental method. Two general categories of quasi-experimental research, and their missing elements, are as follows:

1. *Differential research* involves the comparison of pre-existing groups of subjects. A common example is research comparing men versus women. The "problem" that prevents this type of research from being an experiment is that the researcher has no control over the assignment of subjects to groups. Instead, each subject assigns himself or herself to the appropriate group based on pre-existing subject characteristics.

2. *Time-series research* involves the comparison of observations made at one time versus observations made at a later time. For example, a researcher might observe a group of individuals before a treatment or event and then measure the same individuals after the treatment or event. The "problem" with this type of research is that the researcher has no control over the effects of time. For example, a researcher could record depression scores for a group of patients before and after therapy. If the patients show improvement after therapy, the researcher would like to conclude that the therapy caused the improvement. However, it is possible that the improvement was simply due to the passage of time. Thus, the researcher cannot make an unambiguous cause-and-effect conclusion, and the research study is not a true experiment.

Like an experiment, the quasi-experimental method usually involves the comparison of two (or more) groups of scores. The variable that differentiates the groups is similar to the independent variable in an experiment and often is referred to as an independent variable. More precisely, however, it is called a *quasi-independent variable*. As in an experiment, the score obtained for each subject is called the dependent variable. In a quasi-experimental study comparing attitude scores for men versus women, for example, gender is the quasi-independent variable, and attitude is the dependent variable. Note that the quasi-independent variable consists of antecedent conditions that differentiate groups of subjects prior to making observations of the dependent variable.

DEFINITION   The *quasi-experimental method* examines differences between pre-existing groups of subjects (for example, men versus women) or differences between groups of scores obtained at different times (for example, before treatment versus after treatment). The variable that is used to differentiate the groups is called the *quasi-independent variable,* and the score obtained for each individual is the dependent variable.

Although the quasi-experimental method often is used to address causal questions (for example, Does the therapy cause a change in depression?), you should realize that these studies are not true experiments. Because quasi-experimental research does not rigorously control other variables, it is essentially a correlational strategy, and the results from this type of research cannot be used to establish unambiguous cause-and-effect relationships.

THEORIES AND HYPOTHESES

Theories are a very important part of psychological research. A psychological theory typically consists of a number of statements about the underlying mechanisms of behavior. Theories are important in that they help organize and unify many observations. They may try to account for very large areas of psychology, such as a general theory of learning. However, they may be more specific, such as a theory of the mechanisms involved in just avoidance learning. A theory is especially useful if it directs and promotes future research and provides specific predictions for the outcomes of that research.

When an investigator designs an experiment, there almost always is a specific hypothesis that is addressed. A *hypothesis* is a hunch about the result that will be obtained from the experiment.

DEFINITION

A *hypothesis* is a prediction about the outcome of an experiment. In experimental research, a hypothesis makes a prediction about how the manipulation of the independent variable will affect the dependent variable.

A theory is especially helpful if it generates many testable hypotheses. By testable we mean the hypothesis can be confirmed or disconfirmed by making observations (conducting studies).

Hypotheses are often derived from the theory that the researcher is developing. An experimenter can state the hypothesis as a prediction—specifically, as a relationship between the independent and dependent variables. Simply stated, a hypothesis is a prediction about the effect of the treatment. Therefore, we can think of an experiment as a test of a hypothesis. A very important part of inferential statistics consists of the statistical analysis of hypothesis tests. Much of the book will focus on this topic.

CONSTRUCTS AND OPERATIONAL DEFINITIONS

Theories contain hypothetical concepts, which help describe the mechanisms that underlie behavioral phenomena. These concepts are called *constructs,* and they cannot be observed because they are hypothetical. For example, intelligence, personality types, and motives are hypothetical constructs. They are used in theories to organize observations in terms of underlying mechanisms. If constructs are hypothetical and cannot be observed, then how can they possibly be studied? The answer is that we have to *define* the construct so that it can be studied. An *operational definition* defines a construct in terms of an observable and measurable response. This definition should include the process and operations involved in making the observations. For example, an operational definition for emotionality might be stated as the amount of increase in heart rate after a person is insulted. An operational definition of intelligence might be the score on the Wechsler Adult Intelligence Scale.

DEFINITIONS

Constructs are hypothetical concepts that are used in theories to organize observations in terms of underlying mechanisms.

An *operational definition* defines a construct in terms of specific operations or procedures and the measurements that result from them. Thus, an operational definition consists of two components: First, it describes a set of operations or procedures for measuring a construct. Second, it defines the construct in terms of the resulting measurements.

LEARNING CHECK

1. A researcher would like to compare social interaction skills for kindergarten children who have attended a formal preschool program versus children with no preschool experience.
   a. Does this study use an experimental, correlational, or quasi-experimental strategy?
   b. What is the dependent variable for this study?

2. Cause-and-effect relationships cannot be determined by a correlational method. (True or false?)

3. In a memory experiment, subjects memorize a list of words and then must recall as many words as possible after a 6-hour retention interval. One group

sleeps during the retention interval while people in the other group remain awake and go about their daily routine. The number of words recalled is measured for each subject. The experimenter wants to determine if type of activity during the retention interval has an effect on the number of words recalled. For this study, what is the independent variable? What is the dependent variable?

4. A hypothesis can be stated as a prediction about the effect of _____ on _____.

5. An operational definition defines a construct in terms of _____.

ANSWERS **1. a.** quasi-experimental
b. The dependent variable is social interaction skill.

2. true

3. The independent variable is the type of activity during the retention interval; the dependent variable is the number of words recalled.

4. an independent variable (or treatment); a dependent variable

5. a measurable response

1.4 SCALES OF MEASUREMENT

WHAT IS A MEASUREMENT? It should be obvious by now that data collection requires that we make measurements of our observations. Measurement involves either categorizing events (qualitative measurements) or using numbers to characterize the size of the event (quantitative measurement). Several types of scales are associated with measurements. The distinctions among the scales are important because they underscore the limitations of certain types of measurements and because certain statistical procedures are appropriate for data collected on some scales, but not on others. If you were interested in people's heights, for example, you could measure a group of individuals by simply classifying them into three categories: tall, medium, and short. However, this simple classification would not tell you much about the actual heights of the individuals, and these measurements would not give you enough information to calculate an average height for the group. Although the simple classification would be adequate for some purposes, you would need more-sophisticated measurements before you could answer more-detailed questions. In this section, we examine four different scales of measurement, beginning with the simplest and moving to the most sophisticated.

THE NOMINAL SCALE A *nominal scale* of measurement labels observations so that they fall into different categories.

DEFINITION   A *nominal scale* consists of a set of categories that have different names. Measurements on a nominal scale label and categorize observations, but do not make any quantitative distinctions between observations.

qualitative →

The word *nominal* means "having to do with names." Measurements that are made on this scale involve naming things. For example, if we wish to know the sex of a person responding to a questionnaire, it would be measured on a nominal scale consisting of two categories. A product warranty card might have you check the box that best describes your occupation, and it lists "sales," "professional," "skilled trade," and "other (please specify)." Occupations are being measured in terms of categories; therefore, a nominal scale is being used. A researcher observing the behavior of a group of infant monkeys might categorize responses as playing, grooming, feeding, acting aggressive, or showing submissiveness. Again, this instance typifies a nominal scale of measurement. The nominal scale consists of qualitative distinctions. No attempt is made to measure the size of the event or response. The scales that follow do reflect an attempt to make quantitative distinctions.

THE ORDINAL SCALE   With an *ordinal* scale of measurement, the categories that make up the scale not only have separate names (as in a nominal scale), but also are ranked in terms of magnitude. Thus, as the word *ordinal* implies, observations measured on an ordinal scale are categorized and arranged in rank order.

DEFINITION   An *ordinal scale* consists of a set of categories that are organized in an ordered sequence. Measurements on an ordinal scale rank observations in terms of size or magnitude.

quantitative →

For example, a job supervisor is asked to rank employees in terms of how well they perform their work. The resulting data will tell us who the supervisor considers the best worker, the second best, and so on. However, the data provide no information about the amount that the workers differ in job performance. The data may reveal that Jan, who is ranked second, is viewed as doing better work than Joe, who is ranked third. However, the data do not reveal *how much* better. This is a limitation of measurements on an ordinal scale.

THE INTERVAL AND RATIO SCALES   An *interval scale* of measurement consists of an ordered set of categories (like an ordinal scale) with the additional requirement that the categories form a series of intervals that are all exactly the same size. The additional feature of equal-sized intervals makes it possible to compute distances between values on an interval scale. On a ruler, for example, a 1-inch interval is the same size at every location on the ruler, and a 4-inch distance is exactly the same size no matter where it is measured on the ruler. Thus, an interval scale allows you to measure differences in the size or amount of events. However, an interval scale does not have an absolute zero point that indicates complete absence of the variable being measured. Because there is no absolute zero point on an interval scale, ratios of values are not meaningful. (For example, you cannot compare two values by claiming that one is "twice as large" as another. See Example 1.2)

A *ratio scale* of measurement has all the features of an interval scale, but adds an absolute zero point. That is, on a ratio scale, a value of zero indicates none (a complete absence) of the variable being measured. The advantage of an absolute zero is that ratios of numbers on the scale reflect ratios of magnitude for the variable being measured. The distinction between an interval scale and a ratio scale is demonstrated in Example 1.2.

DEFINITIONS

An *interval scale* consists of ordered categories where all of the categories are intervals of exactly the same size. With an interval scale, equal differences between numbers on the scale reflect equal differences in magnitude. However, ratios of magnitudes are not meaningful.

A *ratio scale* is an interval scale with the additional feature of an absolute zero point. With a ratio scale, ratios of numbers do reflect ratios of magnitude.

EXAMPLE 1.2

good

A researcher obtains measurements of height for a group of 8-year-old boys. Initially, the researcher simply records each child's height in inches, obtaining values such as 44, 51, 49, and so on. These initial measurements constitute a ratio scale. A value of zero represents no height (absolute zero). Also, it is possible to use these measurements to form ratios. For example, a child who is 80 inches tall is twice as tall as a 40-inch-tall child.

Now suppose that the researcher converts the initial measurements into a new scale by calculating the difference between each child's actual height and the average height for this age group. A child who is 1 inch taller than average now gets a score of +1; a child 4 inches taller than average gets a score of +4. Similarly, a child who is 2 inches shorter than average gets a score of −2. The new scores constitute an interval scale of measurement. A score of zero no longer indicates an absence of height; now it simply means average height.

good

Notice that both sets of scores involve measurement in inches, and you can compute differences, or intervals, on either scale. For example, there is a 6-inch difference in height between two boys who measure 57 and 51 inches tall on the first scale. Likewise, there is a 6-inch difference between two boys who measure +9 and +3 on the second scale. However, you should also notice that ratio comparisons are not possible on the second scale. For example, a boy who measures +9 is *not* three times as tall as a boy who measures +3.

---

ex

Most dependent variables we will encounter can be measured on either an interval or a ratio scale. These scales allow basic arithmetic operations that permit us to calculate differences between scores, to sum scores, and to calculate average scores. However, you should know that the distinction between different scales of measurement is often unclear when considering specific measurements. For example, the scores resulting from an IQ test are usually treated as measurements on an interval scale, but many researchers believe that IQ scores are more accurately described as ordinal data. An IQ score of 105 is clearly greater than a score of 100, but there is some question concerning *how much* difference in intelligence is reflected in the 5-point difference between these two scores.

1.5 DISCRETE AND CONTINUOUS VARIABLES

WHAT ARE THEY AND HOW DO THEY DIFFER?

The variables in a study can be characterized by the type of values that can be assigned to them. A *discrete variable* consists of separate, indivisible categories. For this type of variable, there are no intermediate values between two adjacent categories. Consider the values displayed when dice are rolled. Between neighboring values—for example, seven dots and eight dots—no other values can ever be observed.

DEFINITION

A *discrete variable* consists of separate, indivisible categories. No values can exist between two neighboring categories.

A discrete variable is typically restricted to whole countable numbers—for example, the number of children in a family or the number of students attending class. If you observe class attendance from day to day, you may find 18 students one day and 19 students the next day. However, it is impossible ever to observe a value between 18 and 19. A discrete variable may also consist of observations that differ qualitatively. For example, a psychologist observing patients may classify some as having panic disorders, others as having dissociative disorders, and some as having psychotic disorders. The type of disorder is a discrete variable because there are distinct and finite categories that can be observed.

On the other hand, many variables are not discrete. Variables such as time, height, and weight are not limited to a fixed set of separate, indivisible categories. You can measure time, for example, in hours, minutes, seconds, or fractions of seconds. These variables are called *continuous* because they can be divided into an infinite number of fractional parts.

DEFINITION

For a *continuous variable*, there are an infinite number of possible values that fall between any two observed values. A continuous variable is divisible into an infinite number of fractional parts.

For example, subjects are given problems to solve, and a researcher records the amount of time it takes them to find the solutions. One person may take 31 seconds to solve the problems, whereas another may take 32 seconds. Between these two values, it is possible to find any fractional amount—31½, 31¼, 31¹⁄₁₀—provided the measuring instrument is sufficiently accurate. Time is a continuous variable. A continuous variable can be pictured as a number line that is continuous. That is, there are an infinite number of points on the line without any gaps or separations between neighboring points (see Figure 1.4).

CONTINUOUS VARIABLES AND REAL LIMITS

Measurement of a continuous variable typically involves assigning an individual to an *interval* on the number line rather than a single point. For example, if you are measuring time to the nearest second, measurements of $X = 32.8$ seconds and $X = 33.1$ seconds are both rounded to scores of $X = 33$ seconds [see Figure 1.4(a)]. Note that the score $X = 33$ is not a single point on the number line, but instead represents an interval on the line. In this example, a score of 33 corresponds to an interval from 32.5 to 33.5. Any measurement that falls within this interval will be

FIGURE 1.4

When measuring time to the nearest whole second, measurements of 32.8 and 33.1 are assigned the value of 33 seconds. Any measurement in the interval between 32.5 and 33.5 will be assigned the value of 33 (part a). The boundaries that define each interval are called the real limits of the interval (part b).

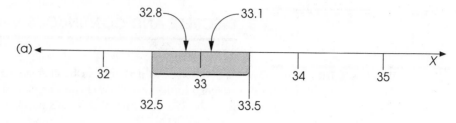

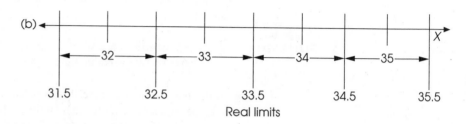

Real limits

assigned a value of $X = 33$ seconds. The boundaries that form the interval are called the *real limits* of the interval. For this example, 32.5 is the *lower real limit* and 33.5 is the *upper real limit* of the interval that corresponds to $X = 33$.*

DEFINITION

For a continuous variable, each score actually corresponds to an interval on the scale. The boundaries that separate these intervals are called *real limits*. The real limit separating two adjacent scores is located exactly halfway between the scores. Each score has two real limits, one at the top of its interval called the *upper real limit* and one at the bottom of its interval called the *lower real limit*. Note that the upper real limit of one interval is also the lower real limit of the next higher interval.

In Figure 1.4(b), note that neighboring X values share a real limit. For example, the score $X = 33$ has an upper limit of 33.5. The value 33.5 is also the lower real limit for $X = 34$. Thus, on a continuous number line such as in Figure 1.4, there are no gaps between adjacent intervals.

The concept of real limits applies to any measurement of a continuous variable, even when the score categories are not whole numbers. For example, if you were measuring time to the nearest tenth of a second, the measurement categories would be 31.0, 31.1, 31.2, and so on. Each of these categories represents an interval on the scale that is bounded by real limits. For example, a score of $X = 31.1$ seconds indicates that the actual measurement is in an interval bounded by a lower real

---

*Technical Note: It is important to distinguish between the *real limits* for an interval and the process of rounding scores. The real limits form boundaries that define an interval on a continuous scale. For example, the real limits 32.5 and 33.5 define an interval that is identified by the score $X = 33$. The real limits, however, are not necessarily a part of the interval. In this example, 32.5 is the lower real limit of the interval. If you are using a rounding process that causes 32.5 to be rounded up, then a measurement of 32.5 would be rounded to 33 and would be included in the 32.5–33.5 interval. On the other hand, if your rounding process causes 32.5 to be rounded down to 32, then this value would not be included in the interval. In general, the question of whether an upper real limit or a lower real limit belongs in an interval is determined by the rounding process that you have adopted.

limit of 31.05 and an upper real limit of 31.15. Remember, the real limits are always halfway between adjacent categories.

Later in this book, real limits are used for constructing graphs and for various calculations with continuous scales. For now, however, you should realize that real limits are a necessity whenever you make measurements of a continuous variable.

LEARNING CHECK

1. An instructor records the order in which students complete their tests—that is, the first to finish, the second to finish, and so on. A(n) _____ scale of measurement is used in this instance.

2. The Scholastic Achievement Test (SAT) most likely measures aptitude on a(n) _____ scale.

3. In a study on perception of facial expressions, subjects must classify the emotions displayed in photographs of people as anger, sadness, joy, disgust, fear, or surprise. Emotional expression is measured on a(n) _____ scale.

4. A researcher studies the factors that determine how many children couples decide to have. The variable, number of children, is a _____ (discrete/continuous) variable.

5. An investigator studies how concept-formation ability changes with age. Age is a _____ (discrete/continuous) variable.

6. **a.** When measuring weight to the nearest pound, what are the real limits for a score of $X = 150$ pounds?

   b. When measuring weight to the nearest ½ pound, what are the real limits for a score of $X = 144.5$ pounds?

ANSWERS   1. ordinal   2. interval   3. nominal   4. discrete   5. continuous

6. **a.** 149.5 and 150.5
   b. 144.25 and 144.75

1.6 STATISTICAL NOTATION

Measurements of behavior usually will provide data composed of numerical values. These numbers form the basis of the computations that are done for statistical analyses. There is a standardized notation system for statistical procedures, and it is used to identify terms in equations and mathematical operations. Some general mathematical operations, notation, and basic algebra are outlined in the review section of Appendix A. There is also a skills assessment exam (p. A-1) to help you determine if you need the basic mathematics review. Here we will introduce some statistical notation that is used throughout this book. In subsequent chapters, additional notation will be introduced as it is needed.

SCORES

Making observations of a dependent variable in a study will typically yield values or scores for each subject. Raw scores are the original, unchanged set of scores obtained in the study. Scores for a particular variable are represented by the letter X. For example, if performance in your statistics course is measured by tests and you obtain a 35 on the first test, then we could state that $X = 35$. A set of scores can be presented in a column that is headed by X. For example, a list of quiz scores from your class might be presented as shown in the margin.

When observations are made for two variables, there will be two scores for each subject. The data can be presented as two lists labeled X and Y for the two variables. For example, observations for people's height in inches (variable X) and weight in pounds (variable Y) can be presented as shown in the margin. Each pair X, Y represents the observations made of a single subject.

It is also useful to specify how many scores are in a set. The number of scores in a data set is represented by the letter N. For populations, we will use an upper-case N, and for samples, we will use a lowercase n. (Throughout the book, notational differences are used to distinguish between samples and populations.) For the height and weight data, $N = 7$ for both variables.

X
37
35
35
30
25
17
16

X	Y
72	165
68	151
67	160
67	160
68	146
70	160
66	133

SUMMATION NOTATION

Many of the computations required in statistics will involve adding up a set of scores. Because this procedure is used so frequently, a special notation is used to refer to the sum of a set of scores. The Greek letter sigma, or Σ, is used to stand for summation. The expression ΣX means to add all the scores for variable X. The summation sign Σ can be read as "the sum of." Thus, ΣX is read "the sum of the scores." For the following set of quiz scores,

$$10, \quad 6, \quad 7, \quad 4$$

$\Sigma X = 27$ and $N = 4$.

To use summation notation, you should realize that the summation sign Σ is always followed by a symbol or mathematical expression. The symbol or expression identifies exactly which values are to be summed. To compute ΣX, for example, the symbol following the summation sign is X, and the task is to find the sum of the X values. On the other hand, to compute $\Sigma(X - 1)^2$, the summation sign is followed by a relatively complex mathematical expression, so your first task is to calculate all of the $(X - 1)^2$ values and then sum the results. In general, the best strategy for using summation notation is to proceed as follows:

1. Identify the symbol or expression following the summation sign.

2. Use the symbol or expression as a column heading and list in the column all of the values corresponding to the symbol or all of the values calculated for the expression.

3. Finally, you sum the values in the column.

If you are not sure how to perform the operations specified by a mathematical expression, you should turn to the section on "Order of Operations" in the Math Review Appendix (p. A-3).

Some specific examples of summation notation and some of the rules for using this notation are summarized as follows. We will illustrate these rules by creating computational tables. These tables contain columns for the variable (or variables) and each computational step.

1. When there are two variables (X and Y), ΣX indicates the sum of the Xs, and ΣY refers to the sum of the Ys. For the following data, $\Sigma X = 16$ and $\Sigma Y = 34$:

X	Y	
3	10	$\Sigma X = 3 + 1 + 7 + 3 + 2 = 16$
1	4	
7	6	$\Sigma Y = 10 + 4 + 6 + 5 + 9 = 34$
3	5	
2	9	

2. All the mathematical operations contained within parentheses are considered parts of one expression and should be completed before summing.

good

   For example, to compute $\Sigma(X - 1)$, you must first subtract 1 point from each score (the operation within parentheses) and then sum the resulting values. This process is demonstrated for the following scores:

X	$(X - 1)$
3	2
1	0
7	6
4	3
	11 $= \Sigma(X - 1)$

Note that we have constructed a computational table to help find the desired sum. The first column lists all the original X values. The second column is added for the $(X - 1)$ values. The sum is obtained by adding the values in the second column.

3. All values that are multiplied together or squared are considered to be parts of one expression. Thus, you should complete all multiplying or squaring before summing.

   When two variables (X and Y) are multiplied together, the product is represented by the symbols XY. Note that the multiplication sign is not written between the symbols ($X \times Y$ can cause confusion). The expression XY is understood to mean "X times Y." The table in the margin shows scores for three individuals. For each person, there is a score for variable X, a score for variable Y, and the product of the two scores, XY.

good

   The total for the X values, $\Sigma X = 9$, is obtained by adding the scores in that column, and the sum of the Y values, $\Sigma Y = 8$, is obtained by adding the Y column. The expression ΣXY means "sum the products of X and Y." The first step is to compute the product for each pair of X and Y scores. These products are displayed in the column headed by XY. In the second step, the products are added together. For this example, the sum of the products is $\Sigma XY = 23$:

X	Y	XY
2	4	8
3	1	3
4	3	12

$$\Sigma XY = 8 + 3 + 12 = 23$$

1.3 COMPUTING ΣX^2 WITH A CALCULATOR

THE SUM of squared scores, ΣX^2, is a common expression in many statistical calculations. The following steps outline the most efficient procedure for using a typical, inexpensive hand calculator to find this sum. We assume that your calculator has one memory where you can store and retrieve information. *Caution:* The following instructions work for most calculators, but not for every single model. If you encounter trouble, don't panic—check your manual or talk with your instructor.

1. Clear the calculator memory. You may press the memory-clear key (usually MC) or simply turn the calculator off and then back on.

2. Enter the first score.

3. Press the multiply key ($\times$); then press the equals key ($=$). The squared score should appear in the display.

(Note that you do not need to enter a number twice to square it. Just follow the sequence: number-times-equals.)

4. Put the squared value into the calculator memory. For most calculators, you press the key labeled M+.

5. Enter the next score, square it, and add it to memory (steps 2, 3, and 4). (Note that you do not need to clear the display between scores.)

6. Continue this process for the full set of scores. Then retrieve the total (ΣX^2) from memory by pressing the memory-recall key (usually labeled MR).

Check this procedure with a simple set of scores, such as 1, 2, 3. You should find $\Sigma X^2 = 14$.

It is very important to note that ΣXY *does not equal* $\Sigma X \Sigma Y$. The latter expression means "the sum of X times the sum of Y." For these data, it is easy to demonstrate that the two expressions are not the same:

$$\Sigma XY \neq \Sigma X \Sigma Y$$

$$23 \neq 9(8)$$

$$23 \neq 72$$

The squared value of a score is represented by the symbol X^2. If every score in the group is squared, then a new column of squared values can be listed as shown in the margin.

The expression ΣX^2 means the sum of the squared scores. Each score is first squared, and then the sum is found for the squared values (see Box 1.3). In this example, adding the X^2 column reveals that

$$\Sigma X^2 = 9 + 1 + 16 + 4 = 30$$

Be careful! The symbol $(\Sigma X)^2$ represents a different order of operations, and the resulting value is not the same as that of ΣX^2. The operations inside the parentheses are performed first. Therefore, the sum of the Xs is determined first. The exponent is outside the parentheses, so the squaring is done last. The expression $(\Sigma X)^2$ means the *squared total*. In the example, this value is

Remember, when a number is squared, it is multiplied by itself. A common mistake is to multiply a number by 2 instead of squaring it.

X	X^2
3	9
1	1
4	16
2	4

$$(\Sigma X)^2 = (10)^2 = 100$$

Therefore, $(\Sigma X)^2$ is *not the same* expression as ΣX^2. It is very important to remember the order of operations for these two expressions. Later we will have to use statistical formulas that contain both of these expressions. It is imperative that you not confuse one with the other.

4. When the expression following a summation sign involves parentheses and multiplication/squaring, you first complete the calculations within the parentheses, then perform the multiplication or squaring, and then sum. Usually it is wise to perform this sequence of mathematical operations in a series of steps using a computational table with a separate column representing each step in the calculation. To compute $\Sigma(X - 1)^2$, for example, the first step is to compute $(X - 1)$ for each individual. The next step is to square each of the $(X - 1)$ values. Finally, you sum the squared values. This process is demonstrated in the following example.

good ex

X	$(X - 1)$	$(X - 1)^2$
3	2	4
1	0	0
7	6	36
4	3	9

The first column lists the original scores. The second column lists the $(X - 1)$ values, and the third column shows the squared values. The problem asks for the sum of the squared values:

$$\Sigma(X - 1)^2 = 4 + 0 + 36 + 9 = 49$$

5. Without parentheses, the mathematical expression following a summation sign *ends at a plus or minus sign (+ or −).*

For example, to compute $\Sigma X - 1$, you would sum only the X values and then subtract 1 point from the total.

good

X
3
1
7
4
$15 = \Sigma X$

For these data, $\Sigma X - 1 = 15 - 1 = 14$

LEARNING CHECK   For the following data, find the values for the listed expressions.

X	Y
3	1
3	2
1	1
2	3
4	5

1. ΣX **2.** ΣX^2 **3.** $(\Sigma X)^2$ **4.** $\Sigma(Y + 3)$ **5.** $(\Sigma Y)^2$

6. $\Sigma X \Sigma Y$ **7.** ΣXY **8.** N for the X scores

ANSWERS   **1.** 13   **2.** 39   **3.** 169   **4.** 27   **5.** 144   **6.** 156   **7.** 36   **8.** 5

A WORD ABOUT COMPUTERS

Long before desktop computers became commonplace at home, they were routinely used in statistics. The computer can make short work of the statistical analysis of large data sets and can eliminate the tedium that goes along with complex and repetitive computations. As the use of computers became widespread, so did the availability of statistical software packages. The typical software package contains a variety of specialized programs, each one capable of performing a specific type of statistical procedure. The user enters the data to be analyzed and then specifies the analysis to be used with one or more software commands.

There are many useful and popular statistical software packages, all differing in their ease of operation, command structure, sophistication, and breadth of coverage of statistical analyses. Two software manuals have been prepared to accompany this book.

Minitab Manual. Minitab is a statistical package that is widely available on large computers as well as desktop (DOS compatible and Macintosh) computers. It is easy to master—or, in computer terms, "user friendly"—and it serves as a good model for many other statistics programs. The manual presents instruction on how to use Minitab and includes demonstrations of Minitab as it is used for many of the specific examples contained in other chapters throughout this book. As you work through the book, you will find computer symbols in the margins (see marginal note) with references to specific sections of the manual. There you will find instructions on how to use Minitab to perform the statistical procedure that is discussed in the text.

Mystat Manual. Mystat is a very easy to use statistical program written for the desktop computer and is available on disk as an optional feature with this text. For courses using this option, the manual provides information and demonstrations for using Mystat. Computer symbols (see marginal note) reference sections of the manual devoted to Mystat.

SPSS Manual. This software is a sophisticated package of programs capable of performing many of the statistical analyses covered in this text and many more-advanced procedures as well. It commonly is used by researchers in the social and behavioral sciences. Again, computer symbols are used to reference the manual.

This computer symbol will be used throughout the book to direct you to additional information or examples for the Minitab, Mystat, and SPSS computer programs. The symbol will be accompanied by a reference to a section in one of the manuals.

While we are on the topic of computers and statistics, the authors cannot resist an editorial comment. Many students have approached us with this question: If computers are so good at doing statistical calculations, why not just teach us how to use the computer and forget about teaching us statistics? This question usually is followed with an accurate observation: If I should get a job where I need to use statistics, I probably will just use a computer anyway.

Although there are many ways to respond to these comments, we will try to limit ourselves to one or two general ideas. The purpose of this book is to help you gain an understanding of statistics. Notice that we used the word *understanding*. Although computers can do statistics with incredible speed and accuracy, they are not capable of exercising any judgment or interpreting the material that you feed into them (input) or the results that they produce (output). Too often students (and researchers) rely on computers to perform difficult calculations and have no idea of what the computer is actually doing. In some fields, this lack of understanding is acceptable—we are all allowed to use the telephone even if we do not understand how it works. But in scientific research, it is critical that you have a complete and accurate understanding of your data. Usually this requires an understanding of the statistical techniques used to summarize and interpret data. So use your computer and enjoy it, but do not rely on it for statistical expertise.

SUMMARY

1. By common usage, the word *statistics* means facts and figures. In this book the word is generally used in reference to techniques and procedures for analyzing data.

2. Science is empirical in that it provides methods for making observations. Statistics consist of methods for organizing and interpreting data.

3. A population is composed of every individual from the group one wishes to study. A sample is a group selected from the population. Samples are drawn from the population for study because the population in question is usually so large that it is not feasible to study every individual in it.

4. Descriptive statistics simplify and summarize data, so that the data are more manageable. Inferential statistics are techniques that allow one to use sample data to make general statements about a population. Meaningful generalizations are possible only if the sample is representative of the population from which it was drawn. Random sampling helps ensure that it is representative.

5. A correlational method looks for interrelationships between variables, but cannot determine the cause-and-effect nature of the relationship. The experimental method is able to establish causes and effects in a relationship. The quasi-experimental method involves comparing different groups where the group differences are based on a pre-existing subject variable or measurements obtained at different times.

6. With the experimental method, one variable (the independent variable) is intentionally manipulated by the experimenter. Then changes are noted in another variable (the dependent variable) as a result of the manipulation.

7. A hypothesis is a prediction about the effect of an independent variable on a dependent variable. Hypotheses are usually derived from theories. Experiments basically involve the test of a hypothesis.

8. Constructs are hypothetical concepts used in theories to describe the mechanisms of behavior. Because they are hypothetical, they cannot be observed. Constructs are studied by providing operational definitions for them. An operational definition defines a construct in terms of an observable and measurable response or event.

9. A nominal scale labels observations so that they fall into different categories. A nominal scale involves making qualitative distinctions. No attempt is made to measure the magnitude of the event.

10. An ordinal scale involves ranking observations in terms of size or magnitude. Although this scale will tell us which observation is larger, it will not tell us how much larger it is.

11. With an interval scale, intervals between numbers reflect differences in magnitude of observations. It is possible to determine which event is of greater magnitude and how much larger it is.

12. A ratio scale has all of the characteristics of an interval scale, and ratios of measurements on this scale reflect ratios of magnitudes. Unlike the interval scale, a ratio scale has an absolute zero point.

13. A discrete variable is one that can have only a finite number of values between any two values. It typically consists of whole numbers that vary in countable steps. A continuous variable can have an infinite number of values between any two values.

14. For a continuous variable, each score corresponds to an interval on the scale. The boundaries that separate intervals are called real limits. The real limits are located exactly halfway between adjacent scores.

15. The letter X is used to represent scores for a variable. If a second variable is used, Y represents its scores. The letter N is used as the symbol for the number of scores in a set. The Greek letter sigma (Σ) is used to stand for summation. Therefore, the expression ΣX is read "the sum of the scores."

KEY TERMS

statistics	random selection	control group	ordinal scale
population	variable	experimental group	interval scale
sample	constant	confounding variable	ratio scale
population parameter	correlational method	quasi-independent variable	discrete variable
sample statistic	experimental method	hypothesis	continuous variable
descriptive statistics	quasi-experimental method	construct	real limits
raw score	independent variable	operational definition	upper real limit
inferential statistics	dependent variable	nominal scale	lower real limit

FOCUS ON PROBLEM SOLVING

1. It may help to simplify summation notation if you observe that the summation sign is always followed by a symbol (or symbolic expression)—for example, ΣX or $\Sigma (X + 3)$. This symbol specifies which values you are to add. If you use the symbol as a column heading and list all the appropriate values in the column, your task is simply to add up the numbers in the column. To find $\Sigma (X + 3)$ for example, start a column headed with $(X + 3)$ next to the column of Xs. List all the $(X + 3)$ values; then find the total for the column.

2. To use summation notation correctly, you must be careful of two other factors:
   a. When you are determining the "symbol" that follows the summation sign, remember that everything within parentheses is part of the same symbol, for example, $\Sigma (X + 3)$, and a string of multiplied values is considered to be a single symbol, for example, ΣXY.
   b. Often it is necessary to use several intermediate columns before you can reach the column of values specified by a particular symbol. To compute $\Sigma (X - 1)^2$, for example, you will need three columns: first, the column of original scores, X's; second, a column of $(X - 1)$ values; third, a column of squared $(X - 1)$ values. It is the third column, headed by $(X - 1)^2$, that you should total.

DEMONSTRATION 1.1

SUMMATION NOTATION

A set of data consists of the following scores:

$$7 \quad 3 \quad 9 \quad 5 \quad 4$$

For these data, find the following values:

    a. ΣX **b.** $(\Sigma X)^2$ **c.** ΣX^2 **d.** $\Sigma X + 5$ **e.** $\Sigma(X - 2)$

Compute ΣX   To compute ΣX, we simply add all of the scores in the group. For these data, we obtain

$$\Sigma X = 7 + 3 + 9 + 5 + 4 = 28$$

Compute $(\Sigma X)^2$ The key to determining the value of $(\Sigma X)^2$ is the presence of parentheses. The rule is to perform the operations that are inside the parentheses first.

STEP 1   Find the sum of the scores, ΣX.

STEP 2   Square the total.
      We have already determined that ΣX is 28. Squaring this total, we obtain

$$(\Sigma X)^2 = (28)^2 = 784$$

Compute ΣX^2   Calculating the sum of the squared scores, ΣX^2, involves two steps.

STEP 1   Square each score.

STEP 2   Sum the squared values.
      These steps are most easily accomplished by constructing a computational table. The first column has the heading X and lists the scores. The second column is labeled X^2 and contains the squared values for each score. For this example, the table is as follows:

X	X^2
7	49
3	9
9	81
5	25
4	16

To find the value for ΣX^2, we sum the X^2 column.

$$\Sigma X^2 = 49 + 9 + 81 + 25 + 16 = 180$$

Compute $\Sigma X + 5$ In this expression, there are no parentheses. Thus, the summation sign is applied only to the X values.

STEP 1   Find the sum of X.

STEP 2   Add the constant 5 to the total from Step 1.

Earlier we found that the sum of the scores is 28. For $\Sigma X + 5$, we obtain the following.

$$\Sigma X + 5 = 28 + 5 = 33$$

Compute $\Sigma(X - 2)$ The summation sign is followed by an expression with parentheses. In this case, $X - 2$ is treated as a single expression, and the summation sign applies to the $(X - 2)$ values.

STEP 1   Subtract 2 from every score.

STEP 2   Sum these new values.

This problem can be done by using a computational table with two columns, headed X and $X - 2$, respectively.

X	$X - 2$
7	5
3	1
9	7
5	3
4	2

To determine the value for $\Sigma(X - 2)$, we sum the $X - 2$ column.

$$\Sigma(X - 2) = 5 + 1 + 7 + 3 + 2 = 18$$

DEMONSTRATION 1.2

SUMMATION NOTATION WITH TWO VARIABLES

The following data consist of pairs of scores (X and Y) for four individuals:

X	Y
5	8
2	10
3	11
7	2

Determine the values for the following expressions:

a. $\Sigma X \Sigma Y$ b. ΣXY

Compute $\Sigma X \Sigma Y$ This expression indicates that we should multiply the sum of X by the sum of Y.

STEP 1 Find the sum of X.

STEP 2 Find the sum of Y.

STEP 3 Multiply the results of steps 1 and 2.
First, we find the sum of X.

$$\Sigma X = 5 + 2 + 3 + 7 = 17$$

Next we compute the sum of Y.

$$\Sigma Y = 8 + 10 + 11 + 2 = 31$$

Finally, we multiply these two totals.

$$\Sigma X \Sigma Y = 17(31) = 527$$

Compute ΣXY Now we are asked to find the sum of the products of X and Y.

STEP 1 Find the XY products.

STEP 2 Sum the products.
The computations are facilitated by using a third column labeled XY.

X	Y	XY
5	8	40
2	10	20
3	11	33
7	2	14

For these data, the sum of the XY products is

$$\Sigma XY = 40 + 20 + 33 + 14 = 107$$

PROBLEMS

*1. Describe the general purposes of descriptive statistics and inferential statistics.

2. Define the terms *population* and *sample,* and explain how each of these is involved in the process of scientific research.

3. Identify the basic characteristics that distinguish the experimental method from other research strategies.

4. Define the concept of *sampling error.* Be sure that your definition includes the concepts of *statistic* and *parameter.*

5. In general, research attempts to establish and explain relationships between variables. What terms are used to identify the two variables in an experiment? Define each term.

6. A researcher reports that individuals given a special diet containing large amounts of oat bran had substantially lower cholesterol levels than individuals placed on a diet with no oat bran. For this study, identify the independent variable and the dependent variable.

7. A developmental psychologist conducts a research study comparing vocabulary skill for 5-year-old boys versus 5-year-old girls.

---

*Solutions for odd-numbered problems are provided in Appendix C.

a. Does this study use the experimental, correlational, or quasi-experimental method?

b. What is the dependent variable for this study?

8. A researcher studying sensory processes manipulates the loudness of a buzzer and measures how quickly subjects respond to the sound at different levels of intensity. Identify the independent and dependent variables for this study.

9. A researcher would like to evaluate the claim that large doses of vitamin C can help prevent the common cold. One group of subjects is given a large dose of the vitamin (500 mg per day), and a second group is given a placebo (sugar pill). The researcher records whether or not each individual experiences a severe cold during the 3-month winter season. For this study:

a. Identify the dependent variable.

b. Is the dependent variable discrete or continuous?

c. What scale of measurement (nominal, ordinal, interval, ratio) is used to measure the dependent variable?

d. What research method is being used (experimental, correlational, quasi-experimental)?

10. A questionnaire asks individuals to report age, sex, eye-color, and height. For each of the four variables,

a. Classify the variable as either discrete or continuous.

b. Identify the scale of measurement that probably would be used.

11. A researcher measures two individuals and then uses the resulting scores to make a statement comparing the two individuals. For each of the following statements, identify the scale of measurement (nominal, ordinal, interval, ratio) that the researcher used.

a. I can only say that the two individuals are different.

b. I can say that one individual scored 6 points higher than the other.

c. I can say that one individual scored higher than the other, but I cannot specify how much higher.

d. I can say that the score for one individual is twice as large as the score for the other individual.

12. Define and differentiate between a discrete variable and a continuous variable.

13. A researcher studying the effects of environment on mood asks subjects to sit alone in a waiting room for 15 minutes at the beginning of an experiment. Half of the subjects are assigned to a room with dark blue walls, and the other half are assigned to a room with bright yellow walls. After 15 minutes in the waiting room, each subject is brought into the lab and given a mood-assessment questionnaire. The scores on the mood questionnaire are then examined.

a. Identify the independent and dependent variables for this study.

b. What scale of measurement is used for the independent variable?

14. Three researchers are evaluating taste preferences among three leading brands of cola. After subjects taste each brand, the first researcher simply asks each subject to identify his/her favorite. The second researcher asks each subject to identify the most preferred, the second most preferred, and the least preferred. The third researcher asks each subject to rate each of the colas on a 10-point scale, where a rating of 1 indicates "terrible taste" and 10 indicates "excellent taste." Identify the scale of measurement used by each researcher.

15. A researcher records the number of errors each subject makes while performing a standardized problem-solving task.

a. Is the researcher measuring a discrete or a continuous variable?

b. What scale of measurement is being used?

16. Define and differentiate between a construct and an operational definition.

17. For the following scores, find the value of each expression:

a. ΣX

b. ΣX^2

c. $(\Sigma X)^2$

d. $\Sigma(X - 1)$

X
4
2
6
1

18. Two scores, X and Y, are recorded for each of $n = 4$ subjects. For these scores, find the value of each expression.

a. ΣX

b. ΣY

c. ΣXY

SUBJECT	X	Y
A	3	2
B	4	1
C	2	3
D	6	4

19. Use summation notation to express each of the following calculations:

a. Sum the scores, and then add 3 points to the total.

b. Subtract 2 points from each score, and square the result. Then sum the squared values.

c. Square each score, and sum the squared values. Then subtract 10 points from the sum.

20. Each of the following summation expressions requires a specific sequence of mathematical operations. For each expression, state in words the sequence of operations necessary to perform the specified calculations. For example, the expression $\Sigma(X + 1)$ instructs you to add 1 point to each score and then sum the resulting values.

a. $\Sigma X - 4$

b. ΣX^2

c. $\Sigma(X + 4)^2$

21. For the following set of scores, find the value of each expression:
  a. ΣX
  b. ΣX^2
  c. $\Sigma(X + 1)$
  d. $\Sigma(X + 1)^2$

X
1
3
0
5

22. For the following set of scores, find the value of each expression:
  a. ΣX
  b. ΣX^2
  c. $\Sigma(X + 3)$

X
3
-2
0
-1
-4

23. For the following set of scores, find the value of each expression:
  a. ΣX
  b. ΣY
  c. ΣXY

X	Y
-2	4
0	5
3	2
-4	3

24. For the following set of scores, find the value of each expression:
  a. ΣX^2
  b. $(\Sigma X)^2$
  c. $\Sigma(X - 5)$
  d. $\Sigma(X - 5)^2$

X
7
4
10
3
1

25. These calculations are examples of formulas that you will encounter in later chapters. Use the following sample of $N = 4$ scores to practice the formulas now.
  a. $\dfrac{\Sigma X}{N}$
  b. $\Sigma(X - 4)$
  c. $\Sigma(X - 4)^2$
  d. $\Sigma X^2 - \dfrac{(\Sigma X)^2}{N}$

X
6
1
4
5

CHAPTER 2

FREQUENCY DISTRIBUTIONS

Reading a textbook is much different from a reading a novel or a newspaper. With a textbook, your goal is to study and to learn the material, not simply to entertain yourself. As a result, you must work to identify and understand the important points. You must take time to digest the material, and it helps to stop and question yourself regularly to be sure that you fully comprehend what you are reading. All this may sound like the same old "how to study" lecture that you probably have heard a hundred times by now. But it is true, and it works.

Experiments have demonstrated that reading strategy can significantly affect comprehension and test performance. In 1974, John Boker presented college students with long passages (2500 words) selected from college-level texts (Boker, 1974). One group of students served as a control group and simply read straight through the material from beginning to end. For the experimental group, the passage was divided into 10 sections, each about 250 words, and the students were presented with questions at the end of each section. A week later, both groups were given a 40-question multiple-choice test covering the passage they had read. Hypothetical data similar to those obtained by Boker are shown in Table 2.1.

From looking at the data in Table 2.1, does it appear that one group did better than the other? Because these data are not organized in any systematic way, you probably find it difficult to discern any differences. This is a basic problem confronting any researcher after data are collected. To make sense of the experiment, you must organize the mass of numbers into a simpler form so that it is possible to "see" what happened. One solution is to present the scores in an organized table or a graph. Figure 2.1 shows the same data that are in Table 2.1, but now they are simplified and organized in a graph. Looking at the figure, does it appear that one group did better than the other?

It should be clear that graphing these data makes it easy to see the difference between two groups. The students who read the passage with interspersed questions performed much better on the test—about 5 points better, which is quite a bit on a 40-question test.

There are two important points to be learned from this discussion. First, you should appreciate the value of simplifying and organizing a set of data. By structuring the data properly, it becomes possible to see at a glance what happened in an experiment. This helps researchers to decide exactly how the data should be analyzed and interpreted, and it helps others to understand the significance of the experiment. In this chapter, we will examine several statistical techniques for organizing data. The second point concerns the implications

TABLE 2.1

Hypothetical Data from an Experiment Comparing Two Strategies for Studying College Textbook Material*

CONTROL GROUP		EXPERIMENTAL GROUP	
25	32	28	29
27	20	25	31
28	23	31	19
17	21	29	35
24	34	30	28
22	29	24	30
24	25	33	27
21	18	34	26
19	22	29	29
30	24	27	32
26	27	30	36
24	23	22	23
23	25	32	33

*The experimental group had questions interspersed through the material as they were reading. The control group read through the material without seeing any questions. One week later both groups were given a 40-item multiple-choice test on the material they had read. The data given are the scores on this test.

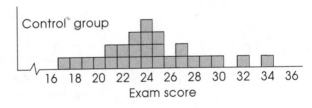

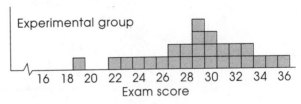

FIGURE 2.1

The two graphs show the same data listed in Table 2.1. In these graphs, each student is represented by a block that is placed directly above his or her exam score. Notice that the experimental group generally performed better than the control group. For students in the experimental group, the exam scores pile up around $X = 29$. For the control group, the scores pile up around $X = 24$.

of Boker's experiment. The way you study can have a tremendous influence on what you learn. As you read through
this book, you will find lots of sample problems in the examples and learning checks that appear in each chapter. Take
time to work through these problems, answer the questions,
and test yourself. A little extra time and effort can increase
your understanding of the material, and it can improve your
grade.

2.1 OVERVIEW

When a researcher finishes the data collection phase of an experiment, the results
usually consist of pages of numbers. The immediate problem for the researcher is
to organize the scores into some comprehensible form so that any trends in the
data can be seen easily and communicated to others. This is the job of descriptive
statistics: to simplify the organization and presentation of data. One of the most
common procedures for organizing a set of data is to place the scores in a frequency distribution.

DEFINITION   A *frequency distribution* is an organized tabulation of the number of individuals located in each category on the scale of measurement.

A frequency distribution takes a disorganized set of scores and places them in
order from highest to lowest, grouping together all individuals who have the same
score. If the highest score is $X = 10$, for example, the frequency distribution groups
together all the 10s, then all the 9s, then the 8s, and so on. Thus, a frequency distribution allows the researcher to see "at a glance" the entire set of scores. It shows
whether the scores are generally high or low and whether they are concentrated in
one area or spread out across the entire scale and generally provides an organized
picture of the data. In addition to providing a picture of the entire set of scores, a
frequency distribution allows you to see the location of any individual score relative to all of the other scores in the set.

Frequency distributions can be structured as either tables or graphs, but both
show the original measurement scale and the frequencies associated with each category. Thus, they present a picture of how the individual scores are distributed on
the measurement scale—hence the name *frequency distribution*.

2.2 FREQUENCY DISTRIBUTION TABLES

It is customary to list scores from highest
to lowest, but this is an arbitrary arrangement. Many computer programs will list
scores from lowest to highest.

The simplest frequency distribution table presents the measurement scale by listing
the different measurement categories (X values) in a column from highest to lowest. Beside each X value, we indicate the frequency, or the number of times that
particular measurement occurred in the data. It is customary to use an X as the
column heading for the scores and an f as the column heading for the frequencies.
An example of a frequency distribution table follows.

EXAMPLE 2.1 The following set of $N = 20$ scores was obtained from a 10-point statistics quiz. We will organize these scores by constructing a frequency distribution table. Scores:

$$8, \quad 9, \quad 8, \quad 7, \quad 10, \quad 9, \quad 6, \quad 4, \quad 9, \quad 8$$

$$7, \quad 8, \quad 10, \quad 9, \quad 8, \quad 6, \quad 9, \quad 7, \quad 8, \quad 8$$

X	f
10	2
9	5
8	7
7	3
6	2
5	0
4	1

1. The highest score is $X = 10$, and the lowest score is $X = 4$. Therefore, the first column of the table will list the scale of measurement (X values) from 10 down to 4. Notice that all of the possible values are listed in the table. For example, no one had a score of $X = 5$, but this value is included. With an ordinal, interval, or ratio scale, the X values are listed in order (usually highest to lowest). For a nominal scale, the X values can be listed in any order.

2. The frequency associated with each score is recorded in the second column. For example, two people had scores of $X = 6$, so there is a 2 in the column f column beside $X = 6$.

Because the table organizes the scores, it is possible to see very quickly the general quiz results. For example, there were only two perfect scores, but most of the class had high grades (8s and 9s). With one exception (the score of $X = 4$), it appears that the class has learned the material fairly well.

Notice that the X values in a frequency distribution table represent the scale of measurement, *not* the actual set of scores. For example, the X column lists the value 10 only one time, but the frequency column indicates that there are actually two values of $X = 10$. Also, the X column lists a value of $X = 5$, but the frequency column indicates that actually there are no scores of $X = 5$.

You also should notice that the frequencies can be used to find the total number of scores in the distribution. By adding up the frequencies, you will obtain the total number of individuals:

$$\Sigma f = N$$

Software Manuals:
Minitab (section 4)
Mystat (section 3)
SPSS (section 6)

OBTAINING ΣX FROM A FREQUENCY DISTRIBUTION TABLE

There may be times when you need to compute the sum of the scores, ΣX, for data in a frequency distribution table. This procedure presents a problem because many students are tempted simply to add the values listed in the X column of the table. However, this practice is incorrect because it ignores the information provided by the frequency (f) column. To calculate ΣX from a frequency distribution table, you must use both the X and the f columns.

Consider the frequency distribution table for Example 2.1. It tells us that the distribution has two 10s, five 9s, seven 8s, and so on. Therefore, you can obtain the total for X by first reconstructing the original distribution and then adding all the X values (compute ΣX): $10 + 10 + 9 + 9 + 9 + 9 + 9 + 8 + 8 + 8 + 8 + 8 + 8 + 8 + \ldots$. For the data in Example 2.1, $\Sigma X = 158$. Try it yourself.

An alternative way to get ΣX from a frequency distribution table is to multiply each X value by its frequency and then add these products. This sum may be expressed in symbols as ΣfX. The computation is summarized as follows for the data in Example 2.1:

X	f	fX	
10	2	20	(The two 10s total 20)
9	5	45	(The five 9s total 45)
8	7	56	(The seven 8s total 56)
7	3	21	(The three 7s total 21)
6	2	12	(The two 6s total 12)
5	0	0	(There are no 5s)
4	1	4	(The one 4 totals 4)

$$\Sigma fX = 158$$

In using either method to find ΣX, by reconstructing the distribution or by computing ΣfX, the important point is that you must use the information given in the frequency column.

PROPORTIONS AND PERCENTAGES

In addition to the two basic columns of a frequency distribution, there are other measures that describe the distribution of scores and can be incorporated into the table. The two most common are proportion and percentage.

Proportion measures the fraction of the total group that is associated with each score. In Example 2.1, there were two individuals with $X = 6$. Thus, 2 out of 20 people had $X = 6$, so the proportion would be $2/20 = 0.10$. In general, the proportion associated with each score is

$$\text{proportion} = p = \frac{f}{N}$$

Because proportions describe the frequency (f) in relation to the total number (N), they often are called *relative frequencies*. Although proportions can be expressed as fractions (for example, $2/20$), they more commonly appear as decimals. A column of proportions, headed with a p, can be added to the basic frequency distribution table (see Example 2.2).

In addition to using frequencies (f) and proportions (p), researchers often describe a distribution of scores with percentages. For example, an instructor might describe the results of an exam by saying that 15% of the class earned *A*s, 23% *B*s, and so on. To compute the percentage associated with each score, you first find the proportion (p) and then multiply by 100:

$$\text{percentage} = p(100) = \frac{f}{N}(100)$$

Percentages can be included in a frequency distribution table by adding a column headed with % (see Example 2.2).

EXAMPLE 2.2

The frequency distribution table from Example 2.1 is repeated here. This time we have added columns showing the proportion (p) and the percentage (%) associated with each score.

X	f	p = f/N	% = p(100)
10	2	2/20 = 0.10	10%
9	5	5/20 = 0.25	25%
8	7	7/20 = 0.35	35%
7	3	3/20 = 0.15	15%
6	2	2/20 = 0.10	10%
5	0	0/20 = 0	0%
4	1	1/20 = 0.05	5%

GROUPED FREQUENCY DISTRIBUTION TABLES

When a set of data covers a wide range of values, it is unreasonable to list all the individual scores in a frequency distribution table. For example, a set of exam scores ranges from a low of $X = 41$ to a high of $X = 96$. These scores cover a range of over 50 points.

If we were to list all the individual scores, it would take 56 rows to complete the frequency distribution table. Although this would organize and simplify the data, the table would be long and cumbersome. Additional simplification would be desirable. This is accomplished by dividing the range of scores into intervals and then listing these intervals in the frequency distribution table. For example, we could construct a table showing the number of students who had scores in the 90s, the number with scores in the 80s, and so on. The result is called a *grouped frequency distribution table* because we are presenting groups of scores, rather than individual values. The groups, or intervals, are called *class intervals*.

There are several rules that help guide you in the construction of a grouped frequency distribution table. These rules should be considered as guidelines, rather than absolute requirements, but they do help produce a simple, well-organized, and easily understood table.

When the X values are whole numbers, the number of rows in the table can be obtained by finding the difference between the highest and the lowest scores and adding 1:

$$rows = highest - lowest + 1$$

RULE 1 The grouped frequency distribution table should have about 10 class intervals. If a table has many more than 10 intervals, it becomes cumbersome and defeats the purpose of a frequency distribution table. On the other hand, if you have too few intervals, you begin to lose information about the distribution of the scores. At the extreme, with only one interval, the table would not tell you anything about how the scores are distributed. Remember, the purpose of a frequency distribution is to help a researcher see the data. With too few or too many intervals, the table will not provide a clear picture. You should note that 10 intervals is a general guide. If you are constructing a table on a blackboard, for example, you probably will want only 5 or 6 intervals. If the table is to be printed in a scientific report, you may want 12 or 15 intervals. In each case, your goal is to present a table that is relatively easy to see and understand.

RULE 2 The width of each interval should be a relatively simple number. For example, 2, 5, 10, or 20 would be a good choice for the interval width. Notice that it is easy to count by 5s or 10s. These numbers are easy to understand and make it possible for someone to see quickly how you have divided the range.

RULE 3 The bottom score in each class interval should be a multiple of the width. If you are using a width of 10 points, for example, the intervals should start with 10, 20, 30, 40, and so on. Again, this makes it easier for someone to understand how the table has been constructed.

RULE 4 All intervals should be the same width. They should cover the range of scores completely with no gaps and no overlaps, so that any particular score belongs in exactly one interval.

The application of these rules is demonstrated in Example 2.3.

EXAMPLE 2.3 An instructor has obtained the set of $N = 25$ exam scores shown here. To help organize these scores, we will place them in a frequency distribution table. Scores:

82, 75, 88, 93, 53, 84, 87, 58, 72, 94, 69, 84, 61

91, 64, 87, 84, 70, 76, 89, 75, 80, 73, 78, 60

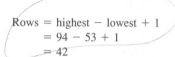

Rows = highest − lowest + 1
     = 94 − 53 + 1
     = 42

The first step is to examine the range of scores. For these data, the smallest score is $X = 53$, and the largest score is $X = 94$, so 42 rows would be needed for a table. Because it would require 42 rows to list each individual score in a frequency distribution table, we will have to group the scores into class intervals.

The best method for determining the appropriate interval width is to use rules 1 and 2 simultaneously. According to Rule 1, we want about 10 intervals; according to Rule 2, we want the width to be a simple number. If we try a width of 2, how many intervals would it take to cover the range of scores? With each interval only 2 points wide, we would need 21 intervals to cover the range. This is too many. What about an interval width of 5? What about a width of 10? The following table shows how many intervals would be needed for these possible widths:

WIDTH	NUMBER OF INTERVALS NEEDED TO COVER A RANGE OF 42 VALUES	
2	21	(too many)
5	9	(OK)
10	5	(too few)

Notice that an interval width of 5 will result in about 10 intervals, which is exactly what we want.

The next step is to actually identify the intervals. The lowest score for these data is $X = 53$, so the lowest interval should contain this value. Because the interval should have a multiple of 5 as its bottom score, the interval would be 50 to 54. Notice that the interval contains five values (50, 51, 52, 53, 54) so it does have a width of 5. The next interval would start at 55 and go to 59. The complete frequency distribution table showing all of the class intervals is presented in Table 2.2.

Once the class intervals are listed, you complete the table by adding a column of frequencies or proportions or percentages. The values in the frequency column indicate the number of individuals whose scores are located in that class interval. For this example, there were three students with scores in the 60–64 interval, so the frequency for this class interval is $f = 3$ (see Table 2.2).

TABLE 2.2

A Grouped Frequency Distribution Table Showing the Data from Example 2.3 The original scores range from a high of $X = 94$ to a low of $X = 53$. This range has been divided into 9 intervals with each interval exactly 5 points wide. The frequency column (f) lists the number of individuals with scores in each of the class intervals.

X	f
90–94	3
85–89	4
80–84	5
75–79	4
70–74	3
65–69	1
60–64	3
55–59	1
50–54	1

REAL LIMITS AND FREQUENCY DISTRIBUTIONS

You should recall from Chapter 1 that a continuous variable has an infinite number of possible values and can be represented by a number line that is continuous and contains an infinite number of points. However, when a continuous variable is measured, the resulting measurements correspond to *intervals* on the number line rather than single points. For example, a score of $X = 8$ for a continuous variable actually represents an interval bounded by the real limits 7.5 and 8.5. Thus, a frequency distribution table showing a frequency of $f = 3$ individuals all assigned a score of $X = 8$ does not mean that all three individuals had exactly the same measurement. Instead, you should realize that the three measurements are simply located in the same interval between 7.5 and 8.5.

The concept of real limits also applies to the class intervals of a grouped frequency distribution table. For example, a class interval of 40–49 contains scores from $X = 40$ to $X = 49$. These values are called the *apparent limits* of the interval because it appears that they form the upper and lower boundaries for the class interval. But $X = 40$ is actually an interval from 39.5 to 40.5. Similarly, $X = 49$ is an interval from 48.5 to 49.5. Therefore, the real limits of the interval are 39.5 (the lower real limit) and 49.5 (the upper real limit). Notice that the next higher class interval would be 50–59, which has a lower real limit of 49.5 Thus, the two intervals meet at the real limit 49.5, so there are no gaps in the scale. You also should notice that the width of each class interval becomes easier to understand when you consider the real limits of an interval. For example, the interval 50–54 has real limits of 49.5 and 54.5. The distance between these two real limits (5 points) is the width of the interval.

LEARNING CHECK

1. Place the following scores in a frequency distribution table that shows the proportion and the percentage as well as the frequency for each score. Scores:

    2, 3, 1, 2, 5, 4, 5, 5, 1, 4, 2, 2, 5, 5, 4, 2, 3, 1, 5, 4

2. A set of scores ranges from a high of $X = 142$ to a low of $X = 65$. If these scores are to be placed in a grouped frequency distribution table, then
    a. What interval width should be used?
    b. What are the apparent limits of the bottom interval?
    c. What are the real limits of the bottom interval?

3. Explain why you should avoid having too many rows in a frequency distribution table. What is the problem with having too few rows?

ANSWERS **1.**

X	f	p	%
5	6	0.30	30%
4	4	0.20	20%
3	2	0.10	10%
2	5	0.25	25%
1	3	0.15	15%

2. a. The range would require 78 rows for a frequency distribution table. With an interval width of 5 points, you would need 16 intervals to cover the range. With an interval width of 10, you would need 8 intervals. For most purposes, a width of 10 points probably is best.

b. With a width of 10, the bottom interval would have apparent limits of 60 and 69.

c. The real limits of the bottom interval would be 59.5 and 69.5.

3. With too many rows, the table is not simple and, therefore, fails to meet the goal of descriptive statistics. With too few rows, you lose information about the distribution.

2.3 FREQUENCY DISTRIBUTION GRAPHS

A frequency distribution graph is basically a picture of the information available in a frequency distribution table. We will consider several different types of graphs, but all start with two perpendicular lines called *axes*. The horizontal line is called the *X*-axis, or the abscissa. The vertical line is called the *Y*-axis, or the ordinate. The measurement scale (set of *X* values) is listed along the *X*-axis in increasing value from left to right. The frequencies are listed on the *Y*-axis in increasing value from bottom to top. As a general rule, the point where the two axes intersect should have a value of zero for both the scores and the frequencies. A final general rule is that the graph should be constructed so that its height (*Y*-axis) is approximately two-thirds to three-quarters of its length (*X*-axis). Violating these guidelines can result in graphs that give a misleading picture of the data (see Box 2.1).

HISTOGRAMS AND BAR GRAPHS

The first type of graph we will consider is called either a histogram or a bar graph. For this type of graph, you simply draw a bar above each *X* value, so that the height of the bar corresponds to the frequency of the score. As you will see, the choice between using a histogram or a bar graph is determined by the scale of measurement.

Software Manuals:
Minitab (section 4)
Mystat (section 3)
SPSS (section 6)

Histograms When a frequency distribution graph is showing data from an interval or a ratio scale, the bars are drawn so that adjacent bars touch each other. The

FIGURE 2.2

An example of a frequency distribution histogram. The same set of data is presented in a frequency distribution table and in a histogram.

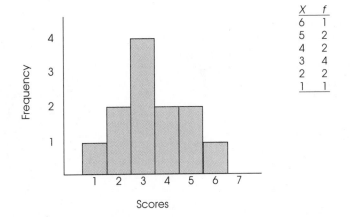

X	f
6	1
5	2
4	2
3	4
2	2
1	1

touching bars produce a continuous figure, which emphasizes the continuity of the variable. This type of frequency distribution graph is called a histogram. An example of a histogram is presented in Figure 2.2.

DEFINITION   For a *histogram,* vertical bars are drawn above each score so that

1. The height of the bar corresponds to the frequency.
2. The width of the bar extends to the real limits of the score.

A histogram is used when the data are measured on an interval or a ratio scale.

When data have been grouped into class intervals, you can construct a frequency distribution histogram by drawing a bar above each interval so that the width of the bar extends to the real limits of the interval. This process is demonstrated in Figure 2.3.

FIGURE 2.3

An example of a frequency distribution histogram for grouped data. The same set of data is presented in a grouped frequency distribution table and in a histogram.

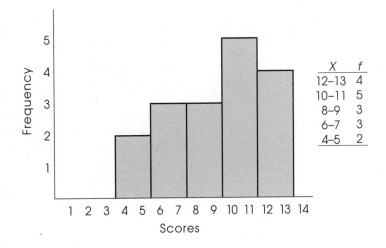

X	f
12–13	4
10–11	5
8–9	3
6–7	3
4–5	2

FIGURE 2.4

A bar graph showing the distribution of personality types in a sample of college students. Because personality type is a discrete variable measured on a nominal scale, the graph is drawn with space between the bars.

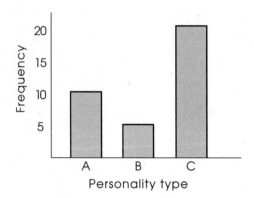

Bar graphs   When you are presenting the frequency distribution for data from a nominal or ordinal scale, the graph is constructed so that there is some space between the bars. In the case of a nominal scale, the separate bars emphasize that the scale consists of separate, distinct categories. For ordinal scales, the bar graph is used because differences between ranks do not provide information about interval size on the *X*-axis. The resulting graph is called a bar graph. An example of a frequency distribution bar graph is given in Figure 2.4.

DEFINITION

For a *bar graph,* a vertical bar is drawn above each score (or category) so that

1. The height of the bar corresponds to the frequency.
2. There is a space separating each bar from the next.

A bar graph is used when the data are measured on a nominal or an ordinal scale.

FREQUENCY DISTRIBUTION POLYGONS

Instead of a histogram, many researchers prefer to display a frequency distribution using a polygon.

DEFINITION

In a *frequency distribution polygon,* a single dot is drawn above each score so that

1. The dot is centered above the score.
2. The height of the dot corresponds to the frequency.

A continuous line is then drawn connecting these dots. The graph is completed by drawing a line down to the *X*-axis (zero frequency) at each end of the range of scores.

As with a histogram, the frequency distribution polygon is intended for use with interval or ratio scales. An example of a polygon is shown in Figure

2.1 THE USE AND MISUSE OF GRAPHS

ALTHOUGH GRAPHS are intended to provide an accurate picture of a set of data, they can be used to exaggerate or misrepresent a set of scores. These misrepresentations generally result from failing to follow the basic rules for graph construction. The following example demonstrates how the same set of data can be presented in two entirely different ways by manipulating the structure of a graph.

For the past several years, the city has kept records of the number of major felonies. The data are summarized as follows:

YEAR	NUMBER OF MAJOR FELONIES
1993	218
1994	225
1995	229

These same data are shown in two different graphs in Figure 2.5. In the first graph, we have exaggerated the height, and we started numbering the Y-axis at 210 rather than at zero. As a result, the graph seems to indicate a rapid rise in the crime rate over the 3-year period. In the second graph, we have stretched out the X-axis and used zero as the starting point for the Y-axis. The result is a graph that shows little change in the crime rate over the 3-year period.

Which graph is correct? The answer is that neither one is very good. Remember that the purpose of a graph is to provide an accurate display of the data. The first graph in figure 2.5 exaggerates the differences between years, and the second graph conceals the differences. Some compromise is needed. You also should note that in some cases a graph may not be the best way to display information. For these data, for example, showing the numbers in a table would be better than either graph.

FIGURE 2.5

Two graphs showing the number of major felonies in a city over a 3-year period. Both graphs are showing exactly the same data. However, the first graph gives the appearance that the crime rate is high and rising rapidly. The second graph gives the impression that the crime rate is low and has not changed over the 3-year period.

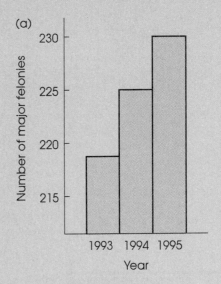

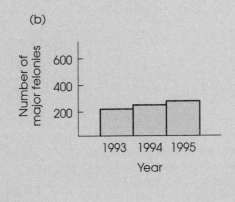

2.6. A polygon also can be used with data that have been grouped into class intervals. In this case, you position each dot directly above the midpoint of a class interval. The midpoint can be found by averaging the apparent limits of the interval or by averaging the real limits of the interval. For example, a class interval of 40–49 would have a midpoint of 44.5.

FIGURE 2.6

An example of a frequency distribution polygon. The same set of data is presented in a frequency distribution table and in a polygon. Note that these data are shown in a histogram in Figure 2.2.

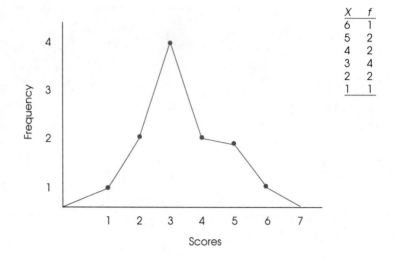

X	f
6	1
5	2
4	2
3	4
2	2
1	1

apparent limits: $\dfrac{40 + 49}{2} = \dfrac{89}{2} = 44.5$

real limits: $\dfrac{39.5 + 49.5}{2} = \dfrac{89}{2} = 44.5$

An example of a frequency distribution polygon with grouped data is shown in Figure 2.7.

RELATIVE FREQUENCIES AND SMOOTH CURVES

Often it is impossible to construct a frequency distribution for a population because there are simply too many individuals for a researcher to obtain measurements and frequencies for the entire group. In this case, it is customary to draw a frequency distribution graph showing *relative frequencies* (proportions) on the vertical axis. For example, a researcher may know that a particular species of animal

FIGURE 2.7

An example of a frequency distribution polygon for grouped data. The same set of data is presented in a grouped frequency distributition table and in a polygon. Note that these data are shown in a histogram in Figure 2.3.

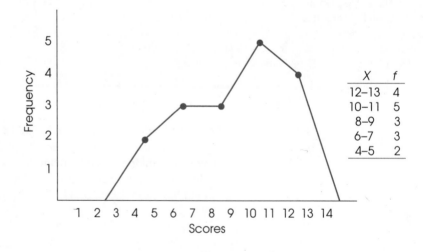

X	f
12–13	4
10–11	5
8–9	3
6–7	3
4–5	2

FIGURE 2.8

The population distribution of IQ scores: an example of a normal distribution.

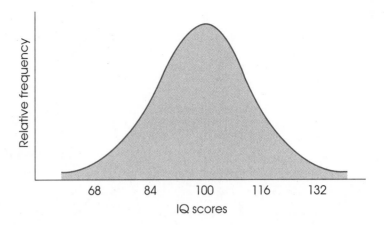

has three times as many females as males in the population. This fact could be displayed in a bar graph by simply making the bar above "female" three times as tall as the bar above "male." Notice that the actual frequencies are unknown, but that the relative frequency of males and females can still be presented in a graph.

It also is possible to use a polygon to show relative frequencies for scores in a population. In this case, it is customary to draw a smooth curve instead of the series of straight lines that normally appears in a polygon. The smooth curve indicates that you are not connecting a series of dots (real frequencies), but rather are showing a distribution that is not limited to one specific set of data. One commonly occurring population distribution is the normal curve. The word *normal* refers to a specific shape that can be precisely defined by an equation. Less precisely, we can describe a normal distribution as being symmetrical, with the greatest frequency in the middle and relatively smaller frequencies as you move toward either extreme. A good example of a normal distribution is the population distribution for IQ scores shown in Figure 2.8. Because normal-shaped distributions occur commonly and because this shape is mathematically guaranteed in certain situations, it will receive extensive attention throughout this book.

In the future, we will be referring to *distributions of scores*. Whenever the term *distribution* appears, you should conjure up an image of a frequency distribution graph. The graph provides a picture showing exactly where the individual scores are located. To make this concept more concrete, you might find it useful to think of the graph as showing a pile of individuals. In Figure 2.8, for example, the pile is highest at an IQ score of around 100 because most people have "average" IQs. There are only a few individuals piled up at an IQ score of 130; it must be lonely at the top.

2.4 THE SHAPE OF A FREQUENCY DISTRIBUTION

Rather than drawing a complete frequency distribution graph, researchers often simply describe a distribution by listing its characteristics. There are three characteristics that completely describe any distribution: shape, central tendency, and variability

FIGURE 2.9

Examples of different shapes for distributions.

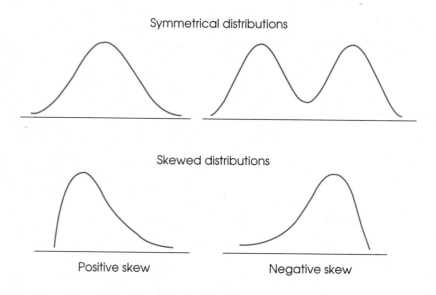

Symmetrical distributions

Skewed distributions

Positive skew   Negative skew

ability. In simple terms, central tendency measures where the center of the distribution is located. Variability tells whether the scores are spread over a wide range or are clustered together. Central tendency and variability will be covered in detail in Chapters 3 and 4. Technically, the shape of a distribution is defined by an equation that prescribes the exact relationship between each X and Y value on the graph. However, we will rely on a few less-precise terms that will serve to describe the shape of most distributions.

Nearly all distributions can be classified as being either symmetrical or skewed.

DEFINITIONS

In a *symmetrical distribution*, it is possible to draw a vertical line through the middle so that one side of the distribution is an exact mirror image of the other (see Figure 2.9).

In a *skewed distribution*, the scores tend to pile up toward one end of the scale and taper off gradually at the other end (see Figure 2.9).

The section where the scores taper off toward one end of a distribution is called the *tail* of the distribution.

A skewed distribution with the tail on the right-hand side is said to be *positively skewed* because the tail points toward the positive (above-zero) end of the X-axis. If the tail points to the left, the distribution is said to be *negatively skewed* (see Figure 2.9).

For a very difficult exam, most scores will tend to be low, with only a few individuals earning high scores. This will produce a positively skewed distribution. Similarly, a very easy exam will tend to produce a negatively skewed distribution, with most of the students earning high scores and only a few with low values.

FIGURE 2.10

Answers to Learning Check Exercise 1.

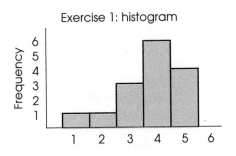

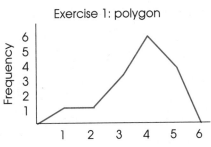

LEARNING CHECK   1. Sketch a frequency distribution histogram and a frequency distribution polygon for the data in the following table:

X	f
5	4
4	6
3	3
2	1
1	1

2. Describe the shape of the distribution in Exercise 1.

3. What type of graph would be appropriate to show the number of gold medals, silver medals, and bronze medals won by the United States during the 1992 Olympics?

4. What shape would you expect for the distribution of salaries for all employees of a major industry?

ANSWERS   1. The graphs are shown in Figure 2.10.

2. The distribution is negatively skewed.

3. A bar graph is appropriate for ordinal data.

4. The distribution probably would be positively skewed, with most employees earning an average salary and a relatively small number of top executives with very large salaries.

2.5 PERCENTILES, PERCENTILE RANKS, AND INTERPOLATION

Although the primary purpose of a frequency distribution is to provide a description of an entire set of scores, it also can be used to describe the position of an individual within the set. Individual scores, or X values, are called raw scores. By themselves, raw scores do not provide much information. For example, if you are told that your score on an exam is $X = 43$, you cannot tell how well you did. To evaluate your score, you need more information such as the average score or the number of people who had scores above and below you. With this additional information, you would be able to determine your relative position in the class. Because raw scores do not provide much information, it is desirable to transform them into a more meaningful form. One transformation that we will consider changes raw scores into percentiles.

DEFINITIONS

The *rank* or *percentile rank* of a particular score is defined as the percentage of individuals in the distribution with scores at or below the particular value.

When a score is identified by its percentile rank, the score is called a *percentile*.

Suppose, for example, that you have a score of $X = 43$ on an exam and that you know that exactly 60% of the class had scores of 43 or lower. Then your score $X = 43$ has a percentile rank of 60%, and your score would be called the 60th percentile. Notice that *percentile rank* refers to a percentage and that *percentile* refers to a score. Also notice that your rank or percentile describes your exact position within the distribution.

CUMULATIVE FREQUENCY AND CUMULATIVE PERCENTAGE

The first step in determining percentiles is to find the number of individuals who are located at or below each point in the distribution. This can be done most easily with a frequency distribution table by simply counting the number who are in or below each category on the scale. The resulting values are called *cumulative frequencies* because they represent the accumulation of individuals as you move up the scale.

EXAMPLE 2.4

In the following frequency distribution table, we have included a cumulative frequency column headed by *cf*. For each row, the cumulative frequency value is obtained by adding up the frequencies in and below that category. For example, the score $X = 3$ has a cumulative frequency of 14 because exactly 14 individuals had scores in this category or in a lower category.

X	f	cf
5	1	20
4	5	19
3	8	14
2	4	6
1	2	2

The cumulative frequencies show the number of individuals located at or below each score. To find percentiles, we must convert these frequencies into percent-

FIGURE 2.11

The relationshp between cumulative frequencies (*cf* values) and upper real limits. Notice that two people has scores of $X = 1$. These two individuals are located between the real limits of 0.5 and 1.5. Although their exact locations are not known, you can be certain that both had scores below the upper real limit of 1.5.

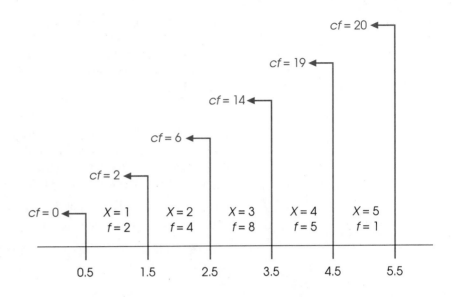

ages. The resulting values are called *cumulative percentages* because they show the percentage of individuals who are accumulated as you move up the scale.

EXAMPLE 2.5 This time we have added a cumulative percentage column (*c%*) to the frequency distribution table from Example 2.4. The values in this column represent the percentage of individuals who are located in and below each category. For example, 70% of the individuals (14 out of 20) had scores of $X = 3$ or lower. Cumulative percentages can be computed by

$$c\% = \frac{cf}{N}(100\%)$$

X	f	cf	c%
5	1	20	100%
4	5	19	95%
3	8	14	70%
2	4	6	30%
1	2	2	10%

The cumulative percentages in a frequency distribution table give the percentage of individuals with scores at or below each X value. However, you must remember that the X values in the table are not points on the scale, but rather intervals. A score of $X = 2$, for example, means that the measurement was somewhere between the real limits of 1.5 and 2.5. Thus, when a table shows that a score of $X = 2$ has a cumulative percentage of 30%, you should interpret this as meaning that 30% of the individuals have been accumulated by the time you reach the top of the interval for $X = 2$. Notice that each cumulative percentage value is associated with the upper real limit of its interval. This point is demonstrated in Figure 2.11, which shows the same data that were used in Example 2.5. Figure 2.11 shows that two people, or 10%, had scores of $X = 1$; that is, two people had scores between 0.5 and 1.5. You cannot be sure that both individuals have been accumulated until you reach 1.5, the upper real limit of the interval. Similarly, a cumulative percentage of 30% is reached at 2.5 on the scale, a percentage of 70% is reached at 3.5, and so on.

INTERPOLATION

It is possible to determine some percentiles and percentile ranks directly from a frequency distribution table, provided that the percentiles are upper real limits and that the ranks are percentages that appear in the table. Using the table in Example 2.5, for example, you should be able to answer the following questions:

1. What is the 95th percentile? (Answer: $X = 4.5$.)
2. What is the percentile rank for $X = 3.5$? (Answer: 70%.)

However, there are many values that do not appear directly in the table, and it is impossible to determine these values precisely. Referring to the table in Example 2.5 again,

1. What is the 50th percentile?
2. What is the percentile rank for $X = 4$?

Because these values are not specifically reported in the table, you cannot answer the questions. However, it is possible to obtain estimates of these intermediate values by using a standard procedure known as interpolation.

    Before we apply the process of interpolation to percentiles and percentile ranks, we will use a simple, commonsense example to introduce this method. Suppose that you hear the weather report at 8 A.M. and again at noon. At 8:00, the temperature was 60°, and at noon, it was 68°. What is your estimate of the temperature at 9:00? To make your task a bit easier, we will create a table showing the time and temperature relationships:

TIME	TEMPERATURE
8:00	60
12:00	68

If you estimated the temperature to be 62° at 9:00, you have done interpolation. You probably went through the following logical steps:

1. The total time from 8:00 to 12:00 is 4 hours.
2. During this time, the temperature changed 8°.
3. 9:00 represents 1 hour, or one-fourth of the total time.
4. Assuming that the temperature went up at a constant rate, it should have increased by 2° during the hour because 2° equals one-fourth of the temperature change.

The process of interpolation is pictured in Figure 2.12. Using the figure, try answering the following questions about other times and temperatures:

1. At what time did the temperature reach 64°?
2. What was the temperature at 11:00?

FIGURE 2.12

A graphic representation of the process of interpolation. The same interval is shown on two separate scales, temperature and time. Only the endpoints of the scales are known—at 8:00, the temperature is 60°, and at 12:00, the temperature is 68°. Interpolational allows you to estimate values within the interval by assuming that fractional portions of one scale correspond to the same fractional portions of the other. For example, it is assumed that halfway through the temperature scale corresponds to halfway through the time scale.

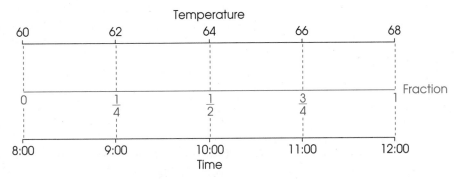

If you got answers of 10:00 and 66°, you have mastered the process of interpolation.

Notice that interpolation provides a method for finding intermediate values, that is, values that are located between two specified numbers. This is exactly the problem we faced with percentiles and percentile ranks. Some values are given in the table, but others are not. Also notice that interpolation only *estimates* the intermediate values. In the time and temperature example, we do not know what the temperature was at 10:00. It may have soared to 80° between 8:00 and noon. The basic assumption underlying interpolation is that the change from one end of the interval to the other is a regular, linear change. We assumed, for example, that the temperature went up consistently at 2° per hour throughout the time period. Because interpolation is based on this assumption, the values we calculate are only estimates. The general process of interpolation can be summarized as follows:

1. A single interval is measured on two separate scales (for example, time and temperature). The endpoints of the interval are known for each scale.

2. You are given an intermediate value on one of the scales. The problem is to find the corresponding intermediate value on the other scale.

3. The interpolation process requires four steps:

   a. Find the width of the interval on both scales.

   b. Locate the position of the intermediate value in the interval. This position corresponds to a fraction of the whole interval:

   $$\text{fraction} = \frac{\text{distance from the top of the interval}}{\text{interval width}}$$

   c. Use this fraction to determine the distance from the top of the interval on the other scale:

   $$\text{distance} = (\text{fraction}) \times (\text{width})$$

   d. Use the distance from the top to determine the position on the other scale.

The following examples demonstrate the process of interpolation as it is applied to percentiles and percentile ranks. The key to successfully working these prob-

Interpolation process

lems is that each cumulative percentage in the table is associated with the upper real limit of its score interval.

You may notice that in each of these problems we use interpolation working from the *top* of the interval. However, this choice is arbitrary, and you should realize that interpolation can be done just as easily working from the bottom of the interval.

E X A M P L E   2 . 6

good →

Using the following distribution of scores, we will find the percentile rank corresponding to $X = 7.0$:

X	f	cf	c%
10	2	25	100%
9	8	23	92%
8	4	15	60%
7	6	11	44%
6	4	5	20%
5	1	1	4%

Notice that $X = 7.0$ is located in the interval bounded by the real limits of 6.5 and 7.5. The cumulative percentages corresponding to these real limits are 20% and 44%, respectively. These values are shown in the following table:

For interpolation problems, it is always helpful to create a table showing the range on both scales.

SCORES (X)	PERCENTAGES
7.5	44%
7.0 ------------------------?	
6.5	20%

S T E P   1   For the scores, the width of the interval is 1 point. For the percentages, the width is 24 points.

S T E P   2   Our particular score is located 0.5 point from the top of the interval. This is exactly halfway down in the interval.

S T E P   3   Halfway down on the percentage scale would be

$$\frac{1}{2}(24 \text{ points}) = 12 \text{ points}$$

S T E P   4   For the percentages, the top of the interval if 44%, so 12 points down would be

$$44\% - 12\% = 32\%$$

This is the answer. A score of $X = 7.0$ correponds to a percentile rank of 32%.

This same interpolation procedure can be used with data that have been grouped into class intervals. Once again, you must remember that the cumulative percentage values are associated with the upper real limits of each interval. The following example demonstrates the calculation of percentiles and percentile ranks using data in a grouped frequency distribution.

EXAMPLE 2.7 Using the following distribution of scores, we will use interpolation to find the 50th percentile:

X	f	cf	c%
20–24	2	20	100%
15–19	3	18	90%
10–14	3	15	75%
5–9	10	12	60%
0–4	2	2	10%

A percentage value of 50% is not given in the table; however, it is located between 10% and 60%, which are given. These two percentage values are associated with the upper real limits of 4.5 and 9.5, respectively. These values are shown in the following table:

SCORES (X)	PERCENTAGES
9.5	60%
? -----------------------	-50%
4.5	10%

STEP 1 For the scores, the width of the interval is 5 points. For the percentages, the width is 50 points.

STEP 2 The value of 50% is located 10 points from the top of the percentage interval. As a fraction of the whole interval, this is 10 out of 50, or ⅕ of the total interval.

STEP 3 Using this same fraction for the scores, we obtain a distance of

$$\frac{1}{5}(5 \text{ points}) = 1 \text{ point}$$

The location we want is 1 point down from the top of the score interval.

STEP 4 Because the top of the interval is 9.5, the position we want is

$$9.5 - 1 = 8.5$$

This is the answer. The 50th percentile is $X = 8.5$.

LEARNING CHECK

1. On a statistics exam, would you rather score at the 80th percentile or at the 40th percentile?

2. For the distribution of scores presented in the following table,
   a. Find the 60th percentile.
   b. Find the percentile rank for $X = 39.5$.

X	f	cf	c%
40–49	4	25	100%
30–39	6	21	84%
20–29	10	15	60%
10–19	3	5	20%
0–9	2	2	8%

3. Using the distribution of scores from Exercise 2 and interpolation,
   a. Find the 40th percentile.
   b. Find the percentile rank for $X = 32$.

ANSWERS

1. The 80th percentile is the higher score.

2. a. $X = 29.5$ is the 60th percentile.
   b. $X = 39.5$ has a rank of 84%.

3. a. Because 40% is between the values of 20% and 60% in the table, you must use interpolation. The score corresponding to a rank of 40% is $X = 24.5$.
   b. Because $X = 32$ is between the real limits of 29.5 and 39.5, you must use interpolation. The percentile rank for $X = 32$ is 66%.

2.6 STEM AND LEAF DISPLAYS

The general term display is used because a stem and leaf display combines the elements of a table and a graph.

In 1977, J.W. Tukey presented a technique for organizing data that provides a simple alternative to a frequency distribution table or graph (Tukey, 1977). This technique, called a *stem and leaf display,* requires that each score be separated into two parts: the first digit (or digits) is called the *stem,* and the last digit (or digits) is called the *leaf.* For example, $X = 85$ would be separated into a stem of 8 and a leaf of 5. Similarly, $X = 42$ would have a stem of 4 and a leaf of 2. To construct a stem and leaf display for a set of data, the first step is to list all the stems in a column. For the data in Table 2.3, for example, the lowest scores are in the 30s and the highest scores are in the 90s, so the list of stems would be

Software Manual:
Minitab (section 4)

STEMS
3
4
5
6
7
8
9

The next step is to go through the data, one score at a time, and write the leaf for each score beside its stem. For the data in Table 2.3, the first score is $X = 83$, so you would write 3 (the leaf) beside the 8 in the column of stems. This process is continued for the entire set of scores. The complete stem and leaf display is shown with the original data in Table 2.3.

COMPARING STEM AND LEAF DISPLAYS WITH FREQUENCY DISTRIBUTIONS

You should notice that the stem and leaf display is very similar to a grouped frequency distribution. Each of the stem values corresponds to a class interval. For example, the stem 3 represents all scores in the 30s, that is, all scores in the interval 30–39. The number of leaves in the display shows the frequency associated with each stem. It also should be clear that the stem and leaf display has several advantages over a traditional frequency distribution:

1. The stem and leaf display is very easy to construct. By going through the data only one time, you can construct a complete display.

2. The stem and leaf display allows you to identify every individual score in the data. In the display shown in Table 2.3, for example, you know that there were three scores in the 60s and you know that the specific values were 62, 68, and 63. A frequency distribution would tell you only the frequency, not the specific values.

3. The stem and leaf display provides both a listing of the scores and a picture of the distribution. If a stem and leaf display is viewed from the side, it is essentially the same as a frequency distribution histogram (see Figure 2.13).

TABLE 2.3

A Set of $N = 24$ Scores Presented as Raw Data and Organized in a Stem and Leaf Display

DATA			STEM AND LEAF DISPLAY	
83	82	63	3	23
62	93	78	4	26
71	68	33	5	6279
76	52	97	6	283
85	42	46	7	1643846
32	57	59	8	3521
56	73	74	9	37
74	81	76		

FIGURE 2.13

A grouped frequency distribution histogram and a stem and leaf display showing the distribution of scores from Table 2.3. The stem and leaf display is placed on its side to demonstrate that the display gives the same information that is provided in the histogram.

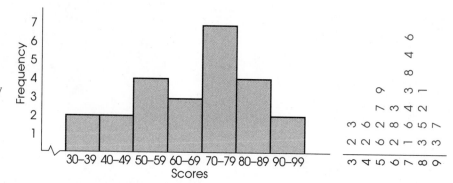

4. Because the stem and leaf display presents the actual value for each score, it is easy to modify a display if you want a more-detailed picture of a distribution. The modification simply requires that each stem be split into two (or more) parts. For example, Table 2.4 shows the same data that were presented in Table 2.3, but now we have split each stem in half. Notice that each stem value is now listed twice in the display. The first half of each stem is associated with the lower leaves (values 0–4), and the second half is associated with the upper leaves (values 5–9). In essence, we have regrouped the distribution using an interval width of 5 points instead of a width of 10 points in the original display.

Although stem and leaf displays are quite useful, you would be warned that they are considered to be a preliminary means for organizing data. Typically, a researcher would use a stem and leaf display to get a first look at experimental data. The final, published report normally would present the distribution of scores in a traditional frequency distribution table or graph.

TABLE 2.4

A Stem and Leaf Display with Each Stem Split into Two Parts
Note that each stem value is listed twice: The first occurrence is associated with the lower leaf values (0–4), and the second occurrence is associated with the upper leaf values (5–9). The data shown in this display are taken from Table 2.3.

3	23
3	
4	2
4	6
5	2
5	679
6	23
6	8
7	1434
7	686
8	321
8	5
9	3
9	7

1. Use a stem and leaf display to organize the following set of scores:

86, 114, 94, 107, 96, 100, 98, 118, 107

132, 106, 127, 124, 108, 112, 119, 125, 115

2. Explain how a stem and leaf display contains more information than a grouped frequency distribution.

1. The stem and leaf display for these data would be

8	6
9	468
10	70768
11	48295
12	745
13	2

2. A grouped frequency distribution table tells only the number of scores in each interval; it does not identify the exact value for each score. The stem and leaf display gives the individual scores as well as the number in each interval.

SUMMARY

1. The goal of descriptive statistics is to simplify the organization and presentation of data. One descriptive technique is to place data in a frequency distribution table or graph that shows how the scores are distributed across the measurement scale.

2. A frequency distribution table lists the scores (from highest to lowest) in one column and the frequency of occurrence for each score in a second column. The table may include a proportion column, showing the relative frequency for each score:

$$\text{proportion} = p = \frac{f}{N}$$

And the table may include a percentage column showing the percentage associated with each score:

$$\text{percentage} = \% = \frac{f}{N}(100)$$

3. When the scores cover a range so broad that it is impractical to list each individual value, it is customary to divide

the range into sections called class intervals. These intervals are then listed in the frequency distribution table along with the frequency or number of individuals that have scores in each interval. The result is called a grouped frequency distribution. The guidelines for constructing a grouped frequency distribution table are as follows:
   a. There should be about 10 intervals.
   b. The width of each interval should be a simple number (e.g., 2, 5, or 10).
   c. The bottom score in each interval should be a multiple of the width.
   d. All intervals should be the same width, and they should cover the range of scores with no gaps.

4. A frequency distribution graph lists scores on the horizontal axis and frequencies on the vertical axis. The type of graph used to display a distribution depends on the scale of measurement used. For interval or ratio scales, you should use a histogram or a polygon. For a histogram, a bar is drawn above each score so that the height of the bar corresponds to the frequency. Each bar extends to the real limits of the score so that adjacent bars touch. For a polygon, a dot is placed above the midpoint of each score or

class interval so that the height of the dot corresponds to the frequency; then lines are drawn to connect the dots. Bar graphs are used with nominal or ordinal scales. Bar graphs are similar to histograms except that gaps are left between adjacent bars.

5. Shape is one of the basic characteristics used to describe a distribution of scores. Most distributions can be classified as either symmetrical or skewed. A skewed distribution that tails off to the right is said to be positively skewed. If it tails off to the left, it is negatively skewed.

6. The cumulative percentage is the percentage of individuals with scores at or below a particular point in the distribution. The cumulative percentage values are associated with the upper real limits of the corresponding scores or intervals.

7. Percentiles and percentile ranks are used to describe the position of individual scores within a distribution. Percentile rank gives a cumulative percentage associated with a particular score. A score that is identified by its rank is called a percentile.

8. When a desired percentile or percentile rank is located between two known values, it is possible to estimate the desired value using the process of interpolation. Interpolation assumes a regular linear change between the two known values.

9. A stem and leaf display is an alternative procedure for organizing data. Each score is separated into a stem (the first digit or digits) and a leaf (the last digit or digits). The display consists of the stems listed in a column with the leaf for each score written beside its stem. A stem and leaf display combines the characteristics of a table and a graph and produces a concise, well-organized picture of the data.

KEY TERMS

frequency distribution	lower real limit	positively skewed distribution	percentile rank
grouped frequency distribution	apparent limits	negatively skewed distribution	cumulative frequency (cf)
range	histogram		cumulative percentage (c%)
class interval	bar graph	tail(s) of a distribution	interpolation
upper real limit	polygon	percentile	stem and leaf display
	symmetrical distribution		

FOCUS ON PROBLEM SOLVING

1. The reason for constructing frequency distributions is to put a disorganized set of raw data into a comprehensible, organized format. Because several different types of frequency distribution tables and graphs are available, one problem is deciding which type should be used. Tables have the advantage of being easier to construct, but graphs generally give a better picture of the data and are easier to understand.

   To help you decide exactly which type of frequency distribution is best, consider the following points:

   a. What is the range of scores? With a wide range, you will need to group the scores into class intervals.

   b. What is the scale of measurement? With an interval or a ratio scale, you can use a polygon or a histogram. With a nominal or an ordinal scale, you must use a bar graph.

2. In setting up class intervals, a common mistake is to determine the interval width by finding the difference between the apparent limits. This is incorrect! To determine the interval width, you must take the difference of the *real limits*. For example, the width for the interval 70–79 is 10 because its real limits are 69.5 and 79.5, and

$$\text{width} = \text{upper real limit} - \text{lower real limit}$$
$$= 79.5 - 69.5 = 10$$

Resist the temptation to state the width is 9. You must use the real limits.

3. Percentiles and percentile ranks are intended to identify specific locations within a distribution of scores. When solving percentile problems, especially with interpolation, it is helpful to sketch a frequency distribution graph. Use the graph to make a preliminary estimate of the answer before you begin any calculations. For example, to find the 60th percentile, you would want to draw a vertical line through the graph so that slightly more than half (60%) of the distribution is on the left-hand side of the line. Locating this position in your sketch will give you a rough estimate of what the final answer should be. When doing interpolation problems, you should keep several points in mind:

   a. Remember that the cumulative percentage values correspond to the upper real limits of each score or interval.

   b. You should always identify the interval with which you are working. The easiest way to do this is to create a table showing the endpoints on both scales (scores and cumulative percentages). This is illustrated in Example 2.6 on page 56.

   c. The word *interpolation* means *between two poles*. Remember, your goal is to find an intermediate value between the two ends of the interval. Check your answer to be sure that it is located between the two endpoints. If not, then check your calculations.

DEMONSTRATION 2.1

A GROUPED FREQUENCY DISTRIBUTION TABLE

For the following set of $N = 20$ scores, construct a grouped frequency distribution table. Use an interval width of 5 points and include columns for f and p. Scores:

14, 8, 27, 16, 10, 22, 9, 13, 16, 12

10, 9, 15, 17, 6, 14, 11, 18, 14, 11

STEP 1   Set up the class intervals.

The largest score in this distribution is $X = 27$, and the lowest is $X = 6$. Therefore, a frequency distribution table for these data would have 22 rows and would be too large. A grouped frequency distribution table would be better. We have asked specifically for an interval width of 5 points, and the resulting table will have five rows.

X
25–29
20–24
15–19
10–14
5–9

Remember, the interval width is determined by the real limits of the interval. For example, the class interval 25–29 has an upper real limit of 29.5 and a lower real limit of 24.5. The difference between these two values is the width of the interval, namely 5.

STEP 2 Determine the frequencies for each interval.

Examine the scores, and count how many fall into the class interval of 25–29. Cross out each score that you have already counted. Record the frequency for this class interval. Now repeat this process for the remaining intervals. The result is the following table:

X	f	
25–29	1	(the score $X = 27$)
20–24	1	($X = 22$)
15–19	5	(the scores $X = 16, 16, 15, 17,$ and 18)
10–14	9	($X = 14, 10, 13, 12, 10, 14, 11, 14,$ and 11)
5–9	4	($X = 8, 9, 9,$ and 6)

STEP 3 Compute the proportions.

The proportion (p) of scores contained in an interval is determined by dividing the frequency (f) of that interval by the number of scores (N) in the distribution. Thus, for each interval, we must compute the following:

$$p = \frac{f}{N}$$

This is demonstrated in the following table:

X	f	p
25–29	1	$f/N = 1/20 = 0.05$
20–24	1	$f/N = 1/20 = 0.05$
15–19	5	$f/N = 5/20 = 0.25$
10–14	9	$f/N = 9/20 = 0.45$
5–9	4	$f/N = 4/20 = 0.20$

DEMONSTRATION 2.2

USING INTERPOLATION TO FIND PERCENTILES AND PERCENTILE RANKS

Find the 50th percentile for the set of scores in the grouped frequency distribution table that was constructed in Demonstration 2.1.

STEP 1 Find the cumulative frequency (cf) and cumulative percentage values, and add these values to the basic frequency distribution table.

Cumulative frequencies indicate the number of individuals located in or below each category (class interval). To find these frequencies, begin with the bottom interval, and then accumulate the frequencies as you move up the scale. For this example, there are 4 individuals who are in or below the 5–9 interval ($cf = 4$). Moving up the scale, the 10–14 interval contains an additional 9 people, so the cumulative value for this interval is $9 + 4 = 13$ (simply add the 9 individuals in the interval to the 4 individuals below). Continue moving up the scale, cumulating frequencies for each interval.

Cumulative percentages are determined from the cumulative frequencies by the relationship

$$c\% = \left(\frac{cf}{N}\right) 100\%$$

For example, the *cf* column shows that 4 individuals (out of the total set of $N = 20$) have scores in or below the 5–9 interval. The corresponding cumulative percentage is

$$c\% = \left(\frac{4}{20}\right) 100\% = \left(\frac{1}{5}\right) 100\% = 20\%$$

The complete set of cumulative frequencies and cumulative percentages is shown in the following table:

X	f	cf	c%
25–29	1	20	100%
20–24	1	19	95%
15–19	5	18	90%
10–14	9	13	65%
5–9	4	4	20%

S T E P 2 Locate the interval that contains the value that you want to calculate.

We are looking for the 50th percentile, which is located between the values of 20% and 65% in the table. The scores (upper real limits) corresponding to these two percentages are 9.5 and 14.5, respectively. The interval, measured in terms of scores and percentages, is shown in the following table:

X	c%
14.5	65%
?? -----------------------	50%
9.5	20%

S T E P 3 Locate the intermediate value as a fraction of the total interval.

Our intermediate value is 50%, which is located in the interval between 65% and 20%. The total width of the interval is 45 points ($65 - 20 = 45$), and the value of 50% is located 15 points down from the top of the interval. As a fraction, the 50th percentile is located $15/45 = 1/3$ down from the top of the interval.

S T E P 4 Use the fraction to determine the corresponding location on the other scale.

Our intermediate value, 50%, is located $1/3$ of the way down from the top of the interval. Our goal is to find the score, the X value, that also is located $1/3$ of the way down from the top of the interval.

On the score (X) side of the interval, the top value is 14.5, and the bottom value is 9.5, so the total interval width is 5 points ($14.5 - 9.5 = 5$). The position we are seeking is ⅓ of the way from the top of the interval. One-third of the total interval is

$$\left(\frac{1}{3}\right)5 = \frac{5}{3} = 1.67 \text{ points}$$

To find this location, begin at the top of the interval, and come down 1.67 points:

$$14.5 - 1.67 = 12.83$$

This is our answer. The 50th percentile is $X = 12.83$.

PROBLEMS

1. Place the following scores in a frequency distribution table. Include columns for proportion (p) and percentage (%) in your table. Scores:

3, 1, 1, 2, 5, 4, 4, 5, 3, 5,

3, 2, 3, 4, 3, 3, 4, 3, 2, 3,

2. Under what circumstances should you use a bar graph instead of a histogram to display a frequency distribution?

3. Sketch a histogram and a polygon showing the distribution of scores presented in the following table:

X	f
5	4
4	6
3	5
2	3
1	2

4. The following are reading comprehension scores for a third-grade class of 18 students:

5, 3, 5, 4, 5, 5, 4, 5, 2

4, 5, 3, 5, 4, 5, 5, 3, 5

a. Place the scores in a frequency distribution table.
b. Sketch a histogram showing the distribution.
c. Using your graph, answer the following questions:
   (1) What is the shape of the distribution?
   (2) If a score of $X = 3$ is considered typical for third-graders, how would you describe the general reading level for this class?

5. An instructor obtained the following set of scores from a 10-point quiz for a class of 26 students:

9, 2, 3, 8, 10, 9, 9, 2, 1, 2, 9, 8, 2

5, 2, 9, 9, 3, 2, 5, 7, 2, 10, 1, 2, 9

a. Place the scores in a frequency distribution table.
b. Sketch a histogram showing the distribution.
c. Using your graph, answer the following questions:
   (1) What is the shape of the distribution?
   (2) As a whole, how did the class do on the quiz? Were most scores high or low? Was the quiz easy or hard?

6. For the set of scores shown in the following frequency distribution table,
a. How many scores are in the distribution? ($N = ?$)
b. Find ΣX for this set of scores.

X	f
4	2
3	4
2	5
1	3

7. A set of scores has been organized into the following frequency distribution table. Find each of the following values for the original set of scores:
a. N
b. ΣX

X	f
5	4
4	3
3	3
2	0
1	2

8. Find each value requested for the set of scores summarized in the following table:
   a. N
   b. ΣX
   c. ΣX^2

X	f
5	2
4	3
3	4
2	1
1	1

9. Find N, ΣX, and ΣX^2 for the set of scores in the following frequency distribution table:

X	f
5	1
4	3
3	5
2	2
1	2

10. Three sets of data are described as follows:

    Set I: highest score is $X = 93$, lowest score is $X = 52$

    Set II: highest score is $X = 35$, lowest score is $X = 26$

    Set III: highest score is $X = 890$, lowest score is $X = 230$

    For each set of data, identify whether a regular table or a grouped table should be used, and if a grouped table is necessary, identify the interval width that would be most appropriate.

11. For each of the following sets of scores:

SET I	SET II
3, 5, 4, 2, 1	3, 9, 14, 10
3, 3, 2, 3, 4	6, 4, 9, 1, 4

    a. Construct a frequency distribution table for each set of data.
    b. Sketch a histogram showing each frequency distribution.
    c. Describe each distribution (separately) using the following characteristics:
       (1) What is the shape of the distribution?
       (2) What score best identifies the center (average) for the distribution?
       (3) Are the scores clustered together around a central point, or are the scores spread out across the scale?

12. For the following set of scores:

    5, 6, 2, 3, 6, 5, 6, 4, 1, 5, 6, 3, 4

    a. Construct a frequency distribution table.
    b. Sketch a polygon showing the distribution.
    c. Describe the distribution using the following characteristics:
       (1) What is the shape of the distribution?
       (2) What score best identifies the center (average) for the distribution?
       (3) Are the scores clustered together, or are they spread out across the scale?

13. For the following set of scores:

    4, 6, 9, 5, 3, 8, 9, 4, 2, 5, 10, 7, 4, 9, 8, 3

    a. Construct a frequency distribution table.
    b. Sketch a polygon showing the distribution
    c. Describe the distribution using the following characteristics:
       (1) What is the shape of the distribution?
       (2) What score best identifies the center (average) for the distribution?
       (3) Are the scores clustered together, or are they spread out across the scale?

14. Place the following 28 scores in a grouped frequency distribution table using
    a. An interval width of 2.
    b. An interval width of 5.

    23, 12, 16, 16, 17, 19, 28

    20, 14, 21, 18, 24, 29, 24

    18, 21, 22, 27, 21, 25, 19

    22, 23, 21, 30, 27, 23, 18

15. Three sets of data are described by identifying the lowest score and the highest score for each set. Describe how a grouped frequency distribution table should be constructed for each set. That is, give the interval width that you would suggest, and make a list of all class intervals.
    a. 3–19
    b. 51–98
    c. 270–660

16. Sketch a frequency distribution histogram for the following data:

X	f
15	2
14	5
13	6
12	3
11	2
10	1

17. For the following set of scores,
  a. Construct a frequency distribution table to organize the scores.
  b. Draw a frequency distribution histogram for these data:
  c. Draw a frequency distribution polygon.

  3, 5, 4, 6, 2, 3, 4, 1, 4, 3

  7, 7, 3, 4, 5, 8, 2, 4, 7, 10

18. Add columns showing cumulative frequency (*cf*) and cumulative percentage (*c%*) to the following frequency distribution table:

X	f
10	3
9	1
8	0
7	4
6	6
5	4
4	2

19. Find each of the requested values for the distribution of scores shown in the following frequency distribution table:

X	f
14–15	2
12–13	5
10–11	6
8–9	7
6–7	4
4–5	1

  a. What is the 20th percentile?
  b. What is the percentile rank for $X = 11.5$?
  c. Use interpolation to find the 60th percentile.
  d. Use interpolation to find the percentile rank for $X = 6$.

20. Complete the cumulative frequency column and the cumulative percentage column for the following table:

X	f	cf	c%
5	7		
4	8		
3	5		
2	3		
1	2		

21. Complete the following frequency distribution table, and find each of the percentiles and percentile ranks requested:

X	f	cf	c%
10	2		
9	3		
8	5		
7	6		
6	2		
5	2		

  a. What is the percentile rank for $X = 6.5$?
  b. What is the percentile rank for $X = 9.5$?
  c. What is the 50th percentile?
  d. What score is needed to be in the top 10% of this distribution?

22. Using the following frequency distribution, find each of the percentiles and percentile ranks requested:

X	f	cf	c%
6	2	20	100%
5	2	18	90%
4	4	16	80%
3	6	12	60%
2	4	6	30%
1	2	2	10%

  a. What is the 60th percentile?
  b. What is the percentile rank for $X = 5.5$?

c. Use interpolation to find the 20th percentile.
d. Use interpolation to find the percentile rank for $X = 5$.
e. What is the minimum score needed to be in the top 25% of this distribution? That is, find the 75th percentile.

23. Find each value requested for the frequency distribution presented in the following table:

X	f	cf	c%
20–24	10	50	100%
15–19	10	40	80%
10–14	15	30	60%
5–9	10	15	30%
0–4	5	5	10%

a. Find the percentile rank for $X = 7$.
b. What is the 75th percentile?
c. Find the percentile rank for $X = 20$.

24. For the set of data shown in the following stem and leaf display:

8	271
7	4586
6	302
5	4169
4	3
3	26
2	5

a. Construct a grouped frequency distribution table using an interval width of 10 to display the data.
b. Place the same data in a frequency distribution histogram, again using an interval width of 10 points.

c. Notice that you can use the information from a stem and leaf display to construct a frequency distribution. If you had started with the frequency distribution, would it provide enough information for you to construct a stem and leaf display? Explain why or why not.

25. Use a stem and leaf display to organize the following scores:

43, 56, 35, 47, 48, 52, 66, 57, 46

39, 43, 47, 61, 55, 50, 49, 39, 40

26. The following data are attitude scores for a sample of 25 students. A high score indicates a positive attitude, and a low score indicates a negative attitude.

ATTITUDE SCORES				
9	73	62	52	14
31	26	74	61	13
79	58	16	62	7
77	9	30	18	23
42	78	10	66	82

a. Construct a stem and leaf display to organize these data.
b. Using your stem and leaf display, construct a grouped frequency distribution table for these scores.
c. Looking at the distribution of scores, which of the following descriptions best fits these data?
  (1) This group has a generally positive attitude.
  (2) This group has a generally negative attitude.
  (3) This group is sharply split with attitudes at both extremes.

27. Using the data from problem 25, construct a grouped frequency distribution table.

CHAPTER 3

CENTRAL TENDENCY

TOOLS YOU WILL NEED

The following items are considered essential background material for this chapter. If you doubt your knowledge of any of these items, you should review the appropriate chapter or section before proceeding.

- Summation notation (Chapter 1)
- Frequency distributions (Chapter 2)

CONTENTS

PREVIEW

In a classic study examining the relationship between heredity and intelligence, Tryon (1940) used a selective breeding program to develop separate strains of "smart" and "dumb" rats. Starting with large samples of rats, Tryon tested each animal on a maze-learning problem. Based on their error scores for the maze, the brightest rats and the dullest rats were selected from this sample. The brightest males were mated with the brightest females. Similarly, the dullest rats were interbred. This process of testing and selectively breeding was continued for several generations until Tryon had established a line of maze-bright rats and a separate line of maze-dull rats. The results obtained by Tryon are shown in Figure 3.1

Notice that after seven generations, there is an obvious difference between the two groups. As a rule, the maze-bright animals outperform the maze-dull animals. It is tempting to describe the results of this experiment by saying that the maze-bright rats are better learners than the maze-dull rats. However, you should notice that there is some overlap between the two groups; not all the dull animals are really dull. In fact, some of the animals bred for brightness are actually poorer learners than some of the animals bred for dullness. What is needed is a simple way of describing the general difference between these two groups while still acknowledging the fact that some individuals may contradict the general trend.

The solution to this problem is to identify the typical or average rat as the representative for each group. Then the experimental results can be described by saying that the typical maze-bright rat is a faster learner than the typical maze-dull rat. On the average, the bright rats really are brighter.

In this chapter, we will introduce the statistical techniques used to identify the typical or average score for a distribution. Although there are several reasons for defining the average score, the primary advantage of an average is that it provides a single number that describes an entire distribution and can be used for comparison with other distributions.

As a footnote, you should know that later research with Tryon's rats revealed that the maze-bright rats were not really more intelligent than the maze-dull rats. Although the bright rats had developed specific abilities that are useful in mazes, the dull rats proved to be just as smart when tested on a variety of other tasks.

Tryon, R.C. (1940). "Genetic differences in maze-learning ability in rats." *The Thirty-ninth Yearbook of the National Society for the Study of Education,* 111–119. Adapted and reprinted with permission of the National Society for the Study of Education.

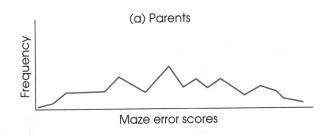

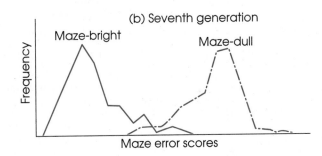

FIGURE 3.1

Distribution of error scores (a) for the original sample of rats (parents) and (b) for the two separate lines that were selectively bred for either good or poor maze performance (maze-bright and maze-dull).

3.1 OVERVIEW

The goal in measuring central tendency is to describe a group of individuals (more accurately, their scores) with a single measurement. Ideally, the value we use to describe the group will be the single value that is most representative of all the individuals.

DEFINITION

Central tendency is a statistical measure that identifies a single score as representative of an entire distribution. The goal of central tendency is to find the single score that is most typical or most representative of the entire group.

Usually we want to choose a value in the middle of the distribution because central scores are often the most representative. In everyday language, the goal of central tendency is to find the "average" or "typical" individual. This average value can then be used to provide a simple description of the entire population or sample. For example, archeological discoveries indicate that the average height for men in the ancient Roman city of Pompeii was 5 feet 7 inches. Obviously, not all the men were exactly 5 feet 7 inches, but this average value provides a general description of the population. Measures of central tendency also are useful for making comparisons between groups of individuals or between sets of figures. For example, suppose that weather data indicate that during the month of December, Seattle averages only 2 hours of sunshine per day, whereas Miami averages over 6 hours. The point of these examples is to demonstrate the great advantage of being able to describe a large set of data with a single, representative number. Central tendency characterizes what is typical for a large population and in doing so makes large amounts of data more digestable. Statisticians sometimes use the expression "number crunching" to illustrate this aspect of data description. That is, we take a distribution consisting of many scores and "crunch" them down to a single value that describes them all.

Unfortunately, there is no single, standard procedure for determining central tendency. The problem is that no single measure will always produce a central, representative value in every situation. The three distributions shown in Figure 3.2 should help demonstrate this fact. Before we discuss the three distributions, take a moment to look at the figure and try to identify the "center" or the "most representative score" for each distribution.

1. The first distribution [Figure 3.2(a)] is symmetrical with the scores forming a distinct pile centered around $X = 5$. For this type of distribution, it is easy to identify the "center," and most people would agree that the value $X = 5$ is an appropriate measure of central tendency.

2. In the second distribution [Figure 3.2(b)], however, problems begin to appear. Now the scores form a negatively skewed distribution, piling up at the high end of the scale around $X = 8$, but tapering off to the left all the way down to $X = 1$. Where is the "center" in this case? Some people might select $X = 8$ as the center because more individuals had this score than any other single value. However, $X = 8$ is clearly not in the middle of the distribution. In fact, the majority of the scores (10 out of 16) have values less than 8, so it seems reasonable that the "center" should be defined by a value that is less than 8.

3. Now consider the third distribution [Figure 3.2(c)]. Again, the distribution is symmetrical, but now there are two distinct piles of scores. Because the distribution is symmetrical with $X = 5$ as the midpoint, you may choose $X = 5$ as the "center." However, none of the scores is located at $X = 5$ (or even close), so this value is not particularly good as a representative score. On the other hand, because there are two separate piles of scores with one group centered at $X = 2$ and the other centered at $X = 8$, it is tempting to say that this distribution has two centers. But can there be two centers?

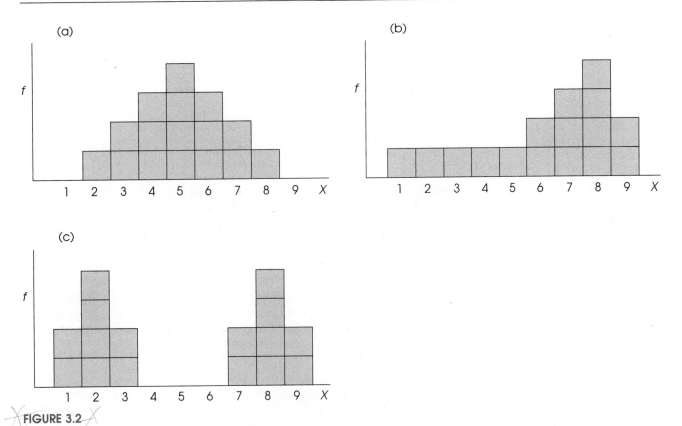

FIGURE 3.2

Three distributions demonstrating the difficulty of defining central tendency. In each case, try to locate the "center" of the distribution.

Clearly, there are problems defining the "center" of a distribution. Occasionally, you will find a nice, neat distribution like the one shown in Figure 3.2(a), where everyone will agree on the center. But you should realize that other distributions are possible and that there may be different opinions concerning the definition of the center. To deal with these problems, statisticians have developed three different methods for measuring central tendency: the mean, the median, and the mode. They are computed differently and have different characteristics. To decide which of the three measures is best for any particular distribution, you should keep in mind that the general purpose of central tendency is to find the single most representative score. Each of the three measures we will present has been developed to work best in a specific situation. We will examine this issue in more detail after we introduce the three measures.

3.2 THE MEAN

The *mean,* commonly known as the arithmetic average, is computed by adding all the scores in the distribution and dividing by the number of scores. The mean for a population will be identified by the Greek letter mu, μ (pronounced "myoo"), and the mean for a sample will be identified by $\overline{X}$ (read "x-bar").

DEFINITION   The *mean* for a distribution is the sum of the scores divided by the number of scores.

The formula for the population mean is

$$\mu = \frac{\Sigma X}{N} \qquad (3.1)$$

First, sum all the scores in the population, and then divide by N. For a sample, the computation is done the same way, but the formula uses symbols that signify sample values:

Software Manuals:
Minitab (section 4)
Mystat (section 3)
SPSS (section 6)

$$\text{sample mean} = \overline{X} = \frac{\Sigma X}{n} \qquad (3.2)$$

In general, we will use Greek letters to identify characteristics of a population and letters of our own alphabet to stand for sample values. If a mean is identified with the symbol $\overline{X}$, you should realize that we are dealing with a sample. Also note that n is used as the symbol for the number of scores in the sample.

EXAMPLE 3.1   For a population of $N = 4$ scores,

3,   7,   4,   6

the mean is

$$\mu = \frac{\Sigma X}{N} = \frac{20}{4} = 5$$

Although the procedure of adding the scores and dividing by the number provides a useful definition of the mean, there are two alternative definitions that may give you a better understanding of this important measure of central tendency.

The first alternative is to think of the mean as the amount each individual would get if the total (ΣX) were divided equally among all the individuals *(N)* in the distribution. This somewhat socialistic viewpoint is particularly useful in problems where you know the mean and must find the total. Consider the following example.

EXAMPLE 3.2   A group of 6 students decided to earn some extra money one weekend picking vegetables at a local farm. At the end of the weekend, the students discovered that their average income was $\mu = \$30$. If they decide to pool their money for a party, how much will they have?

You do not know how much money each student earned. But you do know that the mean is $30. This is the amount that each student would have if the total were divided equally. For each of 6 students to have $30, you must start

FIGURE 3.3

The frequency distribution shown as a
seesaw balanced at the mean.

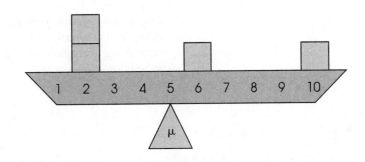

Adapted from *Statistics: An Intuitive Approach,* 4th ed. by G. Weinberg, J. Schumaker, and D. Olt-
man. Copyright © 1981, 1974, 1969, 1962 by Wadsworth Inc. Reprinted by permission of Brooks/
Cole Publishing Co., Monterey, CA 93940.

---

with $6 \times \$30 = \$180$. The total, ΣX, is $180. To check this answer, use the
formula for the mean:

$$\mu = \frac{\Sigma X}{N} = \frac{\$180}{6} = \$30$$

The second alternative definition of the mean describes the mean as a balance
point for a distribution. Consider the population consisting of $N = 4$ scores (2, 2,
6, 10). For this population, $\Sigma X = 20$ and $N = 4$, so $\mu = \frac{20}{4} = 5$.

Imagine that the frequency distribution histogram for this population is drawn so
that the X-axis, or number line, is a seesaw and the scores are boxes of equal weight
that are placed on the seesaw (see Figure 3.3). If the seesaw is positioned so that it
pivots at the value equal to the mean, it will be balanced and will rest level.

The reason the seesaw is balanced over the mean becomes clear when we measure the distance of each box (score) from the mean:

SCORE	DISTANCE FROM THE MEAN
$X = 2$	3 points below the mean
$X = 2$	3 points below the mean
$X = 6$	1 point above the mean
$X = 10$	5 points above the mean

Notice that the mean balances the distances. That is, the total distance below the
mean is the same as the total distance above the mean:

3 points below + 3 points below = 6 points below

1 point above + 5 points above = 6 points above

THE WEIGHTED MEAN   Often it is necessary to combine two sets of scores and then find the overall mean
for the combined group. For example, an instructor teaching two sections of intro-

good ductory psychology obtains an average quiz score of $\overline{X} = 6$ for the 12 students in one section and an average of $\overline{X} = 7$ for the 8 students in the other section. If the two sections are combined, what is the mean for the total group?

The solution to this problem is straightforward if you remember the definition of the mean:

$$\overline{X} = \frac{\Sigma X}{n}$$

To find the overall mean, we must find two values: the total number of students (n) for the combined group and the overall sum of scores for the combined group (ΣX). Finding the number of students is easy. If there are $n = 12$ in one group and $n = 8$ in the other, then there must be $n = 20$ (12 + 8) in the combined group. To find the sum of scores for the combined group, we will use the same method: Find the sum for one group, find the sum for the other, and then add the two sums together.

We know that the first section has $n = 12$ and $\overline{X} = 6$. Using these values in the equation for the mean gives

$$\overline{X} = \frac{\Sigma X}{n}$$

$$6 = \frac{\Sigma X}{12}$$

$$12(6) = \Sigma X \qquad (\text{Note: } n\overline{X} = \Sigma X)$$

$$72 = \Sigma X$$

The second section has $n = 8$ and $\overline{X} = 7$, so ΣX must be equal to 56. When these two groups are combined, the sum of all 20 scores will be

$$72 + 56 = 128$$

Finally, the mean for the combined group is

$$\overline{X} = \frac{\Sigma X}{n} = \frac{128}{20} = 6.4$$

Notice that this value is not obtained by simply averaging the two means. (If we simply averaged $\overline{X} = 6$ and $\overline{X} = 7$, we would obtain a mean of 6.5.) Because the samples are not the same size, one will make a larger contribution to the total group and, therefore, will carry more weight in determining the overall mean. For this reason, the overall mean we have calculated is called the *weighted mean* (see Box 3.1). In this example, the overall mean of $\overline{X} = 6.4$ is closer to the value of $\overline{X} = 6$ (the larger sample) than it is to $\overline{X} = 7$ (the smaller sample). In summary, a weighted mean is obtained by combining the two group sums (ΣXs), then combining the ns for both groups, and finally dividing the combined sum by the combined n. In a formula, it is expressed as

$$\text{weighted mean} = \frac{\Sigma X_1 + \Sigma X_2}{n_1 + n_2} \qquad (3.3)$$

3.1 AN ALTERNATIVE PROCEDURE FOR FINDING THE WEIGHTED MEAN

IN THE text, the weighted mean was obtained by first determining the total number of scores (n) for the two combined samples and then determining the overall sum (ΣX) for the two combined samples. The following example demonstrates how the same result can be obtained using a slightly different conceptual approach.

We will begin with the same two samples that were used in the text: One sample has $\overline{X} = 6$ for $n = 12$ students, and the second sample has $\overline{X} = 7$ for $n = 8$ students. The goal is to determine the mean for the overall group when the two samples are combined.

Logically, when these two samples are combined, the larger sample (with $n = 12$ scores) will make a greater contribution to the combined group than the smaller sample (with $n = 8$ scores). Thus, the larger sample will carry more weight in determining the mean for the combined group. We will accommodate this fact by assigning a weight to each sample mean so that the weight is determined by the size of the sample. To determine how much weight should be assigned to each sample mean,

you simply consider the sample's contribution to the combined group. When the two samples are combined, the resulting group will have a total of 20 scores ($n = 12$ from the first sample and $n = 8$ from the second). The first sample contributes 12 out of 20 scores and, therefore, is assigned a weight of $^{12}/_{20}$. The second sample contributes 8 out of 20 scores, and its weight is $^{8}/_{20}$. Each sample mean is then multiplied by its weight, and the results are summed to find the weighted mean for the combined sample. For this example,

$$\text{weighted mean} = \left(\frac{12}{20}\right)(6) + \left(\frac{8}{20}\right)(7)$$
$$= \frac{72}{20} + \frac{56}{20}$$
$$= 3.6 + 2.8$$
$$= 6.4$$

Note that this is the same result obtained using the method described in the text.

COMPUTING THE MEAN FROM A FREQUENCY DISTRIBUTION TABLE

It is very common for people to make mistakes when determining ΣX from a frequency distribution table. Often the column labeled X is summed while the frequency column is ignored. Be sure to use the information in the f column when determining ΣX. (See Chapter 2, p. 39.) Do not confuse a frequency distribution table with a computational table used in Section 1.6.

Table 3.1 shows the scores on a quiz for a section of statistics students. Instead of listing all of the individual scores, these data are organized into a frequency distribution table. To compute the mean for this sample, you must use all the information in the table, the f values as well as the X values.

To find the mean for this sample, we will need the sum of the scores (ΣX) and the number of scores (n). The number n can be found by summing the frequencies:

$$n = \Sigma f = 8$$

Note that there is one 10, two 9s, four 8s, and one 6 for a total of $n = 8$ scores. To find ΣX, you must be careful to add all eight scores:

$$\Sigma X = 10 + 9 + 9 + 8 + 8 + 8 + 8 + 6 = 66$$

TABLE 3.1

Statistics Quiz Scores for a Section of $n = 8$ Students

QUIZ SCORE (X)	f	fX
10	1	10
9	2	18
8	4	32
7	0	0
6	1	6

This sum also can be found by multiplying each score by its frequency and then adding up the results. This is done in the third column (fX) in Table 3.1. Note, for example, that the two 9s contribute 18 to the total.

Once you have found ΣX and n, you compute the mean as usual:

$$\overline{X} = \frac{\Sigma X}{n} = \frac{\Sigma fX}{\Sigma f} = \frac{66}{8} = 8.25$$

LEARNING CHECK
1. Compute the mean for the sample of scores shown in the following frequency distribution table:

X	f	fX
4	2	8
3	4	12
2	3	6
1	1	1

$\Sigma f = n = 10 \quad \Sigma fX = 27 \qquad \overline{X} = \frac{27}{10} = 2.7$

2. Two samples were obtained from a population. For sample A, $n = 8$ and $\overline{X} = 14$. For sample B, $n = 20$ and $\overline{X} = 6$. If the two samples are combined, will the overall mean be closer to 14 than to 6, closer to 6 than to 14, or halfway between 6 and 14? Explain your answer.

3. A sample of $n = 20$ scores has a mean of $\overline{X} = 5$. What is ΣX for this sample?

ANSWERS
1. $\overline{X} = {}^{27}\!/_{10} = 2.7$

$\overline{X} = \frac{\Sigma X}{n} \qquad 5 = \frac{\Sigma X}{20} = 5(20) = \Sigma X = 100$

2. The mean will be closer to 6. The larger sample will carry more weight in the combined group.

3. $\Sigma X = 100$

CHARACTERISTICS OF THE MEAN

The mean has many characteristics that will be important in future discussions. In general, these characteristics result from the fact that every score in the distribution contributes to the value of the mean. Specifically, every score must be added into the total in order to compute the mean. Three of the more important characteristics will now be discussed.

1. Changing a score or introducing a new score Changing the value of any score, or adding a new score to the distribution, will change the mean. For example, the quiz scores for a psychology lab section consist of

9, 8, 7, 5, and 1

The mean for this sample is

$$\overline{X} = \frac{\Sigma X}{n} = \frac{30}{5} = 6.00$$

Suppose that the student who received the score of $X = 1$ returned a few days later and explained that she was ill on the day of the quiz. In fact, she went straight to the infirmary after class and was admitted for two days with the flu. Out of the goodness of the instructor's heart, the student was given a makeup quiz, and she received an 8. By having changed her score from 1 to 8, the distribution now consists of

$$9, \quad 8, \quad 7, \quad 5, \quad \text{and} \quad 8$$

The new mean is

$$\overline{X} = \frac{\Sigma X}{n} = \frac{37}{5} = 7.40$$

Changing a single score in this sample has given us a different mean.

In general, the mean is determined by two values: ΣX and N (or n). Whenever either of these values is changed, the mean also will be changed. In the preceding example, the value of one score was changed. This produced a change in the total (ΣX) and, therefore, changed the mean. If you add a new score (or take away a score), you will change both ΣX and n, and must compute the new mean using the changed values. The following example demonstrates how the mean is affected when a new score is added to an existing sample (see Box 3.2).

EXAMPLE 3.3 We begin with a sample of $n = 4$ scores with a mean of $\overline{X} = 7$. A new score, $X = 12$, is added to this sample. The problem is to find the mean for the new set of scores.

To find the mean, we must first determine the values for n (the number of scores) and ΣX (the sum of the scores). Finding n is easy: We started with four scores and added one more, so the new value for n is 5 ($n = 5$).

To find the sum for the new sample, you simply begin with the total (ΣX) for the original sample and then add in the value of the new score. The original set of $n = 4$ scores had a mean of $\overline{X} = 7$; therefore, the original total must be $\Sigma X = 28$. Adding a score of $X = 12$ brings the new total to $28 + 12 = 40$.

Finally, the new mean is computed using the values for n and ΣX for the new set: $\overline{X} = \Sigma X/n = {}^{40}\!/_5 = 8$. The entire process can be summarized as follows:

ORIGINAL SAMPLE	NEW SAMPLE ADDING $X = 12$
$n = 4$	$n = 5$
$\Sigma X = 28$	$\Sigma X = 40$
$\overline{X} = {}^{28}\!/_4 = 7$	$\overline{X} = {}^{40}\!/_5 = 8$

2. Adding or subtracting a constant from each score   If a constant value is added to every score in a distribution, the same constant will be added to the mean. Similarly, if you subtract a constant from every score, the same constant will be subtracted from the mean.

3.2 VISUALIZING HOW THE MEAN IS AFFECTED WHEN SCORES ARE CHANGED

THE GENERAL impact of adding a new score, removing a score, or changing a score can be seen if you recall that the mean serves as a balance point for the distribution. Figure 3.4 shows a distribution of $n = 6$ scores presented as a set of boxes on a seesaw that is balanced at $\mu = 10$. Following are three scenarios for adding, removing, and changing scores. As you read each scenario, refer to Figure 3.4 to help you see what happens to the mean.

1. If a new score (box) is added at $X = 3$, what will happen to the seesaw? It should be clear that a new value added on the left side of the distribution, below the mean, will cause the seesaw to tilt to the left. To regain balance, the mean or the balance point must be shifted to the left. Thus, adding a new value that is less than the current mean will cause the mean to be lowered. Similarly, adding a new score (box) on the right-hand end of the seesaw (above the mean) will require that the balance point be shifted to the right.

2. Now consider what will happen to the seesaw if the highest score, $X = 16$, is removed. Clearly, the seesaw will tilt to the left, again requiring that the balance point be shifted to the left in order to restore balance.

3. Finally, what will happen if the score $X = 16$ is changed to $X = 21$? It should be clear that this move will upset the balance and cause the seesaw to tilt to the right. To restore balance, the mean (balance point) will also have to be shifted to the right.

In general, if you visualize a distribution as a set of boxes on a seesaw that is balanced at the mean, it should be easy to see the effect of adding, removing, or changing a score. You will still need to do the arithmetic to determine the exact value for the new mean, but your visual image should help you predict what the new value will be.

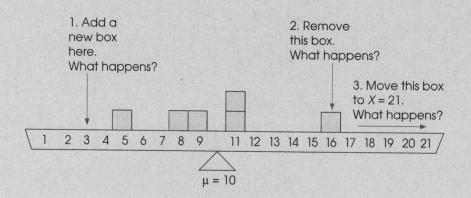

FIGURE 3.4

A set of $N = 6$ scores shown as a set of boxes on a seesaw balanced at the mean, $\mu = 10$. Three scenarios for adding, removing, and changing scores are discussed in the text.

EXAMPLE 3.4 Consider the feeding scores for a sample of $n = 6$ rats. See Table 3.2. These scores are the amounts of food (in grams) they ate during a 24-hour testing session. $\Sigma X = 26$ for $n = 6$ rats, so $\overline{X} = 4.33$. On the following day, each rat is given an experimental drug that reduces appetite. Suppose that this drug has the effect of reducing the meal size by 2 grams for each rat. Note that the effect of the drug is to subtract a constant (2 points) from each rat's feeding score. The new distribution is shown in Table 3.3. Now $\Sigma X = 14$ and n is still 6, so the mean amount of food consumed is $\overline{X} = 2.33$. Subtracting 2

TABLE 3.2

Amount of food (in grams) consumed during baseline session

RAT'S IDENTIFICATION	AMOUNT (X)	
A	6	
B	3	$\Sigma X = 26$
C	5	
D	3	$n = 6$
E	4	$\overline{X} = 4.33$
F	5	

points from each score has changed the mean by the same constant, from $\overline{X} = 4.33$ to $\overline{X} = 2.33$. (It is important to note that experimental effects are practically never so simple as the adding or subtracting of a constant. Nonetheless, the principle of this characteristic of the mean is important and will be addressed in later chapters when we are using statistics to evaluate the effects of experimental manipulations.)

3. Multiplying or dividing each score by a constant If every score in a distribution is multiplied by (or divided by) a constant value, the mean will be changed in the same way.

Multiplying (or dividing) each score by a constant value is a common method for changing the unit of measurement. To change a set of measurements from minutes to seconds, for example, you multiply by 60; to change from inches to feet, you divide by 12. Table 3.4 shows how a sample of $n = 5$ scores originally measured in yards would be transformed into a set of scores measured in feet. The first column shows the original scores which total $\Sigma X = 50$ with $\overline{X} = 10$ yards. In the second column, each of the original values has been multiplied by 3 (to change from yards to feet), and the resulting values total $\Sigma X = 150$ with $\overline{X} = 30$ feet. Multiplying each score by 3 has also caused the mean to be multiplied by 3. You should realize, however, that although the numerical values for the individual scores and the sample mean have been multiplied, the actual measurements are not changed.

LEARNING CHECK

1. **a.** Compute the mean for the following sample of scores:

6, 1, 8, 0, 5

b. Add 4 points to each score, and then compute the mean.

c. Multiply each of the original scores by 5, and then compute the mean.

TABLE 3.3

Amount of food (in grams) consumed after drug injections

RAT'S IDENTIFICATION	BASELINE SCORE MINUS CONSTANT	DRUG SCORE (X)	
A	6 − 2	4	
B	3 − 2	1	$\Sigma X = 14$
C	5 − 2	3	
D	3 − 2	1	$n = 6$
E	4 − 2	2	$\overline{X} = 2.33$
F	5 − 2	3	

TABLE 3.4

Measurement of five pieces of wood

ORIGINAL MEASUREMENT IN YARDS	CONVERSION TO FEET (MULTIPLY BY 3)
10	30
9	27
12	36
8	24
11	33

$\Sigma X = 50$ $\Sigma X = 150$
$\overline{X} = 10$ yards $\overline{X} = 30$ feet

2. After every score in a distribution is multiplied by 3, the mean is calculated to be $\overline{X} = 60$. What was the mean for the original distribution?

ANSWERS   **1. a.** $\overline{X} = {}^{20}\!/_5 = 4$ **b.** $\overline{X} = {}^{40}\!/_5 = 8$ **c.** $\overline{X} = {}^{100}\!/_5 = 20$

2. The original mean was $\overline{X} = 20$.

3.3   THE MEDIAN

The second measure of central tendency we will consider is called the *median*. The median is the score that divides a distribution exactly in half. Exactly one-half of the scores are less than or equal to the median, and exactly one-half are greater than or equal to the median. Because exactly 50% of the scores fall at or below the median, this value is equivalent to the 50th percentile (see Chapter 2).

DEFINITION   The *median* is the score that divides a distribution exactly in half. Exactly 50% of the individuals in a distribution have scores at or below the median. The median is equivalent to the 50th percentile.

Earlier, when we introduced the mean, specific symbols and notation were used to identify the mean and to differentiate a sample mean and a population mean. For the median, however, there are no symbols or notation. Instead, the median is simply identified by the word *median*. In addition, the definition and the computations for the median are identical for a sample and for a population.

By midpoint of the distribution we mean that the area in the graph is divided into two equal parts. We are not locating the midpoint between the highest and lowest X values.

The goal of the median is to determine the precise midpoint of a distribution. The commonsense goal is demonstrated in the following three examples. The three examples are intended to cover all of the different types of data you are likely to encounter.

METHOD 1: WHEN N IS AN ODD NUMBER   With an odd number of scores, you list the scores in order (lowest to highest), and the median is the middle score in the list. Consider the following set of $N = 5$ scores, which have been listed in order:

3,   5,   8,   10,   11

FIGURE 3.5

The median divides the area in the graph exactly in half.

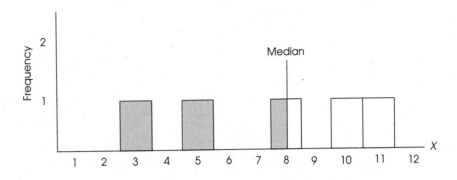

Software Manuals:
Minitab (Section 4)
SPSS (Section 6)

The middle score is $X = 8$, so the median is equal to 8.0. In a graph, the median divides the space or area of the graph in half (Figure 3.5). The amount of area above the median consists of 2½ "boxes," the same as the area below the median (shaded portion).

METHOD 2: WHEN *N* IS AN EVEN NUMBER

With an even number of scores in the distribution, you list the scores in order (lowest to highest) and then locate the median by finding the point halfway between the middle two scores. Consider the following population:

3,　3,　4,　5,　7,　8

Now we select the middle pair of scores (4 and 5), add them together, and divide by 2:

$$\text{median} = \frac{4 + 5}{2} = \frac{9}{2} = 4.5$$

In terms of a graph, we see again that the median divides the area of the distribution exactly in half (Figure 3.6). There are three scores (or boxes) above the median and three below the median.

FIGURE 3.6

The median divides the area in the graph exactly in half.

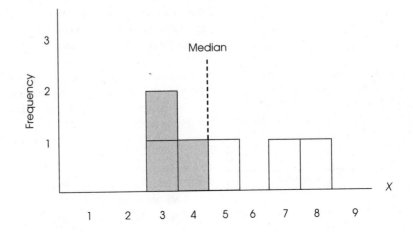

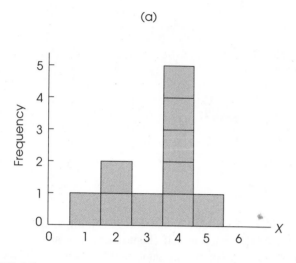

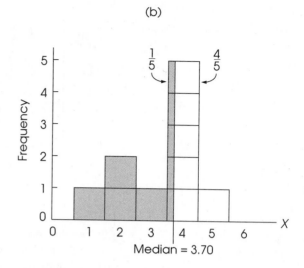

Median = 3.70

FIGURE 3.7

A distribution with several scores clustered at the median. The median for this distribution is positioned so that each of the five blocks above $X = 4$ is divided into two sections, with ⅕ of each block below the median to the left) and ⅘ of each block above the median (to the right).

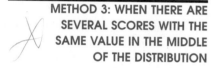

METHOD 3: WHEN THERE ARE SEVERAL SCORES WITH THE SAME VALUE IN THE MIDDLE OF THE DISTRIBUTION

In most cases, one of the two methods already outlined will provide you with a reasonable value for the median. However, when you have more than one individual at the median, these simple procedures may oversimplify the computations. Consider the following set of scores:

1,   2,   2,   3,   4,   4,   4,   4,   4,   5

There are 10 scores (an even number), so you normally would use method 2 and average the middle pair to determine the median. By this method, the median would be 4.

In many ways, this is a perfectly legitimate value for the median. However, when you look closely at the distribution of scores [see Figure 3.7(a)], you probably get the clear impression that $X = 4$ is not in the middle. The problem comes from the tendency to interpret the score of 4 as meaning exactly 4.00 instead of meaning an interval from 3.5 to 4.5. The simple method of computing the median has determined that the value we want is located in this interval. To locate the median with greater precision, it is necessary to use *interpolation* to compute the 50th percentile.

Because the median can be visualized as the midpoint in a graph (dividing the graph into two equal sections), the following graphic demonstration is particularly well suited for finding the median.

The mathematical process of interpolation was introduced in Chapter 2 (see p. 54). Although you can use the mathematical process to compute the 50th percentile (see Box 3.3), the following example demonstrates a simple graphic version of the interpolation process.

EXAMPLE 3.5

For this example, we will use the data shown in Figure 3.7(a). Notice that the figure shows a population of $N = 10$ scores, with each score represented by a block in the histogram. To find the median, we must locate the position of a

3.3   USING INTERPOLATION TO FIND THE MEDIAN

THE SAME data that are used in Example 3.5 (see Figure 3.7) are organized in the following frequency distribution table:

X	f	cf	c%
5	1	10	100%
4	5	9	90%
3	1	4	40%
2	2	3	30%
1	1	1	10%

The goal is to find the 50th percentile, the median, for this distribution. The score corresponding to 50% cannot be read directly from the table, so it will be necessary to use interpolation.

The intermediate value of 50% is located in the interval between the cumulative percentages of 40% and 90%, which correspond to the real limits of 3.5 and 4.5, respectively.

maks sense →

X	c%
4.5	90%
??	50%
3.5	40%

On the percentage scale, the value of 50% is located by 40 percentage points from the top (90%) of the interval, or $^{40}/_{50} = {}^4/_5$ of the total distance down in the interval.

On the X-scale, the total interval is 1.0 point wide, so $^4/_5$ of this total distance would be

$$({}^4/_5)1.00 = 0.80$$

Starting at the top of the X-scale and moving down 0.80 brings us to a score of $X = 4.50 - 0.80 = 3.70$. This is the score corresponding to the 50th percentile. That is, the score $X = 3.70$ is the median. Notice that this is exactly the same answer we obtained using the graphic method of interpolation in Example 3.5

vertical line that will divide the distribution exactly in half, with 5 blocks on the left-hand side and 5 blocks on the right-hand side.

To begin the process, start at the left-hand side of the distribution, and move up the scale of measurement (the X-axis), counting blocks as you go along. The vertical line corresponding to the median should be drawn at the point where you have counted exactly 5 blocks (50% of the total of 10 blocks). By the time you reach a value of 3.5 on the X-axis, you will have gathered a total of 4 blocks, so that only one more block is needed to give you exactly 50% of the distribution. The problem is that there are 5 blocks in the next interval. The solution is to take only a fraction of each of the 5 blocks so that the fractions combine to give you 1 more block. If you take $^1/_5$ of each block, the five fifths will combine to make one whole block. This solution is shown in Figure 3.7(b).

Notice that we have drawn a line separating each of the 5 blocks so that $^1/_5$ is on the left-hand side of the line and $^4/_5$ are on the right-hand side. Thus, the line should be drawn exactly $^1/_5$ of the way into the interval containing the 5 blocks. This interval extends from the lower real limit of 3.5 to the upper real limit of 4.5 on the X-axis and has a width of 1.00 point. One-fifth of the interval would be 0.20 points ($^1/_5$ of 1.00). Therefore, the line should be drawn at the point where $X = 3.70$ (the lower real limit of 3.5 + $^1/_5$ of the interval, or 0.20). This value, $X = 3.70$, is the median and divides the distribution exactly in half.

real limit stuff

The interpolation process demonstrated in Example 3.5 can be summarized in the following four steps, which can be generalized to any situation where several scores are tied at the median.

STEP 1 Count the number of scores (boxes in the graph) below the tied value.

STEP 2 Find the number of additional scores (boxes) needed to make exactly one half of the total distribution.

STEP 3 Form a fraction:

$$\frac{\text{number of boxes needed (step 2)}}{\text{number of tied boxes}}$$

STEP 4 Add the fraction (step 3) to the lower real limit of the interval containing the tied scores.

When these steps are incorporated into a formula, we obtain

$$\text{median} = X_{\text{LRL}} + \left(\frac{0.5N - f_{\text{BELOW LRL}}}{f_{\text{TIED}}} \right) \qquad (3.4)$$

where X_{LRL} is the lower real limit of the tied values, $f_{\text{BELOW LRL}}$ is the frequency of scores with values below X_{LRL}, and f_{TIED} is the frequency for the tied values. Thus, for Example 3.5,

$$\text{median} = 3.5 + \left(\frac{0.5(10) - 4}{5} \right)$$

$$= 3.5 + \left(\frac{5 - 4}{5} \right)$$

$$= 3.5 + \frac{1}{5}$$

$$= 3.5 + 0.2$$

$$= 3.7$$

Rather than using either method of interpolation (Example 3.5 or Box 3.3), you may use this formula for finding the median when there are tied values in the middle of the distribution and the data consist of whole numbers (interval widths of 1).

LEARNING CHECK

1. Find the median for each distribution of scores:
   a. 3, 10, 8, 4, 10, 7, 6
   b. 13, 8, 10, 11, 12, 10
   c. 3, 4, 3, 2, 1, 3, 2, 4

2. A distribution can have more than one median. (True or false?)

3. If you have a score of 52 on an 80-point exam, then you definitely scored above the median. (True or false?)

ANSWERS **1. a.** The median is $X = 7$.

        b. The median is $X = 10.5$.

        c. The median is $X = 2.83$ (by interpolation).

2. False

3. False. The value of the median would depend on where the scores are located.

3.4 THE MODE

The final measure of central tendency that we will consider is called the *mode*. In its common usage, the word *mode* means "the customary fashion" or "a popular style." The statistical definition is similar in that the mode is the most common observation among a group of scores.

DEFINITION
    In a frequency distribution, the *mode* is the score or category that has the greatest frequency.

As with the median, there are no symbols or special notation used to identify the mode or to differentiate between a sample mode and a population mode. In addition, the definition of the mode is the same for a population and for a sample distribution

    The mode can be used to describe what is typical for any scale of measurement (see Chapter 1). Suppose, for example, that you ask a sample of 100 students on campus to name their favorite restaurants in town. Your data might look like the results shown in Table 3.5. These are nominal data because the scale of measurement involves separate, unordered categories (restaurants). For these data, the modal response is Luigi's. This restaurant was named most frequently as a favorite place.

    In a frequency distribution graph, the greatest frequency will appear as the tallest part of the figure. To find the mode, you simply identify the score located directly beneath the highest point in the distribution.

    It is possible for a distribution to have more than one mode. Figure 3.8 shows the number of fish caught at various times during the day. There are two distinct peaks in this distribution, one at 6 A.M. and one at 6 P.M. Each of these values is a mode in the distribution. Note that the two modes do not have identical frequencies. Twelve fish were caught at 6 A.M., and 11 were caught at 6 P.M. Nonetheless, both of these points are called modes. The taller peak is called the *major mode*,

TABLE 3.5

Favorite restaurants named by a sample of $n = 100$ students

CAUTION: The mode is a score or category, not a frequency. For this example, the mode is Luigi's, not $f = 42$.

RESTAURANT	f
College Grill	5
George & Harry's	16
Luigi's	42
Oasis Diner	18
Roxbury Inn	7
Sutter's Mill	12

FIGURE 3.8

The relationship between time of day and number of fish caught.

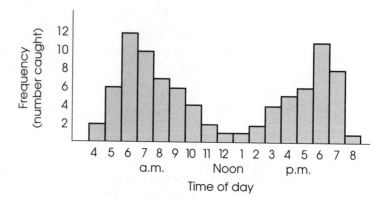

and the shorter one is the *minor mode*. Of course, it also is possible to have a distribution with two (or more) separate peaks that are exactly the same height. A distribution with two modes is said to be *bimodal*. When a distribution has more than two modes, it is called *multimodal*. It also is common for a distribution with several equally high points to be described as having no mode.

LEARNING CHECK

1. Find the mode for the set of scores shown in the following frequency distribution table:

X	f
5	2
4	6
3	4
2	2
1	1

2. In a recent survey comparing picture quality for three brands of color televisions, 63 people preferred brand A, 29 people preferred brand B, and 58 people preferred brand C. What is the mode for this distribution?

3. What is the reason for computing a measure of central tendency?

ANSWERS

1. The mode is $X = 4$.   2. The mode is brand A.

3. The goal of central tendency is to identify a single value to represent an entire distribution.

3.5 SELECTING A MEASURE OF CENTRAL TENDENCY

How do you decide which measure of central tendency to use? The answer to this question depends on several factors. Before we discuss these factors, however, it should be noted that with many sets of data it is possible to compute two or even three different measures of central tendency. Often the three measures will produce similar results, but there are situations where they will be very different (see Section 3.6). Also, it should be noted that the mean is most often the preferred measure of central tendency. Because the mean uses every score in the distribution, it usually is a good representative value. Remember, the goal of central tendency is to find the single value that best represents the entire distribution. Besides being a good representative, the mean has the added advantage of being closely related to variance and standard deviation, the most common measures of variability (Chapter 4). This relationship makes the mean a valuable measure for purposes of inferential statistics. For these reasons, and others, the mean generally is considered to be the best of the three measures of central tendency. But there are specific situations either where it is impossible to compute a mean or where the mean is not particularly representative. It is in these situations that the mode and the median are used.

WHEN TO USE THE MODE

The mode has two distinct advantages over the mean. First, it is easy to compute. Second, it can be used with any scale of measurement (nominal, ordinal, interval, ratio; see Chapter 1).

It is a bit misleading to say that the mode is easy to calculate because actually no calculation is required. When the scores are arranged in a frequency distribution, you identify the mode simply by finding the score with the greatest frequency. Because the value of the mode can be determined "at a glance," it is often included as a supplementary measure along with the mean or median as a no-cost extra. The value of the mode (or modes) in this situation is to give an indication of the shape of the distribution as well as a measure of central tendency. For example, if you are told that a set of exam scores has a mean of 72 and a mode of 80, you should have a better picture of the distribution than would be available from the mean alone (see Section 3.6).

The fact that the mode can be used with any scale of measurement makes it a very flexible value. When scores are measured on a nominal scale, it is impossible or meaningless to calculate either a mean or a median, so the mode is the only way to describe central tendency. Consider the frequency distribution shown in Figure 3.9. These data were obtained by recording the academic major for each student in a psychology lab section. Notice that "academic major" forms a nominal scale that simply classifies individuals into discrete categories.

FIGURE 3.9

Major field of study for $n = 9$ students enrolled in an experimental psychology laboratory section.

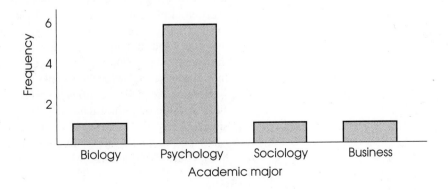

3.4 ## WHAT IS THE "AVERAGE"?

THE WORD *average* is used in everyday speech to describe what is typical and commonplace. Statistically, averages are measured by the mean, median, or mode. U.S. government agencies frequently characterize demographic data, such as average income or average age, with the median. Winners of elections are determined by the mode, the most frequent choice. Scholastic Achievement Test (SAT) scores for large groups of students usually are described with the mean. The important thing to remember about these measures of central tendency (or the "average") is that they describe and summarize a group of individuals rather than any single person. In fact, the "average person" may not actually exist. Figure

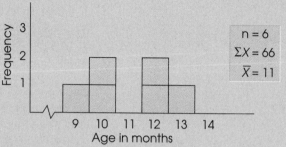

FIGURE 3.12

Frequency distribution showing the age at which each infant in a sample of $n = 6$ uttered his or her first word.

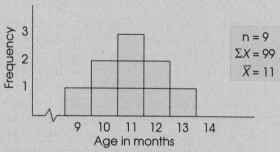

FIGURE 3.11

Frequency distribution showing the age at which each infant in a sample of $n = 9$ uttered his or her first word.

3.11 shows data that were gathered from a sample of $n = 9$ infants. The age at which each infant said his or her first word was recorded by the parents. Note that the mean for this group is $\overline{X} = 11$ months and that three infants uttered their first intelligible words at this age.

Now look at the results of a different study, using a sample of $n = 6$ infants (Figure 3.12). Note that the mean for this group is also $\overline{X} = 11$ months, but that the "average infant" does not exist in this sample. The mean describes the group, not a single individual. It is for this reason that we find humor in statements like "the average American family has 2.4 children," fully knowing that we never will encounter this family.

You cannot compute a mean for these data because it is impossible to determine ΣX. (How much is one biologist plus six psychologists?) Also note that there is no natural ordering for the four categories in this distribution. It is a purely arbitrary decision to place biology on the scale before psychology. Because it is impossible to specify any order for the scores, you cannot determine a median. The mode, on the other hand, provides a very good measure of central tendency. The mode for this sample is psychology. This category describes the typical, or most representative, academic major for the sample.

Because the mode identifies the most typical case, it often produces a more sensible measure of central tendency. The mean, for example, will generate conclusions such as "the average family has 2.4 children and a house with 5.33 rooms." Many people would feel more comfortable saying "the typical, or modal, family has 2 children and a house with 5 rooms" (see Box 3.4).

FIGURE 3.10

Frequency distribution of errors committed before reaching learning criterion.

Notice that the graph in Figure 3.10 shows two *breaks* in the X-axis. Rather than listing all the scores from 0 to 100, the graph jumps directly to the first score, which is $X = 10$, and then jumps directly from $X = 15$ to $X = 100$. The breaks shown in the X-axis are the conventional way of notifying the reader that some values have been omitted.

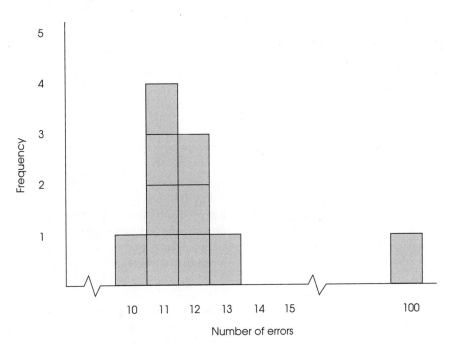

WHEN TO USE THE MEDIAN

There are four specific situations where the median serves as a valuable alternative to the mean. These occur when (1) there are a few extreme scores in the distribution, (2) some scores have undetermined values, (3) there is an open-ended distribution, and (4) the data are measured on an ordinal scale.

Extreme scores or skewed distributions When a distribution has a few extreme scores, scores that are very different in value from most of the others, then the mean may not be a good representative of the majority of the distribution. The problem comes from the fact that one or two extreme values can have a large influence and cause the mean to be displaced. In this situation, the fact that the mean uses all of the scores equally can be a disadvantage. For example, suppose that a sample of $n = 10$ rats is tested in a T-maze for a food reward. The animals must choose the correct arm of the T (right or left) to find the food in the goal box. The experimenter records the number of errors each rat makes before it solves the maze. Hypothetical data are presented in Figure 3.10.

The mean for this sample is

$$\overline{X} = \frac{\Sigma X}{n} = \frac{203}{10} = 20.3$$

Notice that the mean is not very representative of any score in this distribution. Most of the scores are clustered between 10 and 13. The extreme score of $X = 100$ (a slow learner) inflates the value of ΣX and distorts the mean.

The median, on the other hand, is not easily affected by extreme scores. For this sample, $n = 10$, so there should be five scores on either side of the median. The median is 11.50. Notice that this is a very representative value. Also note that

TABLE 3.6

Amount of time to complete puzzle

PERSON	TIME (MIN.)
1	8
2	11
3	12
4	13
5	17
6	Never finished

the median would be unchanged even if the slow learner made 1000 errors instead of only 100. The median commonly is used when reporting the average value for a skewed distribution. For example, the distribution of personal incomes is very skewed, with a small segment of the population earning incomes that are astronomical. These extreme values distort the mean, so that it is not very representative of the salaries that most of us earn. As in the previous example, the median is the preferred measure of central tendency when extreme scores exist.

Undetermined values   Occasionally, you will encounter a situation where an individual has an unknown or undetermined score. In psychology, this often occurs in learning experiments where you are measuring the number of errors (or amount of time) required for an individual to solve a particular problem. For example, suppose that a sample of $n = 6$ people were asked to assemble a wooden puzzle as quickly as possible. The experimenter records how long (in minutes) it takes each individual to arrange all the pieces to complete the puzzle. Table 3.6 presents the outcome of this experiment.

Notice that person 6 never completed the puzzle. After an hour, this person still showed no sign of solving the puzzle, so the experimenter stopped him or her. This person has an undetermined score. (There are two important points to be noted. First, the experimenter should not throw out this individual's score. The whole purpose for using a sample is to gain a picture of the population, and this individual tells us that part of the population cannot solve the puzzle. Second, this person should not be given a score of $X = 60$ minutes. Even though the experimenter stopped the individual after 1 hour, the person did not finish the puzzle. The score that is recorded is the amount of time needed to finish. For this individual, we do not know how long this would be.)

It is impossible to compute the mean for these data because of the undetermined value. We cannot calculate the ΣX part of the formula for the mean. However, it is possible to compute the median. For these data, the median is 12.5. Three scores are below the median, and three scores (including the undetermined value) are above the median.

NUMBER OF CHILDREN (X)	f
5 or more	3
4	2
3	2
2	3
1	6
0	4

Open-ended distributions   A distribution is said to be *open-ended* when there is no upper limit (or lower limit) for one of the categories. The table at the left provides an example of an open-ended distribution, showing the number of children in each family for a sample of $n = 20$ households. The top category in this distribution shows that three of the families have "5 or more" children. This in an open-ended category. Notice that it is impossible to compute a mean for these data because you cannot find ΣX (the total number of children for all 20 families). However, you can find the median. For these data, the median is 1.5 (exactly 50% of the families have fewer than 1.5 children).

Ordinal scale   Many researchers believe that it is not appropriate to use the mean to describe central tendency for ordinal data. When scores are measured on an ordinal scale, the median is always appropriate and is usually the preferred measure of central tendency. The following example demonstrates that although it is possible to compute a "mean rank," the resulting value can be misleading.

EXAMPLE 3.6   Three children held a basketball competition to see who could hit the most baskets in 10 attempts. The contest was held twice; the results are shown in the following table:

| | FIRST CONTEST | | | SECOND CONTEST | |
CHILD	RANK	NUMBER OF BASKETS	CHILD	RANK	NUMBER OF BASKETS
A	1st	10	C	1st	7
B	2nd	4	B	2nd	6
C	3rd	2	A	3rd	5

According to the data, child A finished first in one contest and third in the other, for a "mean rank" of 2. Child C also finished first one time and third one time and also has a mean rank of 2. Although these two children are identical in terms of mean rank, they are different in terms of the total number of baskets: Child A hit a total of 15 baskets, and child C hit only 9. The mean rank does not reflect this difference.

IN THE LITERATURE:
REPORTING MEASURES OF CENTRAL TENDENCY

Measures of central tendency are commonly used in the behavioral sciences to summarize and describe the results of a research study. For example, a researcher may report the sample means from two different treatments or the median score for a large sample. These values may be reported in verbal descriptions of the results, in tables, or in graphs. Typically, measures of central tendency are used to help describe the relationship between an independent variable and a dependent variable. You should recall from Chapter 1 that the independent variable distinguishes the different treatment conditions or groups being compared, and the dependent variable is the score obtained for each subject. A researcher typically computes a measure of central tendency (mean, median, or mode) for the dependent variable and then reports the obtained value for each treatment or group.

In reporting the results, many behavioral science journals use guidelines adopted by the American Psychological Association (APA), as outlined in the *Publication Manual of the American Psychological Association* (1994). We will refer to the APA manual from time to time in describing how data and research

TABLE 3.7

The Mean Number of Errors Made on the Task for Treatment and Control Groups According to Gender

	TREATMENT	CONTROL
Females	1.45	8.36
Males	3.83	14.77

results are reported in the scientific literature. The APA style typically uses the letter *M* as the symbol for the sample mean. Thus, a study might state

> The treatment group showed fewer errors (*M* = 2.56) on the task than the control group (*M* = 11.76).

When there are many means to report, tables with headings provide an organized and more easily understood presentation. Table 3.7 illustrates this point.

The median can be reported using the abbreviation *Mdn,* as in "Mdn = 8.5 errors," or it can simply be reported in narrative text, as follows,

> The median number of errors for the treatment group was 8.5, compared to a median of 13 for the control group.

There is no special symbol or convention for reporting the mode. If mentioned at all, the mode is usually just reported in narrative text.

> The modal hair color was blonde, with 23 out of 50 subjects in this category.

Graphs also can be used to report and compare measures of central tendency. Usually graphs are used to display values obtained for sample means, but occasionally you will see sample medians reported in graphs (modes are rarely, if ever, shown in a graph). The value of a graph is that it allows several means (or medians) to be shown simultaneously so it is possible to make quick comparisons between groups or treatment conditions. When preparing a graph, it is customary to plot the values for the independent variable (the different groups or treatments) on the horizontal axis and the values for the dependent variable (scores) on the vertical axis. The means (or medians) are then displayed using a *line graph,* a *histogram,* or a *bar graph,* depending on the scale of measurement used for the independent variable.

 Figure 3.13 shows an example of a line graph displaying the relationship between drug dose (the independent variable) and mean food consumption (the dependent variable). A line graph is used when the different values of the independent variable are measured on an interval or a ratio scale. The construction of a line graph proceeds in two steps:

1. Directly above each group or treatment shown on the horizontal axis, draw a dot so that the height (vertical position) of the dot corresponds to the mean (or median) for that group or treatment.
2. Draw a line connecting the dots.

The data shown in Figure 3.13 could also be presented in a histogram. To construct a histogram, you would draw a bar above each of the drug-dose values so that the height of the bar corresponds to the mean (or median) for that particular drug dosage. This histogram is drawn so that there are no gaps between bars, which indicates that the independent variable has been measured on an interval or ratio scale.

FIGURE 3.13

The relationship between an independent variable (drug dose) and a dependent variable (food consumption). Because drug dose is a continuous variable, a continuous line is used to connect the different dose levels.

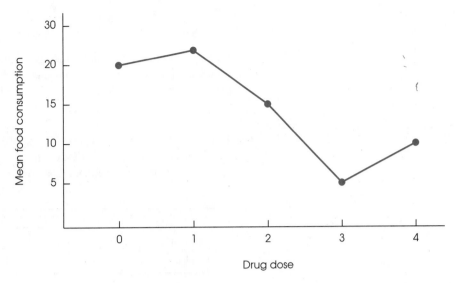

Figure 3.14 shows a bar graph displaying the median selling price for single-family homes in different regions of the United States. Bar graphs are used to present means (or medians) when the independent variable is measured on a nominal or an ordinal scale. To construct a bar graph, you simply draw a bar directly above each group or treatment so that the height of the bar corresponds to the mean (or median) for that group or treatment. For a bar graph, a space is left between adjacent bars to indicate that the scale of measurement is nominal or ordinal.

When constructing graphs of any type, you should recall the basic rules we introduced in Chapter 2:

1. The height of a graph should be approximately two-thirds to three-quarters of its length.

2. Normally, you start numbering both the X-axis and the Y-axis with zero at the point where the two axes intersect. However, when a value of zero is

FIGURE 3.14

Median cost of a new, single-family home by region.

bar graph

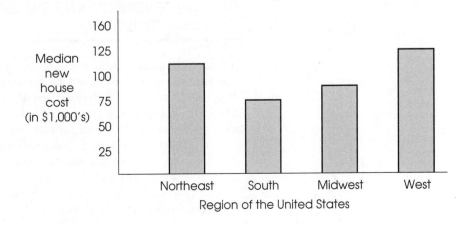

part of the data, it is common to move the zero point away from the intersection so that the graph does not overlap the axes (see Figure 3.13).

More important, you should remember that the purpose of a graph is to give an accurate representation of the information in a set of data. Box 2.1 in Chapter 2 demonstrates what can happen when these basic principles are ignored. ☐

LEARNING CHECK

1. In a study on stress, a researcher exposed groups of rats to signaled shock, unsignaled shock, or no shock. The size (in millimeters) of ulcers for each group was then determined. Construct a graph of the following data:

	NO SHOCK	SIGNALED SHOCK	UNSIGNALED SHOCK
Mean size of ulcers	0	3	7

2. A psychologist studied the effect of sleep deprivation on mood. Groups of clinically depressed subjects were deprived of sleep for 0, 1, 2, or 3 nights. After deprivation, the amount of depression was measured with a depression inventory. Construct a graph of the following data:

NIGHTS OF DEPRIVATION	MEAN DEPRESSION SCORE
0	22
1	17
2	9
3	7

ANSWERS   **1. and 2.** The graphs are shown in Figure 3.15.

3.6 CENTRAL TENDENCY AND THE SHAPE OF THE DISTRIBUTION

We have identified three different measures of central tendency, and often a researcher will calculate all three for a single set of data. Because the mean, the median, and the mode are all trying to measure the same thing (central tendency), it is reasonable to expect that these three values should be related. In fact, there are some consistent and predictable relationships among the three measures of central tendency. Specifically, there are situations where all three measures will have exactly the same value. On the other hand, there are situations where the three measures are guaranteed to be different. In part, the relationships among the mean, median, and mode are determined by the shape of the distribution. We will consider two general types of distributions.

FIGURE 3.15

Answers to Learning Check Exercises 1 and 2.

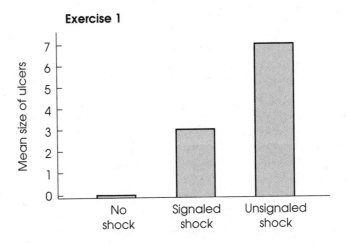

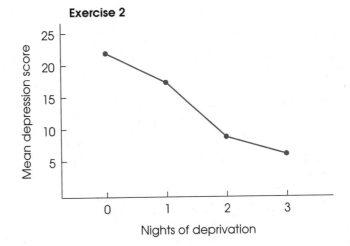

SYMMETRICAL DISTRIBUTIONS

For a *symmetrical distribution*, the right-hand side of the graph will be a mirror image of the left-hand side. By definition, the median will be exactly at the center of a symmetrical distribution because exactly half of the area in the graph will be on either side of the center. The mean also will be exactly at the center of a symmetrical distribution because each individual score in the distribution has a corresponding score on the other side (the mirror image), so that the average of these two values is exactly in the middle. Because all the scores can be paired in this way, the overall average will be exactly at the middle. For any symmetrical distribution, the mean and the median will be the same (Figure 3.16).

If a symmetrical distribution has only one mode, then it must be exactly at the center, so that all three measures of central tendency will have the same value (see Figure 3.16). On the other hand, a bimodal distribution that is symmetrical [Figure 3.16(b)] will have the mean and the median together in the center with the modes on each side. A rectangular distribution [Figure 3.16(c)] has no mode because all X values occur with the same frequency. Still, the mean and the median will be in the center of the distribution and equivalent in value.

FIGURE 3.16

Measures of central tendency for three symmetrical distributions: normal, bimodal, and rectangular.

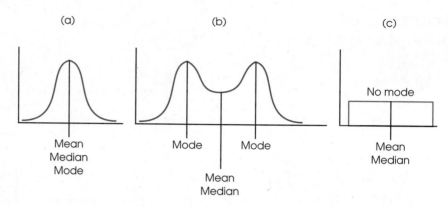

FIGURE 13.17

Measures of central tendency for skewed distributions.

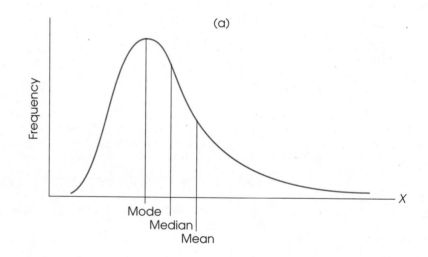

positive skew

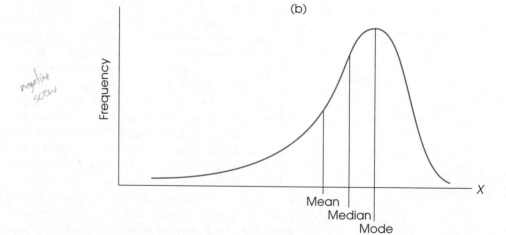

negative skew

SKEWED DISTRIBUTIONS   Distributions are not always symmetrical. In fact, quite often they are lopsided, or *skewed.* For example, Figure 3.17(a) shows a *positively skewed distribution.* In this distribution, the peak (highest frequency) is on the left-hand side. This is the position of the mode. If you examine Figure 3.17(a) carefully, it should be clear that the vertical line drawn at the mode does not divide the distribution into two equal parts. In order to have exactly 50% of the distribution on each side, the median must be located to the right of the mode. Finally, the mean will be located to the right of median because it is influenced most by extreme scores and will be displaced farthest to the right by the scores in the tail. Therefore, in a positively skewed distribution, the mean will have the largest value, followed by the median and then the mode [see Figure 3.17(a)].

Negatively skewed distributions are lopsided in the opposite direction, with the scores piling up on the right-hand side and the tail tapering off to the left. The grades on an easy exam, for example, will tend to form a negatively skewed distribution [see Figure 3.17(b)]. For a distribution with negative skew, the mode is on the right-hand side (with the peak), while the mean is displaced on the left by the extreme scores in the tail. As before, the median is located between the mean and the mode. In order from highest value to lowest value, the three measures of central tendency will be the mode, the median, and the mean.

SUMMARY

1. The purpose of central tendency is to determine the single value that best represents the entire distribution of scores. The three standard measures of central tendency are the mode, the median, and the mean.

2. The mean is the arithmetic average. It is computed by adding all the scores and then dividing by the number of scores. Changing any score in the distribution will cause the mean to be changed. When a constant value is added to (or subtracted from) every score in a distribution, the same constant value is added to (subtracted from) the mean. If every score is multiplied by the same constant, the mean will be multiplied by the same constant. In nearly all cirmunstances, the mean is the best representative value and is the preferred measure of central tendency.

3. The median is the value that divides a distribution exactly in half. The median is the preferred measure of central tendency when a distribution has a few extreme scores that

displace the value of the mean. The median also is used when there are undetermined (infinite) scores that make it impossible to compute a mean.

4. The mode is the most frequently occurring score in a distribution. It is easily located by finding the peak in a frequency distribution graph. For data measured on a nominal scale, the mode is the appropriate measure of central tendency. It is possible for a distribution to have more than one mode.

5. For symmetrical distributions, the mean will equal the median. If there is only one mode, then it will have the same value, too.

6. For skewed distributions, the mode will be located toward the side where the scores pile up, and the mean will be pulled toward the extreme scores in the tail. The median will be located between these two values.

KEY TERMS

central tendency	mode	bimodal distribution	skewed distribution
mean	major mode	multimodal distribution	positive skew
weighted mean	minor mode	symmetrical distribution	negative skew
median			

─────── FOCUS ON PROBLEM SOLVING ───────

1. Because there are three different measures of central tendency, your first problem is to decide which one is best for your specific set of data. Usually the mean is the preferred measure, but the median may provide a more representative value if you are working with a skewed distribution. With data measured on a nominal scale, you must use the mode.

2. Although the three measures of central tendency appear to be very simple to calculate, there is always a chance for errors. The most common sources of error are listed next.

   a. Many students find it very difficult to compute the mean for data presented in a frequency distribution table. They tend to ignore the frequencies in the table and simply average the score values listed in the X column. You must use the frequencies and the scores! Remember, the number of scores is found by $N = \Sigma f$, and the sum of all N scores is found by ΣfX.

   b. The median is the midpoint of the distribution of scores, not the midpoint of the scale of measurement. For a 100-point test, for example, many students incorrectly assume that the median must be $X = 50$. To find the median, you must have the *complete set* of individual scores. The median separates the individuals into two equal-sized groups.

   c. The most common error with the mode is for students to report the highest frequency in a distribution rather than the score with the highest frequency. Remember, the purpose of central tendency is to find the most representative score. Therefore, for the following data, the mode is $X = 3$, not $f = 8$.

X	f
4	3
3	8
2	5
1	2

─────── DEMONSTRATION 3.1 ───────

COMPUTING MEASURES OF CENTRAL TENDENCY

For the following sample data, find the mean, median, and mode. Scores:

$$5, \quad 6, \quad 9, \quad 11, \quad 5, \quad 11, \quad 8, \quad 14, \quad 2, \quad 11$$

Compute the mean   Calculating the mean involves two steps:

1. Obtain the sum of the scores, ΣX.

2. Divide the sum by the number of scores, n.

For these data, the sum of the scores is as follows:

$$\Sigma X = 5 + 6 + 9 + 11 + 5 + 11 + 8 + 14 + 2 + 11 = 82$$

We can also observe that $n = 10$. Therefore, the mean of this sample is obtained by

$$\overline{X} = \frac{\Sigma X}{n} = \frac{82}{10} = 8.2$$

Find the median   The median divides the distribution in half, in that half of the scores are above or equal to the median and half are below or equal to it. In this demonstration, $n = 10$. Thus, the median should be a value that has 5 scores above it and 5 scores below it.

STEP 1   Arrange the scores in order.

$$2, \quad 5, \quad 5, \quad 6, \quad 8, \quad 9, \quad 11, \quad 11, \quad 11, \quad 14$$

STEP 2   With an even number of scores, locate the midpoint between the middle two scores. The middle scores are $X = 8$ and $X = 9$. The median is the midpoint between 8 and 9.

$$\text{median } \frac{8 + 9}{2} = \frac{17}{2} = 8.5$$

Find the mode   The mode is the X value that has the highest frequency. Looking at the data, we can readily determine that $X = 11$ is the score that occurs most frequently.

DEMONSTRATION 3.2

COMPUTING THE MEAN FROM A FREQUENCY DISTRIBUTION TABLE

Compute the mean for the data in the following table:

X	f
6	1
5	0
4	3
3	3
2	2

To compute the mean from a frequency distribution table, you must use the information in *both* the X and the f columns.

STEP 1   Multiply each X value by its frequency.
   You can create a third column labeled fX. For these data,

fX
6
0
12
9
4

STEP 2 Find the sum of the fX values.

$$\Sigma fX = 6 + 0 + 12 + 9 + 4 = 31$$

STEP 3 Find n for these data.
Remember, $n = \Sigma f$.

$$n = \Sigma f = 1 + 0 + 3 + 3 + 2 = 9$$

STEP 4 Divide the sum of fX by n.

$$\overline{X} = \frac{\Sigma fX}{n} = \frac{31}{9} = 3.44$$

PROBLEMS

1. Explain the general purpose for measuring central tendency.

2. Explain why there is more than one method for measuring central tendency. Why not use a single, standardized method for determining the "average" score?

3. Explain what is meant by each of the following statements:
   a. The mean is the *balance point* of the distribution.
   b. The median is the *midpoint* of the distribution.

4. Identify the circumstances where the median instead of the mean is the preferred measure of central tendency.

5. Under what circumstances will the mean, the median, and the mode all have the same value?

6. Under what circumstances is the mode the preferred measure of central tendency?

7. Find the mean, median, and mode for the following sample of scores:

   2, 5, 1, 4, 2, 3, 3, 2

8. For the following set of scores:

   9, 7, 9, 8, 10, 8, 1, 9, 8, 9

   a. Sketch a frequency distribution histogram.
   b. Find the mean, the median, and mode, and locate these values in your graph.

9. In kindergarten, you learned the etiquette of sharing. Now you know the statistics of sharing. Consider the following:
   a. Three boys put all their baseball cards together and find that they have a total of 120 cards. If they divide the cards equally, how many will each boy get?

   b. A sample of $n = 3$ scores has $\Sigma X = 120$. What is $\overline{X}$ for this sample? (Note that this is the same question as in part a.)
   c. Six children bought a bag of candy and divided the pieces equally. If each child got 8 pieces of candy, how many pieces were in the bag?
   d. A sample of $n = 6$ has a mean of $\overline{X} = 8$. What is ΣX for this sample? (Note that this is the same question as in part c.)

10. For the set of scores shown in the following frequency distribution table:
    a. Sketch a histogram showing the distribution, and locate the median in your sketch.
    b. Compute the mean for this set of scores.
    c. Now, suppose that the score $X = 5$ is changed to $X = 45$. How does this change affect the mean and the median? Use your sketch to find the new median, and then compute the new mean.

X	f
5	1
4	2
3	4
2	2
1	1

11. For the set of scores presented in the following frequency distribution:
    a. Find the mean, median, and mode.
    b. Based on your answers from part a, identify the shape of the distribution.

X	f
5	10
4	6
3	2
2	1
1	1

12. A population of $N = 50$ scores has a mean of $\mu = 26$. What is ΣX for this population?

13. A sample has a mean of $\overline{X} = 5$ and $\Sigma X = 320$. How many scores are in this sample? ($n = ?$)

14. A sample has a mean of $\overline{X} = 20$.
   a. If each X value is multiplied by 6, what is the value of the new mean?
   b. If 5 points are added to each of the original X values, what is the value of the new mean?

15. A sample of $n = 8$ scores has a mean of $\overline{X} = 12$. A new score of $X = 4$ is added to the sample.
   a. What is ΣX for the original sample?
   b. What is ΣX for the new sample?
   c. What is n for the new sample?
   d. What is the mean for the new sample?

16. A sample has a mean of $\overline{X} = 40$.
   a. If a new score of $X = 50$ is added to the sample, what will happen to the sample mean (increase, decrease, stay the same)? Explain your answer.
   b. If a new score of $X = 30$, is added the sample, what will happen to the sample mean (increase, decrease, stay the same)? Explain your answer.
   c. If a new score of $X = 40$ is added to the sample, what will happen to the sample mean (increase, decrease, stay the same)? Explain your answer.

17. A sample of $n = 5$ scores has a mean of $\overline{X} = 10$.
   a. If a new score of $X = 4$ is added to the sample, what value will be obtained for the new sample mean?
   b. If one of the scores, $X = 18$, is removed from the original sample, what value will be obtained for the new sample mean?
   c. If one of the scores in the original sample is changed from $X = 5$ to $X = 20$, what value will be obtained for the new sample mean?

18. A sample of $n = 5$ scores has a mean of $\overline{X} = 21$. One new score is added to the sample, and the mean for the resulting new sample is $\overline{X} = 25$. Find the value of the new score. (*Hint:* Find ΣX for the original sample and ΣX for the new sample.)

19. A sample of $n = 10$ scores has a mean of $\overline{X} = 23$. One score is removed from the sample, and the mean for the remaining scores is $\overline{X} = 25$. Find the value of the score that was removed.

20. One sample of $n = 3$ scores has a mean of $\overline{X} = 4$. A second sample of $n = 7$ scores has a mean of $\overline{X} = 10$. If these two samples are combined, what value will be obtained for the mean of the combined sample?

21. For each of the following situations, identify the measure of central tendency (mean, median, mode) that would provide the best description of the "average" score:
   a. A researcher records each individual's favorite TV show for a sample of $n = 50$ 6-year-old children.
   b. A researcher records how much weight is gained or lost for each client during a 6-week diet program.
   c. A researcher studying motivation asks subjects to search through a newspaper for the word "discipline." The researcher records how long (in minutes) each subject works at the task before findng the word or giving up. For a sample of $n = 20$ people, the mean time is $X = 29$ minutes, the median is 17 minutes, and the mode is 15 minutes.

22. A professor computed the mean, median, and mode for the exam scores from a class of $N = 20$ students. Identify which of the following statements *cannot* be true and explain your answer:
   a. 60% of the class had scores greater than the mean.
   b. 60% of the class had scores greater than the median.
   c. 60% of the class had scores greater than the mode.

23. A distribution of exam scores has a mean of 71 and a median of 79. Is it more likely that this distribution is symmetrical, positively skewed, or negatively skewed?

24. The following frequency distribution summarizes the number of absences for each student in a class of $n = 20$:

NUMBER OF ABSENCES (X)	f	cumf	c%f
5 or more	3	20	100%
4	4	17	55%
3	3	13	45%
2	6	10	50%
1	3	4	20%
0	1	1	5%

   a. Find the mode for this distribution.
   b. Find the median number of absences for this class.
   c. Explain why you cannot compute the mean number of absences using the data provided in the table.

25. On a standardized reading achievement test, the nationwide average for seventh grade children is $\mu = 7.0$. A seventh grade teacher is interested in comparing class reading scores with the national average. The scores for the 16 students in this class are as follows:

$$8, \quad 6, \quad 5, \quad 10, \quad 5, \quad 6, \quad 8, \quad 9$$
$$7, \quad 6, \quad 9, \quad 5, \quad 14, \quad 4, \quad 7, \quad 6$$

a. Find the mean and the median reading scores for this class.
b. If the mean is used to define the class average, how does this class compare with the national norm?
c. If the median is used to define the class average, how does this class compare with the national norm?

26. A researcher evaluated the taste of four leading brands of instant coffee by having a sample of individuals taste each coffee and then rate its flavor on a scale from 1 to 5 (1 = very bad and 5 = excellent). The results from this study are summarized as follows:

COFFEE	MEAN RATING
Brand A	2.5
Brand B	4.1
Brand C	3.2
Brand D	3.6

a. Identify the independent variable and the dependent variable for this study. *coffee*
b. What scale of measurement was used for the independent variable (nominal, ordinal, interval, ratio)?
c. If the researcher used a graph to show the obtained relationship between the independent variable and the dependent variable, what kind of graph would be appropriate (line graph, histogram, bar graph)?
d. Sketch a graph showing the results of this experiment.

27. A researcher examined the effect of amount of relaxation training on insomnia. Four treatment groups were used.

Subjects received relaxation training for 2, 4, or 8 sessions. A control group received no training (0 sessions). Following training, the researcher measured how long it took the subjects to fall asleep. The average time for each group is presented in the following table:

TRAINING SESSIONS	AVERAGE TIME (IN MINUTES)
0	72
2	58
4	31
8	14

a. Identify the independent variable and the dependent variable for this study. *relaxation training   time to sleep*
b. What scale of measurement was used for the independent variable nominal, ordinal, interval, ratio?
c. If the researcher used a graph to show the obtained relationship between the independent variable and the dependent variable, what kind of graph would be appropriate (line graph, histogram, bar graph)?
d. Sketch a graph showing the results of this experiment.

28. College officials recently conducted a survey to determine students' attitudes toward extending the library hours. Four different groups of students were surveyed, representing the four major subdivisions of the college. They were asked to give a rating from 1 (leave hours alone) to 10 (definitely extend). The average rating for each group was as follows:

humanities:	7.25
sciences:	5.69
professions:	6.85
fine arts:	5.90

Use a graph to present the results of this survey.

bar graph

CHAPTER 4

VARIABILITY

TOOLS YOU WILL NEED

The following items are considered essential background material for this chapter. If you doubt your knowledge of any of these items, you should review the appropriate chapter or section before proceeding.

- Summation notation (Chapter 1)
- Central tendency (Chapter 3)
  - Mean
  - Median

CONTENTS

good

It's 10 A.M., and Mary L. is washing her hands for the tenth time today. Before she goes to sleep tonight, she will have washed her hands over 60 times. Is this normal?

To differentiate between normal and abnormal behavior, some psychologists have resorted to using a *statistical model*. For example, we could survey a large sample of individuals and record the number of times each person washes his/her hands during a typical day. Because people are different, the scores should be variable, and the data from this survey should produce a distribution similar to the one shown in Figure 4.1. Notice that most people will have average or moderate scores located in the central part of the distribution. Others, such as Mary L., will deviate from the average. According to the statistical model, those who show substantial deviation are abnormal. Note that this model simply defines abnormal as being unusual or different from normal. The model does not imply that abnormal is necessarily negative or undesirable. Mary L. may have a compulsive personality disorder, or she may be a dentist washing her hands between patients.

The statistical model for abnormality requires two statistical concepts: a measure of the average and a measure of deviation from the average. In Chapter 3, we examined the standard techniques for defining the average score for a distribution. In this chapter, we will examine methods for measuring deviations. The fact that scores deviate from average means that they are variable. Variability is one of the most basic statistical concepts. As an introduction to the concept, this chapter will concentrate on defining and measuring variability. In later chapters, we will explore sources of variabil-

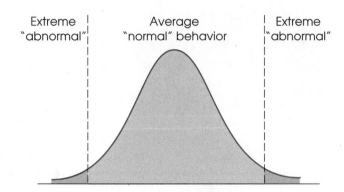

Figure 4.1

The statistical model for defining abnormal behavior. The distribution of behavior scores for the entire population is divided into three sections. Those individuals with average scores are defined as normal, and individuals who show extreme deviation from average are defined as abnormal.

ity and examine how variability affects the interpretation of other statistical measurements.

One additional point should be made before we proceed. You probably have noticed that central tendency and variability are closely related. Whenever one appears, the other usually is close at hand. You should watch for this association throughout the book. The better you understand the relationships between central tendency and variability, the better you will understand statistics.

4.1 OVERVIEW

The term *variability* has much the same meaning in statistics as it has in everyday language; to say that things are variable means that they are not all the same. In statistics, our goal is to measure the amount of variability for a particular set of scores, a distribution. In simple terms, if the scores in a distribution are all the same, then there is no variability. If there are small differences between scores, then the variability is small, and if there are large differences between scores, then the variability is large.

DEFINITION   *Variability* provides a quantitative measure of the degree to which scores in a distribution are spread out or clustered together.

The purpose of measuring variability is to determine how spread out a distribution of scores is. Are the scores all clustered together, or are they scattered over a wide range of values? A good measure of variability should provide an accurate picture of the spread of the distribution. Variability, along with central tendency

4.1 AN EXAMPLE OF VARIABILITY

TO EXAMINE the role of variability, we will consider two games of chance.

For the first game, you pay $1 to play, and you get back 90 cents every time. That's right, you pay me $1, and I give you back 90¢. Notice that this game has no variability; exactly the same thing happens every time. On the average, you lose 10¢ each time you play, and, in this case, the average gives a perfect description of the outcome of the game.

For the second game, the rules are a little different. It still costs $1 to play; but this time you have a 1-out-of-10 chance of winning $9. The rest of the time you win nothing. For this second game, we have added variability; the outcomes will not be all the same. Notice, however, that in the long run you still lose 10¢ each time you play. In 10 games, for example, you would expect to win once ($9), but you would have paid $10 to play. You

expect to lose $1 during 10 games, for an average loss of 10¢ per game.

On the average, these two games are identical. But, in one case, the average perfectly describes every single outcome, and, in the other case, the average is not at all representative of what actually happens on any single trial. The difference between these two games is the variability.

You also should notice the number of times you would need to watch each game in order to understand it. For the first game, any individual outcome (pay $1 and get back 90¢) gives a complete description of the game. After only one or two observations, you know the entire game. For the second game, however, you would need to watch a long time before the nature of the game became clear. In this case, it would take a large sample to provide a good description of the game.

and shape, is one of the three basic descriptive indices that are used to describe distributions of scores.

In addition to providing a description of the distribution, a good measure of variability serves another valuable purpose. A good measure of variability will give an indication of how well an individual score (or group of scores) represents the entire distribution. For example, there are occasions when the population mean is unknown. In these situations, a sample is selected from the population, and the sample is then used to represent the entire distribution. This is particularly important in the area of inferential statistics, where relatively small samples are used to answer general questions about large populations. If the scores in a distribution are all clustered together (small variability), then any individual score will be a reasonably accurate representative of the entire distribution. But if the scores are all spread out, then a single value selected from the distribution often will not be representative of the rest of the group. This point is illustrated by the two "games of chance" described in Box 4.1.

In this chapter, we will consider three different measures of variability: the range, the interquartile range, and the standard deviation. Of these three, the standard deviation (and the related measure of variance) is by far the most important.

4.2 THE RANGE

The range is the distance between the largest score (X_{max}) and the smallest score (X_{min}) in the distribution. In determining this distance, you must also take into account the real limits of the maximum and minimum X values. The range, therefore, is computed as the difference between the upper real limit (URL) for X_{max} and the lower real limit (LRL) for X_{min}.

$$\text{range} = \text{URL } X_{max} - \text{LRL } X_{min}$$

DEFINITION

The *range* is the difference between the upper real limit of the largest (maximum) X value and the lower real limit of the smallest (minimum) X value.

For example, consider the following data:

$$3, \quad 7, \quad 12, \quad 8, \quad 5, \quad 10$$

For these data, $X_{max} = 12$, with an upper real limit of 12.5, and $X_{min} = 3$, with a lower real limit of 2.5. Thus, the range equals

$$\text{range} = \text{URL } X_{max} - \text{LRL } X_{min}$$
$$= 12.5 - 2.5 = 10$$

When the distribution consists of whole numbers, the range also can be obtained as follows:

$$\text{range} = \text{highest } X - \text{lowest } X + 1$$

The range is perhaps the most obvious way of describing how spread out the scores are—simply find the distance between the maximum and minimum scores. The problem with using the range as a measure of variability is that it is completely determined by the two extreme values and ignores the other scores in the distribution. For example, the following two distributions have exactly the same range—10 points in each case. However, the scores in the first distribution are clustered together at one end of the range, whereas the scores in the second distribution are spread out over the entire range.

$$\text{distribution 1:} \quad 1, \quad 8, \quad 9, \quad 9, \quad 10, \quad 10$$

$$\text{distribution 2:} \quad 1, \quad 2, \quad 4, \quad 6, \quad 8, \quad 10$$

If, for example, these were scores on a 10-point quiz for two different class sections, there are clear differences between the two sections. Nearly all the students in the first section have mastered the material, but there is a wide range of achievement for students in the second section. A good measure of variability should show this difference.

Because the range does not consider all the scores in the distribution, it often does not give an accurate description of the variability for the entire distribution. For this reason, the range is considered to be a crude and unreliable measure of variability.

4.3 THE INTERQUARTILE RANGE AND SEMI-INTERQUARTILE RANGE

In Chapter 3, we defined the median as the score that divides a distribution exactly in half. In a similar way, a distribution can be divided into four equal parts using *quartiles*. By definition, the first quartile ($Q1$) is the score that separates the lowest 25% of the distribution from the rest. The second quartile ($Q2$) is the score that has exactly two quarters, or 50%, of the distribution below it. Notice that the sec-

FIGURE 4.2

Frequency distribution for a population of $N = 16$ scores. The first quartile is $Q1 = 4.5$. The third quartile is $Q3 = 8.0$. The interquartile range is 3.5 points. Note that the third quartile ($Q3$) divides the two boxes at $X = 8$ exactly in half, so that a total of 4 boxes is above $Q3$ and 12 boxes are below it.

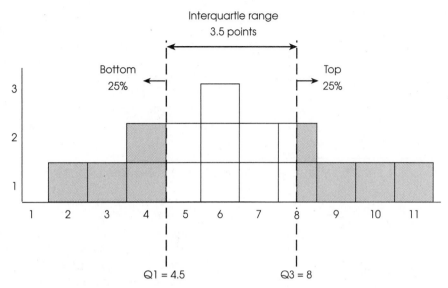

ond quartile and the median are the same. Finally, the third quartile ($Q3$) is the score that divides the bottom three-fourths of the distribution from the top quarter. The interquartile range is defined as the distance between the first and third quartiles. The semi-interquartile range is one-half of the interquartile range. It provides a descriptive measure of the "typical" distance of scores from the median ($Q2$).

DEFINITIONS

The *interquartile range* is the distance between the first quartile and the third quartile:

$$\text{interquartile range} = Q3 - Q1$$

When the interquartile range is used to describe variability, it commonly is transformed into the *semi-interquartile range.* The semi-interquartile range is simply one-half of the interquartile range:

$$\text{semi-interquartile range} = \frac{(Q3 - Q1)}{2}$$

EXAMPLE 4.1

Figure 4.2 shows a frequency distribution histogram for a set of 16 scores. For this distribution, the first quartile is $Q1 = 4.5$. Exactly 25% of the scores (4 out of 16) are located below $X = 4.5$. Similarly, the third quartile $Q3 = 8.0$. Note that this value separates the bottom 75% of the distribution (12 out of 16 scores) from the top 25%. For this set of scores, the interquartile range is

$$Q3 - Q1 = 8.0 - 4.5 = 3.5$$

The semi-interquartile range is simply one-half of this distance:

$$\text{semi-interquartile range} = \frac{3.5}{2} = 1.75$$

Because the semi-interquartile range focuses on the middle 50% of a distribution, it is less likely to be influenced by extreme scores and, therefore, gives a better and more stable measure of variability than the range. Nevertheless, the semi-interquartile range does not take into account the actual distances between individual scores, so it does not give a complete picture of how scattered or clustered the scores are. Like the range, the semi-interquartile range is considered to be a somewhat crude measure of variability. In Chapter 6, we will introduce another method to determine the semi-interquartile range for normal distributions.

LEARNING CHECK

1. For the following data, find the range and the semi-interquartile range:

$$3, \quad 4, \quad 5, \quad 7, \quad 9, \quad 10, \quad 11, \quad 13$$

2. Consider the distribution of Exercise 1, except replace the score of 13 with a score of 100. What are the new values for the range and the semi-interquartile range? In comparing the answer to the one for the previous exercise, what can you conclude about these measures of variability?

ANSWERS

1. Range = URL X_{max} − LRL X_{min} = 13.5 − 2.5 = 11; semi-interquartile range = $(Q3 − Q1)/2$ = (10.5 − 4.5)/2 = 3.

2. Range = 98; semi-interquartile range = 3. The range is greatly affected by extreme scores in the distribution, unlike the semi-interquartile range.

4.4 STANDARD DEVIATION AND VARIANCE FOR A POPULATION

 The standard deviation is the most commonly used and the most important measure of variability. Standard deviation uses the mean of the distribution as a reference point and measures variability by considering the distance between each score and the mean. It determines whether the scores are generally near or far from the mean. That is, are the scores clustered together or scattered? In simple terms, the standard deviation approximates the average distance from the mean.

Although the concept of standard deviation is straightforward, the actual equations will appear complex. Therefore, we will begin by looking at the logic that leads to these equations. If you remember that our goal is to measure the standard, or typical, distance from the mean, then this logic and the equations that follow should be easier to remember.

STEP 1 The first step in finding the standard distance from the mean is to determine the deviation, or distance from the mean, for each individual score. By definition, the deviation for each score is the difference between the score and the mean.

DEFINITION *Deviation* is distance from the mean:

$$\text{deviation score} = X − \mu$$

For a distribution of scores with $\mu = 50$, if your score is $X = 53$, then your deviation score is

$$X - \mu = 53 - 50 = 3$$

If your score is $X = 45$, then your deviation score is

$$X - \mu = 45 - 50 = -5$$

Notice that there are two parts to a deviation score: the sign ($+$ or $-$) and the number. The sign tells the direction from the mean, that is, whether the score is located above ($+$) or below ($-$) the mean. The number gives the actual distance from the mean. For example, a deviation score of -6 corresponds to score that is below the mean by 6 points.

STEP 2 Because our goal is to compute a measure of the standard distance from the mean, the obvious next step is to calculate the mean of the deviation scores. To compute this mean, you first add up the deviation scores and then divide by N. This process is demonstrated in the following example.

EXAMPLE 4.2 We start with the following set of $N = 4$ scores. These scores add up to $\Sigma X = 12$, so the mean is $\mu = {}^{12}\!/_4 = 3$. For each score, we have computed the deviation.

X	$X - \mu$
8	$+5$
1	-2
3	0
0	-3
	$0 = \Sigma(X - \mu)$

Notice that the deviation scores add up to zero. This should not be surprising if you remember that the mean serves as a balance point for the distribution. The distances above the mean are equal to the distances below the mean (see p. 75). Logically, the deviation scores must *always* add up to zero.

Because the mean deviation is always zero, it is of no value as a measure of variability. It is zero whether the scores are grouped together or all scattered out. The mean deviation score provides no information about variability. (You should note, however, that the constant value of zero can be useful in other ways. Whenever you are working with deviation scores, you can check your calculations by making sure that the deviation scores add up to zero.)

STEP 3 The reason that the average of the deviation scores will not work as a measure of variability is that it is always zero. Clearly, this problem results from the positive and negative values canceling each other out. The solution is to get rid of the signs ($+$ and $-$). The standard procedure for accomplishing this is to square each deviation score. Using these squared values, you then compute the *mean squared deviation*, which is called *variance*.

DEFINITION   *Population variance* = mean squared deviation. Variance is the mean of the squared deviation scores.

Note that the process of squaring deviation scores does more than simply get rid of plus and minus signs. It results in a measure of variability based on *squared* distances. Although variance is valuable for some of the *inferential* statistical methods covered later, the mean squared distance is not the best *descriptive* measure for variability.

STEP 4   Remember that our goal is to compute a measure of the standard distance from the mean. Variance, the mean squared deviation, is not exactly what we want. The final step simply makes a correction for having squared all the distances. The new measure, the *standard deviation,* is the square root of the variance.

DEFINITION   *Standard deviation* = $\sqrt{\text{variance}}$.

Technically, standard deviation is the square root of the mean squared deviation. But, conceptually, standard deviation is easier to understand if you think of it as describing the typical distance of scores from the mean (that is, the typical $X - \mu$). As the name implies, standard deviation measures the standard, or typical, deviation score.

The concept of standard deviation (or variance) is the same for a sample as for a population. However, the details of the calculations differ slightly, depending on whether you have data for a sample or a complete population. Therefore, we will first consider the formulas for measures of population variability.

SUM OF SQUARED DEVIATIONS (SS)   Variance, you should recall, is defined as the mean squared deviation. This mean is computed exactly the same way you compute any mean: First find the sum; then divide by the number of scores:

$$\text{variance} = \text{mean squared deviation} = \frac{\text{sum of squared deviations}}{\text{number of scores}}$$

The value in the numerator of this equation, the sum of the squared deviations, is a basic component of variability, and we will focus on it. To simplify things, it is identified by the notation *SS* (for sum of squared deviations), and it generally is referred to as the *sum of squares.*

DEFINITION   *SS,* or *sum of squares,* is the sum of the squared deviation scores.

There are two formulas you will need to know in order to compute *SS*. These formulas are algebraically equivalent (they always produce the same answer), but they look different and are used in different situations.

The first of these formulas is called the *definitional formula* because the terms in the formula literally define the process of adding up the squared deviations:

definitional formula: $SS = \Sigma (X - \mu)^2$ (4.1)

Note that the formula directs you to square each deviation score, $(X - \mu)^2$, and then add them. The result is the sum of the squared deviations, or SS. Following is an example using this formula.

EXAMPLE 4.3

We will compute SS for the following set of $N = 4$ scores. These scores have a sum of $\Sigma X = 8$, so the mean is $\mu = 8/4 = 2$. For each score, we have computed the deviation and the squared deviation. The squared deviations add up to $SS = 22$. These steps are illustrated in the following computational table:

Caution: The definitional formula requires that you first square the deviations and then add them. Note that we have done these computations in a table. Do not confuse this table with a frequency distribution table.

X	$X - \mu$	$(X - \mu)^2$	
1	−1	1	$\Sigma X = 8$
0	−2	4	$\mu = 2$
6	+4	16	
1	−1	1	
		$\overline{22} = \Sigma(X - \mu)^2$	

The second formula for SS is called the *computational formula* (or the machine formula) because it works directly with the scores (X values) and, therefore, is generally easier to use for calculations, especially with an electronic calculator:

$$\text{computational formula:} \quad SS = \Sigma X^2 - \frac{(\Sigma X)^2}{N} \tag{4.2}$$

The first part of this formula directs you to square each score and then sum the squared values (ΣX^2). The second part requires you to add up the scores (ΣX), square this total, and then divide the result by N (see Box 4.2). The use of this formula is shown in Example 4.4 with the same set of scores we used for the definitional formula.

EXAMPLE 4.4

The computational formula is used to calculate SS for the same set of $N = 4$ scores we used in Example 4.3. First, compute ΣX. Then square each score, and compute ΣX^2. These two values are used in the formula.

This table is used to organize the steps of the computations. It lists each individual score. Do not attempt to do these computations with a frequency distribution table.

X	X^2	
1	1	$\Sigma X = 8$
0	0	
6	36	$\Sigma X^2 = 38$
1	1	

$$SS = \Sigma X^2 - \frac{(\Sigma X)^2}{N}$$

$$= 38 - \frac{(8)^2}{4}$$

$$= 38 - \frac{64}{4}$$

$$= 38 - 16$$

$$= 22$$

4.2 COMPUTING *SS* WITH A CALCULATOR

THE COMPUTATIONAL formula for *SS* is intended to simplify calculations, especially when you are using an electronic calculator. The following steps outline the most efficient procedure for using a typical, inexpensive hand calculator to find *SS*. (We assume that your calculator has one memory, where you can store and retrieve information.) The computational formula for *SS* is presented here for easy reference.

$$SS = \Sigma X^2 - \frac{(\Sigma X)^2}{N}$$

STEP 1:   The first term in the computational formula is ΣX^2. The procedure for finding this sum is described in Box 1.3 on page 26. Once you have calculated ΣX^2, write this sum on a piece of paper so you do not lose it. Leave ΣX^2 in the calculator memory, and go to the next step.

STEP 2:   Now you must find the sum of the scores, ΣX. We assume that you can add a set of numbers with your calculator—just be sure to press the equals key (=) after the last score. Write this total on your paper.

(*Note:* You may want to clear the calculator display before you begin this process. It is not necessary, but you may feel more comfortable starting with zero.)

STEP 3:   Now you are ready to plug the sums into the formula. Your calculator should still have the sum of the scores, ΣX, in the display. If not, enter this value.

1. With ΣX in the display, you can compute $(\Sigma X)^2$ simply by pressing the multiply key ($\times$) and then the equals key (=).

2. Now you must divide the squared sum by *N*, the number of scores. Assuming that you have counted the number of scores, just press the divide key ($\div$), enter *N*, and then press the equals key.

Your calculator display now shows $(\Sigma X)^2/N$. Write this number on your paper.

3. Finally, you subtract the value of your calculator display from ΣX^2, which is in the calculator memory. You can do this by simply pressing the memory subtract key (usually M−). The value for *SS* is now in memory, and you can retrieve it by pressing the memory recall key (MR).

Try the whole procedure with a simple set of scores such as 1, 2, 3. You should obtain *SS* = 2 for these scores.

We asked you to write values at several steps during the calculation in case you make a mistake at some point. If you have written the values for ΣX^2, ΣX, and *N*, you should be able to compute *SS* easily even if the contents of memory are lost.

Notice that the two formulas produce exactly the same value for *SS*. Although the formulas look different, they are in fact equivalent. The definitional formula should be very easy to learn if you simply remember that *SS* stands for the sum of the squared deviations. If you use notation to write out "the sum of" (Σ) "squared deviations" $(X - \mu)^2$, then you have the definitional formula. Unfortunately, the terms in the computational formula do not translate directly into "sum of squared deviations," so you simply need to memorize this formula.

The definitional formula for *SS* is the most direct way of calculating the sum of squares, but it can be awkward to use for most sets of data. In particular, if the mean is not a whole number, then the deviation scores will have fractions or decimals, and the calculations become difficult. In addition, calculations with decimals or fractions introduce the opportunity for rounding error, which makes the results less accurate. For these reasons, the computational formula is used most of the time.

If you have a small group of scores and the mean is a whole number, then the definitional formula is fine; otherwise, use the computational formula.

FORMULAS FOR POPULATION STANDARD DEVIATION AND VARIANCE

With the definition and calculation of *SS* behind you, the equations for variance and standard deviation become relatively simple. Remember, variance is defined as the mean squared deviation. The mean is the sum divided by *N*, so the equation for variance is

$$\text{variance} = \frac{SS}{N}$$

In the same way that sum of squares, or *SS*, is used to refer to the sum of squared deviations, the term *mean square*, or *MS*, is often used to refer to variance, which is the mean squared deviation.

Standard deviation is the square root of variance, so the equation for standard deviation is

$$\text{standard deviation} = \sqrt{\frac{SS}{N}}$$

There is one final bit of notation before we work completely through an example computing *SS*, variance, and standard deviation. Like the mean (μ), variance and standard deviation are parameters of a population and will be identified by Greek letters. To identify the standard deviation, we use the Greek letter sigma (the Greek letter *s*, standing for standard deviation). The capital letter sigma (Σ) has been used already, so we now use the lowercase sigma, σ:

$$\text{population standard deviation} = \sigma = \sqrt{\frac{SS}{N}} \tag{4.3}$$

The symbol for population variance should help you remember the relationship between standard deviation and variance. If you square the standard deviation, you will get the variance. The symbol for variance is sigma squared, σ^2:

$$\text{population variance} = \sigma^2 = \frac{SS}{N} \tag{4.4}$$

EXAMPLE 4.5 The following population of scores will be used to demonstrate the calculation of *SS*, variance, and standard deviation:

  1, 9, 5, 8, 7

These five scores add up to $\Sigma X = 30$, so the mean is $30/5 = 6$. Before we do any other calculations, remember that the purpose of variability is to determine how spread out the scores are. Standard deviation accomplishes this by providing a measurement of the standard distance from the mean. The scores we are working with have been placed in a frequency distribution histogram in Figure 4.3 so you can see the variability more easily. Note that the score closest to the mean is $X = 5$ or $X = 7$, both of which are only 1 point away. The score farthest from the mean is $X = 1$, and it is 5 points away. For this distribution, the biggest distance from the mean is 5 points, and the smallest distance is 1 point. The typical, or standard, distance should be somewhere in between 3 or 1

FIGURE 4.3

A frequency distribution histogram for a population of $N = 5$ scores. The mean for this population is $\mu = 6$. The smallest distance from the mean is 1 point, and the largest distance is 5 points. The standard distance (or standard deviation) should be between 1 and 5 points.

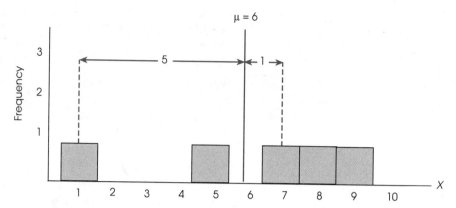

between 1 and 5. By looking quickly at a distribution in this way, you should be able to make a rough estimate of the standard deviation. In this case, the standard deviation should be between 1 and 5, probably around 3 points. Making a preliminary judgment of standard deviation can help you avoid errors in calculation. If, for example, you worked through the formulas and ended up with a value of $\sigma = 12$, you should realize immediately that you have made an error. (If the biggest deviation is only 5 points, then it is impossible for the standard deviation to be 12.)

Now we will start the calculations. The first step is to find SS for this set of scores.

Because the mean is a whole number ($\mu = 6$), we can use the definitional formula for SS:

X	$X - \mu$	$(X - \mu)^2$	
1	−5	25	$\Sigma X = 30$
9	+3	9	$\mu = 6$
5	−1	1	
8	+2	4	
7	+1	1	
		$\overline{40} = \Sigma(X - \mu)^2 = SS$	

$$\sigma^2 = \frac{SS}{N}$$

$$= \frac{40}{5} = 8$$

$$\sigma = \sqrt{8} = 2.83$$

For this set of scores, the variance is $\sigma^2 = 8$, and the standard deviation is $\sigma = \sqrt{8} = 2.83$. Note that the value for the standard deviation is in excellent agreement with our preliminary estimate of the standard distance from the mean.

FIGURE 4.4

The graphic representation of a population with a mean of $\mu = 40$ and a standard deviation of $\sigma = 4$.

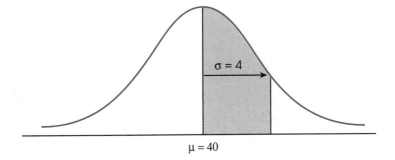

$\sigma = 4$

$\mu = 40$

LEARNING CHECK

1. Write brief definitions of variance and standard deviation.

2. Find *SS*, variance, and standard deviation for the following population of scores: 10, 10, 10, 10, 10. (*Note:* You should be able to answer this question without doing any calculations.)

3. **a.** Sketch a frequency distribution histogram for the following population of scores: 1, 3, 3, 9. Using this histogram, make an estimate of the standard deviation (i.e., the standard distance from the mean).

   b. Calculate *SS*, variance, and standard deviation for these scores. How well does your estimate from part a compare with the real standard deviation?

ANSWERS

1. Variance is the mean squared distance from the mean. Standard deviation is the square root of variance and provides a measure of the standard distance from the mean.

2. Because there is no variability in the population, *SS*, variance, and standard deviation are all equal to zero.

3. **a.** Your sketch should show a mean of $\mu = 4$. The score closest to the mean is $X = 3$, and the farthest score is $X = 9$. The standard deviation should be somewhere between 1 point and 5 points.

   b. For this population, $SS = 36$; the variance is $36/4 = 9$; the standard deviation is $\sqrt{9} = 3$.

GRAPHIC REPRESENTATION OF THE MEAN AND STANDARD DEVIATION

In frequency distribution graphs, we will identify the position of the mean by drawing a vertical line and labeling it with μ or $\overline{X}$ (see Figure 4.4). Because the standard deviation measures distance from the mean, it will be represented by a line drawn from the mean outward for a distance equal to the standard deviation (see Figure 4.4). For rough sketches, you can identify the mean with a vertical line in the middle of the distribution. The standard deviation line should extend approximately halfway from the mean to the most extreme score.

FIGURE 4.5

The population of adult heights forms a normal distribution. If you select a sample from this population, you are most likely to obtain individuals who are near average in height. As a result, the scores in the sample will be less variable (spread out) than the scores in the population.

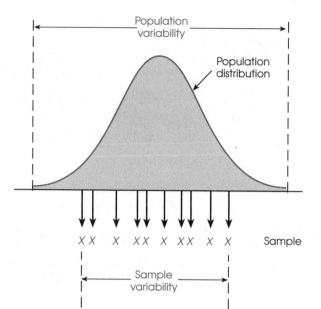

4.5 STANDARD DEVIATION AND VARIANCE FOR SAMPLES

The goal of inferential statistics is to use the limited information from samples to draw general conclusions about populations. The basic assumption of this process is that samples should be representative of the populations from which they come. This assumption poses a special problem for variability because samples consistently tend to be less variable than their populations. An example of this general tendency is shown in Figure 4.5. The fact that a sample tends to be less variable than its population means that sample variability gives a *biased* estimate of population variability. This bias is in the direction of underestimating the population value rather than being right on the mark. To correct for this bias, it is necessary to make an adjustment in the calculation of variability when you are working with sample data. The intent of the adjustment is to make the resulting value for sample variability a more accurate estimate of the population variability.

To compute sample variability, we begin by defining the deviation for each score in the sample. As before, deviation measures the distance from the mean, but now we are using the sample mean in place of the population mean:

A sample statistic is said to be *biased* if, on the average, it consistently overestimates or underestimates the corresponding population parameter.

$$\text{sample deviation score} = X - \overline{X} \tag{4.5}$$

Each deviation score will have a sign and a magnitude. The sign tells the direction from the mean (+ for above, − for below), and the magnitude tells the distance from the mean. The deviation scores always add up to zero.

Variance and standard deviation for sample data have the same basic definitions as they do for populations: Variance measures the average squared distance from the mean, and standard deviation is the square root of variance. To compute the values, we first will need to find SS, the sum of squared deviations. The formulas we use to compute sample SS are essentially identical to the formulas used for populations:

$$\text{definitional formula:} \quad SS = \Sigma(X - \overline{X})^2 \tag{4.6}$$

$$\text{computational formula:} \quad SS = \Sigma X^2 - \frac{(\Sigma X)^2}{n} \tag{4.7}$$

Note that the only difference between these formulas and the population formulas is a minor change in notation. We have substituted $\overline{X}$ in place of μ and n in place of N. For all practical purposes, the population and sample formulas for SS are interchangeable. The difference in notation will have no effect on the calculations.

After you compute SS, however, it becomes critical to differentiate between samples and populations. To correct for the bias in sample variability, it is necessary to make an adjustment in the formulas for sample variance and standard deviation. With this in mind, sample variance (identified by the symbol s^2) is defined as

$$\text{sample variance} = s^2 = \frac{SS}{n-1} \tag{4.8}$$

Sample standard deviation (identified by the symbol s) is simply the square root of the variance.

$$\text{sample standard deviation} = s = \sqrt{\frac{SS}{n-1}} \tag{4.9}$$

Remember, sample variability tends to underestimate population variability unless some correction is made.

Notice that these sample formulas use $n - 1$ instead of n. This is the adjustment that is necessary to correct for the bias in sample variability. The effect of the adjustment is to increase the value you will obtain. Dividing by a smaller number ($n - 1$ instead of n) produces a larger result and makes sample variability an accurate, or unbiased, estimator of population variability.

A complete example showing the calculation of sample variance and standard deviation will now be worked out.

EXAMPLE 4.6   We have selected a sample of $n = 7$ scores from a population. The scores are 1, 6, 4, 3, 8, 7, 6. The frequency distribution histogram for this sample is shown in Figure 4.6. Before we begin any calculations, you should be able to look at the sample distribution and make a preliminary estimate of the outcome. Remember that standard deviation measures the standard distance from the mean. For this sample the mean is $\overline{X} = 5$ ($\frac{35}{7} = 5$). The scores closest to the mean are $X = 4$ and $X = 6$, both of which are exactly 1 point away. The score farthest from the mean is $X = 1$, which is 4 points away. With the smallest distance from the mean equal to 1 and the largest distance equal to 4, we should obtain a standard distance somewhere around 2.5 (between 1 and 4).

Now let's begin the calculations. First, we will find SS for this sample. Because there are only a few scores and the mean is a whole number, the definitional formula will be easy to use. You should try this formula for practice. Meanwhile, we will work with the computational formula.

FIGURE 4.6

The frequency distribution histogram for a sample of $n = 7$ scores. The sample mean is $\bar{X} = 5$. The smallest distance from the mean is 1 point, and the largest distance from the mean is 4 points. The standard distance (standard deviation) should be between 1 and 4 points.

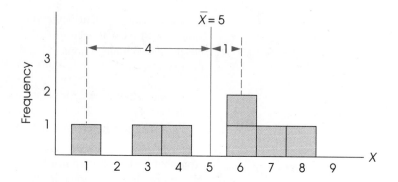

The following computational table illustrates the work:

Caution: For sample variance, you use $n - 1$ after calculating SS. Do not use $n - 1$ in the formula for SS.

X	X^2
1	1
6	36
4	16
3	9
8	64
7	49
6	36

$\Sigma X = 35$
$\Sigma X^2 = 211$

$$SS = \Sigma X^2 - \frac{(\Sigma X)^2}{n}$$

$$= 211 - \frac{(35)^2}{7}$$

$$= 211 - \frac{1225}{7}$$

$$= 211 - 175$$

$$= 36$$

SS for this sample is 36. You should obtain exactly the same answer using the definitional formula. Continuing the calculations,

$$\text{sample variance} = s^2 = \frac{SS}{n-1} = \frac{36}{7-1} = 6$$

Finally, the standard deviation is

$$s = \sqrt{s^2} = \sqrt{6} = 2.45$$

Note that the value we obtained is in excellent agreement with our preliminary prediction.

Software Manuals:
Minitab (section 4)
Mystat (section 3)
SPSS (section 6)

Remember that the formulas for sample variance and standard deviation were constructed so that the sample variability would provide a good estimate of population variability. For this reason, the sample variance is often called *estimated population variance,* and the sample standard deviation is called *estimated population standard deviation.* When you have only a sample to work with, the sample variance and standard deviation provide the best possible estimates of the population variability.

IN THE LITERATURE:
REPORTING THE STANDARD DEVIATION

In reporting the results of a study, the researcher often provides descriptive information for both central tendency and variability. The dependent variables in psychology research frequently involve measures taken on interval or ratio scales. Thus, the mean (central tendency) and the standard deviation (variability) are commonly reported together. In many journals, especially those following APA style, the symbol *SD* is used for the sample standard deviation. For example, the results might state:

> Children who viewed the violent cartoon displayed more aggressive responses (*M* = 12.45, *SD* = 3.7) than those who viewed the control cartoon (*M* = 4.22, *SD* = 1.04).

When reporting the descriptive measures for several groups, the findings may be summarized in a table. Table 4.1 illustrates the results of hypothetical data.

TABLE 4.1

The Number of Aggressive Responses in Male and Female Children After Viewing Cartoons

	TYPE OF CARTOON	
	Violent	Control
Males	*M* = 15.72	*M* = 6.94
	SD = 4.43	*SD* = 2.26
Females	*M* = 3.47	*M* = 2.61
	SD = 1.12	*SD* = 0.98

Sometimes the table will also indicate the sample size, *n*, for each group. You should remember that the purpose of the table is present the data in an organized, concise, and accurate manner.

LEARNING CHECK

1. **a.** Sketch a frequency distribution histogram for the following sample of scores: 1, 1, 9, 1. Using your histogram, make an estimate of the standard deviation for this sample.

   b. Calculate *SS*, variance, and standard deviation for this sample. How well does your estimate from part a compare with the real standard deviation?

2. If the scores in the previous exercise were for a population, what value would you obtain for *SS*?

3. If the scores in Exercise 1 were for a population, would you obtain a larger or a smaller value for the standard deviation? Explain your answer.

ANSWERS 1. **a.** Your graph should show a sample mean of $\overline{X}$ = 3. The score farthest from the mean is *X* = 9, and the closest score is *X* = 1. You should estimate the standard deviation to be between 2 points and 6 points.

   b. For this sample, *SS* = 48; the sample variance is $^{48}/_3$ = 16; the sample standard deviation is $\sqrt{16}$ = 4.

2. $SS = 48$ whether the data are from a sample or a population.

3. Smaller. The formulas for sample data increase the size of variance and standard deviation by dividing by $n - 1$ instead of N. The population formulas will produce smaller values.

SAMPLE VARIABILITY AND DEGREES OF FREEDOM

Although the concept of a deviation score and the calculation of SS are almost exactly the same for samples and populations, the minor differences in notation are really very important. With a population, you can find the exact deviation between any score and μ. With a sample, on the other hand, you can only estimate the deviation scores because $\overline{X}$ is your best estimate for μ. The idea that deviations within a sample are not precise values is demonstrated in the following example.

EXAMPLE 4.7

We will begin with a population with a mean of $\mu = 4$. Two scores are selected from this population, $X = 8$ and $X = 4$, and the deviation score is computed for both X values. The following table shows the deviations and squared deviations for the two scores:

X	$X - \mu$	$(X - \mu)^2$
8	+4	16
4	0	0
		$SS = \overline{16}$

Note that the sum of the squared deviations for the two scores is $SS = 16$.

Now consider what happens if the population mean is unknown. This time we will assume that the sample is being selected in order to learn more about the population. (Note that this is the typical situation for using inferential statistics.) Again, our sample consists of two scores, $X = 8$ and $X = 4$. Without knowing the population mean, how can you find the deviation scores for these X values?

The simple answer is that you cannot compute the deviations, at least not with μ. However, you can *approximate* the deviations. This approximation is accomplished by using the sample mean in place of the unknown population mean. For this sample of $n = 2$ scores, $\Sigma X = 12$ and $\overline{X} = 12/2 = 6$. Using the sample mean, we can now compute a deviation for each score. The following table shows the deviations and squared deviations:

X	$X - \overline{X}$	$(X - \overline{X})^2$
8	+2	4
4	-2	4
		$SS = \overline{8}$

Note that the sum of the squared deviations for the two scores is $SS = 8$.

There are three points to be made from the previous example. First, the deviations computed from a sample mean are not "real" deviations. Instead, they are only approximations of population deviations because you must use the sample mean (instead of the real population mean, μ) as the reference point for computing each deviation.

Second, notice that the sum of the squared deviations (SS) computed with the sample mean is *smaller* than the value of SS computed with the population mean. This is another example of the general point we made earlier: Sample variability tends to underestimate population variability (see p. 118). Although we will not go into the mathematical proof, it is a general fact that SS computed from a sample mean always will be less than or equal to the value of SS computed with the real population mean.

Finally, the fact that you must use the sample mean to compute deviations when the population mean is unknown places a restriction on the variability of scores in a sample The restriction comes from the fact that you must know the value of $\overline{X}$ *before* you can begin to compute deviations and SS. In example 4.7, we had a sample of $n = 2$ with a mean of $\overline{X} = 6$. Given this information, as soon as you know that the first score is $X = 8$, you also know that the second score *must* be $X = 4$. (In order to average $\overline{X} = 6$, the two scores must total $\Sigma X = 12$. If one score is $X = 8$, the other must be $X = 4$.) Thus, the second score in the sample is not free to vary, but rather is restricted by the sample mean.

In general, with a sample of n scores, the first $n - 1$ scores are free to vary, but the final score is restricted by the sample mean. That is, the final score must produce the necessary total, ΣX, to result in the correct sample mean. In statistical terms, the sample is said to have $n - 1$ *degrees of freedom;* that is, n − 1 scores are free to vary, and 1 score is restricted. An analogy for degrees of freedom is presented in Box 4.3.

Alternatively, because $\Sigma(X - \overline{X}) = 0$, the second score must have a deviation score of -2 (which corresponds to $X = 4$).

DEFINITION

Degrees of freedom, or *df,* for a sample are defined as

$$df = n - 1$$

where n is the number of scores in the sample.

The $n - 1$ degrees of freedom for a sample is the same $n - 1$ that is used in the formulas for sample variance and standard deviation. Remember that variance is defined as the mean squared deviation. As always, a mean is computed by finding a sum and dividing by the number of scores:

$$\text{mean} = \frac{\text{sum}}{\text{number}}$$

Thus, variance for the population could be expressed as

$$\text{mean squared deviation} = \frac{\text{sum of squared deviations}}{\text{number}}$$

However, to calculate sample variance (mean squared deviation), we find the sum of the squared deviations (SS) and divide by the number of scores that are free to vary. This number is $n - 1 = df$.

$$s^2 = \frac{\text{sum of squared deviations}}{\text{number of scores free to vary}} = \frac{SS}{n - 1} = \frac{SS}{df}$$

4.3 DEGREES OF FREEDOM, CAFETERIA-STYLE

THE CAFETERIA is an unlikely place to take a discussion of statistics, yet we can make an analogy for degrees of freedom and talk about food a little bit. This analogy, while not truly what we mean by degrees of freedom in statistics, gives you some idea of the general notion that sample variability is restricted.

On any given day, the cafeteria can offer a selection of desserts. This selection is just a sample from a large population of many different types of desserts that could be offered. On this particular afternoon, the cafeteria has five desserts (Figure 4.7). To keep this simple, the cafeteria has only one of each dessert and only five customers. These people work their way down the cafeteria line, piling food on their trays, when they arrive at the dessert section. We will observe their responses to the desserts, which may vary from person to person. How many observations (selections) are free to vary? Consider the following scenario:

The first person in line gets to select from the five desserts and chooses the apple pie.

The second person in line gets to select from the four remaining desserts and chooses the chocolate cake.

The third person gets to select from the three remaining desserts and chooses the sundae.

The fourth person has a choice between the two remaining desserts and takes the fruit.

Each of these observations is free to vary—that is, until we get to the last person, who must settle for the stale cookies. Thus, just as $n - 1$ scores are free to vary for a sample, $n - 1$ choices are free to vary in the cafeteria.

FIGURE 4.7

Of the 5 desserts, $n - 1$ selections are free to vary.

Later in this book, we will use the concept of degrees of freedom in situations involving inferential statistics. For now, you should remember that knowing the sample mean places a restriction on sample variability. Only $n - 1$ of the scores are free to vary. Also, the formula for sample variance (or sample mean squared deviation) is typically expressed as follows:

$$s^2 = \frac{SS}{df}$$

4.6 PROPERTIES OF THE STANDARD DEVIATION

Because standard deviation requires extensive calculations, there is a tendency for many students to get lost in the arithmetic and forget what standard deviation is and why it is useful. Standard deviation is primarily a descriptive measure; it describes how variable, or how spread out, the scores are in a distribution. Remember, standard deviation is a measure of *distance from the mean*. In any distribution, some individual scores will be close to the mean, and others will be relatively far from the mean. Standard deviation provides a measure of the typical, or standard, distance. A small standard deviation indicates that the scores are typically close to the mean, and a large standard deviation indicates that the scores are generally far from the mean. The numerical value for standard deviation should allow you to visualize the distribution: The scores are either clustered close together or spread out over a wide range, depending on the value of the standard deviation (see Box 4.4).

Figure 4.8 shows two distributions of quiz scores. Both distributions have $\mu = 20$, but one distribution has small variability, $\sigma = 2$, and the other has larger varibility, $\sigma = 6$. For one group, the students are all very similar in terms of their quiz performance. For the second group, there are huge differences in performance from one student to the next. You also should recognize that the same score (X value) can have very different meanings in these two distributions. For example, a score of $X = 22$ is one of the highest scores in the low-variability group, but it is only average in the high-variability distribution.

Standard deviation also helps researchers make predictions about sample data. Referring to the two distributions in Figure 4.8, if you were to select a single score from the low-variability population, you could be very confident of obtaining a value close to $\mu = 20$. On the other hand, you have a much greater chance of obtaining an extreme score if you are picking from the high-variability distribution.

The standard deviation also is one of the critical components of inferential statistics. Remember, in inferential statistics we will be using sample data as the basis for drawing general conclusions about populations. You also should remember that a sample generally will not provide a perfectly accurate representation of its population; there will be some discrepancy, or "error," between a sample and the popu-

FIGURE 4.8

Two hypothetical distributions of test scores for a statistics class. For both distributions, $N = 16$ and $\mu = 20$. In distribution (a), where there is little variability, a score of 22 is nearly the top score. In distribution (b), there is more variability, and the same score occupies a more central position in the distribution.

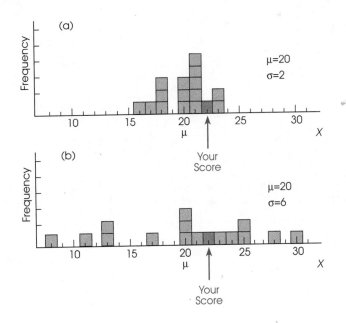

4.4 OBTAINING ROUGH ESTIMATES OF THE MEAN AND STANDARD DEVIATION FOR A DISTRIBUTION

CONCEPTUALLY, THE mean locates the midpoint, or center, of a distribution. Similarly, the standard deviation measures the standard distance from the mean. When a set of scores is organized in a frequency distribution graph, you should be able to visualize the location of the mean and the size of the standard deviation, and thereby obtain rough estimates of these two statistical measures. The following example demonstrates how you can easily and quickly make a commonsense estimates of the mean and standard deviation for any distribution.

Figure 4.9 shows a frequency distribution histogram for a sample of $n = 43$ scores. First, we have drawn a vertical line through the middle of this distribution at the point that "looks like" the mean. Next, we have drawn an arrow representing the standard deviation so that the arrow extends from the mean to a point that is roughly one-half of the total distance between the mean and the highest score. From this graphic representation, we can estimate that the mean is approximately 8 and the standard deviation is roughly 4 points.

We have computed the actual mean and standard deviation for this sample and obtained values of $\overline{X} = 8.35$ and $s = 3.98$. Note that our rough estimates are very close to the actual values.

Finally, notice that we have drawn two additional vertical (dashed) lines located roughly one standard deviation above the mean and one standard deviation below the mean. The vertical lines divide the total distribution into four sections, each corresponding to a distance of approximately one standard deviation. This process of dividing a distribution into four sections demonstrates another easy way to estimate standard deviation: the standard deviation is approximately one-fourth of the total range covered by a set of scores.

The process of making rough estimates of the mean and standard deviation can be very useful, and we encourage you to follow this estimation procedure for any set of data that you encounter. First, making estimates will help you develop a good conceptual understanding of the mean and standard deviation. Also, you can use your rough estimates to help identify computational errors when you actually calculate the mean and standard deviation. For example, if you calculate a value of $s = 27$ for the sample shown in Figure 4.9, you should realize instantly that this value cannot be correct. (*Note:* An alternate method of estimating the standard deviation is shown in Example 4.5 and Figure 4.3.)

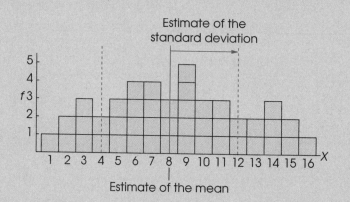

FIGURE 4.9

A frequency distribution histogram showing a sample of $n = 43$ scores. Rough estimates of the mean and standard deviation have been added to the figure based on the conceptual definitions of these two statistical measures.

lation. Standard deviation provides a measure of how big this error will be. For example, suppose that you randomly select a score from a population and obtain a value of $X = 47$. What value would you predict for the population mean? The answer depends on the standard deviation. With $\sigma = 4$, for example, you know that the typical distance between a score and the mean is only 4 points. Thus, you would predict that the population mean is probably within 4 points of $X = 47$. On the other hand, if the standard deviation is $\sigma = 20$, you would predict that the population mean is probably somewhere within 20 points of $X = 47$. In general, the smaller the standard deviation, the more accurately a sample will represent its population. This topic is discussed in more detail in Chapter 7, where we will look at the precise relationship between samples and populations.

In summary, you should realize that standard deviation is a valuable measure for both descriptive and inferential purposes. It appears repeatedly throughout the remainder of this book.

TRANSFORMATIONS OF SCALE

Occasionally, it is convenient to transform a set of scores by adding a constant to each score or by multiplying each score by a constant value. This is done, for example, when you want to "curve" a set of exam scores by adding a fixed amount to each individual's grade or when you want to change the unit of measurement (to convert from minutes to seconds, multiply each X by 60). What happens to the standard deviation when the scores are transformed in this manner?

The easiest way to determine the effect of a transformation is to remember that the standard deviation is a measure of distance. If you select any two scores and see what happens to the distance between them, you also will find out what happens to the standard deviation.

1. **Adding a constant to each score will not change the standard deviation**   If you begin with a distribution that has $\mu = 40$ and $\sigma = 10$, what happens to σ if you add 5 points to every score? Consider any two scores in this distribution: Suppose, for example, that these are exam scores and that you had $X = 41$ and your friend had $X = 43$. The distance between these two scores is $43 - 41 = 2$ points. After adding the constant, 5 points, to each score, your score would be $X = 46$, and your friend would have $X = 48$. The distance between scores is still 2 points. Adding a constant to every score will not affect any of the distances and, therefore, will not change the standard deviation. This fact can be seen clearly if you imagine a frequency distribution graph. If, for example, you add 10 points to each score, then every score in the graph will be moved 10 points to the right. The result is that the entire distribution is shifted to a new position 10 points up the scale. Note that the mean moves along with the scores and is increased by 10 points. However, the variability does not change because each of the deviation scores $(X - \mu)$ does not change.

2. **Multiplying each score by a constant causes the standard deviation to be multiplied by the same constant**   Consider the same distribution of exam scores we looked at earlier. If $\mu = 40$ and $\sigma = 10$, what would happen to σ if each score were multiplied by 2? Again, we will look at two scores, $X = 41$ and $X = 43$, with a distance between them equal to 2 points. After all the scores have been multiplied by 2, these scores would become $X = 82$ and $X = 86$. Now the distance between scores is 4 points, twice the original distance. Multiplying each score causes each distance to be multiplied, so the standard deviation also is multiplied by the same amount.

4.7 COMPARING MEASURES OF VARIABILITY

By far the most commonly used measure of variability is standard deviation (together with the related measure of variance). Nonetheless, there are situations where the range or the semi-interquartile range may be preferred. The advantages and disadvantages of each of these three measures will be discussed.

In simple terms, two considerations determine the value of any statistical measurement:

1. The measure should provide a stable and reliable description of the scores. Specifically, it should not be greatly affected by minor details in the set of data.

2. The measure should have a consistent and predictable relationship with other statistical measurements.

We will examine each of these considerations separately.

FACTORS THAT AFFECT VARIABILITY

1. Extreme scores   Of the three measures of variability, the range is most affected by extreme scores. A single extreme value will have a large influence on the range. In fact, the range is determined exclusively by the two extremes of the distribution. Standard deviation and variance also are influenced by extreme scores. Because these measures are based on squared deviations, a single extreme value can have a disproportionate effect. For example, a score that is 10 points away from the mean will contribute $10^2 = 100$ points to the *SS*. For this reason, standard deviation and variance should be interpreted carefully in distributions with one or two extreme values. Because the semi-interquartile range focuses on the middle of the distribution, it is least affected by extreme values. For this reason, the semi-interquartile range often provides the best measure of variability for distributions that are very skewed or that have a few extreme scores.

2. Sample size   As you increase the number of scores in a sample, you also tend to increase the range because each additional score has the potential to replace the current highest or lowest value in the set. Thus, the range is directly related to sample size. This relationship between sample size and variability is unacceptable. A researcher should not be able to influence variability by manipulating sample size. Standard deviation, variance, and the semi-interquartile range are relatively unaffected by sample size and, therefore, provide better measures.

3. Stability under sampling   If you take several different samples from the same population, you should expect the samples to be similar. Specifically, if you compute variability for each of the separate samples, you should expect to obtain similar values. Because all of the samples come from the same source, it is reasonable that there should be some "family resemblance." When standard deviation and variance are used to measure variability, the samples will tend to have similar variability. For this reason, standard deviation and variance are said to be stable under sampling. The semi-interquartile range also provides a reasonably stable measure of variability. The range, however, will change unpredictably from sample to sample and is said to be unstable under sampling.

4. Open-ended distributions   When a distribution does not have any specific boundary for the highest score or the lowest score, it is open-ended. This can occur when you have infinite or undetermined scores. For example, a subject who cannot solve a problem has taken an undetermined or infinite amount of time to reach the solution. In an open-ended distribution, you cannot compute the range, or the standard deviation, or the variance. In this situation, the only available measure of variability is the semi-interquartile range.

RELATIONSHIP WITH OTHER STATISTICAL MEASURES

As noted earlier, variance and standard deviation are computed from squared deviation scores. Because they are based on squared distances, these measures fit into a coherent system of mathematical relationships that underlies many of the statistical techniques we will examine in this book. Although we generally will not present the underlying mathematics, you will notice that variance and standard deviation appear repeatedly. This is because they are valuable measures of variability. Also, you should notice that variance and standard deviation have a direct relationship to the mean (they are based on deviations from the mean). Therefore, the mean and standard deviation tend to be reported together. Because the mean is the most common measure of central tendency, the standard deviation will be the most common measure of variability.

Because the median and the semi-interquartile range are both based on percentiles, they share a common foundation and tend to be associated. When the median is used to report central tendency, the semi-interquartile range is commonly used to report variability.

The range has no direct relationship to any other statistical measure. For this reason, it is rarely used in conjunction with other statistical techniques.

SUMMARY

1. The purpose of variability is to determine how spread out the scores are in a distribution. There are four basic measures of variability: the range, the semi-interquartile range, the variance, and the standard deviation.

   The range is the distance between the upper real limit of the largest X and the lower real limit of the smallest X in the distribution. The semi-interquartile range is one-half the distance between the first quartile and the third quartile. Variance is defined as the mean squared deviation. Standard deviation is the square root of the variance.

   Standard deviation and variance are by far the most commonly used measures of variability.

2. The logical steps leading to the formulas for variance and standard deviation are summarized as follows. Remember that the purpose of standard deviation is to provide a measure of the standard distance from the mean.
   a. A deviation score is defined as $X - \mu$ and measures the direction and distance from the mean for each score.
   b. Because of the plus and minus signs, the sum of the deviation scores and the average of the deviation scores will always be zero.

   c. To get rid of the signs, we square each deviation and then compute the mean squared deviation, or the variance.
   d. Finally, we correct for having squared all the deviations by taking the square root of the variance. The result is the standard deviation, and it gives a measure of the standard distance from the mean.

3. To calculate either variance or standard deviation, you first need to find the sum of the squared deviations, SS. There are two formulas for SS:

   definitional formula: $SS = \Sigma(X - \mu)^2$

   computational formula: $SS = \Sigma X^2 - \dfrac{(\Sigma X)^2}{N}$

4. Variance is the mean squared deviation and is obtained by finding the sum of the squared deviations and then dividing by the number. For a population, variance is

$$\sigma^2 = \frac{SS}{N}$$

For a sample, only $n - 1$ of the scores are free to vary (degrees of freedom or $df = n - 1$), so sample variance is

$$s^2 = \frac{SS}{n - 1} \quad or \quad s^2 = \frac{SS}{df}$$

$$s = \sqrt{\frac{SS}{n - 1}} \quad or \quad s = \sqrt{\frac{SS}{df}}$$

Using $n - 1$ in the sample formulas makes sample variance and sample standard deviation accurate and unbiased estimates of the corresponding population parameters.

5. Standard deviation is the square root of the variance. For a population, this is

$$\sigma = \sqrt{\frac{SS}{N}}$$

Sample standard deviation is

6. Adding a constant value to every score in a distribution will not change the standard deviation. Multiplying every score by a constant, however, will cause the standard deviation to be multiplied by the same constant.

KEY TERMS

variability	semi-interquartile range	variance	sum of squares (SS)
range	deviation score	standard deviation	degrees of freedom (df)
interquartile range			

———— FOCUS ON PROBLEM SOLVING

1. The purpose of variability is to provide a measure of how spread out the scores are in a distribution. Usually this is described by the standard deviation. Because the calculations are relatively complicated, it is wise to make a preliminary estimate of the standard deviation before you begin. Remember, standard deviation provides a measure of the typical, or standard, distance from the mean. Therefore, the standard deviation must have a value somewhere between the largest and the smallest deviation scores. As a rule of thumb, the standard deviation should be about one-fourth of the range.

2. Rather than trying to memorize all the formulas for SS, variance, and standard deviation, you should focus on the definitions of these values and the logic that relates them to each other:

    SS is the sum of squared deviations.
    Variance is the mean squared deviation.
    Standard deviation is the square root of variance.

    The only formula you should need to memorize is the computational formula for SS.

3. If you heed the warnings in the following list, you may avoid some of the more common mistakes in solving variability problems.
    a. Because the calculation of standard deviation requires several steps of calculation, students often get lost in the arithmetic and forget what they are trying to compute. It helps to examine the data before you begin and make a rough estimate of the mean and the standard deviation.
    b. For SS, a computational table (p. 113) helps organize your work. However, do *not* attempt to compute SS from a frequency distribution table.
    c. The standard deviation formulas for populations and samples are slightly differ-

ent. Be sure that you know whether the data come from a sample or a population before you begin calculations.

d. A common error is to use $n - 1$ in the computational formula for SS when you have scores from a sample. Remember, the SS formula always uses n (or N). After you compute SS for a sample, you must correct for the sample bias by using $n - 1$ in the formulas for variance and standard deviation.

DEMONSTRATION 4.1

COMPUTING MEASURES OF VARIABILITY

For the following sample data, compute the variance and standard deviation. Scores:

$$10, \quad 7, \quad 6, \quad 10, \quad 6, \quad 15$$

Compute the sum of squares   For SS, we will use the definitional formula:

$$SS = \Sigma(X - \overline{X})^2$$

STEP 1   Calculate the sample mean for these data.

$$\overline{X} = \frac{\Sigma X}{n} = \frac{54}{6} = 9$$

STEP 2   Compute the deviation scores, $(X - \overline{X})$, for every X value. This is facilitated by making a computational table listing all the X values in one column and all the deviation scores in another column. Remember, do not use a frequency distribution table.

X	$X - \overline{X}$
10	$10 - 9 = +1$
7	$7 - 9 = -2$
6	$6 - 9 = -3$
10	$10 - 9 = +1$
6	$6 - 9 = -3$
15	$15 - 9 = +6$

STEP 3   Square the deviation scores. This is shown in a new column labeled $(X - \overline{X})^2$.

X	$X - \overline{X}$	$(X - \overline{X})^2$
10	$+1$	1
7	-2	4
6	-3	9
10	$+1$	1
6	-3	9
15	$+6$	36

STEP 4 Sum the squared deviation scores to obtain the value for SS.

$$SS = \Sigma(X - \bar{X})^2 = 1 + 4 + 9 + 1 + 9 + 36 = 60$$

Compute the sample variance   For sample variance, we divide SS by $n - 1$ (also known as degrees of freedom).

STEP 1 Compute degrees of freedom, $n - 1$.

$$\text{degrees of freedom} = df = n - 1 = 6 - 1 = 5$$

STEP 2 Divide SS by df.

$$s^2 = \frac{SS}{n-1} = \frac{60}{5} = 12$$

Compute the sample standard deviation   The sample standard deviation is simply the square root of the sample variance.

$$s = \sqrt{\frac{SS}{n-1}} = \sqrt{\frac{60}{5}} = \sqrt{12} = 3.46$$

PROBLEMS

1. In words, explain what is measured by each of the following:
   a. SS
   b. Variance
   c. Standard deviation

2. Calculate SS, variance, and standard deviation for the following population: 5, 0, 9, 3, 8, 5.

3. Calculate SS, variance, and standard deviation for the following sample: 4, 7, 3, 1, 5.

4. For the following scores: 1, 0, 4, 1
   a. Calculate the mean. (Note that the value of the mean does not depend on whether the set of scores is considered to be a sample or a population.)
   b. Find the deviation for each score, and check that the deviations sum to zero.
   c. Square each deviation, and compute SS. (Again, note that the value of SS is independent of whether the set of scores is a sample or a population.)

5. Describe the circumstances where it is easier to compute SS
   a. Using the definition (or definitional formula).
   b. Using the computational formula.

6. Calculate SS, variance, and standard deviation for the following sample: 0, 3, 0, 3. (*Note:* The computational formula for SS works best with these scores.)

7. Calculate SS, variance, and standard deviation for the following sample: 2, 0, 0, 0, 0, 2, 0, 2, 0. (*Note:* The computational formula for SS works best with these scores.)

8. A population of $N = 10$ scores has a mean of $\mu = 30$ and SS = 200. Find each of the following values for this population:
   a. ΣX
   b. $\Sigma(X - \mu)$
   c. $\Sigma(X - \mu)^2$

9. The standard deviation measures the standard (or typical) distance from the mean. For each of the following two populations, you should be able to use this definition to determine the standard deviation without doing any serious calculations. (*Hint:* Find the mean for each population and then look at the distances between the individual scores and the mean.)
   a. Population 1:   5, 5, 5, 5
   b. Population 2:   4, 6, 4, 6

10. For the following sample of $n = 5$ scores:

    10, 0, 6, 2, 2

   a. Sketch a histogram showing the sample distribution.
   b. Locate the value of the sample mean in your sketch, and make an estimate of the sample standard deviation (as done in Example 4.6).
   c. Compute SS, variance, and standard deviation for the sample. (How well does your estimate compare with the actual value of s?)

11. For the following sample of $n = 5$ scores:

    3, 11, 14, 7, 15

  a. Sketch a histogram showing the sample distribution.
  b. Locate the value of the sample mean in your sketch, and make an estimate of the sample standard deviation (as done in Example 4.6).
  c. Compute SS, variance, and standard deviation for the sample. (How well does your estimate compare with the actual value of s?)

12. For the following population of $N = 5$ scores:

    11, 2, 0, 8, 4

  a. Sketch a histogram showing the population distribution.
  b. Locate the value of the population mean in your sketch, and make an estimate of the standard deviation (as done in Example 4.5).
  c. Compute SS, variance, and standard deviation for the population. (How well does your estimate compare with the actual value of σ?)

13. For the following population of $N = 6$ scores:

    8, 10, 4, 8, 5, 13

  a. Sketch a histogram showing the population distribution.
  b. Locate the value of the population mean in your sketch, and make an estimate of the standard deviation (as done in Example 4.5).
  c. Compute SS, variance, and standard deviation for the population. (How well does your estimate compare with the actual value of σ?)

14. In a study of short-term memory, four samples of subjects read a list of words. The list is removed, and they are tested for recall after a 3-, 6-, 9-, or 12-second retention interval. To eliminate the role of rehearsal, subjects must count backward from 50 by 3s during the retention interval. The number of words remembered for each group is as follows:

RETENTION INTERVAL (SECONDS)			
3	6	9	12
6	5	3	0
7	4	4	3
9	6	3	1
7	3	3	0
8	6	2	2

  a. Compute the mean and standard deviation for each sample. Summarize these values in a table, consistent with APA style.
  b. Draw a line graph of the means for this study.
  c. Looking at the data, describe the relationship between length of retention interval and number of words remembered.

15. A study examines the relationship between level of arousal and problem solving. Three samples are used, consisting of subjects with low, moderate, or high levels of arousal. The researcher measures the number of problems successfully completed during a problem-solving task. The data are as follows:

LEVEL OF AROUSAL		
LOW	MODERATE	HIGH
2	20	9
6	17	8
5	12	8
7	16	6
5	18	7
5	19	10
4	17	6
4	16	8
7	18	7
6	17	8

  a. Compute the mean and standard deviation for each sample. Present these values in a table, using APA style.
  b. Looking at the data, how would you describe the relationship between level of arousal and task performance?

16. Can SS ever have a value less than zero? Explain your answer.

17. A set of $n = 20$ quiz scores has a mean of $\overline{X} = 20$. One person is selected from the class to be the "mystery person." If the deviation scores for the other 19 students in the class add up to $+6$, what score did the mystery person have?

18. For the following population of scores:

    1, 6, 9, 0, 4

  a. Find the mean for the population, and compute the deviation score for each individual.
  b. Show that the deviation scores sum to zero.
  c. Square each deviation, and find the sum of squared deviations (SS).

d. Now assume that the set of scores is a sample instead of a population, and repeat parts a, b, and c. How does the distinction between a sample and a population affect the calculation of *SS*?

19. In general, what does it mean for a sample to have a standard deviation of zero? Describe the scores in such a sample.

20. Sketch a normal distribution with $\mu = 50$ and $\sigma = 20$.
  a. Locate each of the following scores in your sketch, and indicate whether you consider each score to be an extreme value (high or low) or a central value:

  65,   55,   40,   47

  b. Make another sketch showing a distribution with $\mu = 50$, but this time with $\sigma = 2$. Now locate each of the four scores in the new distribution, and indicate whether they are extreme or central.
  (*Note:* The value of the standard deviation can have a dramatic effect on the location of a score within a distribution.

21. For the following population of scores:

  3,   4,   4,   1,   7,   3,   2,   6,   4,   2

  1,   6,   3,   4,   5,   2,   5,   4,   3,   4

  a. Sketch a frequency distribution histogram.
  b. Find the range for the population. (*Hint:* You can use the formula for the range, or you can simply count the boxes or categories across the base of the histogram.)
  c. Find the interquartile range and the semi-interquartile range for the population.

22. For the following population of $N = 4$ scores:

  2,   0,   8,   2

  a. Use the definitional formula to compute *SS*; then find the population variance and the standard deviation.
  b. Add 3 points to each score; then compute *SS*, variance, and standard deviation for the new population.
  c. Multiple each of the original scores by 2; then compute *SS*, variance, and standard deviation for the new population.
  d. When a constant is added to each score, what happens to the deviation scores? What happens to the standard deviation?
  e. When each score is multiplied by a constant, what happens to the deviation scores? What happens to the standard deviation?

23. A population of $N = 10$ scores has a standard deviation of 3.5. What is the variance for this population?

24. A sample of $n = 25$ scores has a variance of 100.
  a. Find the standard deviation for this sample.
  b. Find the value of *SS* for this sample. (Be careful to use the *sample* formula.)

25. For the following population of scores:

  8,   5,   3,   7,   5,   6,   4,   7,   2,   6

  5,   3,   6,   4,   5,   7,   8,   6,   5,   6

  a. Sketch a frequency distribution histogram.
  b. Using the procedures outlined in Box 4.4, estimate the mean and standard deviation on your graph.
  c. Calculate the mean and standard deviation for this population, and compare your estimates with the actual values.

26. Calculate the range, the semi-interquartile range, and the standard deviation for the following sample:

  2,   8,   5,   9,   1,   6,   6,   3,   6,   10,   4,   12

27. Two samples are as follows:

  Sample A: 7,   9,   10,   8,   9,   12

  Sample B: 13,   5,   9,   1,   17,   9

  a. Just by looking at these data, which sample has more variability? Explain your answer.
  b. Compute the mean and the standard deviation for each sample.
  c. In which sample is the mean more representative (more "typical") of its scores? How does the standard deviation affect the interpretation of the mean?

28. The following scores are brain weights in grams for a sample of $n = 5$ fish. Calculate the mean and variance for these data. (*Hint:* Multiply each score by 100 to get rid of the decimal places. Remember to correct for this multiplication before you report your answer.)
Scores:

  0.08,   0.09,   0.08,   0.11,   0.09

29. Calculate *SS*, variance, and standard deviation for the following sample of scores. (*Hint:* The calculations will be easier if you first subtract 430 from each score. For example, $431 - 430 = 1$, and $436 - 430 = 6$. (Remember, subtracting a constant will not affect these measures of variability.) Scores:

431, 432, 435, 432, 436, 431, 434

30. For the data in the following sample:

1, 4, 3, 6, 2, 7, 18, 3, 7, 2, 4, 3

a. Sketch a frequency distribution histogram.
b. Compute the mean and standard deviation.
c. Find the median and the semi-interquartile range.
d. Which measures of central tendency and variability provide a better description of the sample? Explain your answer.

AT THIS point, we have finished the basic elements of descriptive statistics, and it is a good time to pause and consider the material that has been presented thus far. In particular, this is a good time to tie together some of the individual items that have appeared as separate pieces scattered throughout the preceding four chapters. In addition, we will try to direct your attention to specific information that we consider important background material for the chapters that follow.

LOOKING BACK

The goal of descriptive statistics is to summarize or to describe a large set of data in a simple, easy-to-understand form. Commonly, a set of scores will be presented in a summarized form where you are given only the basic descriptive statistics (or parameters) rather than the full set of original scores. In a research report, for example, you will not be given the complete set of data, but rather the report will provide only the mean and standard deviation. You should be able to compute these two statistical measures, but it is equally important that you understand what they represent. One key concept for understanding statistics is the idea of a *distribution of scores*. Although a distribution can be presented as either a table or a graph, the visual image portrayed by a frequency distribution graph is probably the simplest, most concrete way to represent the concept of a distribution.

You should also realize that the concepts of the *mean,* the *standard deviation,* and a *distribution* can all be integrated into a single visual representation. Specifically,

> If you are given the mean and the standard deviation for a set of scores, you should be able to use those two numbers to construct a picture of the distribution.

To help you construct an accurate visual image of a distribution, we suggest that you begin with the following conceptual definitions of the mean and the standard deviation:

> The *mean* identifies the center of the distribution and can be represented by a vertical line drawn through the center of the set of scores.

> In a distribution, the individual scores are scattered on both sides of the mean, with some scores relatively close to the mean and some scores relatively far

away. The *standard deviation* measures the standard distance from the mean and can be represented by an arrow (or arrows) pointing out from the mean for a distance that is roughly halfway to the most extreme scores.

When we talk about a population of scores, we occasionally will show a graph of the distribution. More often, however, we will simply present a few characteristics that describe the population: typically, the shape, the mean, and the standard deviation. Each of these three elements should be meaningful to you, and the combination of all three elements should give you a clear picture of the population distribution. For example, scores on the SAT form a normal distribution with $\mu = 500$ and $\sigma = 100$. From this information, you should be able to sketch (or conjure up) a visual image of the population. The image for this example is shown in Figure TO-1. Notice that the figure not only shows the mean and the standard deviation, but also uses these two values to reconstruct the underlying scale of measurement (the series of X values along the horizontal line). For example, with $\mu = 500$ and $\sigma = 100$, you should realize that a score of $X = 500$ is located exactly in the center of the distribution and that a score of $X = 400$ is located below the mean (to the left) at a distance equal to the standard deviation.

Forming a visual image of a sample distribution follows the same basic procedure that is used for populations. Specifically, the sample *mean* identifies the center

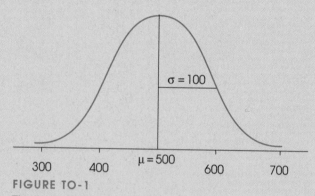

FIGURE TO-1

The distribution of SAT scores. A normal distribution centered at $\mu = 500$ with a standard deviation of $\sigma = 100$.

of the distribution, and the sample *standard deviation* measures the standard distance from the mean. Together, the mean and the standard deviation should allow you to reconstruct the underlying scale of measurement. To differentiate samples from populations, we suggest that you use a histogram to represent sample data and a smooth curve to form the distribution for population data.

LOOKING AHEAD

Throughout the rest of the book, we will constantly discuss samples and populations. Whether or not we specifically mention the word *distribution,* you should think of a sample or a population of scores as a distribution and visualize a graph of the distribution either as a mental image or as a real sketch on paper.

Being able to visualize distributions will be a valuable skill for mastering the material that will be presented in future chapters. For example, an image of a population distribution should enable you to answer a variety of questions about the population. Referring to the image in Figure TO-1: Is a score of $X = 700$ an average score (in the middle), or is it an extreme score (in one of the tails)? Do most individuals in the population have SAT scores less than 700? A good image of the population distribution should make these questions easy to answer. Similarly, a good image of a sample distribution will literally give you a better picture of the sample data and often will clarify more complex statistical analyses that may be done with samples.

In any distribution, the standard deviation provides a *descriptive* measure of how spread out the scores are. However, you should also realize that the standard deviation (or variance) will be an extremely important measure for the *inferential* statistics in later chapters. You should recall that inferential statistics use sample data as the basis for making decisions about populations. In this context, the standard deviation provides a measure of how accurately a sample represents its population. As a simple example, consider the situation where a researcher is selecting a single score (a sample) from a population with $\sigma = 20$. In this situation, you would expect about a 20-point difference between the score and the population mean. A score that was only 10 points away from μ would be considered relatively close and, therefore, a good representative sample. Now imagine that the population standard deviation is $\sigma = 2$ points. In this new distribution, a score that is 10 points away from μ is an extreme value (way out in the tail), and therefore, not a good representative sample. Notice that the standard deviation is used as a benchmark to help judge how much difference there is between a sample score and a population mean. In the future, we will use the standard deviation (and variance) as a measure of *how much error* to expect when we are using sample data as the basis for making inferences about populations.

CHAPTER 5

z-SCORES: LOCATION OF SCORES AND STANDARDIZED DISTRIBUTIONS

TOOLS YOU WILL NEED

The following items are considered essential background material for this chapter. If you doubt your knowledge of any of these items, you should review the appropriate chapter and section before proceeding.

- The mean (Chapter 3)
- The standard deviation (Chapter 4)
- Basic algebra (math review, Appendix A)

CONTENTS

While on vacation recently, 1000 miles from home, I visited a shopping mall. Although I had never been to this particular mall before, I began to realize after a few minutes that it was essentially identical to the old familiar mall where I usually shop at home. The specialty shops were all the same, the food court looked the same, and although some of the department stores had different names, they were basically the same as the stores back home. As the similarities began to sink in, my first response was disappointment. I had traveled 1000 miles to a different city in a different state, only to find that nothing was really different.

On second thought, however, I decided that there are definite advantages to having shopping malls standardized all across the country. First, the new mall was immediately familiar and easily understandable. I did not need to spend much time getting oriented so that I could determine which stores I needed to visit in order to find the items I wanted. Second, because I knew that the items and sizes were standardized, I could be confident that a "large" T-shirt or a pair of size 9½ shoes would fit just as well as the same items purchased back home.

In the same way that shopping malls and shoe sizes are standardized to make them familiar and understandable, researchers often will standardize a set of scores to make them more meaningful and easier to understand. The scores obtained from IQ tests are probably the most familiar example of standardized scores. Specifically, your IQ score is *not* simply a report of the number of questions you answered correctly. In fact, several tests are used to measure IQ (the Stanford-Binet, the WAIS-R, and the WISC-R, for example), some with many questions and some with relatively few. In addition, each test often contains a number of subtests that measure different aspects of IQ. Thus, your actual performance on an IQ test might be reported as follows:

Vocabulary subtext: 8 correct

Arithmetic subtest: 9 correct

General Comprehension subtest: 11 correct

Picture Arrangement subtest: 4 correct

Object Assembly subtest: 4 correct

etc.

Very few people could make much sense of this report. Fortunately, however, IQ scores are standardized, so that each individual's test result can be reported as a single meaningful score. Specifically, the scores are *standardized,* so that they form a distribution with a mean of 100 and a standard deviation of 15. As a result, nearly everyone understands that an IQ of 98 is slightly below average or that an IQ of 150 is substantially above average.

In the preceding chapters, we concentrated on methods for describing entire distributions using the basic parameters of central tendency and variability. In this chapter, we will examine a procedure for *standardizing distributions* and for describing specific locations within a distribution. In particular, we will convert each individual score into a new, *standardized score,* so that the standardized value provides a meaningful description of its exact location within the distribution. We will use the mean as a reference point to determine whether the individual is above or below average. The standard deviation will serve as a yardstick for measuring how much an individual differs from the group average. A good conceptual understanding of the mean and the standard deviation will make this chapter much easier.

5.1 OVERVIEW

This chapter introduces the concept of z-scores or standard scores. The purpose of this statistical technique is to convert each individual score into a standardized z-score, so that the resulting z-score provides a meaningful description of the exact location of the individual score within the distribution. Thus, each individual score will have a corresponding z-score that tells where the individual is located (in the middle of the distribution, at the extreme right-hand tail, at the extreme left-hand tail, and so on).

The process of converting scores into z-scores serves both descriptive statistics and inferential statistics. As a descriptive measure, z-scores give a precise descrip-

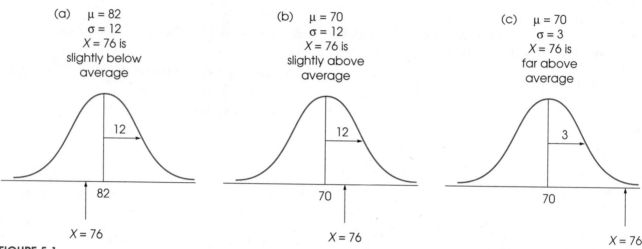

FIGURE 5.1

Three different distributions of test scores showing how the location of a specific score, X = 76, depends on the values for the mean and standard deviation.

tion of location in a distribution. For inferential statistics, z-scores will help determine how well a particular sample represents its population. For example, a sample that is located in the middle of the distribution (according to its z-score) would be considered typical or highly representative. On the other hand, an extreme sample (according to its z-score) would be considered non-representative.

The following example demonstrates the value of standardizing scores and presents the general concept of transforming raw scores (X values) into z-scores.

EXAMPLE 5.1 Suppose that a statistics instructor would like to obtain information about the mathematics background of students entering the statistics course. At the beginning of the course, the instructor administers a mathematics skills test to all students. Suppose that your score on this test is X = 76. How well did you do?

The first point of this example is that a single score, by itself, does not provide much information. For example, your score of X = 76 could be one of the highest in the class or one of the lowest. Without more information, you simply do not know. In particular, your position in the class depends on the mean and the standard deviation for the entire distribution of scores. Figure 5.1 shows three possible distributions.

Figure 5.1(a) shows a distribution with a mean of μ = 82 and a standard deviation of σ = 12. In this distribution, your score, X = 76, is slightly below average.

Your situation improves somewhat in the distribution shown in Figure 5.1(b). In this second distribution, we have lowered the mean to μ = 70 and kept the standard deviation at σ = 12. Now, your score is slightly above average.

Our second point is that the value of the mean plays an important role in determining the location of your score. Having a score that is 6 points *above* the mean is obviously better than having a score that is 6 points *below* the mean.

Finally, consider the distribution shown in Figure 5.1(c). The mean for this distribution is $\mu = 70$, as it was in Figure 5.1(b), but now we have changed the standard deviation to $\sigma = 3$. In this final distribution, your score of $X = 76$ is located in the extreme right-hand tail, one of the highest scores in the class.

Our final point is that the standard deviation is also an important factor in determining where a score is located within a distribution. Your score, $X = 76$, is located 6 points above the mean in Figure 5.1(b) and 5.1(c). However, the 6-point distance is relatively small in Figure 5.1(b) and relatively large in Figure 5.1(c). Thus, both the mean and the standard deviation must be considered to determine the exact location of any particular score, and both μ and σ will be critical factors for determining z-scores.

5.2 z-SCORES AND LOCATION IN A DISTRIBUTION

The goal of z-scores is to provide a simple procedure for standardizing *any distribution*. A z-score takes information about the population mean and standard deviation and uses this information to produce a single numerical value that specifies the location of any raw score within any distribution. The z-score accomplishes this by transforming a raw score into a signed number ($+$ or $-$) so that

1. The *sign* tells whether the score is located above ($+$) or below ($-$) the mean, and

2. The *number* tells the distance between the score and the mean in terms of the number of standard deviations.

Thus, in a distribution of standardized IQ scores with $\mu = 100$ and $\sigma = 15$, a score of $X = 130$ would be transformed into $z = +2.00$. The z value tells that the score is located above the mean ($+$) by a distance of 2 standard deviations (30 points).

DEFINITION

A *z-score* specifies the precise location of each X value within a distribution. The sign of the z-score ($+$ or $-$) signifies whether the score is above the mean (positive) or below the mean (negative). The numerical value of the z-score specifies the distance from the mean by counting the number of standard deviations between X and μ.

Now we can return to the three distributions shown in Figure 5.1 and use a z-score to describe the position of $X = 76$ within each distribution as follows:

In Figure 5.1(a), the score $X = 76$ corresponds to a z-score of $z = -0.50$. That is, the score is located exactly one-half of a standard deviation *below* the mean.

In Figure 5.1(b), the score $X = 76$ corresponds to a z-score of $z = +0.50$. In

FIGURE 5.2

The relationship between *z*-score values
and locations in a population distribution.

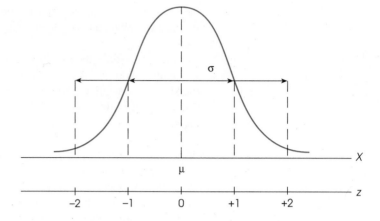

this distribution, the score is located exactly one-half of a standard deviation
above the mean.

Finally, in Figure 5.1(c), the score $X = 76$ corresponds to a *z*-score of $z =$
$+ 2.00$. The score is located *above* the mean by exactly 2 standard deviations.

Notice that a *z*-score always consists of two parts: a sign ($+$ or $-$) and a magnitude. Both parts are necessary to describe completely where a raw score is located within a distribution.

Figure 5.2 shows a population distribution with various positions identified by
their *z*-score values. Notice that all *z*-scores above the mean are positive and all
z-scores below the mean are negative. The sign of a *z*-score tells you immediately
whether the score is located above or below the mean. Also, note that a *z*-score of
$z = +1.00$ corresponds to a position above the mean by exactly 1 standard deviation. A *z*-score of $z = +2.00$ is always located above the mean by exactly 2 standard deviations. The numerical value of the *z*-score tells you the number of standard deviations from the mean (see Box 5.1). Now suppose that the scores from
your statistics test are reported as *z*-scores and you receive a score of $z = -0.50$.
How did you do? From this single value, you should be able to locate your exact
position within the distribution. In this case ($z = -0.50$), you are below the mean
by one-half of the standard deviation. Find this position in Figure 5.2.

The definition of a *z*-score indicates that each *X* value has a corresponding
z-score. The following example demonstrates the relationship between *X* values and
z-scores within a distribution.

Whenever you are working with *z*-scores,
you should imagine or draw a picture
similar to Figure 5.2. Although you
should realize that not all distributions are
normal, we will use the normal shape as
an example when showing *z*-scores.

EXAMPLE 5.2   A distribution of exam scores has a mean (μ) of 50 and a standard deviation
(σ) of 8.

a. For this distribution, what is the *z*-score corresponding to $X = 58$? Because
58 is *above* the mean, the *z*-score has a positive sign. The score is 8 points
greater than the mean. This distance is exactly 1 standard deviation (because $\sigma = 8$), so the *z*-score is

$$z = +1$$

5.1 RELATIVE POSITION WITHIN A DISTRIBUTION: THE ROLE OF STANDARD DEVIATION

WE HAVE now seen that the standard deviation is an essential part of converting any X value to a z-score. Therefore, in a general sense, the amount of variability in a distribution and the relative position of a particular score are interrelated. This can be demonstrated with a simple example of two distributions.

Suppose that in Caribou, Maine, the average snowfall per year is $\mu = 110$ inches with $\sigma = 30$. In Boston, however, let us assume that the yearly average is only $\mu = 24$ inches with $\sigma = 5$. Last year Caribou enjoyed 125 inches of snow, while Boston was blessed with 39 inches. In which city was the winter much worse than average for its residents?

We are essentially asking a question about the relative position of a raw score in its distribution. In particular, we wish to locate the relative position of last year's accumulation for each city. Thus, in the distribution of annual accumulations for Caribou, where does $X = 125$ fall? Similarly, where does $X = 39$ fall within the distribution for Boston?

If we simply consider deviation scores $(X - \mu)$, the snowfall last year was 15 inches above average for both cities. But does this tell the whole story? In this case, it

does not. The distributions for each city differ in terms of variability ($\sigma = 30$ for Caribou, $\sigma = 5$ for Boston). Again, the amount of variability affects the relative standing of a score. Therefore, it is misleading to simply look at deviation scores. When determining the position of a score in a distribution, we should measure distance of a score from the mean in terms of standard deviation units (see the definition of a z-score).

If we look at Caribou, we find that $\mu = 110$ and $\sigma = 30$. A winter with $X = 125$ inches of snow is 15 points above the mean, or 0.5 standard deviations away. For Boston, the distribution has $\mu = 24$ with $\sigma = 5$. Its winter with $X = 39$ inches is also 15 points above the mean, but this is a distance equal to 3 standard deviation units. When we consider the variability in each distribution, we see that it was not an unusual winter for Caribou. Its snowfall was only ½ standard deviation above the mean ($z = +0.5$), close to what we would expect for that town. On the other hand, Boston had an extreme winter. Its snowfall was 3 standard deviations above the mean ($z = +3.0$), much more snow than its residents would expect.

This z-score indicates that the raw score is located 1 standard deviation above the mean.

b. What is the z-score corresponding to $X = 46$? The z-score will be negative because 46 is *below* the mean. The X value is 4 points away from the mean. This distance is exactly one-half of the standard deviation; therefore, the z-score is

$$z = -\frac{1}{2}$$

This z-score tells us that the X value is ½ standard deviation below the mean.

c. For this distribution, what raw score corresponds to a z-score of $+2$? This z-score indicates that the X value is 2 standard deviations above the mean. One standard deviation is 8 points, so 2 standard deviations would be 16 points. Therefore, the score we are looking for is 16 points above the mean. The mean for the distribution is 50, so the X value is

$$X = 50 + 16 = 66$$

FIGURE 5.3

For the population of general psychology test scores, $\mu = 60$ and $\sigma = 4$. A student whose score is 66 is 1.5σ above the mean or has a z-score of $+1.5$.

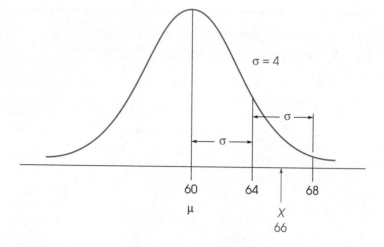

THE z-SCORE FORMULA

The relationship between X values and z-scores can be expressed symbolically in a formula. The formula for transforming raw scores into z-scores is

$$z = \frac{X - \mu}{\sigma}$$

(5.1)

The numerator of the equation, $X - \mu$, is a *deviation score* (Chapter 4, p. 110) and measures the distance in points between X and μ and whether X is located above or below the mean. We divide this difference by σ because we want the z-score to measure distance in terms of standard deviation units. Remember, the purpose of a z-score is to specify an exact location in a distribution. The z-score formula provides a standard procedure for determining a score's location by calculating the direction and distance from the mean.

EXAMPLE 5.3

$$\frac{X - M}{6} \qquad \frac{66 - 60}{4}$$

$$\frac{6}{4} = 1.5$$

A distribution of general psychology test scores has a mean of $\mu = 60$ and a standard deviation of $\sigma = 4$. What is the z-score for a student who received a 66?

Looking at a sketch of the distribution (Figure 5.3), we see that the raw score is above the mean by at least 1 standard deviation, but not quite by 2. Judging from the graph, 66 appears to be $1\frac{1}{2}$ standard deviations from the mean. The computation of the z-score with the formula confirms our estimate:

$$z = \frac{X - \mu}{\sigma} = \frac{66 - 60}{4} = \frac{+6}{4} = +1.5$$

EXAMPLE 5.4

The distribution of SAT verbal scores for high school seniors has a mean of $\mu = 500$ and a standard deviation of $\sigma = 100$. Joe took the SAT and scored 430 on the verbal subtest. Locate his score in the distribution by using a z-score.

Joe's score is 70 points below the mean, so the z-score will be negative. Because 70 points is less than 1 standard deviation, the z-score should have a magnitude that is less than 1. Using the formula, his z-score is

$$z = \frac{X - \mu}{\sigma} = \frac{430 - 500}{100} = \frac{-70}{100} = -0.70$$

DETERMINING A RAW SCORE FROM A z-SCORE

There may be situations in which you have an individual's z-score and would like to determine the corresponding raw score. When you start with a z-score, you can compute the X value by using a different version of the z-score formula. Before we introduce the new formula, let's look at the logic behind converting a z-score back to a raw score.

EXAMPLE 5.5

A distribution has a mean of $\mu = 40$ and a standard deviation of $\sigma = 6$.

What raw score corresponds to $z = +1.5$? The z-score indicates that the X value is located 1.5 standard deviations *above* the mean. Because 1 standard deviation is 6 points, 1.5 standard deviations equal 9 points. Therefore, the raw score is 9 points above the mean, or $X = 49$.

$1.5 = \frac{X - 40}{6}$

$9 = X - 40$

$49 = X$

In Example 5.5, we used the z-score and the standard deviation to determine the deviation for an X value; that is, how much distance lies between the raw score and the mean. The deviation score was then added to or subtracted from the mean (depending on the sign of z) to yield the X value. These steps can be incorporated into a formula so that the X value can be computed directly. This formula is obtained by solving the z-score formula for X:

$$z = \frac{X - \mu}{\sigma}$$

$z\sigma = X - \mu$ (Multiply both sides by σ.)

$X - \mu = z\sigma$ (Transpose the equation.)

$X = \mu + z\sigma$ (Add μ to both sides.)   (5.2)

rearange → formula

Notice that the third equation in this derivation contains the expression $X - \mu$, the definition for a deviation score (Chapter 4, p. 110). Therefore, the deviation score for any raw score can also be found by multiplying the z-score by the standard deviation ($z\sigma$). Essentially, this is the method we used in Example 5.5. If $z\sigma$ provides a deviation score, then we may rewrite equation 5.2 as

raw score = mean + deviation score

In using equation 5.2, always remember that the sign of the z-score ($+$ or $-$) will determine whether the deviation score is added to or subtracted from the mean.

EXAMPLE 5.6 A distribution has a mean of $\mu = 60$ and a standard deviation of $\sigma = 12$.

a. What raw score has $z = +0.25$?

$$X = \mu + z\sigma$$
$$= 60 + 0.25(12)$$
$$= 60 + 3$$
$$= 63$$

b. What X value corresponds to $z = -1.2$?

$$X = \mu + z\sigma$$
$$= 60 + (-1.2)(12)$$
$$= 60 - 14.4$$
$$= 45.6$$

[handwritten annotations in left margin:
$Z = \dfrac{X-M}{6}$ $.25 = \dfrac{X-60}{12}$ $3 = X - 60$

$-1.2 = \dfrac{X-60}{12}$

$-14.4 = X - 60$ *]*

5.3 USING z-SCORES TO STANDARDIZE A DISTRIBUTION

It is possible to describe the location of every raw score in a distribution by assigning z-scores to all of them. The result would be a transformation of the distribution of raw scores into a distribution of z-scores. That is, for each and every X value in the distribution of raw scores, there would be a corresponding z-score in the new distribution. This new distribution has specific characteristics—characteristics that make a *z-score transformation* a very useful tool in statistics. If every X value is transformed into a z-score, then the distribution of z-scores will have the following properties:

THE CHARACTERISTICS OF **1. Shape** The shape of the z-score distribution will be the same as the original
A z-SCORE DISTRIBUTION distribution of raw scores. If the original distribution is negatively skewed, for example, then the z-score distribution will also be negatively skewed. If the original distribution is normal, the distribution of z-scores will also be normal. Transforming raw scores into z-scores does not change anyone's location in the distribution. For example, any raw score that is above the mean by 1 standard deviation will be transformed to a z-score of $z = +1.00$, which is still above the mean by 1 standard deviation. Transforming a distribution from X values to z values does not move scores from one location to another; the procedure simply relabels each score (see Figure 5.4). Because each individual score stays in its same position within the distribution, the overall shape of the distribution does not change.

2. The Mean When raw scores are transformed into z-scores, the resulting z-score distribution will *always* have a mean of zero. This is the case regardless of the value of μ for the raw score distribution. Suppose that a population of scores has $\mu = 100$ and $\sigma = 10$. What is the z-score for the value $X = 100$? Notice that

FIGURE 5.4

Following a z-score transformation, the
X-axis is relabeled in z-score units. The
distance that is equivalent to 1 standard
deviation on the X-axis ($\sigma = 10$ points in
this example) corresponds to 1 point on
the z-score scale.

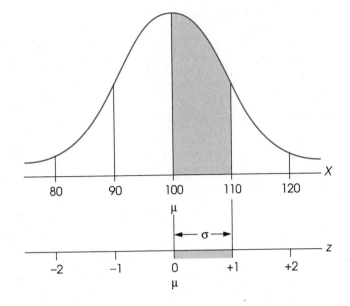

the X value equals the mean of the distribution, so its z-score will also be the z-score
for the mean (see Figure 5.4).

$$z = \frac{X - \mu}{\sigma} = \frac{100 - 100}{10} = \frac{0}{10} = 0$$

The mean of the distribution has a z-score of zero. You will remember that raw
scores that fall below the mean have negative z-scores (that is, z-scores *less than
zero*) and that X values above the mean have positive z-scores (*greater than zero*).
This fact makes the mean a convenient reference point.

The Standard Deviation   When a distribution of X values is transformed into a
distribution of z-scores, the new distribution will have a standard deviation of 1.
For example, a distribution of raw scores has $\mu = 100$ and $\sigma = 10$. In this distribution, a raw score of 110 will have a z-score of +1 (1 standard deviation above
the mean). When X is 90, the z will be −1 (or 1 standard deviation below the
mean). When X is 120, z is +2, and so on. The distribution in Figure 5.4 is labeled
in terms of both X values and their corresponding z-scores. Note that 10 points on
the X scale are the equivalent of 1 standard deviation. Furthermore, the distance of
1 standard deviation on the X scale corresponds to 1 point on the z-score scale.
That is, the X scale has merely been relabeled following a z transformation, so that
1 point on the z scale corresponds to 1 standard deviation unit on the X scale. This
relabeling will give the z-score distribution a standard deviation of 1 point.

Thus, when any distribution of raw scores (X values) is transformed into z-scores,
the resulting z-score distribution will always have a mean of zero and a standard
deviation of 1. Because every z-score distribution has the same mean ($\mu = 0$) and
the same standard deviation ($\sigma = 1$), the z-score distribution is called a *standardized* distribution.

Box 5.2 examines the z-score transformation in terms of the basic properties of
the mean and standard deviation that were discussed in Chapters 3 and 4. In the

z-SCORE TRANSFORMATIONS:
PROPERTIES OF μ AND σ

SOME OF of the properties of the mean (Chapter 3) and standard deviation (Chapter 4) can help explain what happens in a z-score transformation. Consider these two situations:

1. If a constant is subtracted from every score in a distribution, then the mean of the new distribution will equal the old mean minus that constant, but the standard deviation is unchanged.

$$\mu_{new} = \mu_{old} - C$$

$$\sigma_{new} = \sigma_{old} \quad \text{(not changed)}$$

2. If every score in a distribution is divided by a constant, then the mean of the new distribution will equal the old mean divided by that constant, and the standard deviation of the new distribution will equal the old standard deviation divided by that constant.

$$\mu_{new} = \frac{\mu_{old}}{C}$$

$$\sigma_{new} = \frac{\sigma_{old}}{C}$$

Now, let's consider what happens in a z-score transformation. First, for *every raw score* (X), we compute a deviation score. This entails subtracting μ from every score in the distribution. Note that this is basically a situation where a constant value is being subtracted from each score, but here the constant also equals μ. Next, we divide each deviation score by σ to get the z-scores. This last step amounts to nothing more than dividing by a constant value (which in this case happens to equal σ). Considering the characteristics of means and standard deviations that we just reviewed, what will happen to a raw score distribution with $\mu = 100$ and $\sigma = 10$ when a z-score transformation is performed? First, we will look at the mean.

In this case, we are first subtracting a constant of 100 from every raw score to get the deviation scores. Thus, the mean will be reduced by that constant.

$$\mu_{\text{deviation scores}} = \mu_{old} - C = 100 - 100 = 0$$

Next, every deviation score is divided by 10 to get the z-scores, so the mean will now be divided by this constant.

$$\mu_z = \frac{\mu_{\text{deviation scores}}}{C} = \frac{0}{10} = 0$$

Note that the mean for a distribution of z-scores equals zero.

The same logic also applies to the standard deviation during a z-score transformation. First, the deviation scores are obtained by subtracting the constant of 100 from every raw score. However, subtracting a constant from every score does not change the standard deviation.

$$\sigma_{\text{deviation scores}} = \sigma_{old} = 10$$

Then every deviation score is divided by 10 to obtain the z-scores. The standard deviation is also divided by 10.

$$\sigma_z = \frac{\sigma_{\text{deviation scores}}}{C} = \frac{10}{10} = 1$$

Thus, the standard deviation for a z-score distribution equals 1.

following section, we demonstrate the characteristics of a z-score distribution with actual data.

DEMONSTRATING THE PROPERTIES
OF A z-SCORE TRANSFORMATION

By using a small population of raw scores, it is easy to demonstrate the characteristics of a distribution following a z-score transformation. A population of $N = 6$ scores consists of the following values:

$$0, \quad 6, \quad 5, \quad 2, \quad 3, \quad 2$$

The population mean is

$$\mu = \frac{\Sigma X}{N} = \frac{18}{6} = 3$$

The population standard deviation is

$$\sigma = \sqrt{\frac{SS}{N}} = \sqrt{\frac{24}{6}} = \sqrt{4} = 2$$

To demonstrate the characteristics of a z-score distribution, we must transform every raw score into a z-score using equation 5.1:

$$z = \frac{X = \mu}{\sigma}$$

Therefore, for $X = 0$,

$$z = \frac{0 - 3}{2} = -1.5$$

For $X = 6$,

$$z = \frac{6 - 3}{2} = +1.5$$

For $X = 5$,

$$z = \frac{5 - 3}{2} = +1.0$$

For $X = 2$,

$$z = \frac{2 - 3}{2} = -0.5$$

For $X = 3$,

$$z = \frac{3 - 3}{2} = 0$$

For $X = 2$,

$$z = -0.5 \quad \text{(already computed)}$$

The distribution now consists of $N = 6$ z-scores:

$$-1.5, +1.5, +1.0, -0.5, 0, -0.5$$

The distribution of z-scores and the original distribution of raw scores are shown in Figure 5.5. Notice that the shape of the distribution has not been changed by the z-score transformation. All individuals are in the same relative position in the distribution after the transformation to z-scores. For example, the individual with $X = 6$ and $z = +1.5$ has the highest score in both distributions. The X-axis is simply relabeled in z-score units after the transformation.

FIGURE 5.5

Transforming a distribution of raw scores (top) into z-scores (bottom) will not change the shape of the distribution.

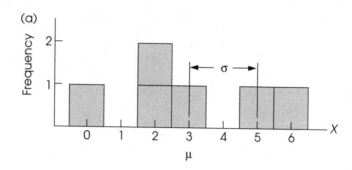

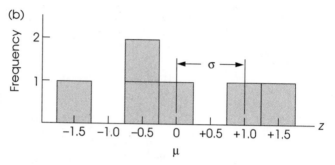

To find the mean of the z distribution, we add all the z-scores and divide by N:

The subscript $_z$ indicates we are computing the mean for the distribution of z-scores.

$$\mu_z = \frac{\Sigma z}{N} = \frac{-1.5 + 1.5 + 1 + (-0.5) + 0 + (-0.5)}{6}$$

$$= \frac{-2.5 + 2.5}{6} = \frac{0}{6} = 0$$

The mean of the distribution of z-scores (μ_z) will always equal zero, regardless of the value of the mean for the raw scores.

To determine the standard deviation of the z-scores, we use the standard deviation formula, but plug in z-scores in place of X values. Therefore, the sum of squares for a z-score distribution is

$$SS_z = \Sigma(z - \mu_z)^2$$

Table 5.1 summarizes the steps for the computation of SS_z. For the standard deviation of the z-score distribution (σ_z), we obtain

$$\sigma_z = \sqrt{\frac{SS_z}{N}} = \sqrt{\frac{6}{6}} = \sqrt{1} = 1$$

In summary, transforming raw scores to z-scores will give us a new distribution with the same shape as the original, a mean of zero, and a standard deviation equal to 1, regardless of the parameters of the distribution of raw scores.

TABLE 5.1

Computation of SS_z for a Distribution of *z*-Scores

For a distribution of *z*-scores, $\mu_z = 0$.
Therefore, $z = z - \mu_z$.

z	$z - \mu_z$	$(z - \mu_z)^2$
-1.5	-1.5	2.25
$+1.5$	$+1.5$	2.25
$+1.0$	$+1.0$	1.00
-0.5	-0.5	0.25
0	0	0
-0.5	-0.5	0.25
		$\overline{6.00} = SS_z = \Sigma(z - \mu_z)^2$

LEARNING CHECK

1. What information does a *z*-score provide?

2. A population of scores has $\mu = 45$ and $\sigma = 5$. Find the *z*-scores for the following raw scores:
   a. $X = 47$ b. $X = 48$ c. $X = 40$ d. $X = 44$
   e. $X = 52$ f. $X = 39$ g. $X = 45$ h. $X = 56$

3. For the same population, determine the raw scores that correspond to the following *z*-scores:
   a. $z = +1.3$ b. $z = -0.4$ c. $z = -3.0$
   d. $z = -1.5$ e. $z - +2.8$ f. $z = 0$

4. What is the advantage of having $\mu = 0$ for a distribution of *z*-scores?

ANSWERS

1. A *z*-score identifies a precise location in a distribution. The sign indicates whether the location is above or below the mean, and the magnitude of *z* indicates the number of standard deviations from the mean.

2. a. $+0.4$ b. $+0.6$ c. -1.0 d. -0.2
   e. $+1.4$ f. -1.2 g. 0   h. $+2.2$

3. a. 51.5   b. 43   c. 30   d. 37.5   e. 59   f. 45

4. With $\mu = 0$, you know immediately that any positive value is above the mean and any negative value is below the mean.

USING *z*-SCORES TO MAKE COMPARISONS

When two scores come from different distributions, it is impossible to make any direct comparison between the two scores. Suppose, for example, that Bob received a score of $X = 60$ on a psychology exam and a score of $X = 56$ on a biology test. For which course should Bob expect the better grade?

Because the two scores come from two different distributions, any comparison would be like the proverbial comparison of apples to oranges. Bob's psychology score might be the lowest score in the class. His biology score could be the highest score in the class. Without more information about the two distributions, you cannot compare the two scores. Specifically, you need to know the mean for each class in order to determine whether Bob is above or below average, and you need to know the two standard deviations to determine how far above the mean (or below the mean) Bob is located in each distribution.

5.2   WHY ARE z-SCORES IMPORTANT?

WE HAVE introduced z-scores as a statistical method for describing a specific location within a distribution. As you have seen, z-scores can be used to determine the precise location of an individual score, and z-scores can be used to compare the relative positions of two or more scores. The ability to describe a location in a distribution is of great value for other statistical purposes. The following is a brief list of some of the ways that z-scores will be used in later chapters.

1. **Probability.** One of the basic goals for statistics is to determine the probability or likelihood of particular events. Often it is possible to use z-scores as a starting point for finding probabilities. In many situations, the most likely outcomes are those that are "typical," or average. In other words, observing an individual with a z-score near zero (in the middle of the distribution) is much more likely than observing an individual with a z-score of +3.00. In Chapter 6, we examine the relationship between z-scores and probability.

2. **Evaluating Treatment Effects.** Many experiments are done to determine whether or not a particular treatment has any effect on a dependent variable. For example, a researcher testing a new stimulant drug would like to know if the drug affects heart rate. One simple test would be to look at the heart rates of individuals who have taken the drug. If these individuals have heart rates that are still average or typical (i.e.,

z-scores around zero), the researcher could conclude that the drug does not seem to influence heart rate. On the other hand, if the individuals had heart rates that were extremely high (i.e., z-scores of +3.00 or +4.00), the researcher might conclude that the drug does increase heart rate. In general, z-scores provide an easy method for determining whether an individual score is average or extreme. We take a closer look at this inferential procedure in Chapters 8 and 18.

3. **Measuring Relationships.** Some statistical methods are intended to describe and measure the relationship between two variables. For example, a psychologist might be interested in the relationship between physical development and mental development for five-year-old children. Are children who are unusually large also unusually bright? In order to examine the relationship, it is first necessary to find the location of each child in the distribution of heights and in the distribution of IQs. Extremely tall children will have large positive z-scores, those of average height will have z-scores near zero, and small children will have negative z-scores. Similarly, each child's IQ can be described as a z-score. The researcher can then determine whether there is a consistent relationship between the z-scores for height and the z-scores for IQ. We examine statistical methods for measuring relationships in Chapter 16.

See Box 5.3 for other examples of how z-scores are useful in statistics.

One way to make a meaningful comparison of Bob's scores is to standardize the distributions for both classes by transforming the exam scores into z-scores. Remember, a z-score transformation will always produce a distribution that has $\mu = 0$ and $\sigma = 1$. Therefore, if every raw score in the psychology and biology classes is transformed into a z-score, the resulting distributions for both classes will have $\mu = 0$ and $\sigma = 1$. All we need to do is compare Bob's z-score for psychology with his z-score for biology to determine which exam score is better. When data transformations are used to make distributions comparable, we are using *standardized distributions*. The z-scores in this instance are often called *standard scores*.

DEFINITIONS

A *standardized distribution* is composed of transformed scores that result in predetermined values for μ and σ, regardless of their values for the raw score distribution. Standardized distributions are used to make dissimilar distributions comparable.

A *standard score* is a transformed score that provides information about its location in a distribution. A z-score is an example of a standard score.

FIGURE 5.6

Distributions of exam scores for a psychology test and a biology test. The scores for one student who took both tests are indicated in the figure.

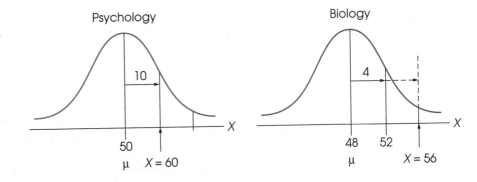

In practice, it is not necessary to transform every score in a distribution in order to compare two scores. We need to transform only the two scores in question. In Bob's case, we must find the z-scores for his psychology and biology scores. To find these two z-scores, you must know the mean and standard deviation for each class. Suppose that the scores for the psychology class had a mean of $\mu = 50$ with $\sigma = 10$, and for biology, the class mean was $\mu = 48$ with $\sigma = 4$. With this information, you can transform Bob's psychology score of $X = 60$ into a z-score as follows:

Be sure to use the μ and σ values for the distribution to which X belongs.

$$z = \frac{X - \mu}{\sigma} = \frac{60 - 50}{10} = \frac{10}{10} = +1.0$$

For biology, Bob's z-score is

$$z = \frac{56 - 48}{4} = \frac{8}{4} = +2.0$$

Note that Bob's z-score for biology is +2.0, which means that his test score is 2 standard deviations above the class mean. On the other hand, his z-score is +1.0 for psychology, or 1 standard deviation above the mean. In terms of relative class standing, Bob is doing much better in the biology class. Notice that it is meaningful to make a direct comparison of the z-scores. A z-score of +2.00 *always* indicates a higher position than a z-score of +1.00 because all z-score values are based on a standardized distribution with a mean of zero and a standard deviation of 1.

Computing the z-scores for Bob's two exam scores is the simplest way to compare the two values. However, an alternative method is to sketch the two distributions and locate the position of Bob's score in each one. Figure 5.6 shows the two exam distributions. A visual comparison of the two distributions confirms what the z-score calculations have already demonstrated: Bob's score is much higher in the biology distribution ($z = +2.00$) than in the psychology distribution ($z = +1.00$).

LEARNING CHECK 1. Why is it possible to compare scores from different distributions after each distribution is transformed into z-scores?

2. For distribution A, $\mu = 20$ and $\sigma = 7$. Distribution B has $\mu = 23$ and $\sigma = 2$. In which distribution will a raw score of 27 have a higher standing?

ANSWERS 1. Comparisons are possible because both distributions will have the same μ and σ ($\mu = 0$, $\sigma = 1$) following a z-score transformation.

2. For distribution A, a raw score of 27 has a *z*-score of + 1.0. For distribution B, a score of 27 corresponds to a *z*-score of +2.0. Therefore, a raw score of 27 has a higher relative standing in distribution B.

5.4 OTHER STANDARDIZED DISTRIBUTIONS BASED ON *z*-SCORES

TRANSFORMING z-SCORES TO A PREDETERMINED μ AND σ

Although *z*-score distributions have distinct advantages, many people find them cumbersome because they contain negative values and decimals. For these reasons, it is common to standardize a distribution by transforming *z*-scores to a distribution with a predetermined mean and standard deviation that are whole round numbers. The goal is to create a new (standardized) distribution that has "simple" values for the mean and standard deviation, but does not change any individual's location within the distribution. Standardized scores of this type are frequently used in psychological testing. For example, raw scores for intelligence tests are frequently converted to standardized scores that have a mean of 100 and a standard deviation of 15. If the same standardized scale is used for several types of intelligence tests, then the exam scores on different tests can be more readily compared because the distributions will have the same mean and standard deviation. Basically, two steps are involved in standardizing a distribution so that it has a pre-specified μ and σ: (1) Each of the raw scores is transformed into a *z*-score, and (2) each of the *z*-scores is then converted into a new *X* value so that a particular μ and σ are achieved. This process assures that each individual has exactly the same *z*-score (location) in the new distribution as in the original distribution.

EXAMPLE 5.7

An instructor gives an exam to a psychology class. For this exam, the distribution of raw scores has a mean of $\mu = 57$ with $\sigma = 14$. The instructor would like to simplify the distribution by transforming all scores into a new standardized distribution with $\mu = 50$ and $\sigma = 10$. To demonstrate this process, we will consider what happens to two specific students: Joe, who has a raw score of $X = 64$ in the original distribution, and Maria, whose original raw score is $X = 43$.

STEP 1

Transform each of the original raw scores into *z*-scores. For Joe, $X = 64$, so his *z*-score is

$$z = \frac{X - \mu}{\sigma} = \frac{64 - 57}{14} = +0.5$$

Remember, the values of μ and σ are for the distribution from which *X* was taken.

For Maria, $X = 43$, and her *z*-score is

$$z = \frac{X - \mu}{\sigma} = \frac{43 - 57}{14} = -1.0$$

STEP 2

Change the *z*-scores to the new standardized scores. The instructor wants to create a standardized distribution with $\mu = 50$ and $\sigma = 10$. Joe's *z*-score, $z =$

TABLE 5.2

	JOE	MARIA
Raw score	$X = 64$	43
Step 1: Compute z-score	$z = +0.5$	-1.0
Step 2: Convert to standardized score	55	40

+0.50, indicates that he is above the mean by exactly one-half standard deviation. In the new distribution, this position would be above the mean by 5 points (½ of 10), so his standardized score would be 55. Maria's score is located 1 standard deviation below the mean ($z = -1.00$). In the new standardized distribution, Maria is located 10 points ($\sigma = 10$) below the mean ($\mu = 50$), so her new score would be $X = 40$.

The results of this two-step transformation process are summarized in Table 5.2 and shown in Figure 5.7. Notice that Joe, for example, has exactly the same z-score ($z = +0.50$) in both the original raw score distribution and the new standardized distribution. This means that Joe's position relative to the other students in the class has not been changed. Similarly, *all* the students stay in the same position relative to the rest of the class. Thus, standardizing a distribution does not change the shape of the overall distribution, and it does not move individuals around within the distribution—the process simply changes the mean and standard deviation.

A FORMULA FOR FINDING THE STANDARDIZED SCORE

Earlier in the chapter, we derived a formula (equation 5.2) to find the raw score that corresponds to a particular z-score:

$$X = \mu + z\sigma$$

For purposes of computing the new standardized score, we can rewrite the equation:

$$\text{standard score} = \mu_{new} + z\sigma_{new} \qquad (5.3)$$

FIGURE 5.7

An original distribution of exam scores (with $\mu = 57$ and $\sigma = 14$) and the standardized distribution (with $\mu = 50$ and $\sigma = 10$). Note that the location of each student is exactly the same within the two distributions.

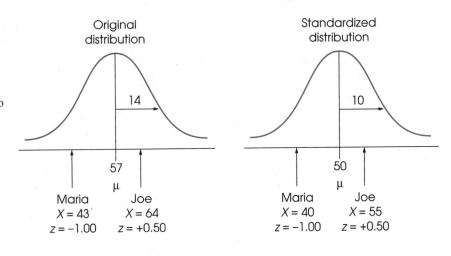

The standardized score equals the mean of the new standardized distribution plus its z-score times the standard deviation of the new standardized distribution. The z-score in the formula is the one computed for the original raw score (step 1). Notice that $z\sigma$ is the deviation score of the standardized score. If the raw score is below the mean, then its z-score and $z\sigma$ will be negative. For scores above the mean, $z\sigma$ is positive.

EXAMPLE 5.8 A psychologist has developed a new intelligence test. For years, the test has been given to a large number of people; for this population, $\mu = 65$ and $\sigma = 10$. The psychologist would like to make the scores of his subjects comparable to scores on other IQ tests, which have $\mu = 100$ and $\sigma = 15$. If the test is standardized so that it is comparable to other tests (with $\mu = 100$ and $\sigma = 15$), what would be the standardized scores for the following individuals?

PERSON	X
1	75
2	45
3	67

STEP 1 Compute the z-score for each individual. Remember, the original distribution has $\mu = 65$ and $\sigma = 10$.

STEP 2 Compute the standardized score for each person. Remember, the standardized distribution will have $\mu = 100$ and $\sigma = 15$. Table 5.3 summarizes the computations for these steps and the results.

TABLE 5.3

	COMPUTATIONS	
	STEP 1: $z = \dfrac{X - \mu}{\sigma}$	STEP 2: $X = \mu + z\sigma$
Person 1	$z = \dfrac{75 - 65}{10} = +1.0$	$X = 100 + 1(15)$ $= 100 + 15 = 115$
Person 2	$z = \dfrac{45 - 65}{10} = -2.0$	$X = 100 - 2(15)$ $= 100 - 30 = 70$
Person 3	$z = \dfrac{67 - 65}{10} = +0.2$	$X = 100 + 0.2(15)$ $= 100 + 3 = 103$

		SUMMARY	
PERSON	X	z	STANDARDIZED SCORE
1	75	+1.00	115
2	45	−2.00	70
3	67	+0.20	103

LEARNING CHECK   **1.** A population has $\mu = 37$ and $\sigma = 2$. If this distribution is transformed into a new distribution with $\mu = 100$ and $\sigma = 20$, what new values will be obtained for each of the following scores: 35, 36, 37, 38, 39?

2. For the following population, $\mu = 7$ and $\sigma = 4$. Scores: 2, 4, 6, 10, 13.
   a. Transform this distribution so $\mu = 50$ and $\sigma = 20$.
   b. Compute μ and σ for the new distribution. (You should obtain $\mu = 50$ and $\sigma = 20$.)

ANSWERS   **1.** The five scores, 35, 36, 37, 38, and 39, are transformed into 80, 90, 100, 110, and 120, respectively.

2. a. The original scores, 2, 4, 6, 10, and 13, are transformed into 25, 35, 45, 65, and 80, respectively.
   b. The new scores add up to $\Sigma X = 250$, so the mean is $^{250}\!/_5 = 50$. The SS for the transformed scores is 2000, the variance is 400, and the new standard deviation is 20.

SUMMARY

1. Each X value can be transformed into a z-score that specifies the exact location of X within the distribution. The sign of the z-score indicates whether the location is above (positive) or below (negative) the mean. The numerical value of the z-score specifies the number of standard deviations between X and μ.

2. The z-score formula is used to transform X values into z-scores:

$$z = \frac{X - \mu}{\sigma}$$

3. To transform z-scores back into X values, solve the z-score equation for X:

$$X = \mu + z\sigma$$

4. When an entire distribution of X values is transformed into z-scores, the result is a distribution of z-scores. The z-score distribution will have the same shape as the distribution of raw scores, and it always will have a mean of 0 and a standard deviation of 1.

5. When comparing raw scores from different distributions, it is necessary to standardize the distributions with a z-score transformation. The distributions will then be comparable because they will have the same parameters ($\mu = 0$, $\sigma = 1$). In practice, it is necessary to transform only those raw scores that are being compared.

6. In certain situations, such as in psychological testing, the z-scores are converted into standardized distributions that have a particular mean and standard deviation.

KEY TERMS

raw score	deviation score	standardized distribution	standard score
z-score	z-score transformation		

———— FOCUS ON PROBLEM SOLVING ————

1. When you are converting an X value to a z-score (or vice versa), do not rely entirely on the formula. You can avoid careless mistakes if you use the definition of a z-score (sign and numerical value) to make a preliminary estimate of the answer before you begin computations. For example, a z-score of $z = -0.85$ identifies a score located *below* the mean by almost 1 standard deviation. When computing the X value for this z-score, be sure that your answer is smaller than the mean, and check that the distance between X and μ is slightly less than the standard deviation.

A common mistake when computing z-scores is to forget to include the sign of the z-score. The sign is determined by the deviation score $(X - \mu)$ and should be carried through all steps of the computation. If, for example, the correct z-score is $z = -2.0$, then an answer of $z = 2.0$ would be wrong. In the first case, the raw score is 2 standard deviations *below* the mean. But the second (and incorrect) answer indicates that the X value is 2 standard deviations *above* the mean. These are clearly different answers, and only one can be correct. What is the best advice to avoid careless errors? Sketch the distribution, showing the mean and the raw score (or z-score) in question. This way you will have a concrete frame of reference for each problem.

2. When comparing scores from distributions that have different standard deviations, it is important to be sure that you use the correct value for σ in the z-score formula. Use the σ value for the distribution from which the raw score in question was taken.

3. Remember, a z-score specifies a relative position within the context of a specific distribution. A z-score is a relative value, not an absolute value. For example, a z-score of $z = -2.0$ does not necessarily suggest a very low raw score—it simply means that the raw score is among the lowest within that specific group.

DEMONSTRATION 5.1

TRANSFORMATING X VALUES INTO z-SCORES

A distribution of scores has a mean of $\mu = 60$ with $\sigma = 12$. Find the z-score for $X = 75$.

STEP 1 Determine the sign of the z-score.

First, determine whether X is above or below the mean. This will determine the sign of the z-score. For this demonstration, X is larger than (above) μ, so the z-score will be positive.

STEP 2 Find the distance between X and μ.

The distance is obtained by computing a deviation score.

$$\text{deviation score} = X - \mu = 75 - 60 = 15$$

Thus, the score, $X = 75$, is 15 points above μ.

STEP 3 Convert the distance to standard deviation units.

Converting the distance from step 2 to σ units is accomplished by dividing the distance by σ. For this demonstration,

$$\frac{15}{12} = 1.25$$

Thus, $X = 75$ is 1.25 standard deviations from the mean.

STEP 4 Combine the sign from step 1 with the number from step 2.

The raw score is above the mean, so the z-score must be positive (step 1). For these data,

$$z = +1.25$$

In using the z-score formula, the sign of the z-score will be determined by the sign of the deviation score, $X - \mu$. If X is larger than μ, then the deviation score will be positive. However, if X is smaller than μ, then the deviation score will be negative. For this demonstration, equation 5.1 is used as follows:

$$z = \frac{X - \mu}{\sigma} = \frac{75 - 60}{12} = \frac{+15}{12} = +1.25$$

DEMONSTRATION 5.2

CONVERTING z-SCORES TO X VALUES

For a population with $\mu = 60$ and $\sigma = 12$, what is the X value corresponding to $z = -0.50$?

Notice that in this situation we know the z-score and must find X.

STEP 1 Locate X in relation to the mean.

The sign of the z-score is negative. This tells us that the X value we are looking for is below μ.

STEP 2 Determine the distance from the mean (deviation score).

The magnitude of the z-score tells us how many standard deviations there are between X and μ. In this case, X is ½ standard deviation from the mean. In this distribution, 1 standard deviation is 12 points ($\sigma = 12$). Therefore, X is one-half of 12 points from the mean, or

$$(0.5)(12) = 6 \text{ points}$$

STEP 3 Find the X value.

Starting with the value of the mean, use the direction (step 1) and the distance (step 2) to determine the X value. For this demonstration, we want to find the score that is 6 points below $\mu = 60$. Therefore,

$$X = 60 - 6 = 54$$

Equation 5.2 is used to convert a z-score to an X value. For this demonstration, we obtain the following using the formula:

$$X = \mu + z\sigma$$

$$= 60 + (-0.50)(12)$$

$$= 60 + (-6) = 60 - 6$$

$$= 54$$

Notice that the sign of the z-score determines whether the deviation score is added to or subtracted from the mean.

PROBLEMS

1. Describe exactly what information is provided by a z-score.

2. A positively skewed distribution has $\mu = 80$ and $\sigma = 12$. If this entire distribution is transformed into z-scores, describe the shape, the mean, and the standard deviation for the resulting distribution of z-scores.

3. A distribution of scores has a mean of $\mu = 200$. In this distribution, a score of $X = 250$ is located 50 points above the mean.
   a. Assume that the standard deviation is $\sigma = 25$. Sketch the distribution, and locate the position of $X = 250$. What is the z-score corresponding to $X = 250$ in this distribution?
   b. Now assume that the standard deviation is $\sigma = 100$. Sketch the distribution, and locate $X = 250$. What is the z-score for $X = 250$ now?

4. For a distribution of raw scores, $\mu = 45$. The z-score for $X = 55$ is computed, and a value of $z = -2.00$ is obtained. Regardless of the value for the standard deviation, why must this z-score be incorrect?

5. For a population with $\mu = 50$ and $\sigma = 16$,
   a. Find the z-scores that corresponds to each of the following X values:
      X = 58   X = 34   X = 82
      X = 46   X = 62   X = 74
   b. Find the raw score (X) for each of the following z-scores:
      z = 2.50   z = -0.50   z = -1.50
      z = 0.25   z = -1.00   z = 0.75

6. For a population with $\mu = 100$ and $\sigma = 10$,
   a. Find the z-score that corresponds to each of the following X values:
      X = 106   X = 125   X = 93
      X = 90   X = 87   X = 118
   b. Find the raw score (X) for each of the following z-scores:
      z = 1.20   z = 2.30   z = -0.80
      z = -0.60   z = 0.40   z = -3.00

7. A population of scores has $\mu = 35$ and $\sigma = 5$. Find the z-score that corresponds to each of the following X values from this population:
   X = 40   X = 42   X = 34
   X = 29   X = 47   X = 26

8. A population of scores has $\mu = 85$ and $\sigma = 20$. Find the raw score (X) for each of the following z-scores in this population:
   z = 1.25   z = -2.30   z = -1.50
   z = 0.60   z = -0.40   z = 2.10

9. For a population with $\mu = 90$, a raw score of $X = 93$ corresponds to $z = +0.50$. What is the standard deviation for this distribution?

10. For a population with $\mu = 50$, a raw score of $X = 44$ corresponds to $z = -1.50$. What is the standard deviation for this distribution?

11. For a population with $\sigma = 8$, a raw score of $X = 43$ corresponds to $z = -0.25$. What is the mean for this distribution?

12. For a population with $\sigma = 20$, a raw score of $X = 110$ corresponds to $z = +1.50$. What is the mean for this distribution?

13. A list of exam scores shows that a raw score of $X = 50$ corresponds to $z = -2.00$ and a raw score of $X = 62$ corresponds to $z = +1.00$. Find the mean and standard deviation for the distribution of the raw scores. (*Hint:* Sketch the distribution, and locate the positions of both scores. How much distance is there between the two scores?)

14. On a statistics exam, you have a score of $X = 73$. If the mean for this exam is $\mu = 65$, would you prefer a standard deviation of $\sigma = 8$ or $\sigma = 16$?

15. Answer the same question as in problem 14, but this time assume that the mean for the exam is $\mu = 81$.

16. On a psychology exam with $\mu = 72$ and $\sigma = 12$, you get a score of $X = 78$. The same day, on an English exam with $\mu = 56$ and $\sigma = 5$, you get a score of $X = 66$. For which of the two exams would you expect to receive the better grade? Explain your answer.

17. The state college requires applicants to submit test scores from either the College Placement Exam (CPE) or the College Board Test (CBT). Scores on the CPE have a mean of $\mu = 200$ with $\sigma = 50$, and scores on the CBT average $\mu = 500$ with $\sigma = 100$. Tom's application includes a CPE score of $X = 235$, and Bill's application reports a CBT score of $X = 540$. Based on these scores, which student is more likely to be admitted? Explain your answer.

18. A distribution of exam scores has $\mu = 90$ and $\sigma = 10$. In this distribution, Sharon's score is 9 points above the mean, Jill has a z-score of $+1.20$, Steve's score is ½ standard deviation above the mean, and Ramon has a score of $X = 110$. List the four students in order from highest to lowest score.

19. The Wechsler Adult Intelligence Scale is composed of a number of subtests. Each subtest is standardized to

create a distribution with $\mu = 10$ and $\sigma = 3$. For one subtest, the raw scores have $\mu = 35$ and $\sigma = 6$. Following are some raw scores for this subtest. What will these scores be when they are standardized?

41, 32, 38, 44, 45, 36, 27

20. A distribution of scores has $\mu = 43$ and $\sigma = 4$. If this distribution is standardized to create a new distribution with $\mu = 60$ and $\sigma = 20$, find the standardized value for each of the following scores from the original distribution:

41, 51, 43, 37, 44, 46

21. A distribution with $\mu = 74$ and $\sigma = 8$ is being standardized to produce a new mean of $\mu = 100$ and a new standard deviation of $\sigma = 20$. Find the standardized value for each of the following scores from the original distribution:

84, 78, 80, 66, 62, 72

22. A population consists of the following scores:

12, 1, 10, 3, 7, 3

a. Compute μ and σ for the population.
b. Find the z-score for each raw score in the population.

23. A population consists of the following $N = 5$ scores:

8, 6, 2, 4, 5

a. Compute μ and σ for the population.
b. Find the z-score for each raw score in the population.
c. Transform the original population into a new population of $N = 5$ scores with $\sigma = 100$ and $\sigma = 20$.

24. A population consists of the following $N = 6$ scores:

14, 3, 12, 5, 9, 5

a. Compute μ and σ for this population.
b. Find the z-score for each raw score in the population.
c. Transform the original population into a new population of $N = 6$ scores with $\mu = 60$ and $\sigma = 8$.

CHAPTER 6 PROBABILITY

TOOLS YOU WILL NEED

The following items are considered essential background material for this chapter. If you doubt your knowledge of any of these items, you should review the appropriate chapter or section before proceeding.

- Proportions (math review, Appendix A)
  - Fractions
  - Decimals
  - Percentages
- Basic algebra (math review, Appendix A)
- Upper and lower real limits (Chapters 1 and 2)
- Percentiles and percentile ranks (Chapter 2)
- Quartiles and semi-interquartile range (Chapter 4)
- z-Scores (Chapter 5)

CONTENTS

If you were to read a novel or a newspaper (or this entire textbook), which of the following would you be more likely to encounter:

1. A word beginning with the letter *K?*
2. A word with a *K* as its third letter?

If you think about this question and answer honestly, you probably will decide that words beginning with a *K* are more probable.

A similar question was asked a group of subjects in an experiment reported by Tversky and Kahneman (1973). Their subjects estimated that words beginning with *K* are twice as likely as words with a *K* as the third letter. In truth, the relationship is just the opposite. There are more than twice as many words with a *K* in the third position as there are words beginning with a *K*. How can people be so wrong? Do they completely misunderstand probability?

When you were deciding which type of *K* words are more likely, you probably searched your memory and tried to estimate which words are more common. How many words can you think of that start with the letter *K?* How many words can you think of that have a *K* as the third letter? Because you have had years of practice alphabetizing words according to their first letter, you should find it much easier to search your memory for words beginning with a *K* than to search for words with a *K* in the third position. Consequently, you would conclude that first-letter *K* words are more common and are, therefore, more likely to occur in a book.

Notice that when you use the strategy of counting words during your search, you are estimating their frequencies. From these frequencies, you estimate the proportions of these words in the population of words. Most people think of probability in this way—as a proportion based on how often an outcome occurs. As you will see in this chapter, this idea is a perfectly reasonable approach to probability. In fact, you will see that probability and proportion often are interchangeable concepts.

As for the Tversky and Kahneman study, your error in judging the relative probabilities of *K* words was not due to a misunderstanding of probability. Instead, you simply were misled by the availability of the two types of words in your memory. If you had actually searched through the words in this text (instead of those in your memory), you probably would have found more third-letter *K* words, and you would have concluded (correctly) that these words are more likely.

6.1 OVERVIEW

Relationships between samples and populations most often are described in terms of probability. Suppose, for example, that you are selecting a sample of 1 marble from a jar that contains 50 black and 50 white marbles. Although you cannot guarantee the exact outcome of your sample, it is possible to talk about the potential outcomes in terms of probabilities. In this case, you have a fifty-fifty chance of getting either color. Now consider another jar (population) that has 90 black and only 10 white marbles. Again, you cannot specify the exact outcome of a sample, but now you know that the sample probably will be a black marble. By knowing the makeup of a population, we can determine the probability of obtaining specific samples. In this way, probability gives us a connection between populations and samples.

You may have noticed that the preceding examples begin with a population and then use probability to describe the samples that could be obtained. This is exactly backward from what we want to do with inferential statistics. Remember, the goal of inferential statistics is to begin with a sample and then answer general questions about the population. We will reach this goal in a two-stage process. In the first stage, we develop probability as a bridge from population to samples. This stage involves identifying the types of samples that probably would be obtained from a specific population. Once this bridge is established, we simply reverse the prob-

FIGURE 6.1

The role of probability in inferential statistics. The goal of inferential statistics is
to use the limited information from
samples to draw general conclusions
about populations. The relationship between samples and populations usually is
defined in terms of probability. Probability allows you to start with a population
and predict what kind of sample is likely
to be obtained. This forms a bridge between populations and samples. Inferential statistics use the *probability bridge* as
a basis for making conclusions about
populations when you have only sample
data.

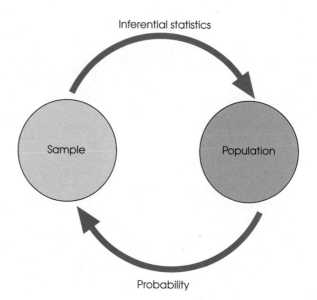

ability rules to allow us to move from samples to populations (see Figure 6.1). The
process of reversing the probability relationship can be demonstrated by considering again the two jars of marbles we looked at earlier. (One jar has 50 black and
50 white marbles; the other jar has 90 black and only 10 white marbles.) This time,
suppose that you are blindfolded when the sample is selected and that your task is
to use the sample to help you to decide which jar was used. If you select a sample
of $n = 4$ marbles and all are black, where did the sample come from? It should be
clear that it would be relatively unlikely (low probability) to obtain this sample
from jar 1; in four draws, you almost certainly would get at least 1 white marble.
On the other hand, this sample would have a high probability of coming from jar
2, where nearly all the marbles are black. Your decision, therefore, is that the sample
probably came from jar 2. Notice that you now are using the sample to make an
inference about the population.

6.2 INTRODUCTION TO PROBABILITY

Probability is a huge topic that extends far beyond the limits of introductory statistics, and we will not attempt to examine it all here. Instead, we will concentrate
on the few concepts and definitions that are needed for an introduction to inferential statistics. We begin with a relatively simple definition of probability.

DEFINITION   In a situation where several different outcomes are possible, we define the
probability for any particular outcome as a fraction or proportion. If the possible outcomes are identified as *A, B, C, D,* and so on, then

$$\text{probability of } A = \frac{\text{number of outcomes classified as } A}{\text{total number of possible outcomes}}$$

For example, when you toss a balanced coin, the outcome will be either heads or tails. Because heads is one of two possible outcomes, the probability of heads is $p = \frac{1}{2}$.

If you are selecting at random 1 card from a complete deck, there are 52 possible outcomes. The probability of selecting the king of hearts is $p = \frac{1}{52}$. The probability of selecting an ace is $p = \frac{4}{52}$ because there are 4 aces in the deck.

To simplify the discussion of probability, we will use a notation system that eliminates a lot of the words. The probability of a specific outcome will be expressed with a lowercase p (for probability) followed by the specific outcome in parentheses. For example, the probability of selecting a king from a deck of cards will be written as p(king). The probability of obtaining heads for a coin toss will be written as p(heads).

You should note that probability is defined as a proportion. This definition makes it possible to restate any probability problem as a proportion problem. For example, the probability problem "What is the probability of obtaining a king from a deck of cards?" can be restated as "Out of the whole deck, what proportion are kings?" In each case, the answer is $\frac{4}{52}$, or "4 out of 52." This translation from probability to proportion may seem trivial now, but it will be a great aid when the probability problems become more complex. In most situations, we are concerned with the probability of obtaining a particular sample from a population. The terminology of *sample* and *population* will not change the basic definition of probability. For example, the whole deck of cards can be considered as a population, and the single card we select is the sample.

The definition we are using identifies probability as a fraction or a proportion. If you work directly from this definition, the probability values you obtain will be expressed as fractions. For example, if you are selecting a card at random,

$$p(\text{spade}) = \frac{13}{52} = \frac{1}{4}$$

Of if you are tossing a coin,

$$p(\text{heads}) = \frac{1}{2}$$

You should be aware that these fractions can be expressed equally well as either decimals or percentages:

If you are unsure how to convert from fractions to decimals or percentages, you should review the section on proportions in the math review, Appendix A.

$$p = \frac{1}{4} = 0.25 = 25\%$$

$$p = \frac{1}{2} = 0.50 = 50\%$$

By convention, probability values most often are expressed as decimal values. But you should realize that any of these three forms is acceptable.

You also should note that all the possible probability values are contained in a limited range. At one extreme, when an event never occurs, the probability is zero or 0% (see Box 6.1). At the other extreme, when an event always occurs, the prob-

6.1 ZERO PROBABILITY

AN EVENT that never occurs has a probability of zero. However, the opposite of this statement is not always true: A probability of zero does not mean that the event is guaranteed never to occur. Whenever there is an extremely large number of possible events, the probability of any specific event is assigned the value zero. This is done because the probability value tends toward zero as the number of possible events get large. Consider, for example, the series

$$\frac{1}{10} \quad \frac{1}{100} \quad \frac{1}{1000} \quad \frac{1}{10,000} \quad \frac{1}{100,000}$$

Note that the value of the fraction is getting smaller and smaller, headed toward zero. At the far extreme, when the number of possible events is so large that it cannot be specified, the probability of a single, specific event is said to be zero.

$$\frac{1}{\text{infinite number}} = 0$$

Consider, for example, the fish in the ocean. If there were only 10 fish, then the probability of selecting any particular one would be $p = \frac{1}{10}$. Note that if you add up the probabilities for all 10 fish, you get a total of 1.00. In reality, the number of fish in the ocean is essentially infinite, and, for all practical purposes, the probability of catching any specific fish would be $p = 0$. However, this does not mean that you are doomed to fail whenever you go fishing. The zero probability simply means that you cannot predict in advance which fish you will catch. Note that each individual fish has a probability near or, practically speaking, equal to zero. However, there are so many fish that when you add up all the "zeros", you still get a total of 1.00. In probability for large populations, a value of zero does not mean never. But, practically speaking, it does mean very, very close to never.

---

 ability is 1, or 100%. For example, suppose that you have a jar containing 10 white marbles. The probability of randomly selecting a black marble would be

$$p(\text{black}) = \frac{0}{10} = 0$$

The probability of selecting a white marble would be

$$p(\text{white}) = \frac{10}{10} = 1$$

Finally, you can determine a probability from a frequency distribution table by computing the proportion for the X value in question. In Chapter 2, we computed this proportion as follows:

$$p = \frac{f}{N}$$

Once again, probability and proportion are equivalent. Also note that this formula is perfectly consistent with the definition of probability. That is, the "number of outcomes classified as A" is the frequency (f) for that particular score, and the "total number of possible outcomes" is the number of scores in the entire distribution, N. Consider the following distribution of scores, which has been summarized in a frequency distribution table.

X	f
9	1
8	3
7	4
6	2

For this distribution of scores, what is the probability of selecting a score of $X = 8$? Stated as a proportion, we may ask, What proportion of all scores in the distribution has a value of 8? There are 10 scores $(N = \Sigma f)$ in the distribution, and 3 of them are $X = 8$. Therefore,

$$p(X = 8) = \frac{f}{N} = \frac{3}{10} = 0.30$$

RANDOM SAMPLING

For the preceding definition of probability to be accurate, it is necessary that the outcomes be obtained by a process called random sampling.

DEFINITION

A *random sample* must satisfy two requirements:

1. Each individual in the population has an *equal chance* of being selected.
2. If more than one individual is to be selected for the sample, there must be *constant probability* for each and every selection.

Each of the two requirements for random sampling has some interesting consequences. The first assures that there is no bias in the selection process. For a population with N individuals, each individual must have the same probability, $p = 1/N$, of being selected. This means, for example, that you would not get a random sample of people in your city by selecting names from a yacht club membership list. Similarly, you would not get a random sample of college students by selecting individuals from your psychology classes. You also should note that the first requirement of random sampling prohibits you from applying the definition of probability to situations where the possible outcomes are not equally likely. Consider, for example, the question of whether or not there is life on Mars. There are only two possible alternatives.

1. There is life on Mars.
2. There is no life on Mars.

However, you cannot conclude that the probability of life on Mars is $p = \frac{1}{2}$.

The second requirement also is more interesting than may be apparent at first glance. Consider, for example, the selection of $n = 2$ cards from a complete deck. For the first draw, what is the probability of obtaining the jack of diamonds?

$$p(\text{jack of diamonds}) = \frac{1}{52}$$

Now, for the second draw, what is the probability of obtaining the jack of diamonds? Assuming that you still are holding the first card, there are two possibilities?

$$p(\text{jack of diamonds}) = \frac{1}{51} \quad \text{if the first card was not the jack of diamonds}$$

or

$$p(\text{jack of diamonds}) = 0 \quad \text{if the first card was the jack of diamonds}$$

In either case, the probability is different from its value for the first draw. This contradicts the requirement for random sampling, which says that the probability must stay constant. To keep the probabilities from changing from one selection to the next, it is necessary to replace each sample before you make the next selection. This is called *sampling with replacement.* The second requirement for random samples (constant probability) demands that you sample with replacement. (*Note:* The definition we are using defines one type of random sampling, often called a *simple random sample* or an *independent random sample.* Other types of random sampling are possible. You also should note that the requirement for replacement becomes relatively unimportant with very large populations. With large populations, the probability values stay essentially constant whether or not you use replacement. For example, in a population of $N = 1,000,001$ individuals, the probability of selecting any one individual is 1/1,000,001. If sampling with replacement is not used, then the probability of selection for the next person will be 1/1,000,000, a negligible change in probability.)

PROBABILITY AND FREQUENCY DISTRIBUTIONS

The situations where we are concerned with probability usually will involve a population of scores that can be displayed in a frequency distribution graph. If you think of the graph as representing the entire population, then different portions of the graph will represent different portions of the population. Because probability and proportion are equivalent, a particular proportion of the graph corresponds to a particular probability in the population. Thus, whenever a population is presented in a frequency distribution graph, it will be possible to represent probabilities as proportions of the graph. The relationship between graphs and probabilities is demonstrated in the following example.

EXAMPLE 6.1

We will use a very simple population that contains only $N = 10$ scores with values 1, 1, 2, 3, 3, 4, 4, 4, 5, 6. This population is shown in the frequency distribution graph in Figure 6.2. If you are taking a random sample of $n = 1$ score from this population, what is the probability of obtaining a score greater than 4? In probability notation,

$$p(X > 4) = ?$$

Using the definition of probability, there are 2 scores that meet this criterion out of the total group of $N = 10$ scores, so the answer would be $p = \frac{2}{10}$. This answer can be obtained directly from the frequency distribution graph if you recall that probability and proportion measure the same thing. Looking at the graph (Figure 6.2), what proportion of the population consists of scores

FIGURE 6.2

A frequency distribution histogram for a population that consists of $N = 10$ scores. The shaded part of the figure indicates the portion of the whole population that corresponds to scores greater than $X = 4$. The shaded portion is two-tenths ($p = \frac{2}{10}$) of the whole distribution.

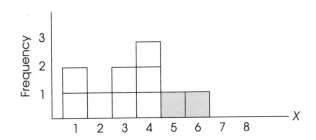

greater than 4? The answer is the shaded part of the distribution, that is, 2 squares out of the total of 10 squares in the distribution. Notice that we now are defining probability as proportion of *area* in the frequency distribution graph. This provides a very concrete and graphic way of representing probability.

Using the same population once again, what is the probability of selecting a score less than 5? In symbols,

$$p(X < 5) = ?$$

Going directly to the distribution in Figure 6.2, we now want to known what part of the graph is not shaded. The unshaded portion consists of 8 out of the 10 blocks ($\frac{8}{10}$ of the area of the graph), so the answer is $p = \frac{8}{10}$.

LEARNING CHECK

1. The animal colony in the psychology department contains 20 male rats and 30 female rats. Of the 20 males, 15 are white and 5 spotted. Of the 30 females, 15 are white, and 15 are spotted. Suppose that you randomly select 1 rat from this colony.

   a. What is the probability of obtaining a female?
   b. What is the probability of obtaining a white male?
   c. Which selection is more likely, a spotted male or a spotted female?

2. What is the purpose of sampling with replacement?

3. Suppose that you are going to select a random sample of $n = 1$ score from the distribution in Figure 6.2. Find the following probabilities:

   a. $p(X > 2)$
   b. $p(X > 5)$
   c. $p(X < 3)$

ANSWERS

1. a. $p = 30/50 = 0.60$ b. $p = 15/50 = 0.30$

   c. A spotted female ($p = 0.30$) is more likely than a spotted male ($p = 0.10$).

2. Sampling with replacement is necessary to maintain constant probabilities for each and every selection.

3. a. $p = 7/10 = 0.70$ b. $p = 1/10 = 0.10$ c. $p = 3/10 = 0.30$

FIGURE 6.3

The normal distribution. The exact shape of the normal distribution is specified by an equation relating each X value (score) with each Y value (frequency). The equation is

$$Y = \frac{1}{\sqrt{2\pi\sigma^2}} e^{-(X-\mu)^2/2\sigma^2}$$

(π and e are mathematical constants.) In simpler terms, the normal distribution is symmetrical with a single mode in the middle. The frequency tapers off as you move farther from the middle in either direction.

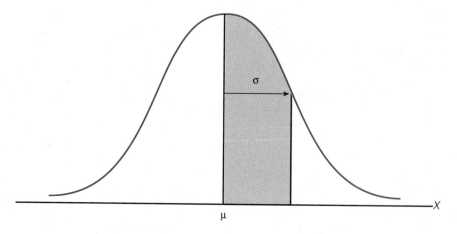

6.3 PROBABILITY AND THE NORMAL DISTRIBUTION

The normal distribution was first introduced in Chapter 2 as an example of a commonly occurring shape for population distributions. An example of a normal distribution is shown in Figure 6.3. Although the exact shape for the normal distribution is precisely defined by an equation (see Figure 6.3), we can easily describe its general characteristics:

1. It is symmetrical. The left side is a mirror image of the right side, and the mean, median, and mode are equal.

2. Fifty percent of the scores are below the mean, and 50 percent above it (mean = median).

3. Most of the scores pile up around the mean (mean = mode), and extreme scores (high or low) are relatively rare (low frequencies).

This shape describes many common variables, such as adult heights, manufacturing tolerances, intelligence scores, personality scores, and so on.

The normal shape also can be described by the proportions of area contained in each section of the distribution. Statisticians often represent these sections by using a normal distribution that has undergone a z-score transformation. Figure 6.4 displays a normal distribution. The sections are marked in z-score units (-2, -1, 0, $+1$, $+2$). Each z-score value indicates the distance from the mean in terms of standard deviations. (Remember, $z = +1$ is one standard deviation above the mean; $z = +2$ is two standard deviations above the mean, and so on.) The graph shows the percentage of scores that fall in each of these sections. For example, the section between the mean ($z = 0$) and the point that is 1 standard deviation above the mean ($z = 1$) makes up 34.13 percent of the scores. Similarly, 13.59 percent of the scores fall between 1 and 2 standard deviations from the mean. The proportions for these sections will be the same for all normal distributions (Figure 6.4). Note that the corresponding sections on the left side of the distribution have the same proportions as the right side because this is a symmetrical distribution. Thus, by

FIGURE 6.4

The normal distribution following a
z-score transformation.

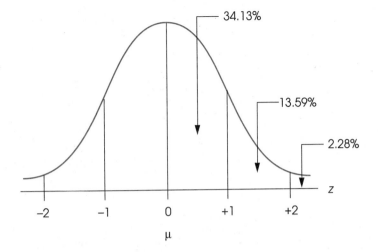

this definition, a distribution is normal if and only if it has all the right proportions.

Because the normal distribution is a good model for many naturally occurring
distributions and because this shape is guaranteed in some circumstances (as you
will see in Chapter 7), we will devote considerable attention to this particular distribution.

The process of answering probability questions about a normal distribution is
introduced in the following example.

EXAMPLE 6.2 Adult heights form a normal distribution with a mean of 68 inches and a standard deviation of 6 inches. Given this information about the population and
the known proportions under the graph (Figure 6.4), we can determine the
probability associated with specific samples. For example, what is the probability of randomly selecting an individual from this population who is taller
than 6 feet 8 inches ($X = 80$ inches)?

Restating this question in probability notation, we get

$$p(X > 80) = ?$$

We will follow a step-by-step process to find the answer to this question.

1. First, the probability question is translated into a proportion question: Out
   of all possible adult heights, what proportion is greater than 80?

2. We know that "all possible adult heights" is simply the population distribution. This population is shown in Figure 6.5(a). The mean is $\mu = 68$, so
   the score $X = 80$ is to the right of the mean. Because we are interested in
   all heights greater than 80, we shade in the area to the right of 80. This
   area represents the proportion we are trying to determine.

3. Statisticians identify sections of the normal distribution in z-score units.
   Remember, any distribution that undergoes a z-score transformation is standardized with $\mu = 0$ and $\sigma = 1$, and it retains the original shape (Chapter
   5). Thus, *any normal* distribution, regardless of its mean and standard de-

FIGURE 6.5

The distribution for Example 6.2.

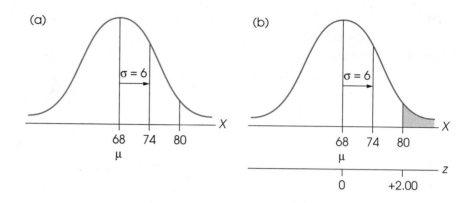

viation, will look like the graph in Figure 6.4. To get the proportion for the shaded area, we locate the X value using a z-score. For this example,

$$z = \frac{X - \mu}{\sigma} = \frac{80 - 68}{6} = \frac{12}{6} = 2$$

That is, a height of 80 inches is 2 standard deviations above the mean.

4. The proportion we are trying to determine may be expressed in terms of its z-score:

$p(z > 2)$

This area is shown in Figure 6.5(b). The shaded area consists of scores beyond 2 standard deviations above the mean. According to Figure 6.4, all normal distributions, regardless of the values for μ and σ, will have 2.28% of the scores in the tail above $z = 2$. Thus, for this population

$p(X > 80) = 2.28\%$

THE UNIT NORMAL TABLE   Before we answer any more probability questions, we need to examine a more useful tool than Figure 6.4. Obviously, the graph of the normal distribution in Figure 6.4 is not sufficient for many situations because it only shows proportions in sections marked by whole standard deviation units. That is, if the height for the previous example had been 1.5 standard deviations (or any fraction of a standard deviation) above the mean, the information in Figure 6.4 would not be adequate for answering probability questions. For this reason, the *unit normal table* was developed. It lists areas, or proportions, for a great many sections of the normal distribution.

To use the unit normal table, you need to transform the distribution of raw scores into z-scores, as was done in Example 6.2 (step 3). The unit normal table basically shows you proportions for sections marked off by a variety of z-score values, more than could be placed in the confined space of a graph.

The complete unit normal table is provided in Appendix B on page A-24; a portion of the table is reproduced in Figure 6.6. The table lists z-score values in column A. Columns B and C are for proportions. Column C represents the proportion

FIGURE 6.6

A portion of the unit normal table. This table lists proportions of the normal distribution corresponding to each z-score value. Column A of the table lists z-scores. Column B lists the proportion in the body of the normal distribution up to the z-score value. Column C lists the proportion of the normal distribution that is located in the tail of the distribution beyond the z-score value.

(A) z	(B) Proportion in Body	(C) Proportion in Tail
0.00	0.5000	0.5000
0.01	0.5040	0.4960
0.02	0.5080	0.4920
0.03	0.5120	0.4880
0.21	0.5832	0.4168
0.22	0.5871	0.4129
0.23	0.5910	0.4090
0.24	0.5948	0.4052
0.25	0.5987	0.4013
0.26	0.6026	0.3974
0.27	0.6064	0.3936
0.28	0.6103	0.3897
0.29	0.6141	0.3859
0.30	0.6179	0.3821
0.31	0.6217	0.3783
0.32	0.6255	0.3745
0.33	0.6293	0.3707
0.34	0.6331	0.3669

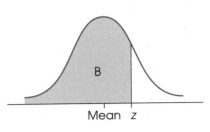

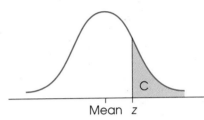

of area in the tail beyond the z-score value. Column B contains the proportion for the remainder or "body" of the distribution. Note that for any specific z-score, column B + column C = 1.000 or 100%. Because the normal distribution is symmetrical, you could imagine negative signs in front of every z-score in the table. Again, column C represents the proportion of the distribution in the tail (this time on the left side) beyond z, and column B provides the remainder. To use the unit normal table for determining probabilities, you should keep two things in mind:

If the area you have shaded is *more* than one-half (50%) of the distribution, then use column B.

If the area is *less* than one-half of the distribution, then use column C.

We will use the phrase "body of the distribution" when referring to a portion that is greater than 50% of the total area and "tail" for the remainder (less than 50%).

Using the unit normal table   The following examples demonstrate several ways the unit normal table can be used to find proportions or probabilities. *Note:* On a graph, *greater than* consists of the area to the *right* of a value, and *less than* refers to the area to the *left* of that value.

EXAMPLE 6.3A   What proportion of the normal distribution corresponds to z-score values greater than z = 1.00? First, you should sketch the distribution and shade in the area you are trying to determine. This is shown in Figure 6.7(a). In this

FIGURE 6.7

The distributions for Examples 6.3A–6.3C.

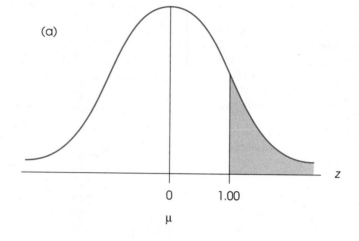

(a)

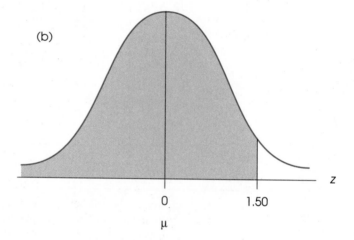

(b)

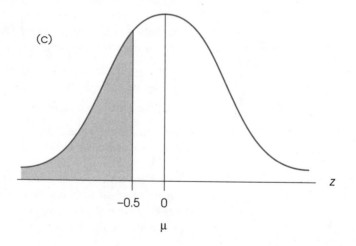

(c)

examples
 ↓

case, the shaded portion is the tail of the distribution beyond $z = 1.00$. To find this shaded area, you simply look up $z = 1.00$ in column A of the unit normal table. Then you read column C (tail) for the proportion. The answer is $p(z > 1.00) = 0.1587$ (or 15.87%).

EXAMPLE 6.3B   What proportion of the normal distribution consists of values less than $z = 1.50$? The distribution is sketched placing $z = 1.50$ to the right of the mean. Then everything to the left of (below) $z = 1.50$ is shaded [Figure 6.7(b)]. This shaded area corresponds to column B of the unit normal table. The z-score of 1.50 is found in column A, and the proportion is taken from column B. The answer is $p(z < 1.50) = 0.9332$ (or 93.32%).

EXAMPLE 6.3C

Moving to the left on the X-axis results in smaller X values and smaller z-scores. Thus, a z-score of -3.00 reflects a smaller value than a z-score of -1.

Many problems will require that you find proportions for negative z-scores. For example, what proportion of the normal distribution corresponds to the tail beyond $z = -0.50$? That is, $p(z < -0.50)$. This portion has been shaded in Figure 6.7(c). To answer questions with negative z-scores, simply remember that the normal distribution is symmetrical with a z-score of zero at the mean, positive values to the right, and negative values to the left. The proportion in the left tail beyond $z = -0.50$ is identical to the proportion in the right tail beyond $z = +0.50$. To find this proportion, look up $z = 0.50$ in column A, and find the proportion in column C (tail). You should get an answer of 0.3085 (30.85%).

EXAMPLE 6.3D   Some problems require that you find the proportion between two z-score values. For example, what proportion of the scores fall between $z = -0.40$ and $z = +1.25$? That is, $p(-0.40 < z < +1.25)$. Figure 6.8(a) shows the normal distribution, with the area between these z-scores shaded. There is no column in the unit normal table that directly gives us the answer. However, note that the unshaded portion of the graph is the two tails beyond $z = -0.40$ and $z = +1.25$. These two tails comprise exactly the area we do *not* want. The solution is to subtract both of these proportions from 1.00 (100%). Thus, for $z = -0.40$, the column C (tail) entry is 0.3446, and for $z = +1.25$, it is 0.1056. Subtracting these two tails from the whole distribution will give us the proportion left over in the shaded area:

$$p(-0.40 < z < +1.25) = 1.0000 - 0.3446 - 0.1056$$

$$= 0.5498 \text{ (or 54.98\%)}$$

EXAMPLE 6.3E   If the proportion we need to find is between two z-scores that are on the same side of the mean, then the solution is a little different. For example, what proportion of the scores fall between $z = +0.35$ and $z = +1.40$? Figure 6.8(b)

FIGURE 6.8

The distributions for Examples 6.3D and
6.3E.

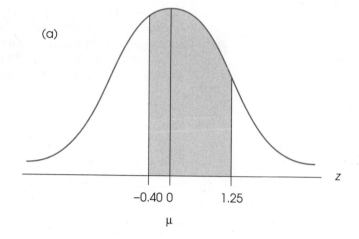

(a)

$-0.40\ 0$ 1.25 z

μ

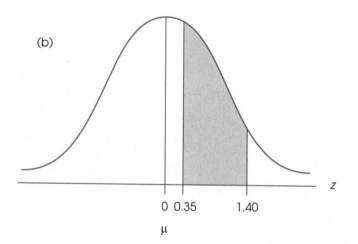

(b)

$0\ 0.35$ 1.40 z

μ

depicts the distribution, with the area between the two *z*-values shaded. Notice that for $z = +0.35$, column C gives us the proportion in the tail beyond this *z*-score. However, this is not exactly what we want. The area in the tail above $z = +1.40$ should be excluded. The solution is to subtract this area from the proportion of scores above $z = +0.35$. Thus, for $z = +0.35$, the proportion from column C is 0.3632, and for $z = +1.40$, it is 0.0808. Subtracting the smaller tail from the larger one will give us the proportion of scores in the shaded area:

$$p(0.35 < z < 1.40) = 0.3632 - 0.0808 = 0.2824 \text{ (or 28.24\%)}$$

You may have noticed that we have sketched distributions for each of the pre-ceding problems. As a general rule, you should always sketch a distribution, locate the mean with a vertical line, and shade in the portion you are trying to determine. Look at your sketch. It will indicate which columns to use in the unit normal table.

If you make a habit of drawing sketches, you will avoid careless errors in using the table.

LEARNING CHECK 1. Find the proportion of the normal distribution that is associated with the following sections of a graph:

   a. $z < +1.00$

   b. $z > +0.80$

   c. $z < -2.00$

   d. $z > -0.33$

   e. $z > -0.50$

   f. $z > -1.50$

   g. $z < +0.67$

   h. $z > +2.00$

2. Find the proportion of the normal distribution that is between the following sets of z-scores:

   a. $p(-0.67 < z < +0.67)$

   b. $p(1.00 < z < 2.00)$

   c. $p(-1.50 < z < +0.50)$

ANSWERS **1. a.** 0.8413   **b.** 0.2119   **c.** 0.0228   **d.** 0.6293

e. 0.6915   **f.** 0.9332   **g.** 0.7486   **h.** 0.0228

2. a. 0.4972   **b.** 0.1359   **c.** 0.6247

ANSWERING PROBABILITY QUESTIONS WITH THE UNIT NORMAL TABLE

The unit normal table provides a listing of proportions (or probability values) corresponding to a great many z-scores in a normal distribution. To use this table to answer probability question, you must first transform the X values into z-scores (standardize the distribution) and then use the table to look up the probability value. This process is discussed in Box 6.2. Finding probabilities with the unit normal table includes these steps:

1. Sketch the distribution, showing the mean and standard deviation.

2. On the sketch, locate the specific score identified in the problem, and draw a vertical line through the distribution at this location. An approximate location is good enough for the sketch, but make sure you place the score and the vertical line on the correct side of the mean and at roughly the correct distance.

3. Read the problem again to determine whether it asks for values *greater than* (to the right side of) or *less than* (to the left of) the specific score. Shade the appropriate section of the distribution. You should be able to make a rough preliminary estimate based on the appearance of your sketch. Does the shaded area look like 10% or 40% or 60%, and so on, of the distribution?

FIGURE 6.9

The distribution for Example 6.4.

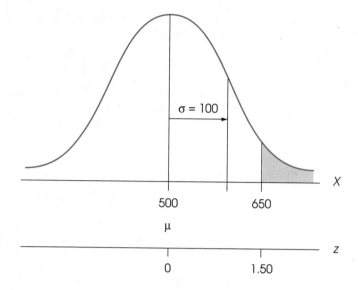

4. Transform the X value from the problem into a z-score. The z-score identifies the precise location in the distribution and will be used to find the proportion in the unit normal table.

5. Look at the shaded area in your sketch to determine which column (B or C) corresponds to the proportion you are trying to find. Ignore the sign of the z-score, and look it up in the unit normal table, taking the proportion from column B or C (whichever is appropriate).

EXAMPLE 6.4 Scores on the Scholastic Achievement Test (SAT) form a normal distribution with $\mu = 500$ and $\sigma = 100$. What is the probability of selecting an individual from the population who scores above 650?

$$p(X > 650) = ?$$

Restated as a proportion question, we want to find out what proportion of the whole distribution has values greater than 650. This distribution is drawn in Figure 6.9, and the part we want has been shaded.

The next step is to change the X values to z-scores. Specifically, the score of $X = 650$ is changed to

You cannot go directly from a score to the unit normal table. You always must go by way of z-scores. (See Box 6.2.)

$$z = \frac{X - \mu}{\sigma} = \frac{650 - 500}{100} = \frac{150}{100} = 1.50$$

Next, you look up this z-score value in the unit normal table. Because we want the proportion of the distribution in the tail beyond 650 (Figure 6.9), the answer will be found in column C. A z-score of 1.5 corresponds to a proportion of 0.0668.

The probability of randomly selecting an individual who scored above 650 is 0.0668:

$$p(X > 650) = p(z > 1.5) = 0.0668 \text{ (or 6.68\%)}$$

FIGURE 6.10

The distribution for Example 6.5.

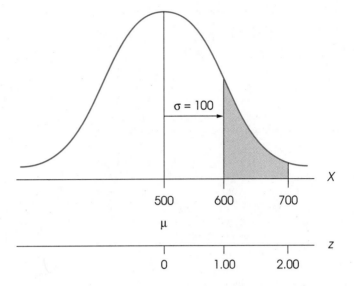

E X A M P L E   6 . 5   This example demonstrates the process of determining the probability associated with a specified range of scores in a normal distribution. We will use the distribution of SAT scores, which is normal with $\mu = 500$ and $\sigma = 100$. For this distribution, what is the probability of randomly selecting an individual with a score between $X = 600$ and $X = 700$? In probability notation, the problem is to find

$$p(600 < X < 700) = ?$$

The distribution of SAT scores is shown in Figure 6.10, with the appropriate area shaded. Remember, finding the probability is the same thing as finding the proportion of the distribution located between 600 and 700. The first step is to transform each X value into a z-score:

$$\text{For } X = 600: z = \frac{X - \mu}{\sigma} = \frac{600 - 500}{100} = \frac{100}{100} = 1.00$$

$$\text{For } X = 700: z = \frac{X - \mu}{\sigma} = \frac{700 - 500}{100} = \frac{200}{100} = 2.00$$

The problem now is to find the proportion of the distribution that is located between $z = +1.00$ and $z = +2.00$. The solution uses the same method as Example 6.3E. That is, you look up the proportions in the tails (column C) for both z-score values and subtract the proportion beyond $z = 2.00$. Using the column C of the table, we find that the area beyond $z = 1.00$ is 0.1587. This includes the shaded portion we want, but also includes the extra area beyond $z = 2.00$. This extra area beyond $z = 2.00$ is 0.0228 (column C) of the entire distribution. Subtracting out this extra portion provides the final answer of

$$p(600 < X < 700) = 0.1587 - 0.0228 = 0.1359 \text{ (or 13.59\%)}$$

6.2   FINDING PROBABILITIES FROM A NORMAL DISTRIBUTION

WORKING WITH probabilities for a normal distribution involves two steps: (1) using a z-score formula and (2) using the unit normal table. However, the order of the steps may vary, depending on the type of probability question you are trying to answer.

In one instance, you may start with a known X value and have to find a probability that is associated with it (as in Example 6.4). First, you must convert the X value to a z-score using equation 5.1 (p. 144). Then you consult the unit normal table to get the probability associated with the particular area of the graph. *Note:* You cannot go directly from the X value to the unit normal table. You must find the z-score first.

However, suppose that you begin with a known probability value and want to find the X value associated with it (as in Example 6.6). In this case, you use the unit normal table first to find the z-score that corresponds with the probability value. Then you convert the z-score into an X value using equation 5.2 (p. 145).

Figure 6.11 illustrated the steps you must take when moving from an X value to a probability or from a probability back to an X value. This chart, much like a map,

guides you through the essential steps as you "travel" between X values and probabilities.

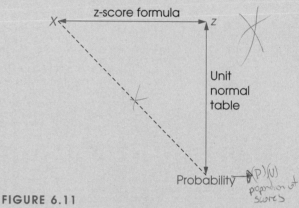

FIGURE 6.11

On this map, the solid lines are the "roads" that you must travel to find a probability value that corresponds to any specific score or to find the score that corresponds to any specific probability value. In taking these routes, you must pass through the intermediate step of finding a z-score value. *Note:* you may *not* travel directly between X values and probability (that is, along the dashed line).

In the previous two examples, we started with an X value and used the unit normal table to find a corresponding probability value. Looking at the map in Box 6.2, we started at X, moved to z, and then on to p. Like most maps, this one can be used to guide travel in either direction; that is, it is possible to start at p and move to X. To move in this direction means that you start with a specific probability value (proportion), find its corresponding z-score, and then determine the X value. The following example demonstrates this type of problem.

EXAMPLE 6.6

Notice that this problem is asking for the 85th percentile.

Scores on the SAT form a normal distribution with $\mu = 500$ and $\sigma = 100$. What is the minimum score necessary to be in the top 15% of the SAT distribution? This problem is shown graphically in Figure 6.12.

In this problem, we begin with a proportion (15% = 0.15), and we are looking for a score. According to the map in Box 6.2, we can move from p (proportion) to X (score) by going via z-scores. The first step is to use the unit normal table to find the z-score that corresponds to a proportion of 0.15. Because the proportion is located beyond z in the tail of the distribution, we will look in column C for a proportion of 0.1500. Note that you may not find 0.1500 exactly, but locate the closest value possible. In this case, the closest value in the table is 0.1492, and the z-score that corresponds to this proportion is $z = 1.04$.

FIGURE 6.12

The distribution of SAT score. The problem is to locate the score that separates the top 15% from the rest of the distribution. A line is drawn to divide the distribution roughly into 15% and 85% sections.

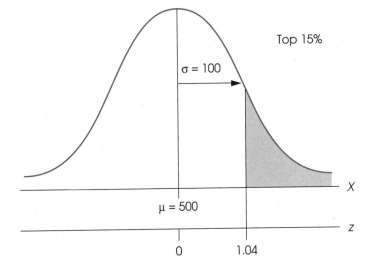

The next step is to determine whether the z-score is positive or negative. Remember, the table does not specify the sign of the z-score. Looking at the graph in Figure 6.12, you should realize that the score we want is above the mean, so the z-score is positive, $z = +1.04$.

Now you are ready for the last stage of the solution, that is, changing the z-score into an X value. Using z-score equation 5.2 (p. 145) and the known values of μ, σ, and z, we obtain

$$X = \mu + z\sigma$$
$$= 500 + 1.04(100)$$
$$= 500 + 104$$
$$= 604$$

The conclusion for this example is that you must have an SAT score of at least 604 to be in the top 15% of the distribution.

LEARNING CHECK

1. For a normal distribution with a mean of 80 and a standard deviation of 10, find each probability value requested.
   a. $p(X > 85) = ?$ **c.** $p(X > 70) = ?$
   b. $p(X < 95) = ?$ **d.** $p(75 < X < 100) = ?$

2. For a normal distribution with a mean of 100 and a standard deviation of 20, find each value requested.
   a. What score separates the top 40% from the bottom 60% of the distribution?
   b. What is the minimum score needed to be in the top 5% of this distribution?
   c. What scores form the boundaries for the middle 60% of this distribution?

3. What is the probability of selecting a score greater than 45 from a positively skewed distribution with $\mu = 40$ and $\sigma = 10$?

ANSWERS **1. a.** $p = 0.3085$ (30.85%)   **c.** $p = 0.8413$ (84.13%)
         b. $p = 0.9332$ (93.32%)   **d.** $p = 0.6687$ (66.87%)

2. a. $z = +0.25$; $X = 105$ **b.** $z = +1.64$; $X = 132.8$
    c. $z = \pm 0.84$; boundaries are 83.2 and 116.8

3. You cannot obtain the answer. The unit normal table cannot be used to answer this question because the distribution is not normal.

6.4 PERCENTILES AND PERCENTILE RANKS

Another useful aspect of the normal distribution is that we can determine percentiles and percentile ranks to answer questions about relative standing.

You should recall from Chapter 2 that the percentile rank of a particular score is defined as the percentage of individuals in the distribution with scores at or below that particular score. The particular score associated with a percentile rank is called a percentile. Suppose, for example, that you have a score of $X = 43$ on an exam and that you know that exactly 60% of the class had scores of 43 or lower. Then your score $X = 43$ has a percentile rank of 60%, and your score would be called the 60th percentile. Remember that percentile ranks refers to a percentage of the distribution, and percentile refers to a score.

FINDING PERCENTILE RANKS

Finding percentile ranks for normal distributions is straightforward if you sketch the distribution. Because a percentile rank is the percentage of the individuals that fall *below* a particular score, we will need to find the proportion of the distribution to the *left* of the score. When finding percentile ranks, we will always be concerned with the percentage on the left-hand side of some X value or, in terms of symbols, $p(X < \text{some value})$. Therefore, if the X value is above the mean, the proportion to the left will be found in column B (the body of the distribution) of the unit normal table. Alternatively, if the X value is below the mean, everything to its left is reflected in column C (the tail). The following examples illustrate these points.

EXAMPLE 6.7A

A population is normally distributed with $\mu = 100$ and $\sigma = 10$. What is the percentile rank for $X = 114$?

Because a percentile rank indicates one's standing relative to all lower scores, we must focus on the area of the distribution to the *left* of $X = 114$. The distribution is shown in Figure 6.13, and the area of the curve containing all scores below $X = 114$ is shaded. The proportion for this shaded area will give us the percentile rank.

Because the distribution is normal, we can use the unit normal table to find this proportion. The first step is to compute the z-score for the X value we are considering.

$$z = \frac{X - \mu}{\sigma} = \frac{114 - 100}{10} = \frac{14}{10} = 1.40$$

FIGURE 6.13

The distribution for Example 6.7A. The proportion for the shaded area provides the percentile rank for X = 114.

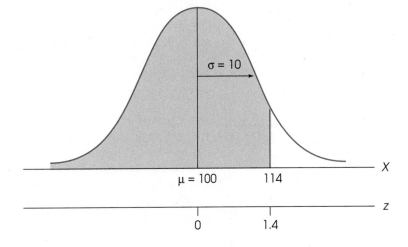

The next step is to consult the unit normal table. Note that the shaded area in Figure 6.13 makes up the large body of the graph. The proportion for this area is presented in column B. For z = 1.40, column B indicates a proportion of 0.9192. The percentile rank for X = 114 is 91.92%.

EXAMPLE 6.7B For the distribution in Example 6.7A, what is the percentile rank for X = 92?

This example is diagramed in Figure 6.14. The score X = 92 is placed in the left side of the distribution because it is below the mean. Again, percentile ranks deal with the area of the distribution below the score in question. Therefore, we have shaded the area to the left of X = 92.

First, the X value is transformed to a z-score:

$$z = \frac{X - \mu}{\sigma} = \frac{92 - 100}{10} = \frac{-8}{10} = -0.80$$

FIGURE 6.14

The distribution for Example 6.7B. The proportion for the shaded area provides the percentile rank for X = 92.

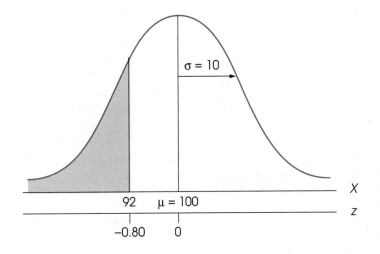

Remember, the normal distribution is symmetrical. Therefore, the proportion in the right-hand tail beyond $z = 0.80$ is identical to that in the left-hand tail beyond $z = -0.80$.

Now the unit normal table can be consulted. The proportion in the left-hand tail beyond $z = -0.80$ can be found in column C. According to the unit normal table, for $z = 0.80$, the proportion in the tail is $p = 0.2119$. This also is the area beyond $z = -0.80$. Thus, the percentile rank for $X = 92$ is 21.19%. That is, a score of 92 is greater than 21.19% of the scores in the distribution.

FINDING PERCENTILES

The process of finding a particular percentile is very similar to the process used in Example 6.6. You are given a percentage (this time a percentile rank), and you must find the corresponding X value (the percentile). You should recall that finding a X value from a percentage requires the intermediate step of determining the z-score for that proportion of the distribution. The following example demonstrates this process for percentiles.

EXAMPLE 6.8

A population is normally distributed with $\mu = 60$ and $\sigma = 5$. For this population, what is the 34th percentile?

In this example, we are looking for an X value (percentile) that has 34% (or $p = 0.3400$) of the distribution below it. This problem is illustrated in Figure 6.15. Note that 34% is roughly equal to one-third of the distribution, so the corresponding shaded area in Figure 6.15 is located entirely on the left-hand side of the mean. In this problem, we begin with a proportion (34% = 0.3400), and we are looking for a score (the percentile). The first step in moving from a proportion to a score is to find the z-score (Box 6.2). You must look at the unit normal table to find the z-score that corresponds to a proportion of 0.3400. Because the proportion is in the tail beyond z, you must look in column C for a proportion of 0.3400. However, there is no entry in the table for the proportion of exactly 0.3400. Instead, we use the closest value, which you will find to be $p = 0.3409$. The z-score corresponding to this value is $z = -0.41$. Note that it is a negative z-score because it is below the mean (Figure 6.15). Thus, the X value for which we are looking has a z of -0.41.

Be careful: The table does not differentiate positive and negative z-scores. You must look at your sketch of the distribution to determine the sign.

The next step is to convert the z-score to an X value. Using the z-score formula solved for X, we obtain

$$X = \mu + z\sigma$$
$$= 60 + (-0.41)(5)$$
$$= 60 - 2.05$$
$$= 57.95$$

The 34th percentile for this distribution is $X = 57.95$. This answer makes sense because the 50th percentile for this example is 60 (the mean and median). Therefore, the 34th percentile has to be a value less than 60.

QUARTILES

Percentiles divide the distribution into 100 equal parts, each corresponding to 1% of the distribution. The area in a distribution can also be divided into four equal parts called quartiles, each corresponding to 25%. We first looked at quartiles in

FIGURE 6.15

The distribution for Example 6.8.

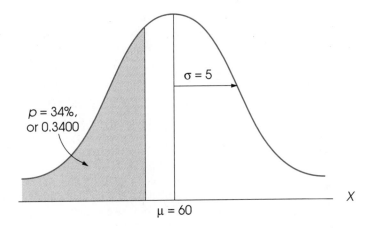

$p = 34\%$,
or 0.3400

$\sigma = 5$

$\mu = 60$

X

Chapter 4 (p. 108) in considering the semi-interquartile range. The first quartile (Q1) is the score that separates the lowest 25% of the distribution from the rest. Thus, the first quartile is the same as the 25th percentile. Similarly, the second quartile (Q2) is the score that has 50% (two quarters) of the distribution below it. You should recognize the Q2 is the median or 50th percentile of the distribution. Finally, the third quartile (Q3) is the X value that has 75% (three quarters) of the distribution below it. The Q3 for a distribution is also the 75% percentile.

For a normal distribution, the first quartile always corresponds to $z = -0.67$, the second quartile corresponds to $z = 0$ (the mean), and the third quartile corresponds to $z = +0.67$ (Figure 6.16). These values can be found by consulting the unit normal table and are true of any normal distribution. This makes finding quartiles and the semi-interquartile range straightforward for normal distributions. The following example demonstrates the use of quartiles.

EXAMPLE 6.9

A population is normally distributed and has a mean of $\mu = 50$ with a standard deviation of $\sigma = 10$. Find the first, second, and third quartile, and compute the semi-interquartile range.

FIGURE 6.16

The z-scores corresponding to the first, second, and third quartiles in a normal distribution.

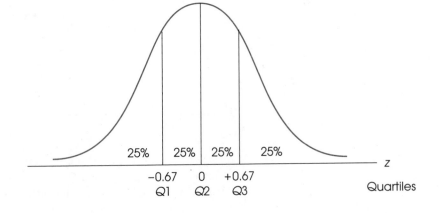

| 25% | 25% | 25% | 25% |

-0.67 0 $+0.67$
Q1   Q2   Q3

z

Quartiles

The first quartile, $Q1$, is the same as the 25th percentile. The 25th percentile has a corresponding z-score of $z = -0.67$. With $\mu = 50$ and $\sigma = 10$, we can determine the X value of $Q1$.

$$X = \mu + z\sigma$$
$$= 50 + (-0.67)(10)$$
$$= 50 - 6.7$$
$$= 43.3$$

The second quartile, $Q2$, is also the 50th percentile, or median. For a normal distribution, the median equals the mean, so $Q2$ is 50. By the formula, with a z-score of 0, we obtain

$$X = \mu + z\sigma$$
$$= 50 + 0(10)$$
$$= 50$$

The third quartile, $Q3$, is also the 75th percentile. It has a corresponding z-score of $z = +0.67$. Using the z-score formula solved for X, we obtain

$$X = \mu + z\sigma$$
$$= 50 + 0.67(10)$$
$$= 50 + 6.7$$
$$= 56.7$$

In Chapter 4 (p. 109), the semi-interquartile range was defined as one-half the distance between the first and third quartile, or

$$\text{semi-interquartile range} = \frac{(Q3 - Q1)}{2}$$

For this example, the semi-interquartile range is

$$\text{semi-interquartile range} = \frac{(Q3 - Q1)}{2}$$
$$= \frac{56.7 - 43.3)}{2}$$
$$= \frac{13.4}{2}$$
$$= 6.7$$

Notice that $Q1$ and $Q3$ are the same distance from the mean (6.7 points in the previous example). $Q1$ and $Q3$ will always be equidistant from the mean for normal distributions because normal distributions are symmetrical. Therefore, one-half

Remember, $z\sigma$ is a deviation score, or distance from the mean (Chapter 5).

of the distance between $Q1$ and $Q3$ (the semi-interquartile range by definition) will also equal the distance of $Q3$ from mean (see Figure 6.16). The distance of $Q3$ from the mean can be obtained simply by multiplying the z-score for $Q3$ ($z = 0.67$) times the standard deviation. Using this shortcut greatly simplifies the computation. For a normal distribution.

$$\text{semi-interquartile range} = 0.67\sigma \qquad (6.1)$$

Remember, this simplified formula is used *only* for normal distributions.

LEARNING CHECK

1. A population is normally distributed and has a mean of $\mu = 90$ with $\sigma = 8$. Find the following values:
   a. The percentile rank for $X = 100$
   b. The percentile rank for $X = 88$
   c. The 85th percentile
   d. The 10th percentile

2. For the population in Exercise 1, find $Q1$, $Q3$, and the semi-interquartile range.

ANSWERS

1. a. 89.44%   b. 40.13%   c. $X = 98.32$ d. $X = 79.76$

2. $Q1 = 84.64$, $Q3 = 95.36$, semi-interquartile range $= 5.36$

6.5 PROBABILITY AND THE BINOMIAL DISTRIBUTION

When a variable is measured on a scale consisting of exactly two categories, the resulting data are called binomial. The term *binomial* can be loosely translated as "two names," referring to the two categories on the measurement scale.

Binomial data can occur when a variable naturally exists with only two categories. For example, people can be classified as male or female, and a coin toss results in either head or tails. It also is common for a researcher to simplify data by collapsing it into two categories. For example, a psychologist may use personality scores to classify people as either high or low in aggression.

In binomial situations, the researcher often knows the probabilities associated with each of the two categories. With a balanced coin, for example, $p(\text{heads}) = p(\text{tails}) = \frac{1}{2}$. The question of interest is the number of times each category occurs in a series of trials or in a sample of individuals. For example:

What is the probability of obtaining 15 heads in 20 tosses of a balanced coin?

What is the probability of obtaining more than 40 introverts in a sampling of 50 college freshmen?

As we shall see, the normal distribution serves as an excellent model for computing probabilities with binomial data.

FIGURE 6.17

The binomial distribution showing the probability for the number of heads in two tosses of a balanced coin.

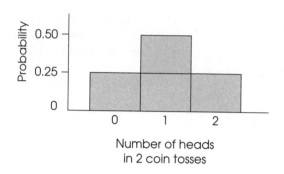

Number of heads
in 2 coin tosses

THE BINOMIAL DISTRIBUTION

To answer probability questions about binomial data, we need to examine the binomial distribution. To define and describe this distribution, we first introduce some notation.

1. The two categories are identified as *A* and *B*.

2. The probabilities (or proportions) associated with each category are identified as

   $p = p(A) = $ the probability of *A*

   $q = p(B) = $ the probability of *B*

   Notice that $p + q = 1.00$ because *A* and *B* are the only two possible outcomes.

3. The number of individuals or observations in the sample is identified by *n*.

4. The variable *X* refers to the number of times category *A* occurs in the sample.

Notice that *X* can have any value from 0 (none of the sample is in category *A*) to *n* (all the sample is in category *A*).

DEFINITION

Using the notation presented here, the *binomial distribution* shows the probability associated with each value of *X* from $X = 0$ to $X = n$.

A simple example of a binomial distribution is presented next.

EXAMPLE 6.10

Figure 6.17 shows the binomial distribution for the number of heads obtained in 2 tosses of a balanced coin. This distribution shows that it is possible to obtain as many as 2 heads or as few as 0 heads in 2 tosses. The most likely outcome (highest probability) is to obtain exactly 1 head in 2 tosses. The construction of this binomial distribution is discussed in detail next.

For this example, the event we are considering is a coin toss. There are two possible outcomes, heads and tails. We assume the coin is balanced, so

$$p = p(\text{heads}) = \frac{1}{2}$$

$$q = p(\text{tails}) = \frac{1}{2}$$

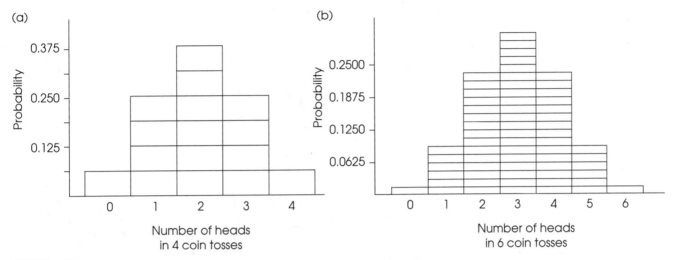

FIGURE 6.18

Binomial distributions showing probabilities for the number of heads (a) in 4 tosses of a balanced coin and (b) in 6 tosses of a balanced coin.

We are looking at a sample of $n = 2$ tosses, and the variable of interest is

$$X = \text{the number of heads}$$

To construct the binomial distribution, we will look at all the possible outcomes from tossing a coin 2 times. The complete set of 4 outcomes is listed below.

1ST TOSS	2ND TOSS	
Heads	Heads	(both heads)
Heads	Tails	(each sequence has
Tails	Heads	exactly 1 head)
Tails	Tails	(no heads)

Notice that there are 4 possible outcomes when you toss a coin 2 times. Only 1 of the 4 outcomes has 2 heads, so the probability of obtaining 2 heads is $p = \frac{1}{4}$. Similarly, 2 of the 4 outcomes have exactly 1 head, so the probability of one head is $p = \frac{2}{4} = \frac{1}{2}$. Finally, the probability of no heads ($X = 0$) is $p = \frac{1}{4}$. These are the probabilities shown in Figure 6.17.

You should notice that this binomial distribution can be used to answer probability questions. For example, what is the probability of obtaining at least 1 head in 2 tosses? According to the distribution shown in Figure 6.17, the answer would be $\frac{3}{4}$.

Similar binomial distributions have been constructed for the number of heads in 4 tosses of a balanced coin and in 6 tosses of a coin (Figure 6.18). It should be obvious from the binomial distributions shown in Figures 6.17 and 6.18 that the

FIGURE 6.19

FIGURE 6.19

The relationship between the binomial distribution and the normal distribution. The binomial distribution is always a discrete histogram, and the normal distribution is a continuous, smooth curve. Each *X* value is represented by a bar in the histogram or a section of the normal distribution.

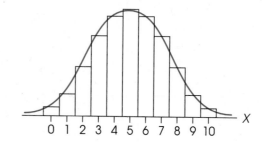

binomial distribution tends toward a normal shape, especially when the sample size (*n*) is relatively large.

It should not be surprising that the binomial distribution tends to be normal. With *n* = 10 coin tosses, for example, the most likely outcome would be to obtain around *X* = 5 heads. On the other hand, values far from 5 would be very unlikely— you would not expect to get all 10 heads or all 10 tails (0 heads) in 10 tosses. Notice that we have described a normal-shaped distribution: The probabilities are highest in the middle (around *X* = 5), and they taper off as you move toward either extreme.

THE NORMAL APPROXIMATION TO THE BINOMIAL DISTRIBUTION

Note: The value of 10 for *pn* or *qn* is a general guide, not an absolute cutoff. Values slightly less than 10 still provide a good approximation. However, with smaller values the normal approximation becomes less accurate as a substitute for the binomial distribution.

We have stated that the binomial distribution tends to approximate a normal distribution, particularly when *n* is large. To be more specific, the binomial distribution will be a nearly perfect normal distribution when *pn* and *qn* are both equal to or greater than 10. Under these circumstances, the binomial distribution will approximate a normal distribution with the following parameters:

$$\text{Mean: } \mu = pn \tag{6.2}$$

$$\text{Standard Deviation: } \sigma = \sqrt{npq} \tag{6.3}$$

Within this normal distribution, each value of *X* has a corresponding *z*-score,

$$z = \frac{X - \mu}{\sigma} = \frac{X - pn}{\sqrt{npq}} \tag{6.4}$$

The fact that the binomial distribution tends to be normal in shape means that we can compute probability values directly from *z*-scores and the unit normal table.

It is important to remember that the normal distribution is only an approximation of a true binomial distribution. Binomial values, such as the number of heads in a series of coin tosses, are *discrete*. The normal distribution is *continuous*. However, the normal approximation provides an extremely accurate model for computing binomial probabilities in many situations. Figure 6.19 shows the difference between the discrete binomial distribution (histogram) and the normal distribution (smooth curve). Although the two distributions are slightly different, the area under the distributions is nearly equivalent. *Remember, it is the area under the distribution that is used to find probabilities.* To gain maximum accuracy when using the normal approximation, you must remember that each *X* value in the binomial distribution is actually an interval, not a point on the scale. In the histogram, this

Note: Coin tosses produce discrete events. In a series of coin tosses, you may observe 1 head, 2 heads, 3 heads, and so on, but no values between them are possible (p. 21).

FIGURE 6.20

The binomial distribution (normal approximation) for the number of answers guessed correctly (X) on a 48-question multiple-choice test. The shaded portion corresponds to the probability of guessing exactly 14 questions. Notice that the score $X = 14$ corresponds to an interval bounded by $X = 13.5$ and $X = 14.5$.

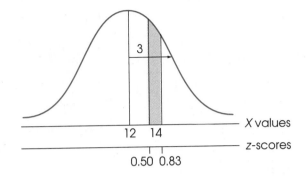

interval is represented by the width of the bar. In Figure 6.19, for example, $X = 6$ is actually an interval bounded by the real limits of 5.5 and 6.5. To find the probability of obtaining a score of $X = 6$, you should find the area of the normal distribution that is contained between the two real limits. If you are using the normal approximation to find the probability of obtaining a score greater than $X = 6$, you should use the area beyond the real limit boundary of 6.5. The following two examples demonstrate how the normal approximation to the binomial distribution is used to compute probability values.

EXAMPLE 6.11   Suppose that you are taking a multiple-choice test where each question has 4 possible answers. If there are 48 questions on the test, what is the probability that you would get exactly 14 questions correct by simply guessing at the answers?

If you are just guessing, then the probability of getting a question correct is $p = \frac{1}{4}$, and the probability of guessing wrong is $q = \frac{3}{4}$. With a sample of $n = 48$ questions, this example meets the criteria for using the normal approximation to the binomial:

$$pn = \frac{1}{4}(48) = 12$$

$$qn = \frac{3}{4}(48) = 36 \quad \text{(both greater than 10)}$$

Therefore, the distribution showing the number correct out of 48 questions will be normal with parameters:

$$\mu = pn = 12$$
$$\sigma = \sqrt{npq} = \sqrt{9} = 3$$

Remember, use the real limits when determining probabilities from the normal approximation to the binomial distribution.

This distribution is shown in Figure 6.20. We want the proportion of this distribution that corresponds to $X = 14$, that is, the portion bounded by $X = 13.5$ and $X = 14.5$. This portion is shaded in Figure 6.20. To find the shaded portion, we first convert each X value into a z-score. For $X = 13.5$,

$$z = \frac{X - \mu}{\sigma} = \frac{13.5 - 12}{3} = 0.50$$

For $X = 14.5$,

$$z = \frac{X - \mu}{\sigma} = \frac{14.5 - 12}{3} = 0.83$$

Looking up these values in the unit normal table, we find
  a. The area beyond $z = 0.50$ is 0.3085.
  b. The area beyond $z = 0.83$ is 0.2033.
Therefore, the area between the two z-scores would be

$$0.3085 - 0.2033 = 0.1052$$

You should remember that this value is an approximation to the exact probability value. However, it is a reasonably accurate approximation. To illustrate the accuracy of the normal approximation, the exact probability of getting $X = 14$ questions correct from the binomial distribution is 0.1015. Notice that the normal approximation value of 0.1052 is very close to the exact probability of 0.1015. As we mentioned earlier, the normal distribution provides an excellent approximation for finding binomial probabilities.

EXAMPLE 6.12

Once again suppose that you are taking a multiple-choice test with 4 possible answers for each of 48 questions. If you simply guess the answer for each question, what is the probability that you would get more than 14 correct?

This is the same binomial situation that we considered in the previous example. For each question, the two categories are "correct" and "incorrect," and the probabilities are

$$p = p(\text{correct}) = \frac{1}{4}$$

$$q = p(\text{incorrect}) = \frac{3}{4}$$

Caution: If the question had asked for the probability of 14 or more correct, you would have used the area beyond 13.5. Read the question carefully.

The normal approximation to this binomial distribution is shown in Figure 6.20. Because we want the probability of obtaining *more than* 14 correct, we must find the area located in the tail of the distribution beyond $X = 14.5$. (Remember, a score of 14 correct corresponds to the interval from 13.5 to 14.5. We want the area beyond this interval.) The first step is to find the z-score corresponding to the boundary $X = 14.5$.

$$z = \frac{X - \mu}{\sigma} = \frac{14.5 - 12}{3} = 0.83$$

Now we can look up the probability in the unit normal table. In this case, we want the proportion in the tail of the distribution beyond $z = 0.83$.

The value from the unit normal table is 0.2033. This is the answer we want. If you are simply guessing on the exam, the probability of getting more than 14 questions correct is $p = 0.2033$, or 20.33%.

1. Under what circumstances is the normal distribution an accurate approximation to the binomial distribution?

2. A multiple-choice test consists of 48 questions with 4 possible answers for each question. What is the probability that you would get more than 20 questions correct just by guessing?

3. If you toss a balanced coin 36 times, you would expect, on the average, to get 18 heads and 18 tails. What is the probability of obtaining exactly 18 heads in 36 tosses?

1. When pn and qn are both greater than 10

2. $p = \frac{1}{4}$, $q = \frac{3}{4}$; $p(X > 20.5) = p(z > 2.83) = 0.0023$

3. $z = \pm 0.17$, $p = 0.1350$

SUMMARY

1. The probability of a particular event A is defined as a fraction or proportion:

$$p(A) = \frac{\text{number of outcomes classified as } A}{\text{total number of possible outcomes}}$$

2. This definition is accurate only for a random sample. There are two requirements that must be satisfied for a random sample:
   a. Every individual in the population has an equal chance of being selected.
   b. When more than one individual is being selected, the probabilities must stay constant. This means there must be sampling with replacement.

3. All probability problems can be restated as proportion problems. The "probability of selecting a king from a deck of cards" is equivalent to the "proportion of the deck that consists of kings." For frequency distributions, probability questions can be answered by determining proportions of area. The "probability of selecting an individual with an IQ greater than 108" is equivalent to the "proportion of the whole population that consists of IQs above 108."

4. For normal distributions, these probabilities (proportions) can be found in the unit normal table. This table provides a listing of the proportions of a normal distribution that correspond to each z-score value. With this table, it is possible to move between X values and probabilities using a two-step procedure:
   a. The z-score formula (Chapter 5) allows you to transform X to z or to change z back to X.

   b. The unit normal table allows you to look up the probability (proportion) corresponding to each z-score or the z-score corresponding to each probability.

5. A percentile rank measures the relative standing of a score in a distribution. Expressed as a percentage, it indicates the proportion of individuals with scores at or below a particular X value. For a normal distribution, you must determine the proportion (percentage) of the distribution that falls to the left of the score in question. This percentage of the distribution is the percentile rank of that score.

6. A percentile is the X value that is associated with a percentile rank. For example, if 80% of the scores in a distribution are less than 250, then X = 250 is the 80th percentile. Note that the 50th percentile is the median of the distribution.

7. Quartiles are the scores that divide the distribution into four areas that make up one-quarter of the distribution in each area. Thus, the first quartile (Q1) is equivalent to the 25th percentile. The second quartile (Q2) is also the 50th percentile (the median), and the third quartile (Q3) is the same as the 75th percentile. For a normal distribution, the semi-interquartile range can be obtained by a special formula:

   $$\text{semi-interquartile range} = 0.67\sigma$$

8. The binomial distribution is used whenever the measurement procedure simply classifies individuals into exactly two categories. The two categories are identified as A and B, with probabilities of

   $$p(A) = p \quad \text{and} \quad p(B) = q$$

9. The binomial distribution gives the probability for each value of X, where X equals the number of occurrences of category A in a series of n events. For example, X equals the number of heads in n = 10 tosses of a coin.

10. When pn and qn are both at least 10, the binomial distribution is closely approximated by a normal distribution with

$$\mu = pn$$
$$\sigma = \sqrt{npq}$$

11. In the normal approximation to the binomial distribution, each value of X has a corresponding z-score:

$$z = \frac{X - \mu}{\sigma} = \frac{X - pn}{\sqrt{npq}}$$

With the z-score and the unit normal table, you can find probability values associated with any value of X. For maximum accuracy, however, you must remember that each X value is actually an interval bounded by real limits. Use the appropriate real limits when computing z-scores and probabilities.

KEY TERMS

probability
random sample
sampling with replacement

percentile rank
unit normal table

binomial distribution
percentile

normal approximation
(binomial)

FOCUS ON PROBLEM SOLVING

1. We have defined probability as being equivalent to a proportion, which means that you can restate every probability problem as a proportion problem. This definition is particularly useful when you are working with frequency distribution graphs where the population is represented by the whole graph and probabilities (proportions) are represented by portions of the graph. When working problems with the normal distribution, you always should start with a sketch of the distribution. You should shade the portion of the graph that reflects the proportion you are looking for.

2. When using the unit normal table, you must remember that the proportions in the table (columns B and C) correspond to specific portions of the distribution. This is important because you will often need to translate the proportions from a problem into specific proportions provided in the table. Also, remember that the table allows you to move back and forth between z-scores and proportions. You can look up a given z to find a proportion, or you can look up a given proportion to find the corresponding z-score. However, you cannot go directly from an X value to a probability in the unit normal table. You must first compute the z-score for X. Likewise, you cannot go directly from a probability value to a raw score. First, you have to find the z-score associated with the probability (see Box 6.2).

3. Remember, the unit normal table shows only positive z-scores in column A. However, since the normal distribution is symmetrical, the probability values in columns B and C also apply to the half of the distribution that is below the mean. To be certain that you have the correct sign for z, it helps to sketch the distribution showing μ and X.

4. A common error for students is to use negative values for proportions on the left-hand side of the normal distribution. Proportions (or probabilities) are always positive: 10% is 10% whether it is in the left or right tail of the distribution.

5. The proportions in the unit normal table are accurate only for normal distributions. If a distribution is not normal, you cannot use the table.

6. When determining percentile ranks, it helps to sketch the distribution first. Remember, shade in the area to the left of the particular X value. Its percentile rank will be the proportion of the distribution in the shaded area. You will need to compute the z-score for the X value to find the proportion in the unit normal table. Percentile ranks are always expressed as a percentage (%) of the distribution.

7. Percentiles are X values. When asked to find the 90th percentile, you are looking for the X value that has 90% (or 0.9000) of the distribution below (to the left of) it. The procedure of finding a percentile requires that you go from a proportion to a z-score, then from z-score to X value (Box 6.2).

8. For maximum accuracy when using the normal approximation to the binomial distribution, you must remember that each X value is an interval bounded by real limits. For example, to find the probability of obtaining an X value greater than 10, you should use the real limit 10.5 in the z-score formula. Similarly, to find the probability of obtaining an X value less than 10, you should use the real limit 9.5.

DEMONSTRATION 6.1

FINDING PROBABILITY FROM THE UNIT NORMAL TABLE

A population is normally distributed with a mean of $\mu = 45$ and a standard deviation of $\sigma = 4$. What is the probability of randomly selecting a score that is greater than 43? In other words, what proportion of the distribution consists of scores greater than 43?

STEP 1   Sketch the distribution

You should always start by sketching the distribution, identifying the mean and standard deviation ($\mu = 45$ and $\sigma = 4$ in this example). You should also find the approximate location of the specified score and draw a vertical line through the distribution at that score. The score of $X = 43$ is lower than the mean, and, therefore, it should be placed somewhere to the left of the mean. Figure 6.21(a) shows the preliminary sketch.

FIGURE 6.21

Sketches of the distribution for Demonstration 6.1.

(a)

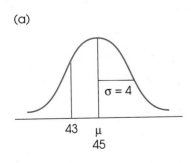

(b)

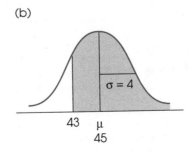

(c)

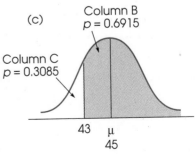

STEP 2   Shade in the distribution.

Read the problem again to determine whether you want the proportion greater than the score (to the right of your vertical line) or less than the score (to the left of the line). Then shade in the appropriate portion of the distribution. In this demonstration, we are considering scores greater than 43. Thus, we shade in the distribution to the right of this score [Figure 6.21(b)]. Notice that if the shaded area covers more than one-half of the distribution, then the probability should be greater than 0.5000.

STEP 3   Transform the X value to a z-score.

Remember, to get a probability from the unit normal table, we must first convert the X value to a z-score.

$$z = \frac{X - \mu}{\sigma} = \frac{43 - 45}{4} = \frac{-2}{4} = -0.5$$

STEP 4   Consult the unit normal table.

Look up the z-score (ignoring the sign) in the unit normal table. Find the two proportions in the table that are associated with the z-score, and write the two proportions in the appropriate regions on the figure. Remember, column B gives the proportion of area in the body of the distribution (more than 50%), and column C gives the area in the tail beyond z. Figure 6.21(c) shows the proportions for different regions of the normal distribution.

STEP 5   Determine the probability.

If one of the proportions in step 4 corresponds exactly to the entire shaded area, then that proportion is your answer. Otherwise, you will need to do some additional arithmetic. In this example, the proportion in the shaded area is given in column B:

$$p(X > 43) = 0.6915$$

──── **DEMONSTRATION 6.2** ────────────────────────────────

PROBABILITY AND THE BINOMIAL DISTRIBUTION

Suppose that you forgot to study for a quiz and now must guess on every question. It is a true-false quiz with $n = 40$ questions. What is the probability that you will get at least 26 questions correct just by chance? Stated in symbols,

$$p(X \geq 26) = ?$$

STEP 1   Identify p and q.

This problem is a binomial situation, where

p = probability of guessing correctly = 0.50

q = probability of guessing incorrectly = 0.50

With $n = 40$ quiz items, both pn and qn are greater than 10. Thus, the criteria for the normal approximation to the binomial distribution are satisfied:

$pn = 0.50(40) = 20$

$qn = 0.50(40) = 20$

FIGURE 6.22

The normal approximation to a binomial distribution with $\mu = 20$ and $\sigma = 3.16$. The proportion of all scores equal to or greater than 26 is shaded. Notice that the real lower limit (25.5) for $X = 26$ is used.

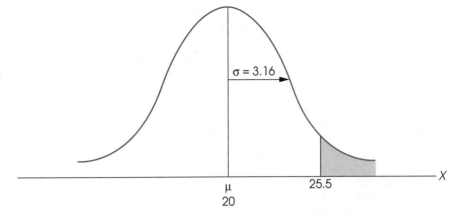

STEP 2   Identify the parameters, and sketch the distribution.

The normal approximation will have a mean and a standard deviation as follows:

$$\mu = pn = 0.5(40) = 20$$

$$\sigma = \sqrt{npq} = \sqrt{10} = 3.16$$

Figure 6.22 shows the distribution. We are looking for the probability of getting $X = 26$ or more questions correct. Remember, when determining probabilities from the binomial distribution, we must use real limits. Because we are interested in scores equal to or greater than 26, we will use the real lower limit for 26 (25.5). By using the real lower limit, we include the entire interval (25.5 to 26.5) that corresponds to $X = 26$. In Figure 6.22, everything to the right of $X = 25.5$ is shaded.

STEP 3   Compute the z-score, and find the probability.

The z-score for $X = 25.5$ is calculated as follows:

$$z = \frac{X - pn}{\sqrt{npq}} = \frac{25.5 - 20}{3.16} = +1.74$$

The shaded area in Figure 6.22 corresponds to column C of the unit normal table. For the z-score of 1.74, the proportion of the shaded area is $P = 0.0409$. Thus, the probability of getting at least 26 questions right just by guessing is

$$p(X \geq 26) = 0.0409 \text{ (or 4.09\%)}$$

PROBLEMS

1. In a psychology class of 60 students, there are 15 males and 45 females. Of the 15 men, only 5 are freshmen. Of the 45 women, 20 are freshmen. If you randomly sample an individual from this class,
   a. What is the probability of obtaining a female?
   b. What is the probability of obtaining a freshman?
   c. What is the probability of obtaining a male freshman?

2. A jar contains 10 black marbles and 20 white marbles.
   a. If you randomly select a marble from the jar, what is the probability that you will get a white marble?
   b. If you are selecting a random sample of $n = 3$ marbles and the first 2 marbles are both white, what is the probability that the third marble will be black?

3. Drawing a vertical line through a normal distribution will separate the distribution into two parts: the section to the right of the line and the section to the left. The size of each section depends on where you draw the line. Sketch a normal distribution, and draw a vertical line for each of the following locations (z-scores). Then find the proportion of the distribution on each side of the line.
   a. $z = 1.00$
   b. $z = -1.50$
   c. $z = 0.25$
   d. $z = -0.50$

4. For each of the following z-score values, sketch a normal distribution, and draw a vertical line through the distribution at the location specified by the z-score. Then find the proportion of the distribution in the tail of the distribution beyond the line.
   a. $z = 0.50$
   b. $z = 1.75$
   c. $z = -1.50$
   d. $z = -0.25$

5. Find the proportion of the normal distribution that lies in the tail beyond each of the following z-scores:
   a. $z = 0.43$ c. $z = -1.35$
   b. $z = 1.68$ d. $z = -0.29$

6. What is sampling with replacement, and why is it used?

7. For a normal distribution, find the z-score location of a vertical line that would separate the distribution into two parts as specified in each of the following:
   a. Where do you draw a line that separates the top 40% (right side) from the bottom 60% (left side)?
   b. Where do you draw a line that separates the top 10% (right side) from the bottom 90% (left side)?
   c. Where do you draw a line that separates the top 80% (right side) from the bottom 20% (left side)?

8. A normal distribution has $\mu = 50$ and $\sigma = 10$. For each of the following locations (X values), draw a sketch of the distribution, and draw a vertical line through the distribution at the location specified by the score. Then find the proportion of the distribution on each side of the line.
   a. $X = 55$
   b. $X = 50$
   c. $X = 48$
   d. $X = 40$

9. For a normal distribution with $\mu = 500$ and $\sigma = 100$, find the X value (location) of a vertical line that would separate the distribution into two parts as specified in each of the following:
   a. Where do you draw a line that separates the top 30% (right side) from the bottom 70% (left side)?
   b. Where do you draw a line that separates the top 25% (right side) from the bottom 75% (left side)?

c. Where do you draw a line that separates the top 90% (right side) from the bottom 10% (left side)?

10. For a normal distribution with $\mu = 100$ and $\sigma = 16$,
    a. What is the probability of randomly selecting a score greater than 104?
    b. What is the probability of randomly selecting a score greater than 96?
    c. What is the probability of randomly selecting a score less than 108?
    d. What is the probability of randomly selecting a score less than 92?

11. Find the proportion of the normal distribution that is located between the following z-score boundaries:
    a. Between $z = 0.25$ and $z = 0.75$
    b. Between $z = -1.00$ and $z = +1.00$
    c. Between $z = 0$ and $z = 1.50$
    d. Between $z = -0.75$ and $z = 2.00$

12. For a normal distribution with a mean of $\mu = 80$ and $\sigma = 12$,
    a. What is the probability of randomly selecting a score greater than 83? $3/12 = .25$ $p < .4013$
    b. What is the probability of randomly selecting a score greater than 74? $6/12 = .50$ $= .6915$
    c. What is the probability of randomly selecting a score less than 92? $12/12 = 1$ $= .84$
    d. What is the probability of randomly selecting a score less than 62? $18/12 = 1.5$

13. One question on a multiple-choice test asked for the probability of selecting a score greater than $X = 50$ from a normal population with $\mu = 60$ and $\sigma = 20$. The answer choices were:
    a. 0.1915   b. 0.3085   c. 0.6915
    Sketch a distribution showing this problem, and without looking at the unit normal table, explain why answers a and b cannot be correct.

14. A normal distribution has a mean of 120 and a standard deviation of 20. For this distribution,
    a. What score separates the top 40% (highest scores) from the rest?
    b. What score corresponds to the 90th percentile?
    c. What range of scores would form the middle 60% of this distribution?

15. A normal distribution has $\mu = 75$ with $\sigma = 9$. Find the following probabilities:
    a. $p(X < 86) = ?$
    b. $p(X > 60) = ?$
    c. $p(X > 80) = ?$
    d. $p(X > 94) = ?$
    e. $p(63 < X < 88) = ?$
    f. The probability of randomly selecting a score within 3 points of the mean.

16. A normal distribution has a mean of 80 and a standard deviation of 10. For this distribution, find each of the following probability values:

    a. $p(X > 75) = ?$ **d.** $p(65 < X < 95) = ?$
    b. $p(X < 65) = ?$ **e.** $p(84 < X = 90)?$
    c. $p(X < 100) = ?$

17. The scores on a psychology exam form a normal distribution with $\mu = 80$ and $\sigma = 8$. On this exam, Tom has a score of $X = 84$. Mary's score is located at the 60th percentile. John's score corresponds to a z-score of $z = 0.75$. If these three students are listed from highest score to lowest score, what is the correct ordering?

18. A normal distribution has a mean of $\mu = 120$ with $\sigma = 15$. Find the following values:

    a. The 15th percentile
    b. The 88th percentile
    c. The percentile rank for $X = 142$
    d. The percentile rank for $X = 102$
    e. The percentile rank for $X = 120$
    f. The semi-interquartile range

19. A positively skewed distribution has a mean of 100 and a standard deviation of 12. What is the probability of randomly selecting a score greater than 106 from this distribution? (Be careful; this is a trick problem.)

20. A normal distribution has a mean of 60 and a standard deviation of 10.

    a. Find the semi-interquartile range for this distribution.
    b. If the standard deviation were 20, what would be the value for the semi-interquartile range?
    c. In general, what is the relationship between the standard deviation and the semi-interquartile range for a normal distribution?

21. For a normal distribution with $\mu = 200$ and $\sigma = 50$,

    a. Find the 90th percentile.
    b. Find the 30th percentile.
    c. Find the 75th percentile.

22. For a normal distribution with $\mu = 500$ and $\sigma = 100$,

    a. What is the percentile rank for $X = 550$?
    b. What is the percentile rank for $X = 650$?
    c. What is the percentile rank for $X = 450$?
    d. What is the percentile rank for $X = 350$?

23. For a normal distribution with $\mu = 100$ and $\sigma = 30$,

    a. Find $Q1$, $Q2$, and $Q3$.
    b. Find the semi-interquartile range.

24. The normal approximation to the binomial distribution is accurate only when both pn and qn are greater than 10.

This requirement is violated in both of the following situations. In each case, explain why the normal distribution is not an appropriate substitute for the real binomial distribution. (*Hint:* Calculate the mean, and sketch each binomial distribution.)

    Situation I: $n = 6, p = .5,$ and $q = .5$

    Situation II: $n = 50, p = .9,$ and $q = .1$

25. One common test for extrasensory perception (ESP) requires subjects to predict the suit of a card that is randomly selected from a complete deck. If a subject has no ESP and is just guessing, find each of the probabilities requested.

    a. What is the probability of a correct prediction on each trial?
    b. What is the probability of correctly predicting more than 18 out of 48 cards?

26. A college dormitory recently sponsored a taste comparison between two major soft drinks. Of the 64 students who participated, 39 selected brand A. If there really is no preference between the two drinks, what is the probability that 39 or more would choose brand A just by chance?

27. A trick coin has been weighted so that the probability of heads is 0.8 and the probability of tails is 0.2.

    a. If you toss the coin 100 times, how many heads would you expect on the average?
    b. What is the probability of obtaining more than 95 heads in 100 tosses?
    c. What is the probability of obtaining less than 95 heads in 100 tosses?
    d. What is the probability of obtaining exactly 95 heads in 100 tosses?

28. **a.** What is the probability of getting more than 30 heads in 50 tosses of a balanced coin?
    b. What is the probability of getting more than 60 heads in 100 tosses of a balanced coin?
    c. Parts a and b of this question both asked for the probability of getting more than 60% heads in a series of coin tosses ($30/50 = 60/100 = 60\%$). Explain why the two probabilities are different.

29. A true-false test has 36 questions. If a passing grade on this test is $X = 24$ (or more) correct, what is the probability of obtaining a passing grade just by guessing?

CHAPTER 7

PROBABILITY AND SAMPLES: THE DISTRIBUTION OF SAMPLE MEANS

TOOLS YOU WILL NEED

The following items are considered essential background material for this chapter. If you doubt your knowledge of any of these items, you should review the appropriate chapter and section before proceeding.

- Random sampling (Chapter 6)
- Probability and the normal distribution (Chapter 6)
- z-Scores (Chapter 5)

CONTENTS

PREVIEW

Now that you have some understanding of probability, consider the following problem

Imagine an urn filled with balls. Two-thirds of the balls are one color, and the remaining one-third is a second color. One individual selects 5 balls from the urn and finds that 4 are red and 1 is white. Another individual selects 20 balls and finds that 12 are red and 8 are white. Which of these two individuals should feel more confident that the urn contains two-thirds red balls and one-third white balls, rather than the opposite?"

When Tversky and Kahneman (1974) presented this problem to a group of experimental subjects, they found that most people felt that the first sample (4 out of 5) provided much stronger evidence and, therefore, should give more confidence. At first glance, it may appear that this is the correct decision. After all, the first sample, contained $\frac{4}{5} = 80\%$ red balls, and the second sample, contained only $\frac{12}{20} = 60\%$ red balls. However, you should also notice that the two samples differ in another important respect: the sample size. One sample contains only $n = 5$, and the other sample contains $n = 20$. The correct answer to the problem is that the larger sample (12 out of 20) gives a much stronger justification for concluding that the balls in the urn are predominately red. It appears that most people tend to focus on the sample proportion and pay very little attention to the sample size.

The importance of sample size may be easier to appreciate if you approach the urn problem from a different perspective.

Suppose that you are the individual assigned responsibility for selecting a sample and then deciding which color is in the majority. Before you select your sample, you are offered a choice of selecting either a sample of 5 balls or a sample of 20 balls. Which would you prefer? It should be clear that the larger sample would be better. With a small number, you risk obtaining an unrepresentative sample. By chance, you could end up with 3 white balls and 2 red balls even though the reds outnumber the whites by 2 to 1. The larger sample is much more likely to provide an accurate representation of the population. This is an example of the *law of large numbers*, which states that large samples will be representative of the population from which they are selected. One final example should help demonstrate this law. If you were tossing a coin, you probably would not be greatly surprised to obtain 3 heads in a row. However, if you obtained a series of 20 heads in a row, you almost certainly would suspect a trick coin. The large sample has more authority.

In this chapter, we will examine the relationship, between samples and populations. More specifically, we will consider the relationship between sample means and the population mean. As you will see, sample size is one of the primary considerations in determining how well a sample mean represents the population mean.

*Adapted from Tversky, A., and Kahneman, D. (1974). Judgments under uncertainty: Heuristics and biases. *Science, 185*, 1124–1131. Copyright 1974 by the AAAS.

7.1 OVERVIEW

The purpose of this chapter is to establish the set of rules that relate samples to populations. These rules, which are of great importance to later topics in inferential statistics, will be based on probabilities. In contrast to Chapter 6, in which we looked at the probability of obtaining a certain score, we will now be looking at samples of more than one score. Therefore, the focus will shift to probability questions involving sample means.

The difficulty of working with samples is that samples generally are not identical to the populations from which they come. More precisely, the statistics calculated for a sample will differ from the corresponding parameters for the population. For example, the sample mean may differ from the population mean. This difference, or *error*, is referred to as *sampling error*.

DEFINITION   *Sampling error* is the discrepancy, or amount of error, between a sample statistic and its corresponding population parameter.

Furthermore, samples are variable; they are not all the same. If you take two separate samples from the same population, the samples will be different. They will contain different individuals, they will have different scores, and they will have different sample means. How can you tell which sample is giving the best description of the population? Can you even predict how well a sample will describe its population? What is the probability of selecting a sample that has a certain sample mean? These questions can be answered once we establish the set of rules that relate samples to populations.

7.2 THE DISTRIBUTION OF SAMPLE MEANS

As noted, two separate samples probably will be different even though they are taken from the same population. The samples will have different individuals, different scores, different means, and the like. In most cases, it is possible to obtain thousands of different samples from one population. With all these different samples coming from the same population, it may seem hopeless to try to establish some simple rules for the relationships between samples and populations. But, fortunately, the huge set of possible samples forms a relatively simple, orderly, and predictable pattern that makes it possible to predict the characteristics of a sample with some accuracy. The ability to predict sample characteristics is based on the *distribution of sample means*.

DEFINITION
The distribution of sample means is the collection of sample means for all the possible random samples of a particular size *(n)* that can be obtained from a population.

You should notice that the distribution of sample means is different from distributions we have considered before. Until now we always have discussed distributions of scores; now the values in the distribution are not scores, but statistics (sample means). Because statistics are obtained from samples, a distribution of statistics is referred to as a sampling distribution.

DEFINITION
A *sampling distribution* is a distribution of statistics obtained by selecting all the possible samples of a specific size from a population.

Thus, the distribution of sample means is an example of a sampling distribution. In fact, it often is called the sampling distribution of $\overline{X}$.

Before we consider the general rules concerning this distribution, we will look at a simple example that provides an opportunity to examine the distribution in detail.

EXAMPLE 7.1   Consider a population that consists of only 4 scores: 2, 4, 6, 8. This population is pictured in the frequency distribution histogram in Figure 7.1.

We are going to use this population as the basis for constructing the distribution of sample means for $n = 2$. Remember, this distribution is the collection of sample means from all the possible random samples of $n = 2$ from

FIGURE 7.1

Frequency distribution histogram for a
population of 4 scores: 2, 4, 6, 8.

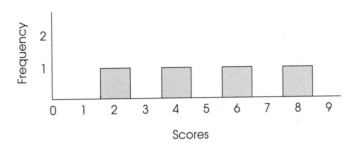

this population. We begin by looking at all the possible samples. Each of the
16 different samples is listed in Table 7.1.

Next, we compute the mean, $\overline{X}$, for each of the 16 samples (see the last column
of Table 7.1). The 16 sample means form the distribution of sample means. These
16 values are organized in a frequency distribution histogram in Figure 7.2.

Notice that the distribution of sample means has some predictable and
some very useful characteristics:

Remember, random sampling requires
sampling with replacement.

1. The sample means tend to pile up around the population mean. For this
   example, the population mean is $\mu = 5$, and the sample means are clustered around a value of 5. It should not surprise you that the sample means
   tend to approximate the population mean. After all, samples are supposed
   to be representative of the population.

2. The distribution of sample means is approximately normal in shape. This is
   a characteristic that will be discussed in detail later and will be extremely
   useful because we already know a great deal about probabilities and the
   normal distribution (Chapter 6).

TABLE 7.1

All the possible samples of $n = 2$ scores
that can be obtained from the population
presented in Figure 7.1

Notice that the table lists *random
samples*. This requires sampling with replacement, so it is possible to select the
same score twice. Also note that samples
are listed systematically. The first four
examples are all the possible samples that
have $X = 2$ as the first score; the next
four samples all have $X = 4$ as the first
score; etc. This way we are sure to have
all the possible samples listed, although
the samples probably would not be selected in this order.

	SCORES		SAMPLE MEAN
SAMPLE	FIRST	SECOND	$(\overline{X})$
1	2	2	2
2	2	4	3
3	2	6	4
4	2	8	5
5	4	2	3
6	4	4	4
7	4	6	5
8	4	8	6
9	6	2	4
10	6	4	5
11	6	6	6
12	6	8	7
13	8	2	5
14	8	4	6
15	8	6	7
16	8	8	8

FIGURE 7.2

The distribution of sample means for $n = 2$. This distribution shows the 16 sample means from Table 7.1.

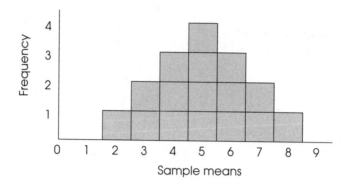

Remember, our goal in this chapter is to answer probability questions about samples with $n > 1$.

3. Finally, you should notice that we can use the distribution of sample means to answer probability questions about sample means (see Box 7.1). For example, if you take a sample of $n = 2$ scores from the original population, what is the probability of obtaining a sample mean greater than 7? In symbols,

$$p(\overline{X} > 7) = ?$$

Because probability is equivalent to proportion, the probability question can be restated as follows: Of all the possible sample means, what proportion has values greater than 7? In this form, the question is easily answered by looking at the distribution of sample means. All the possible sample means are pictured (Figure 7.2), and only 1 out of the 16 means has a value greater than 7. The answer, therefore, is 1 out of 16, or $p = \frac{1}{16}$.

THE CENTRAL LIMIT THEOREM

Example 7.1 demonstrates the construction of the distribution of sample means for a relatively simple, specific situation. In most cases, however, it will not be possible to list all the samples and compute all the possible sample means. Therefore, it is necessary to develop the general characteristics of the distribution of sample means that can be applied in any situation. Fortunately, these characteristics are specified in a mathematical proposition known as the *central limit theorem*. This important and useful theorem serves as a cornerstone for much of inferential statistics. Following is the essence of the theorem:

> *Central Limit Theorem:* For any population with mean μ and standard deviation σ, the distribution of sample means for sample size n will approach a normal distribution with a mean of μ and a standard deviation of $\sigma/\sqrt{n}$ as n approaches infinity.

The value of this theorem comes from two simple facts. First, it describes the distribution of sample means for *any population,* no matter what shape, or mean, or standard deviation. Second, the distribution of sample means "approaches" a normal distribution very rapidly. By the time the sample size reaches $n = 30$, the distribution is almost perfectly normal.

Notice that the central limit theorem describes the distribution of sample means by identifying the three basic characteristics that describe any distribution: shape, central tendency, and variability. Each of these will be examined.

7.1   PROBABILITY AND THE DISTRIBUTION OF SAMPLE MEANS

I HAVE a bad habit of losing playing cards. This habit is compounded by the fact that I always save the old deck in hope that someday I will find the missing cards. As a result, I have a drawer filled with partial decks of playing cards. Suppose that I take one of these almost-complete decks, shuffle the cards carefully, and then randomly select one card. What is the probability that I will draw a king?

You should realize that it is impossible to answer this probability question. To find the probability of selecting a king, you must know how many cards are in the deck and exactly which cards are missing. (It is crucial that you know whether or not any kings are missing.) The point of this simple example is that any probability question requires that you have complete information about the population from which the sample is being selected. In this case, you must know all the possible cards in the deck before you can find the probability for selecting any specific card.

In this chapter, we are examining probability and sample means. In order to find the probability for any specific sample mean, you first must know *all the possible sample means.* Therefore, we begin by defining and describing the set of all possible sample means that can be obtained from a particular population. Once we have specified the complete set of all possible sample means (i.e., the distribution of sample means), we will be able to find the probability of selecting any specific sample mean.

THE SHAPE OF THE DISTRIBUTION OF SAMPLE MEANS

It has been observed that the distribution of sample means tends to be a normal distribution. In fact, this distribution will be almost perfectly normal if either one of the following two conditions is satisfied:

1. The population from which the samples are selected is a normal distribution.
2. The number of scores *(n)* in each sample is relatively large, around 30 or more.

(As *n* gets larger, the distribution of sample means will closely approximate a normal distribution. In most situations when $n > 30$, the distribution is almost perfectly normal regardless of the shape of the original population.)

The fact that the distribution of sample means tends to be normal should not be surprising. Whenever you take a sample from a population, you expect the sample mean to be near to the population mean. When you take lots of different samples, you expect the sample means to "pile up" around μ, resulting in a normal-shaped distribution. You can see this tendency emerging (although it is not yet normal) in Figure 7.2.

THE MEAN OF THE DISTRIBUTION OF SAMPLE MEANS: THE EXPECTED VALUE OF $\overline{X}$

The expected value of $\overline{X}$ is often identified by the symbol $\mu_{\overline{X}}$, signifying the "mean of the sample means." However, $\mu_{\overline{X}}$ is always equal to μ, so we will continue to use the symbol μ to refer to the mean for the population of scores and the mean for the distribution of sample means.

You probably noticed in Example 7.1 that the distribution of sample means is centered around the mean of the population from which the samples were obtained. In fact, the average value of all the sample means is exactly equal to the value of the population mean. This fact should be intuitively reasonable; the sample means are expected to be close to the population mean, and they do tend to pile up around μ. The formal statement of this phenomenon is that the mean of the distribution of sample means always will be identical to the population mean. This mean value is called the *expected value of $\overline{X}$.*

In commonsense terms, a sample mean is "expected" to be near its population mean. When all of the possible sample means are obtained, the average value will be identical to μ.

7.2   THE ERROR BETWEEN $\overline{X}$ AND μ

CONSIDER A population consisting of $N = 3$ scores: 1, 8, 9. The mean for this population is $\mu = 6$. Using this population, try to find a random sample of $n = 2$ scores with a sample mean ($\overline{X}$) exactly equal to the population mean. (Try selecting a few samples; record the scores and the sample mean for each of your samples.)

You may have guessed that we constructed this problem so that it is impossible to obtain a sample

mean that is identical to μ. The point of this exercise is to emphasize the notion of sampling error. Samples are not identical to their populations, and a sample mean generally will not provide a perfect estimate of the population mean. The purpose of standard error is to provide a quantitative measure of the difference (or error) between sample means and the population mean. Standard error is the standard distance between $\overline{X}$ and μ.

DEFINITION   The mean of the distribution of sample means will be equal to μ (the population mean) and is called the *expected value* of $\overline{X}$.

THE STANDARD ERROR OF $\overline{X}$ So far, we have considered the shape and the central tendency of the distribution of sample means. To completely describe this distribution, we need one more characteristic, variability. The value we will be working with is the standard deviation for the distribution of sample means, and it is called the *standard error of $\overline{X}$*.

DEFINITION   The standard deviation of the distribution of sample means is called the *standard error of $\overline{X}$*.

Like any measure of standard deviation, the standard error defines the standard, or typical, distance from the mean. In this case, we are measuring the standard distance between a single sample mean $\overline{X}$ and the population mean μ.

The notation that is used to identify the standard error is $\sigma_{\overline{X}}$. The σ indicates that we are measuring a standard deviation or a standard distance from the mean. The subscript $\overline{x}$ indicates that we are measuring the standard deviation for a distribution of sample means.

$$\text{standard error} = \sigma_{\overline{X}} = \text{standard distance between } \overline{X} \text{ and } \mu$$

The standard error is an extremely valuable measure because it specifies precisely how well a sample mean estimates its population mean, that is, how much error you should expect, on the average, between $\overline{X}$ and μ. Remember, one basic reason for taking samples is to use the sample data to answer questions about the population. Specifically, we can use the sample mean as an estimate of the population mean. Although we do not expect a sample mean to be exactly the same as the population mean, it should provide a good estimate. The standard error tells how good the estimate will be (see Box 7.2).

The numerical value of the standard error is determined by two characteristics: (1) the variability of the population from which the sample is selected and (2) the size of the sample. We will examine each of these separately.

1. The Standard Deviation of the Population. The accuracy with which a sample mean represents its population mean is determined in part by the individual scores in the sample. If the sample contains extreme scores (far from μ), then the sample mean is likely to be very different from μ. On the other hand, if all the individual scores are close to μ, then the sample mean will certainly give an accurate representation of the population mean. Standard deviation measures the standard distance between an individual score (X) and the population mean (μ). When σ is small, each individual score is close to μ, and the sample mean ($\overline{X}$) is also close to μ. With a large standard deviation, you are likely to obtain extreme scores that can increase the distance between $\overline{X}$ and μ.

2. The Sample Size. As a general rule, the larger the sample is, the more accurately the sample represents its population. This rule is also known as the *law of large numbers* (see the Preview).

DEFINITION

The *law of large numbers* states that the larger the sample size (n), the more probable it is that the sample mean will be close to the population mean.

If you were assigned the job of estimating the average IQ for freshmen at your college, you would expect to get a more accurate measure from a group of $n = 100$ than from a sample of $n = 2$. The larger the sample, the smaller the standard error.

These two characteristics are combined in the formula for the standard error:

$$\text{standard error} = \sigma_{\overline{X}} = \frac{\sigma}{\sqrt{n}} \tag{7.1}$$

Notice that when the population standard deviation (σ) is small, the standard error will be small. Also, if the sample size (n) is increased, the standard error will get smaller.

The standard error formula also may be expressed in terms of the population variance, σ^2.

$$\sigma_{\overline{X}} = \sqrt{\frac{\sigma^2}{n}} \tag{7.2}$$

Although we will usually use the population standard deviation to determine the standard error (equation 7.1), the formula based on variance will be useful later (starting in Chapter 9).

LEARNING CHECK

1. What is the difference between a distribution of raw scores and a sampling distribution?

2. Under what circumstances is the distribution of sample means guaranteed to be normal?

3. A population of scores is normal, with $\mu = 50$ and $\sigma = 12$. Describe the distribution of sample means for samples of size $n = 16$ selected from this population. (Describe shape, central tendency, and variability for the distribution.)

4. A population of scores is normal, with $\mu = 100$ and $\sigma = 16$.

   a. If you randomly select one score from this population, then, on the average, how close should the score be to the population mean?

b. If you selected a random sample of $n = 4$ scores, how much error would you expect, on the average, between the sample mean and the population mean?

c. If you selected a random sample of $n = 64$ scores, how much error, on the average, should there be between the sample mean and the population mean?

A N S W E R S   **1.** A distribution of raw scores is composed of original measurements, and a sampling distribution is composed of statistics.

2. The distribution of sample means will be normal if the original population is normal or if the sample size is at least 30.

3. The distribution of sample means will be normal because the population is normal. It has an expected value of $\mu = 50$ and a standard error of $\sigma_{\overline{X}} = 12/\sqrt{16} = 3$

4. **a.** Standard deviation, $\sigma = 16$, measures standard distance from the mean.

b. For a sample of $n = 4$, the standard error would be $16/\sqrt{4} = 8$ points.

c. For a sample of $n = 64$, the standard error would be $16/\sqrt{64} = 2$ points.

7.3 PROBABILITY AND THE DISTRIBUTION OF SAMPLE MEANS

purpose

The primary use of the distribution of sample means is to find the probability associated with any specific sample. You should recall that probability is equivalent to proportion. Because the distribution of sample means presents the entire set of all possible $\overline{X}$'s, we can use proportions of this distribution to determine probabilities. The following example demonstrates this process.

E X A M P L E   7 . 2

Caution: Whenever you have a probability question about a sample mean, you must use the distribution of sample means.

The population of scores on the SAT forms a normal distribution with $\mu = 500$ and $\sigma = 100$. If you take a random sample of $n = 25$ students, what is the probability that the sample mean would be greater than $\overline{X} = 540$?

First, you can restate this probability question as a proportion question: Out of all the possible sample means, what proportion has values greater than 540? You know about "all the possible sample means"; this is simply the distribution of sample means. The problem is to find a specific portion of this distribution. The parameters of this distribution are the following:

a. The distribution is normal because the population of SAT scores is normal.

b. The distribution has a mean of 500 because the population mean is $\mu = 500$.

c. The distribution has a standard error of $\sigma_{\overline{X}} = 20$:

$$\sigma_{\overline{X}} = \frac{\sigma}{\sqrt{n}} = \frac{100}{\sqrt{25}} = \frac{100}{5} = 20$$

This distribution of sample means is shown in Figure 7.3.

FIGURE 7.3

The distribution of sample means for $n = 25$. Samples were selected from a normal population with $\mu = 500$ and $\sigma = 100$.

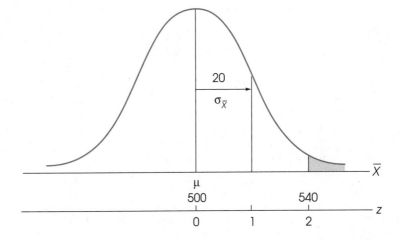

We are interested in sample means greater than 540 (the shaded area in Figure 7.3), so the next step is to use a z-score to locate the exact position of $\overline{X} = 540$ in the distribution. The value 540 is located above the mean by 40 points, which is exactly 2 standard deviations (in this case, exactly 2 standard errors). Thus, the z-score for $\overline{X} = 540$ is $z = +2.00$.

Because this distribution of sample means is normal, you can use the unit normal table to find the probability associated with $z = +2.00$. The table indicates that 0.0228 of the distribution is located in the tail of the distribution beyond $z = +2.00$. Our conclusion is that it is very unlikely, $p = 0.0228$ (2.28%), to obtain a random sample of $n = 25$ students with an average SAT score greater than 540.

As demonstrated in Example 7.2, it is possible to use a z-score to describe the position of any specific sample within the distribution of sample means. The z-score tells exactly where a specific sample is located in relation to all the other possible samples that could have been obtained. A z-score of $z = +2.00$, for example, indicates that the sample mean is much larger than usually would be expected: It is greater than the expected value of $\overline{X}$ by twice the standard distance. The z-score for each sample mean can be computed by using the standard z-score formula with a few minor changes. First, the value we are locating is a sample mean rather than a score, so the formula uses $\overline{X}$ in place of X. Second, the standard deviation for this distribution is measured by the standard error, so the formula uses $\sigma_{\overline{X}}$ in place of σ (see Box 7.3). The resulting formula, giving the z-score value corresponding to any sample mean, is

$$z = \frac{\overline{X} - \mu}{\sigma_{\overline{X}}} \tag{7.3}$$

Every sample mean has a z-score that describes its position in the distribution of sample means. Using z-scores and the unit normal table, it is possible to find the probability associated with any specific sample mean (as in Example 7.2). The following example demonstrates that it also is possible to make quantitative predictions about the kinds of samples that should be obtained from any population.

7.3 THE DIFFERENCE BETWEEN STANDARD DEVIATION AND STANDARD ERROR

A CONSTANT source of confusion for many students is the difference between standard deviation and standard error. You should remember that standard deviation measures the standard distance between a *score* and the population mean, $X - \mu$. Whenever you are working with a distribution of scores, the standard deviation is the appropriate measure of variability. Standard error, on the other hand, measures the standard distance between a *sample mean* and the population mean, $\overline{X} - \mu$. Whenever you have a question concerning a sample, the standard error is the appropriate measure of variability.

If you still find the distinction confusing, there is a simple solution. Namely, if you always use standard error, you always will be right. Consider the formula for standard error:

$$\text{standard error} = \sigma_{\overline{X}} = \frac{\sigma}{\sqrt{n}}$$

If you are working with a single score, then $n = 1$, and the standard error becomes

$$\text{standard error} = \sigma_{\overline{X}} = \frac{\sigma}{\sqrt{n}} = \frac{\sigma}{\sqrt{1}}$$

$$= \sigma = \text{standard deviation}$$

Thus, standard error always measures the standard distance from the population mean, whether you have a sample of $n = 1$ or $n = 100$.

EXAMPLE 7.3

Remember, when answering probability questions, it always is helpful to sketch a distribution and shade in the portion you are trying to find.

Suppose that you simply wanted to predict the kind of value that would be expected for the mean SAT score for a random sample of $n = 25$ students. For example, what range of values would be expected for the sample mean 80% of the time? The simplest way of answering this question is to look at the distribution of sample means. Remember, this distribution is the collection of all the possible sample means, and it will show which samples are likely to be obtained and which are not.

As demonstrated in Example 7.2, the distribution of sample means for $n = 25$ will be normal, will have an expected value of $\mu = 500$, and will have a standard error of $\sigma_{\overline{X}} = 20$. Looking at this distribution, shown again in Figure 7.4, it is clear that the most likely value to expect for a sample mean is around 500. To be more precise, we can identify the range of values that would be expected 80% of the time by locating the middle 80% of the distribution. Because the distribution is normal, we can use the unit normal table. To find the middle 80%, you should notice that 10% of the distribution is in each tail (see Figure 7.4). Thus, we can find the z-scores for each end of the middle 80% by looking up 0.1000 (the decimal equivalent for 10%) in column C of the unit normal table. Here we find a corresponding z-score of 1.28. By definition, a z-score of 1.28 indicates that the score is 1.28 standard error units from the mean. This distance is $1.28 \times 20 = 25.6$ points. The mean is 500, so 25.6 points in either direction would give a range from 474.4 to 525.6. This is the middle 80% of all the possible sample means, so you can expect any particular sample mean to be in this range 80% of the time.

LEARNING CHECK

1. A normal population has $\mu = 80$ and $\sigma = 10$. A sample of $n = 25$ scores has a mean $\overline{X} = 83$. What is the z-score corresponding to this sample mean?

FIGURE 7.4

The middle 80% of the distribution of sample means for $n = 25$. Samples were selected from a normal population with $\mu = 500$ and $\sigma = 100$.

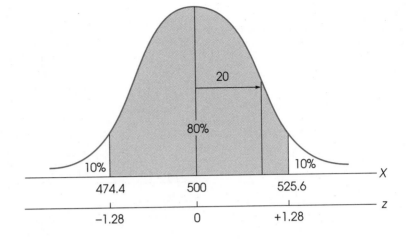

2. A random sample of $n = 9$ scores is selected from a normal population with $\mu = 40$ and $\sigma = 6$.

   a. What is the probability of obtaining a sample mean greater than 41?

   b. What is the probability of obtaining a sample mean less than 46?

3. A skewed distribution has $\mu = 60$ and $\sigma = 8$.

   a. What is the probability of obtaining a sample mean greater than $\overline{X} = 62$ for a sample of $n = 4$? (Be careful.)

   b. What is the probability of obtaining a sample mean greater than $\overline{X} = 62$ for a sample of $n = 64$?

A N S W E R S 1. The standard error is 2. $z = \frac{3}{2} = 1.5$.

2. a. $\overline{X} = 41$ corresponds to $z = +.50$. The probability is 0.3085 (30.85%).

   b. $\overline{X} = 46$ corresponds to $z = +3.0$. The probability is 0.9987 (99.87%).

3. a. Cannot answer because the distribution of sample means is not normal.

   b. With $n = 64$, the distribution of sample means will be normal. $\overline{X} = 62$ corresponds to $z = +2.0$. The probability is 0.0228 (2.28%).

7.4 MORE ABOUT STANDARD ERROR

At the beginning of this chapter, we introduced the idea that it is possible to obtain thousands of different samples from a single population. Each sample will have its own individuals, its own scores, and its own sample mean. The distribution of sample means provides a method for organizing all of the different sample means into a single picture that shows how the sample means are related to each other and how they are related to the overall population mean. Figure 7.5 shows a prototypical distribution of sample means. To emphasize the fact that the distribution contains many different samples, we have constructed this figure so that the distri-

FIGURE 7.5

An example of a typical distribution of sample means. Each of the small boxes represents the mean obtained for one sample.

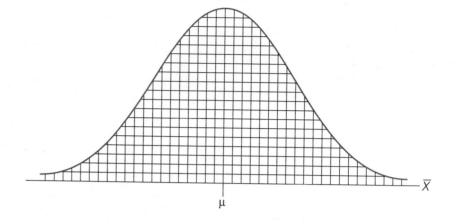

bution is made up of hundreds of small boxes, each box representing a single sample mean. Also notice that the sample means tend to pile up around the population mean (μ), forming a normal-shaped distribution as predicted by the central limit theorem.

The distribution shown in Figure 7.5 provides a concrete example for reviewing the general concepts of *sampling error* and *standard error*. Although the following points may seem obvious, they are intended to provide you with a better understanding of these two statistical concepts.

1. Sampling Error. The general concept of sampling error is that a sample typically will not provide a perfectly accurate representation of its population. More specifically, there typically will be some discrepancy (or error) between a statistic computed for a sample and the corresponding parameter for the population. As you look at Figure 7.5, notice that the individual sample means tend to *underestimate* or *overestimate* the population mean. In fact, 50% of the samples will have means that are smaller than μ (the entire left-hand side of the distribution). Similarly, 50% of the samples will produce means that overestimate the true population mean. In general, there will be some discrepancy, or *sampling error*, between the mean for a sample and the mean for the population from which the sample was obtained.

2. Standard Error. Again, looking at Figure 7.5, notice that most of the sample means are relatively close to the population mean (those in the center of the distribution). These samples provide a fairly accurate representation of the population. On the other hand, some samples will produce means that are out in the tails of the distribution, relatively far away from the population mean. These extreme sample means do not accurately represent the population. For each individual sample, you can measure the error (or distance) between the sample mean and the population mean. For some samples, the error will be relatively small, but for other samples, the error will be relatively large. The *standard error* provides a way to measure the "average" or standard distance between a sample mean and the population mean.

Thus, the standard error provides a method for defining and measuring sampling error. Knowing the standard error gives researchers a good indication of how accurately their sample data represent the populations they are studying. In most research situations, for example, the population mean is unknown, and the researcher selects a sample to help obtain information about the unknown popu-

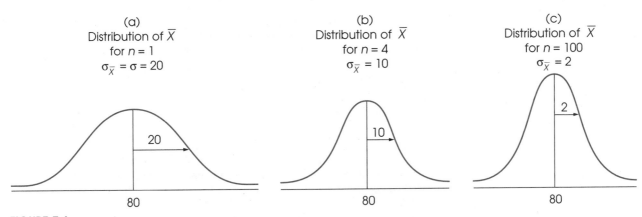

FIGURE 7.6

The distribution of sample means for random samples of size (a) $n = 1$, (b) $n = 4$, and (c) $n = 100$ obtained from a normal population with $\mu = 80$ and $\sigma = 20$. Notice that the size of the standard error decreases as the sample size increases.

lation. Specifically, the sample mean provides information about the value of the unknown population mean. The sample mean is not expected to give a perfectly accurate representation of the population mean; there will be some error, and the standard error tells *exactly how much error,* on the average, should exist between the sample mean and the unknown population mean. The following example demonstrates the use of the standard error and provides additional information about the relationship between standard error and standard deviation.

EXAMPLE 7.4 We will begin with a population that is normally distributed with a mean of $\mu = 80$ and a standard deviation of $\sigma = 20$. Next, we will take a sample from this population and examine how accurately the sample mean represents the population mean. More specifically, we will examine how sample size affects accuracy by considering three different samples: one with $n = 1$ score, one with $n = 4$ scores, and one with $n = 100$ scores.

Figure 7.6 shows the distributions of sample means based on samples of $n = 1$, $n = 4$, and $n = 100$. Each distribution shows the collection of all possible sample means that could be obtained for that particular sample size. Notice that all three sampling distributions are normal (because the original population is normal), and all three have the same mean, $\mu = 80$, which is the expected value of $\overline{X}$. However, the three distributions differ greatly with respect to variability. We will consider each one separately.

The smallest sample size is $n = 1$. When a sample consists of a single score, the mean for the sample will equal the value of that score, $\overline{X} = X$. Thus, when $n = 1$ the distribution of sample means is identical to the original population of scores. In this case, the standard error for the distribution of sample means is equal to the standard deviation for the original population. Equation 7.1 confirms this observation.

$$\sigma_{\overline{X}} = \frac{\sigma}{\sqrt{n}} = \frac{20}{\sqrt{1}} = 20$$

In one sense, the population standard deviation is the "starting point" for the standard error. With the smallest possible sample, $n = 1$, the standard error is equal to the standard deviation [see Figure 7.6(a)].

As the sample size increases, however, the standard error gets smaller. For $n = 4$, the standard error is

$$\sigma_{\overline{X}} = \frac{\sigma}{\sqrt{n}} = \frac{20}{\sqrt{4}} = \frac{20}{2} = 10$$

That is, the typical (or standard) distance between $\overline{X}$ and μ is 10 points. Figure 7.6(b) illustrates this distribution. Notice that the sample means in this distribution approximate the population mean more closely than in the previous distribution where $n = 1$.

With a sample of $n = 100$, the standard error is still smaller.

$$\sigma_{\overline{X}} = \frac{\sigma}{\sqrt{n}} = \frac{20}{\sqrt{100}} = \frac{20}{10} = 2$$

A sample of $n = 100$ scores should provide a sample mean that is a much better estimate of μ than you would obtain with a sample of $n = 4$ or $n = 1$. As shown in Figure 7.6(c), there is very little error between $\overline{X}$ and μ (you would expect only a 2-point error, on the average). The sample means pile up very close to μ.

In summary, this example illustrates that with the smallest possible sample ($n = 1$), the standard error and the population standard deviation are the same. When sample size is increased, the standard error gets smaller, and the sample means tend to approximate μ more closely. Thus, standard error defines the relationship between sample size and the accuracy with which $\overline{X}$ represents μ.

STANDARD ERROR AS A MEASURE OF RELIABILITY

In most research studies, the researcher must rely on a *single* sample to provide an accurate representation of the population being investigated. As we have noted, however, if you take two different samples from the same population, you will get different individuals with different scores and different sample means. Thus, every researcher must face the nagging question, "If I had taken a different sample, would I have obtained different results?"

The importance of this question is directly related to the degree of similarity among all the different samples. For example, if there is a high level of consistency from one sample to another, then a researcher can be reasonably confident that the specific sample being studied will provide a good measurement of the population. That is, when all the samples are similar, then it does not matter which one you have selected. On the other hand, if there are big differences from one sample to another, then the researcher is left with some doubts about the accuracy of his/ her specific sample. In this case, a different sample could have produced vastly different results.

In this context, the standard error can be viewed as a measure of the *reliability* of a sample mean. The term *reliability* refers to the consistency of different measurements of the same thing. More specifically, a measurement procedure is said

reliable

to be reliable if you make two different measurements of the same thing and obtain identical (or nearly identical) values. If you view a sample as a "measurement" of a population, then a sample mean is a "measurement" of a population mean. If the means from different samples are all nearly identical, then the sample mean provides a reliable measure of the population. On the other hand, if there are big differences from one sample to another, then the sample mean is an unreliable measure of the population mean. Figure 7.6 demonstrates how the standard error can be used as a measure of reliability for a sample mean.

ex   Figure 7.6(b) shows a distribution of sample means based on $n = 4$ scores. In this distribution, the standard error is $\sigma_{\overline{X}} = 10$, and it is relatively easy to find two samples with means that differ by 10 or 20 points. In this situation, a researcher cannot be confident that the mean for any individual sample is reliable: That is, a different sample could provide a very different mean.

Now consider what happens when the sample size is increased. Figure 7.6(c) shows the distribution of sample means based on $n = 100$. For this distribution, the standard error is $\sigma_{\overline{X}} = 2$. With a larger sample and a smaller standard error, all of the sample means are clustered close together. With $n = 100$, a researcher can be reasonably confident that the mean for any individual sample is reliable: That is, if a second sample were taken, it would probably produce a sample mean that is essentially equivalent to the mean for the first sample.

STANDARD ERROR AS A
MEASURE OF STABILITY

In Chapter 3, we examined what happens to a sample mean when a new score is added to an existing sample (and when a score is removed or changed). In the context of experimental research, a researcher might wonder what would happen to the research results if one more subject were added to the experiment. As you should recall from Chapter 3 (p. 78), adding a new score will typically change the value of the mean. The value of the standard error provides a good indication of *how much change* a new score is likely to produce. In general, when the standard error is small, adding a new score will typically produce only a small change in the value of $\overline{X}$. On the other hand, if the standard error is large, the act of adding a new score can produce a large change in an existing sample mean. Thus, the value of the standard error provides a measure of the *stability* of a sample mean; that is, how much the sample mean is likely to change if a new score is added (or an existing score is removed or changed).

The relationship between the standard error and the stability of the sample mean should be obvious if you recall that both values are related to the number of scores in the sample. In general, a large sample will be more accurate (have less error) than a small sample. At the same time, a large sample tends to be more stable than a small sample. Adding a new score to a sample of $n = 1000$ probably will have little impact on the sample mean. But adding a new score to a sample of $n = 3$ could produce a drastic change in the sample mean. This point is illustrated in the following example.

EXAMPLE 7.5

good

We will begin with a population with $\sigma = 10$. The following two samples were obtained from this population:

Sample 1: $\overline{X} = 50$ for a sample of $n = 4$ scores

Sample 2: $\overline{X} = 50$ for a sample of $n = 100$ scores

Next, we compute the standard errror for each sample. For sample 1, we obtain

$$\sigma_{\overline{X}} = \frac{\sigma}{\sqrt{n}} = \frac{10}{\sqrt{4}} = \frac{10}{2} = 5$$

And for sample 2, the standard error is

$$\sigma_{\overline{X}} = \frac{\sigma}{\sqrt{n}} = \frac{10}{\sqrt{100}} = \frac{10}{10} = 1$$

Notice that the larger sample has a smaller standard error.

Now consider what happens if we add a new score to each sample. For this example, we will add the same score, $X = 20$, to both samples.

Sample 1 started with $n = 4$ and $\overline{X} = 50$, so $\Sigma X = 200$ for the original sample. With the addition of the new score, we now have $n = 5$ and $\Sigma X = 220$. This results in a new mean of $\overline{X} = 220/5 = 44$. Notice that adding one new score changed the sample mean by 6 points (from $\overline{X} = 50$ to $\overline{X} = 44$). In this case, a relatively large standard error indicates that one new score can produce a relatively large change in the sample mean.

Sample 2 started with $n = 100$ and $\overline{X} = 50$, which means the original sample had $\Sigma X = 5000$. Adding the new score, $X = 20$, produces a sample with $n = 101$ and $\Sigma X = 5020$. The mean for the new sample is $\overline{X} = 5020/101 = 49.70$. In this case, the addition of a new score had almost no effect (the mean changed by 0.30 point, from $\overline{X} = 50$ to $\overline{X} = 49.70$). With $n = 100$ scores, the standard error was relatively small, and the addition of a new score had a relatively small effect on the sample mean.

IN THE LITERATURE:
REPORTING STANDARD ERROR

As we will see later, the standard error plays a very important role in inferential statistics. Because of its crucial role, the standard error for a sample mean, rather than the sample standard deviation, is often reported in scientific papers. Scientific journals vary in how they refer to the standard error, but frequently the symbols *SE* and *SEM* (for standard error of the mean) are used. The standard error is reported in two ways. Much like the standard deviation, it may be reported in a table along with sample means (see Table 7.2). Alternatively, the standard error may be reported in graphs.

TABLE 7.2

The mean self-consciousness scores for subjects who were working in front of a video camera and those who were not (controls)

	n	MEAN	SE
Control	17	32.23	2.31
Camera	15	45.17	2.78

FIGURE 7.7

The mean ($\pm SE$) score for treatment groups A and B.

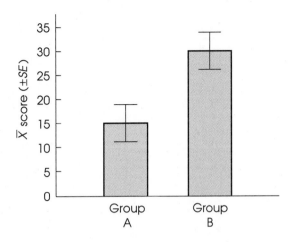

Figure 7.7 illustrates the use of a bar graph to display information about the sample mean and the standard error. In this experiment, two samples (groups A and B) are given different treatments, and then the subjects' scores on a dependent variable are recorded. The mean for group A is $\overline{X} = 15$, and for group B, it is $\overline{X} = 30$. For both samples, the standard error of $\overline{X}$ is $\sigma_{\overline{X}} = 4$. Note that the mean is represented by the height of the bar, and the standard error is depicted on the graph by brackets at the top of each bar. Each bracket extends 1 standard error above and 1 standard error below the sample mean. Thus, the graph illustrates the mean for each group plus or minus 1 standard error ($\overline{X} \pm SE$). When you glance at Figure 7.7, not only do you get a "picture" of the sample means, but also you get an idea of how much error you should expect for those means.

Figure 7.8 shows how sample means and standard error are displayed on a line graph (polygon). In this study, two samples (groups A and B) receive different treatments and then are tested on a task for four trials. The number of mistakes committed on each trial is recorded for all subjects. The graph shows the mean ($\overline{X}$) number of mistakes committed for each group on each trial. The brackets

FIGURE 7.8

The mean ($\pm SE$) number of mistakes made for groups A and B on each trial.

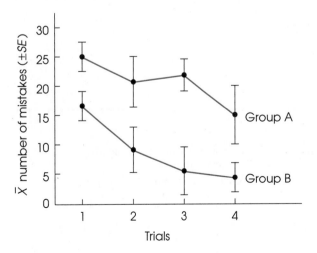

FIGURE 7.9

Answers to Learning Check.

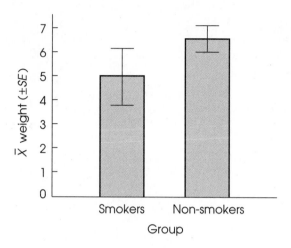

show the size of the standard error for each sample mean. Again, the brackets extend 1 standard error above and below the value of the mean.   ❑

L E A R N I N G   C H E C K   **1.** A researcher examined the effect of smoking during pregnancy on birth weight. One sample consisted of newborns whose mothers smoked cigarettes during the pregnancy. A second sample consisted of newborns of non-smokers. The birth weight of each newborn was recorded, and sample means were computed. The results are summarized in the following table:

The mean birth weights (in pounds) of infants
of smoking and non-smoking mothers

GROUP	MEAN WEIGHT	SE
Smokers	5.0	1.2
Non-smokers	6.5	0.7

Construct a bar graph that incorporates the information provided by the table.

A N S W E R   **1.** See Figure 7.9.

SUMMARY

1. The distribution of sample means is defined as the set of all the possible $\overline{X}$'s for a specific sample size (n) that can be obtained from a given population. The parameters of the distribution of sample means are as follows:

a. Shape. The distribution of sample means will be nor-

mal if either one of the following two conditions is satisfied:

(1) The population from which the samples are selected is normal.

(2) The size of the samples is relatively large (around $n = 30$ or more).

b. **Central Tendency.** The mean of the distribution of sample means will be identical to the mean of the population from which the samples are selected. The mean of the distribution of sample means is called the expected value of $\overline{X}$.

c. **Variability.** The standard deviation of the distribution of sample means is called the standard error of $\overline{X}$ and is defined by the formula

$$\sigma_{\overline{X}} = \frac{\sigma}{\sqrt{n}} \quad \text{or} \quad \sigma_{\overline{X}} = \sqrt{\frac{\sigma^2}{n}}$$

Standard error measures the standard distance between a sample mean ($\overline{X}$) and the population mean μ.

2. One of the most important concepts in this chapter is the standard error. The standard error is the standard deviation of the distribution of sample means. It measures the standard distance between a sample mean ($\overline{X}$) and the popula-

tion mean (μ). The standard error tells how much error to expect if you are using a sample mean to estimate a population mean.

3. The location of each $\overline{X}$ in the distribution of sample means can be specified by a z-score:

$$z = \frac{\overline{X} - \mu}{\sigma_{\overline{X}}}$$

Because the distribution of sample means tends to be normal, we can use these z-scores and the unit normal table to find probabilities for specific sample means. In particular, we can identify which sample means are likely and which are very unlikely to be obtained from any given population. This ability to find probabilities for samples is the basis for the inferential statistics in the chapters ahead.

KEY TERMS

sampling error

distribution of sample means

sampling distribution

central limit theorem

expected value of $\overline{X}$

standard error of $\overline{X}$

law of large numbers

FOCUS ON PROBLEM SOLVING

1. Whenever you are working probability questions about sample means, you must use the distribution of sample means. Remember, every probability question can be restated as a proportion question. Probabilities for sample means are equivalent to proportions of the distribution of sample means.

2. When computing probabilities for sample means, the most common error is to use standard deviation (σ) instead of standard error ($\sigma_{\overline{X}}$) in the z-score formula. Standard deviation measures the typical deviation (or "error") for a single score. Standard error measures the typical deviation (or error) for a sample. Remember, the larger the sample is, the more accurately the sample represents the population—that is, the larger the sample, the smaller the error.

$$\text{standard error} = \sigma_{\overline{X}} = \frac{\sigma}{\sqrt{n}}$$

3. Although the distribution of sample means is often normal, it is not always a normal distribution. Check the criteria to be certain the distribution is normal before you use the unit normal table to find probabilities (see item 1a of the Summary). Remember, all probability problems with the normal distribution are easier if you sketch the distribution and shade in the area of interest.

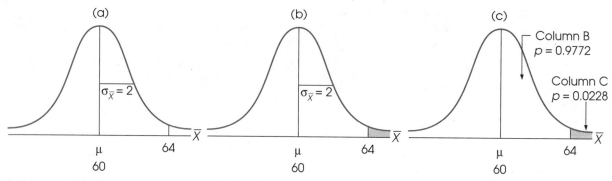

FIGURE 7.10

Sketches of the distributions for Demonstration 7.1

DEMONSTRATION 7.1

PROBABILITY AND THE DISTRIBUTION OF SAMPLE MEANS

For a normally distributed population with $\mu = 60$ and $\sigma = 12$, what is the probability of selecting a random sample of $n = 36$ scores with a sample mean greater than 64?

In symbols, for $n = 36$

$$p(\overline{X} > 64) = ?$$

Notice that we may rephrase the probability question as a proportion question. Out of all the possible sample means for $n = 36$, what proportion has values greater than 64?

STEP 1 Sketch the distribution.

We are looking for a specific proportion of *all possible sample means*. Therefore, we will have to sketch the distribution of sample means. We should include the expected value, the standard error, and the specified sample mean.

The expected value for this demonstration is $\mu = 60$. The standard error is

$$\sigma_{\overline{X}} = \frac{\sigma}{\sqrt{n}} = \frac{12}{\sqrt{36}} = \frac{12}{6} = 2$$

Remember, we must use the standard error, *not* the standard deviation, because we are dealing with the distribution of sample means.

Find the approximate location of the sample mean, and place a vertical line through the distribution. In this demonstration, the sample mean is 64. It is larger than the expected value of $\mu = 60$ and, therefore, is placed on the right side of the distribution. Figure 7.10(a) depicts the preliminary sketch.

STEP 2 Shade the appropriate area of the distribution.

Determine whether the problem asks for a proportion greater than ($>$) or less than ($<$) the specified sample mean. Then shade the appropriate area of the distribution. In this demonstration, we are looking for the area greater than $\overline{X} = 64$, so we shade the area on the right-hand side of the vertical line [Figure 7.10(b)].

STEP 3 Compute the z-score for the sample mean.

Use the z-score formula for sample means. Remember that it uses standard error in the denominator.

$$z = \frac{\overline{X} - \mu}{\sigma_{\overline{X}}} = \frac{64 - 60}{2} = \frac{4}{2} = 2.00$$

STEP 4 Consult the unit normal table.

Look up the z-score in the unit normal table, and note the two proportions in columns B and C. Jot them down in the appropriate areas of the distribution [Figure 7.10(c)]. For this demonstration, the value in column C (the tail beyond z) corresponds exactly to the proportion we want (the shaded area). Thus, for $n = 36$,

$$p(\overline{X} > 64) = p(z > +2.00) = 0.0228$$

PROBLEMS

1. Briefly define each of the following:
   a. The distribution of sample means
   b. The expected value of $\overline{X}$
   c. The standard error of $\overline{X}$

2. Explain the distinction between a *distribution of scores* (a population) and a *sampling distribution.*

3. IQ scores tend to form normal distributions with $\sigma = 15$. However, the mean IQ varies from one population to another. For example, the mean IQ for registered voters is different from the mean for non-registered voters. A researcher would like to use a sample to obtain information about the mean IQ for the population of licensed clinical psychologists in the state of California. Which sample mean should provide a more accurate representation of the population: a sample of $n = 9$ or a sample of $n = 25$? In each case, compute exactly how much error the researcher should expect between the sample mean and the population mean.

4. A distribution of scores has $\sigma = 6$, but the value of the mean is unknown. A researcher plans to select a sample from the population in order to learn more about the unknown mean.
   a. If the sample consists of a single score ($n = 1$), how accurately should the score represent the population mean? That is, how much error, on the average, should the researcher expect between the score and the population mean?
   b. If the sample consists of $n = 9$ scores, how accurately should the sample mean represent the population mean?
   c. If the sample consists of $n = 36$ scores, how much error, on the average, would be expected between the sample mean and the population mean?

5. A population has $\mu = 60$ and $\sigma = 10$. Find the z-score corresponding to each of the following sample means:
   a. A sample of $n = 4$ with $\overline{X} = 55$
   b. A sample of $n = 25$ with $\overline{X} = 64$
   c. A sample of $n = 100$ with $\overline{X} = 62$

6. If you are taking a random sample from a normal population with $\mu = 100$ and $\sigma = 16$, which of the following outcomes is more likely? Explain your answer. (*Hint:* Calculate the z-score for each sample mean.)
   a. A sample mean greater than 106 for a sample of $n = 4$.
   b. A sample mean greater than 103 for a sample of $n = 36$.

7. A normal population has $\mu = 100$ and $\sigma = 20$.
   a. Sketch the distribution of sample means for random samples of $n = 25$.
   b. Using z-scores, find the boundaries that separate the middle 95% of the sample means from the extreme 5% in the tails of the distribution.
   c. A sample mean of $\overline{X} = 106$ is computed for a sample of $n = 25$ scores. Is this sample mean in the extreme 5%?

8. A normal population has $\mu = 80$ and $\sigma = 12$.
   a. Using this population, sketch the distribution of sample means for $n = 4$. Mark the location of the mean (the expected value), and show the standard error in your sketch.
   b. Using your sketch from part a, what proportion of samples of $n = 4$ will have sample means greater than 86? (Locate the position of $\overline{X} = 86$, find the corresponding z-score, and use the unit normal table to determine the proportion.)
   c. Sketch the distribution of sample means based on $n = 16$.

d. Using your sketch from part c, what proportion of samples of $n = 16$ will have sample means greater than 86?

9. A normal population has $\mu = 55$ and $\sigma = 8$.
  a. Sketch the distribution of sample means for samples of size $n = 16$ selected from this population.
  b. What proportion of samples based on $n = 16$ will have sample means greater than 59?
  c. What proportion of samples with $n = 16$ will have sample means less than 56?
  d. What proportion of samples with $n = 16$ will have sample means between 53 and 57?

10. A normal population has $\mu = 70$ and $\sigma = 12$.
  a. Sketch the population distribution. What proportion of the scores has values greater than $X = 73$.
  b. Sketch the distribution of sample means for samples of size $n = 16$. What proportion of the sample means has values greater than 73?

11. A normal population has $\mu = 50$ and $\sigma = 10$.
  a. Sketch the population distribution. What proportion of the scores have values within 5 points of the population mean? That is, find $p(45 < X < 55)$.
  b. Sketch the distribution of sample means for samples of size $n = 25$. What proportion of the sample means will have values within 5 points of the population mean? That is, find $p(45 < \overline{X} < 55)$ for $n = 25$.

12. Scores on a personality test form a normal distribution with $\mu = 80$ and $\sigma = 12$. If a random sample of $n = 16$ people is selected and the mean score is computed for this sample, then
  a. Sketch the distribution of all the possible sample means that could be obtained.
  b. Of all the possible sample means, what proportion will be greater than 85?
  c. What proportion of the sample means will be less than 83?
  d. What proportion of the sample means will be less than 74?
  e. Of all the possible sample means, what proportion will be within 4 points of the population mean? (That is, what proportion will be between 76 and 84?)

13. For a normal population with $\mu = 70$ and $\sigma = 20$, what is the probability of obtaining a sample mean greater than 75
  a. For a random sample of $n = 4$ scores?
  b. For a random sample of $n = 16$ scores?
  c. For a random sample of $n = 100$ scores?

14. For a negatively skewed population with $\mu = 85$ and $\sigma = 18$, what is the probability of obtaining a sample mean greater than 88

a. For a random sample of $n = 4$ scores? (*Caution:* This is a trick question.)
b. For a random sample of $n = 36$ scores?

15. A population of scores forms a normal distribution with $\mu = 75$ and $\sigma = 12$.
  a. What is the probability of obtaining a random sample of $n = 4$ scores with a sample mean that is within 5 points of the population mean? That is, find $p(70 < \overline{X} < 80)$.
  b. For a sample of $n = 16$ scores, what is the probability of obtaining a sample mean that is within 5 points of the population mean?

16. In addition to describing the standard distance between $\overline{X}$ and μ, the standard error provides a measure of the "stability" of a sample mean. As sample size increases, the standard error of $\overline{X}$ decreases. One consequence of this relationship is that larger samples are not only more accurate in representing their populations, but also more stable. Consider the following two samples that were obtained from a population with $\mu = 42$ and $\sigma = 10$.

  Sample 1: $n = 4$, with $\overline{X} = 40$

  Sample 2: $n = 25$, with $\overline{X} = 40$

  a. Compute the standard error for each sample mean.
  b. Suppose that a new score, $X = 60$, is added to each sample. How will the new score affect each sample mean? Compute the new mean for each of the two samples.
  c. Adding a new score, the extreme value $X = 60$, changed the mean for both samples. Describe how the impact of the new score is related to the standard error for the two sample means.

17. A population has $\mu = 300$ and $\sigma = 80$.
  a. If a random sample of $n = 25$ scores is selected from this population, how much error would be expected between the sample mean and the population mean?
  b. If the sample size were 4 times larger, $n = 100$, how much error would be expected?
  c. If the sample size were increased again by a factor of 4 to $n = 400$, how much error would be expected?
  d. Comparing your answers to parts a, b, and c, what is the relationship between sample size and standard error. (Note that the sample size was increased by a factor of 4 each time.)

18. Standard error measures the standard distance between a sample mean and the population mean. For a population with $\sigma = 20$,
  a. How large a sample would be needed to obtain a standard error less than 10 points?

b. How large a sample would be needed to have a standard error smaller than 5 points?

c. If you wanted your sample mean to be within 1 point of the population mean (on the average), how large a sample should you use?

19. The local hardware store sells screws in 1-pound bags. Because the screws are not identical, the number of screws varies from bag to bag, with $\mu = 140$ and $\sigma = 10$. A carpenter needs a total of 600 screws for a project. What is the probability that the carpenter will get enough screws if only 4 bags are purchased? Assume that the distribution is normal. *Note:* In order to obtain a total of 600 screws, the 4 bags must average at least $\overline{X} = 150$.

20. The average age for registered voters in the county is $\mu = 39.7$ years with $\sigma = 11.8$. The distribution of ages is approximately normal. During a recent jury trial in the county courthouse, a statistician noted that the average age for the 12 jurors was $\overline{X} = 50.4$ years.

a. How likely is it to obtain a jury this old or older by chance?

b. Is it reasonable to conclude that this jury is not a random sample of registered voters?

21. Boxes of sugar are filled by machine with considerable accuracy. The distribution of box weights is normal and has a mean of 32 ounces with a standard deviation of only 2 ounces. A quality control inspector takes a sample of $n = 16$ boxes and finds the sample contains, on the average, $\overline{X} = 31$ ounces of sugar. What is the probability of obtaining a sample with this much or more short-changing in its boxes? Should the inspector suspect that the filling machinery needs repair?

22. A researcher evaluated the effectiveness of relaxation training in reducing anxiety. One sample of anxiety-ridden people received relaxation training, while a second sample did not. Then anxiety scores were measured for all subjects, using a standardized test. Use the information that is summarized in the following table to complete this exercise:

The effect of relaxation training on anxiety scores

GROUP	MEAN ANXIETY SCORE	SE
Control group	36	7
Relaxation training	18	5

a. Construct a bar graph that incorporates all of the information in the table.

b. Looking at your graph, do you think the relaxation training really worked? Explain your answer.

23. Suppose that a researcher did the same study described in Problem 22. This time the results of the experiment were as follows:

The effect of relaxation training on anxiety scores

GROUP	MEAN ANXIETY SCORE	SE
Control group	36	12
Relaxation training	18	10

a. Construct a bar graph that incorporates all of the information in the table.

b. Looking at your graph, do you think the relaxation training really worked? Explain your answer.

24. A researcher assessed the effects of a new drug on migraine headaches. One sample of migraine sufferers received a placebo pill (0 milligrams of the drug) every day for a month. A second sample received a 10-mg dose of the drug daily for a month, and a third sample received daily doses of 20 mg. The number of headaches each person had during the month was recorded. The results are summarized in the following table:

The mean number of migraines during drug treatment

DOSE OF DRUG (mg)	MEAN NUMBER OF MIGRAINES	SE
0	28	5
10	12	4
20	5	2

Draw a line graph (polygon) that illustrates the information provided by the table.

TIME OUT

AT THIS point, we have finished the material that serves as a foundation for the inferential statistics in future chapters. Before we move on, it is time to stop for a moment, look back at what you should know so far, and consider how this knowledge will be used in the statistical procedures that follow.

LOOKING BACK

We have seen that *z-scores* (Chapter 5) are useful for describing the location of an individual within a distribution. This is accomplished by determining how many standard deviations an X value is from the mean of the distribution, or

$$z = \frac{X - \mu}{\sigma}$$

When every X value is transformed into a z-score, the resulting distribution of z-scores will have a mean of $\mu = 0$ and a standard deviation of $\sigma = 1$. Thus, a z-score value near zero indicates that the X value is close to the mean. Alternatively, a large z-score value (near ± 2, for example) indicates that the X value is extreme.

The distribution of z-scores was then used to answer probability questions about a normal distribution (Chapter 6). An X value is first converted to (located with) a z-score. Then the z-score is used with the unit normal table to determine a probability. An X value with a z-score near zero is a likely occurrence (has a high probability). An X value with a large z-score is more extreme and less likely (has a low probability).

In Chapter 7, we used z-scores and probability to determine which *sample means* are likely and which are extreme. This task requires that we look at the *distribution of sample means,* which has an expected value equal to μ and a standard error of $\sigma_{\overline{X}} = \sigma/\sqrt{n}$. Standard error measures how much we can expect sample means to deviate from the population mean. To determine probability, we use another z-score:

$$z = \frac{\overline{X} - \mu}{\sigma_{\overline{X}}}$$

and the unit normal table to determine the probability for a sample mean. A sample mean with a z-score near zero is likely to be observed (has a high probability). Conversely, a sample mean with a large z-score is extreme and has a low probability.

Thus, whether you are selecting a sample that consists of a single score ($n = 1$) or a number of scores, you should be able to determine whether the sample is representative of the population (has a high probability) or whether the sample is substantially different from the population (has a low probability)

LOOKING AHEAD

In the next eight chapters, we will be using sample means to make inferences about population means. The major concern in this process is *sampling error*. Remember, the limited information from a sample provides an incomplete and potentially inaccurate picture of a population. This introduces uncertainty into statistical inference. Yet, in a research situation, you must rely on sample data to answer questions about populations. How can a researcher be confident that the sample data in a research study accurately represent the population? Fortunately, the standard error allows us to measure the standard amount of error between a sample mean and the population mean. Specifically, by using the standard error, it is possible to compute a z-score and a probability for any sample mean. Thus, we can determine which samples are likely and which are extreme. The standard error, z-scores, and probability will bridge the gap between a sample and a population.

CHAPTER 8

INTRODUCTION TO HYPOTHESIS TESTING

TOOLS YOU WILL NEED

The following items are considered essential background material for this chapter. If you doubt your knowledge of any of these items, you should review the appropriate chapter or section before proceeding.

- z-Scores (Chapter 5)
- Distribution of sample means (Chapter 7)
  - Expected value
  - Standard error
  - Probability of sample means

CONTENTS

PREVIEW

The label on the back of this wine bottle I am holding has an ominous warning:

> According to the surgeon general, women should not drink alcoholic beverages during pregnancy. . . .

There is good reason for the warning: Alcohol may result in birth defects that include anatomical malformations of the face, heart, and brain, as well as cognitive deficits and retarded growth. These effects are known as fetal alcohol syndrome (FAS), and many of them are obvious at the time of birth. Let's look at one of these effects. A researcher, who is interested in FAS, would like to determine if prenatal exposure to alcohol results in low birth weight as well. This researcher might propose the following hypothesis:

> For the population of subjects, prenatal exposure to alcohol has an effect on birth weight.

Notice that the hypothesis is making a prediction about the relationship between the independent variable (alcohol exposure) and the dependent variable (birth weight). Because the hypothesis identifies specific variables, it can be evaluated in an experiment. Also note that the hypothesis refers to the entire population.

Of course, it would be unethical to conduct an experiment with humans because it may very well produce injury to the unborn, so the hypothesis will be tested with an animal model using laboratory rats. Also, even though the hypothesis is made about a population, it would be impossible to test the entire population of subjects in an experiment. Instead, it is reasonable to test the effects of prenatal alcohol exposure on a subset of the population—namely, a relatively small sample of laboratory rats. Thus, a random sample of rats is selected, and these animals are given daily doses of alcohol during pregnancy. When the rat pups are born, they are weighed immediately. The researcher then uses data from the sample to evaluate the hypothesis about the population. For this example, the researcher would determine whether or not the weight of the rat pups given prenatal alcohol exposure is substantially different from what is normally expected for untreated rat pups.

In this example, as in most scientific research, the investigator is using data from a sample to evaluate a hypothesis about a population. You should recall that the general technique of using sample data as the basis for making conclusions about a population is called inferential statistics. The process of testing hypotheses is one of the standard inferential procedures in statistics. In this chapter, we will introduce the logic, the notation, and the general mechanics of hypothesis testing. We also spend a lot of time discussing errors in hypothesis testing. You should realize that any inferential procedure is subject to errors. When making conclusions about a population based on a single sample, there is a chance that you will make the wrong decision and reach the wrong conclusion. One of the general goals in the process of hypothesis testing will be to limit or control the probability of errors.

8.1 OVERVIEW

It is usually impossible or impractical for a researcher to observe every individual in a population. Therefore, researchers usually collect data from a sample. Hypothesis testing is a statistical procedure that allows scientists to use sample data to draw inferences about the population of interest.

DEFINITION   *Hypothesis testing* is an inferential procedure that uses sample data to evaluate the credibility of a hypothesis about a population.

In very simple terms, the logic underlying the hypothesis-testing procedure is as follows:

1. First, we state a hypothesis about a population. Usually the hypothesis concerns the value of a population parameter. For example, we might hypothesize that the mean age for first-time drug use among students is $\mu = 15$ years.

FIGURE 8.1

The basic experimental situation for hypothesis testing. It is assumed that the parameter μ is known for the population before treatment. The purpose of the experiment is to determine whether or not the treatment has an effect on the population mean.

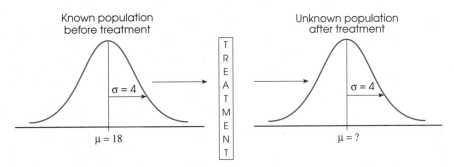

2. Next, we obtain a random sample from the population. For example, we might select a random sample of $n = 200$ students who have tried a drug at one time or another.

3. Finally, we compare the sample data with the hypothesis. If the data are consistent with the hypothesis, we will conclude that the hypothesis was reasonable. But if there is a big discrepancy between the data and the hypothesis, we will decide that the hypothesis was wrong.

Although the general logic of hypothesis testing is relatively simple, there are many details involved in standardizing and quantifying the hypothesis-testing procedure. In this chapter, we will examine these details and develop the general technique of hypothesis testing.

8.2 THE LOGIC OF HYPOTHESIS TESTING

The hypothesis-testing procedure usually begins with an unknown population, specifically, a population with an unknown mean. Often this situation arises after a treatment is administered to a known population (see Figure 8.1). In this case, the researcher begins with an original population with known parameters. For example, suppose that the original population is known to be normal with $\mu = 18$ and $\sigma = 4$. The researcher's questions concerns what effect the treatment will have on this population. Will the treatment cause the scores to increase or decrease, or will the treatment have no effect whatsoever? The specific question is, What happens to the population mean after treatment? Hypothesis testing is a procedure that will help the researcher determine whether or not a treatment effect occurred. This situation is illustrated in Figure 8.1.

To simplify the hypothesis-testing situation, one basic assumption is made about the effect of the treatment: If the treatment has any effect, it is simply to add (or subtract) a constant amount to (or from) each individual's score. You should recall from Chapters 3 and 4 that adding (or subtracting) a constant will not change the shape of the population, nor will it change the standard deviation. Thus, we will assume that the population after treatment has the same shape and the same standard deviation as the original population. This assumption is incorporated into the situation shown in Figure 8.1.

The first step in the hypothesis-testing procedure involves stating a hypothesis about the unknown population mean. We could, for example, hypothesize that the treatment has no effect, so that the population mean after treatment is the same as the mean for the original population. Or we might hypothesize that the treatment will increase each individual's score by 10 points, so that the mean for the treated population will be 10 points higher than the mean for the original population. Notice that the hypothesis concerns the entire population.

Next, the researcher would collect sample data. A sample of individuals is selected from the treated population. That is, the researcher obtains a sample of individuals who have received the treatment. The sample data are then used to evaluate the hypothesis. Specifically, the researcher must determine if the sample data are consistent with the hypothesis or if the sample data contradict the hypothesis. Notice that the researcher is using the information from a sample to evaluate a hypothesis about a population. This is the basis of inferential statistics: using sample data to draw inferences about populations.

In this overview of the hypothesis-testing procedure, you can think of the researcher as a police detective gathering evidence. The sample is the evidence that the researcher uses to build a case for or against the hypothesis. Sometimes the evidence is overwhelming, and the researcher can make confident conclusions about the hypothesis. Often the evidence is not very convincing, and the researcher is uncertain about a conclusion. There is always a possibility that the evidence is misleading and the researcher will reach the wrong conclusion.

Because the process of hypothesis testing involves some uncertainty and can lead to errors, the procedure has been formalized to a standard series of operations. In this way, the researcher has a standardized method for evaluating the evidence from an experiment. Other researchers will recognize and understand exactly how the data were evaluated and how conclusions were reached. In addition, the hypothesis-testing procedure is developed so that a researcher can identify and partially control the risk of an error. Throughout this book, we will present hypothesis testing as a four-step procedure. We now examine these steps in more detail, using the research example described in the Preview.

STEP 1: STATING THE HYPOTHESES

Suppose that our researcher knows, from information given by the laboratory suppliers, that the mean birth weight of the laboratory rat is $\mu = 18$ grams. That is, in a controlled environment, the *untreated* rat pup should weigh around 18 grams at birth. To determine whether prenatal exposure to alcohol has any effect, the researcher must compare the sample birth weights of *treated* rats to the mean weight (μ) provided by the supplier. To begin this process, the researcher states two opposing hypotheses. Note that both hypotheses are stated in terms of population parameters.

The first is the *null hypothesis,* or H_0. This hypothesis states that the treatment has *no effect*. (The null hypothesis, often pronounced "H-naught," always says that there is no effect, no change, no difference, nothing happened—hence the name *null*.) In this example, the null hypothesis states that prenatal exposure to alcohol will have *no effect* on birth weight for the population of laboratory rats. In symbols, this hypothesis would be

H_0: $\mu_{\text{prenatal exposure}} = 18$ grams   (Even with prenatal exposure to alcohol, the mean birth weight of rat pups is still 18 grams.)

The goal of inferential statistics is to make general statements about the population by using sample data. Therefore, when testing hypotheses, we make our predictions about the population parameters.

DEFINITION   The *null hypothesis* (H_0) predicts that the independent variable (treatment) has no effect on the dependent variable for the population.

The second hypothesis is called the *scientific* or *alternative hypothesis* (H_1). This hypothesis states that the treatment will have an effect on the dependent variable. For this example, it predicts that prenatal alcohol exposure does alter birth weight for the population. In symbols, it is represented as

$$H_1: \mu_{\text{prenatal exposure}} \neq 18 \text{ grams} \quad \text{(With prenatal alcohol exposure, the mean will be different from 18 grams.)}$$

DEFINITION   The *alternative hypothesis* (H_1) predicts that the independent variable (treatment) will have an effect on the dependent variable for the population.

Notice that the alternative hypothesis simply states that there will be some type of change. It does not specify whether the effect will be increased or decreased birth weight. In some circumstances, it is appropriate to specify the direction of the effect in H_1. For example, the researcher might hypothesize that prenatal exposure to alcohol will decrease birth weight ($\mu < 18$ grams). This type of hypothesis results in a directional hypothesis test, which will be examined in detail later in this chapter. For now we will concentrate on non-directional tests, where the hypothesis always state that the treatment has some effect (H_1) or has no effect (H_0). For this example, we are examining whether prenatal alcohol exposure does alter birth weight in some way (H_1) or has no effect (H_0). You should also realize that both hypotheses refer to a population whose mean is unknown—namely, the population of rats that received prenatal alcohol exposure. Once again, Figure 8.1 illustrates this point.

STEP 2: SETTING THE CRITERIA FOR A DECISION

The researcher will eventually use the data from the sample to evaluate the credibility of the null hypothesis. For this example, the null hypothesis states that the mean for the treated population will still be $\mu = 18$ (the same as the original untreated population). Thus, if our sample of treated rat pups showed a mean birth weight close to 18 grams, we could conclude that the treatment (prenatal alcohol exposure) does not seem to have any effect. On the other hand, if the rat pups in our sample weighed much more or less than 18 grams, we could conclude that the prenatal alcohol exposure does seem to have an effect on birth weight.

Notice that the final decision is based on a comparison of the sample data versus the null hypothesis. Whenever there is a big discrepancy between the data and the hypothesis, we can conclude that the hypothesis is wrong. However, you should also notice that we are comparing a sample (the data) versus a population (the null hypothesis). You should recall from Chapter 7 that a sample mean generally will not be identical to the population mean. There will almost always be some discrepancy between $\overline{X}$ and μ due to sampling error (measured by standard error, $\sigma_{\overline{X}}$). The problem for the researcher is to determine whether the difference between the sample data and the null hypothesis is the result of the treatment effect or is simply due to sampling error. When does the sample provide sufficient evidence to conclude that the treatment really does have an effect? To solve this problem, the researcher must establish criteria (or "cutoffs") that define precisely how much difference must exist between the data and the null hypothesis to justify a decision that the null hypothesis is false. The procedure for establishing criteria is consid-

8.1   REJECTING THE NULL HYPOTHESIS VERSUS PROVING THE ALTERNATIVE HYPOTHESIS

IT MAY seem awkward to pay so much attention to the null hypothesis. After all, the purpose of most experiments is to show that a treatment does have an effect, and the null hypothesis states that there is no effect. The reason for focusing on the null hypothesis rather than the alternative hypothesis comes from the limitations of inferential logic. Remember, we want to use the sample data to draw conclusions, or inferences, about a population. Logically, it is much easier to demonstrate that a universal (population) hypothesis is false than to demonstrate that it is true. This principle is shown more clearly in a simple example. Suppose that you make the universal statement "all dogs have four legs" and you intend to test this hypothesis by using a sample of one dog. If the dog in your sample does have four legs, have you proved

the statement? It should be clear that one four-legged dog does not prove the general statement to be true. On the other hand, suppose that the dog in your sample has only three legs. In this case, you have proved the statement to be false. Again, it is much easier to show that something is false than to prove that it is true.

Hypothesis testing uses this logical principle to achieve its goals. It would be difficult to state "the treatment has an effect" as the hypothesis and then try to prove that this is true. Therefore, we state the null hypothesis, "the treatment has no effect," and try to show that it is false. The end result still is to demonstrate that the treatment does have an effect. That is, we find support for the alternative hypothesis by disproving (rejecting) the null hypothesis.

ered in Section 8.3. For now, you should recognize that criteria are essential for a researcher to make an objective decision about the hypotheses.

STEP 3: COLLECTING SAMPLE DATA

The next step in hypothesis testing is to obtain the sample data. A random sample of rats receives daily doses of alcohol during pregnancy. At birth, the sample of newborn pups is weighed. Usually the raw data from the sample are summarized in a single statistic, such as the sample mean (X) or a z-score. Of course, selecting a sample randomly is important because it helps ensure that the sample is representative of the population. For example, it would help avoid the selection of a group of rats that would have pups with unusually high or low birth weights, regardless of the treatment.

You also should note that the data are collected only after the researcher has stated hypotheses and established criteria for making a decision. This sequence of events helps ensure that a researcher makes an honest, objective evaluation of the data and does not tamper with the decision criteria after the experiment outcome is known.

STEP 4: EVALUATING THE NULL HYPOTHESIS

In the final step, the researcher compares the data ($\overline{X}$) with the null hypothesis (μ) and makes a decision according to the criteria and cutoffs that were established in step 2. There are two possible decisions, and both are stated in terms of the null hypothesis.

One possibility is that the researcher decides to *reject the null hypothesis*. This decision is made whenever the sample data are substantially different from what the null hypothesis predicts. In this case, the data provide strong evidence that the treatment does have an effect.

The second possibility occurs when the data do not provide convincing evidence of a treatment effect. In this case, the sample data are consistent with the null hypothesis, and the statistical decision is to *fail to reject the null hypothesis*. The term *fail to reject* is used because the experiment failed to produce evidence that H_0 is wrong. (See Box 8.1.)

ERRORS IN HYPOTHESIS TESTING   The problem in hypothesis testing is deciding whether or not the sample data are consistent with the null hypothesis. In the second step of the hypothesis-testing procedure, we identify the kind of data that are expected if the null hypothesis is true. If the outcome of the experiment is consistent with this prediction, then there is no need to be suspicious about the credibility of the null hypothesis. If, on the other hand, the outcome of the experiment is very different from this prediction, then we would reject the null hypothesis because the evidence is overwhelmingly against it. In either case, it is possible that the data obtained from a single experiment can be misleading and cause a researcher to make an incorrect decision. The two possibilities are presented here and in Box 8.2.

Type I errors   It is possible to reject the null hypothesis when in reality the treatment has no effect. The outcome of the experiment could be different from what H_0 predicted just by chance. After all, unusual events do occur. For example, it is possible, although unlikely, to toss a balanced coin five times and have it turn up heads every time. In the experiment we have been considering, it is possible just by chance to select a sample of exceptional rat pups who display unusual (much less or much greater than normal) birthweights even though the prenatal alcohol exposure has no effect. In this situation, the data would lead us to reject the null hypothesis even though it is correct. This kind of mistake is called a *Type I error* (see Table 8.1), and in psychology, it is very serious mistake. A Type I error results in the investigator making a false report of a treatment effect. In the prenatal alcohol experiment, the researcher would claim that alcohol exposure alters birth weight when in fact no such effect exists.

DEFINITION   A *Type I error* consists of rejecting the null hypothesis when H_0 is actually true.

Type II errors   It also is possible for the data to be consistent with the null hypothesis even when H_0 is false. Suppose that prenatal alcohol has a small effect on birth weight, so that even with alcohol exposure our sample averages slightly below 18 grams. However, the difference between the sample and the predicted (H_0) data is too small to reject H_0 confidently. Still another possibility is that the sample of rat pups would have had exceptionally high birth weights just by chance (sampling error). Then prenatal alcohol exposure decreases birth weight, but only to the extent that the rat pups reach the expected (according to H_0) birth weight of 18 grams. In these cases, we would decide to retain the null hypothesis when in reality it is false, a *Type II error* (Table 8.1). That is, we conclude the treatment has no effect when in fact it does.

TABLE 8.1

Possible outcomes of a statistical decision

		ACTUAL SITUATION	
		No Effect, H_0 True	Effect Exists, H_0 False
Experimenter's decision	Reject H_0	Type I error	Decision correct
	Retain H_0	Decision correct	Type II error

8.2 A SUMMARY OF STATISTICAL ERRORS

Definitions:

A Type I error is rejecting a true null hypothesis.
A Type II error is failing to reject a false null hypothesis.

Interpretation:

Type I error: The researcher concludes that the treatment does have an effect when in fact there is no treatment effect.

Type II error: The researcher concludes that there is no evidence for a treatment effect when in fact the treatment does have an effect.

How does it happen?:

Type I error: By chance the sample consists of individuals with extreme scores. As a result, the sample looks different from what we would have expected according to H_0. Note that the treatment has not actually affected the individuals in the sample—they were different from average from the start of the experiment.

Type II error: Although there are several explanations for a type II error, the simplest is that the treatment effect was too small to have a noticeable effect on the sample. As a result, the sample does not appear to have been affected by the treatment. It is also possible that, just by chance, the sample was extreme to start with and in the opposite direction of the treatment effect. The treatment effect, in turn, restores the sample to the average that is expected by H_0. A treatment effect does not appear to have occurred even though it did.

Consequences:

Type I error: Because the sample data appear to demonstrate a treatment effect, the researcher may claim in a published report that the treatment has an effect. This is a false report and can have serious consequences. For one, other researchers may spend precious time and resources trying to replicate the findings to no avail. In addition, the false report creates a false data base upon which other workers develop theories and plan new experiments. In reality, they may be taking a journey down an experimental and theoretical dead end.

Type II error: In this case, the sample data do not provide sufficient evidence to say that the treatment has any effect—that is, the experiment has failed to detect the treatment effect. The researcher can interpret this finding in two different ways:

First, the researcher can conclude that the treatment probably does have an effect, but the experiment was not good enough to find it. Perhaps an improved experiment (larger sample, better measurement, more potent treatment, etc.) would be able to demonstrate the treatment effect. The consequence is that refined experiments may be capable of detecting the effect.

Second, the researcher may believe that the statistical decision is correct. Either the treatment has no effect, or the effect is too small to be important. In this case, the experiment is abandoned. Note that this interpretation can have serious consequences. It means that the researcher is giving up a line of research that might have otherwise provided important findings.

DEFINITION   In a *Type II error,* the investigator fails to reject a null hypothesis that is really false.

Most experiments in psychology are done with the hope of rejecting the null hypothesis. Remember, the null hypothesis states that the treatment has no effect on the dependent variable. However, we face a dilemma in reaching a decision about H_0. On one hand, we would like to establish that there is a treatment effect (reject H_0). But we also would like to avoid a Type I error (rejecting H_0 when it really is true).

TABLE 8.2

Possible outcomes of a jury's decision

		ACTUAL SITUATION	
		Did Not Commit Crime	Committed Crime
Jury's Verdict	Guilty	Type I error	Verdict correct
	Innocent	Verdict correct	Type II error

Adapted from *Essence of Statistics*, by G.R. Loftus and E.F. Loftus. Copyright © 1982 by Wadsworth Inc. Reprinted by permission of Brooks/Cole Publishing Company, Monterey, Calif.

A similar dilemma occurs in the "hypothesis testing" that is done in the courtroom. Just as we assume H_0 is true before we collect our data, the jury is instructed to assume that the accused person is innocent of a crime—innocent until proven guilty. A Type I error would occur if the jury decides a person is guilty when in reality that person did not commit the crime (see Table 8.2). A Type I error is serious: An innocent person would be sent to prison. Just as in scientific research, it is desirable to avoid making a Type I error. This may mean that the jury will let a guilty person off the hook, a Type II error (Table 8.2). To deal with the dilemma of testing a person's innocence while avoiding a Type I error, the judge instructs the jury that the accused individual should be found guilty only if the evidence is conclusive "beyond a reasonable doubt." This guideline will reduce the chance that the jury will commit a Type I error and punish an innocent person.

Likewise, it is important for scientists to minimize the likelihood of making a Type I error in their investigations. It is highly desirable to avoid making a false report that a treatment effect exists. This creates a false data base upon which other researchers will try to build their theories and test their hypotheses. To be sure a Type I error is avoided, the H_0 is rejected only when the sample data are very extreme, indicating it is unlikely for H_0 to be true. That is, the evidence must be so overwhelming against H_0 that the researcher can reject the null hypothesis with the confidence that the "verdict" is correct "beyond a reasonable doubt." How unlikely or overwhelming must the sample data be before the researcher can confidently reject H_0 and conclude there is an effect? The guideline is provided by the level of significance that the investigator uses in testing the hypothesis. We examine this guideline in Section 8.3.

LEARNING CHECK

1. What does the null hypothesis predict about a population?

2. Why do we evaluate (decide to reject or not reject) the null hypothesis instead of evaluating the alternative hypothesis?

3. What is a Type I error? A Type II error?

4. Is it possible to commit a Type II error when H_0 is rejected? Explain your answer.

5. Why do we state hypotheses in terms of population parameters?

ANSWERS

1. The null hypothesis predicts that the treatment will have no effect on the dependent variable for the population.

2. It is much easier to disprove a universal (population) statement than to prove one. Therefore, to find support for a treatment effect in the population, we must obtain sample data that suggest we should reject H_0. That is, we support the presence of a treatment effect when we disprove the null hypothesis.

3. A Type I error occurs when the experimenter rejects a null hypothesis that is actually true. An effect is reported when none exists. A Type II error occurs when the decision is "fail to reject H_0," but the null hypothesis is really false. One fails to report an effect that does exist.

4. No. A Type II error results from *failing to reject* a false H_0. Therefore, it cannot result from rejecting the null hypothesis.

5. We make predictions about the population because the goal of inferential statistics is to make general statements about the *population* based on the sample data.

8.3 EVALUATING HYPOTHESES

As previously noted, there is always the possibility for error in making an inference. As a result, we can never be absolutely positive that a hypothesis test has produced the correct decision. Although we cannot know for certain if our decision is right or wrong, we can know the probabilities for being right or wrong. Specifically, the hypothesis-testing procedure is structured so that a researcher can specify and control the probability of making a Type I error. By keeping this probability small, a researcher can be confident that the risk of error is very low whenever the null hypothesis is rejected.

ALPHA LEVEL: MINIMIZING THE RISK OF A TYPE I ERROR

The final decision in a hypothesis test is based on a comparison of the sample data versus the null hypothesis. Specifically, a big discrepancy between the data ($\overline{X}$) and the null hypothesis (μ) will lead us to reject the null hypothesis. To formalize this decision process, it is necessary to determine what data are expected if H_0 is true and what data are very unlikely. This is accomplished by examining the distribution of all possible outcomes if the null hypothesis is true. Usually, this is the distribution of sample means for the sample size (n) that was used in the experiment. This distribution is then separated into two parts:

1. Those sample means that are expected (high probability) if H_0 is true—that is, sample data that are consistent with the null hypothesis.

2. Those sample means that are very unlikely (low probability) if H_0 is true—that is, sample data that are very different from the null hypothesis.

In using statistical symbols and notation for hypothesis testing, we will follow APA style as outlined in the *Publication Manual of the American Psychological Association* (1994). The APA style does not use a leading zero in a decimal value for an alpha level. The expression $\alpha = .05$ is traditionally read "alpha equals point oh-five."

The *level of significance,* also called the *alpha level,* is simply a probability value that is used to define the term *very unlikely.* By convention, alpha (α) levels are very small probabilities, commonly .05 (5%), .01 (1%), or .001 (0.1%). With an alpha level of $\alpha = .05$, for example, the extreme 5% of the distribution of sample means ("very unlikely" outcomes) would be separated from the rest of the distribution (see Figure 8.2). Thus, the alpha level is used to divide the distribution of sample means into two sections: (1) sample means that are compatible with the

FIGURE 8.2

The alpha level separates the extreme and unlikely sample means from the rest of the distribution.

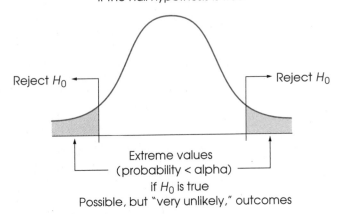

The distribution of sample means
(all possible experimental outcomes)
if the null hypothesis is true

Reject H_0 ←   → Reject H_0

Extreme values
(probability < alpha)
if H_0 is true
Possible, but "very unlikely," outcomes

null hypothesis (the center of the distribution) and (2) sample means that are significantly different from the null hypothesis (the very unlikely values in the extreme tails). Whenever we obtain sample data in the extreme tails of the distribution, we will conclude that there is a significant discrepancy between the data and the hypothesis, and we will reject the null hypothesis.

Although extreme data, as defined by alpha, are very unlikely to be obtained if H_0 is true, there is still a slim probability (equal to α) that such data will be obtained. That is, when the null hypothesis is true, it is still possible to obtain extreme data that will lead us to reject the null hypothesis. Thus, it is possible to reject a true null hypothesis and thereby commit a Type I error. However, the probability of this error occurring is determined by the alpha level. With $\alpha = .05$, for example, there is a 5% chance of obtaining extreme sample data that will lead us to reject H_0 even when H_0 is true. Thus, with $\alpha = .05$, there is a 5% risk of committing a Type I error.

DEFINITION   The *alpha level* or *level of significance*, is a probability value that defines the very unlikely sample outcomes when the null hypothesis is true. Whenever an experiment produces very unlikely data (as defined by the alpha level), we will reject the null hypothesis. Thus, the alpha level also defines the probability of a Type I error—that is, the probability of rejecting H_0 when it is actually true.

We will examine the role that alpha plays in the hypothesis-testing procedure by returning to the example of the effects of prenatal exposure to alcohol.

PROCEDURES AND STEPS   Recall that the study examines the effect of prenatal exposure to alcohol on birth weight. We will assume that the researcher's sample consists of $n = 16$ rat pups that have been exposed to alcohol prior to birth by giving the mother rats daily doses of alcohol. Also, we are assuming (based on information provided by the rat supplier) that birth weights are normally distributed with $\mu = 18$ grams and $\sigma = 4$ for the population of untreated rats (no prenatal exposure to alcohol). There are four steps to hypothesis testing: (1) State the hypotheses and select an alpha level, (2) use the alpha level to define what kind of sample data would warrant rejection of H_0, (3) analyze the sample data, and (4) make a decision about H_0. We will use these steps to assess the effect of prenatal alcohol exposure on birth weight.

STEP 1   We must state the hypotheses and select an alpha level. The null hypothesis predicts that no effect will occur. That is, even though the rats were prenatally exposed to alcohol, their mean weight will still be 18 grams. In symbols, this hypothesis is stated as follows:

$$H_0\text{: } \mu_{\text{prenatal exposure}} = 18 \text{ grams}$$

The alternative hypothesis states that the alcohol treatment will change the mean birth weight for the population. In symbols, this hypothesis would state the following:

$$H_1\text{: } \mu_{\text{prenatal exposure}} \neq 18 \text{ grams}$$

We will select an alpha level of 5% or, in terms of a proportion, $\alpha = .05$. This means that in order to reject the null hypothesis, the sample data must be extremely convincing—the data must be in the most extreme 5% of the distribution. By setting α to this level, we are limiting the probability of a Type I error to only 5%.

STEP 2   We establish criteria that define what kind of sample data would warrant rejection of the null hypothesis. We begin by looking at all the possible data that could be obtained if the null hypothesis were true. Our researcher is taking a random sample of $n = 16$. If the null hypothesis is true, it is possible to examine the distribution of all the possible sample means that could be obtained from this experiment. This distribution is the distribution of sample means based on samples of $n = 16$. It will be normal and have an expected value of $\mu = 18$ if H_0 is true. Furthermore, this distribution will have a standard error of

$$\sigma_{\overline{X}} = \frac{\sigma}{\sqrt{n}} = \frac{4}{\sqrt{16}} = \frac{4}{4} = 1$$

This distribution is shown in Figure 8.3.

If H_0 is true, we expect to obtain a sample mean near the population mean, $\mu = 18$. Extreme values in the tails of the distribution would be extremely unlikely.

We have selected the value of $\alpha = .05$ for the level of significance. This proportion is divided evenly between the two tails of the distribution (see Figure 8.3). It is very unlikely that we would obtain a sample mean from this area of the distribution if H_0 is true. The area between the tails is the middle 95% of the distribution. This area contains the most likely sample means, and it is very likely that we would obtain a sample from this region if H_0 is true.

Notice that the boundaries that separate the middle 95% from the extreme 5% (2.5% in each tail) are located at the z-score values of $+1.96$ and -1.96 (from the unit normal table in Appendix B). A z-score of 1.96 indicates that the corresponding sample mean is 1.96 standard errors away from μ. For this example, the standard error is $\sigma_{\overline{X}} = 1$, so the z-score of $+1.96$ corresponds to a sample mean of 19.96 and the z-score of -1.96 corresponds to a sample mean of 16.04. These values mark off the boundaries between the middle 95% and the extreme tails of the distribution (see Figure 8.3).

Because we are splitting $\alpha = .05$ evenly between two tails, look up .0250 in column C of the unit normal table.

FIGURE 8.3

The distribution of all the possible sample means for $n = 16$ that could be obtained if H_0 is true. The boundaries separate the middle 95% from the most extreme 5% ($\alpha = .05$).

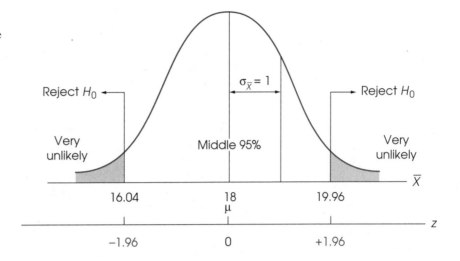

APA style does not use a leading zero in a probability value that refers to a level of significance.

If the treatment has no effect (H_0 is true), then we would expect to observe a sample mean near 18 grams. Most of the time (95% to be exact) we would expect the sample to be in the middle section of the distribution. It is very improbable that we would obtain a sample mean that is out in the extreme tails of the distribution if H_0 is true. These extreme tails, the shaded areas in Figure 8.3, are called the *critical region* of the distribution. If H_0 is true, then it would be extremely unlikely to obtain a sample in the critical region. Notice that we have defined "extremely unlikely" as meaning "having a probability less than alpha." For this example, H_0 is rejected only when the sample data are really extreme—when the probability of our sample observation is less than the alpha level ($p < .05$). In other words, H_0 is rejected when the sample data fall in the critical region. Thus, it may be helpful to consider critical regions as "regions of rejection."

DEFINITION

The *critical region* is composed of extreme sample values that are very unlikely to be obtained if the null hypothesis is true. The size of the critical region is determined by the alpha level. Sample data that fall in the critical region will warrant the rejection of the null hypothesis.

STEP 3 Now we turn our attention to the sample data. Following the prenatal treatment with alcohol, the researcher weighs the $n = 16$ rat pups immediately after they are born. Suppose that the mean weight for this sample is $\overline{X} = 13$ grams. What can we conclude about the relationship between prenatal alcohol exposure and birth weight?

STEP 4 We must make a decision about the null hypothesis. The result we obtained from the sample, $\overline{X} = 13$, lies in the critical region—specifically, the left tail (Figure 8.3). The sample is not what we expected if the null hypothesis is true. It is an extremely unlikely outcome ($p < .05$) for a true H_0. Therefore, we decide to reject the null hypothesis and conclude that prenatal alcohol exposure did have a statistically significant effect on birth weight. With this statistical decision, we are risking a Type I error. That is, we could be rejecting a true null hypothesis. It is possible that the treatment had no effect on birth weight and the rats we

Always state your conclusion in terms of the independent variable and the dependent variable for the particular experiment being examined.

A RECIPE FOR A TEST STATISTIC

THE Z-SCORE formula, like any formula, can be thought of as a recipe. If you follow the instructions and use all the right ingredients, the formula will always produce a z-score. In hypothesis-testing situations, however, you do not have all the necessary ingredients. Specifically, you do not know the value for the population mean (μ), which is one component (or ingredient) in the formula.

This situation is similar to trying to follow a cake recipe where one of the ingredients is not clearly listed. For example, a cake recipe may call for flour, but not specify exactly how much flour is needed. In this situation, you could proceed with the recipe and just add whatever amount of flour you think is appropriate. Your "hypothesis" about the amount of flour would be confirmed or rejected depending on the outcome of the cake.

If the cake was good, you could reasonably assume that your hypothesis was correct. But if the cake was horrid, you would conclude that your hypothesis was wrong.

When using the z-score in a hypothesis test, you do not know the value for μ. Therefore, you take a hypothesized value from H_0, plug it into the z-score formula, and see how it works. If your hypothesized value produces a reasonable outcome (a z-score near zero), you conclude that the hypothesis was acceptable. But if the formula produces an extreme z value (in the critical region), you conclude that the hypothesis was wrong. This recipe concept applies not only to hypothesis tests with z-scores, but also to some of the other test statistics that follow in later chapters.

---

sampled would have averaged 13 grams anyway. However, this error is very unlikely. If H_0 is true, then the probability of getting any sample, just by chance, in the critical region is less than 5%, the alpha level selected. The maximum probability of committing a Type I error is equal to alpha.

z-SCORES AND HYPOTHESIS TESTING

In the prenatal alcohol example, our decision to reject H_0 was based on the obtained sample mean of $\overline{X} = 13$, which falls within the critical region. We could have based this decision entirely on z-scores. For this example, the critical region consists of any z value greater than $+1.96$ or less than -1.96 (Figure 8.3). We can simply convert the obtained $\overline{X}$ value into a z-score to determine its location. That is, we determine whether or not it is in the critical region. For the obtained sample,

$$z = \frac{\overline{X} - \mu}{\sigma_{\overline{X}}} = \frac{13 - 18}{1} = -5.00$$

The obtained z-score is less than -1.96 and thus lies in the critical region. The statistical decision would be the same: H_0 is rejected. Notice that the z-score is being used to test a hypothesis. In this use, the z-score is often called a *test statistic* (see Box 8.3). We examine other types of test statistics that are used in hypothesis testing in later chapters.

THE STRUCTURE OF THE z-SCORE FORMULA

It is useful to define the z-score formula

$$z = \frac{\overline{X} - \mu}{\sigma_{\overline{X}}}$$

in terms of the important steps and elements of hypothesis testing. The null hypothesis is represented in the formula by μ. The value of μ that we use in the formula is the value predicted by H_0. We test H_0 by collecting sample data, which are represented by the sample mean $(\overline{X})$ in the formula. Thus, the numerator of the z formula can be rewritten as

$$\overline{X} - \mu = \text{sample data} - \text{population hypothesis}$$

You should recall that the standard error $(\sigma_{\overline{X}})$ measures the standard distance between a sample mean and the population mean. Thus, standard error measures the expected difference (due to chance) between $\overline{X}$ and μ. Now we can restate the entire z-score test statistic as

$$z = \frac{\text{sample mean} - \text{hypothesized population mean}}{\text{standard error between } \overline{X} \text{ and } \mu}$$

Notice that the difference between the sample data and the null hypothesis must be substantially larger than would be expected by chance in order to obtain a z-score that is large enough to fall in the critical region. The structure of this z-score formula will form the basis for some of the test statistics to follow in later chapters.

LEARNING CHECK

1. Define alpha.

2. If H_0 is rejected when alpha is .05, will it necessarily be rejected when alpha has been set at .01?

3. What is the critical region? How is it used?

4. Experimenter 1 typically sets alpha to .10, whereas experimenter 2 always uses an alpha level of .05. In the long run, which experimenter will make more Type I errors?

ANSWERS

1. Alpha is the risk an investigator takes of committing a Type I error. The alpha level determines the level of significance of a statistical test.

2. Not necessarily. The data may be extreme enough to warrant rejecting H_0 at the 5% level of significance, but not extreme enough for the same decision at the 1% level.

3. The critical region consists of extreme sample values that are very unlikely to be obtained (probability less than α) if the null hypothesis is true. If sample data fall in the critical region, we reject H_0.

4. Experimenter 1 is taking a greater risk (10%) of committing a Type I error.

FAILURES TO REJECT THE NULL HYPOTHESIS

Using the prenatal alcohol example again, let us suppose that our sample of $n = 16$ rat pups weighed an average of $\overline{X} = 16.5$ grams at birth. Steps 1 and 2 (stating the hypotheses and locating the critical region) remain the same. For step 3, we can compute the z-score for this sample mean. If $\overline{X} = 16.5$, then

$$z = \frac{\overline{X} - \mu}{\sigma_{\overline{X}}} = \frac{16.5 - 18}{1} = -1.50$$

In the final step, the statistical decision is made. The z-score for the obtained sample score is not in the critical region. This is the kind of outcome we would expect if

Limitations in the logic of inference make it easier to disprove a hypothesis about the population (Box 8.1).

H_0 were true. It is important to note that we have not proved that the null hypothesis is true. The sample provides only limited information about the entire population, and, in this case, we did not obtain sufficient evidence to claim that prenatal alcohol exposure does or does not have an effect on birthweight. For this reason, researchers avoid using the phrase "accepting the null hypothesis," opting instead for "failing to reject the null hypothesis." The latter phrase is more consistent with the logic of hypothesis testing. When the data are not overwhelmingly contrary to H_0, at best all we can say is that the data do not provide sufficient evidence to reject the null hypothesis.

Our decision to "fail to reject" H_0 means that we are risking a Type II error. For this example, a Type II error would mean that the prenatal alcohol exposure actually did have some effect and yet we failed to discover it. A Type II error generally is not as serious a mistake as a Type I error. The consequences of a Type II error would be that a real effect is not reported. If a researcher suspects that a Type II error has occurred, there is always the option of repeating the experiment, usually with some refinements or modifications (see Box 8.4).

α is for Type I, and β is for Type II.

Unlike Type I errors, where the exact amount of risk is specified by the alpha level (α), there is no simple way to determine the probability of a Type II error. In fact, this probability is not a single value, but rather depends on the size of the treatment effect. Although the exact probability of committing a Type II error is not easily calculated, it is identified by the Greek letter *beta*, β. We have more to say about Type II errors and β in Section 8.4.

IN THE LITERATURE:
REPORTING THE RESULTS OF THE STATISTICAL TEST

A special jargon and notational system are used in published reports of hypothesis tests. When you are reading a scientific journal, for example, you typically will not be told explicitly that the researcher evaluated the data using a *z*-score as a test statistic with an alpha level of .05. Nor will you be told that "the null hypothesis is rejected." Instead, you will see a statement such as

> The treatment with medication had a significant effect on people's depression scores, $z = 3.85$, $p < .05$.

Let us examine this statement piece by piece. First, what is meant by the term *significant?* In statistical tests, this word indicates that the result is different from what would be expected due to chance. A significant result means that the null hypothesis has been rejected. (Note that the null hypothesis for this study would state that the medication *has no effect* on depression scores for the population.) That is, the data are significant because the sample mean falls in the critical region and is not what we would have expected to obtain if H_0 were true.

DEFINITION

Findings are said to be *statistically significant* when the null hypothesis has been rejected. Thus, if results achieve statistical significance, the researcher concludes that a treatment effect occurred.

Next, what is the meaning of $z = 3.85$? The *z* indicates that a *z*-score was used as the test statistic to evaluate the sample data and that its value is 3.85. Finally,

8.4 PROBLEMS IN REPLICATION

WHAT CAN a researcher conclude when new experiments do not replicate an earlier finding in his or her own laboratory? This dilemma faced Dr. Neal E. Miller, a very prominent psychologist, who for years did outstanding research at Yale University and later Rockefeller University. He wanted to see if rats could learn to control their involuntary vital responses by operant conditioning and do so without the aid of voluntary movements. For example, if a rat is given a reward (pleasurable brain stimulation) for slowing down its heart rate, would it learn to control its heart and make it beat slower to get more reward? There was a "catch" to the experiment. The rats had to learn to control heart rate without voluntary movements (such as becoming very relaxed) that could slow the heart. So rats were temporarily paralyzed with a drug called curare. Sure enough, even though their muscles were paralyzed, the rats could still learn to control how fast their hearts would beat. Miller and the scientific community in general were excited by the findings and the possible applications for treating psychosomatic disorders. However, after reporting the results of the first few experiments, Miller and his coworkers found that they could no longer get the same effects. He could not replicate the conditioning of involuntary responses by use of reward.

Were the original findings actually nothing more than a Type I error? Or were the more recent findings a Type II error? Miller assumed that his original findings were correct and instead focused on the second question. He assumed that something had gone wrong in the laboratory during the later studies. Perhaps the newer batch of rats was somehow different from the previous animals? So Miller tried a different kind of rat, to no avail. Perhaps the paralyzing drug had gone bad and interfered with the conditioning of heart rates? He tried a new sample of curare, but nothing changed. Perhaps the reward was no longer as effective as before, or perhaps changes in the laboratory diet caused general physiological changes in the animals that prevent the effect? The list of possible reasons why the conditioning effect could not be replicated seems endless. As Miller and Dworkin (1974, p. 315) noted,

> The problem is that, whereas there often are millions of ways of doing something wrong, there may be only one or two ways of doing it right. Thus, one positive result can yield vastly more information than many negative ones.

Whenever a Type II error is suspected, a researcher will typically repeat the study with some modifications and improvements. Assuming a Type II error did occur, perhaps using the right combination of treatment conditions in the experiment (repeating the experiment the "one or two ways of doing it right") will result in evidence for an effect.

On the other hand, maybe Miller's assumptions were wrong. Perhaps the original finding was indeed a Type I error (there was no effect, but H_0 was rejected anyway). If a great many attempts are made to replicate the original finding and they all fail to find evidence for an effect, then it would be reasonable to suspect that a Type I error occurred in the first study.

what is meant by $p < .05$? This part of the statement is a conventional way of specifying the alpha level that was used for the hypothesis test. More specifically, we are being told that the result of the experiment would occur by chance with a probability (p) that is less than .05 (alpha).

In circumstances where the statistical decision is to *fail to reject H_0*, the report might state that

> There was no evidence that the medication had an effect on depression scores, $z = 1.30$, $p > .05$.

In this case, we are saying that the obtained result, $z = 1.30$, is not unusual (not in the critical region) and is relatively likely to occur by chance (the probability is greater than .05). Thus, H_0 was not rejected.

Sometimes students become confused when trying to determine whether $p >$

FIGURE 8.4

Sample means that fall in the critical region (shaded areas) have a probability *less than* alpha ($p < \alpha$). H_0 should be rejected. Sample means that do not fall in the critical region have a probability *greater than* alpha ($p > \alpha$).

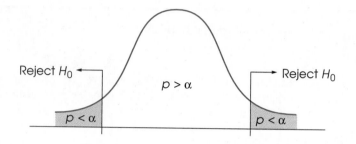

.05 or $p < .05$. Note that if H_0 were really true, then it would be extremely unlikely to obtain a test statistic (z) that falls in the critical region. Therefore, we reject H_0. Now we are defining *extremely unlikely* as meaning "having a probability less than alpha." With this idea in mind, whenever we reject H_0, we are saying that the results are unlikely, or $p < \alpha$ that we got these results just by chance. On the other hand, when we fail to reject H_0, we are stating that the results are not unusual; they are what we would expect by chance alone and $p > \alpha$. Thus, when the results are in the critical region, H_0 is rejected, and $p < \alpha$. When the data do not fall in the critical region, H_0 is not rejected, and $p > \alpha$. Figure 8.4 illustrates this point.

Finally, you should notice that in scientific reports, the researcher does not actually state that "the null hypothesis was rejected." Instead, the researcher reports that the effect of the treatment was statistically significant. Likewise, when H_0 is not rejected, one simply states that the treatment effect was not statistically significant or that there was no evidence for a treatment effect. In fact, when you read scientific reports, you will note that the terms *null hypothesis* and *alternative hypothesis* are rarely mentioned. Nevertheless, H_0 and H_1 are part of the logic of hypothesis testing even if they are not formally stated in a scientific report. Because of their central role in the process of hypothesis testing, you should be able to identify and state these hypotheses.   ❑

MORE ABOUT ALPHA—THE LEVEL OF SIGNIFICANCE

As you have seen, the alpha level for a hypothesis test serves two very important functions. First, alpha determines the risk of a Type I error. Second, alpha helps determine the boundaries for the critical region. As you might expect, these two functions interact with each other. When you lower the alpha level—for example, from .05 to .01—you reduce the risk of a Type I error. To gain this extra margin of safety, you must demand more evidence from the data before you are willing to reject H_0. This is accomplished by moving the boundaries for the critical region. With $\alpha = .05$, for example, the z-score boundaries are located at ± 1.96. For $\alpha = .01$, the boundaries move to $z = \pm 2.58$, and with $\alpha = .001$, the boundaries move all the way out to $z = \pm 3.30$ (see Figure 8.5). With $\alpha = .001$, it would take a huge difference between the data and the hypothesis to be significant. In general, as you lower the alpha level, the critical boundaries become more and more extreme, and it becomes increasingly more difficult to obtain a sample that is located in the critical region. Thus, sample data that are sufficient to reject H_0 at the .05 level of significance may not provide sufficient evidence to reject H_0 at the .01 level. If you push alpha to an extremely low level, it can become essentially impossible for an experiment ever to demonstrate a significant treatment effect.

FIGURE 8.5

The location of the critical region boundaries for three different levels of significance: $\alpha = .05$, $\alpha = .01$, and $\alpha = .001$.

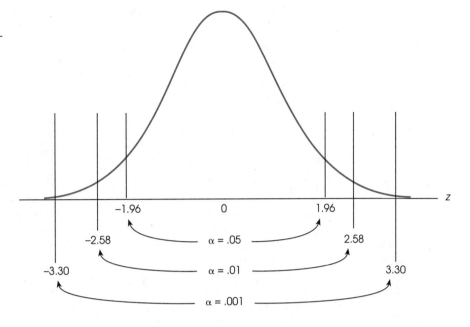

good stuff

Where do you set the critical boundaries so that your experiment has some chance of being successful and (at the same time) you can minimize your risk of a Type I error? Historically, the answer is to use an alpha level of .05. This value was first suggested in 1925 by a well-known statistician named Sir Ronald A. Fisher. Fisher noted that it is convenient to use the .05 level as a limit in judging whether a result is considered to be significant or not, and he suggested that researchers ignore all results that fail to reach this limit. Although Fisher selected $\alpha = .05$ as a personal, arbitrary standard, it has become recognized as the minimum level of significance that is acceptable for publication of research in many journals. In fact, some of the more prestigious journals require an alpha level of .01 for their published results. For most research, an alpha level of .05 is appropriate and is generally defined as *statistically significant*. The .01 level of significance is used in situations where you have special reason to fear a Type I error or where you want to make an exceptionally strong demonstration of a treatment effect. The .01 alpha level is generally defined as *highly statistically significant*. (For more information on the origins of the .05 level of significance, see the excellent short article by Cowles and Davis, 1982.)

ASSUMPTIONS FOR HYPOTHESIS TESTS WITH z-SCORES

It will become evident in later chapters that certain conditions must be present for each type of hypothesis test to be an appropriate and accurate procedure. These conditions are assumed to be satisfied when the results of a hypothesis test are interpreted. However, the decisions based on the test statistic (that is, rejecting or not rejecting H_0) may be compromised if these assumptions are not satisfied. In practice, researchers are not overly concerned with the conditions of a statistical test unless they have strong suspicions that the assumptions have been violated. Nevertheless, it is crucial to keep in mind the fundamental conditions that are associated with each type of statistical test to ensure that it is being used appropri-

8.5

INDEPENDENT OBSERVATIONS

INDEPENDENT OBSERVATIONS are a basic requirement for nearly all hypothesis tests. The critical concern is that the observation or score obtained for one individual is not influenced by the observation or score obtained for another individual. The concept of independent observations is best demonstrated by counterexample. The following two situations demonstrate circumstances where observations are *not* independent.

1. A researcher is interested in examining television preferences for children. To obtain a sample of $n = 20$ children, the researcher selects 4 children from family A, 3 children from family B, 5 children from family C, 2 children from family D, and 6 children from family E.

   It should be obvious that the researcher does *not* have 20 independent observations. Within each family, the children probably share television preference (at least they watch the same shows). Thus,

the response for each child is likely to be related to the responses of his or her siblings.

2. A researcher is interested in people's ability to judge distances. A sample of 20 people is obtained. All 20 subjects are gathered together in the same room. The researcher asks the first subject to estimate the distance between New York and Miami. The second subject is asked the same question, then the third subject, fourth subject, and so on.

   Again, the observations that the researcher obtains are not independent: The response of each subject is probably influenced by the responses of the previous subjects. For example, consistently low estimates by the first few subjects could create pressure to conform and thereby increase the probability that the following subjects would also produce low estimates.

ately. The assumptions for hypothesis tests with z-scores that involve one sample are summarized below.

Random sampling   It is assumed that the subjects used to obtain the sample data were selected randomly. Remember, we wish to generalize our findings from the sample to the population. This task is accomplished when we use sample data to test a hypothesis about the population. Therefore, the sample must be representative of the population from which it has been drawn. Random samplings helps to ensure that it is representative.

Independent observations   The values in the sample must consist of *independent* observations. In everyday terms, two observations are independent if there is no consistent, predictable relationship between the first observation and the second. More precisely, two events (or observations) are independent if the occurrence of the first event has no effect on the probability of the second event. Specific examples of independence and non-independence are examined in Box 8.5. Usually this assumption is satisfied by using a *random* sample, which also helps ensure that the sample is representative of the population and that the results can be generalized to the population.

The value of σ **is unchanged by the treatment**   The general purpose of hypothesis testing is to determine whether or not a treatment (independent variable) produces a change in the population mean. The null hypothesis, the critical region, and the z-score statistic all are concerned with the treated population. In the z-score formula, we use $\overline{X}$ from the treated sample, a hypothesized value of μ for the treated population, and a standard error that indicates how close $\overline{X}$ should be to μ. However, you may have noticed that when we compute the standard error, we use the standard deviation from the untreated population. Thus, the z-score appears to be using values from two different populations: $\overline{X}$ and μ from the treated population and σ from the untreated population. To justify this apparent contradiction, we must make an assumption. Specifically, we must assume that the value of σ is the same after treatment as it was before treatment.

Actually, this assumption is the consequence of a more general assumption that is part of many statistical procedures. This general assumption states that the effect of the treatment is to add (or subtract) a constant amount to every score in the population. You should recall that adding (or subtracting) a constant will change the mean, but will have no effect on the standard deviation. You also should note that this assumption is a theoretical ideal. In actual experiments, a treatment generally will not show a perfect and consistent additive effect.

Normal sampling distribution To evaluate hypotheses with z-scores, we have used the unit normal table to identify the critical region. This table can be used only if the distribution of sample means is normal.

LEARNING CHECK   **1.** An instructor has been teaching large sections of general psychology for the past 10 semesters. As a group, final exam scores are normally distributed with $\mu = 42$ and $\sigma = 9$. With the current class of $n = 100$ students, the instructor tries a different teaching format. Once a week, the class breaks down into smaller groups that meet with the instructor for discussion of recent lecture and reading material. At the end of the semester, the instructor notes that the mean for this section on the final exam was $\overline{X} = 46.5$. Did the teaching format have a significant effect on performance on the final exam? Test with alpha set at .05.

a. State the hypotheses.

b. Locate the critical region.

c. Compute the test statistic.

d. Make a decision regarding H_0.

e. For this example, identify the independent and the dependent variables.

ANSWER   **1. a.** H_0: $\mu_{\text{discussion groups}} = 42$; H_1: $\mu_{\text{discussion groups}} \neq 42$

b. The critical region consists of z-score values greater than $+1.96$ or less than -1.96.

c. $\sigma_{\overline{X}} = 0.9$; $z = +5.0$

d. Reject H_0, and conclude that teaching format does affect scores on the final exam.

e. The independent variable is teaching format. The dependent variable is the score on the final exam.

8.4 DIRECTIONAL (ONE-TAILED) HYPOTHESIS TESTS

The hypothesis testing procedure presented in Section 8.2 was the standard, or *two-tailed*, test format. The *two-tailed* comes from the fact that the critical region is located in both tails of the distribution. This format is by far the most widely accepted procedure for hypothesis testing. Nonetheless, there is an alternative that will be discussed in this section.

Usually a researcher begins an experiment with a specific prediction about the direction of the treatment effect. For example, a special training program is expected to *increase* student performance, or alcohol consumption is expected to *slow* reaction times. In these situations, it is possible to state the statistical hypotheses in a manner that incorporates the directional prediction into the statement of H_0 and H_1. The result is a directional test, or what commonly is called a *one-tailed test*.

DEFINITION   In a *directional hypothesis test*, or a *one-tailed test*, the statistical hypotheses (H_0 and H_1) specify either an increase or a decrease in the population mean score.

Suppose, for example, that a researcher is using a sample of $n = 16$ laboratory rats to examine the effect of a new diet drug. It is known that under regular circumstances these rats eat an average of 10 grams of food each day. The distribution of food consumption is normal with $\sigma = 4$. The expected effect of the drug is to reduce food consumption. The purpose of the experiment is to determine whether or not the drug really works.

THE HYPOTHESES FOR A DIRECTIONAL TEST   Because a specific direction is expected for the treatment effect, it is possible for the researcher to perform a directional test. The first step (and the most critical step) is to state the statistical hypotheses. Remember that the null hypothesis states that there is no treatment effect and that the alternative hypothesis says that there is an effect. For directional tests, it is easier to begin with the alternative hypothesis. In words, this hypothesis says that with the drug the mean food consumption is *less than* 10 grams per day; that is, the drug does reduce food consumption. In symbols, H_1 would say the following:

H_1: $\mu_{\text{with drug}} < 10$ (mean food consumption is reduced)

The null hypothesis states that the treatment did not work (the opposite of H_1). In this case, H_0 states that the drug does not reduce food consumption. That is, even with the drug, the rats still will eat at least 10 grams per day. In symbols, H_0 would say the following:

H_0: $\mu_{\text{with drug}} \geq 10$ (the mean is at least 10 grams per day)

For a one-tailed test, how do you know which tail to shade for the critical region? You can get a clue by looking at the alternative hypothesis. If H_1 states that μ is less than ($<$) some value, then you shade the left tail (the left side of the distribution has scores below the mean). On the other hand, if H_1 states that μ is greater than ($>$) some value, then you place the entire critical region in the right tail.

FIGURE 8.6

The distribution of sample means for $n = 16$ if H_0 is true. The null hypothesis states that the diet pill has no effect, so the population mean will be $\mu = 10$ or larger.

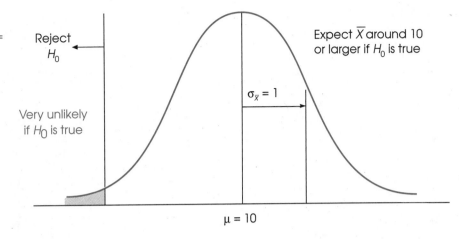

Reject
H_0

Very unlikely
if H_0 is true

$\sigma_{\bar{x}} = 1$

Expect $\bar{X}$ around 10
or larger if H_0 is true

$\mu = 10$

THE CRITICAL REGION FOR DIRECTIONAL TESTS

The critical region is determined by sample values that are very unlikely if the null hypothesis is true; that is, sample values that refute H_0 and provide evidence that the treatment really does work. In this example, the treatment is intended to reduce food consumption. Therefore, only sample values that are substantially less than $\mu = 10$ would indicate that the treatment worked and thereby lead to rejecting H_0. Thus, the critical region is located entirely in one tail of the distribution (see Figure 8.6). This is why the directional test commonly is called one-tailed.

A complete example of a one-tailed test is presented next.

EXAMPLE 8.1

phonetic instruction

A researcher would like to assess the "miraculous" claims of improvement made in a TV advertisement about a phonetic reading instruction package. It is known that the scores on a standardized reading test for nine-year-olds form a normal distribution with $\mu = 45$ and $\sigma = 10$. A random sample of $n = 25$ eight-year olds is given the reading package for a year, and the manufacturer's instructions are followed by their parents. At age nine, this sample is given the standardized reading test. The mean score for the sample is $\bar{X} = 48.6$.

STEP 1

State the hypotheses. Because the researcher wants to assess the claims of improvement, it is possible to do a directional test. It usually is easier to begin with H_1, the alternative hypothesis, which states that the reading package does increase reading scores. In symbols, this hypothesized effect is

$$H_1: \mu > 45 \quad \text{(there is improvement in reading scores)}$$

Simply because you can do a directional test does not mean that you must use a directional test. A two-tailed test is always acceptable.

The null hypothesis states that the treatment (the reading package) does not increase test scores. In symbols,

$$H_0: \mu \leq 45 \quad \text{(there is no improvement)}$$

Alpha will be set at the .05 level of significance for one tail.

FIGURE 8.7

Critical region for Example 8.1.

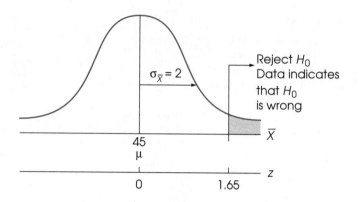

STEP 2   *Locate the critical region.* To find the critical region, we look at all possible sample means for $n = 25$ that could be obtained if H_0 were true. This is the distribution of sample means. It will be normal (because the population is normal), it will have a standard error of $\sigma_{\overline{X}} = 10/\sqrt{25} = 2$, and it will have a mean of $\mu = 45$ if the null hypothesis is true. The distribution is shown in Figure 8.7.

If H_0 is true and the reading package does not increase reading scores, we would expect the sample to average around 45 or less on the test. Only sample means that are large would provide evidence that H_0 is wrong and that the reading package does increase test scores. With $\alpha = .05$, the most likely 95% of the distribution is separated from the most unlikely 5% by a z-score of $z = +1.65$ (see Figure 8.7).

STEP 3   *Analyze the sample data.* The mean for the sample is $\overline{X} = 48.6$. This value corresponds to a z-score of

$$z = \frac{\overline{X} - \mu}{\sigma_{\overline{X}}} = \frac{48.6 - 45}{2} = \frac{3.6}{2} = +1.80$$

STEP 4   *Make a statistical decision.* A z-score of $z = +1.80$ indicates that our sample mean is in the critical region. This is a very unlikely outcome if H_0 is true, so the statistical decision is to reject H_0. The conclusion is that the reading package improved reading test scores.

COMPARISON OF ONE-TAILED VERSUS TWO-TAILED TESTS

The general goal of hypothesis testing is to determine whether or not a particular treatment has any effect on a population. The test is performed by selecting a sample, administering the treatment to the sample, and then comparing the result with the original population. If the treated sample is noticeably different from the original population, then we conclude that the treatment has an effect, and we reject H_0. On the other hand, if the treated sample is still similar to the original population, then we conclude that there is no evidence for a treatment effect, and we fail to reject H_0. A critical factor in this decision is the *size of the difference* between the treated sample and the original population. A large difference is evidence that the treatment worked; a small difference is not sufficient to say that the treatment has any effect.

A potential problem with one-tailed tests is in the criteria they use for rejecting H_0. A one-tailed test allows you to reject the null hypothesis when the difference between the sample and the population is relatively small, provided the difference is in the specified direction. A two-tailed test, on the other hand, requires a relatively large difference independent of direction. This point is illustrated in the following example.

EXAMPLE 8.2

Consider again the experiment examining the reading package and test scores (see Example 8.1). If we had used a standard two-tailed test, then the hypotheses would have been

H_0: $\mu = 45$ (no treatment effect)

H_1: $\mu \neq 45$ (reading package does affect test scores)

With $\alpha = .05$, the critical region would consist of any z-score beyond the $z = \pm 1.96$ boundaries.

If we obtained the same sample data, $\overline{X} = 48.6$, which corresponds to a z-score of $z = 1.80$, our statistical decision would be "fail to reject H_0."

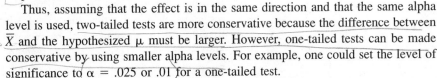

Notice that with the two-tailed test (Example 8.2), the difference between the data ($\overline{X} = 48.6$) and the hypothesis ($\mu = 45$) is not big enough to conclude that the hypothesis is wrong. In this case, we are saying that the data do not provide sufficient evidence to justify rejecting H_0. However, with the one-tailed test (Example 8.1), the same data led us to reject H_0.

Thus, assuming that the effect is in the same direction and that the same alpha level is used, two-tailed tests are more conservative because the difference between $\overline{X}$ and the hypothesized μ must be larger. However, one-tailed tests can be made conservative by using smaller alpha levels. For example, one could set the level of significance to $\alpha = .025$ or .01 for a one-tailed test.

There should be some justification for using a one-tailed test prior to doing the study. That is, a theory or hypothesis might predict directional effects, or previous studies might indicate the direction you should expect. However, you should note that one-tailed tests can be misused, or even abused. For example, a researcher might set alpha to .05 for a two-tailed test. The critical z-scores are ± 1.96, but the z-score for the sample mean is 1.90. The null hypothesis would not be rejected. The researcher might try to remedy the outcome by switching to a one-tailed test with alpha still set at the .05 level. With a critical z-score now at 1.65, H_0 would be rejected. One problem, among others, with this approach is that it lacks objectivity. Of course, this kind of abuse can occur for two-tailed tests in situations where the alpha level is raised above what is commonly acceptable just so H_0 can be rejected. Remember, while we would like to find evidence for an effect (reject H_0), we also want to *reduce the likelihood* of a Type I error. Two tailed tests should be used in situations where competing theories predict opposite effects. Finally, it is always acceptable to use a two-tailed test, even in situations where a directional hypothesis could have been made. One could argue that there is also some chance that the unexpected might happen.

LEARNING CHECK

1. A researcher predicts that a treatment will lower scores. If this researcher uses a one-tailed test, will the critical region be in the right- or left-hand tail of the distribution?

2. A psychologist is examining the effects of early sensory deprivation on the development of perceptual discrimination. A sample of $n = 9$ newborn kittens is obtained. These kittens are raised in a completely dark environment for four weeks, after which they receive normal visual stimulation. At age six months, the kittens are tested on a visual discrimination task. The average score for this sample is $\overline{X} = 32$. It is known that under normal circumstances cats score an average of $\mu = 40$ on this task. The distribution of scores is normal with $\sigma = 12$. The researcher is predicting that the early sensory deprivation will reduce the kittens' performance on the discrimination task. Use a one-tailed test with $\alpha = .01$ to test this hypothesis.

ANSWERS

1. The left-hand tail.

2. The hypotheses are H_0: $\mu \geq 40$ and H_1: $\mu < 40$. The critical region is determined by z-scores less than -2.33. The z-score for these sample data is $z = -2.00$. Fail to reject H_0.

8.5 STATISTICAL POWER

The purpose of a hypothesis test is to determine whether or not a particular treatment has an effect. The null hypothesis states that there is no effect, and the researcher is hoping that the sample data will provide evidence to reject this hypothesis. In previous sections, we saw that the hypothesis-testing procedure always involves some risk of reaching a wrong conclusion. Specifically, a researcher may commit a Type I error by rejecting a true null hypothesis. This risk is minimized by selecting an alpha level (usually .05 or .01) that determines the maximum probability of committing a Type I error. You should also recall that every hypothesis test has the potential for resulting in a Type II error, failing to reject a false null hypothesis. In simple terms, a Type II error means that the treatment really does have an effect, but the hypothesis test failed to discover it.

 In this section, we reverse our perspective on hypothesis testing. Rather than examining the potential for making an error, we examine the probability of reaching the correct decision. Remember that the researcher's goal is to demonstrate that the experimental treatment actually does have an effect. This is the purpose of conducting the experiment in the first place. If the researcher is correct and the treatment really does have an effect, then what is the probability that the hypothesis test will correctly identify it? This is a question concerning the *power* of a statistical test.

DEFINITION

The *power* of a statistical test is the probability that the test will correctly reject a false null hypothesis.

As the definition implies, the more powerful a statistical test is, the more readily it will detect a treatment effect when one really exists (correctly rejecting H_0). It should be clear that the concepts of power and Type II error are closely related. *When a treatment effect exists,* the hypothesis test will have one of two results:

1. It can fail to discover the existing treatment effect (a Type II error).

2. It can correctly detect the presence of a treatment effect (rejecting a false null hypothesis).

We already have noted that the probability of a Type II error is identified by the symbol beta, β. Thus, the probability of correctly rejecting a false H_0 must be $1 - \beta$. If, for example, a hypothesis test has a probability of .20 (20% chance) of failing to detect a treatment effect (Type II error), then it must have a probability of .80 (80% chance) of successfully detecting it. Thus, the power of a statistical test is determined by

Remember, the probabilities for all events must add up to 1.00 (100%).

$$\text{power} = p(\text{reject a false } H_0) = 1 - \beta \qquad (8.1)$$

POWER AND THE SIZE OF THE TREATMENT EFFECT

Although we have defined power, we have not attempted to compute a value for this probability. The difficulty in specifying this value comes from the fact that power depends on the size of the treatment effect. Therefore, it does not have a single value for every hypothesis test. When a treatment has a large effect, it will be easy to detect this effect, and power will be high. On the other hand, when the treatment effect is very small, it will be difficult to detect, and power will be low. Thus, rather than talking about power as a single value, we must examine the different values of power associated with different magnitudes of treatment effect. We can illustrate this in a set of graphs that represent different treatment effects, but, first, one more reminder is necessary. Remember, the null hypothesis is rejected whenever sample data are in the critical region. With this in mind, we can restate the definition of power as follows:

DEFINITION

Power is the probability of obtaining sample data in the critical region when the null hypothesis is false.

Note: Because "data in the critical region" is equivalent to "rejecting the null hypothesis," this definition is equivalent to our original definition of power.

Consider the following situation. A researcher is interested in whether caffeine affects reaction time. It is known that for untreated subjects, reaction times are normally distributed with a mean of $\mu = 200$ milliseconds. Note that the null hypothesis would state

H_0: $\mu = 200$ (Even with caffeine, the average reaction time is still 200 milliseconds.)

Let's assume that caffeine actually has an effect and that the size of the treatment effect is 20 points (subjects receiving caffeine have an average reaction time 20 milliseconds lower). Figure 8.8 shows two distributions of sample means:

1. A null distribution (on the right, Figure 8.8) that corresponds to a situation in which H_0 is true and the treatment has no effect ($\mu = 200$).

FIGURE 8.8

Two distributions of sample means: when H_0 is true (null distribution, right) and when there is a 20-point treatment effect (treatment distribution, left). Statistical power is determined by the proportion of the shaded area, $1 - \beta$, in the treatment distribution.

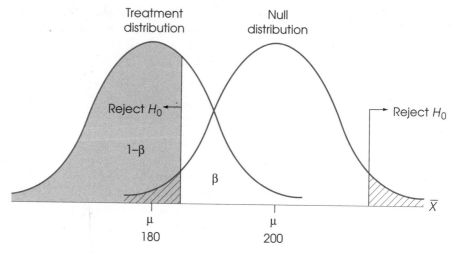

2. A treatment distribution (on the left, Figure 8.8) that reflects the actual effect of the treatment (an average reduction in reaction time of 20 points).

Remember, it is the null hypothesis (H_0: $\mu = 200$) that is being tested. Therefore, the critical region is determined by extreme, unlikely sample means in the tails of the null distribution. The treatment distribution (left) shows all the sample means that are possible, given a 20-point treatment effect. Notice that many of these sample means (shaded area) fall beyond the boundary for the critical region of the null distribution. Obtaining a sample mean from this shaded area would result in the researcher correctly rejecting H_0. The proportion for this shaded area would indicate the probability of correctly rejecting a false null hypothesis—that is, the amount of power. Thus, the shaded portion of the treatment distribution represents $1 - \beta$. However, not all the sample means in the treatment distribution fall beyond the cutoff for the critical region (unshaded part of treatment distribution). Obtaining one of these sample means would result in the researcher failing to reject a false H_0, which is a Type II error. The proportion of area in this part of the treatment distribution provides the value for β, the probability of committing a Type II error.

Now let's assume that the treatment effect is only 10 points. What happens to statistical power? Figure 8.9 illustrates the null and treatment distributions, showing an average reaction time reduction of 10 points ($\mu = 190$ for subjects who receive caffeine). Notice that the treatment distribution for a 10-point effect is closer to the null distribution (Figure 8.9), compared with the situation when the treatment produces a 20-point effect (Figure 8.8). Thus, fewer sample means from the treatment distribution fall beyond the boundary of the critical region. The shaded area is smaller, and statistical power, $1 - \beta$, also is diminished (Figure 8.9). On the other hand, the probability of a Type II error, β, is now larger, as shown by the larger unshaded area of the treatment distribution (Figure 8.9).

Thus, when an experiment produces a large treatment effect, statistical power is large (you are more likely to correctly identify that effect). Alternatively, when an experiment produces a small treatment effect, statistical power is small (you are less likely to detect the effect).

FIGURE 8.9

Two distributions of sample means: when H_0 is true (null distribution, right) and when there is a 10-point treatment effect (treatment distribution, left). When the treatment effect is smaller, statistical power is also smaller (shaded area, $1 - \beta$).

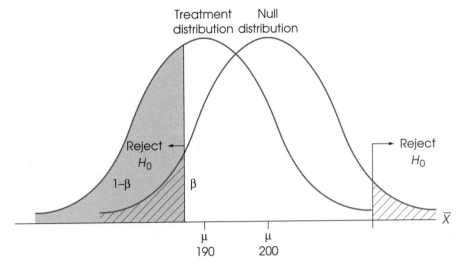

FACTORS AFFECTING POWER   As we have seen, the size of the treatment effect is one factor that influences statistical power. Although it is an important factor, a researcher typically will not know before a study is done how much of a treatment effect, if any, exists. There are, however, three factors that affect power that are under the direct control of the experimenter. These factors are the alpha level, the type of test (one- versus two-tailed), and the sample size.

Alpha level   Reducing the alpha level will reduce the power of a statistical test. For example, reducing α from .05 to .01 moves the critical region boundaries from $z = \pm 1.96$ to $z = \pm 2.58$. The result is that the smaller alpha level makes it harder to reject the null hypothesis. Thus, you are less likely to reject a true H_0 (a Type I error), but you also are less likely to reject a false H_0 (power). Figure 8.10 illustrates the role of alpha level in determining power using the caffeine and reaction time example. Figure 8.10(a) shows the treatment and null distributions for a 20-point effect with an alpha level of $\alpha = .05$, Figure 8.10(b) depicts the same situation, except that the alpha level is now $\alpha = .01$. Note that when alpha is .05, there are more sample means in the treatment distribution that fall beyond the boundary of the critical region. This area is shaded, and its proportion of the total distribution is $1 - \beta$, or the amount of power. When the alpha level is smaller [Figure 8.10(b)], this shaded area is smaller, indicating lower power.

One-tailed versus two-tailed tests   You should recall that one-tailed tests make it easier to reject the null hypothesis. Thus, one-tailed tests should increase power. Again, let's consider the experiment assessing the effects of caffeine on reaction time. With $\alpha = .05$, for example, the critical boundary for a one-tailed test is located at $z = -1.65$. For a two-tailed test, the boundaries would be at $z = \pm 1.96$. Therefore, the critical region for the one-tailed test is larger, and its critical boundary is not as extreme. A greater portion of the sample means from the treatment distribution will fall beyond this boundary. Statistical power is greater.

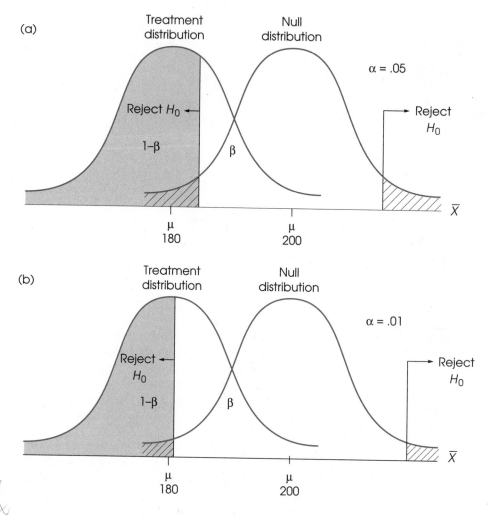

FIGURE 8.10

Statistical power (a) when the level of significance is $\alpha = .05$ and (b) when it is $\alpha = .01$. A 20-point treatment effect is assumed in both cases. The proportion of shaded area, $1 - \beta$, is smaller in (b), indicating lower statistical power.

Sample size   In general, the larger the sample is, the better it will represent the population. If there actually is a treatment effect in the population, you are more likely to find it with a large sample than with a small sample. Thus, the power of a test can be increased by using larger samples. Once again, we will look at the experiment on caffeine and reaction time. For the untreated population, $\mu = 200$. We will assume that the size of the treatment effect is 20 points. Let's compare two situations: one in which a sample of $n = 25$ subjects is used and a second study where $n = 100$.

Figure 8.11 shows the set of distributions for samples of $n = 25$ and $n = 100$. The standard error for these distributions will be larger when $n = 25$ and smaller when $n = 100$. Note that when the standard error is small (when $n = 100$), nearly all the sample means in the treatment distribution fall beyond the critical region boundary [Figure 8.11(b)]. The proportion for this shaded area is nearly 100% and

Remember, $\sigma_{\bar{x}} = \sigma/\sqrt{n}$.

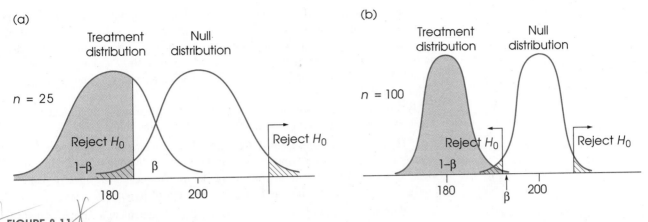

FIGURE 8.11

Statistical power (a) when the sample size is $n = 25$ and (b) when it is $n = 100$. The treatment effect is 20 points in both figures. The proportion of the shaded area is greater in (b), reflecting greater power for larger samples.

the statistical power is extremely high (you are almost guaranteed to detect the treatment effect). On the other hand, when sample size is small and standard error is large, a small proportion of the sample means in the treatment distribution falls beyond the boundary of the critical region. Therefore, there is less power with the smaller sample.

LEARNING CHECK

1. For a particular hypothesis test, $1 - \beta$, equals .50 for a 5-point treatment effect. Will the power be greater or lesser for a 10-point treatment effect?

2. As the power of a test increases, what happens to the probability of a Type II error?

3. If a researcher uses $\alpha = .01$ rather than $\alpha = .05$, then power will increase. (True or false?)

4. What is the effect of increasing sample size on power?

ANSWERS

1. The hypothesis test is more likely to detect a 10-point effect, so power will be greater.

2. As power increases, the probability of a Type II error decreases.

3. False. 4. Power increases as sample size gets larger.

8.6 THE GENERAL ELEMENTS OF HYPOTHESIS TESTING: A REVIEW

The z-score hypothesis test presented in this chapter is one specific example of the general process of hypothesis testing. In later chapters, we will examine many other hypothesis tests. Although the details of the hypothesis test will vary from one situation to another, all of the different tests use the same basic logic and consist of the same elements. In this section, we will present a generic hypothesis test that outlines the basic elements and logic common to all tests. The better you understand the general process of a hypothesis test, the better you will understand inferential statistics.

Hypothesis tests consist of five basic elements organized in a logical pattern. The elements and their relationships to each other are as follows:

1. Hypothesized Population Parameter. The first step in a hypothesis test is to state a null hypothesis. You will notice that the null hypothesis typically provides a specific value for an unknown population parameter. The specific value predicted by the null hypothesis is the first element of hypothesis testing.

2. Sample Statistic. The sample data are used to calculate a sample statistic that corresponds to the hypothesized population parameter. If the null hypothesis specifies a value for the population mean, then the appropriate sample statistic would be the sample mean. Similarly, if the hypothesis specified a value for the population variance, then the appropriate statistic would be the sample variance.

3. Estimate of Error. To evaluate our findings, we must know what types of sample data are likely to occur simply due to chance. Typically, a measure of standard error is used to provide this information. The general purpose of standard error is to provide a measure of how much difference is expected between a sample statistic and the corresponding population parameter. You should remember that samples (statistics) are not expected to provide a perfectly accurate picture of populations (parameters). There always will be some error or discrepancy between a statistic and a parameter; this is the concept of sampling error. The standard error tells how much error is expected just by chance.

In Chapter 7, we introduced the standard error of $\overline{X}$. This is the first specific example of the general concept of standard error, and it provides a measure of how much error is expected between a sample mean (statistic) and the corresponding population mean (parameter). In later chapters, you will encounter other examples of standard error, each of which measures the standard distance (expected by chance) between a specific statistic and its corresponding parameter. Although the exact formula for standard error will change from one situation to another, you should recall that standard error is basically determined by two factors:

a. The variability of the scores. Standard error is directly related to the variability of the scores: The larger the variability, the larger the standard error.

b. The size of the sample. Standard error is inversely related to sample size: The larger the sample, the smaller the standard error.

4. Test Statistic. In this chapter, the test statistic is a *z*-score:

$$z = \frac{\overline{X} - \mu}{\sigma_{\overline{X}}}$$

This *z*-score statistic provides a model for other test statistics that will follow. In particular, a test statistic typically forms a *ratio*. The numerator of the ratio is simply the obtained difference between the sample statistic and the hypothesized parameter. The denominator of the ratio is the standard error measuring how much difference is expected by chance. Thus, the generic form of a test statistic is

$$\text{test statistic} = \frac{\text{obtained difference}}{\text{difference expected by chance}}$$

In general, the purpose of a test statistic is to determine whether or not the result of an experiment (the obtained difference) is more than expected by chance alone. Thus, a test statistic that has a value greater than 1.00 indicates that the obtained result (numerator) is greater than chance (denominator). In addition, the test statistic provides a measure of how much greater than chance. A value of 3.00, for example, indicates that the obtained difference is three times greater than would be expected by chance.

5. Alpha Level. The final element in a hypothesis test is the alpha level, or level of significance. The alpha level provides a criterion for interpreting the test statistic. As we noted, a test statistic greater than 1.00 indicates that the obtained result is greater than expected by chance. However, researchers demand that the likelihood of a result be not simply "more than chance," but *significantly more than chance.* The alpha level provides a criterion for "significance."

Earlier in this chapter (page 240), we noted that when a significant result is reported in the literature, it always is accompanied by a *p* value; for example, *p* < .05 means that there is less than a 5% probability that the result occurred by chance. In general, a *significant* result means that the researcher is very confident that the result is not simply due to chance. A result that is significant at the .05 (5%) level, for example, means that the researcher is 95% confident that the obtained difference is greater than what one would expect by chance alone. Similarly, the .01 (1%) level indicates 99% confidence, and the .001 (.1%) level indicates 99.9% confidence.

To gain more confidence (rejecting H_0 with a smaller alpha), the results must demonstrate a larger difference (treatment effect). As you know, the alpha level is used to obtain a critical value for the test statistic. With the *z*-score test, for example, $\alpha = .05$ produces a critical value of ± 1.96. In general, the alpha level determines how big the test statistic ratio must be before you can claim a *significant* result. The following values are *not* intended to be precise, but rather they should provide you with a *rough idea* of how the alpha level is related to the test statistic:

a. For $\alpha = .05$, the criterion for significance is a test statistic ratio of at least 2.00. That is, the obtained difference (numerator) must be at least *twice as big* as chance (denominator). *Note:* The exact value for the *z*-score test is 1.96.

b. For $\alpha = .01$, the criterion for significance is a test statistic ratio of at least 2.50. That is, the obtained difference must be at least *two and one-half times bigger* than chance. *Note:* The exact value for the *z*-score test is 2.58.

c. For $\alpha = .001$, the criterion for significance is a test statistic ratio of at least 3.00. That is, the obtained difference must be at least *three times bigger* than chance. *Note:* The exact value for the *z*-score test is 3.30.

Again, these values are *approximate* and provide a rough "rule of thumb." You always will need to consult a statistical table (for example, the unit normal table) to determine the exact critical values for your hypothesis test. Finally, we remind you to watch for the five basic elements described in this section as you encounter different examples of hypothesis testing throughout the rest of the book.

SUMMARY

1. Hypothesis testing is an inferential procedure for using the limited data from a sample to draw a general conclusion about a population. It begins with hypothesizing values for the mean of an unknown population, generally a population that has received a treatment (Figure 8.1).

2. The null hypothesis (H_0) states that the treatment has not changed the mean. That is, it is the same as the mean for a known and untreated population. At this stage, we also select an alpha level, usually $\alpha = .05$ or $.01$, which sets the risk of committing a Type I error. Alpha determines the level of significance of a statistical test.

3. The second step involves locating the critical region. We examine all the possible experimental outcomes if the null hypothesis is true and then identify the most unlikely values. We define "unlikely according to H_0" as the outcomes with a probability less than alpha. Thus, the selected alpha level determines the critical z-scores that are associated with the critical region. Sample data that produce a z-score that falls within the critical region would imply that H_0 is not tenable.

4. The sample data are collected. Specifically, the sample mean $\overline{X}$ is used to test a hypothesis about μ. To determine how unlikely the obtained sample mean is, we must locate it within the distribution of sample means. This is accomplished by computing a z-score for $\overline{X}$:

$$z = \frac{\overline{X} - \mu}{\sigma_{\overline{X}}}$$

When a z-score is used in the test of a hypothesis, it is called a test statistic.

5. The z-score equation can be expressed as

$$z = \frac{\text{sample mean} - \text{hypothesized population mean}}{\text{standard error between } \overline{X} \text{ and } \mu}$$

That is, the difference between the sample mean and the hypothesized population mean (according to H_0) is compared to (divided by) the amount of error we would expect between $\overline{X}$ and μ.

6. In the fourth step, we compare the obtained data to the set of possible results that were outlined in the second step. That is, if the obtained z-score falls in the critical region, we reject H_0 because it is very unlikely that these data would be obtained if H_0 were true. We would conclude that a treatment effect occurred. If the data are not in the critical region, then there is not sufficient evidence to reject H_0. The statistical decision is "fail to reject H_0."

We conclude that we failed to find sufficient evidence for an effect.

7. Whatever decision is reached in a hypothesis test, there is always a risk of making the incorrect decision. There are two types of errors that can be committed.

   A Type I error is defined as rejecting a true H_0. This is a serious error because it results in falsely reporting a treatment effect. The risk of a Type I error is determined by the alpha level and, therefore, is under the experimenter's control.

   A Type II error is defined as failing to reject a false H_0. In this case, the experiment fails to report an effect that actually occurred. The probability of a Type II error cannot be specified as a single value and depends in part on the size of the treatment effect. It is identified by the symbol β (beta).

8. When a researcher predicts that a treatment effect will be in a particular direction (increase or decrease), it is possible to do a directional or one-tailed test. The first step in this procedure is to state the alternative hypothesis (H_1). This hypothesis states that the treatment works and, for directional tests, specifies the direction of the predicted treatment effect. The null hypothesis is the opposite of H_1. To locate the critical region, you must identify the kind of experimental outcome that refutes the null hypothesis and demonstrates that the treatment works. These outcomes will be located entirely in one tail of the distribution. The entire critical region (5% or 1%, depending on α) will be in one tail.

9. Directional tests should be used with caution because they may allow the rejection of H_0 when the experimental evidence is relatively weak. Even though a researcher may have a specific directional prediction for an experiment, it is never inappropriate to use a non-directional (two-tailed) test.

10. The power of a hypothesis test is defined as the probability that the test will correctly reject the null hypothesis. Power is identified as

$$\text{power} = 1 - \beta$$

where β is the probability of a Type II error.

11. To illustrate the power for a hypothesis test, you must first identify the treatment and null distributions. Also, you must specify the magnitude of the treatment effect. Next, you locate the critical region in the null distribution. The power of the hypothesis test is the portion of the treatment distribution that is located beyond the boundary (critical value) of the critical region.

12. As the size of the treatment effect increases, statistical power increases. Also, power is influenced by several factors that can be controlled by the experimenter:

a. Increasing the alpha level will increase power.

b. A one-tailed test will have greater power than a two-tailed test.

c. A large sample will result in more power than a small sample.

KEY TERMS

hypothesis testing	Type II error	critical region	directional test
null hypothesis	level of significance	test statistic	one-tailed test
alternative hypothesis	alpha level	beta	power
Type I error			

FOCUS ON PROBLEM SOLVING

1. Hypothesis testing involves a set of logical procedures and rules that enable us to make general statements about a population when all we have are sample data. This logic is reflected in the four steps that have been used throughout this chapter. Hypothesis-testing problems will become easier to tackle when you learn to follow the steps.

STEP 1 State the hypotheses, and set the alpha level.

STEP 2 Locate the critical region.

STEP 3 Compute the z-score for the sample statistic.

STEP 4 Make a decision about H_0 based on the result of step 3.

A nice benefit of mastering these steps is that all hypothesis tests that will follow use the same basic logic outlined in this chapter.

2. Students often ask, "What alpha level should I use?" Or a student may ask, "Why is an alpha of .05 used?" as opposed to something else. There is no single correct answer to either of these questions. Keep in mind the idea of setting an alpha level in the first place: *to reduce the risk of committing a Type I error.* Therefore, you would not want to set α to something like .20. In that case, you would be taking a 20% risk of committing a Type I error—reporting an effect when one actually does not exist. Most researchers would find this level of risk unacceptable. Instead, researchers generally agree to the convention that $\alpha = .05$ is the greatest risk one should take in making a Type I error. Thus, the .05 level of significance is frequently used and has become the "standard" alpha level. However, some researchers prefer to take even less risk and use alpha levels of .01 and smaller.

3. Take time to consider the implications of your decision about the null hypothesis. The null hypothesis states that there is no effect. Therefore, if your decision is to reject H_0, you should conclude that the sample data provide evidence for a treatment effect. However, it is an entirely different matter if your decision is to fail to reject H_0. Remember that when you fail to reject the null hypothesis, the results are inconclusive. It is impossible to *prove* that H_0 is correct; therefore, you cannot state with

certainty that "there is no effect" when H_0 is not rejected. At best, all you can state is that "there is insufficient evidence for an effect" (see Box 8.1).

4. It is very important that you understand the structure of the z-score formula (page 239). It will help you understand many of the other hypothesis tests that will be covered later.

5. When you are doing a directional hypothesis test, read the problem carefully, and watch for key words (such as increase or decrease, raise or lower, and more or less) that tell you which direction the researcher is predicting. The predicted direction will determine the alternative hypothesis (H_1) and the critical region. For example, if a treatment is expected to *increase* scores, H_1 would contain a *greater than* symbol, and the critical region would be in the tail associated with high scores.

DEMONSTRATION 8.1

HYPOTHESIS TEST WITH z

A researcher begins with a known population—in this case, scores on a standardized test that are normally distributed with $\mu = 65$ and $\sigma = 15$. The researcher suspects that special training in reading skills will produce a change in the scores for the individuals in the population. Because it is not feasible to administer the treatment (the special training) to everyone in the population, a sample of $n = 25$ individuals is selected, and the treatment is given to this sample. Following treatment, the average score for this sample is $\overline{X} = 70$. Is there evidence that the training has an effect on test scores?

STEP 1 State the hypothesis and select an alpha level.

Remember, the goal of hypothesis testing is to use sample data to make general conclusions about a population. The hypothesis always concerns an unknown population. For this demonstration, the researcher does not know what would happen if the entire population were given the treatment. Nevertheless, it is possible to make hypotheses about the treated population.

Specifically, the null hypothesis says that the treatment has no effect. According to H_0, the unknown population (after treatment) is identical to the original population (before treatment). In symbols,

$$H_0: \mu = 65 \quad \text{(After special training, the mean is still 65.)}$$

The alternative hypothesis states that the treatment does have an effect that causes a change in the population mean. In symbols,

$$H_1: \mu \neq 65 \quad \text{(After special training, the mean is different from 65.)}$$

At this time, you also select the alpha level. Traditionally, α is set at .05 or .01. If there is particular concern about a Type I Error, or if a researcher desires to present overwhelming evidence for a treatment effect, a smaller alpha level can be used (such as $\alpha = .001$). For this demonstration, we will set alpha to .05. Thus, we are taking a 5% risk of committing a Type I error.

STEP 2 Locate the critical region.

You should recall that the critical region is defined as the set of outcomes that is

FIGURE 8.12

The critical region for Demonstration 8.1 consists of the extreme tails with boundaries of $z = -1.96$ and $z = +1.96$.

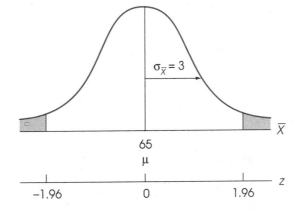

$\sigma_{\bar{X}} = 3$

65
μ

$\bar{X}$

-1.96   0   1.96 z

very unlikely to be obtained if the null hypothesis is true. Therefore, obtaining sample data from this region would lead us to reject the null hypothesis and conclude there is an effect. Remember, the critical region is a region of rejection.

We begin by looking at all possible outcomes that could be obtained and then use the alpha level to determine the outcomes that are unlikely. For this demonstration, we look at the distribution of sample means for samples of $n = 25$ — that is, all possible sample means that could be obtained if H_0 were true. The distribution of sample means will be normal because the original population is normal. It will have an expected value of $\mu = 65$ and a standard error of

$$\sigma_{\bar{X}} = \frac{\sigma}{\sqrt{n}} = \frac{15}{\sqrt{25}} = \frac{15}{5} = 3$$

With $\alpha = .05$, we want to identify the most unlikely 5% of this distribution. The most unlikely part of a normal distribution is in the tails. Therefore, we divide our alpha level evenly between the two tails, 2.5% or $p = .0250$ per tail. In column C of the unit normal table, find $p = .0250$. Then find its corresponding z-score in column A. The entry is $z = 1.96$. The boundaries for the critical region are -1.96 (on the left side) and $+1.96$ (on the right side). The distribution with its critical region is shown in Figure 8.12.

STEP 3 Obtain the sample data, and compute the test statistic.

For this demonstration, the researcher obtained a sample mean of $\bar{X} = 70$. This sample mean corresponds to a z-score of

$$z = \frac{\bar{X} - \mu}{\sigma_{\bar{X}}} = \frac{70 - 65}{3} = \frac{5}{3} = +1.67$$

STEP 4 Make a decision about H_0, and state the conclusion.

The z-score we obtained is not in the critical region. This indicates that our sample mean of $\bar{X} = 70$ is not an extreme or unusual value to be obtained from a population with $\mu = 65$. Therefore, our statistical decision is to *fail to reject* H_0. Our conclusion for the study is that the data do not provide sufficient evidence that the special training changes test scores.

PROBLEMS

1. Discuss the errors that can be made in hypothesis testing.
   a. What is a Type I error? Why might it occur?
   b. What is a Type II error? How does it happen?

2. Why do we test H_0 to establish an effect instead of H_1?

3. After several years of studying human performance in flight simulators, a psychologist knows that reaction times to an overhead emergency indicator form a normal distribution with $\mu = 200$ milliseconds and $\sigma = 20$. The psychologist would like to determine if placing the indicator in front of the person at eye level has any effect on reaction time. A random sample of $n = 25$ people is selected, they are tested in a simulator with the indicator light at eye level, and their reaction times are recorded.
   a. Identify the dependent variable and the independent variable.
   b. State the null hypothesis using a sentence that includes the dependent and independent variables.
   c. Using symbols, state the hypotheses (H_0 and H_1) that the psychologist is testing.
   d. Sketch the appropriate distribution, and locate the critical region for the .05 level of significance.
   e. If the psychologist obtained an average reaction time of $\overline{X} = 195$ milliseconds for this sample, then what decision would be made about the null hypothesis?
   f. If the psychologist had used a sample of $n = 100$ subjects and had obtained an average reaction time of $\overline{X} = 195$, then what decision would be made about the effects of the position of the indicator? Explain why this conclusion is different from the one in part e.

4. Suppose that scores on the Scholastic Achievement Test (SAT) form a normal distribution with $\mu = 500$ and $\sigma = 100$. A high school counselor has developed a special course designed to boost SAT scores. A random sample of $n = 16$ students is selected to take the course and then the SAT. The sample had an average score of $\overline{X} = 554$. Does the course have an effect on SAT scores?
   a. What are the dependent and independent variables for this experiment?
   b. Perform the hypothesis test using the four steps outlined in the chapter. Use $\alpha = .05$.
   c. If $\alpha = .01$ were used instead, what z-score values would be associated with the critical region?
   d. For part c, what decision should be made regarding H_0? Compare to part b, and explain the difference.

5. Explain the structure of the z-score formula as it is used for hypothesis testing.
   a. What does $\overline{X} - \mu$ tell us in a hypothesis-testing situation?
   b. What does the standard error indicate?

6. IQ scores for the general population form a normal distribution with $\mu = 100$ and $\sigma = 15$. However, there are data that indicate that children's intelligence can be affected if their mothers have German measles during pregnancy. Using hospital records, a researcher obtained a sample of $n = 20$ school children whose mothers all had German measles during their pregnancies. The average IQ for this sample was $\overline{X} = 97.3$. Do these data indicate that German measles have a significant effect on IQ? Test with $\alpha = .05$.

7. A pegboard task requires that subjects place small metal pegs into a board with holes arranged in rows. Normative data show that when people work as fast as possible, the scores are normally distributed, and the mean time to complete the task is $\mu = 185$ seconds with $\sigma = 16$. Because this task measures eye-hand coordination, the researcher tests a sample of $n = 18$ subjects that have recently been diagnosed with multiple sclerosis (MS). For the sample of subjects with MS, the mean completion time is $\overline{X} = 212$ seconds. Is eye-hand coordination significantly different for those newly diagnosed with MS? Test with $\alpha = .01$ for two tails.

8. On a perceptual task, subjects must sort cards with shapes (star, cross, triangle, or square) into separate piles. Normative data reveal a normal distribution with an average completion time of $\mu = 92$ seconds and $\sigma = 11$. A sample of $n = 5$ subjects with frontal lobe damage is tested on the task. For these subjects, the average time to complete the task is $\overline{X} = 115$ seconds. Do these people differ significantly from the norm? Use the .01 level of significance for two tails.

9. For the past two years, the vending machine in the psychology department has charged 70¢ for a soft drink. During this time, company records indicate that an average of $\mu = 185$ cans of soft drinks were sold each week. The distribution of sales is approximately normal with $\sigma = 23$. Recently, the company increased the price to 80¢ a can. The weekly sales for the first 8 weeks after the price increase are as follows: 148, 135, 142, 181, 164, 159, 192, 173. Do these data indicate that there was a significant change in sales after the price increase? Test at the .05 level of significance for two tails.

10. A researcher is trying to assess some of the physical changes that occur in addicts during drug withdrawal. For the population, suppose that the average body temperature is $\mu = 98.6°F$ with $\sigma = 0.56$. The following data consist of the body temperatures of a sample of heroin addicts during drug withdrawal: 98.6, 99.0, 99.4, 100.1, 98.7, 99.3, 99.9, 101.0, 99.6, 99.5, 99.4, 100.3. Is there a

significant change in body temperature during withdrawal? Test at the .01 level of significance for two tails. Show all four steps of the hypothesis test.

11. In 1965, a nationwide survey revealed that U.S. grade school children spent an average of $\mu = 8.4$ hours per week doing homework. The distribution of homework times was normal with $\sigma = 3.3$. Last year a sample of $n = 200$ students was given the same survey. For this sample, the average number of homework hours was $\overline{X} = 7.1$.
   a. Do these data indicate a significant change in the amount of homework hours for American grade school children? Test at the .01 level of significance for two tails.
   b. If there had been only $n = 20$ students in the sample, would the data still indicate a significant change? Use the same sample mean, $\overline{X} = 7.1$, and use $\alpha = .01$ for two tails.
   c. Explain the different findings in parts a and b. What is the role of standard error?

12. Researchers have often noted increases in violent crimes when it is very hot. In fact, Reifman, Larrick, and Fein (1991) noted that this relationship even extends to baseball. That is, there is a much greater chance of a batter being hit by a pitch when the temperature increases. Consider the following hypothetical data. Suppose that over the past 30 years, during any given week of the major league season, an average of $\mu = 12$ players are hit by wild pitches. Assume that the distribution is nearly normal with $\sigma = 3$. For a sample of $n = 4$ weeks in which the daily temperature was extremely hot, the weekly average of hit-by-pitch players was $\overline{X} = 15.5$. Are players more likely to get hit by pitches during hot weeks? Set alpha to .05 for two tails.

13. A psychologist develops a new inventory to measure depression. Using a very large standardization group of "normal" individuals, the mean score on this test is $\mu = 55$ with $\sigma = 12$, and the scores are normally distributed. To determine if the test is sensitive in detecting those individuals that are severely depressed, a random sample of patients who are described as depressed by a therapist is selected and given the test. Presumably, the higher the score on the inventory is, the more depressed the patient is. The data are as follows: 59, 60, 60, 67, 65, 90, 89, 73, 74, 81, 71, 71, 83, 83, 88, 83, 84, 86, 85, 78, 79. Do patients score significantly differently on the test? Test with the .01 level of significance for two tails.

14. On a vocational/interest inventory that measures interest in several categories, a very large standardization group of adults has an average score on the "literary" scale of $\mu = 22$ with $\sigma = 4$. A researcher would like to determine if scientists differ from the general population in terms of writing interests. A random sample of scientists is selected from the directory of a national scientific society. The scientists are given the inventory, and their test scores on the literary scale are as follows: 21, 20, 23, 28, 30, 24, 23, 19. Do scientists differ from the general population in their writing interests? Test at the .05 level of significance for two tails.

15. Suppose that during impersonal social interactions (that is, with business or casual acquaintances) people in the United States maintain a mean social distance of $\mu = 7$ feet from the other individual. This distribution is normal and has a standard deviation of $\sigma = 1.5$. A researcher examines whether or not this is true for other cultures. A random sample of $n = 8$ individuals of Middle Eastern culture is observed in an impersonal interaction. For this sample, the mean distance is $\overline{X} = 4.5$ feet. Is there a cultural difference in social distance? Use an alpha of .05 for two tails.

16. Assuming the same population parameters from Problem 15 ($\mu = 7$ feet with $\sigma = 1.5$ for people in the United States), suppose that social distance in impersonal interactions is measured for people in England. A random sample of $n = 9$ individuals is selected. For these subjects, the mean social distance is $\overline{X} = 8$. Is there a significant difference in social distance? Set alpha at .05 for two tails.

17. A developmental psychologist has prepared a training program that, according to a psychological theory, should improve problem-solving ability. For the population of six-year-olds, the average score on a standardized problem-solving test is known to be $\mu = 80$ with $\sigma = 10$. To test the effectiveness of the training program, a random sample of $n = 18$ six-year-old children is selected. After training, the average score for this sample is $\overline{X} = 84.44$. Can the experimenter conclude that the program has an effect? Test with alpha set at .05.
   a. Perform the hypothesis test showing all four steps. When you state the hypotheses, explain what they predict in terms of the independent and dependent variables used in this experiment.
   b. Would the same decision have been made about H_0 if a one-tailed had been used with $\alpha = .05$? How about $\alpha = .025$?

18. On a standardized anagram task (anagrams are sets of scrambled letters that must be arranged to form words), people successfully complete an average of $\mu = 26$ anagrams with $\sigma = 4$. This distribution is normal. A researcher would like to demonstrate that the arousal from anxiety is distracting and will decrease task performance. A sample of $n = 14$ anxiety-ridden subjects is tested on the task. The average number of anagrams solved is $\overline{X} = 23.36$.

a. Do the anxiety-ridden subjects show a decrease in task performance? Test with alpha set at .01 for one tail.

b. If a two-tailed test with $\alpha = .01$ was used, what conclusion should be drawn?

19. A researcher did a one-tailed hypothesis test using an alpha level of .01. For this test, H_0 was rejected. A colleague analyzed the same data, but used a two-tailed test with $\alpha = .05$. In this test, H_0 was *not* rejected. Can both analyses be correct? Explain your answer.

20. What happens to power as the treatment distribution gets farther from the null distribution?

21. Suppose that a researcher normally uses an alpha level of .01 for hypothesis tests, but this time used an alpha level of .05. What does this change in alpha level do to the amount of power? What does it do to the risk of a Type I error?

22. Explain why power for a hypothesis test can never be less than the alpha level for the test. (*Hint:* Sketch a null distribution, and then add several different treatment distributions to your sketch. What happens to power as the treatment distribution gets very close to the null distribution?)

23. A researcher wants a statistical test to be powerful, yet would also like to avoid a Type I error. Which of the following approaches would achieve these goals? Explain your answer.

a. Increase the alpha level (for example, from .05 to .10).

b. Use a small alpha level, but increase the sample size.

c. Use a one-tailed test.

24. A psychologist is examining the effect of chronic alcohol abuse on memory. In this experiment, a standardized memory test is used. Scores on this test for the general population form a normal distribution with $\mu = 50$ and $\sigma = 6$. A sample of $n = 22$ alcohol abusers has an average score of $\overline{X} = 47$. Is there evidence for memory impairment among alcoholics? Use $\alpha = .01$ for a one-tailed test.

25. Performance scores on a motor skills task form a normal distribution with $\mu = 20$ and $\sigma = 4$. A psychologist is using this task to determine the extent to which increased self-awareness affects performance. The prediction for this experiment is that increased self-awareness will reduce a subject's concentration and result in lower performance scores. A sample of $n = 16$ subjects is obtained, and each subject is tested on the motor skills task while seated in front of a large mirror. The purpose of the mirror is to make the subjects more self-aware. The average score for this sample is $\overline{X} = 15.5$. Use a one-tailed test with $\alpha = .05$ to test the psychologist's prediction.

26. A psychological theory predicts that individuals who grow up as an only child will have above-average IQs. A sample of $n = 64$ people from single-child families is obtained. The average IQ for this sample is $\overline{X} = 104.9$. In the general population, IQs form a normal distribution with $\mu = 100$ and $\sigma = 15$. Use a one-tailed test with $\alpha = .01$ to evaluate the theory.

27. A psychologist is interested in the long-term effects of a divorce on the children in a family. A sample is obtained of $n = 10$ children whose parents were divorced at least five years ago. Each child is given a personality questionnaire measuring depression. In the general population, the scores on this questionnaire form a normal distribution with $\mu = 80$ and $\sigma = 12$. The scores for this sample are as follows: 83, 81, 75, 92, 84, 107, 63, 112, 92, 88. The psychologist is predicting that children from divorced families will be more depressed than children in the general population. Use a one-tailed test with $\alpha = .05$ to test this hypothesis.

25) $H_0: \mu \geq 20$ $\quad CU = \pm 1.65$ $\quad z = \frac{15.5 - 20}{4} = -1.125$ fail to reject
$H_1: \mu < 20$

CHAPTER 9

INTRODUCTION TO THE *t* STATISTIC

TOOLS YOU WILL NEED

The following items are considered essential background material for this chapter. If you doubt your knowledge of any of these items, you should review the appropriate chapter or section before proceeding.

- Sample standard deviation (Chapter 4)
- Degrees of freedom (Chapter 4)
- Hypothesis testing (Chapter 8)

CONTENTS

PREVIEW

Numerous accounts suggest that for many animals, including humans, direct stare from another animal is aversive (e.g., Cook, 1977). Try it out for yourself. Make direct eye contact with a stranger in a cafeteria. Chances are the person will display avoidance by averting his or her gaze or turning away from you. Some insects, such as moths, have even developed eye-spot patterns on the wings or body to ward off predators (mostly birds) who may have a natural fear of eyes (Blest, 1957). Suppose that a comparative psychologist is interested in determining whether or not the birds that feed on these insects show an avoidance of eye-spot patterns.

Using methods similar to those of Scaife (1976), the researcher performed the following experiment. A sample of $n = 16$ moth-eating birds is selected. The animals are tested in an apparatus that consists of a two-chambered box. The birds are free to roam from one side of the box to the other through a doorway in the partition that separates the two chambers. In one chamber, there are two eye-spot patterns painted on the wall. The other side of the box has plain walls. One at a time, the researcher tests each bird by placing it in the doorway between the chambers. Each subject is left in the apparatus for 60 minutes, and the amount of time spent in the plain chamber is recorded.

What kind of data should the experimenter expect if the null hypothesis is true? If the animals show no aversion to

the eye spots, they should spend, on the average, half of the time in the plain side. Therefore, the null hypothesis would predict that

$$H_0: \mu_{\text{plain side}} = 30 \text{ minutes}$$

Suppose that the researcher collected data for the sample and found that the amount of time spent on the plain side was $\overline{X} = 35$ minutes. The researcher now has two of the needed pieces of information to compute a *z*-score test statistic—the sample data ($\overline{X}$) and the hypothesized mean (according to H_0). All that is needed is the population standard deviation so that the standard error can be computed. Note that the investigator does not have this information about the population. All that is known is that the population of animals should, on the average, spend half of the 60-minute period in the plain chamber if the eye spots have no effect on behavior. Without complete information about the population, how can the comparative psychologist test the hypothesis with a *z*-score? The answer is simple—*z* cannot be used for the test statistic because the standard error cannot be computed. However, it is possible to estimate the standard error using the sample data and to compute a test statistic that is similar in structure to the *z*-score. This new test statistic is called the *t* statistic.

9.1 OVERVIEW

In the previous chapter, we presented the statistical procedures that permit researchers to use a sample mean to test hypotheses about a population. These statistical procedures were based on a few basic notions, which we summarize as follows:

Remember, the expected value of the distribution of sample means is μ, the population mean.

1. A sample mean ($\overline{X}$) is expected more or less to approximate its population mean (μ). This permits us to use the sample mean to test a hypothesis about the population mean.

2. The standard error provides a measure of how well a sample mean approximates the population mean.

$$\sigma_{\overline{X}} = \frac{\sigma}{\sqrt{n}} \qquad \text{or} \qquad \sigma_{\overline{X}} = \sqrt{\frac{\sigma^2}{n}}$$

3. To quantify our inferences about the population, we compare the obtained sample mean ($\overline{X}$) with the hypothesized population mean (μ) by computing a *z*-score test statistic.

$$z = \frac{\overline{X} - \mu}{\sigma_{\overline{X}}} = \frac{\text{obtained difference between data and hypothesis}}{\text{standard distance expected by chance}}$$

When the *z*-scores form a normal distribution, we are able to use the unit normal table (Appendix B) to find the critical region for the hypothesis test.

The shortcoming of using the *z*-score as an inferential statistic is that the *z*-score formula requires more information than is usually available. Specifically, *z*-scores require that we know the value of the population standard deviation (or variance), which is needed to compute the standard error. Most often the standard deviation of the population is not known, and the standard error of sample means cannot be computed. Without the standard error, we have no way of quantifying the expected amount of distance (or error) between $\overline{X}$ and μ. We have no way of making precise, quantitative inferences about the population based on *z*-scores. For situations in which the population standard deviation is not known, we use the *t* statistic rather than a *z*-score.

9.2 THE *t* STATISTIC—A SUBSTITUTE FOR *z*

As previously noted, the limitation of *z*-scores in hypothesis testing is that the population standard deviation (or variance) must be known. More often than not, however, the variability of the scores in the population is not known. In fact, the whole reason for conducting a hypothesis test is to gain knowledge about an *unknown* population. This situation appears to create a paradox: You want to use a *z*-score to find out about an unknown population, but you must know about the population before you can compute a *z*-score. Fortunately, there is a relatively simple solution to this problem. When the variability for the population is not known, we use the sample variability in its place.

In Chapter 4, the sample variance and sample standard deviation were developed specifically to provide unbiased estimates of the corresponding population variance and standard deviation. You should recall the formulas as follows:

$$\text{sample variance} = \frac{SS}{n - 1} = \frac{SS}{df}$$

$$\text{sample standard deviation} = \sqrt{\frac{SS}{n - 1}} = \sqrt{\frac{SS}{df}}$$

Using the sample values, we can now *estimate* the standard error. You should recall from Chapters 7 and 8 that the value of the standard error can be computed using either standard deviation or variance:

$$\sigma_{\overline{X}} = \frac{\sigma}{\sqrt{n}} = \sqrt{\frac{\sigma^2}{n}}$$

The process of estimating the standard error simply involves substituting the sample variance or standard deviation in place of the unknown population value:

$$s_{\overline{X}} = \frac{s}{\sqrt{n}} = \sqrt{\frac{s^2}{n}} \tag{9.1}$$

Notice that the symbol for the estimated standard error is $s_{\overline{X}}$ instead of $\sigma_{\overline{X}}$, indicating that the estimated value is computed from sample data rather than the actual population parameter.

Finally, you should realize that the standard error (actual or estimated) can be computed using either the standard deviation or the variance. In the past (Chapters 7 and 8), we have concentrated on the formula using standard deviation. However, the formula based on variance is better suited to the variety of inferential statistics that we will encounter in later chapters. Therefore, we will now shift our focus to the variance-based formula. Throughout the remainder of this chapter, and in following chapters, the *estimated standard error of* $\overline{X}$ typically will be presented and computed using

$$ s_{\overline{X}} = \sqrt{\frac{s^2}{n}} $$

DEFINITION   The *estimated standard error* $(s_{\overline{X}})$ is used as an estimate of $\sigma_{\overline{X}}$ when the value of σ is unknown. It is computed from the sample variance and provides an estimate of the standard distance between a sample mean $\overline{X}$ and the population mean μ.

Now we can substitute the estimated standard error in the denominator of the *z*-score formula. This new test statistic is called a *t* statistic:

$$ t = \frac{\overline{X} - \mu}{s_{\overline{X}}} \tag{9.2} $$

The only difference between the *t* formula and the *z*-score formula is that the *z*-score formula uses the actual population variance (σ^2) and the *t* statistic uses the sample variance as an estimate when σ^2 is unknown. Structurally, the two formulas have the same form:

$$ z \text{ or } t = \frac{\text{sample mean} - \text{population mean}}{\text{(estimated) standard error}} $$

Because both *z* and *t* formulas are used for hypothesis testing, there is one rule to remember:

RULE   When you know the value of σ^2, use a *z*-score. If σ^2 is unknown, use the *t* statistic.

DEFINITION   The *t statistic* is used to test hypotheses about μ when the value for σ^2 is not known. The formula for the *t* statistic is similar in structure to that for the *z*-score, except that the *t* statistic uses estimated standard error.

DEGREES OF FREEDOM AND THE *t* STATISTIC

In this chapter, we have introduced the *t* statistic as a substitute for a *z*-score. The basic difference between these two is that the *t* statistic uses sample variance (s^2) and the *z*-score uses the population variance (σ^2). To determine how well a *t* statistic approximates a *z*-score, we must determine how well the sample variance approximates the population variance.

In Chapter 4, we introduced the concept of degrees of freedom. Reviewing briefly, you must know the sample mean before you can compute sample variance.

FIGURE 9.1

Distributions of the *t* statistic for different values of degrees of freedom are compared to a normal *z*-score distribution. Like the normal distribution, *t* distributions are bell-shaped and symmetrical and have a mean of zero. However, *t* distributions have more variability, indicated by the flatter and more spread-out shape. The larger the value of *df* is, the more closely the *t* distribution approximates a normal distribution.

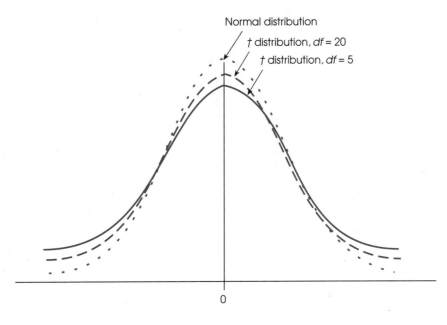

Normal distribution

t distribution, *df* = 20

t distribution, *df* = 5

0

This places a restriction on sample variability such that only $n - 1$ scores in a sample are free to vary. The value $n - 1$ is called the *degrees of freedom* (or *df*) for the sample variance.

$$\text{degrees of freedom} = df = n - 1 \qquad (9.3)$$

DEFINITION

Degrees of freedom describe the number of scores in a sample that are free to vary. Because the sample mean places a restriction on the value of one score in the sample, there are $n - 1$ degrees of freedom for the sample (see Chapter 4).

The greater the value of *df* is for a sample, the better s^2 represents σ^2, and the better the *t* statistic approximates the *z*-score. This should make sense because the larger the sample (*n*) is, the better the sample represents its population. Thus, the degrees of freedom associated with s^2 also describe how well *t* represents *z*.

THE *t* DISTRIBUTIONS

Every sample from a population can be used to compute a *z*-score or a *t* statistic. If you select all the possible samples of a particular size (*n*), then the entire set of resulting *z*-scores will form a *z*-score distribution. In the same way, the set of all possible *t* statistics will form a *t* distribution. As we saw in Chapter 7, the distribution of *z*-scores computed from sample means tends to be a normal distribution. For this reason, we consulted the unit normal table to find the critical region when using *z*-scores to test hypotheses about a population. The *t* distribution will approximate a normal distribution in the same way that a *t* statistic approximates a *z*-score. How well a *t* distribution approximates a normal distribution is determined by degrees of freedom. In general, the greater the sample size (*n*) is, the larger the degrees of freedom ($n - 1$) are, and the better the *t* distribution approximates the normal distribution (see Figure 9.1).

9.1 THE CRITICAL VALUES IN A NORMAL *z* DISTRIBUTION AND A *t* DISTRIBUTION: THE INFLUENCE OF DEGREES OF FREEDOM

AS PREVIOUSLY noted, a *t* distribution approximates a normal *z* distribution. How well it approximates a normal distribution depends on the value of *df*. This can be seen by simply comparing critical values for *z* with critical values of *t* at various degrees of freedom. For example, if we test a hypothesis with a *z*-score using a two-tailed test and α = .05, the critical *z*-scores will be +1.96 and −1.96. However, suppose that the population standard deviation was not known and we conducted this hypothesis test with a *t* statistic. For a sample of *n* = 4, the *t* statistic would have *df* = 3. For 3 degrees of freedom, the critical values of *t* would be +3.182 and −3.182 (with alpha still set at .05). When *df* is small, the *t* distribution is flatter and more spread out. Consequently, the tails have a greater area for the *t* distribution compared to a normal distribution (see Figure 9.1). The extreme 5% of the distribution will be farther than the mean and have a larger critical value in the *t* distribution. If, however, we use a sample of *n* = 31, then *df* = 30, and the critical *t* values will be +2.042 and −2.042. These values are very close to the critical *z*-score values (±1.96). If the sample is made even larger—say, *n* = 121—the critical values get even closer to the *z* values. For 120 degrees of freedom, the critical values of *t* are +1.980 and −1.980 when α = .05. Thus, the difference between a *t* distribution and normal *z*-distribution becomes negligible when a sample of more than 30 individuals is used. (*Note:* Determining critical values for *t* is discussed on pages 270–272.)

THE SHAPE OF THE *t* DISTRIBUTION

The exact shape of a *t* distribution changes with degrees of freedom. In fact, statisticians speak of a "family" of *t* distributions. That is, there is a different sampling distribution of *t* (a distribution of all possible sample *t* values) for each possible number of degrees of freedom. As *df* gets very large, the *t* distribution gets closer in shape to a normal *z*-score distribution (see Box 9.1). A quick glance at Figure 9.1 reveals that distributions of *t* are bell-shaped and symmetrical and have a mean of zero. However, the *t* distribution has more variability than a normal *z* distribution, especially when *df* values are small (Figure 9.1). The *t* distribution tends to be flatter and more spread out, whereas the normal *z* distribution has more of a central peak.

Why is the *t* distribution flatter and more variable than a normal *z* distribution? For a particular population, the top of the *z*-score formula, $\overline{X} - \mu$, can take on different values because $\overline{X}$ will vary from one sample to another. However, the value of the bottom of the *z*-score formula, $\sigma_{\overline{X}}$, is constant. The standard error will not vary from sample to sample because it is derived from the population variance. The implication is that samples that have the same value for $\overline{X}$ should also have the same *z*-score.

On the other hand, the standard error in the *t* formula is not a constant because it is estimated. That is, $s_{\overline{X}}$ is based on the sample variance, which will vary in value from sample to sample. The result is that samples can have the same value for $\overline{X}$, yet different values of *t* because the estimated error will vary from one sample to another. Therefore, a *t* distribution will have more variability than the normal *z* distribution. It will look flatter and more spread out. When the value of *df* increases, the variability in the *t* distribution decreases, and it more closely resembles the normal distribution because with greater *df*, $s_{\overline{X}}$ will more closely estimate $\sigma_{\overline{X}}$, and when *df* is very large, they are nearly the same.

DETERMINING PROPORTIONS AND PROBABILITIES FOR *t* DISTRIBUTIONS

Just as we used the unit normal table to locate proportions associated with *z*-scores, we will use a *t* distribution table to find proportions for *t* statistics. The complete *t* distribution table is presented in Appendix B, page A-27, and a portion of this table is reproduced in Table 9.1. The two rows at the top of the table show propor-

TABLE 9.1

A portion of the *t* distribution table

The numbers in the table are the values of *t* that separate the tail from the main body of the distribution. Proportions for one or two tails are listed at the top of the table, and *df* values for *t* are listed in the first column.

	PROPORTION IN ONE TAIL					
	0.25	0.10	0.05	0.025	0.01	0.005
	PROPORTION IN TWO TAILS					
df	0.50	0.20	0.10	0.05	0.02	0.01
1	1.000	3.078	6.314	12.706	31.821	63.657
2	0.816	1.886	2.920	4.303	6.965	9.925
3	0.765	1.638	2.353	3.182	4.541	5.841
4	0.741	1.533	2.132	2.776	3.747	4.604
5	0.727	1.476	2.015	2.571	3.365	4.032
6	0.718	1.440	1.943	2.447	3.143	3.707

tions of the *t* distribution contained in either one or two tails, depending on which row is used. The first column of the table lists degrees of freedom for the *t* statistic. Finally, the numbers in the body of the table are the *t* values that mark the boundary between the tails and the rest of the *t* distribution.

For example, with *df* = 3, exactly 5% of the *t* distribution is located in the tail beyond *t* = 2.353 (see Figure 9.2). To find this value, you locate *df* = 3 in the first column and locate 0.05 (5%) in the one-tail proportion row. When you line up these two values in the table, you should find *t* = 2.353. Similarly, 5% of the *t* distribution is located in the tail beyond *t* = −2.343 (see Figure 9.2). Finally, you should notice that a total of 10% is contained in the two tails beyond *t* = ±2.353 (check the proportion value in the "two-tails" row at the top of the table).

A close inspection of the *t* distribution table in Appendix B will demonstrate a point we made earlier: As the value for *df* increases, the *t* distribution becomes more and more similar to a normal distribution. For example, examine the column containing *t* values for a 0.05 proportion in two tails. You will find that when *df* = 1, the *t* values that separate the extreme 5% (0.05) from the rest of the distribution are *t* = ±12.706. As you read down the column, however, you should find that the critical *t* values become smaller and smaller, ultimately reaching ±1.96. You should

FIGURE 9.2

The *t* distribution with *df* = 3. Note that 5% of the distribution is located in the tail beyond *t* = 2.353. Also, 5% is in the tail beyond *t* = −2.353. Thus, a total proportion of 10% (0.10) is in the two tails beyond *t* = ±2.353.

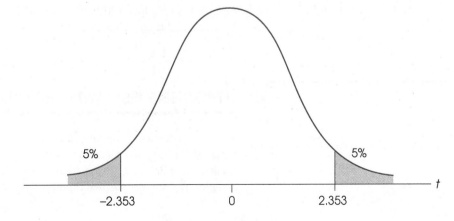

recognize ± 1.96 as the *z*-score values that separate the extreme 5% in a normal distribution. Thus, as *df* increases, the proportions in a *t* distribution become more like the proportions in a normal distribution. When the sample size (and degrees of freedom) is sufficiently large, the difference between a *t* distribution and the normal distribution becomes negligible.

Caution: The *t* distribution table printed in this book has been abridged and does not include entries for every possible *df* value. For example, the table lists *t* values for *df* = 40 and for *df* = 60, but does not list any entries for *df* values between 40 and 60. Occasionally, you will encounter a situation where your *t* statistic has a *df* value that is not listed in the table. In these situations, you should look up the critical *t* for both of the surrounding *df* values listed and then use the *larger* value for *t*. If, for example, you have *df* = 53 (not listed), you should look up the critical *t* value for *both df* = 40 and *df* = 60 and then use the larger *t* value. If your sample *t* statistic is greater than the larger value listed, you can be certain that the data are in the critical region, and you can confidently reject the null hypothesis.

LEARNING CHECK

1. A hypothesis test with a *z*-score can be performed only when the population variance is known. (True or false?)

2. To compute estimated standard error, $s_{\overline{X}}$, you must know the value for the population variance. (True or false?)

3. As the value for *df* get smaller, the *t* distribution resembles a normal distribution more and more. (True or false?)

4. As the value for *df* gets larger, s^2 provides a better estimate of σ^2. (True or false?)

5. For *df* = 10, what *t* value(s) are associated with

   a. The top 1% of the *t* distribution?
   b. The bottom 5% of the *t* distribution?
   c. The most extreme 1% of the distribution?

ANSWERS

1. True (With large samples, *z*-scores and *t* statistics are very similar. For this reason, some statisticians allow the use of a *z*-score instead of *t* when the sample size is at least *n* = 30. However, there is always some difference between *z* and *t*, so we recommend that you use a *z*-score only when the population variance is known.)

2. False   3. False   4. True

5. a. +2.764   b. −1.812   c. +3.169 and −3.169

9.3 HYPOTHESIS TESTS WITH THE *t* STATISTIC

In the hypothesis-testing situation, we begin with a population with an unknown mean and an unknown variance, often a population that has received some treatment (Figure 9.3). The goal is to use a sample from the treated population (a treated sample) as the basis for determining whether or not the treatment has any effect.

FIGURE 9.3

The basic experimental situation for using the *t* statistic or the *z*-score is presented. It is assumed that the parameter μ is known for the population before treatment. The purpose of the experiment is to determine whether or not the treatment has an effect. We ask, Is the population mean after treatment the same as or different from the mean before treatment? A sample is selected from the treated population to help answer this question.

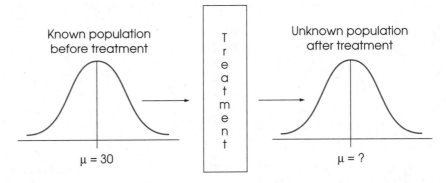

As always, the null hypothesis states that the treatment has no effect; specifically, H_0 states that the population mean is unchanged. Thus, the null hypothesis provides a specific value for the unknown population mean. The sample data provide a value for the sample mean. Finally, the variance and estimated standard error are computed from the sample data. When these values are used in the *t* formula, the result becomes

$$t = \frac{\substack{\text{sample mean} \\ \text{(from the data)}} - \substack{\text{population mean} \\ \text{(hypothesized from } H_0\text{)}}}{\text{estimated standard error}}$$

As with the *z*-score formula, the *t* statistic forms a ratio. The numerator measures the actual difference between the sample data ($\overline{X}$) and the population hypothesis (μ). The denominator measures how much difference is expected just by chance (error). When the obtained difference between the data and the hypothesis (numerator) is much greater than chance (denominator), we will obtain a large value for *t* (either large positive or large negative). In this case, we conclude that the data are not consistent with the hypothesis, and our decision is to "reject H_0." On the other hand, when the difference between the data and the hypothesis is small relative to the standard error, we will obtain a *t* statistic near zero, and our decision will be "fail to reject H_0."

The basic steps of the hypothesis-testing procedure will now be reviewed.

STEPS AND PROCEDURES For hypothesis tests with a *t* statistic, we use the same steps that we used with *z*-scores (Chapter 8). The major difference is that we are now required to estimate standard error because σ^2 is unknown. Consequently, we compute a *t* statistic rather than a *z*-score and consult the *t* distribution table rather than the unit normal table to find the critical region.

STEP 1 The hypotheses are stated, and the alpha level is set. The experimenter states the null hypothesis, that is, what should happen if no treatment effect exists. On the other hand, the alternative hypothesis predicts the outcome if an effect does occur. These hypotheses are always stated in terms of the population parameter, μ.

STEP 2 The critical region is located. The exact shape of the *t* distribution and, therefore, the critical *t* values vary with degrees of freedom. Thus, to find a critical region

9.2 COMPARING *z*-SCORES AND *t* STATISTICS AS TEST STATISTICS

CONCEPTUALLY, THE *z*-score and the *t* statistic are used similarly in hypothesis-testing situations:

$$z \text{ or } t = \frac{\text{sample data} - \text{population hypothesis}}{\text{amount of error between } \overline{X} \text{ and } \mu}$$

That is, in the numerator, we find the difference between the obtained sample data ($\overline{X}$) and the hypothesized population mean according to H_0. This discrepancy is compared to (divided by) the amount of error between $\overline{X}$ and μ that we would expect due to chance (the standard error). Thus, the discrepancy between the sample data and the null hypothesis would have to be much larger than chance (sampling error) in order to obtain a large test statistic (*z* or *t*) that falls in the critical region. The *t* statistics that follow in later chapters also have this same basic conceptual structure

in a *t* distribution, it is necessary to determine the value for *df*. Then the critical region can be located by consulting the *t* distribution table (Appendix B).

STEP 3 The sample data are collected, and the test statistic is computed. When σ^2 is unknown, the test statistic is a *t* statistic (equation 9.2).

STEP 4 The null hypothesis is evaluated. If the *t* statistic we obtained in step 3 falls within the critical region (exceeds the value of a critical *t*), then H_0 is rejected. It can be concluded that a treatment effect exists. However, if the obtained *t* value does not lie in the critical region, then we fail to reject H_0, and we conclude that we failed to observe evidence for an effect in our study (see Box 9.2).

HYPOTHESIS-TESTING EXAMPLE

eye-contact example again

Let us return to the research problem posed in the Preview to demonstrate the steps and procedures of hypothesis testing. Recall that direct eye contact is avoided by many animals. Some animals, such as moths, have evolved large eye-spot patterns, presumably to ward off predators that have a natural aversion to direct gaze. The experiment will assess the effect of exposure to eye-spot patterns on the behavior of moth-eating birds, using procedures similar to Scaife's (1976) study.

EXAMPLE 9.1

Software manuals:
Minitab (Section 5).

To test the effectiveness of eye-spot patterns in deterring predation, a sample of $n = 16$ insectivorous birds is selected. The animals are tested in a box that has two separate chambers (see Figure 9.4). The birds are free to roam from one chamber to another through a doorway in a partition. On the wall of one

FIGURE 9.4

Apparatus used in Example 9.1.

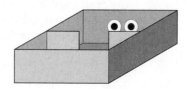

FIGURE 9.5

The critical region in the *t* distribution for $\alpha = .05$ and $df = 15$.

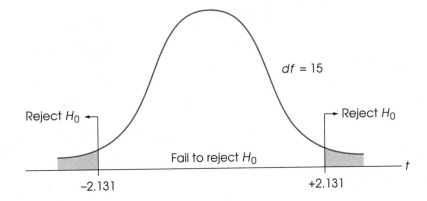

chamber, two large eye-spot patterns have been painted. The other chamber has plain walls. The birds are tested one at a time by placing them in the doorway in the center of the apparatus. Each animal is left in the box for 60 minutes, and the amount of time spent in the plain chamber is recorded. Suppose that the sample of $n = 16$ birds spent an average of $\overline{X} = 35$ minutes in the plain side, with $SS = 1215$. Can we conclude that eye-spot patterns have an effect on behavior? Note that while it is possible to predict a value for μ, we have no information about the population variance.

STEP 1 State the hypotheses, and select an alpha level. If the null hypothesis were true, then the eye-spot patterns would have no effect on behavior. The animals should show no preference for either side of the box. That is, they should spend half of the 60-minute test period in the plain chamber. In symbols, the null hypothesis would state that

$$H_0: \mu_{\text{plain side}} = 30 \text{ minutes}$$

The alternative hypothesis would state that the eye patterns have an effect on behavior. There are two possibilities: (1) The animals may avoid staying in the chamber with the eye spots as we suspect, or (2) maybe for some reason the animals may show a preference for the patterns painted on the wall. A non-directional hypothesis (for a two-tailed test) would be represented in symbols as follows:

Directional hypotheses could be used and would specify whether the average time on the plain side is more or less than 30 minutes.

$$H_1: \mu_{\text{plain side}} \neq 30 \text{ minutes}$$

We will set the level of significance at $\alpha = .05$ for two tails.

STEP 2 Locate the critical region. The test statistic is a *t* statistic because the population variance is not known. The exact shape of the *t* distribution and, therefore, the proportions under the *t* distribution depend on the number of degrees of freedom associated with the sample. To find the critical region, *df* must be computed:

$$df = n - 1 = 16 - 1 = 15$$

For a two-tailed test at the .05 level of significance and with 15 degrees of freedom, the critical region consists of *t* values greater than $+2.131$ or less than -2.131. Figure 9.5 depicts the critical region in this *t* distribution.

STEP 3 Calculate the test statistic. The *t* statistic typically requires much more computation than is necessary for a *z*-score. Therefore, we recommend that you divide the calculations into a three-stage process as follows.

    a. First, calculate the sample variance. Remember, the population variance is unknown, and you must use the sample value in its place. (This is why we are using a *t* statistic instead of a *z*-score.)

$$s^2 = \frac{SS}{n-1} = \frac{SS}{df}$$

$$= \frac{1215}{15}$$

$$= 81$$

    b. Next, use, the sample variance (s^2) to compute the estimated standard error. This value will be the denominator of the *t* statistic and measures how much error is expected by chance between a sample mean and the corresponding population mean.

$$s_{\overline{X}} = \sqrt{\frac{s^2}{n}}$$

$$= \sqrt{\frac{81}{16}}$$

$$= 2.25$$

    c. Finally, compute the *t* statistic for the sample data.

$$t = \frac{\overline{X} - \mu}{s_{\overline{X}}}$$

$$= \frac{35 - 30}{2.25}$$

$$= \frac{5}{2.25}$$

$$= 2.22$$

STEP 4 Make a decision regarding H_0. The obtained *t* statistic of 2.22 falls into the critical region on the right-hand side of the *t* distribution (Figure 9.5). Our statistical decision is to reject H_0 and conclude that the presence of eye-spot patterns does influence behavior. As can be seen from the sample mean, there is a tendency for animals to avoid the eyes and spend more time on the plain side of the box.

IN THE LITERATURE:
REPORTING THE RESULTS OF A *t* TEST

In Chapter 8, we noted the conventional style for reporting the results of a hypothesis test, according to APA format. First, you should recall that a scientific report typically uses the term *significant* to indicate that the null hypothesis has been rejected and the term *not significant* to indicate failure to reject H_0. Additionally, there is a prescribed format for reporting the calculated value of the test statistic, degrees of freedom, and alpha level for a *t* test. This format parallels the style introduced in Chapter 8 (p. 240). For Example 9.1, we calculated a *t* statistic of $+2.22$ with $df = 15$ and decided to reject H_0 with alpha set at .05. In a scientific report, this information is conveyed in a concise statement, as follows:

> The subjects spent more time on the plain side of the apparatus ($M = 35$, $SD = 9$). Statistical analysis revealed that the birds spent significantly more time in the chamber without eye-spot patterns; $t(15) = +2.22$, $p < .05$, two-tailed.

The statement $p < .05$ was explained in Chapter 8, page 241.

In the first statement, the mean ($M = 35$) and the standard deviation ($SD = 9$) are reported as previously noted (Chapter 4, p. 121). The next statement provides the results of the statistical analysis. Note that the degrees of freedom are reported in parentheses immediately after the symbol *t*. The value for the obtained *t* statistic follows (2.22), and next is the probability of committing a Type I error (less than 5%). Finally, the type of test (one versus two-tailed) is noted. ❑

DIRECTIONAL HYPOTHESES AND ONE-TAILED TESTS

As we noted in Chapter 8, the non-directional (two-tailed) test is most commonly used. On the other hand, a directional (one-tailed) test may be used in some research situations, such as exploratory investigations or pilot studies or where there is *a priori* justification (for example, a theory or previous findings). Even though a researcher may have a specific directional prediction for an experiment, it is still acceptable to use a non-directional (two-tailed) test. The following example demonstrates a directional hypothesis test with a *t* statistic, using the same experimental situation that was presented in Example 9.1.

EXAMPLE 9.2

The research question is whether eye-spot patterns will affect the behavior of birds placed in a special testing box. The researcher is expecting the birds to avoid the eye-spot patterns. Therefore, the researcher predicts that the birds will spend most of the hour on the plain side of the box.

STEP 1 State the hypotheses, and select an alpha level. With most directional tests, it is easier to begin by stating the alternative hypothesis. Remember, H_1 states that the treatment does have an effect. For this example, the eye patterns should cause the birds to spend most of their time on the plain side, In symbols,

$$H_1: \mu_{\text{plain side}} > 30 \text{ minutes}$$

The null hypothesis states that the treatment will not have the predicted effect. In this case, H_0 says that the eye patterns will not cause the birds to spend more time on the plain side. In symbols,

$$H_0: \mu_{\text{plain side}} \leq 30 \text{ minutes} \quad \text{(not greater than 30 minutes)}$$

We will set the level of significance at $\alpha = .05$.

STEP 2 Locate the critical region. In this example, the researcher is predicting that the same mean ($\overline{X}$) will be greater than 30. The null hypothesis states that the population mean is $\mu = 30$ (or less). If you examine the structure of the *t* statistic

FIGURE 9.6

The critical region in the t distribution for $\alpha = .05$, $df = 15$, one-tailed test.

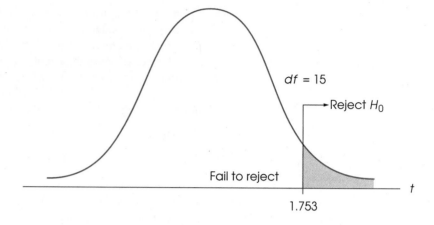

formula, it should be clear that a positive t statistic would support the researcher's prediction and refute the null hypothesis.

$$t = \frac{\overline{X} - \mu}{s_{\overline{X}}}$$

The problem is to determine how large a positive value is necessary to reject H_0. To find the critical value, you must look in the t distribution table using the one-tail proportions. With a sample of $n = 16$, the t statistic will have $df = 15$; using $\alpha = .05$, you should find a critical t value of 1.753. Figure 9.6 depicts the critical region in the t distribution.

STEP 3   Calculate the test statistic. The computation of the t statistic is the same for either a one-tailed or a two-tailed test. Earlier (in Example 9.1), we found that the data for this experiment produce a test statistic of $t = 2.22$.

STEP 4   Make a decision. The test statistic is in the critical region, so we reject H_0. In terms of the experimental variables, we have decided that the birds spent significantly more time on the plain side of the box than on the side with eye-spot patterns.

ASSUMPTIONS OF THE t TEST   There are two basic assumptions necessary for hypothesis tests with the t statistic.

1. The values in the sample must consist of *independent* observations.
   In everyday terms, two observations are independent if there is no consistent, predictable relationship between the first observation and the second. More precisely, two events (or observations) are independent if the occurrence of the first event has no effect on the probability of the second event. Specific examples of independence and non-independence were presented in Box 8.3. Usually this assumption is satisfied by using a *random* sample, which also helps ensure that the sample is representative of the population and that the results can be generalized to the population.

2. The population sampled must be normal

This assumption is a necessary part of the mathematics underlying the development of the *t* statistic and the *t* distribution table. However, violating this assumption has little practical effect on the results obtained for a *t* statistic, especially when the sample size is relatively large. With very small samples, a normal population is important. With larger samples, this assumption can be violated without affecting the validity of the hypothesis test. If you have reason to suspect that the population is not normal, use a large sample to be safe.

THE VERSATILITY OF THE *t* TEST The obvious advantage of hypothesis testing with the *t* statistic (as compared to *z*-scores) is that you do not need to know the value of the population variance. This means that we still can do a hypothesis test even though we have little or no information about the population. One result of this extra versatility is that it is possible to do *t* tests in circumstances where hypothesis tests with *z*-scores would not even allow for the statement of a null hypothesis.

Both the *t* statistic and the *z*-score tests were introduced as a means of determining whether or not a treatment has any effect on a dependent variable. For both tests, we assumed that you start with a *known* population mean before treatment and the research question (hypotheses) concerned the *unknown* population mean after treatment (see Figures 8.1 and 9.3). For example, if the population mean is known to be $\mu = 80$ before treatment, the null hypothesis would state that the population mean is still $\mu = 80$ after treatment. For the *z*-score test, a known population is essential to determine the value for σ and to determine the hypothesized mean for H_0. Although the *t* statistic can be used in this "before and after" type of experiment, the *t* test also permits hypothesis testing in situations where you do not have a "known" population mean to serve as a standard. Specifically, the *t* test does not require any prior knowledge about the population mean or the population variance. All you need to compute a *t* statistic is a sensible null hypothesis and a sample from the unknown population. Thus, a *t* test can be used in situations where the value for the null hypothesis can be obtained from a theory, a logical prediction, or just wishful thinking. You may have noticed in the preceding examples (9.1 and 9.2) that there was no "known" value for the mean time that birds spend in each side of the box. For both examples, the null hypothesis was based on logic: If the eye-spot patterns have no effect, then the birds should show no preference between the two sides of the box. Some similar examples follow. Notice that in each case the hypothesis is not dependent on knowing the actual population mean before treatment and that the rest of the *t* statistic can be computed entirely from the obtained sample data.

1. A researcher would like to examine the accuracy of people's judgment of time when they are distracted. Individuals are placed in a waiting room where many distracting events occur for a period of 12 minutes. The researcher then asks each person to judge how much time has passed. The null hypothesis would state that distraction has no effect and that time judgments are accurate. That is,

H_0: $\mu = 12$ minutes

2. A local fund-raising organization has set a goal of receiving $25 per contributor. After 1 week, a sample of contributions is selected to see if they

deviate significantly from the goal. The null hypothesis would state that the contributions do not deviate from the goal of the organization. In symbols, it is

$$H_0: \mu = \$25.00$$

3. A soft-drink company has developed a new, improved formula for its product and would like to determine how consumers respond to the new formula. A sample is obtained, and each individual is asked to taste the original soft drink and the new formula. After tasting, the subjects are required to state whether the new formula is better or worse than the original formula using a 7-point scale. A rating of 4 indicates no preference between the old and new formulas. Ratings above 4 indicate that the new formula is better (5 = slightly better, 6 = better, and 7 = much better). Similarly, ratings below 4 indicate that the new formula tastes worse than the old formula. The null hypothesis states that there is no perceived difference between the two formulas. In symbols, the new formula would receive an average rating of

$$H_0: \mu = 4$$

LEARNING CHECK

1. A professor of philosophy hypothesizes that an introductory course in logic will help college students with their other studies. To test this hypothesis, a random sample of $n = 25$ freshmen is selected. These students are required to complete a logic course during their freshman year. At the time of graduation, the final grade point average is computed for each of these students. The mean GPA for this sample is $\overline{X} = 2.83$ with $SS = 6$. Can the professor conclude that the grades for the sample were significantly different from the rest of the graduating class, which had an average GPA of $\mu = 2.58$? Test with a two-tailed test at $\alpha = .05$.

do this

a. State the hypotheses.

b. Determine the value for df, and locate the critical region.

c. Compute the test statistic.

d. Make a decision regarding H_0.

ANSWERS

1. a. $H_0: \mu_{\text{with logic course}} = 2.58$ (even with the logic course, the population mean GPA will still be 2.58)

$H_1: \mu_{\text{with logic course}} \neq 2.58$ (for the population, the logic course has an effect on GPA)

b. $df = 24$; the critical region begins at t values of $+2.064$ and -2.064.

c. $s^2 = 0.25$; $s_{\overline{X}} = 0.1$; $t = +2.5$.   d. Reject H_0.

SUMMARY

1. When σ is unknown, the standard error cannot be computed, and a hypothesis test based on a z-score is impossible.

2. In order to test a hypothesis about μ when σ^2 (or σ) is unknown, σ^2 must first be estimated using the sample variance, s^2.

$$s^2 = \frac{SS}{n-1} = \frac{SS}{df}$$

Next, the standard error is estimated by substituting s^2 for σ^2 in the standard error formula. The estimated standard error ($s_{\bar{X}}$) is calculated in the following manner:

$$s_{\bar{X}} = \sqrt{\frac{s^2}{n}}$$

Finally, a t statistic is computed using the estimated standard error. The t statistic serves as a substitute for a z-score, which cannot be computed because σ^2 is unknown.

$$t = \frac{\bar{X} - \mu}{s_{\bar{X}}}$$

3. The structure of the t formula is similar to that of the z-score in that

$$z \text{ or } t = \frac{\text{sample mean} - \text{population mean}}{\text{(estimated) standard error}}$$

4. The t distribution is an approximation of the normal z distribution. To evaluate a t statistic that is obtained for a sample mean, the critical region must be located in a t distribution. There is a family of t distributions, with the exact shape of a particular distribution of t values depending on degrees of freedom ($n - 1$). Therefore, the critical t values will depend on the value for df associated with the t test. As df increases, the shape of the t distribution approaches a normal distribution.

KEY TERMS

estimated standard error t statistic   degrees of freedom t distribution

independent observations

FOCUS ON PROBLEM SOLVING

1. The first problem we confront in analyzing data is determining the appropriate statistical test. Remember, you can use a z-score for the test statistic only when the value for σ is known. If the value for σ is not provided, then you must use the t statistic.

2. For a t test, students sometimes use the unit normal table to locate the critical region. This, of course, is a mistake. The critical region for a t test is obtained by consulting the t distribution table. Notice that to use this table you first must compute the value for degrees of freedom (df).

3. For the t test, the sample variance is used to find the value for estimated standard error. Remember, when computing the sample variance, use $n - 1$ in the denominator (see Chapter 4). When computing estimated standard error, use n in the denominator.

DEMONSTRATION 9.1

A HYPOTHESIS TEST WITH THE t STATISTIC

A psychologist has prepared an "Optimism Test" that is administered yearly to graduating college seniors. The test measures how each graduating class feels about its future—the higher the score, the more optimistic the class. Last year's class had a mean score of $\mu = 15$. A sample of $n = 9$ seniors from this year's class was selected and tested. The scores for these seniors are as follows:

$$7 \quad 12 \quad 11 \quad 15 \quad 7 \quad 8 \quad 15 \quad 9 \quad 6$$

On the basis of this sample, can the psychologist conclude that this year's class has a different level of optimism than last year's class?

Note that this hypothesis test will use a t statistic because the population variance (σ^2) is not known.

STEP 1   State the hypotheses, and select an alpha level.

The statements for the null hypothesis and the alternative hypothesis follow the same form for the t statistic and the z-score test.

$$H_0: \mu = 15 \quad \text{(there is no change)}$$

$$H_1: \mu \neq 15 \quad \text{(this year's mean is different)}$$

For this demonstration, we will use $\alpha = .05$, two tails.

STEP 2   Locate the critical region.

Remember, for hypothesis tests with the t statistic, we must now consult the t distribution table to find the critical t values. With a sample of $n = 9$ students, the t statistic will have degrees of freedom equal to

$$df = n - 1 = 9 - 1 = 8$$

For a two-tailed test with $\alpha = .05$ and $df = 8$, the critical t values are $t = \pm 2.306$. These critical t values define the boundaries of the critical region. The obtained t value must be more extreme that either of these critical values to reject H_0.

STEP 3   Obtain the sample data, and compute the test statistic.

For the t formula, we need to determine the values for the following:

1. The sample mean, $\overline{X}$
2. The estimated standard error, $s_{\overline{X}}$

We will also have to compute sums of squares (*SS*) and the variance (s^2) for the sample in order to get the estimated standard error.

The sample mean. For these data, the sum of the scores is

$$\Sigma X = 7 + 12 + 11 + 15 + 7 + 8 + 15 + 9 + 6 = 90$$

Therefore, the sample mean is

$$\overline{X} = \frac{\Sigma X}{n} = \frac{90}{9} = 10$$

Sum of squares. We will use the definitional formula for sum of squares,

$$SS = \Sigma (X - \overline{X})^2$$

The following table summarizes the steps in the computation of *SS*:

X	$X - \bar{X}$	$(X - \bar{X})^2$
7	$7 - 10 = -3$	9
12	$12 - 10 = +2$	4
11	$11 - 10 = +1$	1
15	$15 - 10 = +5$	25
7	$7 - 10 = -3$	9
8	$8 - 10 = -2$	4
15	$15 - 10 = +5$	25
9	$9 - 10 = -1$	1
6	$6 - 10 = -4$	16

For this demonstration problem, the sum of squares value is

$$SS = \Sigma(X - \bar{X})^2 = 9 + 4 + 1 + 25 + 9 + 4 + 25 + 1 + 16$$
$$= 94$$

Sample variance.

$$s^2 = \frac{SS}{n - 1} = \frac{94}{8} = 11.75$$

Estimated standard error. The estimated standard error for these data is

$$s_{\bar{X}} = \sqrt{\frac{s^2}{n}} = \sqrt{\frac{11.75}{9}} = 1.14$$

The t statistic. Now that we have the estimated standard error and the sample mean, we can compute the *t* statistic. For this demonstration,

$$t = \frac{\bar{X} - \mu}{s_{\bar{X}}} = \frac{10 - 15}{1.14} = \frac{-5}{1.14} = -4.39$$

STEP 4 Make a decision about H_0, and state a conclusion.

The *t* statistic we obtained ($t = -4.39$) is in the critical region. Thus, our sample data are unusual enough to reject the null hypothesis at the .05 level of significance. We can conclude that there is a significant difference in level of optimism between this year's and last year's graduating classes, $t(8) = -4.39$, $p < .05$, two-tailed.

PROBLEMS

1. Why is it necessary to *estimate* the standard error when a *t* statistic is used?

2. Briefly describe what is measured by the sample standard deviation, *s*, and what is measured by the estimated standard error, $s_{\bar{X}}$.

3. Several different factors influence the value obtained for a *t* statistic. For each of the following, describe how the value of *t* is affected. In each case, assume that all other factors are held constant.
   a. What happens to the value of *t* when the variability of the scores in the sample increases?

b. What happens to the value of *t* when the number of scores in the sample is increased?

c. What happens to the value of *t* when the difference between the sample mean and the hypothesized population mean increases?

4. Why is the *t* statistic more versatile for inferential statistics than the *z*-score?

5. What assumptions (or set of conditions) must be satisfied for a *t* test to be valid?

6. Why is a *t* distribution generally more variable than a normal distribution?

7. What is the relationship between the value for degrees of freedom and the shape of the *t* distribution? What happens to the critical value of *t* for a particular alpha level when *df* increases in value?

8. The following sample was obtained from a population with unknown parameters. Scores:

$$15 \quad 3 \quad 15 \quad 7$$

a. Find the sample mean, the sample variance, and the sample standard deviation. (Note that these values are descriptive statistics that summarize the sample data.)

b. How accurately does the sample mean represent the unknown population mean? Compute the estimated standard error for $\overline{X}$. (Note that this value is an inferential statistic that allows you to use the sample data to answer questions about the population.)

9. A developmental psychologist would like to know whether success in one specific area can affect a person's general self-esteem. The psychologist selects a sample of $n = 25$ 10-year-old children who all excel in athletics. These children are given a standardized self-esteem test for which the general population of 10-year-old children averages $\mu = 70$. The average score for the sample is $\overline{X} = 73$ with $SS = 2400$. On the basis of these data, can the psychologist conclude that excelling in athletics has a general effect on self-esteem? Use $\alpha = .05$.

10. For a standard set of discrimination problems that have been used for years in primate research, it is known that monkeys require an average of $\mu = 20$ trials before they can successfully reach the criterion (five consecutive correct solutions). A psychologist hypothesizes that the animals can learn the task vicariously—that is, simply by watching other animals perform the task. To test this hypothesis, the researcher selects a random sample of $n = 4$ monkeys. These animals are placed in neighboring enclosures from which they can watch another animal learn the task. After a week of viewing other animals, the 4 monkeys in the sample are tested on the problem. These

animals require an average of $\overline{X} = 15$ trials to solve the problem with $SS = 300$. On the basis of these data, can the psychologist conclude that there is evidence that the animals perform significantly better after viewing others? Use a one-tailed test at the .01 level of significance

a. State the hypotheses using symbols. Explain what they predict for this experiment.

b. Sketch the distribution, and locate the critical region.

c. Calculate the test statistic.

d. Make a decision regarding H_0, and state your conclusion.

11. Educational administrators have complained for years that American high school students have little knowledge of world geography. To evaluate this complaint, a history teacher prepared a 40-question, multiple-choice geography test. Each question had 4 choices for the answer, so the probability of guessing correctly is $p = \frac{1}{4}$. Thus, chance performance would result in an average score of $\mu = 10$ out of 40. The test was administered to a random sample of $n = 36$ students, and the mean score for the sample was $\overline{X} = 13.5$ with $s^2 = 144$. On the basis of these data, can the teacher conclude that the students' scores are significantly different from what would be expected by chance? Use a two-tailed test with $\alpha = .05$.

12. A recent survey of college seniors evaluated how the students view the "real world" that they are about to enter. One question asked the seniors to evaluate the future job market on a 10-point scale from 1 (dismal) to 10 (excellent). The average score for the sample of $n = 100$ students was $\overline{X} = 7.3$ with $SS = 99$. Ten years ago, the same survey produced an average score of $\mu = 7.9$ for this question. Do the sample data indicate a significant change in the perceived job market during the past 10 years? Test at the .01 level of significance.

13. A random sample has a mean of $\overline{X} = 81$ with $s = 10$. Use this sample to test the null hypothesis that $\mu = 85$ for each of the following situations:

a. Assume that the sample size in $n = 25$, and use $\alpha = .05$ for the hypothesis test.

b. Assume that the sample size is $n = 400$, and use $\alpha = .05$ for the hypothesis test.

c. In general, how does sample size affect the outcome of a hypothesis test?

14. A population has a mean of $\mu = 50$. A sample of $n = 16$ individuals is selected from the population, and a treatment is administered to the sample.

a. After treatment, the sample mean is computed to be $\overline{X} = 55$ with $SS = 60$. Compute the sample standard deviation (*s*), and draw a sketch of the sample distribution. Sketch a normal-shaped distribution using the values for $\overline{X}$ and *s* to determine the mean and standard deviation (see Figure 4.3). Locate the position of $\mu =$

50 on your sketch. Does it appear from your sketch that the sample is centered around $\mu = 50$, or does it appear that the sample scores pile up around a location significantly different from $\mu = 50$?

b. Now use a hypothesis test to determine whether these data provide sufficient evidence to conclude that the treatment has a significant effect? Test at the .05 level of significance. Are the results of the hypothesis test consistent with the appearance of your sketch?

c. Now assume that the sample mean is $\overline{X} = 55$ with $SS = 6000$. Compute the sample standard deviation, and sketch the sample distribution as you did in part a. Does it appear that this sample is centered near $\mu = 50$, or is the sample piled up at a location significantly different from $\mu = 50$?

d. Using the new sample data, test the hypothesis that $\mu = 50$ with $\alpha = .05$. Once again, is the result of the hypothesis test consistent with the appearance of your sketch?

e. Based on the preceding parts of this problem, how does sample variability affect the outcome of a hypothesis test?

15. The local grocery store sells potatoes in 5-pound bags. Because potatoes come in unpredictable sizes, it is almost impossible to get a bag that weighs exactly 5 pounds. Therefore, the store advertises that the bags *average* five pounds. To check this claim, a sample of $n = 25$ bags was randomly selected. The average weight for the sample was $\overline{X} = 5.20$ pounds with a standard deviation of $s = 0.50$. On the basis of this sample,

a. Can you conclude that the average weight for a bag of potatoes is *significantly different* from $\mu = 5$ pounds. Use $\alpha = .05$.

b. Can you conclude that the average weight for a bag of potatoes is *significantly more* than $\mu = 5$ pounds? Use a one-tailed test with $\alpha = .05$.

16. A researcher would like to examine the effects of humidity on eating behavior. It is known that laboratory rats normally eat an average of $\mu = 21$ grams of food each day. The researcher selects a random sample of $n = 100$ rats and places them in a controlled atmosphere room where the relative humidity is maintained at 90%. The daily food consumption for the sample averages $\overline{X} = 18.7$ with $SS = 2475$. On the basis of this sample, can the researcher conclude that humidity affects eating behavior? Test at the .05 level.

17. A psychologist would like to determine whether there is a relationship between depression and aging. It is known that the general population averages $\mu = 40$ on a standardized depression test. The psychologist obtains a sample of $n = 36$ individuals who are all over the age of 70. The average depression score for this sample is

$\overline{X} = 44.5$ with $SS = 5040$. On the basis of this sample, can the psychologist conclude that depression for elderly people is significantly different from depression in the general population? Test at the .05 level of significance.

18. A social psychologist recently developed a childhood-memories test that is intended to measure how people recall pleasant and unpleasant experiences from childhood. Scores on the test range from 1 (very unpleasant) to 100 (very pleasant). The psychologist standardized the test with a large group of college students (aged 18–25), so that the mean score was $\mu = 60$. The test was then given to a sample of $n = 25$ individuals who were all between the ages of 40 and 45. The average score for this sample was $\overline{X} = 64.3$ with $SS = 600$. Does this sample provide sufficient evidence to conclude that childhood memories for older adults (aged 40–45) are significantly more pleasant than memories for college students? Use a one-tailed test with $\alpha = .05$.

19. Fifteen years ago, the average weight of American men between the ages of 30 and 50 was $\mu = 166$ pounds. A researcher would like to determine whether there has been any change in this figure during the past 15 years. A sample of $n = 100$ men is obtained. The average weight for this sample is $\overline{X} = 173$ with a standard deviation of $s = 23$. On the basis of these data, can the researcher conclude that there has been a significant change in weight? Use a two-tailed test with $\alpha = .01$.

20. A fund raiser for a charitable organization has set a goal of averaging at least $25 per donation. To see if the goal is being met, a random sample of recent donations is selected. The data for this sample are as follows: 20, 50, 30, 25, 15, 20, 40, 50, 10, 20. Use a one-tailed test with $\alpha = .05$ to determine whether the donations are averaging significantly more than $25.

21. One of the original tests of extrasensory perception (ESP) involves using Zener cards. Each card shows one of five different symbols (square, circle, star, wavy lines, cross). One person randomly picks a card and concentrates on the symbol it shows. A second person, in a different room, attempts to identify the symbol that was selected. Chance performance on this task (just guessing) should lead to correct identification of one out of five cards. A psychologist used the Zener cards to evaluate a sample of $n = 9$ subjects who claimed to have ESP. Each subject was tested on a series of 100 cards, and the number correct for each individual is as follows: 18, 23, 24, 22, 19, 28, 15, 26, 25.

Chance performance on a series of 100 cards would be $\mu = 20$ correct. Did this sample perform significantly better than chance? Use a one-tailed test at the .05 level of significance.

$\alpha = .05$
$c_v = 1.86$
$df = 8$
$\mu = 20$
$\overline{X} = 22.22$
$n = 9$

$\overline{X} = 22.22 \quad \Sigma x = 200 \quad \Sigma x^2 = 4584 \quad (\Sigma x)^2 = 40,000$

21) $H_0: \mu_T \leq 20$
$H_1: \mu_T > 20$

$\alpha = .05$
t

$s = \sqrt{4584 - \dfrac{40,000}{9}} \Big/ \sqrt{9-1} = 4.18$

$s_{\overline{x}} = \dfrac{4.18}{\sqrt{9}} = 1.39$

$t = \dfrac{22.22 - 20}{1.39} = 1.597 \quad \text{reject } H_0$

22. A recent national survey reports that the general population gives the president an average approval rating of $\mu = 62$ on a scale of 1 to 100. A researcher suspects that college students are likely to be more critical of the president than people in the general population. To test this suspicion, a random sample of college students is selected and asked to rate the president. The data for this sample are as follows: 44, 52, 24, 45, 39, 57, 20, 38, 78, 74, 61, 56, 49, 66, 53, 49, 47, 88, 38, 51, 65, 47, 35, 59, 23, 41, 50, 19. On the basis of this sample, can the researcher conclude that college students rate the president differently? Test at the .01 level of significance, two tails.

23. On a standardized spatial skills task, normative data reveal that people typically get $\mu = 15$ correct solutions. A psychologist tests $n = 7$ individuals who have brain injuries in the right cerebral hemisphere. For the following data, determine whether or not right-hemisphere damage results in significantly reduced performance on the spatial skills task. Test with alpha set at .05 with one tail. The data are as follows: 12, 16, 9, 8, 10, 17, 10.

24. After many studies of memory, a psychologist has determined that when a standard list of 40 words is presented at a rate of 2 words per second, college students can recall an average of $\mu = 17.5$ words from the list. The psychologist would like to determine if the rate of presentation affects memory. A random sample of $n = 15$ students is selected, and each is given the standard list of words at a rate of only 1 word per second. At the end of the presentation of the list, each student is tested for recall. The numbers of words recalled are as follows: 14, 21, 23, 19, 17, 20, 24, 16, 27, 17, 20, 21, 18, 20, 19.
   a. Is there evidence for an effect of presentation rate? Test at the .05 level of significance and with two tails.
   b. Would you arrive at the same conclusion had the .01 level of significance been used?

25. A family therapist states that parents talk to their teenagers an average of 27 minutes per week. Surprised by that

claim, a psychologist decided to collect some data on the amount of time parents spend in conversation with their teenage children. For $n = 12$ parents, the study revealed the following times (in minutes) devoted to conversation in a week:

29   22   19   25   27   28

21   22   24   26   30   22

Do the psychologist's findings differ significantly from the therapist's claim? If so, is the family expert's claim an overestimate or underestimate of actual time spent talking to children? Use the .05 level of significance with two tails.

26. A psychologist assesses the effect of distraction on time perception. Subjects are asked to judge the length of time between signals given by the experimenter. The actual interval of time is 10 minutes. During this period, the subjects are distracted by noises, conversation between the experimenter and his assistant, and questions from the assistant. The experimenter expects that the subjects' judgments will average around 10 minutes if the distraction has no effect. The data are as follows:

11   9.5   14   8

8   14   15   15

12   7.5   15   18

15   12   11   10

20   10   9   14

Is there a significant effect? Test at the .05 level of significance. What conclusion can be made?

CHAPTER 10

HYPOTHESIS TESTS WITH TWO INDEPENDENT SAMPLES

CONTENTS

PREVIEW

In a classic study in the area of problem solving, Katona (1940) compared the effectiveness of two methods of instruction. One group of subjects was shown the exact, step-by-step procedure for solving a problem, and then these subjects were required to memorize the solution. This method was called *learning by memorization* (later called the *expository* method). Subjects in a second group were encouraged to study the problem and find the solution on their own. Although these subjects were given helpful hints and clues, the exact solution was never explained. This method was called *learning by understanding* (later called the *discovery* method).

Katona's experiment included the problem shown in Figure 10.1. This figure shows a pattern of five squares made of matchsticks. The problem is to change the pattern into exactly four squares by moving only three matches. (All matches must be used, none can be removed, and all the squares must be the same size.) Two groups of subjects learned the solution to this problem. One group learned by understanding, and the other group learned by memorization. After 3 weeks, both groups returned to be tested again. The two groups did equally well on the matchstick problem they had learned earlier. But when they were given two new problems (similar to the matchstick problem), the *understanding* group performed much better than the *memorization* group.

The outcome of Katona's experiment probably is no surprise. However, you should realize that the experimental design is different from any we have considered before. This experiment involved *two separate samples*. Previously, we have examined statistical techniques for evaluating the data

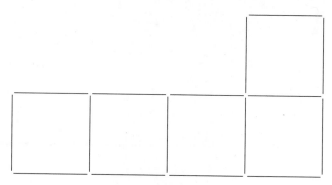

FIGURE 10.1

A pattern of five squares made of matchsticks. The problem is to change the pattern into exactly four squares by moving only three matchsticks.

from only one sample. In this chapter, we will present the statistical procedures that allow a researcher to use two samples to evaluate the difference between two experimental treatment conditions.

Incidentally, if you still have not discovered the solution to the matchstick problem, keep trying. According to Katona's results, it would be very poor teaching strategy for us to give you the answer.

Katona, G. (1940) *Organizing and Memorizing.* New York: Columbia University Press. Reprinted by permission.

10.1 OVERVIEW

Until this point, all the inferential statistics we have considered have involved using one sample as the basis for drawing conclusions about one population. Although these *single-sample* techniques are used occasionally in real research, most of the interesting experiments require two (or more) sets of data in order to compare two (or more) populations. For example, a social psychologist may want to compare men and women in terms of their attitudes toward abortion, or an educational psychologist may want to compare two methods for teaching mathematics. In both of these examples, the basic question concerns a mean difference between two populations or between two treatments. Is the average attitude for men any different from the average attitude for women? Do children who are taught math by method A score higher than children who are taught by method B?

FIGURE 10.2

Do the achievement scores for children taught by method A differ from the scores for children taught by method B? In statistical terms, are the two population means the same or different? Because neither of the two population means is known, it will be necessary to take two samples, one from each population. The first sample will provide information about the mean for the first population, and the second sample will provide information about the second population.

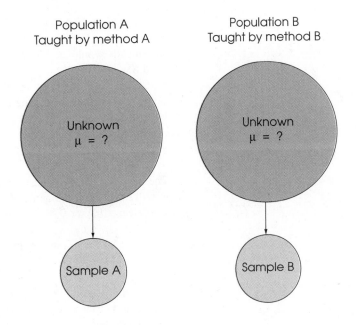

In most experimental situations, a researcher will not have prior knowledge about either of the two populations being compared. This means that the researcher has a question about two unknown populations. One way to examine two unknown populations is to take two separate samples (see Figure 10.2). In this chapter, we will present the statistical techniques that permit a researcher to examine the data obtained from two separate samples. More specifically, our goal is to use the data from two samples as the basis for evaluating the mean difference between two populations.

DEFINITION   An experiment that uses a separate sample for each treatment condition (or each population) is called an *independent-measures* research design.

The term *independent-measures* comes from the fact that the data consist of two *independent* sets of measurements, that is, two separate samples. On occasion, you will see an independent-measures experiment referred to as a *between-subjects* or a *between-groups* design. This terminology reflects the fact that an independent-measures design evaluates differences between treatments by looking at differences between the groups of subjects.

10.2 THE *t* STATISTIC FOR AN INDEPENDENT-MEASURES RESEARCH DESIGN

Because an independent-measures study involves two separate samples, we will need some special notation to help specify which data go with which sample. This notation involves the use of subscripts, which are small numbers written beside a sample statistic. For example, the number of scores in the first sample would be identified by n_1; for the second sample, the number of scores would be n_2. The sample means would be identified by $\overline{X}_1$ and $\overline{X}_2$. The sums of squares would be SS_1 and SS_2.

Recall that our goal is to evaluate the mean difference between two populations (or between two treatment conditions). In symbols, the mean difference between the two populations can be written as $\mu_1 - \mu_2$. For hypothesis tests, we will hypothesize a value for this mean difference. Generally, the null hypothesis says there is no difference between the two population means: $\mu_1 - \mu_2 = 0$.

The basis for the hypothesis test will be a t statistic. The formula for this t statistic will have the same general structure as the single-sample t formula that was introduced in Chapter 9.

$$ t = \frac{\overline{X} - \mu}{s_{\overline{X}}} = \frac{\text{sample statistic} - \text{population parameter}}{\text{estimated standard error}} $$

However, the details of the formula must be modified to accommodate the independent-measures research design. Now the population parameter of interest is the difference between the two population means ($\mu_1 - \mu_2$). The corresponding sample statistic will be the difference between the two sample means ($\overline{X}_1 - \overline{X}_2$). The standard error in the denominator of the formula measures the standard distance between the sample statistic ($\overline{X}_1 - \overline{X}_2$) and the population parameter ($\mu_1 - \mu_2$). As always, standard error tells how well a sample value is expected to approximate the corresponding population value. In this case, the standard error tells how well the sample mean difference should approximate the population mean difference. The symbol for this standard error is $s_{\overline{X}_1 - \overline{X}_2}$. The s indicates an estimated standard distance, and the subscript $\overline{X}_1 - \overline{X}_2$ simply indicates that our sample value is the difference between two sample means. Substituting these values into the general t formula gives

$$ t = \frac{(\overline{X}_1 - \overline{X}_2) - (\mu_1 - \mu_2)}{s_{\overline{X}_1 - \overline{X}_2}} $$

This is the t formula that will be used with data from an independent-measures study. You should note that this is still a t statistic; it has the same basic structure as the original t formula that was introduced in Chapter 9. However, to distinguish between these two t formulas, we will occasionally refer to the original formula as the *single-sample t statistic* and this new formula as the *independent-measures t statistic*. To complete the independent-measures t formula, we must define more precisely the calculations needed for the standard error, $s_{\overline{X}_1 - \overline{X}_2}$.

THE STANDARD ERROR FOR A SAMPLE MEAN DIFFERENCE

In general, the purpose of standard error is to provide a measure of how accurately a sample statistic approximates the population parameter. In the independent-measures t formula, the sample statistic consists of two sample means, and the population parameter consists of two population means. We expect the sample statistic ($\overline{X}_1 - \overline{X}_2$) to be close to the population parameter ($\mu_1 - \mu_2$), but there will be some error. Our goal is to determine how much error. To develop the formula for this standard error, we will consider three points:

1. There are two sources of error because each of the two samples provides an estimate of its own population mean.

   $\overline{X}_1$ approximates μ_1 with some error.

   $\overline{X}_2$ approximates μ_2 with some error.

2. The amount of error associated with each sample mean can be measured by the standard error of $\overline{X}$. In Chapter 9, we calculated this standard error from sample variance (equation 9.1) as follows:

$$s_{\overline{X}} = \sqrt{\frac{s^2}{n}}$$

3. For the independent-measures t statistic, we want to know the total amount of error involved in using *two* sample means to approximate *two* population means. To do this, we will find the error from each sample separately and then add the two errors together. The resulting formula for standard error is

$$s_{\overline{X}_1 - \overline{X}_2} = \sqrt{\frac{s_1^2}{n_1} + \frac{s_2^2}{n_2}} \qquad (10.1)$$

Because the sample statistic $(\overline{X}_1 - \overline{X}_2)$ consists of two sample means and the corresponding parameter $(\mu_1 - \mu_2)$ consists of two population means, we have now accounted for the two sources of error (see Box 10.1).

POOLED VARIANCE

Although equation 10.1 accurately presents the concept of standard error for the independent-measures t statistic, this formula is limited to situations where the two samples are exactly the same size (that is, $n_1 = n_2$). In situations where the two sample sizes are different, the formula is *biased* and, therefore, inappropriate. The bias comes from the fact that equation 10.1 treats the two sample variances equally. However, when the sample sizes are different, the two sample variances are not equally good and should not be treated equally. In Chapter 7, we introduced the law of large numbers, which states that statistics obtained from large samples tend to be better (more accurate) estimates of population parameters than statistics obtained from small samples. This same fact holds for sample variances: The variance obtained from a large sample will be a more accurate estimate of σ^2 than the variance obtained from a small sample.

To correct for the bias in the sample variances, the independent-measures t statistic will combine the two sample variances into a single value called the *pooled variance*. The pooled variance is obtained by averaging or "pooling" the two sample variances using a procedure that allows the bigger sample to carry more weight in determining the final value. This process is demonstrated in the following example.

EXAMPLE 10.1

Suppose that we have two samples from the same population. The first sample has $n = 4$ scores and $SS = 36$. For the second sample, $n = 8$ and $SS = 56$. From these data, we can compute a variance for each sample.

10.1   THE VARIABILITY OF DIFFERENCE SCORES

IT MAY seem odd that the independent-measures *t* statistic *adds* together the two sample errors when it *subtracts* to find the difference between the two sample means. The logic behind this apparently unusual procedure is demonstrated here.

We begin with two populations, I and II (see Figure 10.3). The scores in population I range from a high of 70 to a low of 50. The scores in population II range from 30 to 20. We will use the range as a measure of how spread out (variable) each population is:

For population I, the scores cover a range of 20 points.

For population II, the scores cover a range of 10 points

If we randomly select a score from population I and a score from population II and compute the difference between these two scores ($X_1 - X_2$), what range of values is possible for these differences? To answer this question,

we need to find the biggest possible difference and the smallest possible difference. Look at Figure 10.3; the biggest difference occurs when $X_1 = 70$ and $X_2 = 20$. This is a difference of $X_1 - X_2 = 50$ points. The smallest difference occurs when $X_1 = 50$ and $X_2 = 30$. This is a difference of $X_1 - X_2 = 20$ points. Notice that the differences go from a high of 50 to a low of 20. This is a range of 30 points:

range for population I (X_1 scores) = 20 points

range for population II (X_2 scores) = 10 points

range for the differences ($X_1 - X_2$) = 30 points

The variability for the difference scores is found by *adding* together the variabilities for the two populations.

In the independent-measures *t* statistics, we are computing the variability (standard error) for a sample mean difference. To compute this value, we add together the variability for each of the two sample means.

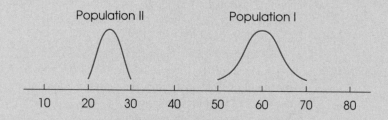

Population II   Population I

10	20	30	40	50	60	70	80

FIGURE 10.3

Two population distributions. The scores in population I vary from 50 to 70 (a 20-point spread), and the scores in population II range from 20 to 30 (a 10-point spread). If you select one score from each of these two populations, the closest two values are $X_1 = 50$ and $X_2 = 30$. The two values that are farthest apart are $X_1 = 70$ and $X_2 = 20$.

For sample 1,

$$s_1^2 = \frac{SS}{n-1} = \frac{36}{3} = 12$$

For sample 2,

$$s_2^2 = \frac{SS}{n-1} = \frac{56}{7} = 8$$

Because these two samples are from the same population, each of the sample variances provides an estimate of the same population variance. Therefore, it is reasonable somehow to average these two estimates together in order to get a better estimate. Before we average the two variances, however, you should notice that one of the samples is much bigger than the other. Because bigger samples tend to give better estimates of the population, we would expect the sample variance based on $n = 8$ to be a better value than the variance based on $n = 4$. When we pool the two variances, we will let the "better" value carry more weight.

To compute the pooled variance, we will weight each of the sample variances by its degrees of freedom ($df = n - 1$). The degrees of freedom indicate how well the sample variance approximates the population variance (the bigger the sample, the bigger the df, and the better the estimate). To find the pooled variance, or the weighted mean for two sample variances, you follow two steps:

1. Multiply each s^2 by its df and then add the results together (this weights each variance).

2. Divide this total by the sum of the two df values.

The equation for this process is

$$\text{pooled variance} = s_p^2 = \frac{df_1 s_1^2 + df_2 s_2^2}{df_1 + df_2} \tag{10.2}$$

For this example, the calculation can be described in words as follows: You take 3 of the first variance ($df = 3$) and 7 of the second variance ($df = 7$). This gives you a total of 10 variances ($df_1 + df_2 = 10$). To find the average, you must divide by 10. For example,

$$\text{pooled variance} = \frac{3(12) + 7(8)}{3 + 7} = \frac{36 + 56}{10} = 9.2$$

Notice that the value we obtained is not halfway between the two sample variances. Rather, it is closer to $s^2 = 8$ (the big sample) than it is to $s^2 = 12$ (the small sample) because the larger sample carried more weight in computing the average.

You may have noticed that the calculation of the pooled variance in Example 10.1 can be simplified greatly. In the numerator of the formula, each sample variance is multiplied by its df. When you do this, you always obtain *SS*:

$$df(s^2) = df\frac{SS}{df} = SS$$

Therefore, we can use *SS* in place of $df(s^2)$ in the formula. The simplified result is

$$\text{pooled variance} = s_p^2 = \frac{SS_1 + SS_2}{df_1 + df_2} \tag{10.3}$$

Using the pooled variance (equation 10.3), we can now obtain an unbiased measure of the standard error for a sample mean difference. The resulting formula for the independent-measures standard error is

10.2 POOLED VARIANCE: THE WEIGHTED MEAN SQUARE

IN CHAPTER 3 (p. 75), we introduced the weighted mean. This enabled us to take two samples, combine them, and determine the new mean. The mean for this combined group is weighted in the direction of the mean from the larger sample. We demonstrated that the weighted mean can be obtained as follows:

$$\text{weighted mean} = \frac{\Sigma X_1 + \Sigma X_2}{n_1 + n_2}$$

or, more simply,

$$\text{weighted mean} = \frac{\text{sum for sample 1} + \text{sum for sample 2}}{n_1 + n_2}$$

$$= \frac{\text{combined sum}}{\text{combined } n}$$

In Chapter 4, we introduced the notion that variance is *the mean of the squared deviation scores*; hence, the term *mean square* (or *MS*). If we were to compute the combined mean square for two samples, we would need to know

1. The *sum* of the squared deviations for each sample (*SS*).
2. The *number* of scores free to vary for each sample (*df*).

Because a weighted (or "pooled") mean requires that you combine two sums and combine two *ns* (in this case, the number of scores free to vary), the pooled variance can be expressed as

$$s_p^2 = \frac{SS_1 + SS_2}{df_1 + df_2} = \frac{\text{combined } SS}{\text{combined } df}$$

$$s_{\overline{X}_1 - \overline{X}_2} = \sqrt{\frac{s_p^2}{n_1} + \frac{s_p^2}{n_2}} \qquad (10.4)$$

In this formula, s_p^2/n_1 represents the error from the first sample, and s_p^2/n_2 is the error from the second sample. Because we now have two sample means approximating two population means, we now have two sources of error. The formula for the standard error for the independent-measures *t* statistic simply adds together the two sources of error. Also note that the standard error formula uses the pooled variance, s_p^2, as the measure of variability for the scores. Box 10.2 shows how the pooled variance calculation (equation 10.3) is similar to a weighted mean.

THE FINAL FORMULA AND DEGREES OF FREEDOM

The complete equation for the independent-measures *t* statistic is as follows:

$$t = \frac{(\overline{X}_1 - \overline{X}_2) - (\mu_1 - \mu_2)}{s_{\overline{X}_1 - \overline{X}_2}} = \frac{(\overline{X}_1 - \overline{X}_2) - (\mu_1 - \mu_2)}{\sqrt{\frac{s_p^2}{n_1} + \frac{s_p^2}{n_2}}} \qquad (10.5)$$

with the pooled variance, s_p^2, defined by either equation 10.2 or equation 10.3.

The degrees of freedom for this *t* statistic are determined by the *df* values for the two separate samples:

Remember, we pooled the two sample variances to compute the *t* statistic. Now we combine the two *df* values to obtain the overall *df* for the *t* statistic.

$$df = df \text{ for first sample} + df \text{ for second example} \qquad (10.6)$$

$$= df_1 + df_2$$

Occasionally, you will see degrees of freedom written in terms of the number of scores in each sample:

$$df = (n_1 - 1) + (n_2 - 1) \qquad (10.7)$$
$$= n_1 + n_2 - 2$$

This *t* formula will be used for hypothesis testing. We will use the sample statistic $(\overline{X}_1 - \overline{X}_2)$ as the basis for testing hypotheses about the population parameter $(\mu_1 - \mu_2)$.

LEARNING CHECK

1. Describe the general experimental situation in which an independent-measures statistic would be used.

2. Identify the two sources of error that are reflected in the standard error for the independent-measures *t* statistic.

3. Sample 1 of an experiment has dozens of subjects, and $s_1^2 = 32$. On the other hand, sample 2 has fewer than 10 subjects, and its variance is $s_2^2 = 57$. When these variances are pooled, which sample variance will s_p^2 more closely resemble?

ANSWERS

1. Independent-measures statistics are used whenever an experiment uses separate samples to represent the different treatment conditions or populations being compared.

2. The two sources of error come from the differences between the means of both samples and their respective population means. That is, $\overline{X}_1$ approximates μ_1 with some error, and $\overline{X}_2$ approximates μ_2 with some error.

3. The value for s_p^2 will be closer to $s_1^2 = 32$ because the size of sample 1 is larger.

10.3 HYPOTHESIS TESTS WITH THE INDEPENDENT-MEASURES *t* STATISTIC

The independent-measures *t* statistic can be used to test a hypothesis about the mean difference between two populations (or between two treatments). As always, the null hypothesis states that there is no difference:

$$H_0: \mu_1 - \mu_2 = 0$$

The alternative hypothesis says that there is a mean difference:

$$H_1: \mu_1 - \mu_2 \neq 0$$

The hypothesis-testing procedure will determine whether or not the data provide evidence for a mean difference between the two populations. At the conclusion of the hypothesis test, we will decide either to

a. Reject H_0 (We conclude that the data indicate a significant difference between the two populations.) or to

FIGURE 10.4

The *t* distribution with *df* = 18. The critical region for α = .05 is shown.

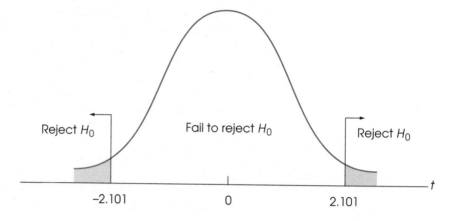

Reject H_0 Fail to reject H_0 Reject H_0

−2.101   0   2.101

t

b. Fail to reject H_0 (The data do not provide sufficient evidence to conclude that a difference exists.).

For hypothesis tests, we will use the *t* formula as follows:

$$t = \frac{\text{sample statistic} - \text{hypothesized population parameter}}{\text{estimated standard error}}$$

Notice that the independent-measures *t* statistic forms a ratio, just like the *z*-score or single-sample *t*. The numerator of the ratio measures the obtained difference between the sample statistic (the data) and the hypothesized population parameter (from H_0). The denominator of the ratio is the standard error, which measures how much difference is expected just by chance. Thus, the basic structure of the independent-measures *t* is the same as we have encountered earlier:

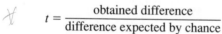

$$t = \frac{\text{obtained difference}}{\text{difference expected by chance}}$$

As always, a large value for *t* provides evidence that the obtained difference (from the data) is caused by more than chance (see Figure 10.4).

A complete example of a hypothesis test with two independent samples follows. Notice that the hypothesis-testing procedure follows the same four steps that we have used before.

STEP 1 State the hypotheses H_0 and H_1, and select an alpha level. For the independent-measures *t* test, the hypotheses concern the difference between two population means.

STEP 2 Locate the critical region. The critical region is defined as sample data that would be extremely unlikely ($p < α$) if the null hypothesis were true. In this case, we will be locating extremely unlikely *t* values.

STEP 3 Get the data, and compute the test statistic. Here we compute the *t* value for our data using the value from H_0 in the formula.

STEP 4 Make a decision. If the *t* statistic we compute is in the critical region, we reject H_0. Otherwise, we conclude that the data do not provide sufficient evidence that the two populations are different.

EXAMPLE 10.2

Remember, an independent-measures design means that there are separate samples for each treatment condition.

In recent years, psychologists have demonstrated repeatedly that using mental images can greatly improve memory. A hypothetical experiment, designed to examine this phenomenon, is presented here.

The psychologist first prepares a list of 40 pairs of nouns (for example, dog/bicycle, grass/door, lamp/piano). Next, two groups of subjects are obtained (two separate samples). Subjects in the first group are given the list for 5 minutes and instructed to memorize the 40 noun pairs. Subjects in the second group receive the same list of words, but in addition to the regular instructions, these people are told to form a mental image for each pair of nouns (imagine a dog riding a bicycle, for example). Notice that the two samples are identical except that the second group is using mental images to help learn the list.

Later each group is given a memory test, and the psychologist records the number of words correctly recalled for each individual. The data from this experiment are as follows. On the basis of these data, can the psychologist conclude that mental images affected memory?

Software manuals:
Minitab (Section 5)
Mystat (Section 3)
SPSS (Section 6)

DATA (NUMBER OF WORDS RECALLED)			
GROUP 1 (NO IMAGES)		GROUP 2 (IMAGES)	
24	13	18	31
23	17	19	29
16	20	23	26
17	15	29	21
19	26	30	24
$n = 10$		$n = 10$	
$\overline{X} = 19$		$\overline{X} = 25$	
$SS = 160$		$SS = 200$	

(handwritten: 576, 529, 256, 289, 361, 169, 289, 400, 225, 676, 3770, 3770-3610 / 160, 190/36180)

STEP 1 State the hypotheses, and select the alpha level.

Directional hypotheses could be used and would specify whether imagery should increase or decrease recall scores.

H_0: $\mu_1 - \mu_2 = 0$ (no difference; imagery has no effect)

H_1: $\mu_1 - \mu_2 \neq 0$ (imagery produces a difference)

We will set $\alpha = .05$.

STEP 2 This is an independent-measures design. The *t* statistic for these data will have degrees of freedom determined by

$$df = df_1 + df_2$$
$$= (n_1 - 1) + (n_2 - 1)$$
$$= 9 + 9$$
$$= 18$$

The *t* distribution for $df = 18$ is presented in Figure 10.4. For $\alpha = .05$, the critical region consists of the extreme 5% of the distribution and has boundaries of $t = +2.101$ and $t = -2.101$.

STEP 3 Obtain the data, and compute the test statistic. The data are as given, so all that remains is to compute the t statistic. Because the independent-measures t formula is relatively complex, the calculations can be simplified by dividing the process into three parts.

First, find the pooled variance for the two samples:

Caution: The pooled variance combines the two samples to obtain a single estimate of variance. In the formula, the two samples are combined in a single fraction. You divide the combined SS by the combined df.

$$s_p^2 = \frac{SS_1 + SS_2}{df_1 + df_2}$$

$$= \frac{160 + 200}{9 + 9}$$

$$= \frac{360}{18}$$

$$= 20$$

Second, use the pooled variance to compute the standard error:

Caution: The standard error adds the errors from two separate samples. In the formula, these two errors are added as two separate fractions.

$$s_{\overline{X}_1 - \overline{X}_2} = \sqrt{\frac{s_p^2}{n_1} + \frac{s_p^2}{n_2}}$$

$$= \sqrt{\frac{20}{10} + \frac{20}{10}}$$

$$= \sqrt{4}$$

$$= 2$$

Third, compute the t statistic:

$$t = \frac{(\overline{X}_1 - \overline{X}_2) - (\mu_1 - \mu_2)}{s_{\overline{X}_1 - \overline{X}_2}} = \frac{(19 - 25) - 0}{2}$$

$$= \frac{-6}{2}$$

$$= -3.00$$

STEP 4 Make a decision. The obtained value ($t = -3.00$) is in the critical region. In this example, the obtained sample mean difference is three times greater than would be expected by chance (the standard error). This result is very unlikely if H_0 is true. Therefore, we reject H_0 and conclude that using mental images produced a significant difference in memory performance. More specifically, the group using images recalled significantly more words than the group with no images.

IN THE LITERATURE:
REPORTING THE RESULTS OF AN INDEPENDENT-MEASURES *t* TEST

In Chapter 4 (p. 121), we demonstrated how the mean and the standard deviation are reported in APA format. In Chapter 9 (p. 277), we illustrated the APA style for reporting the results of a *t* test. Now we will use the APA format to report the results of Example 10.2, an independent-measures *t* test. A concise statement might read as follows:

> The group using mental images recalled more words ($M = 25$, $SD = 4.71$) than the group that did not use mental images ($M = 19$, $SD = 4.22$). This difference was significant, $t(18) = -3.00$, $p < .05$, two-tailed.

You should note that standard deviation is not a step in the computations for the independent-measures *t* test. Yet it is useful when providing descriptive statistics for each treatment group. It is easily computed when doing the *t* test because you need *SS* and *df* for both groups to determine the pooled variance. Note that the format for reporting *t* is exactly the same as that described in Chapter 9.   ❑

DIRECTIONAL HYPOTHESES AND ONE-TAILED TESTS

When planning an independent-measures experiment, a researcher usually has some expectation or specific prediction for the outcome. For the memory experiment described in Example 10.2, the psychologist clearly expects the group using images to have higher memory scores than the group without images. This kind of directional prediction can be incorporated into the statement of the hypotheses, resulting in a directional, or one-tailed, test. You should recall from Chapter 8 that one-tailed tests can be less conservative than two-tailed tests, and should be used when clearly justified by theory or previous findings. The following example demonstrates the procedure for stating hypotheses and locating the critical region for a one-tailed test using the independent-measures *t* statistic.

EXAMPLE 10.3

We will use the same experimental situation that was described in Example 10.2. The researcher is using an independent-measures design to examine the effect of mental images on memory. The prediction is that the imagery group will have higher memory scores.

STEP 1

State the hypotheses, and select α. As always, the null hypothesis says that there is no effect, and H_1 says that there is a difference between the treatments. With a one-tailed test, it usually is easier to begin with the statement of H_1.

For this example, we will identify the no-imagery condition as treatment 1 and the imagery condition as treatment 2. Because images are expected to produce higher scores, the alternative hypothesis would be

$$H_1: \quad \mu_1 - \mu_2 < 0 \quad \text{(imagery produces higher scores)}$$

The null hypothesis states that the treatment does not work. For this example,

$$H_0: \quad \mu_1 - \mu_2 \geq 0 \quad \text{(imagery scores are not higher)}$$

We will set $\alpha = .05$.

STEP 2

Locate the critical region. The researcher predicts that the imagery group (sample 2) will have higher scores. If this is correct, then $\overline{X}_2$ will be greater than $\overline{X}_1$, and the data will produce a negative *t* statistic.

$$t = \frac{(\overline{X}_1 - \overline{X}_2) - (\mu_1 - \mu_2)}{s_{\overline{X}_1 - \overline{X}_2}}$$

FIGURE 10.5

The critical region in the t distribution for $\alpha = .05$, $df = 18$, one-tailed test.

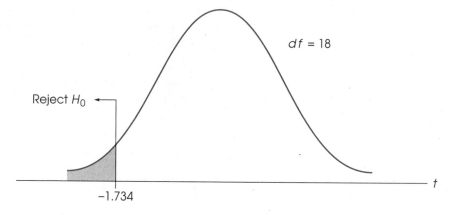

Thus, a negative value for t will tend to support the researcher's prediction and refute H_0. The question is, How large a negative t value is needed to reject H_0? With $n = 10$ scores in each sample, the data will produce an independent-measures t statistic with $df = 18$. To find the critical value, look in the t distribution table with $df = 18$ and $\alpha = .05$ for a one-tailed test. You will find a critical t value of 1.734, and this value should be negative. Figure 10.5 shows the one-tailed critical region in the t distribution. The data from this example produce a test statistic of $t = -3.00$ (see Example 10.2). This value is in the critical region, so we reject H_0 and conclude that recall is significantly better in the imagery condition than in the no-imagery condition.

The table lists critical values without signs. You must determine whether the sign is positive or negative.

THE t STATISTIC AS A RATIO

You should note that the magnitude of the t statistic is determined not only by the mean difference between the two samples, but also by the sample variability. The bigger the difference between the sample means (the numerator of the t formula), the bigger the t value. This relationship is reasonable because a big difference between the samples is a clear indication of a difference between the two populations. However, the sample variability (in the denominator of the t formula) is just as important. If the variability is large, t will tend to be small. The role of variability becomes clearer if you consider a simplified version of the t formula:

$$t = \frac{\text{sample mean difference}}{\text{variability}}$$

Notice that we have left out the population mean difference because the null hypothesis says that this is zero. Also, we have used the general term *variability* in place of standard error. In this simplified form, t becomes a ratio involving only the sample mean difference and the sample variability. It should be clear that large variability will make the t value smaller (or small variability will make t larger). Thus, variability plays an important role in determining whether or not a t statistic is significant. When variability is large, even a big difference between the two sample means may not be enough to make the t statistic significant. On the other hand, when variability is low, even a small difference between the two sample

FIGURE 10.6

Data from experiment I comparing attitude scores for men versus women. The independent-measures t test for these data gives a t statistic of $t = 9.17$. This value is in the critical region, so we reject H_0 and conclude that the two samples come from different populations.

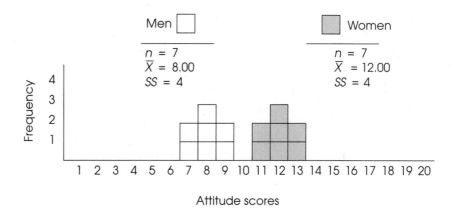

means may be enough to produce a significant t statistic. The importance of sample variability is demonstrated in the following example.

EXAMPLE 10.4   The following two hypothetical experiments demonstrate the influence of variability in the computation and interpretation of an independent-measures t statistic. Each of these experiments compares attitude scores for men versus women. Both experiments use a sample of $n = 7$ individuals from each of the populations, and both experiments obtain the same sample mean values ($\overline{X} = 8$ for the men and $\overline{X} = 12$ for the women). The only difference between the two experiments is in the amount of sample variability.

The data from experiment I are pictured in Figure 10.6. In this experiment, the scores in each sample are clustered around the mean, so the sample variability is relatively small. The hypothesis test using these data gives a t statistic of $t = 9.17$. With $df = 12$, this value is in the critical region, so we would reject H_0 and conclude that the population mean for men is different from the population mean for women.

If you look at the data in Figure 10.6, the statistical decision should be easy to understand. The two samples look like they come from different populations. By visually examining a graph of the data, you often can predict the outcome of a statistical test.

Now consider the data from experiment II, which are shown in Figure 10.7. Do these two samples look like they came from two separate populations? It should be clear that it is no longer easy to see a difference between the two samples. The scores completely overlap, and it appears likely that all 14 scores could have come from the same population.

The impression that the two samples do not look different is supported by the hypothesis test. The data from experiment II give a t statistic of $t = 1.18$. This value is not in the critical region, so we fail to reject H_0. In this case, we conclude that there is not enough evidence to say that the samples come from two different populations.

There are two general points to be made from this example. First, variability plays an important role in the independent-measures hypothesis test. In both experiments, there was a 4-point difference between the two sample

FIGURE 10.7

Data from experiment II comparing attitude scores for men versus women. The independent-measures t test for these data gives a t statistic of $t = 1.18$. This value is not in the critical region, so we fail to reject H_0 and conclude that there is not sufficient evidence to say that the two samples come from different populations.

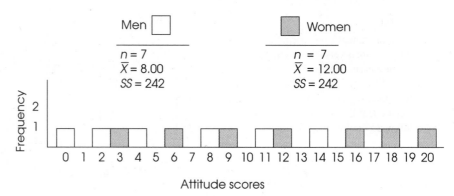

means. In experiment I, this difference was easy to see, and it was statistically significant. In experiment II, this 4-point difference gets lost in all the variability.

The second point is that the t statistic you obtain from a hypothesis test should be intuitively reasonable. In the first experiment, it looks like there are two separate populations, and the t statistic supports this appearance. In the second experiment, there does not appear to be any difference, and the t statistic says that there is no difference. The t value should not be a mysterious number; it simply is a precise, mathematical way of determining whether or not it "looks like" there is a difference between two samples.

LEARNING CHECK

1. A developmental psychologist would like to examine the difference in mathematical skills for 10-year-old boys versus 10-year-old girls. A sample of 10 boys and 10 girls is obtained, and each child is given a standardized mathematical abilities test. The data from this experiment are as follows:

BOYS	GIRLS
$\overline{X} = 37$	$\overline{X} = 31$
$SS = 150$	$SS = 210$

Do these data indicate a significant difference in mathematical skills for boys versus girls? Test at the .05 level of significance.

2. A psychologist is interested in the effect of aging on memory. A sample of 10 college graduates is obtained. Five of these people are between 30 and 35 years old. The other 5 are between 60 and 65 years old. Each person is given a list of 40 words to memorize. An hour later, each person is asked to recall as many of the words as possible. The data from this experiment are as follows:

30-YEARS-OLD	60-YEARS-OLD
$\overline{X} = 21$	$\overline{X} = 16$
$SS = 130$	$SS = 190$

Do these data provide evidence for a significant change in recall ability with age? Test at the .05 level of significance.

ANSWERS **1.** Pooled variance = 20; standard error = 2; $t = 3.00$. With $df = 18$, this value is in the critical region, so the decision is to reject H_0: There is a significant difference.

  2. Pooled variance = 40; standard error = 4; $t = 1.25$. With $df = 8$, this value is not in the critical region, so the decision is to fail to reject H_0: These data do not provide evidence for a significant difference.

10.4 ASSUMPTIONS UNDERLYING THE INDEPENDENT-MEASURES *t* FORMULA

There are three assumptions that should be satisfied before you use the independent-measures *t* formula for hypothesis testing:

1. The observations within each sample must be independent (see p. 244).
2. The two populations from which the samples are selected must be normal.
3. The two populations from which the samples are selected must have equal variances.

The first two assumptions should be familiar from the single-sample *t* hypothesis test presented in Chapter 9. As before, the normality assumption is the less important of the two, especially with large samples. When there is reason to suspect that the populations are far from normal, you should compensate by ensuring that the samples are relatively large.

The third assumption is referred to as *homogeneity of variance* and states that the two populations being compared must have the same variance. You may recall a similar assumption for both the *z*-score and the single-sample *t*. For those tests, we assumed that the effect of the treatment was to add (or subtract) a constant amount to each individual score. As a result, the population standard deviation after treatment was the same as it had been before treatment. We now are making essentially the same assumption, but phrasing it in terms of variances.

> Remember, adding a constant to (or subtracting a constant from) each score does not change the standard deviation.

You should recall that the pooled variance in the *t* statistic formula is obtained by averaging together the two sample variances. It makes sense to average these two values only if they both are estimating the same population variance—i.e., if the homogeneity of variance assumption is satisfied. If the two sample variances represent different population variances, then the average would be meaningless. (*Note:* There is no meaning to the value obtained by averaging two unrelated numbers. For example, what is the significance of the number obtained by averaging your shoe size and the last two digits of your social security number?)

> The importance of the homogeneity assumption increases when there is a large discrepancy between the sample sizes. With equal (or nearly equal) sample sizes, this assumption is less critical, but still important.

The homogeneity of variance assumption is quite important because violating this assumption can negate any meaningful interpretation of the data from an independent-measures experiment. Specifically, when you compute the *t* statistic in a hypothesis test, all the numbers in the formula come from the data except for the population mean difference, which you get from H_0. Thus, you are sure of all the numbers in the formula except for one. If you obtain an extreme result for the

HARTLEY'S *F*-MAX TEST FOR HOMOGENEITY OF VARIANCE

ALTHOUGH THERE are many different statistical methods for determining whether or not the homogeneity of variance assumption has been satisfied, Hartley's *F*-max test is one of the simplest to compute and to understand. An additional advantage is that this test can be used to check homogeneity of variance with two or more independent samples. In Chapter 13, we will examine statistical methods involving several samples, and Hartley's test will be useful again.

The *F*-max test is based on the principle that a sample variance provides an unbiased estimate of the population variance. Therefore, if the population variances are the same, the sample variances should be very similar. The procedure for using the *F*-max test is as follows:

1. Compute the sample variance, $s^2 = SS/df$, for each of the separate samples.

2. Select the largest and the smallest of these sample variances, and compute

$$F\text{-max} = \frac{s^2(\text{largest})}{s^2(\text{smallest})}$$

A relatively large value for *F*-max indicates a large difference between the sample variances. In this case, the data suggest that the population variances are different and that the homogeneity assumption has been violated. On the other hand, a small value of *F*-max (near 1.00) indicates that the sample variances are similar and that the homogeneity assumption is reasonable.

3. The *F*-max value computed for the sample data is compared with the critical value found in Table B3 (Appendix B). If the sample value is larger than the table value, then you conclude that the variances are different and that the homogeneity assumption is not valid.

To locate the critical value in the table, you need to know

a. k = number of separate samples. (For the independent-measures *t* test, $k = 2$.)

b. $df = n - 1$ for each sample variance. The Hartley test assumes that all samples are the same size.

c. The α level. The table provides critical values for $\alpha = .05$ and $\alpha = .01$. Generally, a test for homogeneity would use the larger alpha level.

Example: Two independent samples each have $n = 10$. The sample variances are 12.34 and 9.15. For these data,

$$F\text{-max} = \frac{s^2(\text{largest})}{s^2(\text{smallest})} = \frac{12.34}{9.15} = 1.35$$

With $\alpha = .05$, $k = 2$, and $df = n - 1 = 9$, the critical value from the table is 4.03. Because the obtained *F*-max is smaller than this critical value, you conclude that the data do not provide evidence that the homogeneity of variance assumption has been violated.

t statistic (a value in the critical region), you conclude that the hypothesized value was wrong. But consider what happens when you violate the homogeneity of variance assumption. In this case, you have two questionable values in the formula (the hypothesized population value and the meaningless average of the two variances). Now if you obtain an extreme *t* statistic, you do not know which of these two values is responsible. Specifically, you cannot reject the hypothesis because it may have been the pooled variance that produced the extreme *t* statistic. Without satisfying the homogeneity of variance requirement, you cannot accurately interpret a *t* statistic, and the hypothesis test becomes meaningless.

How do you know whether or not the homogeneity of variance requirement is satisfied? There are statistical tests that can be used to determine if the two population variances are the same or different (see Box 10.3), but there is a simple rule of thumb that works most of the time. If the two population variances are the same, then the two sample variances should be very similar. You can just look at the two sample variances to see whether or not they are close. For small samples ($n < 10$), if one of the sample variances is more than four times larger than the other, you probably have violated the homogeneity of variance requirement. For larger samples, there is reason for concern if one variance is more than two times larger than the other. Otherwise, the two population variances are close enough to proceed with the hypothesis test.

SUMMARY

1. The independent-measures t statistic is used to draw inferences about the mean difference between two populations or between two treatment conditions. The term *independent* is used because this t statistic requires data from two separate (or independent) samples.

2. The formula for the independent measures t statistic has the same structure as the original z-score or the single-sample t:

$$t = \frac{\text{sample statistic} - \text{population parameter}}{\text{estimated standard error}}$$

For the independent-measures statistic, the sample statistic consists of the difference between the two sample means $(\overline{X}_1 - \overline{X}_2)$. The population parameter of interest is the difference between the two population means $(\mu_1 - \mu_2)$. The standard error is computed by combining the errors for the two sample means. The resulting formula is

$$t = \frac{(\overline{X}_1 - \overline{X}_2) - (\mu_1 - \mu_2)}{s_{\overline{X}_1 - \overline{X}_2}}$$

$$= \frac{(\overline{X}_1 - \overline{X}_2) - (\mu_1 - \mu_2)}{\sqrt{\dfrac{s_p^2}{n_1} + \dfrac{s_p^2}{n_2}}}$$

The pooled variance in the formula, s_p^2, is the weighted mean of the two sample variances:

$$s_p^2 = \frac{SS_1 + SS_2}{df_1 + df_2}$$

This t statistic has degrees of freedom determined by the sum of the df values for the two samples:

$$df = df_1 + df_2$$

$$= (n_1 - 1) + (n_2 - 1)$$

3. For hypothesis testing, the formula has the following structure:

$$t = \frac{\text{sample statistic} - \text{population hypothesis}}{\text{estimated standard error}}$$

The null hypothesis normally states that there is no difference between the two population means:

$$H_0: \mu_1 = \mu_2 \quad \text{or} \quad \mu_1 - \mu_2 = 0$$

4. Appropriate use and interpretation of the t statistic require that the data satisfy the homogeneity of variance assumption. This assumption stipulates that the two populations have equal variances. An informal test of this assumption can be made by simply comparing the two sample variances: If the two sample variances are approximately equal, the t test is justified. Hartley's F-max test provides a statistical technique for determining whether or not the data satisfy the homogeneity assumption.

KEY TERMS

independent-measures research design

between-subjects research design

pooled variance

homogeneity of variance

FOCUS ON PROBLEM SOLVING

1. As you learn more about different statistical methods, one basic problem will be deciding which method is appropriate for a particular set of data. Fortunately, it is easy

to identify situations where the independent-measures t statistic is used. First, the data will always consist of two separate samples (two ns, two $\overline{X}$s, two SSs, and so on). Second, this t statistic always is used to answer questions about a mean difference: On the average, is one group different (better, faster, smarter) than the other group? If you examine the data and identify the type of question that a researcher is asking, you should be able to decide whether or not an independent-measures t is appropriate.

2. When computing an independent-measures t statistic from sample data, we suggest that you routinely divide the formula into separate stages rather than trying to do all the calculations at once. First, find the pooled variance. Second, compute the standard error. Third, compute the t statistic.

3. One of the most common errors for students involves confusing the formulas for pooled variance and standard error. When computing pooled variance, you are "pooling" the two samples together into a single variance. This variance is computed as a *single fraction,* with two SS values in the numerator and two df values in the denominator. When computing the standard error, you are adding the error from the first sample and the error from the second sample. These two separate errors add as *two separate fractions* under the square root symbol.

——— DEMONSTRATION 10.1 ———

THE INDEPENDENT-MEASURES *t* TEST

In a study of jury behavior, two samples of subjects were provided details about a trial in which the defendant was obviously guilty. Although group 2 received the same details as group 1, the second group was also told that some evidence had been withheld from the jury by the judge. Later the subjects were asked to recommend a jail sentence. The length of term suggested by each subject is presented here. Is there a significant difference between the two groups in their responses?

group 1 scores: 4   4   3   2   5   1   1   4

group 2 scores: 3   7   8   5   4   7   6   8

There are two separate samples in this study. Therefore, the analysis will use the independent-measures t test.

STEP 1   State the hypothesis, and select an alpha level.

H_0: $\mu_1 - \mu_2 = 0$ (For the population, knowing evidence has been withheld has no effect on the suggested sentence.)

H_1: $\mu_1 - \mu_2 \neq 0$ (For the population, knowledge of withheld evidence has an effect on the jury's response.)

We will set the level of significance to $\alpha = .05$, two tails.

STEP 2   Identify the critical region.

For the independent-measures t statistic, degrees of freedom are determined by

$$df = n_1 + n_2 - 2$$
$$= 8 + 8 - 2$$
$$= 14$$

The t distribution table is consulted, for a two-tailed test with $\alpha = .05$ and $df = 14$. The critical t values are $+2.145$ and -2.145.

STEP 3 Compute the test statistic.

We are computing an independent-measures t statistic. To do this, we will need the mean and SS for each sample, pooled variance, and estimated standard error.

Sample means and sums of squares. The means $(\overline{X})$ and sums of squares (SS) for the samples are computed as follows:

SAMPLE 1		SAMPLE 2	
X	X^2	X	X^2
4	16	3	9
4	16	7	49
3	9	8	64
2	4	5	25
5	25	4	16
1	1	7	49
1	1	6	36
4	16	8	64
$\Sigma X = 24$	$\Sigma X^2 = 88$	$\Sigma X = 48$	$\Sigma X^2 = 312$

$$n_1 = 8 \qquad n_2 = 8$$

$$\overline{X}_1 = \frac{\Sigma X}{n} = \frac{24}{8} = 3 \qquad \overline{X}_2 = \frac{\Sigma X}{n} = \frac{48}{8} = 6$$

$$SS_1 = \Sigma X^2 - \frac{(\Sigma X)^2}{n} \qquad SS_2 = \Sigma X^2 - \frac{(\Sigma X)^2}{n}$$

$$= 88 - \frac{(24)^2}{8} \qquad = 312 - \frac{(48)^2}{8}$$

$$= 88 - \frac{576}{8} \qquad = 312 - \frac{2304}{8}$$

$$= 88 - 72 \qquad = 312 - 288$$

$$SS_1 = 16 \qquad SS_2 = 24$$

Pooled variance. For these data, the pooled variance equals

$$s_p^2 = \frac{SS_1 + SS_2}{df_1 + df_2} = \frac{16 + 24}{7 + 7} = \frac{40}{14} = 2.86$$

Estimated standard error. Now we can calculate the estimated standard error for mean differences.

$$s_{\overline{X}_1-\overline{X}_2} = \sqrt{\frac{s_p^2}{n_1} + \frac{s_p^2}{n_2}} = \sqrt{\frac{2.86}{8} + \frac{2.86}{8}} = \sqrt{0.358 + 0.358}$$

$$= \sqrt{0.716} = 0.85$$

The t statistic. Finally, the *t* statistic can be computed.

$$t = \frac{(\overline{X}_1 - \overline{X}_2) - (\mu_1 - \mu_2)}{s_{\overline{X}_1-\overline{X}_2}} = \frac{(3-6) - 0}{0.85} = \frac{-3}{0.85}$$

$$= -3.53$$

STEP 4 Make a decision about H_0, and state a conclusion.

The obtained *t* value of -3.53 falls in the critical region of the left tail (critical $t = \pm 2.145$). Therefore, the null hypothesis is rejected. The subjects that were informed about the withheld evidence gave significantly longer sentences, $t(14) = -3.53$, $p < .05$, two tails.

PROBLEMS

1. Describe the general characteristics of a research study for which an independent-measures *t* statistic would be the appropriate test statistic.

2. What is measured by the estimated standard error that is used for the independent-measures *t* statistic?

3. Describe the homogeneity of variance assumption, and explain why it is important for the independent-measures hypothesis test.

4. What happens to the value of the independent-measures *t* statistic as the difference between the two sample means increases? What happens to the *t* value as the variability of the scores in the two samples increases?

5. The following data are from two separate independent-measures experiments. Without doing any calculation, which experiment is more likely to demonstrate a significant difference between treatments A and B? Explain your answer. *Note:* You do not need to compute the *t* statistics; just look carefully at the data.

6. A person's gender can have a tremendous influence on his/her personality and behavior. Psychologists classify individuals as masculine, feminine, or androgynous. Androgynous individuals possess both masculine and feminine traits. Among other things, androgynous individuals appear to cope better with stress than do traditionally masculine or feminine people. In a typical study, depression scores are recorded for a sample of traditionally masculine or feminine subjects and for a sample of androgynous subjects all of whom have recently experienced a series of strongly negative events. The average depression score for the sample of $n = 10$ androgynous subjects is $\overline{X} = 63$ with $SS = 700$. The sample of $n = 10$ traditional sex-typed subjects averaged $\overline{X} = 71$ with $SS = 740$. Do these data indicate that the traditional subjects experienced significantly more depression than the androgynous subjects? Use a one-tailed test with $\alpha = .05$.

7. Extensive data indicate that first-born children develop different characteristics than later-born children. For example, first-borns tend to be more responsible, more hardworking, higher achieving, and more self-disciplined than their later-born siblings. The following data represent scores on a test measuring self-esteem and pride. Samples of $n = 10$ first-born college freshmen and $n = 20$ later-born freshmen were each given the self-esteem test. The first-borns averaged $\overline{X} = 48$ with $SS = 670$, and the later-borns averaged $\overline{X} = 41$ with $SS = 1010$. Do these data indicate a significant difference between the two groups? Test at the .01 level of significance.

EXPERIMENT I		EXPERIMENT II	
TREATMENT A	TREATMENT B	TREATMENT A	TREATMENT B
$n = 10$	$n = 10$	$n = 10$	$n = 10$
$\overline{X} = 42$	$\overline{X} = 52$	$\overline{X} = 61$	$\overline{X} = 71$
$SS = 180$	$SS = 120$	$SS = 986$	$SS = 1042$

8. A researcher reports an independent-measures t statistic of $t = 2.53$ with $df = 24$.
   a. How many subjects participated in the researcher's experiment?
   b. Can the researcher conclude that there is a significant difference between the two samples with $\alpha = .05$?
   c. Can the researcher conclude that the mean difference is significant at the .01 level?

9. A researcher would like to compare the political attitudes for college freshmen versus college seniors. Samples of $n = 10$ freshmen and $n = 10$ seniors are obtained, and each student is given a questionnaire measuring political attitude on a scale from 0 (very conservative) to 100 (very liberal). The average score for the freshmen is $\overline{X} = 52$ with $SS = 4800$, and the seniors average $\overline{X} = 39$ with $SS = 4200$. Do these data indicate a significant difference in political attitude for freshmen versus seniors? Test at the .05 level of significance.

10. A psychologist would like to examine the effects of fatigue on mental alertness. An attention test is prepared that requires subjects to sit in front of a blank TV screen and press a response button each time a dot appears on the screen. A total of 110 dots is presented during a 90-minute period, and the psychologist records the number of errors for each subject. Two groups of subjects are selected. The first group of subjects ($n = 5$) is tested after they have been kept awake for 24 hours. The second group ($n = 10$) is tested in the morning after a full night's sleep. The data for these two samples are as follows:

AWAKE 24 HOURS	RESTED
$\overline{X} = 35$	$\overline{X} = 24$
$SS = 120$	$SS = 270$

On the basis of these data, can the psychologist conclude that fatigue significantly increases errors on an attention task? Use a one-tailed test with $\alpha = .05$.

11. A researcher would like to compare the effectiveness of video versus reading for communicating information to adolescents. A sample of $n = 10$ adolescents is given a pamphlet explaining nuclear energy and told that they will be tested on the information. A separate sample of $n = 10$ adolescents is shown a video that contains the same information presented in a fast-paced visual form and told that they will be tested. One week later, all 20 subjects take a test on nuclear energy. The average score for the pamphlet group is $\overline{X} = 49$ with $SS = 160$. The video group averages $\overline{X} = 46$ with $SS = 200$. Do these data indicate a significant difference between the two modes of presentation? Perform the appropriate test using $\alpha = .05$.

12. Friedman and Rosenman (1974) have classified people into two categories: Type A personalities and Type B personalities. Type As are hard-driving, competitive, and ambitious. Type Bs are more relaxed, easy-going people. One factor that differentiates these two groups is the chronically high level of frustration experienced by Type As. To demonstrate this phenomenon, separate samples of Type As and Type Bs are obtained with $n = 8$ in each sample. The individual subjects are all given a frustration inventory measuring level of frustration. The average score for the Type As is $\overline{X} = 84$ with $SS = 740$, and the Type Bs average $\overline{X} = 71$ with $SS = 660$. Do these data indicate a significant difference between the two groups? Test at the .01 level of significance.

13. Anagrams are words that have had their letters scrambled into a different order. The task is to unscramble the letters and determine the correct word. One factor that influences performance on this task is the appearance of the scrambled letters. For example, the word SHORE could be presented as OSHER (a pronounceable form) or as HRSOE (an unpronounceable, random-looking sequence). Typically, the pronounceable form is more difficult, probably because it already looks "good," which makes it difficult for people to change the letters around. A researcher studying this phenomenon presented one group of $n = 8$ subjects with a series of pronounceable anagrams and a second group of $n = 8$ with unpronounceable versions of the same anagrams. The amount of time needed to solve the set was recorded for each subject. For the pronounceable condition, the mean time was $\overline{X} = 48$ seconds with $SS = 3100$, and for the unpronounceable condition, the mean was $\overline{X} = 27$ seconds with $SS = 2500$. Is there a significant difference between the two conditions? Test with $\alpha = .01$.

14. In a study examining the power of imagination, Cervone (1989) asked subjects to think about factors that could influence performance on solving maze-like puzzles. In one condition, subjects imagined positive factors that could make the task easier, and in another condition, subjects imagined negative factors that would make the task more difficult. Later Cervone measured task persistence: how long the subjects continued working on the task, or how quickly they gave up. Hypothetical data, similar to Cervone's, are as follows: positive condition, $n = 12$, $\overline{X} = 28$ with $SS = 280$; negative condition, $n = 12$, $\overline{X} = 22$ with $SS = 248$. Do these data support the conclusion that imagination can have a significant effect on task persistence? Test at the .05 level of significance.

15. In a test of cognitive dissonance theory, Festinger and Carlsmith (1959) had college students participate in a really boring experiment. Later these students were asked to recruit other subjects for the same experiment by pretending that it was an interesting experience. Some of these students were paid $20 to recruit others, and some were paid only $1. Afterward, each student was asked to report how he or she really felt about the experiment. Hypothetical data representing these reports are as follows:

STUDENTS PAID $1				STUDENTS PAID $20			
3	3	4	6	1	2	5	2
5	5	5	7	3	5	4	5
8	5	4	8	2	3	4	4
2	6	4	4	1	2	3	3
6	7	5	5	5	1	1	3

Cognitive dissonance theory predicts that those paid only $1 would come to believe that the experiment really was interesting. It must have been, or they would not have worked so hard for only $1. The students paid $20 were working for money, not for the experiment, so they would have no reason to change their opinions. Do the preceding data support this prediction? Test for a significant difference between the two groups with $\alpha = .01$.

16. A researcher would like to measure the effects of air pollution on life expectancy. Two samples of newborn rats are selected. The first sample of 10 rats is housed in cages where the atmosphere is equivalent to the air in a severely polluted city. The second sample of $n = 20$ is placed in cages with clean air. The average life span for the first group is $\overline{X} = 478$ days with $SS = 5020$ and for the second group $\overline{X} = 511$ with $SS = 10,100$. Does pollution cause a difference in life expectancy? Test with $\alpha = .01$.

17. Siegel (1990) found that elderly people who owned dogs were less likely to pay visits to their doctors after upsetting events than those who did not own pets. Similarly, consider the following hypothetical data. A sample of elderly dog owners is compared to a similar group (in terms of age and health) who do not own dogs. The researcher records the number of visits to the doctor during the past year for each person. For the following data, is there a significant difference in the number of doctor visits between dog owners and control subjects? Use the .05 level of significance.

CONTROL GROUP	DOG OWNERS
12	8
10	5
6	9
9	4
15	6
12	
14	

18. In a classic study examining the effects of environment on development, Kretch and his colleagues (1962) divided a sample of infant rats into two groups. One group was housed for a *stimulus-rich* environment containing ladders, platforms, tunnels, and colorful decorations. The second group was housed in *stimulus-poor* conditions consisting of plain grey cages. At maturity, maze-learning performance was measured for all the rats. The following hypothetical data simulate Kretch's results. Each score indicates the number of errors committed by a rat before it successfully solved the maze:

rich rats: 18 24 27 23 31 29 20 33 25 30

poor rats: 37 27 26 31 35 43 40 36 28 39

Do these data indicate a significant difference between the two groups? Test at the .01 level of significance.

19. A personality *trait* is defined as a long-lasting, relatively stable characteristic of a individual's personality. Traits such as honesty, optimism, sensitivity, and seriousness help define your personality. Cattell (1973) identified 16 basic traits that serve to differentiate individuals. One of these traits, relaxed/tense, has been shown to be a consistent factor differentiating creative artists from airline pilots. The following data, similar to Cattell's, represent relaxed/tense scores for two groups of subjects. Lower scores indicate a more relaxed personality.

artists: 7 7 6 9 8 8 7 9 5 3 6 8 7 9

pilots: 4 2 2 3 1 5 4 3 2 2 6 2 5 3

Do these data indicate a significant difference between the two professions? Test at the .05 level of significance.

20. In a classic study of problem solving, Duncker (1945) asked subjects to mount a candle on a wall in an upright position so that it would burn normally. One group of subjects was given a candle, a book of matches, and a box of tacks. A second group was given the same items, except the tacks and the box were presented separately as two distinct items. The solution to this problem involves using the tacks to mount the box on the wall, which creates a shelf for the candle. Duncker reasoned that the first group of subjects would have trouble seeing a "new" function for the box (a shelf) because it was already serving a function (holding tacks). For each subject, the amount of time needed to solve the problem was recorded. Data similar to Duncker's are as follows. Do these data indicate a significant difference between the two conditions? Test at the .01 level of significance.

TIME TO SOLVE PROBLEM (IN SEC.)	
BOX OF TACKS	TACKS & BOX SEPARATE
128	42
160	24
53	68
101	35
94	47

t- because est. σ^2

pilots   creative artists

$\alpha = \dfrac{.05}{2} = .025$ $df = 26$

(α) $H_0 : \mu_{pi} = \mu_a$ $\bar{x}_{pi} = 3.14$ $\bar{x}_a = 7.07$

$H_1 : \mu_{pi} \neq \mu_a$ $\Sigma x^2 = 166$ $\Sigma x^2 = 737$ $CV_{df=26} = \pm 2.056$

$\Sigma x = 44$ $\Sigma x = 99$

$s^2_{pi} = \dfrac{166 - \frac{(44^2)}{14}}{14-1} = 2.13$ $s^2_a = \dfrac{737 - \frac{99^2}{14}}{14-1} = 2.84$

$S_p^2 = \dfrac{(13)(2.13) + (13)(2.84)}{26} = 2.485$ $s_{\bar{x}_1 - \bar{x}_2} = \sqrt{\dfrac{2.485}{13} + \dfrac{2.485}{13}} = .6183$

$t_{(26)} = \dfrac{(7.07 - 3.14) - (0)}{.6183} = 6.356$ reject H_0

\# is slightly wrong

CHAPTER 11

HYPOTHESIS TESTS WITH RELATED SAMPLES

TOOLS YOU WILL NEED

The following items are considered essential background material for this chapter. If you doubt your knowledge of any of these items, you should review the appropriate chapter or section before proceeding.

- Introduction to the *t* statistic (Chapter 9)
  - Estimated standard error
  - Degrees of freedom
  - *t* distribution
  - Hypothesis tests with the *t* statistic
- Independent-measures design (Chapter 10)

CONTENTS

At the Olympic level of competition, even the smallest factors can make the difference between winning and losing. Pelton (1983) reports on one study demonstrating this point. The study recorded the scores obtained by Olympic marksmen when firing *during* heartbeats compared with the scores for shots fired *between* heartbeats. The results show the marksmen had significantly higher scores when they shot between heartbeats. Apparently the small vibrations caused by a heartbeat were enough to disturb the marksmen's aim.

To conduct this study, the researchers monitored each individual's heart during a shooting session (see Figure 11.1). The shots fired during heartbeats were then separated from the shots fired between heartbeats, and two separate scores were computed for each marksman. Thus, the study involved only one sample of subjects, but produced two sets of scores. The goal of the study is to look for a mean difference between the two sets of scores.

In the previous chapter, we introduced a statistical procedure for evaluating the mean difference between two sets of data (the independent-measures *t* statistic). However, the independent-measures *t* statistic is intended for research situations involving two separate and independent samples. You should realize that the two sets of shooting scores are not independent samples. In fact, for each subject, the score for shots fired during a heartbeat is *directly related,* one to one, to the score for shots fired between heartbeats because both scores come from the same individual. This kind of study is called a repeated-measures (or related-samples) design because the data are obtained by literally repeating measurements, under different conditions, for the same sample. Because the two sets of measurements are related, rather than independent, a different statistical analysis will be required. In this chapter, we will introduce the statistical methods used to evaluate and interpret mean differences for two related samples.

A repeated-measures study (like that of the Olympic shooters) provides an excellent example of a distinction we made in Chapter 1. Specifically, we noted that the term *sample* is used in two different ways. First, the word is used to refer to a set of individuals selected to participate in a research study. For this example, the study involved one sample of Olympic marksmen. However, the term *sample* is also used to refer to a set of scores. By this definition, the marksmen produced two samples of scores. To help clarify the distinction between individual subjects and their scores, the generic term *sample* is often modified, so that the group of individuals is called a *subject sample* and the set of scores is called a *statistical sample.* Using this terminology, a repeated-measures study involves one subject sample and produces two statistical samples.

Finally, we should note that independent measures and repeated measures are two basic research strategies that are available whenever a researcher is planning a study that will compare treatment conditions. That is, a researcher may choose to use two separate samples, one for each of the treatments, or a researcher may choose to use one sample and measure each individual in both of the treatment conditions. Later in this chapter, we will take a closer look at the differences between independent-measures and repeated-measures designs and discuss the advantages and disadvantages of each.

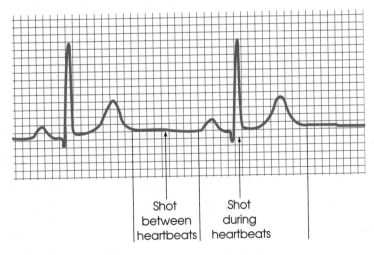

FIGURE 11.1

Illustration of the timing of shots taken between or during a heartbeat.

11.1 OVERVIEW

Previously, we discussed inferential techniques using two separate samples to examine the mean difference between two populations. Usually our goal was to evaluate the difference between two treatment conditions. For example, if a researcher would like to assess the effect of a new drug on depression, he or she might use two treatment conditions: a drug treatment and a no-drug treatment. With an independent-measures design (Chapter 10), one sample of patients receives the drug, and the other sample receives an ineffective placebo. Depression can be measured by the subjects' scores on a depression inventory. Differences in the severity of depression between these two samples can then be used to test the effectiveness of the new drug. This independent-measures design can be recognized by the assignment of separate, or "independent," samples of subjects for each treatment condition.

It should be obvious that there is a different experimental technique that could be used to evaluate the drug. Specifically, you could use a single sample of subjects and measure their depression scores while they are taking the placebo; then you could switch to the real drug and repeat the measurements. This experimental design is called a *repeated-measures* study. By repeating measurements on a single sample of subjects, we are looking for differences *within* the same subjects from one measurement to the next. Sometimes this type of study is also called a *within-subjects* design.

DEFINITION

A *repeated-measures* study is one in which a single sample of subjects is used to compare two (or more) different treatment conditions. Each individual is measured in one treatment, and then the same individual is measured again in the second treatment. Thus, a repeated-measures study produces two (or more) sets of scores, but each set is obtained from the same sample of subjects.

The main advantage of a repeated-measures study is that it uses exactly the same subjects in all treatment conditions. Thus, there is no risk that the subjects in one treatment are substantially different from the subjects in another. With an independent-measures design, on the other hand, there is always a risk that the results are biased by the fact that one sample was much different (smarter, faster, more extroverted, and so on) than the other.

Occasionally, researchers will try to approximate the advantages of a repeated-measures study by using a technique known as *matched subjects*. For example, suppose that a researcher is testing the effectiveness of a special reading program. One sample of fourth graders take the reading course, and a second sample serves as the control group. The researcher plans to compare these two groups in terms of reading comprehension. However, the researcher is concerned that the subjects in one sample may have higher IQs than the subjects in the second sample. If this occurs, then the low IQ sample may end up with lower reading scores no matter which reading program they receive. Thus, the IQ difference between samples could obscure (or exaggerate) the effects of the special reading program. One solution to this problem is to match the subjects in terms of IQ. That is, if a person assigned to the control group has an IQ of 120, the researcher assigns another individual

TABLE 11.1

Group assignment of subjects matched for IQ

CONTROL		READING PROGRAM	
SUBJECT	IQ	SUBJECT	IQ
A	120	E	120
B	105	F	105
C	110	G	110
D	95	H	95

with the same IQ to the treatment group (see Table 11.1). The result is called a *matched-subjects* study.

DEFINITION

In a *matched-subjects* study, each individual in one sample is matched with a subject in the other sample. The matching is done so that the two individuals are equivalent (or nearly equivalent) with respect to a specific variable that the researcher would like to control.

In a repeated-measures, or a matched-subjects, design, all the subjects in one treatment are directly related, one to one, with the subjects in another treatment. For this reason, these two experimental designs are often called *related-samples* designs (or correlated-samples designs). In this chapter, we will focus our discussion on repeated-measures designs because they are overwhelmingly the more common example of related-groups designs. However, you should realize that the statistical techniques used for repeated-measures studies can be applied directly to data from a matched-subjects study.

A matched-subjects study occasionally is called a *matched-samples design*. But the subjects in the samples must be matched one to one before you can use the statistical techniques in this chapter.

Now we will examine the statistical techniques that allow a researcher to use the sample data from a repeated-measures study to draw inferences about the general population.

11.2 THE *t* STATISTIC FOR RELATED SAMPLES

The *t* statistic for related samples is structurally similar to the other *t* statistics we have examined. As we shall see, it is essentially the same as the single-sample *t* statistic covered in Chapter 9. One major distinction of the related-samples *t* is that it is based on difference scores rather than raw scores (X values). In this section, we examine difference scores and develop the *t* statistic for related samples.

DIFFERENCE SCORES

Table 11.2 presents hypothetical data for a drug evaluation study. The first score for each person (X_1) is the score obtained on the depression inventory before the drug treatment. The second score (X_2) was obtained after the drug treatment. Because we are interested in how much change occurs as a result of the treatment, each person's scores are summarized as a single difference score. This is accomplished by subtracting the first score (before treatment) from the second score (after treatment) for each person:

$$\text{difference score} = D = X_2 - X_1 \tag{11.1}$$

TABLE 11.2

Scores on a depression inventory before and after treatment

PERSON	BEFORE TREATMENT, X_1	AFTER TREATMENT, X_2	D
A	72	64	−8
B	68	60	−8
C	60	50	−10
D	71	66	−5
E	55	56	+1
			$\Sigma D = -30$

$$\overline{D} = \frac{\Sigma D}{n} = \frac{-30}{5} = -6$$

In a matched-subjects design, D is the difference between scores for two matched subjects.

The difference scores, or D values, are shown in the last column of the table. Note that the sign of each D score tells you the direction of change. For example, person A showed a decrease in depression, as indicated by the negative difference score.

The researcher's goal is to use this sample of difference scores to answer questions about the general population. Notice that we are interested in a population of *difference scores*. More specifically, we are interested in the mean for this population of difference scores. We will identify this population mean difference with the symbol μ_D (using the subscript letter D to indicate that we are dealing with D values rather than X scores). Because populations usually are too large to test in an experiment, investigators must rely on the data from samples. Do these data indicate that the drug has a significant effect (more than chance)? Our problem is to use the limited data from a sample to test hypotheses about the population. This problem is diagrammed in Figure 11.2.

Notice that the problem we are facing here is essentially identical to the situation we encountered in Chapter 9. We have a single sample of scores that must be used to test hypotheses about a single population. In Chapter 9, we introduced a t statistic that allowed us to use the sample mean as a basis for testing hypotheses about the population mean. This t statistic formula will be used again here to develop the repeated-measures t test.

THE t STATISTIC

To refresh your memory, the single-sample t statistic (Chapter 9) is defined by the formula

$$t = \frac{\overline{X} - \mu}{s_{\overline{X}}}$$

The sample mean, $\overline{X}$, comes from the data. The standard error, $s_{\overline{X}}$ (also computed from the sample data), gives a measure of the error between the sample mean and the population mean, μ.

For the repeated-measures design, the sample data are difference scores and are identified by the letter D rather than X. Therefore, we will substitute Ds in the formula in place of Xs to emphasize that we are dealing with difference scores instead of X values. Also, the population mean that is of interest to us is the population mean difference (the mean amount of change for the entire population), and we identify this parameter with the symbol μ_D. With these simple changes, the t *formula for the repeated-measures design* becomes

FIGURE 11.2

Because populations are usually too large to test in a study, the researcher selects a random sample from the population. The sample data are used to make inferences about the population mean, μ_D. The data of interest in the repeated-measures study are difference scores (D scores) for each subject.

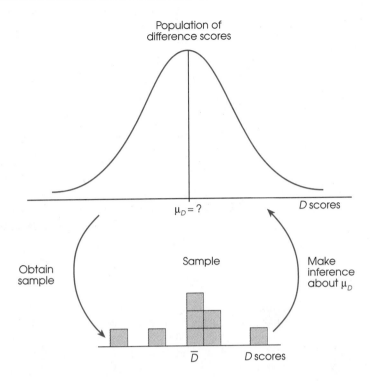

In this formula, the estimated standard error for $\bar{D}$, $s_{\bar{D}}$, is computed exactly as it was in the original single-sample t statistic. First, we compute the variance for the sample (this time a sample of D scores):

$$s^2 = \frac{SS}{n-1} = \frac{SS}{df}$$

Note that the sample data consist of difference scores with only one D value per subject (or one D value per matched pair in a matched-subjects design). Because there are exactly n difference scores in the sample, the sample variance and the t statistic will have $df = n - 1$. However, you should note that n refers to the number of D values, not the number of X values in the raw data.

Then we use the sample variance to compute the estimated standard error:

$$s_{\bar{D}} = \sqrt{\frac{s^2}{n}} \tag{11.3}$$

You should also note that the repeated-measures t statistic is conceptually similar to the t statistics we have previously examined:

$$t = \frac{\text{sample statistic} - \text{population parameter}}{\text{estimated standard error}}$$

In this case, the sample data are represented by the sample mean of the difference scores ($\bar{D}$), the population hypothesis is the value predicted by H_0 for μ_D, and the amount of sampling error is measured by the standard error of sample mean differences ($s_{\overline{D}}$).

11.3   HYPOTHESIS TESTS FOR THE REPEATED-MEASURES DESIGN

In a repeated-measures study, we are interested in whether or not any difference exists between scores in the first treatment and scores in the second treatment. In statistical terms, we are interested in the population mean difference, μ_D. Is the population mean difference equal to zero (no change), or has a change occurred? As always, the null hypothesis states that there is no treatment effect. In symbols, this is

$$H_0\text{: } \mu_D = 0$$

PROCEDURES AND STEPS

As we saw in previous tests, the level of significance defines what values are sufficiently "far away" to reject H_0.

As a statistician, your job is to determine whether the sample data support or refute the null hypothesis. In simple terms, we must decide whether the sample mean difference is close to zero (indicating no change) or far from zero (indicating there is a change). The t statistic helps us determine if the sample data are "close to" or "far from" zero.

The repeated-measures t test procedure follows the same outline we have used in other situations. The basic steps for hypothesis testing are reviewed here.

STEP 1   State the hypotheses, and select an alpha level. For the repeated-measures experiment, the null hypothesis is stated symbolically as

$$H_0\text{: } \mu_D = 0$$

Directional hypotheses can be used as well and would predict whether μ_D is greater or smaller than zero. A one-tailed test is used in those instances.

The alternative hypothesis states that there is a difference between the treatments. In symbols, this is

$$H_1\text{: } \mu_D \neq 0$$

STEP 2   Locate the critical region. As before, the critical region is defined as values that would be very unlikely (probability less than alpha) if H_0 is true. Because the repeated-measures test uses a t statistic with $df = n - 1$, we simply compute df and look up the critical values in the t distribution table.

STEP 3   Compute the test statistic—in this case, the t statistic for repeated measures. We first must find the sample mean, $\overline{D}$, for the set of difference scores. This sample statistic along with the hypothesized value of μ_D from H_0 will form the numerator of the t statistic. Then compute the variance for the sample of difference scores, and use this value to compute the standard error, $s_{\overline{D}}$. As with the z-score and other t statistics, the repeated-measures t forms a ratio. The numerator measures the obtained difference between the data ($\overline{D}$) and the hypothesis (μ_D), and the denominator measures the standard difference that is expected by chance.

$$t = \frac{\overline{D} - \mu_D}{s_{\overline{D}}} = \frac{\text{obtained difference}}{\text{difference expected by chance}}$$

TABLE 11.3

The number of doses of medication needed for asthma attacks before and after relaxation training

PATIENT	WEEK BEFORE TRAINING	WEEK AFTER TRAINING	D	D^2
A	9	4	-5	25
B	4	1	-3	9
C	5	5	0	0
D	4	0	-4	16
E	5	1	-4	16

$$\Sigma D = -16 \quad \Sigma D^2 = 66$$

Because the data consist of difference scores (D values) instead of X scores, the formulas for the mean and SS also use D in place of X. However, you should recognize the computational formula for SS that was introduced in Chapter 4.

$$\bar{D} = \frac{\Sigma D}{n} = \frac{-16}{5} = -3.2$$

$$SS = \Sigma D^2 - \frac{(\Sigma D)^2}{n} = 66 - \frac{(-16)^2}{5}$$

$$= 66 - 51.2 = 14.8$$

As always, a large value for the test-statistic ratio indicates that the obtained difference is more than chance.

STEP 4 Make a decision. If the obtained value falls in the critical region, we reject H_0 and conclude that there is a significant treatment effect. Remember, it is very unlikely for the t value to be in the critical region if H_0 is true. On the other hand, if the obtained t is not in the critical region, then we fail to reject H_0 and conclude that the sample data do not provide sufficient evidence for a treatment effect.

The complete hypothesis-testing procedure is demonstrated in Example 11.1

EXAMPLE 11.1

asthma

Software manuals:
Minitab (Section 5)
Mystat (Section 3)
SPSS (Section 6)

A researcher in behavioral medicine believes that stress often makes asthma symptoms worse for people who suffer from this respiratory disorder. Because of the suspected role of stress, the investigator decides to examine the effect of relaxation training on the severity of asthma symptoms. A sample of five patients is selected for the study. During the week before treatment, the investigator records the severity of their symptoms by measuring how many doses of medication are needed for asthma attacks. Then the patients receive relaxation training. For the week following training, the researcher once again records the number of doses required by each patient. Table 11.3 shows the data and summarizes the findings. Do these data indicate that relaxation training alters the severity of symptoms?

STEP 1 State the hypotheses, and select the alpha level.

H_0: $\mu_D = 0$ (no change in symptoms)

H_1: $\mu_D \neq 0$ (there is a change)

The level of significance is set at $\alpha = .05$ for a two-tailed test.

STEP 2 Locate the critical region. For this example, $n = 5$, so the t statistic will have $df = n - 1 = 4$. From the t distribution table, you should find that the critical values are $+2.776$ and -2.776. These values are shown in Figure 11.3.

FIGURE 11.3

The critical regions with $\alpha = .05$ and $df = 4$ begin at $+2.776$ and -2.776 in the t distribution. Obtained values of t that are more extreme than these values will lie in a critical region. In that case, the null hypothesis would be rejected.

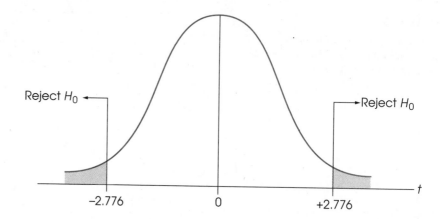

STEP 3   Calculate the t statistic. Table 11.3 shows the sample data and the calculations for $\overline{D} = -3.2$ and $SS = 14.8$. As we have done with the other t statistics, we will present the computation of the t statistic as a three-step process.

First, compute the variance for the sample. Remember, the population variance (σ^2) is unknown, and we must use the sample value in its place.

$$s^2 = \frac{SS}{n-1} = \frac{14.8}{4} = 3.7$$

Next, use the sample variance to compute the estimated standard error.

$$s_{\overline{D}} = \sqrt{\frac{s^2}{n}} = \sqrt{\frac{3.7}{5}} = \sqrt{0.74} = 0.86$$

Finally, use the sample mean ($\overline{D}$) and the hypothesized population mean (μ_D) along with the estimated standard error to find the value for the t statistic.

$$t = \frac{\overline{D} - \mu_D}{s_{\overline{D}}} = \frac{-3.2 - 0}{0.86} = -3.72$$

STEP 4   Make a decision. The t value we obtained falls in the critical region (see Figure 11.3). The investigator rejects the null hypothesis and concludes that relaxation training does affect the amount of medication needed to control the asthma symptoms.

IN THE LITERATURE:

REPORTING THE RESULTS OF A REPEATED-MEASURES t TEST

As we have seen in Chapters 9 and 10, the APA format for reporting the results of t tests consists of a concise statement that incorporates the t value, degrees of freedom, and alpha level. One typically includes values for means and standard deviations, either in a statement or in a table (Chapter 4). For Example 11.1, we observed a mean difference of $\overline{D} = -3.2$ with $s = \sqrt{3.7} = 1.92$. Also, we obtained a t statistic of $t = -3.72$ with $df = 4$, and our decision was to reject the null hypothesis at the .05 level of significance. A published report of this study might summarize the conclusion as follows:

> Relaxation training resulted in a decrease ($M = 3.2$, $SD = 1.92$) in the number of doses of medication needed to control asthma symptoms. This reduction was statistically significant, $t(4) = -3.72$, $p < .05$, two-tailed.

In reporting the mean change, we did not bother to include the negative sign because we explicitly noted that the change was a decrease. ❑

DIRECTIONAL HYPOTHESES AND ONE-TAILED TESTS

In many repeated-measures and matched-subjects experiments, the researcher has a specific prediction concerning the direction of the treatment effect. For example, in the study described in Example 11.1, the researcher expects relaxation training to reduce the severity of asthma symptoms and, therefore, to reduce the amount of medication needed for asthma attacks. This kind of directional prediction can be incorporated into the statement of hypotheses, resulting in a directional, or one-tailed, hypothesis test. You should recall that directional tests should be used with caution. The standard two-tailed test often is preferred and is always appropriate, even in situations where the researcher has a specific directional prediction. The following example demonstrates how the hypotheses and critical region are determined in a directional test.

EXAMPLE 11.2

We will reexamine the experiment presented in Example 11.1. The researcher is using a repeated-measures design to investigate the effect of relaxation training on the severity of asthma symptoms. The researcher predicts that people will need less medication after training than before, which will produce negative difference scores.

$$D = X_2 - X_1 = \text{after} - \text{before}$$

STEP 1 State the hypotheses, and select the alpha level. With most one-tailed tests, it is easiest to incorporate the researcher's prediction directly into H_1. In this example, the researcher predicts a negative difference, so

$$H_1: \mu_D < 0 \text{ (medication is reduced after training)}$$

The null hypothesis states that the treatment does not have the predicted effect. In this example,

$$H_0: \mu_D \geq 0 \text{ (medication is not reduced after training)}$$

STEP 2 Locate the critical region. The researcher is predicting negative difference scores if the treatment works. Hence, a negative t statistic would tend to support the experimental prediction and refute H_0. With a sample of $n = 5$ subjects, the t statistic will have $df = 4$. Looking in the t distribution table for $df = 4$ and $\alpha = .05$ for a one-tailed test, we find a critical value of 2.132. Thus, a t statistic that is more extreme than -2.132 would be sufficient to reject H_0. The t distribution with the one-tailed critical region is shown in Figure 11.4. For this example, the

FIGURE 11.4

The one-tailed critical region for $\alpha = .05$ in the t distribution with $df = 4$.

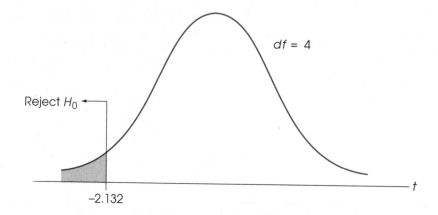

Reject H_0

$df = 4$

-2.132

t

data produce a t statistic of $t = -3.72$ (see Example 11.1). Therefore, we reject H_0 and conclude that the relaxation training did significantly reduce the amount of medication needed for asthma attacks.

LEARNING CHECK   **1.** A researcher would like to examine the effect of hypnosis on cigarette smoking. A sample of smokers ($n = 4$) is selected for the study. The number of cigarettes smoked on the day prior to treatment is recorded. The subjects are then hypnotized and given the posthypnotic suggestion that each time they light a cigarette, they will experience a horrible taste and feel nauseous. The data are as follows:

THE NUMBER OF CIGARETTES SMOKED BEFORE AND AFTER HYPNOSIS		
SUBJECT	BEFORE TREATMENT	AFTER TREATMENT
1	19	13
2	35	37
3	20	14
4	31	25

a. Find the difference scores (D values) for this sample.

b. The difference scores have $\overline{D} = -4$ and $SS = 48$. Do these data indicate that hypnosis has a significant effect on cigarette smoking? Test with $\alpha = .05$.

ANSWERS   **1. a.** The difference scores are $-6, 2, -6, -6$.

b. For these data, $s^2 = 16$, $s_{\overline{D}} = 2$, and $t = -2.00$. With $\alpha = .05$, we fail to reject H_0; these data do not provide sufficient evidence to conclude that hypnosis has a significant effect on cigarette smoking.

TABLE 11.4

Reading comprehension scores for children in a matched-subjects study of a new reading program

	CONTROL	READING PROGRAM	D	D^2
Matched pair A	6	15	+9	81
Matched pair B	5	15	+10	100
Matched pair C	11	17	+6	36
Matched pair D	6	13	+7	49

$$\Sigma D = +32 \quad \Sigma D^2 = 266$$

$$\overline{D} = \frac{\Sigma D}{n} = \frac{+32}{4} = +8$$

$$SS = \Sigma D^2 - \frac{(\Sigma D)^2}{n} = 266 - \frac{(32)^2}{4}$$

$$= 266 - \frac{1024}{4}$$

$$= 266 - 256 = 10$$

11.4 HYPOTHESIS TESTING WITH A MATCHED-SUBJECTS DESIGN

As noted in Section 11.1, matched-subjects studies involve two related samples. Each subject in the second sample has been matched to a subject in the first sample on some variable that the researcher wishes to control. In this way, the researcher attempts to make the groups equivalent at the start of the study, so that any differences observed can be attributed to the treatment (independent variable). As noted earlier, data from the matched-subjects design may be analyzed using the related-samples t test. The following example illustrates this analysis.

EXAMPLE 11.3   A psychologist studies the effectiveness of a newly developed reading program. One sample of students takes the new reading course. A second sample serves as a control group and takes the regular coursework. The groups are later tested in reading comprehension to assess the effectiveness of the new program. However, the researcher is concerned with the possibility that differences in intelligence between the two groups (rather than the new reading program) will cause differences in reading comprehension. Therefore, when assigning subjects to treatment groups, each subject in the first group is matched to one in the second group in terms of IQ score. That is, if a child in the first group has an IQ of 110, then another child with the same IQ is assigned to the second group. Thus, the study consists of *matched pairs* of children, with one child of each pair serving in the control group and the other participating in the reading program. The data are summarized in Table 11.4. Is there evidence for a significant effect of the new reading program?

STEP 1   State the hypotheses, and select an alpha level.

H_0: $\mu_D = 0$ (no effect on reading comprehension)

H_1: $\mu_D \neq 0$ (there is an effect)

We will set the alpha level to .01 for a two-tailed test.

STEP 2   Locate the critical region. For this example, $df = n - 1 = 3$. The t distribution table indicates the critical values are $+5.841$ and -5.841.

STEP 3   Calculate the t statistic. This study used a matched-subjects design; thus, a related-samples t statistic is appropriate. The values for SS and $\overline{D}$ were calculated in Table 11.4.

Calculation of the t statistic proceeds in a three-step process: First, compute the variance for the sample of D scores.

$$s^2 = \frac{SS}{n-1} = \frac{10}{3} = 3.33$$

Next, use the sample variance to compute the estimated standard error.

$$s_{\overline{D}} = \sqrt{\frac{s^2}{n}} = \sqrt{\frac{3.33}{4}} = \sqrt{0.83} = 0.91$$

Finally, compute the t statistic.

$$t = \frac{\overline{D} - \mu_D}{s_{\overline{D}}} = \frac{8 - 0}{0.91} = 8.79$$

STEP 4   Make a decision. The obtained t value of $t = 8.79$ is more extreme than the critical value of $+5.841$. Therefore, it falls within the critical region on the right side of the t distribution. The null hypothesis can be rejected, and it can be concluded that the new reading program has a significant effect on reading comprehension, $t(3) = 8.79$, $p < .01$, two tails.

11.5   USES AND ASSUMPTIONS FOR RELATED-SAMPLES t TESTS

USES OF RELATED-SAMPLE STUDIES

The repeated-measures study differs from an independent-measures study in a fundamental way. In the latter type of study, a separate sample is used for each treatment. In the repeated-measures design, only one sample of subjects is used, and measurements are repeated for the same sample in each treatment. There are many situations where it is possible to examine the effect of a treatment by using either type of study. However, there are situations where one type of design is more desirable or appropriate than the other. For example, if a researcher would like to study a particular type of subject (a rare species, people with an unusual illness, etc.) that is not commonly found, a repeated-measures study will be more economical in the sense that fewer subjects are needed. Rather than selecting several samples for the study (one sample per treatment), a single sample can be used for the entire study.

Another factor in determining the type of design is the specific question being asked by the researcher. Some questions are better studied with a repeated-measures design, especially those concerning changes in response across time. For example, a psychologist may wish to study the effect of practice on how well a person performs a task. To show that practice is improving a person's performance, the researcher would typically measure the person's responses very early in the study (when there is little or no practice) and repeat the measurement later when the person has had a certain amount of practice. Most studies of skill acquisition examine practice effects by using a repeated-measures design. Another situation where a repeated-measures study is useful is in developmental psychology. By repeating observations of the same individuals at various points in time, an investigator can watch behavior unfold and obtain a better understanding of developmental processes.

Finally, there are situations where a repeated-measures design cannot be used. Specifically, when you are comparing two different populations (men versus women, first-born versus second-born children, and the like), you must use separate samples from each population. Typically, these situations require an independent-measures design, but it is occasionally possible to match subjects with respect to a critical variable and conduct a matched-subjects study.

INDIVIDUAL DIFFERENCES

There are certain statistical advantages to repeated-measures designs, particularly when you are studying a population with large differences from one individual to the next. One of the sources of variability that contributes to the standard error is these individual differences—that is, subjects all respond differently because they enter the experiment with different abilities, experiences, and the like. Large individual differences would produce larger standard errors, which might mask a mean difference. A repeated-measures design reduces the amount of this error variability in the analysis by using the same subjects for every treatment. The result is that the size of the standard error is reduced, and the *t* test will be more likely to detect the presence of a treatment effect.

The following example is intended to demonstrate the role of individual differences in both independent-measures and repeated-measures designs.

EXAMPLE 11.4

Consider the following set of data showing the results of a research study comparing two treatment conditions:

SUBJECT	TREATMENT I	TREATMENT II	DIFFERENCE SCORES
A	10	16	+6
B	20	24	+4
C	30	35	+5
D	40	46	+6
E	50	54	+4
	$\bar{X} = 30$	$\bar{X} = 35$	$\bar{X} = +5$
	$SS = 1000$	$SS = 964$	$SS = 4$

First, direct your attention to the scores in treatment I and treatment II. We have deliberately created these data to produce large differences between subjects. For example, the scores for subject B are consistently 10 points higher than the scores for subject A. Similarly, subject C has scores 10 points higher than those for subject B, and subject D is 10 points higher than subject C. These consistent differences from one subject to another are called *individual differences*. Also notice that the large individual differences contribute to the variability of the scores, producing SS values of approximately 1000 for both treatment conditions.

Now look at the set of difference scores. Suddenly the big differences from one subject to another are gone. The D scores are all clustered close together (small variability), producing an SS value of only 4. The process of subtracting to obtain the difference scores has eliminated the absolute level of performance for each subject (10 versus 20, etc.) and thus has eliminated the individual differences.

By removing the individual differences, we have drastically reduced the variability of the scores from $SS = 1000$ for the original X values to $SS = 4$ for the difference scores. The advantage of reducing variability in this manner can be demonstrated by comparing the independent-measures and the repeated-measures hypothesis tests.

For both tests, the t statistic forms a ratio with the following general structure:

$$t = \frac{\text{sample mean difference}}{\text{difference expected by chance}} = \frac{\text{sample mean difference}}{\text{standard error}}$$

For the data we are considering, the sample mean difference is 5 points, and this value will form the numerator for both the independent-measures and the repeated-measures t statistics. However, the two t statistics will have very different values for the standard error.

We will begin by treating the data as if they are from an independent-measures study; that is, we will ignore the column of difference scores and assume that there is a separate sample of $n = 5$ individuals for each treatment. To find the denominator of the t statistic, we begin with the two SS values, then compute the pooled variance, and finally compute the standard error. For these data, the standard error is 9.91. (You can check the arithmetic for yourself, but you should realize that this value is consistent with the 10-point differences from one score to another in the data.) With a standard error of 9.91, the formula produces a t statistic of

$$t = \frac{(\overline{X}_1 - \overline{X}_2) - (\mu_1 - \mu_2)}{s_{\overline{X}_1 - \overline{X}_2}} = \frac{-5 - 0}{9.91} = -0.50$$

You should realize immediately that a t value near zero indicates that you should fail to reject the null hypothesis and conclude that there is no significant difference between the two treatments. In this case, the individual differences are included in the data, and they contribute to the variability of the scores. The result is a standard error of more than 9 points, which completely overwhelms the 5-point mean difference found in the experiment.

Now consider the result when the data are viewed as coming from a *repeated-measures* study. To find the standard error for the repeated-measures t statistic, we begin with the SS for the difference scores, then compute the variance, and finally compute the standard error. Beginning with $SS = 4$, we obtain a standard error of $s_{\overline{D}} = 0.45$. (Again, you can check the arithmetic, but notice that this value is consistent with the small differences from one score to another among the *D* values.) Using this value, the repeated-measures *t* statistic is

$$t = \frac{\bar{D} - \mu_D}{s_{\bar{D}}} = \frac{5 - 0}{0.45} = 11.11$$

For the repeated-measures test, the 5-point mean difference is significant (reject H_0 with $\alpha = .05$), and we conclude that there is a significant difference between the two treatments.

As a final demonstration of how the individual differences are removed in a repeated-measured design, we will reconstruct the original data with the individual differences taken out. Specifically, we will make all of the individual subjects the same by starting each one with a score of zero in treatment I. For example, subject A, who started with a low score of $X = 10$, now begins with $X = 0$. Similarly, subject E, who started with a high score of $X = 50$, now begins with $X = 0$. With all of the subjects beginning with $X = 0$, there are no longer any differences between subjects; that is, we have removed the individual differences. The following table shows the result of this operation:

SUBJECT	TREATMENT I	TREATMENT II	DIFFERENCE SCORES
A	0	6	+6
B	0	4	+4
C	0	5	+5
D	0	6	+6
E	0	4	+4
	$\bar{X} = 0$	$\bar{X} = 5$	$\bar{D} = +5$
	$SS = 0$	$SS = 4$	$SS = 4$

Notice that the scores for treatment II show the same treatment effect that was observed for each subject in the original data. For example, in the original data, subject A went from $X = 10$ to $X = 16$ (an increase of 6 points), and now this subject's scores go from $X = 0$ to $X = 6$ (again, an increase of 6 points).

Notice that removing the individual differences from the data drastically reduces the variability of the scores in treatment I and treatment II. In the original data, each treatment had an SS value of approximately 1000. With the individual differences removed, the *SS* values are down to 0 and 4. In fact, for these reconstructed data, the variability within the treatments is exactly the same as the variability for the difference scores: $SS_1 + SS_2 = 4$, which is exactly the same as SS for the *D* scores. Furthermore, once the individual differences have been removed, the independent-measures *t* test and the repeated-measures *t* test *will produce exactly the same value for the t statistic.* (Try it for yourself, using the reconstructed data. You should find that both tests produce a standard error of 0.45 and a *t* statistic of $t = 11.11$.)

As demonstrated in Example 11.4, removing the individual differences from a set of data can greatly reduce the variability of the scores and thereby reduce the standard error. As a result, the removal of individual differences usually produces a more sensitive test that is more likely to detect a treatment effect. In Example 11.4, the 5-point mean difference shows up clearly as a significant difference in the repeated-measures study where individual differences are removed, but the same 5-point mean difference is not significant in the independent-measures study. Thus, a repeated-measures study often is more powerful (more likely to find a significant result) than an independent-measures study. However, there are two notes of caution that must accompany this general claim.

1. The removal of individual differences occurs only in a repeated-measures or matched-subjects design. In these designs, the scores are paired one to one so that each pair of scores comes from identical or matched subjects. In these situations, it is possible to measure the absolute level of response for each individual and then evaluate the size of the individual differences. In an independent-measures design, on the other hand, the scores in one treatment come from different individuals than the scores in the second treatment. In this case, it is impossible to separate the individual differences from the treatment differences. Thus, for an independent-measures design, the individual differences must be left in the data as part of the variability of the scores.

2. In research situations where there are relatively large differences from one individual to another, the process of removing individual differences can be extremely valuable. For example, if a researcher is measuring reaction time, which varies tremendously from one person to another, removing the individual differences will often make the results easier to see. In this case, a repeated-measures design would have a large advantage over an independent-measures design. On the other hand, if all the subjects in an experiment are similar, so that individual differences are relatively small, then there is not much to be gained by removing the individual differences, and the repeated-measures design has no real advantage over the independent-measures design.

CARRY-OVER EFFECTS AND PROGRESSIVE ERROR

The general goal of a repeated-measures t test is to demonstrate that two different treatment conditions result in two different means. However, the outcome of a repeated-measures study may be contaminated by other factors that can cause the two means to be different when there actually is no difference between the two treatments. Two such factors specifically associated with repeated-measures designs are *carry-over effects* and *progressive error.*

A carry-over effect occurs when a subject's response in the second treatment is altered by lingering aftereffects from the first treatment. Examples of carry-over effects include the following:

1. Imagine that a researcher is comparing the effectiveness of two drugs by testing both drugs, one after the other, on the same group of subjects. If the second drug is tested too soon after the first, there may be some of the first drug still in the subject's system, and this residual could exaggerate or minimize the effects of the second drug.

2. Imagine that a researcher is comparing performance on two tasks that vary in difficulty. If subjects are given a very difficult task first, their poor performance may cause them to lose motivation, so that performance suffers when they get to the second task.

In each of these examples, the researcher will observe a difference between the two treatment means. However, the difference in performance is not caused by the treatments; instead, it is caused by carry-over effects.

Progressive error occurs when a subject's performance or response changes consistently over time. For example, a subject's performance may decline over time as a result of fatigue. Or a subject's performance may improve over time as a result of practice. In either case, a researcher will observe a mean difference in performance between the first treatment and the second treatment, but the change in performance is not due to the treatments; instead, it is caused by progressive error.

To help distinguish between carry-over effects and progressive error, remember that carry-over effects are related directly to the first treatment. Progressive error, on the other hand, occurs as a function of time, independent of which treatment condition is presented first or second. Both of these factors, however, can influence the outcome of a repeated-measures study, and they can make it difficult for a researcher to interpret the results: Is the mean difference caused by the treatments, or is it caused by other factors?

One way to deal with carry-over effects or progressive error is to *counterbalance* the order of presentation of treatments. That is, the subjects are randomly divided into two groups, with one group receiving treatment 1 followed by treatment 2 and the other group receiving treatment 2 followed by treatment 1. When there is reason to expect strong carry-over effects or large progressive error, your best strategy is not to use a repeated-measures design. Instead, use an independent-measures design with a separate sample for each treatment condition, or use a matched-subjects design so that each individual participates in only one treatment condition.

ASSUMPTIONS OF THE RELATED-SAMPLES *t* TEST

The related-samples *t* statistic requires two basic assumptions:

1. The observations within each treatment condition must be independent (see p. 244).
2. The population distribution of difference scores (D values) must be normal.

As before, the normality assumption is not a cause for concern unless the sample size is relatively small. In the case of severe departures from normality, the validity of the *t* test may be compromised with small samples. However, with relatively large samples ($n > 30$), this assumption can be ignored.

LEARNING CHECK

1. What assumptions must be satisfied for the repeated-measures *t* tests to be valid?

2. Describe some situations for which a repeated-measures design is well suited.

3. How is a matched-subjects design similar to a repeated-measures design? How do they differ?

good?

4. The data from a research study consist of 8 scores for each of two different treatment conditions. How many individual subjects would be needed to produce these data

   a. For an independent-measures design?

   b. For a repeated-measures design?

   c. For a matched-subjects design?

ANSWERS 1. The observations within a treatment are independent. The population distribution of D scores is assumed to be normal. *or ≥ 30*

good answers

2. The repeated-measures design is suited to situations where a particular type of subject is not readily available for study. This design is helpful because it uses fewer subjects (only one sample is needed). Certain questions are addressed more adequately by a repeated-measures design—for example, anytime one would like to study changes across time in the same individuals. Also, when individual differences are large, a repeated-measures design is helpful because it reduces the amount of this type of error in the statistical analysis.

3. They are similar in that the role of individual differences in the experiment is reduced. They differ in that there are two samples in a matched-subjects design and only one in a repeated-measures study.

4. a. The independent-measures design would require 16 subjects (two separate samples with $n = 8$ in each).

   b. The repeated-measures design would require 8 subjects (the same 8 individuals are measured in both treatments).

   c. The matched-subjects design would require 16 subjects (8 matched pairs).

SUMMARY

1. In a repeated-measures study, a single sample of subjects is randomly selected, and measurements are repeated on this sample for each treatment condition. This type of experiment may take the form of a before-and-after study.

2. The data analysis for a repeated-measures t test is done on the basis of the difference between the first and second measurements for each subject. These difference scores (D scores) are obtained by

$$D = X_2 - X_1$$

3. The formula for the repeated-measures t statistic is

$$t = \frac{\overline{D} - \mu_D}{s_{\overline{D}}}$$

where the sample mean is

$$\overline{D} = \frac{\Sigma D}{n}$$

the estimated standard error is

$$s_{\overline{D}} = \sqrt{\frac{s^2}{n}}$$

and the value of degrees of freedom is obtained by

$$df = n - 1$$

4. A repeated-measures design may be more useful than an independent-measures study when one wants to observe changes in behavior in the same subjects, as in learning or developmental studies. An important advantage of the repeated-measures design is that it removes or reduces individual differences, thus lowering sample variability and tending to increase the chances for obtaining a significant result.

5. A related-samples study may consist of two samples in which subjects have been matched on some variable. The repeated-measures t test may be used in this situation.

KEY TERMS

repeated-measures design

within-subjects design

matched-subjects design

difference scores

repeated-measures t statistic

estimated standard error
  for $\overline{D}$

individual differences

carry-over effects

progressive error

FOCUS ON PROBLEM SOLVING

1. Once data have been collected, we must then select the appropriate statistical analysis. How can you tell if the data call for a repeated-measures t test? Look at the experiment carefully. Is there only one sample of subjects? Are the same subjects tested a second time? If your answers are yes to both of these questions, then a repeated-measures t test should be done. There is only one situation in which the repeated-measures t can be used for data from two samples, and that is for *matched-subjects* studies (p. 323).

2. The repeated-measures t test is based on difference scores. In finding difference scores, be sure you are consistent with your method. That is, you may use either $X_2 - X_1$ or $X_1 - X_2$ to find D scores, but you must use the same method for all subjects.

DEMONSTRATION 11.1

A REPEATED-MEASURES *t* TEST

A major oil company would like to improve its tarnished image following a large oil spill. Its marketing department develops a short television commercial and tests it on a sample of $n = 7$ subjects. People's attitudes about the company are measured with a short questionnaire, both before and after viewing the commercial. The data are as follows:

PERSON	X_1 (BEFORE)	X_2 (AFTER)
A	15	15
B	11	13
C	10	18
D	11	12
E	14	16
F	10	10
G	11	19

Was there a significant change?

Note that subjects are being tested twice—once before and once after viewing the commercial. Therefore, we have a repeated-measures experiment.

STEP 1   State the hypotheses, and select an alpha level.

The null hypothesis states that the commercial has no effect on people's attitude, or in symbols,

$$H_0: \mu_D = 0 \quad \text{(the mean difference is zero)}$$

The alternative hypothesis states that the commercial does alter attitudes about the company, or

$$H_1: \mu_D \neq 0 \quad \text{(there is a mean change in attitudes)}$$

For this demonstration, we will use an alpha level of .05 for a two-tailed test.

STEP 2   Locate the critical region.

Degrees of freedom for the repeated-measures t test are obtained by the formula

$$df = n - 1$$

For these data, degrees of freedom equal

$$df = 7 - 1 = 6$$

The t distribution table is consulted for a two-tailed test with $\alpha = .05$ for $df = 6$. The critical t values for the critical region are $t = \pm 2.447$.

STEP 3   Obtain the sample data, and compute the test statistic.

The first step in computing the repeated-measures t statistic is to calculate basic descriptive statistics for the sample data. This involves finding the difference scores (D values) and then computing the sample mean and SS for the D scores.

The difference scores.   The following table illustrates the computations of the D values for our sample data. Remember, $D = X_2 - X_1$.

X_1	X_2	D
15	15	$15 - 15 = \ \ 0$
11	13	$13 - 11 = +2$
10	18	$18 - 10 = +8$
11	12	$12 - 11 = +1$
14	16	$16 - 14 = +2$
10	10	$10 - 10 = \ \ 0$
11	19	$19 - 11 = +8$

The sample mean of D values.   The sample mean for the difference scores is equal to the sum of the D values divided by n. For these data,

$$\Sigma D = 0 + 2 + 8 + 1 + 2 + 0 + 8 = 21$$

$$\bar{D} = \frac{\Sigma D}{n} = \frac{21}{7} = 3$$

Sum of squares for D scores.   We will use the computational formula for SS. The following table summarizes the calculations:

D	D^2
0	0
2	4
8	64
1	1
2	4
0	0
8	64

$\Sigma D = 21$

$\Sigma D^2 = 0 + 4 + 64 + 1 + 4 + 0 + 64 = 137$

$$SS = \Sigma D^2 - \frac{(\Sigma D)^2}{n} = 137 - \frac{(21)^2}{7}$$

$$SS = 137 - \frac{441}{7} = 137 - 63 = 74$$

Variance for the D *scores.* The variance for the sample of D scores equals

$$s^2 = \frac{SS}{n-1} = \frac{74}{6} = 12.33$$

Estimated standard error for $\overline{D}$. The estimated standard error for the sample mean difference is computed as follows:

$$s_{\overline{D}} = \sqrt{\frac{s^2}{n}} = \sqrt{\frac{12.33}{7}} = \sqrt{1.76} = 1.33$$

The repeated-measures t *statistic.* Now we have the information required to calculate the *t* statistic.

$$t = \frac{\overline{D} - \mu_D}{s_{\overline{D}}} = \frac{3 - 0}{1.33} = 2.26$$

STEP 4 Make a decision about H_0, and state the conclusion.

The obtained *t* value is not extreme enough to fall in the critical region. Therefore, we fail to reject the null hypothesis. We conclude that there is no evidence that the commercial will change people's attitudes, $t(6) = 2.26$, $p > .05$, two-tailed. (Note that we state that p is *greater than* .05 because we failed to reject H_0.)

PROBLEMS

1. For the following studies, indicate whether or not a repeated-measures *t* test is the appropriate analysis. Explain your answers.
   a. A researcher examines the effect of relaxation training on test anxiety. One sample of subjects receives relaxation training for three weeks. A second sample serves as a control group and does not receive the treatment. The researcher then measures anxiety levels for both groups in a test-taking situation.
   b. Another researcher does a similar study. Baseline levels of test anxiety are recorded for a sample of subjects. Then all subjects receive relaxation training for three weeks, and their anxiety levels are measured again.
   c. In a test-anxiety study, two samples are used. Subjects are assigned to groups, so that they are matched for self-esteem and for grade-point average. One sample receives relaxation training for three weeks, and the second serves as a no-treatment control group. Test anxiety is measured for both groups at the end of three weeks.

2. What is the primary advantage of a repeated-measures design over an independent-measures design?

3. Explain the difference between a matched-subjects design and a repeated-measures design.

4. A researcher conducts an experiment comparing two treatment conditions and obtains data with 10 scores for each treatment condition.
   a. If the researcher used an independent-measures design, how many subjects participated in the experiment?

b. If the researcher used a repeated-measures design, how many subjects participated in the experiment?

c. If the researcher used a matched-subjects design, how many subjects participated in the experiment?

5. Many people who are trying to quit smoking will switch to a lighter brand of cigarettes to reduce their intake of tar and nicotine. However, there is some evidence that switching to a lighter brand simply results in people smoking more cigarettes. A researcher examining this phenomenon records the number of cigarettes smoked each day for a sample of $n = 16$ subjects before and after they switched to a lighter brand. On average, the subjects smoke $\overline{D} = 3.2$ more cigarettes after switching with $SS = 375$. Do these data indicate a significant change in the number of cigarettes smoked per day? Test at the .05 level of significance.

6. The Pollyanna effect is a basic phenomenon observed by cognitive psychologists. Simply stated, the Pollyanna effect says that pleasant information is processed more efficiently and recalled better than unpleasant information. To demonstrate this phenomenon, a researcher prepares a list of 40 words consisting of 20 pleasant words (e.g., clown, sunshine, smile) and 20 unpleasant words (e.g., flood, disease, dirt) presented in a scrambled order. A sample of $n = 36$ subjects is obtained, and the entire list of 40 words is read to the subjects. Thirty minutes later, each subject is asked to recall as many words as possible from the entire list. The number of pleasant words and the number of unpleasant words are recorded for each subject. On average, this sample recalls $\overline{D} = 6.3$ more of the pleasant words than the unpleasant words with $SS = 560$. Do these data indicate a significant difference in recall for pleasant versus unpleasant words? Test with $\alpha = .01$.

7. Many over-the-counter cold medications come with a warning that the medicine may cause drowsiness. To evaluate this effect, a researcher measures reaction time for a sample of $n = 36$ subjects. Each subject is then given a dose of a popular cold medicine, and reaction time is measured again. For this sample, reaction time increases by an average of $\overline{D} = 24$ milliseconds with $s = 8$ after the medication. Do these data indicate that the cold medicine has a significant effect on reaction time? Use a two-tailed test with $\alpha = .05$.

8. Following are data from two repeated-measures experiments. In each experiment, a sample of $n = 4$ subjects is tested before treatment and again after treatment. For both experiments, the scores after treatment average $\overline{D} = 5$ points higher than the scores before treatment. However, in the first experiment, the treatment effect is fairly consistent across subjects; that is, all 4 subjects show an increase of about 5 points. In the second experiment,

there is no consistent effect; some subjects show an increase, some show a decrease, and some show no change at all.

EXPERIMENT 1		EXPERIMENT 2	
BEFORE TREATMENT	AFTER TREATMENT	BEFORE TREATMENT	AFTER TREATMENT
8	13	8	25
10	14	10	10
14	19	14	21
11	17	11	7

a. For each experiment, find the difference scores, and compute the mean and variance for the D values.

b. For each experiment, use a repeated-measures t test to determine whether or not the treatment has a significant effect. In each case, use a two-tailed test with $\alpha = .05$.

c. Explain why the two experiments lead to different conclusions about the significance of the treatment effect.

9. The following data are from an experiment comparing two treatments:

TREATMENT 1	TREATMENT 2	DIFFERENCE
10	11	1
2	5	3
1	2	1
15	18	3
7	9	2
$\overline{X} = 7$	$\overline{X} = 9$	$\overline{X} = 2$
$SS = 134$	$SS = 150$	$SS = 4$

a. Ignoring the difference scores, assume that the data are from an independent-measures experiment, and use a t test to determine whether there is a significant difference between the two treatments. Test with $\alpha = .05$.

b. Now assume that the data are from a repeated-measures experiment. Again, test for a significant mean difference using $\alpha = .05$.

c. How do you explain the different outcomes from parts a and b? *Hint:* Look at the variability (SS) for the two different tests. This is an example of the general idea that a repeated-measures experiment removes the variability due to individual differences.

10. One of the benefits of aerobic exercise is the release of endorphins, which are natural chemicals in the brain that produce a feeling of general well-being. A sample of $n = 16$ subjects is obtained, and each person's tolerance for pain is tested before and after a 50-minute session of aerobic exercise. On average, the pain tolerance for this sample is $\bar{D} = 10.5$ points higher after exercise than it was before. The SS for the sample of difference scores is $SS = 960$. Do these data indicate a significant increase in pain tolerance following exercise? Use a one-tailed test with $\alpha = .01$.

11. A researcher for a dog food manufacturer would like to determine whether animals show any preference between two new food mixes that the company has recently developed. A sample of $n = 9$ dogs is obtained. The dogs are deprived of food overnight and then presented simultaneously with two bowls of food, one with each mix, the next morning. After 10 minutes, the bowls are removed, and the amount of food consumed (in ounces) is determined for each mix. The researcher computes the difference between the two mixes for each dog. The data show that the dogs ate $\bar{D} = 6$ ounces more of the first mix than of the second with $SS = 288$. Do these data indicate a significant difference between the two food mixes? Test with $\alpha = .05$.

12. A psychologist is testing a new drug for its pain-killing effects. The pain threshold is measured for a sample of $n = 9$ subjects by determining the intensity of an electric shock that causes discomfort. After the initial baseline is established, each subject receives the drug, and the pain threshold is measured once again. For this sample, the pain threshold has increased by an average of $\bar{D} = 1.6$ milliamperes with $s = 0.4$ after receiving the drug. Do these data indicate that the drug produces a significant increase in pain tolerance? Use a one-tailed test with $\alpha = .05$.

13. Although psychologists do not completely understand the phenomenon of dreaming, it does appear that people need to dream. One experiment demonstrating this fact shows that people who are deprived of dreaming one night will tend to have extra dreams the following night, as if they are trying to make up for the lost dreams. In a typical version of this study, the psychologist first records the number of dreams (by monitoring rapid eye movements—REMs) during a normal night's sleep. Then subjects are prevented from dreaming one night by being awakened as soon as they begin a dream. Following the night of deprivation, the psychologist once again records the number of dreams. Data from a sample of $n = 16$ subjects show an increase of $\bar{D} = 4.3$ dreams per night after deprivation with $SS = 60$. Do the data indicate that one night of dream deprivation has a significant effect on the number of dreams? Test at the .05 level of significance.

14. A consumer protection agency is testing the effectiveness of a new gasoline additive that claims to improve gas mileage. A sample of $n = 10$ cars is obtained, and each car is driven over a standard 100-mile course with and without the additive. The cars in this test average $\bar{D} = 2.7$ miles per gallon higher with the additive than without, with $s = 1.4$. Are these data sufficient to conclude that the additive significantly increases gas mileage? Use a one-tailed test with $\alpha = .05$.

15. Although it is generally assumed that routine exercise will improve overall health, there is some question about how much exercise is necessary to produce the benefits. To address this question, a researcher obtained $n = 7$ pairs of subjects, matched one to one for age, sex, and weight. All subjects exercised regularly, but one subject within each pair exercised less than two hours per week, and the other spent more than five hours per week exercising. Each subject was evaluated by a physician and given an overall health rating. The data from this study are as follows:

SUBJECT PAIR	TWO HOURS PER WEEK	FIVE HOURS PER WEEK
A	15	18
B	12	14
C	16	12
D	9	11
E	13	14
F	16	16
G	17	16

Do these data indicate that the amount of regular exercise has an effect on health? Test for a significant difference using $\alpha = .05$.

16. In the Preview section of this chapter, we discussed a report describing how the accuracy of Olympic marksmen can be affected by heartbeats. Pelton (1983) reported that Olympic-level marksmen shoot much better if they fire between heartbeats rather than squeezing the trigger during a heartbeat. The small vibration caused by a heartbeat seems to be sufficient to affect the marksmen's aim. The following hypothetical data demonstrate this phenomenon. A sample of $n = 6$ Olympic marksmen fires a series of rounds while a researcher records heartbeats. For each marksman, the total score is recorded for shots fired during heartbeats and for shots fired between heartbeats. Do these data indicate a significant difference? Test with $\alpha = .05$.

SUBJECT	DURING HEARTBEAT	BETWEEN HEARTBEAT
A	93	98
B	90	94
C	95	96
D	92	91
E	95	97
F	91	97

17. Sensory isolation chambers are used to examine the effects of mild sensory deprivation. The chamber is a dark, silent tank where subjects float on heavily salted water and are thereby deprived of nearly all external stimulation. Sensory deprivation produces deep relaxation and has been shown to produce temporary increases in sensitivity for vision, hearing, touch, and even taste. The following data represent hearing threshold scores for a group of subjects who were tested before and immediately after one hour of deprivation. A lower score indicates more sensitive hearing. Do these data indicate that deprivation has a significant effect on hearing threshold? Test at the .05 level of significance.

SUBJECT	BEFORE	AFTER
A	31	30
B	34	31
C	29	29
D	33	29
E	35	32
F	32	34
G	35	28

18. The level of lymphocytes (white blood cells) in the blood is associated with susceptibility to disease—lower levels indicate greater susceptibility. In a study of the effects of stress on physical well-being, Schleifer and his colleagues (1983) recorded the lymphocyte counts for men who were going through a period of extreme emotional stress (the death of a spouse). For a sample of $n = 20$ men, the lymphocyte counts dropped an average of $\bar{D} = 0.09$ with $s = 0.08$. Do these data indicate a significant change? Test at the .05 level of significance.

19. It has been demonstrated that memory for a list of items can be improved if you make meaningful associations with each item. In one demonstration of this phenom-enon, Craik and Tulving (1975) presented subjects with a list of words to be remembered. Each word was presented in the context of a sentence. For some words, the sentences were very simple, and for others, the sentences were more elaborate. For the word *rabbit,* for example, a simple sentence would be "She cooked the rabbit." An elaborate sentence would be "The great bird swooped down and carried off the struggling rabbit." The researchers recorded the number of words recalled for each type of sentence to determine whether the more elaborate sentences produced richer associations and better memory. Hypothetical data, similar to the experimental results, are as follows. Do these data indicate a significant difference between the two types of sentences? Test at the .01 level of significance.

SUBJECT	SIMPLE SENTENCE	ELABORATE SENTENCE
A	14	22
B	15	17
C	19	24
D	12	19
E	17	28
F	15	20

20. There are two supermarkets in town, and a student would like to determine whether there is any significant difference in the prices they charge. The student identifies a sample of 9 basic grocery items and records the prices of the items at each store. Do these sample data indicate a significant difference in prices between the two stores? Test at the .05 level of significance.

ITEM	STORE A	STORE B
paper towels	$1.09	$1.05
½ gallon of milk	1.09	1.29
bread	1.29	1.05
5 pounds of potatoes	1.79	1.60
corn flakes	2.65	2.65
1 dozen eggs	.99	.85
1 pound of coffee	3.29	3.19
1 pound of ground beef	1.85	1.79
peanut butter	2.50	2.35

$\Sigma D = -6.33$

19) $H_0: \mu_1 = \mu_2$ $\alpha = \frac{.01}{2} = .005$ Simple — Elaborate

$H_1: \mu_1 \neq \mu_2$

D's -8
-2
-5
-7
-11
-5

$n = 6$

$CV_{df=5} = \pm 4.032$

$\Sigma D = -38$
$\Sigma D^2 = 288$

$S_D^2 = 288 - \frac{-38^2}{6} = 9.467$

$\frac{}{6-1}$

$S_D = \sqrt{9.467} = 3.07$

$S_{\bar{D}} = \frac{9.467}{\sqrt{6}} = 1.26$

$t = \frac{-6.33 - 0}{1.26} = -5.02$

reject H_0

3 TIME OUT

THE PROCESS of using sample means to answer questions about population means has been the central topic for the preceding four chapters and will continue to be the primary focus for the next four chapters. Thus, we are half-way into a sequence of eight similar chapters, and it is a good time to pause before we move on.

LOOKING BACK

The preceding four chapters have all involved inferential statistical methods using either a z-score or a t statistic. In each case, the z or t value is determined by a formula with the following basic structure:

$$z \text{ or } t = \frac{\text{sample statistic} - \text{population parameter}}{\text{standard error}}$$

As we have stated repeatedly, the z or t formula forms a *ratio*. The numerator of the ratio measures the observed difference between a sample statistic and the corresponding population parameter. The denominator is the standard error, which measures the standard or typical amount of difference between the statistic and the parameter. Thus, the z or t ratio measures the discrepancy between the sample and the population in *multiples of the standard error*. For example, if the obtained difference between the sample statistic and the population parameter is 10 points and the standard error is 5 points, then the value for z or t is $^{10}/_5 = 2$. The value of 2 indicates that the obtained difference is *two times* the standard error. Thus, the standard error serves as a benchmark or margin of error for evaluating the outcome of a research study.

In the preceding four chapters, we presented four examples of standard error, each measuring the standard distance between a sample mean (or means) and the corresponding population mean (or means). To review, the four standard errors are as follows:

1. The standard error of $\overline{X}$ when σ is known:

$$\sigma_{\overline{X}} = \frac{\sigma}{\sqrt{n}} \quad \text{or} \quad \sigma_{\overline{X}} = \sqrt{\frac{\sigma^2}{n}}$$

2. The standard error of $\overline{X}$ when σ is not known:

$$s_{\overline{X}} = \frac{s}{\sqrt{n}} \quad \text{or} \quad s_{\overline{X}} = \sqrt{\frac{s^2}{n}}$$

3. The standard error of $\overline{D}$ (the mean for a sample of difference scores):

$$s_{\overline{D}} = \sqrt{\frac{s^2}{n}}$$

4. The standard error of $(\overline{X}_1 - \overline{X}_2)$ (the difference between two sample means):

$$s_{\overline{X}_1 - \overline{X}_2} = \sqrt{\frac{s_p^2}{n_1} + \frac{s_p^2}{n_2}}$$

(Note that when there are two sample means, you simply add the error for the first mean and the error for the second mean.)

Although the exact formula for standard error changes from one situation to another, you should recognize the similarities among the formulas. All four formulas have the same structure and involve the same two elements:

1. s^2 (or σ^2), the variance of the scores. As the variance increases, the error also increases.

2. n, the sample size. The bigger the sample is, the smaller the error is.

At this point, you should understand how researchers use statistics to evaluate the sample mean(s) obtained in research studies. Specifically, you should know how to calculate the amount of error that ought to exist between a sample mean and a population mean, and you should understand how scientists use standard error to determine whether or not their research results are significant.

LOOKING AHEAD

In the next chapter, we will continue to use the z-score and the three t statisics you have learned. However, the formulas will be applied in a new technique called *estimation*. Like the hypothesis tests in the preceding four chapters, estimation will use sample means as the basis for drawing inferences about population means. In addition to introducing a new statistical method, Chapter 12 provides an excellent opportunity to review the z-score and t formulas from Chapters 8 through 11.

Continued

TIME OUT—continued

After Chapter 12 (estimation), we will begin a three-chapter sequence introducing a hypothesis-testing procedure called *analysis of variance*. Although this statistical technique will involve different terminology and formulas, you should find that analysis of variance is very similar to the independent-measures *t* and the repeated-measures *t* tests you have just completed. Specifically, analysis of variance will still use differences between sample means to evaluate hypotheses about the differences between population means. Also, the new test statistic will be structured as a ratio, comparing the obtained mean differences with the differences that would be expected by error.

$$\text{test statistic} = \frac{\text{differences between treatment means}}{\text{error}}$$

One of the changes you will notice as you begin the analysis of variance chapters is a shift in emphasis from the concept of *standard error* to the concept of *error variance*. Although the terminology is new, the error variance, like the standard error, is intended to measure the unexplained, unpredicted differences that occur naturally within any set of data.

For an independent-measures design, the error is computed by simply measuring the variance (differences) *within each treatment*. The rationale for this procedure is that the individuals within each treatment are all selected from the same population and are all treated exactly the same. In other words, nothing is done to *cause* the scores to be different, so any differences that exist are simply due to error. Thus, for an independent measures design, the error variance is

$$\text{error} = \text{variance within treatments}$$

Although the term *within treatments* is new, you should realize that the variance within treatments is essentially identical to the pooled variance that is calculated as part of the independent-measures *t* statistic.

With a repeated-measures design, the calculation of *error* changes somewhat. You should recall that one of the primary advantages of a repeated-measures study is that it removes variability due to individual differences. With this in mind, the error variance for a repeated-measures test becomes

$$\text{error} = \text{variance within treatments} - \text{individual differences}$$

Again, you should recognize this definition as essentially equivalent to the variance (s^2) that is calculated as part of the repeated-measures *t* statistic. In the *t* formula, the variance is computed for the *D* scores, which have already eliminated the individual differences.

Finally, you should keep in mind that the general goal of a hypothesis test is to determine whether the results from a research study are significantly greater than chance; that is, are the results caused by the treatment, or can the result be explained by error? For all of the hypothesis tests we have considered thus far, and for the hypothesis tests in future chapters, the test statistic provides a means of comparing the obtained result (numerator) with naturally occurring error (denominator).

look &
think

ESTIMATION

CONTENTS

PREVIEW

Suppose that we asked you to describe the "typical" college student in the United States. For example, what is the mean age of this population? On the average, how many hours per week do members of this population study? What is the mean amount of money students spend on "junk food" each year? On the average, how many hours of sleep do they get each night? Notice we are asking questions about values for population parameters (mean age, mean money spent, and so on).

When you attempt to describe the typical college student, you probably will take a look at the students you know on your campus. From this group, you can begin to describe what the population of college students might be like. Notice that you are starting with a sample (the students you know) and then you are making some general statements about the population (for example, the mean age is around 21, the mean hours per week studying is 18, and so on). The process

of using sample data to estimate the values for population parameters is called *estimation*. It is used to make inferences about unknown populations and often serves as a follow-up to hypothesis tests.

As the term *estimation* implies, the sample data provide values that are only approximations (estimates) of population parameters. Many factors can influence these estimates. One obvious factor is sample size. Suppose that you knew only two other students. How might this affect your estimate? Another factor is the type of estimate used. For example, why limit our estimate to a single value? Instead of estimating the population mean age of students at precisely 21, why not estimate it to be somewhere in an interval between 20 and 23 years? In this chapter, we address these and many other questions as we closely examine the process of estimation.

12.1 OVERVIEW

In Chapter 8, we introduced hypothesis testing as a statistical procedure that allows researchers to use sample data to draw inferences about populations. Hypothesis testing is probably the most frequently used inferential technique, but it is not the only one. In this chapter, we will examine the process of estimation, which provides researchers with an additional method for using samples as the basis for drawing general conclusions about populations.

The basic principle underlying all of inferential statistics is that samples are representative of the populations from which they come. The most direct application of this principle is the use of sample values as estimators of the corresponding population values, that is, using statistics to estimate parameters. This process is called estimation.

DEFINITION   The inferential process of using sample data to estimate population parameters is called *estimation*.

The use of samples to estimate populations is quite common. For example, you often hear news reports such as "Sixty percent of the general public approves of the president's new budget plan." Clearly, the percentage that is reported was obtained from a sample (they don't ask everyone's opinion), and this sample statistic is being used as an estimate of the population parameter.

We already have encountered estimation in earlier sections of this book. For example, the formulas for sample variance and estimated standard error were developed so that the sample statistics would give an accurate and unbiased estimate of the corresponding population parameters. Now we will examine the process of using sample means as the basis for estimating population means.

PRECISION AND CONFIDENCE IN ESTIMATION

Before we begin the actual process of estimation, there are a few general points that should be kept in mind. First, a sample will not give a perfect picture of the whole population. A sample is expected to be representative of the population, but there always will be some differences between the sample and the entire population. These differences are referred to as *sampling error* and are measured by standard error. Second, there are two distinct ways of making estimates. Suppose, for example, that you are asked to estimate the weight of this book. You could pick a single value (say, 2 pounds), or you could choose a range of values (say, between 1.5 pounds and 2.5 pounds). The first estimate, using a single number, is called a *point estimate*. Point estimates have the advantage of being very precise; they specify a single value. On the other hand, you generally do not have much confidence that a point estimate is actually correct. You would not bet your paycheck on it, for example.

DEFINITION

For a *point estimate*, you use a single number as your estimate of an unknown quantity.   *good precision less confidence*

The second type of estimate, using a range of values, is called an *interval estimate*. Interval estimates do not have the precision of point estimates, but they do give you more confidence. You would feel more comfortable, for example, saying that this book weighs "around 2 pounds." At the extreme, you would be very confident in estimating that this book weighs between 0.5 and 10 pounds. (Maybe you would feel more comfortable betting your paycheck that *this* estimate is correct.) Notice that there is a trade-off between precision and confidence. As the interval gets wider and wider, your confidence grows. But, at the same time, the precision of the estimate gets worse. We will be using samples to make both point and interval estimates of a population mean. Because the interval estimates are associated with confidence, they usually are called *confidence intervals*.

DEFINITIONS

For an *interval estimate*, you use a range of values as your estimate of an unknown quantity.   *confidence but less precision*

When an interval estimate is accompanied with a specific level of confidence (or probability), it is called a *confidence interval*.

Estimation is used in the same general situations in which we have already used hypothesis testing. In fact, there is an estimation procedure that accompanies each of the hypothesis tests we presented in the preceding four chapters. Although the details of the estimation process will differ from one experiment to the next, the general experimental situation is shown in Figure 12.1. The figure shows a population with an unknown mean (the population after treatment). A sample is selected from the unknown population. The goal of estimation is to use the sample data to obtain an estimate of the unknown population mean.

COMPARISON OF HYPOTHESIS TESTS AND ESTIMATION

You should recognize that the situation shown in Figure 12.1 is the same situation in which we have used hypothesis tests in the past. In many ways, hypothesis testing and estimation are similar. They both make use of sample data and either z-scores or t statistics to make inferences about unknown populations. But these two inferential procedures are designed to answer different questions. Using the situation shown in Figure 12.1 as an example, we could use a hypothesis test to

FIGURE 12.1

The basic experimental situation for estimation. The purpose is to use the sample data to obtain an estimate of the population mean after treatment.

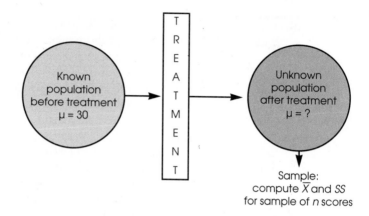

evaluate the effect of the treatment. The test would determine whether or not the treatment has any effect. Notice that this is a yes-no question. The null hypothesis says, "No, there is no treatment effect." The alternative hypothesis says, "Yes, there is a treatment effect."

 The goal of estimation, on the other hand, is to determine the value of the unknown population mean after treatment. Essentially, estimation will determine *how much* effect the treatment has (see Box 12.1). If, for example, we obtained a point estimate of $\mu = 38$ for the population after treatment, we could conclude that the effect of the treatment is to increase scores by an average of 8 points (from the original mean of $\mu = 30$ to the post-treatment mean of $\mu = 38$).

WHEN TO USE ESTIMATION

There are three situations where estimation commonly is used:

1. Estimation is used after a hypothesis test where H_0 is rejected. Remember that when H_0 is rejected, the conclusion is that the treatment does have an effect. The next logical question would be, How much effect? This is exactly the question that estimation is designed to answer.

2. Estimation is used when you already know that there is an effect and simply want to find out how much. For example, the city school board probably knows that a special reading program will help students. However, they want to be sure that the effect is big enough to justify the cost. Estimation is used to determine the size of the treatment effect.

3. Estimation is used when you simply want some basic information about an unknown population. Suppose, for example, that you want to know about the political attitudes of students at your college. You could use a sample of students as the basis for estimating the population mean.

THE LOGIC OF ESTIMATION

As we have noted, estimation and hypothesis testing are both *inferential* statistical techniques that involve using sample data as the basis for drawing conclusions about an unknown population. More specifically, a researcher begins with a question about an unknown population parameter. To answer the question, a sample is obtained, and a sample statistic is computed. In general, *statistical inference* involves using

12.1 HYPOTHESIS TESTING VERSUS ESTIMATION: STATISTICAL SIGNIFICANCE VERSUS PRACTICAL SIGNIFICANCE

As WE already noted, hypothesis tests tend to involve a yes-no decision. Either we decide to reject H_0, or we fail to reject H_0. The language of hypothesis testing reflects this process. The outcome of the hypothesis test is one of two conclusions:

There is no evidence for a treatment effect (fail to reject H_0)

or

There is a statistically significant effect (H_0 is rejected).

For example, a researcher studies the effect of a new drug on people with high cholesterol. In hypothesis testing, the question is whether or not the drug has a significant effect on cholesterol levels. Suppose that the hypothesis test revealed that the drug did produce a significant decrease in cholesterol. The next question might be, How much of a reduction occurs? This question calls for estimation, in which the size of a treatment effect for the population is estimated.

Estimation can be of great practical importance because the presence of a "statistically significant" effect does not necessarily mean the results are large enough for use in practical applications. Consider the following possibility: Before drug treatment, the sample of patients had a mean cholesterol level of 225. After drug treatment, their cholesterol reading was 210. When analyzed, this 15-point change reached statistical significance (H_0 was rejected). Although the hypothesis test revealed that the drug produced a *statistically significant* change, it may not be *clinically significant*. That is, a cholesterol level of 210 is still quite high. In estimation, we would estimate the population mean cholesterol level for patients who are treated with the drug. This estimated value may reveal that even though the drug does in fact reduce cholesterol levels, it does not produce a large enough change (notice we are looking at a "how much" question) to make it of any practical value. Thus, the hypothesis test might reveal that an effect occurred, but estimation indicates it is small and of little *practical significance* in real-world applications.

sample statistics to help answer questions about population parameters. The general logic underlying the processes of estimation and hypothesis testing is based on the fact that each population parameter has a corresponding sample statistic. In addition, you usually can compute a standard error that measures how much discrepancy is expected, on the average, between the statistic and the parameter. For example, a sample mean, $\overline{X}$, corresponds to the population mean, μ, with a standard error measured by $\sigma_{\overline{X}}$ or $s_{\overline{X}}$.

In the preceding four chapters, we examined four hypothesis-testing situations involving sample statistics, parameters, and standard errors. The four situations are summarized in Table 12.1.

The statistic, the parameter, and the standard error can all be combined into a single formula to compute a z-score or a t statistic. For example,

$$z = \frac{\overline{X} - \mu}{\sigma_{\overline{X}}} \quad \text{or} \quad t = \frac{\overline{X} - \mu}{s_{\overline{X}}}$$

For estimation and for hypothesis testing, the population parameter is unknown, and the z-score or t statistic formula has the general structure

$$z \text{ or } t = \frac{\text{sample statistic} - \text{unknown population parameter}}{\text{standard error}}$$

TABLE 12.1

A summary of research situations where a sample statistic is used to draw inferences about the corresponding population parameter

SAMPLE STATISTIC	POPULATION PARAMETER	STANDARD ERROR*	
$\overline{X}$	μ	$\sigma_{\overline{X}}$	(Chapter 8)
$\overline{X}$	μ	$s_{\overline{X}}$	(Chapter 9)
$\overline{X}_1 - \overline{X}_2$	$\mu_1 - \mu_2$	$s_{\overline{X}_1 - \overline{X}_2}$	(Chapter 10)
$\overline{D}$	μ_D	$s_{\overline{D}}$	(Chapter 11)

*In each case, the standard error provides a measure of the standard distance or error between the statistic and the parameter.

In previous chapters, we used this general formula to test hypotheses about the unknown parameter. Now we will use the same formula as the basis for *estimating* the value of an unknown parameter. Although hypothesis tests and estimation use the same basic formula, these two inferential procedures follow different logical paths because they have different goals. The two different paths are developed as follows:

different logic for estimation

HYPOTHESIS TEST	ESTIMATION
Goal: To test a hypothesis about a population parameter—usually the null hypothesis, which states that the treatment has no effect.	*Goal:* To estimate the value of an unknown population parameter—usually the value for an unknown population mean.
A. For a hypothesis test, you begin by hypothesizing a value for the unknown population parameter. This value is specified in the null hypothesis.	A. For estimation, you do not attempt to calculate z or t. Instead, you begin by estimating what the z or t value ought to be. The strategy for making this estimate is to select a "reasonable" value for z or t. (*Note:* You are not just picking a value for z or t, but rather you are estimating where the sample is located in the distribution.)
B. The hypothesized value is substituted into the formula, and *the value for z or t is computed.*	
C. If the hypothesized value produces a "reasonable" value for z or t, we conclude that the hypothesis was "reasonable," and we fail to reject H_0. If the result is an "unreasonable" value for z or t, H_0 is rejected.	B. As with hypothesis testing, a "reasonable" value for z or t is defined as a high-probability outcome located near the center of the distribution (see Figure 12.2).
D. A "reasonable" value for z or t is defined by its location in a distribution. In general, "reasonable values are high-probability outcomes in the center of the distribution. Extreme values with low probability are considered "unreasonable" (see Figure 12.2).	C. The "reasonable" value for z or t is substituted into the formula, and *the value for the unknown population parameter is computed.*
	D. Because you used a "reasonable" value for z or t in the formula, it is assumed that the computation will produce a "reasonable" estimate of the population parameter.

FIGURE 12.2

For estimation or hypothesis testing, the distribution of *z*-scores or *t* statistics is divided into two sections: the middle of the distribution, consisting of high-probability outcomes that are considered "reasonable," and the extreme tails of the distribution, consisting of low-probability, "unreasonable" outcomes.

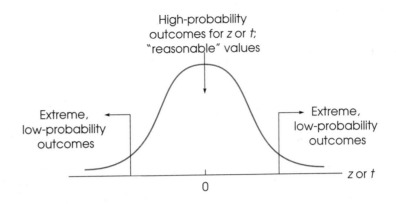

High-probability
outcomes for *z* or *t*;
"reasonable" values

Extreme,
low-probability
outcomes

Extreme,
low-probability
outcomes

z or *t*

0

Because the goal of the estimation process is to compute a value for an unknown population parameter, it usually is easier to regroup the terms in the *z* or *t* formula so that the population parameter is isolated on one side of the equation. In algebraic terms, we simply solve the equation for the unknown parameter. The result takes the following form:

$$\text{unknown population parameter} = \text{sample statistic} \pm [(z \text{ or } t)(\text{standard error})] \qquad (12.1)$$

This is the general equation that we will use for estimation. Consider the following four points about equation 12.1:

1. In this formula, the values for the sample mean and the standard error can be computed directly from the sample data. Only the value for the *z*-score (or *t* statistic) cannot be computed. If we can determine this missing value, then the equation can be used to compute the unknown population parameter.

2. Although the specific value for the *z*-score (or *t* statistic) cannot be computed, you do know what the entire distribution of *z*-scores (or *t* statistics) looks like. For example, the *z*-scores may be normally distributed and always have a mean of zero. Likewise, the *t* distribution is bell-shaped with its exact shape determined by the value of *df*, and it also will have a mean of zero.

3. While you cannot compute the specific value for the *z*-score (or *t* statistic) for the sample data, you can *estimate* the location of the sample data in the sampling distribution. The procedure involves selecting "reasonable" values for the *z*-scores (or *t* statistics) to estimate the location of the sample.

4. For a point estimate, your best bet is to estimate that the sample statistic (for example, $\bar{X}$) is located in the exact center of its sampling distribution (distribution of sample means), that is, the location that corresponds to $z = 0$ (or $t = 0$). This is a reasonable estimate for location because sample statistics become increasingly unlikely as you move toward the tails of the distribution.

For an interval estimate, your best bet is to predict that the sample statistic is in the middle section of the sampling distribution. For example, to be

FIGURE 12.3

A population distribution before the treatment is administered and the same population after treatment. Note that the effect of the treatment is to add a constant amount to each score. The goal of estimation is to determine how large the treatment effect is; i.e., what the new population mean is (μ = ?).

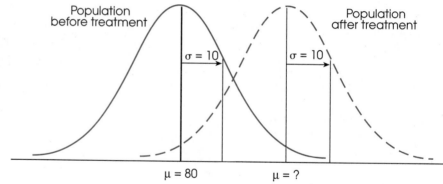

90% confident that μ is in your interval, you would use the z-score (or t statistic) values that mark off the middle 90% of the distribution of sample means.

Notice that by estimating the location of a sample statistic ($\overline{X}$) within its sampling distribution (distribution of sample means) and by taking the standard error into account, we can arrive at an estimate of μ using equation 12.1.

12.2 ESTIMATION WITH z-SCORES

The z-score statistic is used in situations where the population standard deviation is known, but the population mean is unknown. Often this is a population that has received some treatment. Suppose that you are examining the effect of a special summer reading program for grade school children. Using a standard reading achievement test, you know that the scores for second-graders in the city school district from a normal distribution with μ = 80 and σ = 10. It is reasonable to assume that a special reading program would increase the students' scores. The question is, How much?

The example we are considering is shown graphically in Figure 12.3. Notice that we have assumed that the effect of the treatment (the special program) is to add a constant amount to each student's reading score. As a result, after the summer reading program the entire distribution would be shifted to a new location with a larger mean. This new mean is what we want to estimate.

Because it would not be reasonable to put all the students in the special program, we cannot measure this mean directly. However, we can get a sample and use the sample mean to estimate the population value for μ. For this example, assume that a random sample of n = 25 students is selected to participate in the summer program. At the end of the summer, each student takes the reading test, and we compute a mean reading score of $\overline{X}$ = 88. Note that this sample represents the population after the special program. The goal of estimation is to use this sample mean as the basis for estimating the unknown population mean.

The procedure for estimating μ is based on the distribution of sample means (see Chapter 7). You should recall that this distribution is the set of all the possible

If the treatment simply adds a constant to each score, the standard deviation will not be changed. Although it is common practice to assume that a treatment will add a constant amount, you should realize that in most real-life situations there is a general tendency for variability to increase when the mean increases.

FIGURE 12.4

The distribution of sample means based on $n = 25$. Samples were selected from the unknown population (after treatment) shown in Figure 12.3.

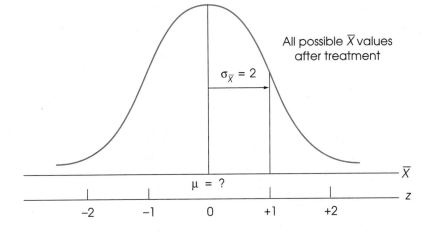

$\sigma_{\overline{X}} = 2$

All possible $\overline{X}$ values after treatment

$\mu = \,?$

$\overline{X}$

z

$-2 \qquad -1 \qquad 0 \qquad +1 \qquad +2$

$\overline{X}$ values for a specified sample size (n). The parameters of this distribution are the following:

1. The mean (called expected value) is equal to the population mean.

Because the value for σ is known, it is easiest to use this equation rather than the one based on variance: $\sqrt{\sigma^2/n}$

2. The standard deviation for this distribution (called standard error) is equal to $\sigma/\sqrt{n}$.

3. The distribution of sample means will be normal if either

   a. The population is normal, or

   b. The sample size is at least $n = 30$.

For the example we are considering, the distribution of sample means for $n = 25$ will be normal (because the population is normal), it will have a standard error of $\sigma/\sqrt{n} = 10/\sqrt{25} = 10/5 = 2$, and it will have a mean that is equal to the unknown population mean ($\mu = \,?$). This distribution is shown in Figure 12.4.

Our sample mean, $\overline{X} = 88$, is somewhere in this distribution; that is, we have one value out of all the possible sample means. Unfortunately, we do not know where our sample mean is located in the distribution. Nonetheless, we can specify different locations by using *z*-scores. The *z*-score values and their locations have been identified in Figure 12.4.

Our sample mean, $\overline{X} = 88$, has a *z*-score given by the formula

$$z = \frac{\overline{X} - \mu}{\sigma_{\overline{X}}}$$

Because our goal is to find the population mean (μ), we will solve this *z*-score equation for μ. The algebra in this process is as follows:

$$z\sigma_{\overline{X}} = \overline{X} - \mu \qquad \text{(Multiply both sides of the equation by } \sigma_{\overline{X}}.\text{)}$$

$$\mu + z\sigma_{\overline{X}} = \overline{X} \qquad \text{(Add } \mu \text{ to both sides of the equation.)}$$

$$\mu = \overline{X} - z\sigma_{\overline{X}} \qquad \text{(Subtract } z\sigma_{\overline{X}} \text{ from both sides of the equation.)} \quad (12.2)$$

To use this equation, we begin with the values we know: $\overline{X} = 88$ and $\sigma_{\overline{X}} = 2$. To complete the equation, we must obtain a value for *z*. The value we will use for *z* is determined by estimating the z-score for our sample mean. More precisely, we are estimating the location of our sample mean within the distribution of sample means. The estimated position will determine a z-score value that can be used in the equation to compute μ. It is important to note that the z-score value we will be using is an *estimate;* therefore, the population mean that we compute will also be an estimate.

POINT ESTIMATES

For a point estimate, you must select a single value for the z-score. It should be clear that your best bet is to select the exact middle of the distribution—that is, $z = 0$. It would be unwise to pick an extreme value such as $z = 2$ because there are relatively few samples that far away from the population mean. Most of the sample means pile up around $z = 0$, so this is your best choice. When this z-value is used in the equation, we get

$$\mu = \overline{X} - z\sigma_{\overline{X}}$$
$$\mu = 88 - 0(2)$$
$$= 88$$

This is our point estimate of the population mean. You should notice that we simply have used the sample mean, $\overline{X}$, to estimate the population mean, μ. The sample is the *only* information we have about the population, and you should recall from Chapter 7 that sample means tend to approximate μ (central limit theorem). Our conclusion is that the special summer program will increase reading scores from an average of $\mu = 80$ to an average of $\mu = 88$. We are estimating that the program will have an 8-point effect on reading scores.

INTERVAL ESTIMATES

To make an interval estimate, you select a range of z-score values rather than a single point. Looking again at the distribution of sample means in Figure 12.3, where would you estimate our sample mean is located? Remember, you now can pick a range of values. As before, your best bet is to predict that the sample mean is located somewhere in the center of the distribution. There is a good chance, for example, that our sample mean is located somewhere between $z = +1$ and $z = -1$. You would be almost certain that $\overline{X}$ is between $z = +3$ and $z = -3$. How do you know what range to use? Because several different ranges are possible and each range has its own degree of confidence, the first step is to determine the amount of confidence we want and then use this value to determine the range. Commonly used levels of confidence start at about 60% and go up. For this example, we will use 90%. This means that we want to be 90% confident that our interval estimate of μ is correct.

There are no strict rules for choosing a level of confidence. Researchers must decide how much precision and how much confidence are needed in each specific situation.

To be 90% confident, we simply estimate that our sample mean is somewhere in the middle 90% of the distribution of sample means. This section of the distribution is bounded by z-scores of $z = +1.65$ and $z = -1.65$. (Five percent of the distribution is in each tail. Check column C the unit normal table.) We are 90% confident that our particular sample mean ($\overline{X} = 88$) is in this range because 90% of all the possible means are there.

The next step is to use this range of z-score values in the estimation equation. We use the two ends of the z-score range to compute the two ends of the interval estimate for μ.

At one extreme, $z = +1.65$, which gives

$$\mu = \overline{X} - z\sigma_{\overline{X}}$$
$$= 88 - 1.65(2)$$
$$= 88 - 3.30$$
$$= 84.70$$

At the other extreme, $z = -1.65$, which gives

$$\mu = \overline{X} - z\sigma_{\overline{X}}$$
$$= 88 - (-1.65)(2)$$
$$= 88 + 3.30$$
$$= 91.30$$

Software manuals:
Minitab (Section 6)

The result is an interval estimate for μ. We are estimating that the population mean after the special summer program is between 84.70 and 91.30. If the mean is as small as 84.70, then the effect of the special program would be to increase reading scores by an average of 4.70 points (from $\mu = 80$ to $\mu = 84.70$). If the mean is as large as 91.30, the program would have increased scores by an average of 11.30 points (from $\mu = 80$ to $\mu = 91.30$). Thus, we conclude that the special summer program will increase reading scores, and we estimate that the magnitude of the increase will be between 4.7 and 11.3 points.

INTERPRETATION OF THE CONFIDENCE INTERVAL

In the preceding example, we computed the 90% confidence interval for μ. The interval ranges from 84.7 to 91.3, and we are 90% confident that the true (unknown) population mean is located somewhere in this interval. The logic that allows us to be 90% confident in this estimate proceeds as follows:

1. The sample mean, $\overline{X} = 88$, is located somewhere within the distribution of sample means. The exact location is determined by a z-score.

2. Although we do not know the exact location of the sample mean, or its z-score, we can be 90% confident that the z-score is between 1.65 and -1.65 because 90% of all the possible z-scores are contained in this range (see Figure 12.5).

3. Therefore, we *estimate* that our sample mean is located between $z = 1.65$ and $z = -1.65$. If this estimate is correct, and it will be correct 90% of the time, then the sample mean is guaranteed to be within a specific distance of the unknown population mean (see Figure 12.5). This distance is determined by z times the standard error: In this example,

$$z\sigma_{\overline{X}} = (1.65)(2) = 3.30 \text{ points}$$

This distance is then used to construct the confidence interval. As long as the sample mean falls within the z-score boundaries, you are guaranteed that the population mean will fall within the limits of the confidence interval.

In Chapter 5 (p. 145), we noted that $z\sigma$ is a deviation score.

FIGURE 12.5

The distribution of sample means for samples of size $n = 25$ selected from a normal population with $\sigma = 10$ and an unknown mean ($\mu = ?$). Note that 90% of all the possible sample means are located between $z = 1.65$ and $z = -1.65$. Also note that any sample mean located within these z-score boundaries will be within $(1.65)(2) = 3.30$ points of the population mean.

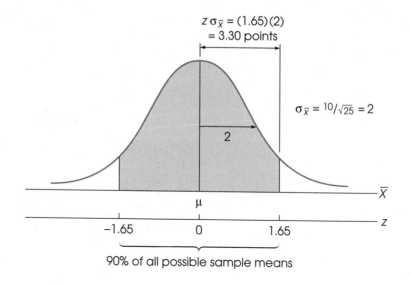

$z\sigma_{\bar{X}} = (1.65)(2)$
$= 3.30$ points

$\sigma_{\bar{X}} = 10/\sqrt{25} = 2$

2

$\bar{X}$

μ

z

−1.65   0   1.65

90% of all possible sample means

4. If we took additional samples and computed each sample mean, then we would have a variety of values for $\bar{X}$ and could compute a variety of different confidence intervals. However, 90% of all the different sample means would be located between $z = 1.65$ and $z = -1.65$ (see Figure 12.5). Thus, 90% of the sample means would be located within a distance of 3.30 points of the unknown population mean. Because each confidence interval extends 3.30 points in either direction from the sample mean, 90% of the different confidence intervals would contain the true population mean. As long as the sample mean is located in the middle 90% of the distribution, the 90% confidence interval will contain μ.

Notice that the confidence interval sets up a range of values with the sample mean in the middle. As with point estimates, we are using the sample mean to estimate the population mean, but now we are saying that the value of μ should be *around* $\bar{X}$ rather than exactly equal to $\bar{X}$. Because the confidence interval is built around $\bar{X}$, adding in one direction and subtracting in the other, we will modify the estimation equation in order to simplify the arithmetic.

$$\mu = \bar{X} \pm z\sigma_{\bar{X}} \tag{12.3}$$

To build the confidence interval, start with the sample mean, and add $z\sigma_{\bar{X}}$ to get the boundary in one direction; then subtract $z\sigma_{\bar{X}}$ to get the other boundary. Translated into words, the formula says that

population mean = sample mean ± some error

The sample mean is expected to be representative of the population mean with some margin of error. Although it may seem obvious that the sample mean is used as the basis for estimating the population mean, you should not overlook the reason for this result. Sample means, on the average, provide an accurate, unbiased representation of the population mean. You should recognize this fact as one of the characteristics of the distribution of sample means: The mean (expected value) of the distribution of sample means is μ.

LEARNING CHECK **1.** A cattle rancher is interested in using a newly developed hormone to increase the weight of beef cattle. Before investing in this hormone, the rancher would like to obtain some estimate of its effect. Without the hormone, the cattle weigh an average of $\mu = 250$ pounds when they are sold at 8 months. The distribution of weights is approximately normal with $\sigma = 80$. A sample of 16 calves is selected to test the hormone. At age 8 months, the average weight for this sample is $\overline{X} = 340$ pounds.

   a. Use these data to make a point estimate of the population mean weight if all the cattle were given the hormone.

   b. Make an interval estimate of the population mean so that you are 95% confident that the true mean is in your interval.

ANSWERS **1. a.** For a point estimate, use the sample mean: $\overline{X} = 340$ pounds.

   b. For the 95% confidence interval, $z = \pm 1.96$ and $\sigma_{\overline{X}} = 20$. The interval would be

$$\mu = 340 \pm 39.20$$

The interval ranges from 300.80 to 379.20 pounds.

12.3 ESTIMATION WITH THE SINGLE-SAMPLE *t* STATISTIC

The single-sample *t* statistic is used in situations where you have a population with an unknown mean ($\mu = ?$) and an unknown standard deviation ($\sigma = ?$). The goal of estimation is to use the sample data to obtain an estimate of the unknown population mean. As you will see, the process of estimation with *t* statistics is nearly identical to the process described for *z*-scores in Section 12.2. However, in situations where σ is unknown, we must use a *t* statistic instead of a *z*-score.

Because the purpose of estimation is to find the approximate value for the population mean, μ, we begin with the *t* statistic.

$$t = \frac{\overline{X} - \mu}{s_{\overline{X}}}$$

Solving for μ, we obtain

$$\mu = \overline{X} - t s_{\overline{X}}$$

Because *t* can have a positive or negative value in interval estimates, we can simplify the arithmetic of the formula:

$$\mu = \overline{X} \pm t s_{\overline{X}} \qquad\qquad \text{(12.4)}$$

This is the basic formula for estimation using the t statistic. You should notice that this formula is very similar to the z-score formula used for estimation (equation 12.3). Also note that either formula (using t or z) can be expressed conceptually in words as

$$\text{population mean} = \text{sample mean} \pm \text{some error}$$

PROCEDURES OF ESTIMATION USING A t STATISTIC

To obtain an estimate of μ using equation 12.4, we first find the value for the sample mean (from the sample data) and calculate the estimated standard error (also computed from the sample data). Next, we must obtain a value for t. Remember that you cannot calculate t because you do not know the population mean, μ. However, you know that every sample has a corresponding t value, and this t value is located somewhere within the t distribution. Therefore, the next step is to estimate where your particular sample is located in the t distribution. For a point estimate, you use the most likely value in the distribution, namely, $t = 0$. For an interval estimate, you use a range of t values determined by the level of confidence you have selected (for example, 95% or 99%). Because the t value in the formula is an estimate, the result we obtain is an estimate for the value of μ. The process of estimation is demonstrated in the following example.

EXAMPLE 12.1

In this example, we are simply trying to estimate the value of μ. Because no particular treatment is involved here, we are not trying to determine the size of a treatment effect.

A marketing researcher for a major U.S. jeans manufacturer would like to estimate the mean age for the population of people who buy its products. This information will be valuable in making decisions about how to spend advertising dollars. For example, should the company place more advertisements in *Seventeen* magazine or in *Cosmopolitan?* These represent publications that are directed at different age groups. It would be too costly and time consuming to record the age of every person in the population of their consumers, so a random sample is taken to estimate the value of μ. A sample of $n = 30$ people is drawn from the consumers who purchase the jeans from several major clothing outlets. The mean age of this sample is $\overline{X} = 30.5$ years with $SS = 709$. The marketing researcher wishes to make a point estimate and to determine the 95% confidence interval for μ.

Notice that nothing is known about the population parameters. Estimation of the value for μ will be based solely on the sample data. Because σ is unknown, a t statistic will be used for the estimation. The confidence level has been selected (95%), and the sample data have been collected. Now we can turn our attention to the computational steps of estimation.

Compute s^2 and $s_{\overline{X}}$ The population standard deviation is not known; therefore, to estimate μ, it is necessary to use the estimated standard error. In chapters 7 and 9, we introduced ways to compute standard errors with variance. To obtain $s_{\overline{X}}$, we must first compute the sample variance. Using the information provided, we obtain

$$s^2 = \frac{SS}{n-1}$$

$$= \frac{709}{29}$$

$$= 24.45$$

For estimated standard error, we obtain

$$s_{\overline{X}} = \sqrt{\frac{s^2}{n}}$$

$$= \sqrt{\frac{24.45}{30}}$$

$$= \sqrt{0.81}$$

$$= 0.90$$

Compute the point estimate   The value for *t* that is used depends on the type of estimate being made. A single *t* value is used for a point estimate, and an interval of values is used for the confidence interval. Just as we observed with the *z*-score distribution, *t* values are symmetrically distributed with a mean of zero. Therefore, we will use $t = 0$, the center of the distribution, as the best choice for the point estimate. Using the sample data, the estimation formula yields a point estimate of

$$\mu = \overline{X} \pm ts_{\overline{X}}$$

$$= 30.5 \pm 0(0.90)$$

$$= 30.5 \pm 0$$

$$= 30.5$$

As noted before, the sample mean is the most appropriate point estimate of the population mean.

Construct an interval estimate   For an interval estimate of μ, we construct an interval around the sample mean in which the value for μ probably falls. We now use a range of *t* values to define this interval. For example, there is a good chance that the sample has a *t* value somewhere between $t = +2$ and $t = -2$ and even a much better chance it is between $t = +4$ and $t = -4$. The level of confidence (percentage of confidence) will determine the *t* values that mark off the boundaries of this interval. However, unlike the normal *z* distribution, there is a family of *t* distributions in which the exact shape of the distribution depends on the value of degrees of freedom. Therefore, the value of *df* that is associated with the sample is another determining factor of the *t* values to be used in the interval estimate. For this example,

$$df = n - 1 = 30 - 1 = 29$$

The marketing researcher selected the 95% confidence interval. Figure 12.6 depicts the *t* distribution for *df* = 29. To obtain the *t* values associated with the 95% confidence interval, we must consult the *t* distribution table. We look under the heading of proportions in *two tails*. If the middle 95% of the distribution is of interest to us, then both tails outside of the interval together will contain 5% of the *t* values. Therefore, to find the *t* values associated with the 95% confidence interval, we look for the entry under $p = .05$, two tails, for *df* = 29. The values of *t* used for the boundaries of this confidence interval are -2.045 and $+2.045$ (Figure 12.6). Using these values in the formula for μ, we obtain, for one end of the confidence interval.

We do not know the actual *t* value associated with the $\overline{X}$ we obtained. For that information, we would need the value for μ—which we are trying to estimate. So we use values of *t*, just as we did with *z*, to define an interval around $\overline{X}$ that probably contains the value of μ.

FIGURE 12.6

The 95% confidence interval for $df = 29$ will have boundaries that range from $t = -2.045$ to $+2.045$. Because the t distribution table presents proportions in both tails of the distribution, for the 95% confidence interval you find the t values under $p = 0.05$ (proportions of t-scores in two tails) for $df = 29$.

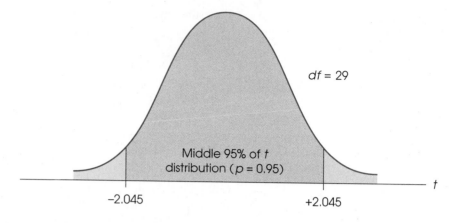

$$df = 29$$

Middle 95% of t
distribution ($p = 0.95$)

-2.045 $+2.045$

$$\mu = \overline{X} - ts_{\overline{X}}$$

$$= 30.5 - 2.045(.90)$$

$$= 30.5 - 1.84$$

$$= 28.66$$

 Software manuals:
Minitab (Section 6)

For the other end of the interval,

$$\mu = \overline{X} + ts_{\overline{X}}$$

$$= 30.5 + 2.045(0.90)$$

$$= 30.5 + 1.84$$

$$= 32.34$$

Therefore, the marketing researcher can be 95% confident that the population mean age for consumers of his product is between 28.66 and 32.34 years. The confidence level (%) determines the range of t values used in constructing the interval. As long as the obtained sample really does have a t value that falls within the estimated range of t values, the population mean will be included in the confidence interval.

LEARNING CHECK

1. A professor of philosophy hypothesizes that an introductory course in logic will help college students with their other studies. To test this hypothesis, a random sample of $n = 25$ freshmen is selected. These students are required to complete a logic course during their freshman year. At the time of graduation, the final grade point average is computed for each of these students. The mean GPA for this sample is $\overline{X} = 2.83$ with $SS = 6$. Using the sample data, make a point estimate and an interval estimate for the mean GPA of the population of students that take the course. Use a confidence level of 99%.

2. Suppose that the sample data consisted of $\overline{X} = 2.83$, $SS = 6$, and $n = 16$. Make a point estimate, and construct the 99% confidence interval.

ANSWERS   **1.** Point estimate: $\mu = 2.83$. 99% confidence interval: μ is between 3.11 and 2.55.

           2. Point estimate: $\mu = 2.83$. 99% confidence interval: $s^2 = 0.40$; $s_{\overline{X}} = 0.16$; μ is between 3.30 and 2.36.

12.4 ESTIMATION WITH THE INDEPENDENT-MEASURES *t* STATISTIC

The independent-measures *t* statistic can be used for estimation as well as for hypothesis testing. In either case, the *t* statistic provides a means for using sample data to draw inferences about the difference between two population means. For the hypothesis test, the goal is to answer a yes-no question: Is there any mean difference between the two populations? For estimation, the goal is to determine *how much* difference.

Recall that the basic structure of the independent-measures *t* formula is the same as we observed for the initial *z*-score or single-sample *t*:

$$t = \frac{\text{sample statistic} - \text{population parameter}}{\text{estimated standard error}}$$

Because we are interested in finding the population parameter, we will rewrite this equation as follows:

$$\text{population parameter} = \text{sample statistic} \pm t \times \text{estimated standard error}$$

This is the basic formula for estimation. With an independent-measures experimental design, we must solve equation 10.4 for $\mu_1 - \mu_2$. The formula we obtain for estimation is

$$\mu_1 - \mu_2 = (\overline{X}_1 - \overline{X}_2) \pm ts_{\overline{X}_1 - \overline{X}_2} \qquad (12.5)$$

In words, we are using the sample mean difference, plus or minus some error, to estimate the population mean difference. To use this equation to estimate $\mu_1 - \mu_2$ requires two steps:

1. Use the sample data to compute the sample mean difference $(\overline{X}_1 - \overline{X}_2)$ and the standard error $(s_{\overline{X}_1 - \overline{X}_2})$.
2. Estimate the *t* value that is associated with the sample data. This is accomplished by selecting a *t* value that is appropriate for the type of estimate we are using. That is, we can either make a point estimate, in which case $t = 0$, or select a level of confidence and use a range of *t* values for the estimate. With 90% confidence, for example, you would estimate that the *t* statistic for $\overline{X}_1 - \overline{X}_2$ is located somewhere in the middle 90% of the *t* distribution.

Remember, we are not simply choosing a *t* value but are estimating the location of our sample data within the *t* distribution.

At this point, you have all the values on the right-hand side of the equation (equation 12.5), and you can compute the value for $\mu_1 - \mu_2$. If you have used a single number to estimate the location of *t*, you will get a single point estimate for $\mu_1 - \mu_2$. If you have used a range of values for *t*, you will compute a confidence interval for $\mu_1 - \mu_2$. A complete example of this estimation procedure follows.

EXAMPLE 12.2   Studies have allowed neuroscientists to establish definite links between specific foods and specific brain functions. For example, lecithin (found in soybeans, eggs, liver) has been shown to increase the concentration of certain brain chemicals that help regulate memory and motor coordination. This experiment is designed to demonstrate the importance of this particular food substance.

lecithin help brain

The experiment involves two separate samples of newborn rats (an independent-measures experiment). The 10 rats in the first sample are given a normal diet containing standard amounts of lecithin. The 5 rats in the other sample are fed a special diet, which contains almost no lecithin. After 6 months, each of the rats is tested on a specially designed learning problem that requires both memory and motor coordination. The purpose of the experiment is to demonstrate the deficit in performance that results from lecithin deprivation. The score for each animal is the number of errors before the learning problem was solved. The data from this experiment are as follows:

REGULAR DIET	NO-LECITHIN DIET
$n = 10$	$n = 5$
$\bar{X} = 25$	$\bar{X} = 33$
$SS = 250$	$SS = 140$

Because we fully expect that there will be a significant difference between these two treatments, we will not do the hypothesis test (although you should be able to do it). We want to use these data to obtain an estimate of the size of the difference between the two population means; that is, how much does lecithin affect learning performance? We will use a point estimate and the 80% confidence interval.

The basic equation for estimation with an independent-measures experiment is

$$\mu_1 - \mu_2 = (\bar{X}_1 - \bar{X}_2) \pm t s_{\bar{X}_1 - \bar{X}_2}$$

The first step is to obtain the known values from the sample data. The sample mean difference is easy; one group averaged $\bar{X} = 25$, and the other averaged $\bar{X} = 33$, so there is an 8-point difference. Notice that it is not important whether we call this a $+8$ or a -8 difference. In either case, the size of the difference is 8 points, and the regular diet group scored lower. Because it is easier to do arithmetic with positive numbers, we will use

$$\bar{X}_1 - \bar{X}_2 = 8$$

Compute the standard error   To find the standard error, we first must pool the two variances:

$$s_p^2 = \frac{SS_1 + SS_2}{df_1 + df_2} = \frac{250 + 140}{9 + 4}$$

$$= \frac{390}{13}$$

$$= 30$$

FIGURE 12.7

The distribution of *t* values with *df* = 13. Note that *t* values pile up around zero and that 80% of the values are between +1.350 and −1.350.

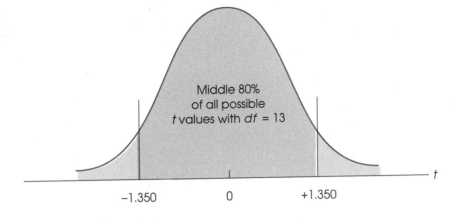

Middle 80%
of all possible
t values with *df* = 13

−1.350   0   +1.350   *t*

Next, the pooled variance is used to compute the standard error:

$$s_{\bar{X}_1 - \bar{X}_2} = \sqrt{\frac{s_p^2}{n_1} + \frac{s_p^2}{n_2}} = \sqrt{\frac{30}{10} + \frac{30}{5}} = \sqrt{3 + 6} = \sqrt{9} = 3$$

You should recall that this standard error combines the error from the first sample and the error from the second sample. Because the first sample is much larger, *n* = 10, it should have less error. This difference shows up in the formula. The larger sample contributes an error of 3 points, and the smaller sample contributes 6 points, which combine for a total error of 9 points under the square root.

Sample 1 has *df* = 9, and sample 2 has *df* = 4. The *t* statistic has *df* = 9 + 4 = 13.

The final value needed on the right-hand side of the equation is *t*. The data from this experiment would produce a *t* statistic with *df* = 13. With 13 degrees of freedom, we can sketch the distribution of all the possible *t* values. This distribution is shown in Figure 12.7. The *t* statistic for our data is somewhere in this distribution. The problem is to estimate where. For a point estimate, the best bet is to use *t* = 0. This is the most likely value, located exactly in the middle of the distribution. To gain more confidence in the estimate, you can select a range of *t* values. For 80% confidence, for example, you would estimate that the *t* statistic is somewhere in the middle 80% of the distribution. Checking the table, you find that the middle 80% is bounded by values of *t* = +1.350 and *t* = −1.350.

Using these *t* values and the sample values computed earlier, we now can estimate the magnitude of the performance deficit caused by lecithin deprivation.

Compute the point estimate For a point estimate, use the single-value (point) estimate of *t* = 0:

$$\mu_1 - \mu_2 = (\bar{X}_1 - \bar{X}_2) \pm ts_{\bar{X}_1 - \bar{X}_2}$$

$$= 8 \pm 0(3)$$

$$= 8$$

Notice that the result simply uses the sample mean difference to estimate the population mean difference. The conclusion is that lecithin deprivation produces an average of 8 more errors on the learning task. (Based on the fact that the normal animals averaged around 25 errors, an 8-point increase would mean a performance deficit of approximately 30%.)

Construct the interval estimate   For an interval estimate, or confidence interval, use the range of t values. With 80% confidence, at one extreme,

$$\mu_1 - \mu_2 = (\overline{X}_1 - \overline{X}_2) + ts_{\overline{X}_1 - \overline{X}_2}$$

$$= 8 + 1.350(3)$$

$$= 8 + 4.05$$

$$= 12.05$$

Software manuals:
Minitab (Section 6).

and at the other extreme,

$$\mu_1 - \mu_2 = (\overline{X}_1 - \overline{X}_2) - ts_{\overline{X}_1 - \overline{X}_2}$$

$$= 8 - 1.350(3)$$

$$= 8 - 4.05$$

$$= 3.95$$

This time we are concluding that the effect of lecithin deprivation is to increase errors with an average increase somewhere between 3.95 and 12.05 errors. We are 80% confident of this estimate because the only thing estimated was the location of the t statistic, and we used the middle 80% of all the possible t values.

Note that the result of the point estimate is to say that lecithin deprivation will increase errors by exactly 8. To gain confidence, you must lose precision and say that errors will increase by around 8 (for 80% confidence, we say that the average increase will be 8 ± 4.05).

gain confidence
lose precision

LEARNING CHECK   **1.** In families with several children, the first-born children tend to be more reserved and serious, whereas the last-born children tend to be more outgoing and happy-go-lucky. A psychologist is using a standardized personality inventory to measure the magnitude of this difference. A sample of eight first-born and eight last-born children is obtained. Each child is given the personality test. The results of this test are as follows:

FIRST-BORN	LAST-BORN
$\overline{X} = 11.4$	$\overline{X} = 13.9$
$SS = 26$	$SS = 30$

a. Use these sample data to make a point estimate of the population mean difference in personality for first-born versus last-born children.

b. Make an interval estimate of the population mean difference so that you are 80% confident that the true mean difference is in your interval.

ANSWERS 1. a. For a point estimate, use the sample mean difference: $\overline{X}_1 - \overline{X}_2 = 2.5$ points.

        b. With $df = 14$, the middle 80% of all possible *t* statistics is bounded by $t = +1.345$ and $t = -1.345$. For these data, the pooled variance is 4, and the standard error is 1. The 80% confidence interval is 1.155 to 3.845.

12.5 ESTIMATION WITH THE REPEATED-MEASURES *t* STATISTIC

In a repeated-measures experiment, a single sample of subjects is measured in two different treatment conditions. For each subject, a difference score is computed by subtracting the first score (treatment 1) from the second score (treatment 2).

$$D = X_2 - X_1$$

The resulting sample of difference scores can be used to draw inferences about the mean difference for the general population, μ_D. The repeated-measures *t* statistic allows researchers to use the sample mean difference, $\overline{D}$, to estimate the value of μ_D. Once again, the repeated-measures *t* formula is

$$t = \frac{\overline{D} - \mu_D}{s_{\overline{D}}}$$

Because we want to estimate the value of the population mean difference, this formula is solved for μ_D:

$$\mu_D = \overline{D} \pm ts_{\overline{D}} \tag{12.6}$$

In words, this formula may be stated as

        population mean difference = sample mean difference ± some error

That is, to estimate the mean difference for the population, we use the sample mean difference plus or minus some error.

PROCEDURE FOR ESTIMATION OF μ_D The process of estimation with the repeated-measures *t* statistic follows the same steps that were used for estimation with the single-sample *t* statistic. First, you calculate the sample mean ($\overline{D}$) and the estimated standard error ($s_{\overline{D}}$) using the sample of difference scores. Next, you determine the appropriate values for *t* ($t = 0$ for a point estimate or a range of values from the *t* distribution for an interval estimate). Finally, these values are used in the estimation formula (equation 12.6) to compute an estimate of μ_D. The following example demonstrates this process.

EXAMPLE 12.3   A school psychologist has determined that a remedial reading course increases scores on a reading comprehension test. The psychologist now would like to estimate how much improvement might be expected for the whole population of students in his city. A random sample of $n = 16$ children is obtained.

FIGURE 12.8

The t values for the 90% confidence interval are obtained by consulting the t table for $df = 15$, $p = 0.10$ for two tails.

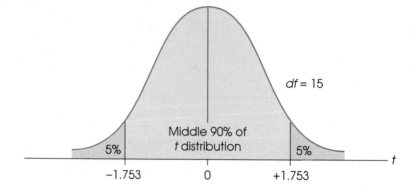

df = 15

Middle 90% of
t distribution

5%   5%

−1.753   0   +1.753   t

These children are first tested for level of reading comprehension and then enrolled in the course. At the completion of the remedial reading course, the students are tested again, and the difference between the second score and the first score is recorded for each child. For this sample, the average difference was $\bar{D} = +21$, and the SS for the difference scores was $SS = 1215$. The psychologist would like to use these data to make a point estimate and a 90% confidence interval estimate of μ_D.

The formula for estimation requires that we know the values of $\bar{D}$, $s_{\bar{D}}$, and t. We know that $\bar{D} = +21$ points for this sample, so all that remains is to compute $s_{\bar{D}}$ and look up the value of t in the t distribution table.

Compute the standard error   To find the standard error, we first must compute the sample variance:

$$s^2 = \frac{SS}{n-1} = \frac{1215}{15} = 81$$

Now the estimated standard error is

$$s_{\bar{D}} = \sqrt{\frac{s^2}{n}} = \sqrt{\frac{81}{16}} = \frac{9}{4} = 2.25$$

To complete the estimate of μ_D, we must identify the value of t. We will consider the point estimate and the interval estimate separately.

Compute the point estimate   To obtain a point estimate, a single value of t is selected to approximate the location of $\bar{D}$. Remember that the t distribution is symmetrical and bell-shaped with a mean of zero (see Figure 12.8). Because $t = 0$ is the most frequently occurring value in the distribution, this is the t value that is used for the point estimate. Using this value in the estimation formula gives

$$\mu_D = \bar{D} \pm t s_{\bar{D}}$$
$$= 21 \pm 0(2.25)$$
$$= 21$$

As noted several times before, the sample mean, $\overline{D} = 21$, provides the best point estimate of μ_D.

Construct the interval estimate   The psychologist also wanted to make an interval estimate in order to be 90% confident that the interval contains the value of μ_D. To get the interval, it is necessary to determine what *t* values form the boundaries of the middle 90% of the *t* distribution. To use the *t* distribution table, we first must determine the proportion associated with the tails of this distribution. With 90% in the middle, the remaining area in both tails must be 10%, or $p = .10$. Also note that our sample has $n = 16$ scores, so the *t* statistic will have $df = n - 1 = 15$. Using $df = 15$ and $p = 0.10$ for two tails, you should find the values $+1.753$ and -1.753 in the *t* table. These values form the boundaries for the middle 90% of the *t* distribution. (See Figure 12.8.) We are confident that the *t* value for our sample is in this range because 90% of all the possible *t* values are there. Using these values in the estimation formula, we obtain the following: On one end of the interval,

$$\mu_D = \overline{D} - ts_{\overline{D}}$$

$$= 21 - 1.753(2.25)$$

$$= 21 - 3.94$$

$$= 17.06$$

← 2 ends of interval

Software manuals:
Minitab (Section 6).

and on the other end of the interval,

$$\mu_D = 21 + 1.753(2.25)$$

$$= 21 + 3.94$$

$$= 24.94$$

Therefore, the school psychologist can be 90% confident that the average amount of improvement in reading comprehension for the population (μ_D) will be somewhere between 17.06 and 24.94 points.

LEARNING CHECK   **1.** A government researcher believes that driving and automotive tips will result in energy-saving habits. A sample of nine subjects is given a brochure containing energy-saving tips and is asked to follow this advice. Before and after using the tips, the subjects maintain gasoline consumption records for their automobiles. For this sample, the average improvement in gasoline mileage (in miles per gallon) was $\overline{D} = 6.50$ with $SS = 72$. A repeated-measures *t* test indicated that the mean change was statistically significant. However, before the government prints millions of copies of the brochure, the researcher is requested to estimate how much mean change can be expected for the population of drivers. The investigator decides to report the 95% confidence interval. What will this interval be?

ANSWER   **1.** For this sample, $s^2 = 9$ and $s_{\overline{D}} = 1$. For the 95% confidence interval with $df = 8$, $t = \pm 2.306$; the 95% confidence interval for μ_D is from 4.194 to 8.806.

12.6 FACTORS AFFECTING THE WIDTH OF A CONFIDENCE INTERVAL

There are two characteristics of the confidence interval that should be noted. First, notice what happens to the width of the interval when you change the level of confidence (the percentage of confidence). To gain more confidence in your estimate, you must increase the width of the interval. Conversely, to have a smaller interval, you must give up confidence. This is the basic trade-off between precision and confidence that was discussed earlier. In the estimation formula, the percent confidence influences the width of the interval by way of the z-score or t value. The larger the level of confidence (the percentage), the larger the z or t value, and the larger the interval. This relationship can be seen in Figure 12.8. In the figure, we have identified the middle 90% of the t distribution in order to find a 90% confidence interval. It should be obvious that if we were to increase the confidence level to 95%, it would be necessary to increase the range of t values and thereby increase the width of the interval.

Second, notice what would happen to the interval width if you had a different sample size. This time, the basic rule is as follows: The bigger the sample (n), the smaller the interval. This relationship is straightforward if you consider the sample size as a measure of the amount of information. A bigger sample gives you more information about the population and allows you to make a more precise estimate (a narrower interval). The sample size controls the magnitude of the standard error in the estimation formula. As the sample size increases, the standard error decreases, and the interval gets smaller.

With t statistics, the sample size has an additional effect on the width of a confidence interval. Remember that the exact shape of the t distribution depends on degrees of freedom. As the sample size gets larger, df also get larger, and the t values associated with any specific percentage of confidence get smaller. This fact simply enhances the general relationship that the larger a sample, the smaller a confidence interval.

SUMMARY

1. Estimation is a procedure that uses sample data to obtain an estimate of a population mean. The estimate can be either a point estimate (single value) or an interval estimate (range of values). Point estimates have the advantage of precision, but they do not give much confidence. Interval estimates provide confidence, but you lose precision as the interval grows wider.

2. Estimation and hypothesis testing are similar processes: Both use sample data to answer questions about populations. However, these two procedures are designed to answer different questions. Hypothesis testing will tell you whether or not a treatment effect exists (yes or no). Estimation will tell you how much treatment effect there is.

3. The z-score or t formula can be used to estimate a population mean using the data from a single sample. The

z-score formula is used when the population standard deviation is known, and the t formula is used when σ is unknown. The two formulas are

$$\mu = \overline{X} \pm z\sigma_{\overline{X}} \quad \text{and} \quad \mu = \overline{X} \pm ts_{\overline{X}}$$

To use either formula, first calculate the sample mean and the standard error ($\sigma_{\overline{X}}$ or $s_{\overline{X}}$) from the sample data. Next, obtain an estimate of the value of z or t by estimating the location of the sample mean within its sampling distribution. For a point estimate, use $z = 0$ or $t = 0$. For an interval estimate, first select a level of confidence (percentage of confidence) and then look up the range of z-scores or t values in the appropriate table.

4. For an independent-measures experiment, the formula for estimation is

$$\mu_1 - \mu_2 = (\overline{X}_1 - \overline{X}_2) \pm ts_{\overline{X}_1 - \overline{X}_2}$$

To use this formula, you first decide on a degree of precision and a level of confidence desired for the estimate. If your primary concern is precision, use $t = 0$ to make a point estimate of the mean difference. Otherwise, you select a level of confidence (percentage of confidence) that determines a range of t values to be used in the formula.

5. For a repeated-measures experiment, estimation of the amount of mean change for the population is accomplished by solving the t statistic formula for μ_D:

$$\mu_D = \overline{D} \pm ts_{\overline{D}}$$

For a point estimate, a t value of zero is used. A range of t values is used to construct an interval around $\overline{D}$. As in previous estimation problems, the t values that mark the interval boundaries are determined by the confidence level that is selected and by degrees of freedom.

6. The width of a confidence interval is an indication of its precision: A narrow interval is more precise than a wide interval. The interval width is influenced by sample size and the level of confidence.
   a. As sample size (n) gets larger, the interval width gets smaller (greater precision).
   b. As the percentage of confidence increases, the interval width gets greater (less precision).

KEY TERMS

estimation   point estimate   interval estimate   confidence interval

FOCUS ON PROBLEM SOLVING

1. Although hypothesis tests and estimation are similar in some respects, you should remember that they are separate statistical techniques. A hypothesis test is used to determine whether or not there is evidence for a treatment effect. Estimation is used to determine how much effect a treatment has.

2. When students perform a hypothesis test and estimation with the same set of data, a common error is to take the z-score or t statistic from the hypothesis test and use it in the estimation formula. For estimation, the z-score or t statistic value is determined by the level of confidence and must be looked up in the appropriate table.

3. Now that you are familiar with several different formulas for hypothesis tests and estimation, one problem will be determining which formula is appropriate for each set of data. When the data consist of a single sample selected from a single population, the appropriate statistic will be either z or the single-sample t, depending on whether σ is known or unknown, respectively. For an independent-measures design, you will always have two separate samples. In a repeated-measures design, there is only one sample, but each individual is measured twice so that difference scores can be computed.

DEMONSTRATION 12.1

ESTIMATION WITH A SINGLE-SAMPLE t STATISTIC

A sample of $n = 16$ is randomly selected from a population with unknown parameters. For the following sample data, estimate the value of μ using a point estimate and a 90% confidence interval. Sample data:

13   10   8   13   9   14   12   10

11   10   15   13   7   6   15   10

Note that we have a single sample and we do not know the value for σ. Thus, the single-sample t statistic should be used for these data. The formula for estimation is

$$\mu = \overline{X} \pm ts_{\overline{X}}$$

STEP 1 Compute the sample mean.

The sample mean is the basis for our estimate of μ. For these data,

$$\Sigma X = 13 + 10 + 8 + 13 + 9 + 14 + 12 + 10 +$$

$$11 + 10 + 15 + 13 + 7 + 6 + 15 + 10$$

$$= 176$$

$$\overline{X} = \frac{\Sigma X}{n} = \frac{176}{16} = 11$$

STEP 2 Compute the estimated standard error, $s_{\overline{X}}$.

To compute the estimated standard error, we must first find the value for SS and the sample variance.

Sum of squares. We will use the definitional formula for SS. The following table demonstrates the computations:

X	$X - \overline{X}$	$(X - \overline{X})^2$
13	$13 - 11 = +2$	4
10	$10 - 11 = -1$	1
8	$8 - 11 = -3$	9
13	$13 - 11 = +2$	4
9	$9 - 11 = -2$	4
14	$14 - 11 = +3$	9
12	$12 - 11 = +1$	1
10	$10 - 11 = -1$	1
11	$11 - 11 = \ \ 0$	0
10	$10 - 11 = -1$	1
15	$15 - 11 = +4$	16
13	$13 - 11 = +2$	4
7	$7 - 11 = -4$	16
6	$6 - 11 = -5$	25
15	$15 - 11 = +4$	16
10	$10 - 11 = -1$	1

To obtain SS, we sum the squared deviation scores in the last column.

$$SS = \Sigma(X - \overline{X})^2 = 112$$

Variance. The sample variance is computed for these data.

$$s^2 = \frac{SS}{n - 1} = \frac{112}{16 - 1} = \frac{112}{15} = 7.47$$

Estimated standard error. The estimated standard error can now be determined.

$$s_{\overline{X}} = \sqrt{\frac{s^2}{n}} = \sqrt{\frac{7.47}{16}} = \sqrt{0.467} = 0.68$$

STEP 3 Compute the point estimate for μ.

For a point estimate, we use $t = 0$. Using the estimation formula, we obtain

$$\mu = \overline{X} \pm ts_{\overline{X}}$$
$$= 11 \pm 0(0.68)$$
$$= 11 \pm 0 = 11$$

The point estimate for the population mean is $\mu = 11$.

STEP 4 Determine the confidence interval for μ.

For these data, we want the 90% confidence interval. Therefore, we will use a range of t values that form the middle 90% of the distribution. For this demonstration, degrees of freedom are

$$df = n - 1 = 16 - 1 = 15$$

If we are looking for the middle 90% of the distribution, then 10% ($p = 0.10$) would lie in both tails outside of the interval. To find the t values, we look up $p = 0.10$, two tails, for $df = 15$ in the t distribution table. The t values for the 90% confidence interval are $t = \pm 1.753$.

Using the estimation formula, one end of the confidence interval is

$$\mu = \overline{X} - ts_{\overline{X}}$$
$$= 11 - 1.753(0.68)$$
$$= 11 - 1.19 = 9.81$$

For the other end of the confidence interval, we obtain

$$\mu = \overline{X} + ts_{\overline{X}}$$
$$= 11 + 1.753(0.68)$$
$$= 11 + 1.19 = 12.19$$

Thus, the 90% confidence interval for μ is 9.81 to 12.19.

DEMONSTRATION 12.2

ESTIMATION WITH THE INDEPENDENT-MEASURES *t* STATISTIC

Samples are taken from two school districts, and knowledge of American history is tested with a short questionnaire. For the following sample data, estimate the amount of mean difference between the students of these two districts. Specifically, provide a point estimate and a 95% confidence interval for $\mu_1 - \mu_2$.

district A scores: 18   15   24   15

district B scores: 9   12   13   6

STEP 1 Compute the sample means.

The estimate of population mean difference $(\mu_1 - \mu_2)$ is based on the sample mean difference $(\bar{X}_1 - \bar{X}_2)$.

For district A,

$$\Sigma X = 18 + 15 + 24 + 15 = 72$$

$$\bar{X}_1 = \frac{\Sigma X}{n} = \frac{72}{4} = 18$$

For district B,

$$\Sigma X = 9 + 12 + 13 + 6 = 40$$

$$\bar{X}_2 = \frac{\Sigma X}{n} = \frac{40}{4} = 10$$

STEP 2 Calculate the estimated standard error for mean difference, $s_{\bar{X}_1 - \bar{X}_2}$.

To compute the estimated standard error, we first need to determine the values of SS for both samples and pooled variance.

Sum of squares. The computations for sum of squares, using the definitional formula, are shown for both samples in the following tables:

	DISTRICT A	
X	$X - \bar{X}$	$(X - \bar{X})^2$
18	$18 - 18 = 0$	0
15	$15 - 18 = -3$	9
24	$24 - 18 = +6$	36
15	$15 - 18 = -3$	9

	DISTRICT B	
X	$X - \bar{X}$	$(X - \bar{X})^2$
9	$9 - 10 = -1$	1
12	$12 - 10 = +2$	4
13	$13 - 10 = +3$	9
6	$6 - 10 = -4$	16

For district A,

$$SS_1 = \Sigma(X - \bar{X})^2 = 0 + 9 + 36 + 9 = 54$$

For district B,

$$SS_2 = \Sigma(X - \bar{X})^2 = 1 + 4 + 9 + 16 = 30$$

Pooled variance. For pooled variance, we use the SS and df values from both samples. For district A, $df_1 = n_1 - 1 = 3$. For district B, $df_2 = n_2 - 1 = 3$. Pooled variance is

$$s_p^2 = \frac{SS_1 + SS_2}{df_1 + df_2} = \frac{54 + 30}{3 + 3} = \frac{84}{6} = 14$$

Estimated standard error. The estimated standard error for mean difference can now be calculated.

$$s_{\overline{X}_1 - \overline{X}_2} = \sqrt{\frac{s_p^2}{n_1} + \frac{s_p^2}{n_2}} = \sqrt{\frac{14}{4} + \frac{14}{4}} = \sqrt{3.5 + 3.5}$$

$$= \sqrt{7} = 2.65$$

STEP 3 Compute the point estimate for $\mu_1 - \mu_2$.

For the point estimate, we use a t value of zero. Using the sample means and estimated standard error from previous steps, we obtain

$$\mu_1 - \mu_2 = (\overline{X}_1 - \overline{X}_2) \pm ts_{\overline{X}_1 - \overline{X}_2}$$

$$= (18 - 10) \pm 0(2.65)$$

$$= 8 \pm 0 = 8$$

STEP 4 Determine the confidence interval for $\mu_1 - \mu_2$.

For the independent measures t statistic, degrees of freedom are determined by

$$df = n_1 + n_2 - 2$$

For these data, df is

$$df = 4 + 4 - 2 = 6$$

With a 95% level of confidence, 5% of the distribution falls in the tails outside the interval. Therefore, we consult the t distribution table for $p = 0.05$, two tails, with $df = 6$. The t values from the table are $t = \pm 2.447$. On one end of the confidence interval, $\mu_1 - \mu_2$ is

$$\mu_1 - \mu_2 = (\overline{X}_1 - \overline{X}_2) - ts_{\overline{X}_1 - \overline{X}_2}$$

$$= (18 - 10) - 2.447(2.65)$$

$$= 8 - 6.48$$

$$= 1.52$$

On the other end of the confidence interval, the population mean difference is

$$\mu_1 - \mu_2 = (\overline{X}_1 - \overline{X}_2) + ts_{\overline{X}_1 - \overline{X}_2}$$

$$= (18 - 10) + 2.447(2.65)$$

$$= 8 + 6.48$$

$$= 14.48$$

Thus, the 95% confidence interval for population mean difference is from 1.52 to 14.48.

PROBLEMS

1. Explain how the purpose of estimation differs from the purpose of a hypothesis test.

2. Explain why it would *not* be reasonable to use estimation after a hypothesis test where the decision was "fail to reject H_0."

3. Explain how each of the following factors affects the width of a confidence interval:
   a. Increasing the sample size
   b. Increasing the sample variability
   c. Increasing the level of confidence (the percentage of confidence)

4. For the following studies, state whether estimation or hypothesis testing is required. Also, is an independent- or a repeated-measures *t* statistic appropriate?
   a. An educator wants to determine how much mean difference can be expected for the population in SAT scores following an intensive review course. Two samples are selected. The first group takes the review course, and the second receives no treatment. SAT scores are subsequently measured for both groups.
   b. A psychiatrist would like to test the effectiveness of a new antipsychotic medication. A sample of patients is first assessed for the severity of psychotic symptoms. Then the patients are placed on drug therapy for two weeks. The severity of their symptoms is assessed again at the end of the treatment.

5. In 1985, an extensive survey indicated that fifth-grade students in the city school district spent an average of $\mu = 5.5$ hours per week doing homework. The distribution of homework times was approximately normal with $\sigma = 1$. Last year, a sample of $n = 100$ fifth-grade students produced a mean of $\overline{X} = 5.1$ hours of homework each week.
   a. Use the data to make a point estimate of the population mean for last year. Assume that there was no change in the standard deviation.
   b. Based on your point estimate, how much change has occurred in homework time since 1985?
   c. Make an interval estimate of last year's homework time so that you are 80% confident that the true population mean is in your interval.

6. A researcher has constructed a 90% confidence interval of 87 ± 10, based on a sample of $n = 25$ scores. Note that this interval is 20 points wide (from 77 to 97). How large a sample would be needed to produce a 90% interval that is only 10 points wide?

7. Researchers have developed a filament that should add to the life expectancy of light bulbs. The standard 60-watt bulb burns for an average of $\mu = 750$ hours with $\sigma = 20$. A sample of $n = 100$ bulbs is prepared using the new filament. The average life for this sample is $\overline{X} = 820$ hours.
   a. Use these sample data to make a point estimate of the mean life expectancy for the new filament.
   b. Make an interval estimate so that you are 80% confident that the true mean is in your interval.
   c. Make an interval estimate so that you are 99% confident that the true mean is in your interval.

8. A toy manufacturer asks a developmental psychologist to test children's responses to a new product. Specifically, the manufacturer wants to know how long, on the average, the toy captures children's attention. The psychologist tests a sample of $n = 9$ children and measures how long they play with the toy before they get bored. This sample had a mean of $\overline{X} = 31$ minutes with $SS = 648$.
   a. Make a point estimate for μ.
   b. Make an interval estimate for μ using a confidence level of 95%.

9. A random sample of $n = 11$ scores is selected from a population with unknown parameters. The scores in the sample are as follows: 12, 5, 9, 9, 10, 14, 7, 10, 14, 13, 8.
   a. Provide an unbiased estimate of the population standard deviation.
   b. Use the sample data to make a point estimate for μ and to construct the 95% confidence interval for μ.

10. A psychologist has developed a new personality questionnaire for measuring self-esteem and would like to estimate the population parameters for the test scores. The questionnaire is administered to a sample of $n = 25$ subjects. This sample has an average score of $\overline{X} = 43$ with $SS = 2400$.
   a. Provide an estimate for the population standard deviation.
   b. Make a point estimate for the population mean.
   c. Make an interval estimate for μ so that you are 90% confident that the value for μ is in your interval.

11. Most adolescents experience a growth spurt when they are between 12 and 15 years old. This period of dramatic growth generally occurs around age 12 for girls and around age 14 for boys. A researcher studying physical development selected a random sample of $n = 9$ girls and a second sample of $n = 16$ boys and recorded the gain in height (in millimeters) between the 14th birthday and 15th birthday for each subject. The girls showed an average gain of $\overline{X} = 40$ millimeters with $SS = 1152$, and the boys gained an average of $\overline{X} = 95$ millimeters with $SS = 2160$.

a. Estimate the population mean growth in one year for 14-year-old boys. Make a point estimate and an 80% confidence interval estimate.

b. Estimate the population mean growth in one year for 14-year-old girls. Make a point estimate and an 80% confidence interval estimate.

c. Estimate the mean difference in growth for boys versus girls during this one-year period. Again, make a point estimate and an 80% confidence interval estimate.

12. A therapist has demonstrated that five sessions of relaxation training significantly reduced anxiety levels for a sample of $n = 16$ clients. However, the therapist is concerned about the long-term effects of the training. Six months after therapy is completed, the patients are recalled, and their anxiety levels are measured again. On the average, the anxiety scores for these patients are $\overline{D} = 5.5$ points higher after six months than they had been at the end of therapy. The difference scores had $SS = 960$. Use these data to estimate the mean amount of relapse that occurs after therapy ends. Make a point estimate and an 80% confidence interval estimate of the population mean difference.

13. An educational psychologist has observed that children seem to lose interest and enthusiasm for school as they progress through the elementary grades. To measure the extent of this phenomenon, the psychologist selects a sample of $n = 15$ second-grade children and a sample of $n = 15$ fifth-graders. Each child is given a questionnaire measuring his/her attitude toward school. Higher scores indicate a more positive attitude. The second-grade children average $\overline{X} = 85$ with $SS = 1620$, and the fifth-graders average $\overline{X} = 71$ with $SS = 1740$. Use these data to estimate how much the enthusiasm for school declines from second to fifth grade. Make a point estimate and a 90% confidence interval estimate of the mean difference.

14. The counseling center at the college offers a short course in study skills for students who are having academic difficulty. To evaluate the effectiveness of this course, a sample of $n = 25$ students is selected, and each student's grade-point average is recorded for the semester before the course and for the semester immediately following the course. On the average, these students show an increase of $\overline{D} = 0.72$ with $SS = 24$. Use these data to estimate how much effect the course has on grade-point average. Make a point estimate and a 95% confidence interval estimate of the mean difference.

15. Clinical trials have demonstrated that a new sleeping medication for insomniacs reduces the amount of time needed to fall asleep by an average of $\mu = 23$ minutes. However, a researcher suspects that part of the drug's effectiveness is simply a placebo effect; that is, the pa-

tients expect the drug to be effective so they relax and are less worried about falling asleep. To determine how much of the effect is due to the medication and how much is simply a placebo effect, the researcher selects a sample of $n = 9$ insomniacs. The time needed to fall asleep is measured for each individual for a week, and then they are given a placebo instead of the real drug. For the following week, the amount of time needed to fall asleep is recorded for each person. On the average, the people in this experiment fall asleep $\overline{D} = 8$ minutes faster with the placebo than they had before, with $SS = 288$. Use these data to make a point estimate and an 80% confidence interval estimate of the placebo effect.

16. "Encoding specificity" is a psychological principle that states that a person's recall performance will be best if memory is tested under the same conditions that existed when the person originally learned the material. To evaluate the magnitude of this effect, a researcher obtains a sample of 50 subjects. The subjects all listen to a lecture on river pollution and are warned that they will be tested on the information. One week later, the subjects are reassembled. Twenty-five subjects are assigned to the same room where they heard the lecture, and the other 25 are assigned to a different room. All subjects take the same test. The average score for the same-room subjects is $\overline{X} = 38$ with $SS = 1040$, and the different-room subjects average $\overline{X} = 26$ with $SS = 1360$. Use these data to estimate how much memory is affected by having memory tested in the same room as learning. Make a point estimate and a 90% confidence interval estimate of the mean difference.

17. Many researchers have reported that exposure to violence on television can result in increased violent or aggressive behavior in children. To evaluate this effect a researcher obtains a sample of $n = 4$ children in a preschool setting. The group of children is observed for two hours one afternoon, and the number of violent or aggressive acts is recorded for each child. The following morning the children are shown a video cartoon with several violent and aggressive scenes. That afternoon the children's behavior is observed again. On the average, the children exhibit $\overline{D} = 4.2$ more violent/aggressive behaviors after viewing the video than they did the previous day. The sample difference scores had $SS = 12$. Use these data to estimate the effects of viewing television violence. Make a point estimate and a 95% confidence interval estimate of the mean effect.

18. Problem 19 at the end of Chapter 10 presents data from a study comparing personality traits for artists versus airline pilots. The data from this study showed that pilots are significantly more relaxed than artists. Use the same data to estimate how much difference there is in relax-

ation scores between the two professions. Make a point estimate and a 90% confidence interval estimate of the mean difference.

19. Problem 16 at the end of Chapter 11 compares shooting scores for Olympic marksmen for shots fired during heartbeats versus shots fired between heartbeats. The data indicate that the marksmen have significantly higher scores for shots fired between heartbeats. Use the same data to estimate how much scores are affected by firing during a heartbeat. Make a point estimate and an 80% confidence interval estimate of the mean difference.

20. A vocabulary skills test designed for six-year-old children has been standardized to produce a mean score of $\mu = 50$. A researcher would like to use this test in an experiment with five-year-old children. Before beginning the experiment, however, the researcher would like some indication of how well five-year-olds can perform on this test. Therefore, a sample of $n = 21$ five-year-old children is given the test. The data for this sample are as follows:

VOCABULARY TEST SCORES						
42	56	49	37	43	46	47
48	57	39	40	51	49	50
36	45	52	47	49	40	53

a. Use the data to make a point estimate of the population mean for five-year-old children.

b. Make an interval estimate of the mean so that you are 95% confident that the true mean is in your interval.

c. On the basis of your confidence interval, can the researcher be 95% confident that the population mean for five-year-olds is lower than the mean for six-year-olds?

CHAPTER 13

INTRODUCTION TO ANALYSIS OF VARIANCE

CONTENTS

PREVIEW

"But I read the chapter four times! How could I possibly have failed the exam!"

Most of you probably have had the experience of reading a textbook and suddenly realizing that you have no idea of what was said on the past few pages. Although you have been reading the words, your mind has wandered off, and the meaning of the words has never reached memory. In an influential paper on human memory, Craik and Lockhart (1972) proposed a *levels of processing* theory of memory that can account for this phenomenon. In general terms, this theory says that all perceptual and mental processing leaves behind a memory trace. However, the quality of the memory trace depends on the level or the depth of the processing. If you superficially skim the words in a book, your memory also will be superficial. On the other hand, when you think about the meaning of the words and try to understand what you are reading, the result will be a good, substantial memory that should serve you well on exams. In general, deeper processing results in better memory.

Rogers, Kuiper, and Kirker (1977) conducted an experiment demonstrating the effect of levels of processing. Subjects in this experiment were shown lists of words and asked to answer questions about each word. The questions were designed to require different levels of processing, from superficial to deep. In one experimental condition, subjects were

simply asked to judge the physical characteristics of each printed word ("Is it printed in capital letters or small letters?") A second condition asked about the sound of each word ("Does it rhyme with 'boat'?"). In a third condition, subjects were required to process the meaning of each word ("Does it have the same meaning as 'attractive'?"). The final condition required subjects to understand each word and relate its meaning to themselves ("Does this word describe you?"). After going through the complete list, all subjects were given a surprise memory test. As you can see in Figure 13.1, deeper processing resulted in better memory. Remember, these subjects were not trying to memorize the words; they were simply reading through the list answering questions. However, the more they processed and understood the words, the better they recalled the words on the test.

In terms of human memory, the Rogers, Kuiper, and Kirker experiment is notable because it demonstrates the importance of "self" in memory. You are most likely to remember material that is directly related to you. In terms of statistics, however, this study is notable because it compares four different treatment conditions in a single experiment. Although it may seem like a small step to go from two treatments (as in the *t* tests in Chapters 10 and 11) to four treatments, there is a tremendous gain in experimental sophistication. Suppose, for example, that Rogers, Kuiper, and Kirker had decided to examine only two levels of processing: one

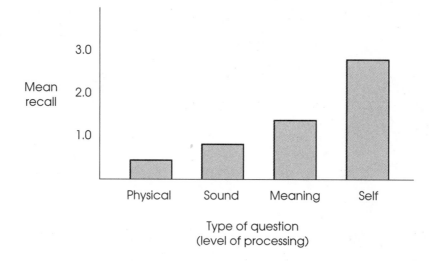

FIGURE 13.1

Mean recall as a function of the level of processing.
Rogers, T.B., Kuiper, N.A., & Kirker, W.S. (1977). Self-reference and the encoding of personal information. *Journal of Personality and Social Psychology, 35,* 677–688. Copyright (1977) by the American Psychological Association. Adapted by permission of the author.

based on physical characteristics and one based on sound. In this simplified experiment, they would have made only *one* comparison: physical versus sound. In the real experiment, however, they used four conditions and were able to make *six* different comparisons:

Physical versus sound
Physical versus meaning
Physical versus self
Sound versus meaning
Sound versus self
Meaning versus self

To gain this experimental sophistication, there is some cost. Specifically, you no longer can use the familiar *t* tests we encountered in Chapters 10 and 11. Instead, you now must learn a new statistical technique that is designed for experiments consisting of two or more sets of data. This new, general-purpose procedure is called analysis of variance.

13.1 INTRODUCTION

Analysis of variance (ANOVA) is a hypothesis-testing procedure that is used to evaluate mean differences between two or more treatments (or populations). As with all inferential procedures, ANOVA uses sample data as the basis for drawing general conclusions about populations. It may appear that analysis of variance and *t* tests are simply two different ways of doing exactly the same job: testing for mean differences. In some respects, this is true—both tests use sample data to test hypotheses about population means. However, ANOVA has a tremendous advantage over *t* tests. Specifically, *t* tests are limited to situations where there are only two treatments to compare. The major advantage of ANOVA is that it can be used to compare *two or more treatments*. Thus, ANOVA provides researchers with much greater flexibility in designing experiments and interpreting results (see Figure 13.2).

Like the *t* tests presented in Chapters 10 and 11, ANOVA can be used with either an independent-measures or a repeated-measures design. You should recall that an independent-measures design means that there is a separate sample for each of the treatments (or populations) being compared. In a repeated-measures design, on the other hand, the same sample is tested in all of the different treatment conditions. In addition, ANOVA can be used to evaluate the results from a research study that involves more than one independent variable. For example, an educational psychologist might want to compare the effectiveness of two different teaching methods (independent variable 1) for three different class sizes (independent variable 2). The dependent variable for this study would be each student's score on a standardized achievement test. The structure of this experiment, which involves comparing sample means from six different treatment conditions, is shown in Figure 13.2 (b).

As you can see, analysis of variances provides researchers with an extremely flexible data-analysis technique. It can be used to evaluate the significance of mean differences in a wide variety of research situations and is one of the most commonly used hypothesis-testing procedures.

In this chapter, we will introduce analysis of variance in its simplest form. Specifically, we will limit our discussion of ANOVA to independent-measures research designs involving only one independent variable. These situations are often called *single-factor, independent-measures designs*. In the terminology of analysis of variance, an independent variable is called a *factor*. Thus, a design with only one in-

FIGURE 13.2

Research designs for which ANOVA would be appropriate. Note that each design involves comparisons of more than two sample means. (a) A research study comparing vocabulary skill (dependent variable) for three different age groups (independent variable). Note that this study could be done as an independent-measures design using three separate samples or as a repeated-measures design testing the same sample at three different times. In either case, the analysis would compare the three sample means. (b) The structure of a research design with two independent variables. The effects of two different teaching methods and three different class sizes are evaluated in a single experiment. The dependent variable is the standardized-achievement-test score for each student. Note that this study involves comparing six different sample means.

(a)

INDEPENDENT VARIABLE: AGE		
4 YEARS	5 YEARS	6 YEARS
Vocabulary scores for sample 1	Vocabulary scores for sample 2	Vocabulary scores for sample 3

(b)

		INDEPENDENT VARIABLE 1: CLASS SIZE		
		SMALL CLASS	MEDIUM CLASS	LARGE CLASS
INDEPENDENT VARIABLE 2: TEACHING METHOD	METHOD A	Sample 1	Sample 2	Sample 3
	METHOD B	Sample 4	Sample 5	Sample 6

dependent variable is called a *single-factor design*. Research designs with more than one independent variable [like the teaching-method/class-size study in Figure 13.2(b)] are called *factorial designs*. The next two chapters will explore the flexibility of ANOVA by examining repeated-measures designs (Chapter 14) and factorial designs with two independent variables (Chapter 15).

DEFINITIONS

In analysis of variance, a *factor* is an independent variable. A research study that involves only one independent variable is called a *single-factor design*. A study with more than one independent variable is called a *factorial design*.

The basic logic and procedures for analysis of variance that are presented in this chapter form the foundation for more complex applications of ANOVA (for example, repeated-measures or factorial designs). However, the details of the analysis will differ from one situation to another, as you will discover in the following chapters.

THE SINGLE-FACTOR, INDEPENDENT-MEASURES DESIGN

A diagram of a single-factor, independent-measures research design is shown in Figure 13.3. Notice that a separate sample is taken for each of the three treatment conditions. Also notice that the three samples have different scores and different means. The goal of ANOVA is to help the researcher decide between the following two interpretations:

1. There really are no differences between the populations (or treatments). The observed differences between samples are simply due to chance (sampling error).

FIGURE 13.3

A typical situation where ANOVA would be used. Three separate samples are obtained to evaluate the mean differences among three populations (or treatments) with unknown means.

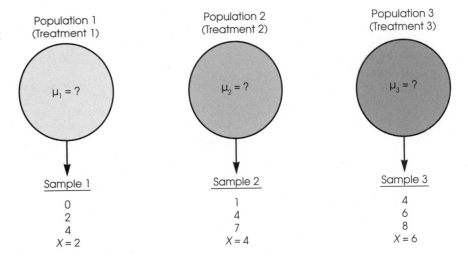

2. The differences between the sample means represent real differences between the populations. That is, the populations (or treatments) really do have different means, and the sample data accurately reflect these differences.

You should recognize these two interpretations as corresponding to the two hypotheses (null hypothesis and alternative hypothesis) that are part of the general hypothesis-testing procedure.

STATISTICAL HYPOTHESES FOR ANOVA

The following example will be used to introduce the statistical hypotheses for ANOVA. Suppose that a psychologist examined learning performance under three temperature conditions: 50°, 70°, and 90°. Three samples of subjects are selected, one sample for each treatment condition. The purpose of the study is to determine whether room temperature affects learning performance. In statistical terms, we want to decide between two hypotheses: the null hypothesis (H_0), which says that temperature has no effect, and the alternative hypothesis (H_1), which states that temperature does affect learning. In symbols, the null hypothesis states

$$H_0: \mu_1 = \mu_2 = \mu_3$$

That is, there are no differences among the means of the populations that receive the three treatments. The population means are all the same. Once again, notice that hypotheses are always stated in terms of population parameters, even though we use sample data to test them.

For the alternative hypothesis, we may state that

H_1: At least one population mean is different from the others.

Notice that we have not given any specific alternative hypothesis. This is because many different alternatives are possible, and it would be tedious to list them all. One alternative, for example, would be that the first two populations are identical, but that the third is different. Another alternative states that the last two means are the same, but that the first is different. Other alternatives might be

H_1: $\mu_1 \neq \mu_2 \neq \mu_3$ (all three means are different)

H_1: $\mu_1 = \mu_3$ but μ_2 is different

It should be pointed out that a researcher typically entertains only one (or at most a few) of these alternative hypotheses. Usually a theory or the outcomes of previous studies will dictate a specific prediction concerning the treatment effect. For the sake of simplicity, we will state a general alternative hypothesis rather than try to list all the possible specific alternatives.

THE TEST STATISTIC FOR ANOVA

The test statistic for ANOVA is very similar to the t statistics used in earlier chapters. For the t statistic, we computed a ratio with the following structure:

$$t = \frac{\text{obtained difference between sample means}}{\text{difference expected by chance (error)}}$$

For analysis of variance, the test statistic is called an F-ratio and has the following structure:

$$F = \frac{\text{variance (differences) between sample means}}{\text{variance (differences) expected by chance (error)}}$$

Notice that the F-ratio is based on *variance* instead of sample mean *difference*. The reason for this change is that ANOVA is used in situations where there are more than two sample means. For example, when you have only two means, it is easy to find the difference between them. If two samples have means of $\overline{X} = 20$ and $\overline{X} = 30$, there is a 10-point difference between sample means. However, if we add a third sample mean, $\overline{X} = 35$, it becomes more difficult to describe the "difference" between samples. The solution to this problem is to compute the variance for the set of sample means. If the sample means are all clustered close together (small differences), then the variance will be small. On the other hand, if the sample means are spread over a wide range of values (big differences), then the variance will be large. Thus, the variance in the numerator of the F-ratio provides a single number that describes the differences between all the sample means.

In much the same way, the variance in the denominator of the F-ratio and the standard error in the denominator of the t statistic both measure the differences that would be expected by chance. In the t statistic, the standard error measures standard distance or standard deviation. In the F-ratio, this standard deviation *(s)* is simply converted to a variance (s^2). In fact, the denominator of the F-ratio is often called *error variance* in order to stress its relationship to the "standard error" in the t statistic.

Finally, you should realize that the t statistic and the F-ratio provide the same basic information. In each case, the numerator of the ratio measures the actual difference obtained from the sample data, and the denominator measures the difference that would be expected by chance. With either the F-ratio or the t statistic, a large value provides evidence that the sample mean difference is more than chance (see Box 13.1).

TYPE I ERRORS AND
MULTIPLE–HYPOTHESIS TESTS

IF WE already have *t* tests for comparing mean differences, you might wonder why analysis of variance is necessary. Why create a whole new hypothesis-testing procedure that simply duplicates what the *t* tests can already do? The answer to this question is based in a concern about Type I errors.

Remember, each time you do a hypothesis test, you select an alpha level that determines the risk of a Type I error. With $\alpha = .05$, for example, there is a 5%, or a 1-in-20, risk of a Type I error. Thus, for every 20 hypothesis tests, you expect to make one Type I error. The more tests you do, the more risk there is of a Type I error. For this reason, researchers often make a distinction between the *testwise* alpha level and the *experimentwise* alpha level. The testwise alpha level is simply the alpha level you select for each individual hypothesis test. The experimentwise alpha level is the total probability of a Type I error accumulated from all of the separate tests in the experiment. As the number of separate tests increases, so does the experimentwise alpha level.

For an experiment involving three treatments, you would need three separate *t* tests to compare all of the mean differences:

Test 1 compares treatment I versus treatment II.

Test 2 compares treatment I versus treatment III.

Test 3 compares treatment II versus treatment III.

The three separate tests accumulate to produce a relatively large experimentwise alpha level. The advantage of analysis of variance is that it performs all three comparisons simultaneously in the same hypothesis test. Thus, no matter how many different means are being compared, ANOVA uses one test with one alpha level to evaluate the mean differences and thereby avoids the problem of an inflated experimentwise alpha level.

13.2 THE LOGIC OF ANALYSIS OF VARIANCE

The formulas and calculations required in ANOVA are somewhat complicated, but the logic that underlies the whole procedure is fairly straightforward. Therefore, this section will give a general picture of analysis of variance before we start looking at the details. We will introduce the logic of ANOVA with the help of the hypothetical data in Table 13.1. These data represent the results of an independent-measures experiment comparing learning performance under three temperature conditions.

One obvious characteristic of the data in Table 13.1 is that the scores are not all the same. In everyday language, the scores are different; in statistical terms, the scores are variable. Our goal is to measure the amount of variability (the size of the differences) and to explain where it comes from.

The first step is to determine the total variability for the entire set of data. To compute the total variability, we will combine all the scores from all the separate samples to obtain one general measure of variability for the complete experiment. Once we have measured the total variability, we can begin to break it apart into separate components. The word *analysis* means dividing into smaller parts. Because we are going to analyze variability, the process is called *analysis of variance*. This analysis process divides the total variability into two basic components.

1. Between-Treatments Variability. Looking at the data in the Table 13.1, we clearly see that much of the variability in the scores is due to general differences between treatment conditions. For example, the scores in the 70° condition tend to be much higher ($\overline{X} = 4$) than the scores in the 50° condition ($\overline{X} = 1$). We will calculate the variability between treatments to provide a measure of the

TABLE 13.1

Hypothetical data from an experiment examining learning performance under three temperature conditions*

TREATMENT 1 50° (SAMPLE 1)	TREATMENT 2 70° (SAMPLE 2)	TREATMENT 3 90° (SAMPLE 3)
0	4	1
1	3	2
3	6	2
1	3	0
0	4	0
$\overline{X} = 1$	$\overline{X} = 4$	$\overline{X} = 1$

*Note that there are three separate samples, with $n = 5$ in each sample. The dependent variable is the number of problems solved correctly.

overall differences between treatment conditions—that is, the differences between sample means.

2. Within-Treatment Variability. In addition to the general differences between treatment conditions, there is variability within each sample. Looking again at Table 13.1, the scores in the 70° condition are not all the same; they are variable. The within-treatments variability will provide a measure of the variability inside each treatment condition.

Analyzing the total variability into these two components is the heart of analysis of variance. We will now examine each of the components in more detail.

BETWEEN-TREATMENTS VARIABILITY

Whenever you compare two samples representing two treatment conditions, there are three possible explanations for the differences (variability) between sample means:

1. Treatment Effect. It is possible that the different treatments have caused the samples to be different. In Table 13.1, the scores in sample 1 were obtained in a 50° room, and the scores in sample 2 were obtained in a 70° room. It is possible that the difference between these two samples is due in part to the different temperatures.

2. Individual Differences. Subjects enter an experiment with different backgrounds, abilities, and attitudes; that is, they are unique individuals. Whenever you compare separate samples (different groups of individuals), it is possible that the differences between samples are simply the result of individual differences.

3. Experimental Error. Whenever you make a measurement, there is a chance of error. The error could be caused by poor equipment, lack of attention, or unpredictable changes in the event you are measuring. This kind of uncontrolled and unexplained difference is called *experimental error,* and it can cause two samples to be different.

Thus, when we compute the variability between treatments, we are measuring differences that could be due to any of these three factors or any combination of the three.

WITHIN-TREATMENTS VARIABILITY

There are only two possible explanations for variability within a treatment condition:

1. Individual Differences. The scores are obtained from different individuals, which could explain why the scores are variable.

FIGURE 13.4

The independent-measures analysis of variance partitions, or analyzes, the total variability into two components: variability between treatments and variability within treatments.

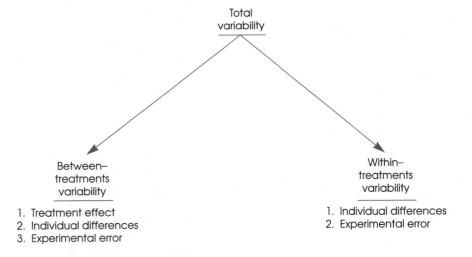

2. Experimental Error. There always is a chance that the differences are caused by experimental error.

Notice that the variability inside a treatment condition cannot be attributed to any treatment effect because all subjects within a treatment condition are treated exactly the same. Thus, the differences within a treatment are not systematic or predictable, but rather are due to chance. The analysis, or partitioning, of variability is diagrammed in Figure 13.4.

THE *F*-RATIO: THE TEST STATISTIC FOR ANOVA

Once we have analyzed the total variability into two basic components (between treatments and within treatments), we simply compare them. The comparison is made by computing a statistic called an *F-ratio*. For the independent-measures ANOVA, the *F*-ratio has the following structure:

$$F = \frac{\text{variance between treatments}}{\text{variance within treatments}} \tag{13.1}$$

When we express each component of variability in terms of its sources (see Figure 13.4), the structure of the *F*-ratio is

$$F = \frac{\text{treatment effect} + \text{individual differences} + \text{experimental error}}{\text{individual differences} + \text{experimental error}} \tag{13.2}$$

You should note that the between-treatments variability and the within-treatments variability differ in only one respect: the variability (mean differences) caused by the treatment effect. This single difference between the numerator and denominator of the *F*-ratio is crucial in determining if a treatment effect has occurred. Remember, the whole purpose for doing the experiment and the analysis is to find out whether or not the treatment has any effect. Let's consider the two possibilities:

1. H_0 is true, and there is no treatment effect. In this case, the numerator and denominator of the *F*-ratio are measuring the same variance:

$$F = \frac{0 + \text{individual differences} + \text{experimental error}}{\text{individual differences} + \text{experimental error}}$$

When H_0 is true and the treatment effect is zero, the F-ratio is expected to equal 1.

2. If H_0 is false, then a treatment effect does exist, and the F-ratio becomes

$$F = \frac{\text{treatment effect} + \text{individual differences} + \text{experimental error}}{\text{individual differences} + \text{experimental error}}$$

The numerator of the ratio should be larger than the denominator, and the F-ratio is expected to be larger than 1.00. Ordinarily, the presence of a large treatment effect is reflected in a large value for the F-ratio.

In more general terms, the denominator of the F-ratio measures only uncontrolled and unexplained (often called *unsystematic*) variability. For this reason, the denominator of the F-ratio is called the *error term*. The numerator of the F-ratio always includes the same unsystematic variability as in the error term, but it also includes any systematic differences caused by the treatment effect. The goal of ANOVA is to find out whether or not a treatment effect exists.

DEFINITION   For ANOVA, the denominator of the F-ratio is called the *error term*. The error term provides a measure of the variance due to chance. When the treatment effect is zero (H_0 is true), the error term measures the same sources of variance as the numerator of the F-ratio, so the value of the F-ratio is expected to be nearly equal to 1.00.

LEARNING CHECK   1. ANOVA is a statistical procedure that compares two or more treatment conditions for differences in variance. (True or false?)

2. In ANOVA, what value is expected, on the average, for the F-ratio when the null hypothesis is true?

3. What happens to the value of the F-ratio if differences between treatments are increased? What happens to the F-ratio if variability inside the treatments is increased?

4. In ANOVA, the total variability is partitioned into two parts. What are these two variability components called, and how are they used in the F-ratio?

ANSWERS   1. False. Although ANOVA uses variability in the computations, the purpose of the test is to evaluate differences in *means* between treatments.

2. When H_0 is true, the expected value for the F-ratio is 1.00 because the top and bottom of the ratio are both measuring the same variance.

3. As differences between treatments increase, the F-ratio will increase. As variability within treatments increases, the F-ratio will decrease.

4. The two components are between-treatments variability and within-treatments variability. Between-treatments variability is the numerator of the F-ratio, and within-treatments variability is the denominator.

TABLE 13.2

Hypothetical data from an experiment examining learning performance under three temperature conditions*

TEMPERATURE CONDITIONS			
1 50°	2 70°	3 90°	
0	4	1	$\Sigma X^2 = 106$
1	3	2	$G = 30$
3	6	2	$N = 15$
1	3	0	$k = 3$
0	4	0	
$T_1 = 5$	$T_2 = 20$	$T_3 = 5$	
$SS_1 = 6$	$SS_2 = 6$	$SS_3 = 4$	
$n_1 = 5$	$n_2 = 5$	$n_3 = 5$	
$\overline{X}_1 = 1$	$\overline{X}_2 = 4$	$\overline{X}_3 = 1$	

*Summary values and notation for an analysis of variance are also presented.

13.3 ANOVA VOCABULARY, NOTATION, AND FORMULAS

Before we introduce the notation, we will look at some special terminology that is used for ANOVA. As noted earlier, in analysis of variance an independent variable is a factor. Therefore, for the experiment shown in Table 13.1, the factor is temperature. Because this experiment has only one independent variable, it is a single-factor experiment. The next term you need to know is *levels*. The levels in an experiment consist of the different values used for the independent variable (factor). For example, in the learning experiment (Table 13.1) we are using three values of temperature. Therefore, the temperature factor has three levels.

DEFINITION   The individual treatment conditions that make up a factor are called *levels* of the factor.

Because ANOVA most often is used to examine data from more than two treatment conditions (and more than two samples), we will need a notational system to help keep track of all the individual scores and totals. To help introduce this notational system, we will use the hypothetical data from Table 13.1 again. The data are reproduced in Table 13.2 along with some of the notation and statistics that will be described.

1. The letter k is used to identify the number of treatment conditions, that is, the number of levels of the factor. For an independent-measures experiment, k also specifies the number of separate samples. For the data in Table 13.2, there are three treatments, so $k = 3$.

2. The number of scores in each treatment is identified by a lowercase letter n. For the example in Table 13.2, $n = 5$ for all the treatments. If the samples are of different sizes, you can identify a specific sample by using a subscript. For example, n_2 is the number of scores in treatment 2.

3. The total number of scores in the entire experiment is specified by a capital letter N. When all the samples are the same size (n is constant), $N = kn$. For the data in Table 13.2, there are $n = 5$ scores in each of the $k = 3$ treatments, so $N = 3(5) = 15$.

Because ANOVA formulas require ΣX for each treatment and ΣX for the entire set of scores, we have introduced new notation (T and G) to help identify which ΣX is being used. Remember, T stands for *treatment total,* and G stands for *grand total.*

4. The total (ΣX) for each treatment condition is identified by the capital letter T. The total for a specific treatment can be identified by adding a numerical subscript to the T. For example, the total for the second treatment in Table 13.2 is $T_2 = 20$.

5. The sum of all the scores in the experiment (the grand total) is identified by G. You can compute G by adding up all N scores or by adding up the treatment totals: $G = \Sigma T$.

6. Although there is no new notation involved, we also have computed SS and $\overline{X}$ for each sample, and we have calculated ΣX^2 for the entire set of $N = 15$ scores in the experiment. These values are given in Table 13.2 and will be important in the formulas and calculations for ANOVA.

ANOVA FORMULAS

Because analysis of variance requires extensive calculations and many formulas, one common problem for students is simply keeping track of the different formulas and numbers. Therefore, we will examine the general structure of the procedure and look at the organization of the calculations before we introduce the individual formulas.

1. The final calculation for ANOVA is the F-ratio, which is composed of two variances:

$$F = \frac{\text{variance between treatments}}{\text{variance within treatments}}$$

2. You should recall that variance for sample data has been defined as

$$\text{sample variance} = s^2 = \frac{SS}{df}$$

Therefore, we will need to compute an SS and a df for the variance between treatments (numerator of F), and we will need another SS and df for the variance within treatments (denominator of F). To obtain these SS and df values, we must go through two separate analyses: First, compute SS for the total experiment, and analyze it into two components (between and within). Then compute df for the total experiment, and analyze it into two components (between and within).

Thus, the entire process of analysis of variance will require nine calculations: three values for SS, three values for df, two variances (between and within), and a final F-ratio. However, these nine calculations are all logically related and are all directed toward finding the final F-ratio. Figure 13.5 shows the logical structure of ANOVA calculations.

ANALYSIS OF SUM OF SQUARES (SS)

The ANOVA requires that we first compute a total variability and then partition this value into two components: between treatments and within treatments. This

FIGURE 13.5

The structure of ANOVA calculations.

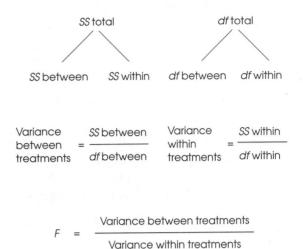

analysis is outlined in Figure 13.6. We will examine each of the three components separately.

1. Total Sum of Squares, SS_{total}. As the name implies, SS_{total} is simply the sum of squares for the entire set of N scores. We calculate this value by using the computational formula for SS:

$$SS = \Sigma X^2 - \frac{(\Sigma X)^2}{N}$$

To make this formula consistent with the ANOVA notation, we substitute the letter G in place of ΣX and obtain

$$SS_{total} = \Sigma X^2 - \frac{G^2}{N} \tag{13.3}$$

FIGURE 13.6

Partitioning the sum of squares *(SS)* for the independent-measures analysis of variance.

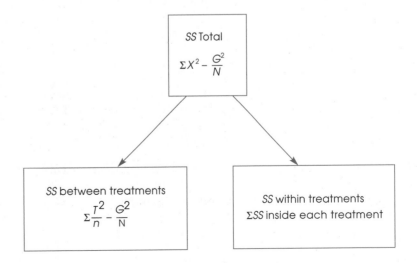

Applying this formula to the set of data in Table 13.2, we obtain

$$SS_{\text{total}} = 106 - \frac{30^2}{15}$$

$$= 106 - 60$$

$$= 46$$

2. Within-Treatments Sum of Squares, SS_{within}. Now we are looking at the variability inside each of the treatment conditions. We already have computed the SS within each of the three treatment conditions (Table 13.2): $SS_1 = 6$, $SS_2 = 6$, and $SS_3 = 4$. To find the overall within-treatment sum of squares, we simply add these values together:

$$SS_{\text{within}} = \Sigma SS_{\text{inside each treatment}} \tag{13.4}$$

For the data in Table 13.2, this formula gives

$$SS_{\text{within}} = 6 + 6 + 4$$

$$= 16$$

3. Between-Treatments Sum of Squares, SS_{between}. Before we introduce the equation for SS_{between}, consider what we have found so far. The total variability for the data in Table 13.2 is $SS_{\text{total}} = 46$. We intend to partition this total into two parts (see Figure 13.6). One part, SS_{within}, has been found to be equal to 16. This means that SS_{between} must be equal to 30 in order for the two parts (16 and 30) to add up to the total (46). The equation for the between-treatments sum of squares should produce a value of $SS_{\text{between}} = 30$. You should recall that the variability between treatments is measuring the differences between treatment means. Conceptually, the most direct way of measuring the amount of variability among the treatment means is to compute the sum of squares for the set of means. To do this, we begin by computing the overall mean for the entire set of N scores in the experiment. This overall mean will be identified by the symbol $\overline{G}$, indicating the grand mean. For the data in Table 13.2, the grand total is $G = 30$ for a set of $N = 15$ scores, so the grand mean is $\overline{G} = {}^{30}\!/_{15} = 2$. Next, we measure the extent to which each individual sample mean deviates from the grand mean:

$$\text{deviation} = (\overline{X} - \overline{G})$$

Then we square these deviations and sum the results to obtain the sum of squared deviations *(SS)* for the set of sample means

$$SS_{\text{means}} = \Sigma(\overline{X} - \overline{G})^2$$

Because each individual treatment mean represents a sample of n scores, each of the squared deviations is multiplied by n to obtain a complete measure of the between-treatments sum of squares:

$$SS_{\text{between}} = \Sigma n(\overline{X} - \overline{G})^2 \tag{13.5}$$

Applying this formula to the data in Table 13.2, we obtain

$$SS_{between} = 5(1 - 2)^2 + 5(4 - 2)^2 + 5(1 - 2)^2$$
$$= 5 + 20 + 5$$
$$= 30$$

Notice that the result, $SS_{between} = 30$, is exactly what we predicted. The two parts from the analysis (between and within) add up to the total:

$$SS_{total} = SS_{within} + SS_{between}$$
$$46 = 16 + 30$$

Although equation 13.5 is conceptually the most direct way of computing the amount of variability among the treatment means, this formula can be awkward to use, especially when the means are not whole numbers. For this reason, we generally will use an algebraically equivalent formula that uses the treatment totals (T values) instead of the means:

$$SS_{between} = \Sigma \frac{T^2}{n} - \frac{G^2}{N} \tag{13.6}$$

Using this new formula with the data in Table 13.2, we obtain

$$SS_{between} = \frac{5^2}{5} + \frac{20^2}{5} + \frac{5^2}{5} - \frac{30^2}{15}$$
$$= 5 + 80 + 5 - 60$$
$$= 90 - 60$$
$$= 30$$

At this point of the analysis, the work may be checked to see if total SS equals between-treatments SS plus within-treatments SS.

Notice that this result is identical to the value we obtained using equation 13.5.

The formula for each SS and the relationships among these three values are shown in Figure 13.6.

THE ANALYSIS OF DEGREES OF FREEDOM (DF)

The analysis of degrees of freedom (*df*) follows the same pattern as the analysis of SS. First, we will find *df* for the total set of N scores, and then we will partition this value into two components: degrees of freedom between treatments and degrees of freedom within treatments. In computing degrees of freedom, there are two important considerations to keep in mind:

1. Each *df* value is associated with a specific SS value.
2. Normally, the value of *df* is obtained by counting the number of items that were used to calculate SS and then subtracting 1. For example, if you compute SS for a set of n scores, then $df = n - 1$.

With this in mind, we will examine the degrees of freedom for each part of the analysis.

1. Total Degrees of Freedom, df_{total}. To find the df associated with SS_{total}, you must first recall that this SS value measures variability for the entire set of N scores. Therefore, the df value will be

$$df_{total} = N - 1 \qquad\qquad (13.7)$$

For the data in Table 13.2, the total number of scores is $N = 15$, so the total degrees of freedom would be

$$df_{total} = 15 - 1$$
$$= 14$$

2. Within-Treatments Degrees of Freedom, df_{within}. To find the df associated with SS_{within}, we must look at how this SS value is computed. Remember, we first find SS inside of each of the treatments and then add these values together. Each of the treatment SS values measures variability for the n scores in the treatment, so each SS will have $df = n - 1$. When all these individual treatment values are added together, we obtain

$$df_{within} = \Sigma(n - 1) \qquad\qquad (13.8)$$

For the experiment we have been considering, each treatment has $n = 5$ scores. This means there are $n - 1 = 4$ degrees of freedom inside each treatment. Because there are three different treatment conditions, this gives a total of 12 for the within-treatments degrees of freedom. Notice that this formula for df simply adds up the number of scores in each treatment (the n values) and subtracts 1 for each treatment. If these two stages are done separately, you obtain

$$df_{within} = N - k \qquad\qquad (13.9)$$

(Adding up all the n values gives N. If you subtract 1 for each treatment, then altogether you have subtracted k because there are k treatments.) For the data in Table 13.2, $N = 15$ and $k = 3$, so

$$df_{within} = 15 - 3$$
$$= 12$$

3. Between-Treatments Degrees of Freedom, $df_{between}$. The df associated with $SS_{between}$ can be found by considering the SS formula. This SS formula measures the variability among the treatment means or totals. To find $df_{between}$, simply count the number of T values (or means) and subtract 1. Because the number of treatments is specified by the letter k, the formula for df is

$$df_{between} = k - 1 \qquad\qquad (13.10)$$

For the data in Table 13.2, there are three different treatment conditions (three T values), so the between-treatments degrees of freedom are computed as follows:

$$df_{between} = 3 - 1$$
$$= 2$$

FIGURE 13.7

Partitioning degrees of freedom *(df)* for the independent-measures analysis of variance.

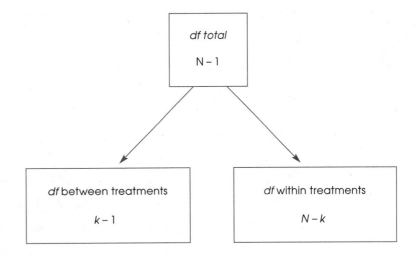

Notice that the two parts we obtained from this analysis of degrees of freedom add up to equal the total degrees of freedom:

$$df_{total} = df_{within} + df_{between}$$

$$14 = 12 + 2$$

The complete analysis of degrees of freedom is shown in Figure 13.7.

CALCULATION OF VARIANCES (MS) AND THE F-RATIO

The final step in the analysis of variance procedure is to compute the variance between treatments and the variance within treatments in order to calculate the *F*-ratio (see Figure 13.5). You should recall (from Chapter 4) that variance is defined as the average squared deviation. For a sample, you compute this average by the following formula:

$$\text{variance} = \frac{SS}{n-1} = \frac{SS}{df}$$

In ANOVA, it is customary to use the term *mean square,* or simply *MS,* in place of the term *variance.* Note that variance is the *mean squared* deviation, so this terminology is quite sensible. For the final *F*-ratio, you will need an *MS* between treatments and an *MS* within treatments. In each case,

$$MS = \frac{SS}{df} \tag{13.11}$$

For the data we have been considering,

$$MS_{between} = \frac{SS_{between}}{df_{between}} = \frac{30}{2} = 15$$

VARIANCE, POOLED VARIANCE, AND MS_{within}

13.2

BACK IN Chapter 4, we defined the variance for a single sample as follows:

$$\text{variance} = s^2 = \frac{SS}{df}$$

More recently, in Chapter 10 (independent-measures t), we combined the variances from two separate samples to calculate a value we called *pooled variance:*

$$\text{pooled variance} = s^2 = \frac{SS_1 + SS_2}{df_1 + df_2}$$

Now, with analysis of variance, we are using the same method to combine the variances from two or more separate samples. Specifically,

$$MS_{\text{within}} = \frac{SS_1 + SS_2 + SS_3 + \ldots}{df_1 + df_2 + df_3 + \ldots}$$

This may appear to be a completely new formula for MS_{within}, but you should realize that it simply combines three formulas that were presented separately in this chapter. In particular, you should recall that

$$MS_{\text{within}} = \frac{SS_{\text{within}}}{df_{\text{within}}}$$

where

$$SS_{\text{within}} = \Sigma SS = SS_1 + SS_2 + SS_3 + \ldots$$

and

$$df_{\text{within}} = \Sigma df = df_1 + df_2 + df_3 + \ldots$$

Finally, you should realize that the concept of MS_{within} and the concept of pooled variance are equivalent. Specifically, MS_{within} is measuring the variance within the separate treatment conditions, that is, the variance inside the separate samples. The formula for MS_{within} simply combines the separate sample variances into a single pooled variance, exactly as we have done in the past.

and

An alternative view of MS_{within} is presented in Box 13.2.

$$MS_{\text{within}} = \frac{SS_{\text{within}}}{df_{\text{within}}} = \frac{16}{12} = 1.33$$

We now have a measure of the variance (or differences) between the treatments and a measure of the variance within the treatments. The F-ratio simply compares these two variances:

$$F = \frac{MS_{\text{between}}}{MS_{\text{within}}} \tag{13.12}$$

For the experiment we have been examining, the data give an F-ratio of

$$F = \frac{15}{1.33} = 11.28$$

It is useful to organize the results of the analysis in one table called an *ANOVA summary table.* The table shows the source of variability (between treatments, within treatments, and total variability), SS, df, MS, and F. For the previous computations, the ANOVA summary table is constructed as follows:

SOURCE	SS	df	MS	
Between treatments	30	2	15	$F = 11.28$
Within treatments	16	12	1.33	
Total	46	14		

Although these tables are no longer commonly used in published reports, they do provide a concise method for presenting the results of an analysis. (Note that you can conveniently check your work: Adding the first two entries in the SS column $(30 + 16)$ yields the total SS. The same applies to the df column.) When using analysis of variance, you might start with a blank ANOVA summary table and then fill in the values as they are calculated. With this method, you will be less likely to "get lost" in the analysis, wondering what to do next.

For this example, the obtained value of $F = 11.28$ indicates that the numerator of the F-ratio is substantially bigger than the denominator. If you recall the conceptual structure of the F-ratio as presented in equations 13.1 and 13.2, the F value we obtained indicates that the differences between treatments are substantially greater than would be expected by chance, providing evidence that a treatment effect really exists. Stated in terms of the experimental variables, it appears that temperature does have an effect on learning performance. However, to properly evaluate the F-ratio, we must examine the F distribution.

13.4 THE DISTRIBUTION OF F-RATIOS

In analysis of variance, the F-ratio is constructed so that the numerator and denominator of the ratio are measuring exactly the same variance when the null hypothesis is true (see equation 13.2). In this situation, we expect the value of F to be around 1.00. The problem now is to define precisely what we mean by "around 1.00." What values are considered to be close to 1.00, and what values are far away? To answer this question, we need to look at all the possible F values, that is, the *distribution of F-ratios*.

Before we examine this distribution in detail, you should note two obvious characteristics:

1. Because F-ratios are computed from two variances (the numerator and denominator of the ratio), F values always will be positive numbers. Remember, variance is always positive.

2. When H_0 is true, the numerator and denominator of the F-ratio are measuring the same variance. In this case, the two sample variances should be about the same size, so the ratio should be near 1. In other words, the distribution of F-ratios should pile up around 1.00.

With these two factors in mind, we can sketch the distribution of F-ratios. The distribution is cut off at zero (all positive values), piles up around 1.00, and then tapers off to the right (see Figure 13.8). The exact shape of the F distribution depends on the degrees of freedom for the two variances in the F-ratio. You should

FIGURE 13.8

The distribution of *F*-ratios with $df = 2$, 12. Of all the values in the distribution, only 5% are larger than $F = 3.88$, and only 1% are larger than $F = 6.93$.

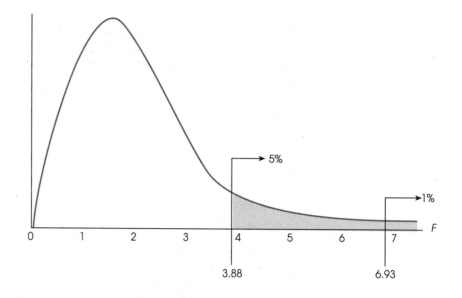

recall that the precision of a sample variance depends on the number of scores or the degrees of freedom. In general, the variance for a large sample (large *df*) provides a more accurate estimate of the population variance. Because the precision of the *MS* values depends on *df,* the shape of the *F* distribution also will depend on the *df* values for the numerator and denominator of the *F*-ratio. With very large *df* values, nearly all the *F*-ratios will be clustered very near to 1.00. With the smaller *df* values, the *F* distribution is more spread out.

For analysis of variance, we expect *F* near 1.00 if H_0 is true, and we expect a large value for *F* if H_0 is not true. In the *F* distribution, we need to separate those values that are reasonably near 1.00 from the values that are significantly greater than 1.00. These critical values are presented in an *F* distribution table in Appendix B, page A-29. To use the table, you must know the *df* values for the *F*-ratio (numerator and denominator), and you must know the alpha level for the hypothesis test. It is customary for an *F* table to have the *df* values for the numerator of the *F*-ratio printed across the top of the table. The *df* values for the denominator of *F* are printed in a column on the left-hand side. A portion of the *F* distribution table is shown in Table 13.3. For the temperature experiment we have been considering, the numerator of the *F*-ratio (between treatments) has $df = 2$, and the denominator of the *F*-ratio (within treatments) has $df = 12$. This *F*-ratio is said to have "degrees of freedom equal to 2 and 12." The degrees of freedom would be written as $df = 2$, 12. To use the table, you would first find $df = 2$ across the top of the table and $df = 12$ in the first column. When you line up these two values, they point to a pair of numbers in the middle of the table. These numbers give the critical cutoffs for $\alpha = .05$ and $\alpha = .01$. With $df = 2$, 12, for example, the numbers in the table are 3.88 and 6.93. These values indicate that the most unlikely 5% of the distribution ($\alpha = .05$) begins at a value of 3.88. The most extreme 1% of the distribution begins at a value of 6.93 (see Figure 13.8).

In the temperature experiment, we obtained an *F*-ratio of 11.28. According to the critical cutoffs in Figure 13.8, this value is extremely unlikely (it is in the most extreme 1%). Therefore, we would reject H_0 with α set at either .05 or .01 and conclude that temperature does have a significant effect on learning performance.

TABLE 13.3

A portion of the F distribution table (Entries in roman type are critical values for the .05 level of significance, and bold type values are for the .01 level of significance.)

DEGREES OF FREEDOM: DENOMINATOR	DEGREES OF FREEDOM: NUMERATOR					
	1	2	3	4	5	6
10	4.96	4.10	3.71	3.48	3.33	3.22
	10.04	**7.56**	**6.55**	**5.99**	**5.64**	**5.39**
11	4.84	3.98	3.59	3.36	3.20	3.09
	9.65	**7.20**	**6.22**	**5.67**	**5.32**	**5.07**
12	4.75	3.88	3.49	3.26	3.11	3.00
	9.33	**6.93**	**5.95**	**5.41**	**5.06**	**4.82**
13	4.67	3.80	3.41	3.18	3.02	2.92
	9.07	**6.70**	**5.74**	**5.20**	**4.86**	**4.62**
14	4.60	3.74	3.34	3.11	2.96	2.85
	8.86	**6.51**	**5.56**	**5.03**	**4.69**	**4.46**

LEARNING CHECK

1. Calculate SS_{total}, $SS_{between}$, and SS_{within} for the following set of data:

TREATMENT 1	TREATMENT 2	TREATMENT 3	
$n = 10$	$n = 10$	$n = 10$	$N = 30$
$T = 10$	$T = 20$	$T = 30$	$G = 60$
$SS = 27$	$SS = 16$	$SS = 23$	$\Sigma X^2 = 206$

2. A researcher uses an ANOVA to compare three treatment conditions with a sample of $n = 8$ in each treatment. For this analysis, find df_{total}, $df_{between}$, and df_{within}.

3. With $\alpha = .05$, what value forms the boundary for the critical region in the distribution and F-ratios with $df = 2, 24$?

ANSWERS

1. $SS_{total} = 86$; $SS_{between} = 20$; $SS_{within} = 66$

2. $df_{total} = 23$; $df_{between} = 2$; $df_{within} = 21$

3. The critical value is 3.40.

13.5 EXAMPLES OF HYPOTHESIS TESTING WITH ANOVA

Although we have seen all the individual components of ANOVA, the following example demonstrates the complete ANOVA process using the standard four-step procedure for hypothesis testing.

EXAMPLE 13.1

The data depicted in Table 13.4 were obtained from an independent-measures experiment designed to measure the effectiveness of three pain relievers (A, B, and C). A fourth group that received a placebo (sugar pill) also was tested.

TABLE 13.4

The effect of drug treatment on the amount of time (in seconds) a stimulus is endured

PLACEBO	DRUG A	DRUG B	DRUG C	
0	0	3	8	$N = 12$
0	1	4	5	$G = 36$
3	2	5	5	$\Sigma X^2 = 178$
$T = 3$	$T = 3$	$T = 12$	$T = 18$	
$SS = 6$	$SS = 2$	$SS = 2$	$SS = 6$	

Software Manuals:
Minitab (Section 7)
Mystat (Section 3)
SPSS (Section 6)

The purpose of the analysis is to determine whether these sample data provide evidence of any significant differences among the four drugs. The dependent variable is the amount of time (in seconds) that subjects can withstand a painfully hot stimulus.

Before we begin the hypothesis test, note that we already have computed a variety of summary statistics for the data in Table 13.4. Specifically, the treatment totals *(T)* and *SS* values are shown for each sample, and the grand total *(G)* as well as *N* and ΣX^2 are shown for the entire set of data. Having these summary values will simplify the computations in the hypothesis test, and we suggest that you always compute these summary statistics before you begin an analysis of variance.

STEP 1   The first step is to state the hypotheses and select an alpha level:

H_0: $\mu_1 = \mu_2 = \mu_3 = \mu_4$ (no treatment effect)

H_1:   At least one of the treatment means is different.

We will use $\alpha = .05$.

STEP 2   To locate the critical region for the *F*-ratio, we first must determine degrees of freedom for $MS_{between}$ and MS_{within} (the numerator and denominator of *F*). For these data, the total degrees of freedom would be

Often it is easier to postpone finding the critical region until after step 3 where you compute the df values as part of the calculations for the F-ratio.

$$df_{total} = N - 1$$
$$= 12 - 1$$
$$= 11$$

Analyzing this total into two components, we obtain

$$df_{between} = k - 1$$
$$= 4 - 1$$
$$= 3$$
$$df_{within} = N - k$$
$$= 12 - 4$$
$$= 8$$

FIGURE 13.9

The distribution of F-ratios with $df = 3$, 8. The critical value for $\alpha = .05$ is $F = 4.07$.

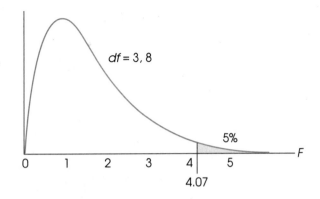

The F-ratio for these data will have $df = 3, 8$. The distribution of all the possible F-ratios with $df = 3, 8$ is presented in Figure 13.9. Almost always (95% of the time) we should obtain an F-ratio less than 4.07 if H_0 is true.

STEP 3 To compute the F-ratio for these data, you must go through the series of calculations outlined in Figure 13.5. The calculations can be summarized as follows:

a. Analyze the SS to obtain $SS_{between}$ and SS_{within}.

b. Use the SS values and the df values (from step 2) to calculate $MS_{between}$ and MS_{within}.

c. Finally, use the two MS values (variances) to compute the F-ratio.

Analysis of SS. First, we will compute the total SS and then the two components as indicated in Figure 13.5:

$$SS_{total} = \Sigma X^2 - \frac{G^2}{N}$$

$$= 178 - \frac{36^2}{12}$$

$$= 178 - 108$$

$$= 70$$

$$SS_{within} = \Sigma SS_{inside\ each\ treatment}$$

$$= 6 + 2 + 2 + 6$$

$$= 16$$

$$SS_{between} = \Sigma \frac{T^2}{n} - \frac{G^2}{N}$$

$$= \frac{3^2}{3} + \frac{3^2}{3} + \frac{12^2}{3} + \frac{18^2}{3} - \frac{36^2}{12}$$

$$= 3 + 3 + 48 + 108 - 108$$

$$= 54$$

Calculation of mean squares. Now we must compute the variance or *MS* for each of the two components:

The *df* values ($df_{between} = 3$ and $df_{within} = 8$) were computed in step 2 when we located the critical region.

$$MS_{between} = \frac{SS_{between}}{df_{between}} = \frac{54}{3} = 18$$

$$MS_{within} = \frac{SS_{within}}{df_{within}} = \frac{16}{8} = 2$$

Calculation of F. Finally, we compute the *F*-ratio:

$$F = \frac{MS_{between}}{MS_{within}} = \frac{18}{2} = 9.00$$

STEP 4 Finally, we make the statistical decision. The *F* value we obtained, $F = 9.00$, is in the critical region (see Figure 13.9). It is very unlikely ($p < .05$) that we will obtain a value this large if H_0 is true. Therefore, we reject H_0 and conclude that there is a significant treatment effect.

Example 13.1 demonstrated the complete, step-by-step application of the ANOVA procedure. There are two additional points that can be made using this example.

First, you should look carefully at the statistical decision. We have rejected H_0 and concluded that not all the treatments are the same. But we have not determined which ones are different. Is drug A different from the placebo? Is drug A different from drug B? Unfortunately, these questions remain unanswered. We do know that at least one difference exists (we rejected H_0), but additional analysis is necessary to find out exactly where this difference is. This problem is addressed in Section 13.6.

Second, as noted earlier, all of the components of the analysis (the *SS, df, MS,* and *F*) can be presented together in one summary table. The summary table for the analysis in Example 13.1 is as follows:

SOURCE	SS	DF	MS	
Between treatments	54	3	18	$F = 9.00$
Within treatments	16	8	2	
Total	70	11		

Although these tables are very useful for organizing the components of an analysis of variance, they are not commonly used in published reports. The current method for reporting the results from an ANOVA is presented in the following section.

IN THE LITERATURE:
REPORTING THE RESULTS OF ANALYSIS OF VARIANCE

The APA format for reporting the results of ANOVA begins with a presentation of the treatment means and standard deviations in the narrative of the article, a table, or a graph. These descriptive statistics are not needed in the calculations of the actual analysis of variance, but you can easily determine the treatment means from n and T $(\overline{X} = T/n)$ and the standard deviations from the SS of each treatment $[s = \sqrt{SS/(n-1)}]$. Next, the results of the ANOVA are reported. For the study described in Example 13.1, the report might state

---

The means and standard deviations are presented in Table 1. The analysis of variance revealed a significant difference, $F(3, 8) = 9.00$, $p < .05$.

TABLE 1

Amount of time (seconds) the stimulus was endured

| | TREATMENT CONDITION | | | |
	PLACEBO	DRUG A	DRUG B	DRUG C
M	1.0	1.0	4.0	6.0
SD	1.73	1.00	1.00	1.73

Notice how the F-ratio is reported. In this example, degrees of freedom for between and within treatments are $df = 3, 8$, respectively. These values are placed in parentheses immediately following the symbol F. Next, the calculated value for F is reported, followed by the probability of committing a Type I error. Because H_0 has been rejected and alpha was set at .05, p is *less than* .05.

We have rejected the null hypothesis; thus, we are concluding that not all treatments are the same. However, the analysis has not determined which ones are different. Is drug A different from the placebo? Is drug A different from drug B? Is drug B different from drug C, and so on? Unfortunately, these questions remain unanswered. However, we do know that at least one difference exists [H_0 was rejected with $F(3, 8) = 9.00$, $p < .05$]. Additional analysis is necessary to determine exactly which groups differ. This additional analysis is addressed in Section 13.6. ❑

A CONCEPTUAL VIEW OF ANOVA

Because analysis of variance requires relatively complex calculations, students encountering this statistical technique for the first time often tend to be overwhelmed by the formulas and arithmetic and lose sight of the general purpose for the analysis. The following two examples are intended to minimize the role of the formulas and shift attention back to the conceptual goal of the ANOVA process.

EXAMPLE 13.2

The following data represent the outcome of an experiment using two separate samples to evaluate the mean difference between two treatment conditions. Take a minute to look at the data and, without doing any calculations, try to predict the outcome of an ANOVA for these values. Specifically, predict what values should be obtained for $SS_{between}$, $MS_{between}$, and the F-ratio. If you do not "see" the answer after 20 or 30 seconds, try reading the hints that follow the data.

TREATMENT I	TREATMENT II	
4	2	$N = 8$
0	1	$G = 16$
1	0	$\Sigma X^2 = 56$
3	5	
$T = 8$	$T = 8$	
$SS = 10$	$SS = 14$	

If you are having trouble predicting the outcome of the ANOVA, read the following hints, and then go back and look at the data.

Hint 1: Remember, $SS_{between}$ and $MS_{between}$ provide a measure of how much difference there is *between* treatment conditions.

Hint 2: Find the mean for each treatment, and determine how much difference there is between the two means.

You should realize by now that the data have been constructed so that there is zero difference between treatments. The two sample means (and totals) are identical, so $SS_{between} = 0$, $MS_{between} = 0$, and the F-ratio is zero.

Conceptually, the numerator of the F-ratio always measures how much difference exists between treatments. In Example 13.2, we constructed an extreme set of scores with zero difference. However, you should be able to look at any set of data and quickly compare the means (or totals) to determine whether there are big differences between treatments or small differences between treatments.

Being able to estimate the magnitude of between-treatment differences is a good first step in understanding ANOVA and should help you to predict the outcome of an analysis of variance. However, the *between-treatment* differences are only one part of the analysis. You must also understand the *within-treatment* differences that form the denominator of the F-ratio. The following example is intended to demonstrate the concepts underlying SS_{within} and MS_{within}. In addition, the example should give you a better understanding of how the between-treatment differences and the within-treatment differences act together within the ANOVA.

EXAMPLE 13.3   The purpose of this example is to present a visual image for the concepts of between-treatments variability and within-treatments variability. In the example, we will compare two hypothetical outcomes for the same experiment. In each case, the experiment uses two separate samples to evaluate the mean difference between two treatments. The following data represent the two outcomes, which we will call case 1 and case 2.

FIGURE 13.10

A visual representation of the between-treatments variability and the within-treatments variability that form the numerator and denominator, respectively, of the *F*-ratio. In (a), the between-treatments variability is relatively large and easy to see. In (b), the same 5-point difference between treatments is relatively small and is overwhelmed by the within-treatments variability.

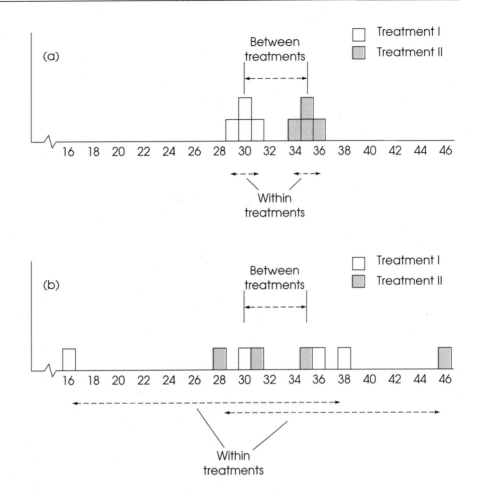

	CASE 1			CASE 2	
	TREATMENT			TREATMENT	
I		II		I	II
29		34		16	28
30		35		30	31
30		35		36	35
31		36		38	46
$\bar{X} = 30$		$\bar{X} = 35$		$\bar{X} = 30$	$\bar{X} = 35$
$SS = 2$		$SS = 2$		$SS = 296$	$SS = 186$

The data from case 1 are displayed in a frequency distribution graph in Figure 13.10(a). In the figure, we have indicated the *between treatments* difference by showing the distance between the two means. We also have represented the *within-treatment* differences by using the range of scores for each separate sample. Clearly, the between-treatments value is substantially greater than the within-treatments value. This observation is confirmed by computing the

F-ratio for case 1. (You may check the calculations by performing the ANOVA yourself.)

$$F = \frac{\text{between-treatments difference}}{\text{within-treatments differences}} = \frac{MS_{\text{between}}}{MS_{\text{within}}} = \frac{50}{0.667} = 75.0$$

An F-ratio of $F = 75$ is sufficient to reject the null hypothesis with $\alpha = .05$, so we conclude that there is a significant difference between the two treatments. Notice that the statistical conclusion agrees with the simple observation that the data [Figure 13.10(a)] show two distinct sets of scores, and it is easy to see that there is a clear difference between the two treatment conditions.

The data from case 2 present a very different picture. These data are shown in Figure 13.10(b). Again, the *between-treatments* difference is represented by the distance between the treatment means, and the *within-treatment* differences are indicated by the range of scores within each treatment condition. Now, the between-treatments value is small in comparison to the within-treatments differences. Calculating the F-ratio confirms this observation.

$$F = \frac{\text{between-treatments difference}}{\text{within-treatments differences}} = \frac{MS_{\text{between}}}{MS_{\text{within}}} = \frac{50}{80.33} = 0.62$$

For case 2, the F-ratio is not large enough to reject the null hypothesis, so we conclude that there is no significant difference between the two treatments. Once again, the statistical conclusion is consistent with the appearance of the data in Figure 13.10(b). Looking at the figure, the scores from the two samples appear to be intermixed randomly with no clear distinction between treatments.

Although Example 13.3 presents a somewhat simplified demonstration with exaggerated data, the general point of the example is to help you *see* what happens when you perform an analysis of variance. Specifically:

1. The numerator of the F-ratio (MS_{between}) simply measures how much difference exists between the treatment means. The bigger the mean differences, the bigger the F-ratio.

2. The denominator of the F-ratio (MS_{within}) measures the variability of the scores inside each treatment. As seen in Example 13.3, a large amount of variability can make it difficult to see a mean difference. In general, the greater the variability, the smaller the F-ratio.

Finally, one last bit of terminology before we move on. In analysis of variance, the denominator of the F-ratio is commonly called the *error term*. This terminology is based on the fact that the denominator measures the amount of variability that is unexplained and unpredictable, that is, the amount of variability due to "error." For an independent-measures design, the error term is always determined by the amount of variability *within treatments*. Within each treatment, all the subjects are treated exactly the same. In other words, the researcher does not do anything to cause variability among the scores within a treatment condition. Therefore, any dif-

TABLE 13.5

The performance of different species of monkeys on a delayed-response task

VERVET	RHESUS	BABOON	
$n = 4$	$n = 10$	$n = 6$	$N = 20$
$\overline{X} = 9$	$\overline{X} = 14$	$\overline{X} = 4$	$G = 200$
$T = 36$	$T = 140$	$T = 24$	$\Sigma X^2 = 3400$
$SS = 200$	$SS = 500$	$SS = 320$	

ferences that exist within a treatment can only be explained by chance or error. By contrast, a researcher hopes to obtain systematic and predictable differences between treatments. The error term is used by the researcher as a benchmark or standard for evaluating the differences between treatments. If the between-treatments differences ($MS_{between}$) are substantially greater than the error term, then the researcher can confidently conclude that the differences between treatments are more than chance.

DEFINITION

In analysis of variance, the MS value in the denominator of the F-ratio is called the *error term*. This MS value is intended to measure the amount of error variability; that is, variability in the data for which there is no systematic or predictable explanation. These unexplained differences from one score to another are assumed to be the result of chance. The error term is used as a standard for determining whether or not the differences between treatments (measured by $MS_{between}$) are greater than would be expected just by chance.

AN EXAMPLE WITH UNEQUAL SAMPLE SIZES

In the previous examples, all the samples were exactly the same size (equal ns). However, the formulas for ANOVA can be used when the sample size varies within an experiment. With unequal sample sizes, you must take care to be sure that each value of n is matched with the proper T value in the equations. You also should note that the general ANOVA procedure is most accurate when used to examine experimental data with equal sample sizes. Therefore, researchers generally try to plan experiments with equal ns. However, there are circumstances where it is impossible or impractical to have an equal number of subjects in every treatment condition. In these situations, ANOVA still provides a valid test, especially when the samples are relatively large and when the discrepancy between sample sizes is not extreme.

EXAMPLE 13.4

A psychologist conducts an experiment to compare learning performance for three species of monkeys. The animals are tested individually on a delayed-response task. A raisin is hidden in one of three containers while the animal is viewing from its cage window. A shade is then pulled over the window for 1 minute to block the view. After this delay period, the monkey is allowed to respond by tipping over one container. If its response is correct, the monkey is rewarded with the raisin. The number of trials it takes before the animal makes five consecutive correct responses is recorded. The experimenter used all of the available animals from each species, which resulted in unequal sample sizes (n). The data are summarized in Table 13.5.

STEP 1 State the hypotheses, and select the alpha level.

$$H_0: \quad \mu_1 = \mu_2 = \mu_3$$

$H_1:$ At least one population is different from the others.

$$\alpha = .05$$

STEP 2 Locate the critical region. To find the critical region, we first must determine the df values for the F-ratio:

$$df_{\text{total}} = N - 1 = 20 - 1 = 19$$

$$df_{\text{between}} = k - 1 = 3 - 1 = 2$$

$$df_{\text{within}} = N - k = 20 - 3 = 17$$

The F-ratio for these data will have $df = 2, 17$. With $\alpha = .05$, the critical value for the F-ratio is 3.59.

STEP 3 Compute the F-ratio. First, compute SS for all three parts of the analysis:

$$SS_{\text{total}} = \Sigma X^2 - \frac{G^2}{N}$$

$$= 3400 - \frac{200^2}{20}$$

$$= 3400 - 2000$$

$$= 1400$$

$$SS_{\text{between}} = \Sigma \frac{T^2}{n} - \frac{G^2}{N} = \frac{T_1^2}{n_1} + \frac{T_2^2}{n_2} + \frac{T_3^2}{n_3} - \frac{G^2}{N}$$

$$= \frac{36^2}{4} + \frac{140^2}{10} + \frac{24^2}{6} - \frac{200^2}{20}$$

$$= 324 + 1960 + 96 - 2000$$

$$= 380$$

$$SS_{\text{within}} = \Sigma SS_{\text{inside each treatment}}$$

$$= 200 + 500 + 320$$

$$= 1020$$

Finally, compute the MS values and the F-ratio:

$$MS_{\text{between}} = \frac{SS}{df} = \frac{380}{2} = 190$$

$$MS_{\text{within}} = \frac{SS}{df} = \frac{1020}{17} = 60$$

$$F = \frac{MS_{\text{between}}}{MS_{\text{within}}} = \frac{190}{60} = 3.17$$

STEP 4 Make a decision. Because the obtained F-ratio is not in the critical region, we fail to reject H_0 and conclude that these data do not provide evidence of significant differences among the three populations of monkeys in terms of average learning performance.

1. The following data summarize the results of an experiment using three separate samples to compare three treatment conditions:

TREATMENT 1	TREATMENT 2	TREATMENT 3	
$n = 5$	$n = 5$	$n = 5$	
$T = 5$	$T = 10$	$T = 30$	$\Sigma X^2 = 325$
$SS = 45$	$SS = 25$	$SS = 50$	

Do these data provide evidence of any significant mean differences among the treatments? Test with $\alpha = .05$.

2. A researcher reports an F-ratio with $df = 2, 30$ for an independent-measures analysis of variance. How many treatment conditions were compared in the experiment? How many subjects participated in the experiment?

1. The following summary table presents the results of the analysis:

SOURCE	SS	DF	MS	
Between	70	2	35	$F = 3.5$
Within	120	12	10	
Total	190	14		

The critical value for F is 3.88. The obtained value for F is not in the critical region, and we fail to reject H_0.

2. There were 3 treatment conditions ($df_{between} = k - 1 = 2$). A total of $N = 33$ individuals participated ($df_{within} = 30 = N - k$).

13.6 POST HOC TESTS

In analysis of variance, the null hypothesis states that there is no treatment effect:

$$H_0: \mu_1 = \mu_2 = \mu_3 = \ldots$$

When you reject the null hypothesis, you conclude that the means are not all the same. Although this appears to be a simple conclusion, in most cases it actually creates more questions than it answers. When there are only two treatments in an experiment, H_0 will state that $\mu_1 = \mu_2$. If you reject this hypothesis, the conclusion is quite straightforward; that is, the two means are not equal ($\mu_1 \neq \mu_2$). However, when you have more than two treatments, the situation immediately becomes more complex. With $k = 3$, for example, rejecting H_0 indicates that not all the means are the same. Now you must decide which ones are different. Is μ_1 different from μ_2? If μ_1 is different from μ_3? Is μ_2 different from μ_3? Are all three different? The purpose of *post hoc tests* is to answer these questions.

As the name implies, post hoc tests are done after an analysis of variance. More specifically, these tests are done after ANOVA when

1. You reject H_0 and
2. There are 3 or more treatments ($k \geq 3$).

Rejecting H_0 indicates that at least one difference exists among the treatments. With $k = 3$ or more, the problem is to find where the differences are.

In general, a post hoc test enables you to go back through the data and compare the individual treatments two at a time. In statistical terms, this is called making *pairwise comparisons*. For example, with $k = 3$, we would compare μ_1 versus μ_2, then μ_2 versus μ_3, and then μ_1 versus μ_3. In each case, we are looking for a significant mean difference. The process of conducting pairwise comparisons involves performing a series of separate hypothesis tests, and each of these tests includes the risk of a Type I error. As you do more and more separate tests, the risk of a Type I error accumulates and is called the *experimentwise alpha level* (see Box 13.1).

DEFINITION

The *experimentwise alpha level* is the overall probability of a Type I error that is accumulated over a series of separate hypothesis tests. Typically, the experimentwise alpha level is substantially greater than the value of alpha used for any one of the individual tests.

When conducting a series of post hoc tests, you must always be concerned about the experimentwise alpha level. The more comparisons you make, the greater the experimentwise alpha level is, and the greater the risk of a Type I error is. Fortunately, many post hoc tests have been developed that attempt to control the experimentwise alpha level. We will examine two of the commonly used procedures: Tukey's HSD test and the Scheffé test.

TUKEY'S HONESTLY SIGNIFICANT DIFFERENCE (HSD) TEST

The first post hoc test we will consider is Tukey's HSD test. We have selected Tukey's HSD test because it is a commonly used test in psychological research. Tukey's test allows you to compute a single value that determines the minimum difference between treatment means that is necessary for significance. This value, called the *honestly significant difference,* or HSD, is then used to compare any two treatment conditions. If the mean difference exceeds Tukey's HSD, you conclude that there is a significant difference between the treatments. Otherwise, you cannot conclude that the treatments are significantly different. The formula for Tukey's HSD is

$$\text{HSD} = q\sqrt{\frac{MS_{\text{within}}}{n}} \tag{13.13}$$

The q value used in Tukey's HSD test is called a Studentized range statistic.

where the value of q is found in Table B.5 (Appendix B, p. A-32), MS_{within} is the within-treatments variance from the ANOVA, and n is the number of scores in each treatment. Tukey's test requires that the sample size, n, be the same for all treat-

TABLE 13.6

Pain threshold data for four different pain relievers.

1 PLACEBO	2 DRUG A	3 DRUG B	4 DRUG C
$n = 3$	$n = 3$	$n = 3$	$n = 3$
$T = 3$	$T = 3$	$T = 12$	$T = 18$
$\overline{X} = 1$	$\overline{X} = 1$	$\overline{X} = 4$	$\overline{X} = 6$

ments. To locate the appropriate value of q, you must know the number of treatments in the overall experiment (k) and the degrees of freedom for MS_{within} (the error term in the F-ratio) and select an alpha level (generally the same α used for the ANOVA).

EXAMPLE 13.5 To outline the procedure for conducting post hoc tests with Tukey's HSD, we will use the data from the pain-reliever study in Example 13.1. The data are reproduced in summary form in Table 13.6. The within-treatments variance for these data is $MS_{within} = 2.00$ with $df = 8$.

With $\alpha = .05$ and $k = 4$, the value of q for these data is $q = 4.53$. Tukey's HSD is

$$HSD = q \sqrt{\frac{MS_{within}}{n}}$$

$$= 4.53 \sqrt{\frac{2.00}{3}}$$

$$= 3.70$$

Therefore, the mean difference between any two samples must be at least 3.70 to be significant. Using this value, we can make the following four conclusions:

1. Drug A is not significantly different from the placebo (both have $\overline{X} = 1$).
2. Drug B is not significantly different from either the placebo or drug A ($\overline{X} = 4$ versus $\overline{X} = 1$).
3. Drug C is significantly different from both the placebo and drug A ($\overline{X} = 6$ versus $\overline{X} = 1$).
4. Drug C is not significantly different from drug B ($\overline{X} = 6$ versus $\overline{X} = 4$).

Thus, drug C is the only one that produced significantly more pain relief than the placebo, and drug C is significantly better than drug A.

You also should notice that post-tests can lead to apparently contradictory results. In this case, for example, we have found that there is no significant difference between drug A and drug B, and we have found that there is no significant difference between drug B and drug C. This combination of outcomes might lead you to expect that there is no significant difference between drug A and drug C. However, the test did show a significant difference. The answer to this apparent contradiction lies in the criterion of statistical significance. The differences between A and B and between B and C are too small to satisfy the criterion of significance. However, when these differences are combined, the total difference between A and C is large enough to meet the criterion of statistical significance.

THE SCHEFFÉ TEST

Because it uses an extremely cautious method for reducing the risk of a Type I error, the *Scheffé test* has the distinction of being one of the safest of all possible post hoc tests. The Scheffé test uses an *F*-ratio to test for a significant difference between any two treatment conditions. The numerator of the *F*-ratio is an *MS* between treatments that is calculated using *only the two treatments you want to compare*. The denominator is the same *MS* within treatments that was used for the overall ANOVA. The "safety factor" for the Scheffé test comes from the following two considerations:

1. Although you are comparing only two treatments, the Scheffé test uses the value of *k* from the original experiment to compute *df* between treatments. Thus, *df* for the numerator of the *F*-ratio is $k - 1$.

2. The critical value for the Scheffé *F*-ratio is the same as was used to evaluate the *F*-ratio from the overall ANOVA. Thus, Scheffé requires that every post-test satisfy the same criteria used for the complete analysis of variance. The following example uses the data from Example 13.1 (Table 13.7) to demonstrate the Scheffé post-test procedure.

EXAMPLE 13.6

Rather than test all the possible comparisons of the four treatment conditions shown in Table 13.7, we will begin with the largest mean difference and then test progressively smaller differences until we find one that is not significant. For these data, the largest difference is between the placebo ($T = 3$) and drug C ($T = 18$). The first step is to compute $SS_{between}$ for these two treatments.

The grand total, *G*, for these two treatments is found by adding the two treatment totals ($G = 3 + 18$), and *N* is found by adding the number of scores in the two treatments ($N = 3 + 3$).

$$SS_{between} = \Sigma \frac{T^2}{n} - \frac{G^2}{N}$$

$$= \frac{3^2}{3} + \frac{18^2}{3} - \frac{21^2}{6}$$

$$= 37.5$$

Although we are comparing only two treatments, these two were selected from an experiment consisting of $k = 4$ treatments. The Scheffé test uses the overall experiment ($k = 4$) to determine the degrees of freedom between treatments. Therefore, $df_{between} = k - 1 = 3$, and the *MS* between treatments is

$$MS_{between} = \frac{SS_{between}}{df_{between}} = \frac{37.5}{3} = 12.5$$

Scheffé also uses the within-treatments variance from the complete experiment, $MS_{within} = 2.00$ with $df = 8$, so the Scheffé *F*-ratio is

$$F = \frac{MS_{between}}{MS_{within}} = \frac{12.5}{2} = 6.25$$

With $df = 3, 8$ and $\alpha = .05$, the critical value for F is 4.07 (see Table B.4). Therefore, our F-ratio is in the critical region, and we conclude that there is a significant difference between the placebo and drug C. Because the data for drug A and the placebo are equivalent (both have $T = 3$), we also conclude that drug C is significantly different from drug A.

Next, we consider the second largest mean difference for the data: drug B ($T = 12$) versus the placebo ($T = 3$). Again, we compute $SS_{between}$ using only these two treatment groups.

$$SS_{between} = \Sigma \frac{T^2}{n} - \frac{G^2}{N}$$

$$= \frac{3^2}{3} + \frac{12^2}{3} - \frac{15^2}{6}$$

$$= 13.5$$

As before, the Scheffé test uses the overall experiment ($k = 4$) to determine df between treatments. Thus, $df_{between} = k - 1 = 3$, and $MS_{between}$ for this comparison is

$$MS_{between} = \frac{SS_{between}}{df_{between}} = \frac{13.5}{3} = 4.5$$

Using $MS_{within} = 2$ with $df = 8$, we obtain a Scheffé F-ratio of

$$F = \frac{MS_{between}}{MS_{within}} = \frac{4.5}{2} = 2.25$$

With $df = 3, 8$ and $\alpha = .05$, the obtained F-ratio is less than the critical value of 4.07. Because the F-ratio is not in the critical region, our decision is that these data do not provide sufficient evidence to conclude that there is a significant difference between the placebo and drug B. Because the mean difference between the placebo and drug B is larger than that for any of the remaining pairs of treatments, we can conclude that none of the other pairwise comparisons would be significant with the Scheffé test.

Thus, the conclusion from the Scheffé post-test is that drug C is significantly different from both the placebo and drug A. These are the only significant differences for this experiment (using Scheffé), and these differences are the source of the significant F-ratio obtained for the overall ANOVA.

13.7 THE RELATIONSHIP BETWEEN ANOVA AND t TESTS

When you have data from an independent-measures experiment with only two treatment conditions, you can use either a t test (Chapter 10) or an independent-measures ANOVA. In practical terms, it makes no difference which you choose. These two statistical techniques always will result in the same statistical decision. In fact the two methods use many of the same calculations and are very closely related in several other respects. The basic relationship between t statistics and F-ratios can be stated in an equation:

$$F = t^2$$

This relationship can be explained by first looking at the structure of the formulas for F and t.

The structure of the t statistic compares the actual difference between the samples (numerator) with the standard difference that would be expected by chance (denominator).

$$t = \frac{\text{obtained difference between sample means}}{\text{difference expected by chance (error)}}$$

The structure of the F-ratio also compares differences between sample means versus differences due to chance or error.

$$F = \frac{\text{variance (differences) between sample means}}{\text{variance (differences) expected by chance (error)}}$$

However, the numerator and denominator of the F-ratio measure variances, or mean squared differences. Therefore, we can express the F-ratio as follows:

$$F = \frac{(\text{differences between samples})^2}{(\text{differences expected by chance})^2}$$

The fact that the t statistic is based on differences and the F-ratio is based on *squared* differences leads to the basic relationship $F = t^2$.

There are several other points to consider in comparing the t statistic to the F-ratio.

1. It should be obvious that you will be testing the same hypotheses whether you choose a t test or an ANOVA. With only two treatments, the hypotheses for either test are

    H_0: $\mu_1 = \mu_2$

    H_1: $\mu_1 \neq \mu_2$

2. The degrees of freedom for the t statistic and the df for the denominator of the F-ratio (df_{within}) are identical. For example, if you have two samples, each with six scores, the independent-measures t statistic will have $df = 10$, and the F-ratio will have $df = 1, 10$. In each case, you are adding the df from the first sample ($n - 1$) and the df from the second sample.

3. The distribution of t and the distribution of F-ratios match perfectly if you take into consideration the relationship $F = t^2$. Consider the t distribution with $df = 18$ and the corresponding F distribution with $df = 1, 18$ that are presented in Figure 13.11. Notice the following relationships:

    a. If each of the t values is squared, then all of the negative values will become positive. As a result, the whole left-hand side of the t distribution (below zero) will be flipped over to the positive side. This creates a non-symmetrical, positively skewed distribution, that is, the F distribution.

FIGURE 13.11

The distribution of *t* statistics with *df* = 18 and the corresponding distribution of *F*-ratios with *df* = 1, 18. Notice that the critical values for $\alpha = .05$ are $t = \pm 2.101$ and that $F = 2.101^2 = 4.41$.

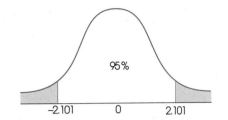

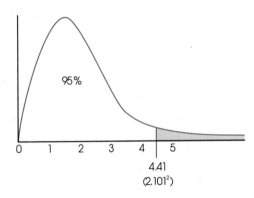

b. For $\alpha = .05$, the critical region for *t* is determined by values greater than $+2.101$ or less than -2.101. When these boundaries are squared, you get

$$\pm 2.101^2 = 4.41$$

Notice that 4.41 is the critical value for $\alpha = .05$ in the *F* distribution. Any value that is in the critical region for *t* will end up in the critical region for *F*-ratios after it is squared.

ASSUMPTIONS FOR THE INDEPENDENT-MEASURES ANOVA

The independent-measures ANOVA requires the same three assumptions that were necessary for the independent-measures *t* hypothesis test:

1. The observations within each sample must be independent (see p. 244).

2. The populations from which the samples are selected must be normal.

3. The populations from which the samples are selected must have equal variances (homogeneity of variance).

Ordinarily, researchers are not overly concerned with the assumption of normality, especially when large samples are used, unless there are strong reasons to suspect the assumption has not been satisfied. The assumption of homogeneity of variance is an important one. If a researcher suspects it has been violated, it can be tested by Hartley's *F*-max test for homogeneity of variance (Chapter 10, p. 304).

LEARNING CHECK

1. The Scheffé post hoc test uses between-treatments *df* from the original ANOVA even though $SS_{between}$ is calculated for a pair of treatments. (True or false?)

2. An ANOVA produces an F-ratio with $df = 1, 34$. Could the data have been analyzed with a t test? What would be the degrees of freedom for the t statistic?

3. With $k = 2$ treatments, are post hoc tests necessary when the null hypothesis is rejected? Explain why or why not.

ANSWERS **1.** True

2. If the F-ratio has $df = 1, 34$, then the experiment compared only two treatments, and you could use a t statistic to evaluate the data. The t statistic would have $df = 34$.

3. No. Post hoc tests are used to determine which treatments are different. With only two treatment conditions, there is no uncertainty as to which two treatments are different.

SUMMARY

1. Analysis of variance is a statistical technique that is used to test for mean differences among two or more treatment conditions or among two or more populations. The null hypothesis for this test states that there are no differences among the population means. The alternative hypothesis states that at least one mean is different from the others. Although analysis of variance can be used with either an independent- or a repeated-measures experiment, this chapter examined only independent-measures designs, that is, experiments with a separate sample for each treatment condition.

2. The test statistic for analysis of variance is a ratio of two variances called an F-ratio. The F-ratio is structured so that the numerator and denominator measure the same variance when the null hypothesis is true. In this way, the existence of a significant treatment effect is apparent if the data produce an "unbalanced" F-ratio. The variances in the F-ratio are called mean squares, or MS values. Each MS is computed by

$$MS = \frac{SS}{df}$$

3. For the independent-measures analysis of variance, the F-ratio is

$$F = \frac{MS_{between}}{MS_{within}}$$

The $MS_{between}$ measures differences among the treatments by computing the variability of the treatment means or totals. These differences are assumed to be produced by three factors:

a. Treatment effects (if they exist)

b. Individual differences

c. Experimental error

The MS_{within} measures variability inside each of the treatment conditions. This variability is assumed to be produced by two factors:

a. Individual differences

b. Experimental error

With these factors in mind, the F-ratio has the following structure:

$$F = \frac{\text{treatment effect} + \text{individual diff's.} + \text{experimental error}}{\text{individual diff's.} + \text{experimental error}}$$

When there is no treatment effect (H_0 is true), the numerator and denominator of the F-ratio are measuring the same variance, and the obtained ratio should be near 1.00. If there is a significant treatment effect, the numerator of the ratio should be larger than the denominator, and the obtained F value should be much greater than 1.00

4. The formulas for computing each SS, df, and MS value are presented in Figure 13.12, which also shows the general structure for the analysis of variance.

5. The F-ratio has two values for degrees of freedom, one associated with the MS in the numerator and one associated with the MS in the denominator. These df values are used to find the critical value for the F-ratio in the F distribution table.

6. When the decision from an analysis of variance is to reject the null hypothesis and when the experiment contained more than two treatment conditions, it is necessary to continue the analysis with a post hoc test such as Tukey's HSD test or the Scheffé test. The purpose of these tests is to determine exactly which treatments are significantly different and which are not.

FIGURE 13.12

Formulas for ANOVA.

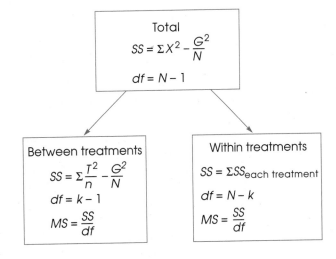

$$F\text{-ratio} = \frac{MS \text{ between treatments}}{MS \text{ within treatments}}$$

KEY TERMS

analysis of variance (ANOVA)

between-treatments variability

within-treatments variability

treatment effect

individual differences

experimental error

F-ratio

error term

factor

levels

mean square *(MS)*

ANOVA summary table

distribution of *F*-ratios

post hoc tests

Scheffé test

Tukey's HSD test

FOCUS ON PROBLEM SOLVING

1. The words and labels used to describe the different components of variance can help you remember the ANOVA formulas. For example, *total* refers to the total experiment. Therefore, the SS_{total} and df_{total} values are based on the whole set of N scores. The word *within* refers to the variability inside (within) the treatment groups. Thus, the value for SS_{within} is based on an SS value from each group, computed from the scores *within* each group. Finally, *between* refers to the variability (or differences) between treatments. The $SS_{between}$ component measures the differences between treatments (T_1 versus T_2, and so on), and $df_{between}$ is simply the number of T values (k) minus 1.

2. When you are computing SS and df values, always calculate all three components (total, between, and within) separately; then check your work by making sure that the *between-treatments* and *within-treatments* components add up to the *total*.

3. Because ANOVA requires a fairly lengthy series of calculations, it helps to organize your work. We suggest that you compute all of the SS values first, followed by the df values, then the two MS values, and finally the F-ratio. If you use the same sys-

tem all the time (practice it!), you will be less likely to get lost in the middle of a problem.

4. The previous two focus points are facilitated by using an ANOVA summary table (for example, see p. 394). The first column has the heading *Source*. Listed below the heading are the three sources of variability (between, within, and total). The second and third columns have the headings *SS* and *df*. These can be filled in as you perform the appropriate computations. The last column is headed *MS* for the mean square values.

5. Remember that an *F*-ratio has two separate values for *df*: a value for the numerator and one for the denominator. Properly reported, the $df_{between}$ value is stated first. You will need both *df* values when consulting the *F* distribution table for the critical *F* value. You should recognize immediately that an error has been made if you see an *F*-ratio reported with a single value for *df*.

6. When you encounter an *F*-ratio and its *df* values reported in the literature, you should be able to reconstruct much of the original experiment. For example, if you see "$F(2, 36) = 4.80$," you should realize that the experiment compared $k = 3$ treatment groups (because $df_{between} = k - 1 = 2$), with a total of $N = 39$ subjects participating in the experiment (because $df_{within} = N - k = 36$).

7. Keep in mind that a large value for *F* indicates evidence for a treatment effect. A combination of factors will yield a large *F* value. One such factor is a large value for $MS_{between}$ in the numerator of the ratio. This will occur when there are large differences between groups, as would be expected when a treatment effect occurs. Another factor that contributes to a large *F* value would be a small value for MS_{within} on the bottom of the *F* ratio. This will occur when there is a little error variability, reflected in low variability within groups.

DEMONSTRATION 13.1

ANALYSIS OF VARIANCE

A human factors psychologist studied three computer keyboard designs. Three samples of individuals were given material to type on a particular keyboard, and the number of errors committed by each subject was recorded. The data are as follows:

keyboard A: 0   4   0   1   0

keyboard B: 6   8   5   4   2

keyboard C: 6   5   9   4   6

Does typing performance differ significantly among the three types of keyboards?

STEP 1   State the hypotheses, and specify the alpha level.
The null hypothesis states that there is no difference among the keyboards in terms of number of errors committed. In symbols, we would state

H_0: $\mu_1 = \mu_2 = \mu_3$ (there is no effect of type of keyboard used)

As noted previously in this chapter, there are a number of possible statements for the alternative hypothesis. Here we state the general alternative hypothesis.

H_1:   At least one of the treatment means is different.

That is, there is an effect of the type of keyboard on typing performance. We will set alpha at $\alpha = .05$.

STEP 2 Locate the critical region.

To locate the critical region, we must obtain the values for $df_{between}$ and df_{within}.

$$df_{between} = k - 1 = 3 - 1 = 2$$

$$df_{within} = N - k = 15 - 3 = 12$$

The F-ratio for this problem will have $df = 2, 12$. The F distribution table is consulted for $df = 2$ in the numerator and $df = 12$ in the denominator. The critical F value for $\alpha = .05$ is $F = 3.88$. The obtained F ratio must exceed this value to reject H_0.

STEP 3 Perform the analysis.

The analysis involves the following steps:

1. Compute T and SS for each sample, and obtain G and ΣX^2 for all ($N = 15$) scores.

2. Perform the analysis of SS.

3. Perform the analysis of df.

4. Calculate mean squares.

5. Calculate the F-ratio.

Compute T, SS, G, and ΣX^2. We will use the computational formula for the SS of each sample. The calculations are illustrated with the following tables:

KEYBOARD A		KEYBOARD B		KEYBOARD C	
X	X^2	X	X^2	X	X^2
0	0	6	36	6	36
4	16	8	64	5	25
0	0	5	25	9	81
1	1	4	16	4	16
0	0	2	4	6	36
$\Sigma X = 5$	$\Sigma X^2 = 17$	$\Sigma X = 25$	$\Sigma X^2 = 145$	$\Sigma X = 30$	$\Sigma X^2 = 194$

For keyboard A, T and SS are computed using only the $n = 5$ scores of this sample:

$$T_1 = \Sigma X = 0 + 4 + 0 + 1 + 0 = 5$$

$$SS_1 = \Sigma X^2 - \frac{(\Sigma X)^2}{n} = 17 - \frac{(5)^2}{5} = 17 - \frac{25}{5} = 17 - 5$$

$$= 12$$

For keyboard B, T and SS are computed for its $n = 5$ scores:

$$T_2 = \Sigma X = 25$$

$$SS_2 = \Sigma X^2 - \frac{(\Sigma X)^2}{n} = 145 - \frac{(25)^2}{5} = 145 - \frac{625}{5} = 145 - 125$$

$$= 20$$

For the last sample, keyboard C, we obtain

$$T_3 = \Sigma X = 30$$

$$SS_3 = \Sigma X^2 - \frac{(\Sigma X)^2}{n} = 194 - \frac{(30)^2}{5} = 194 - \frac{900}{5} = 194 - 180$$

$$= 14$$

The grand total *(G)* for $N = 15$ scores is

$$G = \Sigma T = 5 + 25 + 30 = 60$$

The ΣX^2 for all $N = 15$ scores in this study can be obtained by summing the X^2 columns for the three samples. For these data, we obtain

$$\Sigma X^2 = 17 + 145 + 194 = 356$$

Perform the analysis of SS. We will compute SS_{total} followed by its two components.

$$SS_{total} = \Sigma X^2 - \frac{G^2}{N} = 356 - \frac{60^2}{15} = 356 - \frac{3600}{15}$$

$$= 356 - 240 = 116$$

$$SS_{within} = \Sigma SS_{inside\ each\ treatment}$$

$$= 12 + 20 + 14$$

$$= 46$$

$$SS_{between} = \Sigma \frac{T^2}{n} - \frac{G^2}{N}$$

$$= \frac{5^2}{5} + \frac{25^2}{5} + \frac{30^2}{5} - \frac{60^2}{15}$$

$$= \frac{25}{5} + \frac{625}{5} + \frac{900}{5} - \frac{3600}{15}$$

$$= 5 + 125 + 180 - 240$$

$$= 70$$

Analyze degrees of freedom. We will compute df_{total}. Its components, $df_{between}$ and df_{within}, were previously calculated (step 2).

$$df_{total} = N - 1 = 15 - 1 = 14$$

$$df_{between} = 2$$

$$df_{within} = 12$$

Calculate the MS values. The values for $MS_{between}$ and MS_{within} are determined.

$$MS_{between} = \frac{SS_{between}}{df_{between}} = \frac{70}{2} = 35$$

$$MS_{within} = \frac{SS_{within}}{df_{within}} = \frac{46}{12} = 3.83$$

Compute the F-ratio. Finally, we can compute F.

$$F = \frac{MS_{between}}{MS_{within}} = \frac{35}{3.83} = 9.14$$

STEP 4 Make a decision about H_0, and state a conclusion.

The obtained F of 9.14 exceeds the critical value of 3.88. Therefore, we can reject the null hypothesis. The type of keyboard used has a significant effect of the number of errors committed, $F(2, 12) = 9.14$, $p < .05$. The following table summarizes the results of the analysis:

SOURCE	SS	df	MS	
Between treatments	70	2	35	$F = 9.14$
Within treatments	46	12	3.83	
Total	116	14		

PROBLEMS

1. Explain why the expected value for an F-ratio is equal to 1.00 when there is no treatment effect.

2. Describe the similarities between an F-ratio and a t statistic.

3. What happens to the value of the F-ratio in analysis of variance if the difference between sample means increases? What happens to the value of F if the sample variability increases?

4. Explain why you should use ANOVA instead of several t tests to evaluate mean differences when an experiment consists of three or more treatment conditions.

5. Describe *when* and *why* post hoc tests are used. Explain why you would not need to do post hoc tests for an experiment with only $k = 2$ treatment conditions.

6. Use the following set of data.
   a. Without doing any calculations (just look at the data), what value should be obtained for the variance between treatments? ($MS_{between} = ?$)

   b. Based on your answer to part a, what value would be obtained for the F-ratio for these data?
   c. Calculate $SS_{between}$ and $MS_{between}$ to verify your answers.

TREATMENTS		
I	II	
1	2	
4	5	$G = 16$
0	0	$\Sigma X^2 = 56$
3	1	
$T = 8$	$T = 8$	
$SS = 10$	$SS = 14$	

7. For the following set of data, without doing any calculations (just look at the data), what value should be obtained for the variance within treatments? ($MS_{within} = ?$)

TREATMENTS		
I	II	
1	3	
1	3	$G = 16$
1	3	$\Sigma X^2 = 40$
1	3	
$T = 4$	$T = 12$	

8. The following data are from an experiment comparing three treatment conditions with a separate sample of $n = 4$ in each treatment

TREATMENTS			
I	II	III	
0	1	8	$G = 48$
4	5	5	
0	4	6	$\Sigma X^2 = 284$
4	2	9	
$T = 8$	$T = 12$	$T = 28$	
$SS = 16$	$SS = 10$	$SS = 10$	

a. Use an ANOVA with $\alpha = .05$ to determine whether there are any significant differences among the three treatments.

b. Use Tukey's HSD test to find exactly which treatments are different from each other. Again, use the .05 level of significance.

9. A developmental psychologist is examining problem-solving ability for grade school children. Random samples of 5-year-old, 6-year-old, and 7-year-old children are obtained with $n = 3$ in each sample. Each child is given a standardized problem-solving task, and the psychologist records the number of errors. The data are as follows:

5-YEAR-OLDS	6-YEAR-OLDS	7-YEAR-OLDS	
5	6	0	
4	4	1	$G = 30$
6	2	2	$\Sigma X^2 = 138$
$T = 15$	$T = 12$	$T = 3$	
$SS = 2$	$SS = 8$	$SS = 2$	

a. Use these data to test whether there are any significant differences among the three age groups. Use $\alpha = .05$.

b. Use the Scheffé test to determine which groups are different.

10. The extent to which a person's attitude can be changed depends in part on how big a change you are trying to produce. In a classic study on persuasion, Aronson, Turner, and Carlsmith (1985) obtained three groups of subjects. One group listened to a persuasive message that differed only slightly from the subjects' original attitudes. For the second group, there was a moderate discrepancy between the message and the original attitudes. For the third group, there was a large discrepancy between the message and the original attitudes. For each subject, the amount of attitude change was measured. Hypothetical data, similar to the experimental results, are as follows:

SIZE OF DISCREPANCY			
SMALL	MODERATE	LARGE	
1	3	0	
0	4	2	$G = 36$
0	6	0	$\Sigma X^2 = 138$
2	3	4	
3	5	0	
0	3	0	
$T = 6$	$T = 24$	$T = 6$	
$SS = 8$	$SS = 8$	$SS = 14$	

a. Use an analysis of variance with $\alpha = .01$ to determine whether the amount of discrepancy between the original attitude and the persuasive argument has a significant effect on the amount of attitude change.

b. For these data, describe how the effectiveness of a persuasive argument is related to the discrepancy between the argument and a person's original attitude.

11. There have been a number of studies on the adjustment problems (that is, "jetlag") people experience when traveling across time zones (see Moore-Ede, Sulzman, and Fuller, 1982). Jetlag always seems to be worse when traveling east. Consider this hypothetical study. A researcher examines how many days it takes a person to adjust after taking a long flight. One group flies east across time zones (California to New York), a second group travels west (New York to California), and a third group takes a long flight within one time zone (San Diego to Seattle). For the following data, create a table that displays the mean and the standard deviation for each sample. Then perform an analysis of variance to determine if jetlag varies for type of travel. Use the .05 level of significance.

WESTBOUND	EASTBOUND	SAME TIME ZONE
2	6	1
1	4	0
3	6	1
3	8	1
2	5	0
4	7	0

12. Several studies indicate that handedness (left-handed/ right-handed) is related to differences in brain function. Because different parts of the brain are specialized for specific behaviors, this means that left- and right-handed people should show different skills or talents. To test this hypothesis, a psychologist tested pitch discrimination (a component of musical ability) for three groups of subjects: left-handed, right-handed, and ambidextrous. The data from this study are as follows:

RIGHT-HANDED	LEFT-HANDED	AMBIDEXTROUS	
6	1	2	
4	0	0	
3	1	0	$G = 30$
4	1	2	$\Sigma X^2 = 102$
3	2	1	
$T = 20$	$T = 5$	$T = 5$	
$SS = 6$	$SS = 2$	$SS = 4$	

Each score represents the number of errors during a series of pitch discrimination trials.
a. Do these data indicate any differences among the three groups? Test with $\alpha = .05$.
b. Use the F-max test to determine whether these data satisfy the homogeneity of variance assumption (see Chapter 10).

13. The following data represent three separate samples tested in three different treatment conditions.
a. Using only the first two samples (treatments I and II), use an ANOVA with $\alpha = .05$ to test for a mean difference between the two treatments.
b. Now use all three samples to test for mean differences among the three treatment conditions, again using $\alpha = .05$.
c. You should find that the first two treatments are significantly different (part a), but that there are no significant differences when the third treatment is included in the analysis (part b). How can you explain this outcome? (*Hint:* Compute the three sample

means. How large is the mean difference when you are comparing only treatment I versus treatment II? How large are the mean differences, on the average, when you are comparing all three treatments?)

	TREATMENTS	
I	II	III
0	6	4
4	6	0
0	2	4
0	6	4
$T = 4$	$T = 20$	$T = 12$
$SS = 12$	$SS = 12$	$SS = 12$

14. A pharmaceutical company has developed a drug that is expected to reduce hunger. To test the drug, three samples of rats are selected with $n = 10$ in each sample. The first sample receives the drug every day. The second sample is given the drug once a week, and the third sample receives no drug at all. The dependent variable is the amount of food eaten by each rat over a one-month period. These data are analyzed by an analysis of variance, and the results are reported in the following summary table. Fill in all missing values in the table. (*Hint:* Start with the df column.)

SOURCE	SS	df	MS	
Between treatments	___	___	___	$F = 12$
Within treatments	54	___	___	
Total	___	___		

15. The following summary table presents the results of an ANOVA from an experiment comparing four treatment conditions with a sample of $n = 10$ in each treatment. Complete all missing values in the table.

SOURCE	SS	df	MS	
Between treatments	___	___	15	$F = $ ___
Within treatments	108	___	___	
Total	___	___		

16. A common science-fair project involves testing the effects of music on the growth of plants. For one of these projects, a sample of 24 newly sprouted bean plants is

obtained. These plants are randomly assigned to four treatments, with $n = 6$ in each group. The four conditions are rock, heavy metal, country, and classical music. The dependent variable is the height of each plant after two weeks. The data from this experiment were examined using an ANOVA, and the results are summarized in the following table. Fill in all missing values.

SOURCE	SS	df	MS	
Between treatments	____	____	10	$F = $ ____
Within treatments	40	____	____	
Total	____	____		

17. One way to define and measure the capacity of immediate memory is to show subjects a series of objects one at a time and then ask them to report the items they just saw. We begin with only one or two items and gradually increase the number until the subject begins to make errors. Most adults perform perfectly up to seven or eight items before memory begins to fail. (For example, you can recall a 7-digit phone number after hearing it once, but most of us have trouble if presented with a list of 9 or 10 digits to be recalled.) This basic memory ability appears to develop gradually during childhood. The following data represent immediate memory performance for 2-year-old, 6-year-old, and 10-year-old children. Use an analysis of variance with $\alpha = .05$ to test for mean differences among the three age groups. (*Note:* You will need to convert means to totals and standard deviations to SS values before you can use the normal ANOVA formulas. Also, these summarized data do not provide enough information for direct calculation of SS_{total}.)

2-year-olds: $n = 20, \overline{X} = 2.1, s = 1.3$

6-year-olds: $n = 20, \overline{X} = 4.3, s = 1.5$

10-year-olds: $n = 20, \overline{X} = 6.9, s = 1.8$

18. Use an analysis of variance with $\alpha = .05$ to determine whether the following data provide evidence of any significant differences among the three treatments:

TREATMENT 1	TREATMENT 2	TREATMENT 3	
$n = 4$	$n = 5$	$n = 6$	$N = 15$
$T = 2$	$T = 10$	$T = 18$	$G = 30$
$SS = 13$	$SS = 21$	$SS = 26$	$\Sigma X^2 = 135$

19. The following data represent the results of an independent-measures experiment comparing two treatment conditions:

TREATMENT 1	TREATMENT 2
1	5
2	4
2	3
4	2
1	6

a. Use an analysis of variance with $\alpha = .05$ to test for a significant difference between the two treatment means.

b. Use an independent-measures t statistic to test for a significant difference. (Remember, you should find the basic relationship $F = t^2$.)

20. Sheldon (1940) examined the relationship between personality characteristics and physical characteristics (body shape). He identified three categories of body shape: endomorph, ectomorph, and mesomorph corresponding to rounded, thin, and muscular, respectively. He then evaluated personality characteristics that tend to be associated with each body type. One relationship Sheldon examined involved sociability and body type. Specifically, endomorphs tend to be more social, and ectomorphs tend to be more private. The following hypothetical data represent an attempt to demonstrate this relationship. Sociability scores were obtained for three separate samples representing the three different body types. Do these data indicate significant differences in personality between groups with different physical characteristics? Test with $\alpha = .05$.

ENDOMORPHS	ECTOMORPHS	MESOMORPHS
23	19	18
25	17	14
19	16	15
20	21	11
23	15	17

21. First-born children tend to develop language skills faster than their younger siblings. One possible explanation for the phenomenon is that first-borns have undivided attention from their parents. If this explanation is correct, then it is also reasonable that twins should show slower language development than single children and that triplets

should be even slower. Davis (1937) found exactly this result. The following hypothetical data demonstrate the relationship. The dependent variable is a measure of language skill at age three for each child. Do the data indicate any significant differences? Test with $\alpha = .05$.

SINGLE CHILD	TWIN	TRIPLET
8	4	4
7	6	4
10	7	7
6	4	2
9	9	3

22. Betz and Thomas (1979) have reported a distinct connection between personality and health. They identified three personality types who differ in their susceptibility to serious, stress-related illness (heart attack, high blood pressure, etc.). The three personality types are alphas, who are cautious and steady; betas, who are carefree and outgoing; and gammas, who tend toward extremes of behavior such as being overly cautious or very careless. Sample data representing general health scores for each of these three groups are as follows. A low score indicates poor health.

ALPHAS		BETAS		GAMMAS	
43	44	41	52	36	29
41	56	40	57	38	36
49	42	36	48	45	42
52	53	51	55	25	40
41	21	52	39	41	36

a. Compute the mean for each personality type. Do these data indicate a significant difference among the three types? Test with $\alpha = .05$.

b. Use the Scheffé test to determine which groups are different. Explain what happened in this study.

23. A psychologist is interested in the extent to which physical attractiveness can influence judgment of other personal characteristics such as intelligence or ability. The psychologist selected three groups of subjects who were to play the role of a company personnel manager. Each subject was given a stack of job applications, each of which included a photograph of the applicant. One of these applications was previously selected as the test stimulus. For one group of subjects, this application contained a photograph of a very attractive person. For the second group, the photograph was of an average-looking person. For the third group, a photo of a very unattractive person was attached to the application. The subjects were instructed to rate the quality of each job applicant (0 = "very poor" to 10 = "excellent"). The psychologist recorded the rating of the test stimulus for each subject. These data are as follows:

ATTRACTIVE			AVERAGE			UNATTRACTIVE		
5	4	4	6	5	3	4	3	1
3	5	6	6	6	7	3	1	2
4	3	8	5	4	6	2	4	3
3	5	4	8	7	8	2	1	2

a. Compute the means of the groups, and draw a graph showing the results.

b. Use an ANOVA with $\alpha = .05$ to determine whether there are any significant differences among these three groups.

CHAPTER 14

REPEATED-MEASURES ANALYSIS OF VARIANCE (ANOVA)

TOOLS YOU WILL NEED

The following items are considered essential background material for this chapter. If you doubt your knowledge of any of these items, you should review the appropriate chapter or section before proceeding.

- Introduction to analysis of variance (Chapter 13)
- The logic of analysis of variance
- ANOVA notation and formulas
- Distribution of *F*-ratios
- Repeated-measures design (Chapter 11)

CONTENTS

PREVIEW

In the early 1970s, it was discovered that the brain manufactures and releases morphinelike substances called endorphins (see Snyder, 1977). Among many possible functions, these substances are thought to act as natural painkillers. For example, acupuncture may relieve pain because the acupuncture needles stimulate a release of endorphins in the brain. It also is thought that endorphins are responsible for reducing pain for long-distance runners and may produce the "runner's high."

Gintzler (1980) studied changes in pain threshold during pregnancy and examined how these changes are related to endorphin activity. Gintzler tested pregnant rats in several sessions spaced at regular intervals throughout their pregnancies (a rat's pregnancy lasts only three weeks). In a test session, a rat received a series of foot shocks that increased in intensity. The intensity of shock that elicited a jump response was recorded as the index of pain threshold. In general, the rats showed less sensitivity to shock (increased thresholds) as the pregnancy progressed. The change in threshold from one session to another was gradual, up until just a day or two before birth of the pups. At that point, there was an abrupt increase in pain threshold. Gintzler also found evidence that the change in pain sensitivity was due to enhanced activity of

endorphins. Perhaps a natural pain-killing mechanism prepares these animals for the stress of giving birth.

You should recognize Gintzler's experiment as an example of a repeated-measures design: Each rat was observed repeatedly at several different times during the course of pregnancy. You also should recognize that it would be inappropriate to use the repeated-measures t statistic to evaluate the data because each subject is measured in *more than* two conditions. As noted in Chapter 13, whenever the number of levels of a treatment is greater than two, analysis of variance (ANOVA) should be performed rather than multiple t tests. Because each t test has a risk of Type I error, doing several t tests would result in an unacceptably large experimentwise alpha level, making the probability of a Type I error for the entire set of tests undesirably high. The ANOVA, on the other hand, provides a single test statistic (the F-ratio) for the experiment.

In this chapter, we will examine how the repeated-measures design is analyzed with ANOVA. As you will see, many of the notational symbols and computations are the same as those used for the independent-measures ANOVA. In fact, your best preparation for this chapter is a good understanding of the basic ANOVA procedure presented in Chapter 13.

14.1 OVERVIEW

In the previous chapter, we introduced the statistical technique of analysis of variance, and we examined how this hypothesis-testing procedure is used for independent-measures experimental designs. In this chapter, we will examine how data from a repeated-measures experiment are evaluated using ANOVA. You should recall that an independent-measures design uses a separate sample for each treatment condition. A repeated-measures experiment, on the other hand, uses a single sample, so that the same individuals are measured in each of the treatment conditions. In both experimental designs, ANOVA is used to determine whether or not the sample data provide evidence of mean differences between two or more treatment conditions. As always, the null hypothesis states that there are no mean differences among the treatments: In symbols,

$$H_0: \mu_1 = \mu_2 = \mu_3 = \ldots$$

The alternative hypothesis states that the treatments are not all the same. As before, we will not list all the possible alternative hypotheses, but rather will simply state

H_1:   At least one treatment mean is different from the others.

When repeated-measures designs were first introduced in Chapter 11, we noted that this type of experiment is particularly useful when a researcher wants to examine how behavior changes over time or across different treatment conditions in the same individuals. As a result, repeated-measures designs are used commonly to examine development (over time), to chart the course of learning (at different levels of practice), or simply to examine performance under different conditions. We also noted in Chapter 11 that a repeated-measures experiment has the advantage of being more powerful than an independent-measures design because it eliminates individual differences. Because the same individuals are tested in each treatment condition, differences between treatments cannot be attributed to differences between groups of subjects.

As we shall see, many of the notational symbols and computations for repeated-measures ANOVA are identical to those used for the independent-measures design. In fact, the repeated-measures ANOVA can be viewed as a two-stage process where the first stage is exactly the same analysis that was used for the independent-measures analysis (Chapter 13). However, the fact that the repeated-measures analysis eliminates individual differences will produce a fundamental change in the structure of the final F-ratio. To introduce this change, we will begin with the general logic of the repeated-measures ANOVA and then look at the details of notation and formulas.

14.2   THE LOGIC OF REPEATED-MEASURES ANOVA

ANOVA evaluates mean differences between two or more treatments by comparing the actual differences versus the amount of difference that would be expected by chance. This comparison is made in an F-ratio, which is a ratio of two variances.

$$F = \frac{\text{variance between treatments}}{\text{variance due to chance}} \qquad (14.1)$$

$$= \frac{\text{variance (differences) between treatments}}{\text{variance (differences) expected by sampling error}}$$

As with the independent-measures ANOVA, a large value for the F-ratio indicates that the sample mean differences are more than would be expected by chance. We will examine in more detail the two variance components that comprise the numerator and denominator of the F-ratio.

VARIANCE BETWEEN TREATMENTS   The variance between treatments provides a measure of the actual mean differences between treatment conditions in an experiment. What might cause the scores in one treatment to be different from the scores in another treatment? For a repeated-measures design, there are only two answers to this question.

1. Treatment Effect. It is possible that the different treatment conditions actually do produce different effects and, therefore, cause the individuals' scores to be higher (or lower) in one condition than in another. Remember, the purpose of the experiment is to determine whether or not a treatment effect exists.

2. Experimental Error. Any time behavior is measured, error may be introduced. The error may be inherent in the accuracy of the measurement tools, or it might be attributed to uncontrolled conditions in the laboratory, such as noises or changes in room temperature. This kind of uncontrolled and unsystematic error may cause the individuals' scores in one condition to be different from their scores in another condition.

Notice that we have not listed "individual differences" as a possible explanation for variance between treatments. Remember, a repeated-measures design uses the *same* individuals in every treatment condition, so any differences between treatments cannot be attributed to individual differences.

VARIANCE DUE TO CHANCE: THE ERROR TERM

The error term (denominator of the *F*-ratio) is intended to provide a measure of the amount of variance expected by chance. In addition, the error term is intended to produce a balanced *F*-ratio when the null hypothesis is true and there is no treatment effect. That is, the only difference between the components of the numerator and those of the denominator is the presence of a treatment-effect component in the numerator. Because variance between treatments has two components, the treatment effect and experimental error, the denominator should have only experimental error. The *F*-ratio for the repeated-measures ANOVA will have the following structure:

$$F = \frac{\text{treatment effect} + \text{experimental error}}{\text{experimental error}} \qquad (14.2)$$

Now when the treatment effect is zero (H_0 is true), the top and bottom of the *F*-ratio are measuring the same variance (the *F*-ratio is balanced). Just as we saw in Chapter 13 (pp. 379–380), when there is no treatment effect, the expected value of *F* is 1.00. To obtain a measure of variance due to experimental error, we begin with the variance within treatments. You should recall from Chapter 13 that the differences (or variance) inside each treatment condition come from two sources:

1. Individual Differences. Within each treatment, the scores come from different individuals.

2. Experimental Error. This uncontrolled and unsystematic error always could be the source of differences between scores.

The denominator of the repeated-measures *F*-ratio requires a measure of variance that is due *only* to experimental error (equation 14.2). To obtain this measure, we will analyze the within-treatments variability into two separate components: the variance from individual differences and the variance from experimental error.

Figure 14.1 summarizes the complete analysis of variance for a repeated-measures design. Note that the analysis consists of a two-stage process. In the first stage, the total variance is partitioned into two components: (1) variance between treatments and (2) variance within treatments. This stage is identical to the analysis we conducted for an independent-measures design (see Chapter 13). The second stage of the analysis is necessary to separate individual differences and experimental error. This is accomplished by computing the variance between subjects and

FIGURE 14.1

The partitioning of variability for a
repeated-measures experiment.

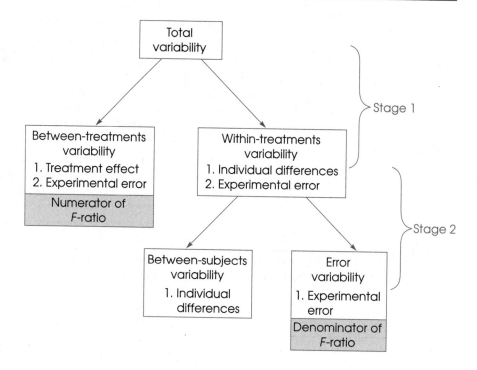

The term *residual* is often used in place
of *error.*

subtracting it from the variance within treatments. The residual, error variance,
provides a measure of experimental error and is used as the error term in the
F ratio.

LEARNING CHECK

1. What sources contribute to between-treatments variability for the repeated-measures design?

2. What sources of variability contribute to within-treatments variability?

3. **a.** Describe the structure of the *F*-ratio for a repeated-measures ANOVA.

   b. Compare it to the *F*-ratio structure for the independent-measures ANOVA (Chapter 13). How do they differ?

4. In the second stage of analysis, within-treatments variability is partitioned into _____ variability and _____ variability.

ANSWERS

1. Treatment effect, experimental error

2. Individual differences, experimental error

3. **a.** $F = \dfrac{\text{treatment effect} + \text{experimental error}}{\text{experimental error}}$

   b. For the independent-measures ANOVA, individual differences contribute variability to both between-treatments variability and the error term of the *F*-ratio.

4. Between-subjects variability, error variability

TABLE 14.1

Manual dexterity scores as a function of amount of practice (test session)

PERSON	TEST SESSION			P
	SESSION 1	SESSION 2	SESSION 3	
A	3	3	6	12
B	2	2	2	6
C	1	1	4	6
D	2	4	6	12

$$T_1 = 8 \qquad T_2 = 10 \qquad T_3 = 18$$
$$SS_1 = 2 \qquad SS_2 = 5 \qquad SS_3 = 11$$
$$G = 36 \quad \Sigma X^2 = 140 \quad k = 3 \quad n = 4 \quad N = 12$$

14.3 NOTATION AND FORMULAS FOR REPEATED-MEASURES ANOVA

We will use the data in Table 14.1 to help introduce the notation and formulas for the repeated-measures ANOVA. The data represent manual dexterity scores for a sample of $n = 4$ people measured over a series of three practice sessions. The goal of the experiment is to examine changes in manual dexterity performance (dependent variable) as a function of practice (independent variable). Most of the notation for a repeated-measures study is identical to the notation used in an independent-measures experiment. The following list reviews the notation system:

1. The letter k identifies the number of treatment conditions. For Table 14.1, $k = 3$.

2. The number of scores in each treatment is identified by the lowercase letter n. For a repeated-measures study, n is the same for all treatments because the same sample is used in all treatments. In Table 14.1, $n = 4$.

3. The total number of scores in the entire study is identified by an uppercase N. For these data, $N = 12$.

4. The sum of all the scores in the study is G. The value of G corresponds to ΣX for all N scores and specifies the grand total for the experiment. For Table 14.1, $G = 36$.

5. The sum of the scores in each treatment condition is identified by the letter T, for treatment total.

6. We also identify the sum of squares for each treatment (SS) and the sum of the squared scores (ΣX^2) for the entire study.

7. The repeated-measures design includes one new notational symbol. The total of the scores for each individual is identified by the letter P, for "person total." In Table 14.1, person A has scores of 3, 3, and 6, so the total for this person is $P = 12$. The P values are used to help measure individual differences in the analysis.

Remember, we are using T and G to help differentiate ΣX for treatments and ΣX for the entire set of scores.

FORMULAS FOR REPEATED-MEASURES ANOVA

The F-ratio for ANOVA requires two measures of sample variance: between-treatments variance and error variance. As always, sample variance is computed by

FIGURE 14.2

The partitioning of sum of squares (SS) for a repeated-measures analysis of variance.

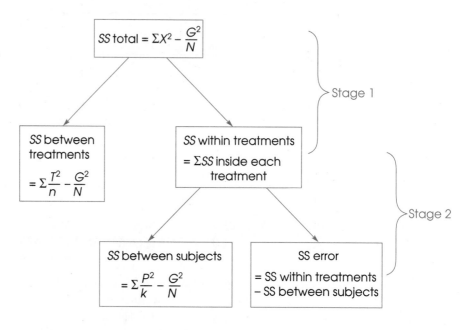

$$SS\text{ total} = \Sigma X^2 - \frac{G^2}{N}$$

Stage 1

$$SS\text{ between treatments} = \Sigma\frac{T^2}{n} - \frac{G^2}{N}$$

$$SS\text{ within treatments} = \Sigma SS\text{ inside each treatment}$$

Stage 2

$$SS\text{ between subjects} = \Sigma\frac{P^2}{k} - \frac{G^2}{N}$$

SS error = SS within treatments − SS between subjects

$$\text{sample variance} = s^2 = \frac{SS}{df}$$

To compute each of the variances (mean squares) in the F-ratio, we will need an SS value and a df value. These values are obtained by conducting a complete analysis of the sum of squares following the outline shown in Figure 14.1 and a separate analysis of degrees of freedom. These two analyses are described in detail in the following sections.

ANALYSIS OF THE SUM OF SQUARES (SS)

We will continue to use the data in Table 14.1 to demonstrate the ANOVA formulas. As shown in Figure 14.2, the repeated-measures ANOVA can be viewed as a two-stage process. The first stage of the analysis separates the total variability into two components: between treatments and within treatments. This stage of the analysis is exactly the same as the process used for an independent-measures experiment (Chapter 13).

Stage 1   The first step in the analysis of SS is to compute SS_{total}, which measures the total variability for the entire set of N scores.

$$SS_{\text{total}} = \Sigma X^2 - \frac{G^2}{N} \tag{14.3}$$

Using this formula for the data in Table 14.1, we obtain

$$SS_{\text{total}} = 140 - \frac{(36)^2}{12}$$

$$= 140 - 108 = 32$$

The next step is to partition SS_{total} into two components: between treatments and within treatments (see Figure 14.2). The $SS_{\text{between treatments}}$ measures the mean differences among the treatment conditions and is computed using the treatment totals (Ts). The formula for this SS value is

$$SS_{\text{between treatments}} = \Sigma \frac{T^2}{n} - \frac{G^2}{N} \tag{14.4}$$

For the data in Table 14.1, we obtain

$$SS_{\text{between treatments}} = \frac{8^2}{4} + \frac{10^2}{4} + \frac{18^2}{4} - \frac{36^2}{12}$$

$$= 16 + 25 + 81 - 108$$

$$= 14$$

The $SS_{\text{within treatments}}$ measures the variability inside the treatment conditions. To compute this value, we simply add the SS values from each of the separate treatment conditions.

$$SS_{\text{within treatments}} = \Sigma SS_{\text{inside each treatment}} \tag{14.5}$$

For the experiment in Table 14.1, we obtain

$$SS_{\text{within treatments}} = 2 + 5 + 11$$

$$= 18$$

To check your calculations, you should always compute all three SS values and verify that the two components add up to the total.

This completes the first stage of the analysis (see Figure 14.2). You should notice that the formulas and computations up to this point are identical to those of the independent-measures ANOVA. You also should note that the two SS components (between and within) add up to the total SS.

Stage 2   The second stage of the analysis involves partitioning the SS_{within} into two components: $SS_{\text{between subjects}}$ and SS_{error} (see Figure 14.2). As you will see, we actually compute only $SS_{\text{between subjects}}$ and then subtract this value from SS_{within}. The residual is SS_{error}.

Because the same individuals are used in every treatment in a repeated-measures study, it is possible to measure the variability due to individual differences. If you examine the data in Table 14.1, you will notice that some individuals tend to have higher scores than others. These individual differences are reflected in the P values, or person totals. To evaluate the individual differences, we compute an $SS_{\text{between subjects}}$ that measures the variability among the person totals, the P values. The formula for $SS_{\text{between subjects}}$ is

$$SS_{\text{between subjects}} = \Sigma \frac{P^2}{k} - \frac{G^2}{N} \tag{14.6}$$

Notice that the formula for $SS_{\text{between subjects}}$ is similar in structure to the formula for $SS_{\text{between treatments}}$ (see Box 14.1). The person totals (P values) are used instead of treatment totals (T values). Each P value is divided by the number of scores that were added together to obtain P or by k. Remember, each person was measured

14.1

THE RELATIONSHIP BETWEEN
$SS_{\text{BETWEEN SUBJECTS}}$ AND $SS_{\text{BETWEEN TREATMENTS}}$

THE DATA for a repeated-measures study are normally presented in a matrix, with the treatment conditions determining the columns and the subjects defining the rows. The data in Table 14.1 provide an example of this normal presentation. The calculation of $SS_{\text{between treatments}}$ is intended to provide a measure of the variability, or differences between the treatments—that is, a measure of the mean differences between *columns* in the data matrix. For the data in Table 14.1, the column totals are 8, 10, and 18. These values are variable, and $SS_{\text{between treatments}}$ measures the amount of variability.

The following table reproduces the data from Table 14.1, but now we have turned the data matrix sideways so that the subjects define the columns and the treatment conditions define the rows:

In this new form, the variability, or differences between the columns, represents the between-subject variability. The calculation of $SS_{\text{between subjects}}$ now has exactly the same structure as the original calculation of $SS_{\text{between treatments}}$. The column totals are now P values (instead of T values), and the number of scores in each column is now identified by k (instead of n); except for this change in notation, the formula for $SS_{\text{between subjects}}$ is exactly the same as the formula for $SS_{\text{between treatments}}$. For these data, person totals (column totals) are 12, 6, 6, and 12. These values are variable, and $SS_{\text{between subjects}}$ measures the amount of variability.

		PERSON			
SESSION	A	B	C	D	
1	3	2	1	2	$T = 8$
2	3	2	1	4	$T = 10$
3	6	2	4	6	$T = 18$
	$P = 12$	$P = 6$	$P = 6$	$P = 12$	

repeatedly, once for each treatment. There are k treatment conditions, and thus k scores are used to get a person total. For the example, $SS_{\text{between subjects}}$ is

$$SS_{\text{between subjects}} = \Sigma \frac{P^2}{k} - \frac{G^2}{N}$$

$$= \frac{12^2}{3} + \frac{6^2}{3} + \frac{6^2}{3} + \frac{12^2}{3} - \frac{36^2}{12}$$

$$= 48 + 12 + 12 + 48 - 108$$

$$= 120 - 108$$

$$= 12$$

The final step in the analysis is to obtain SS_{error} by subtracting $SS_{\text{between subjects}}$ from SS_{within} (see Figure 14.2).

$$SS_{\text{error}} = SS_{\text{within treatments}} - SS_{\text{between subjects}} \tag{14.7}$$

Substituting the values we have already obtained for SS_{within} and $SS_{\text{between subjects}}$ into the formula, we obtain

FIGURE 14.3

The partitioning of degrees of freedom for a repeated-measures experiment.

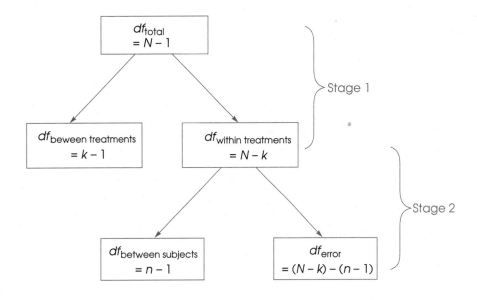

$$SS_{error} = 18 - 12$$

$$= 6$$

Subtracting the variability due to individual differences from $SS_{within\ treatments}$ is the easiest way to compute SS_{error}.

ANALYSIS OF DEGREES OF FREEDOM (*DF*)

Each of the *SS* values in analysis of variance has a corresponding degrees of freedom. In general terms, *SS* measures the variability for a set of items, such as scores, treatment totals, person totals, and so on, and the *df* value for each *SS* is determined by the number of items minus one. Thus, for a set of *n* scores, $df = n - 1$. The *df* formulas for the first stage of the repeated-measures analysis are identical to those in the independent-measures ANOVA. Figure 14.3 presents the complete analysis of degrees of freedom. You may want to refer to this figure as you read the following section on *df* formulas.

Stage 1   Remember, the total *SS* measures the variability for the entire set of *N* scores. The total *df* is computed by

$$df_{total} = N - 1 \tag{14.8}$$

For the data in Table 14.1,

$$df_{total} = 12 - 1$$

$$= 11$$

The between-treatments *SS* is based on the *k* treatment totals (*T*s), and the corresponding *df* is

$$df_{between\ treatments} = k - 1 \tag{14.9}$$

For the data in Table 14.1,

$$df_{\text{between treatments}} = 3 - 1$$
$$= 2$$

The within-treatments SS was obtained by summing the SS values for each of the treatment conditions. Each of these SS values has $df = n - 1$, and $df_{\text{within treatments}}$ is obtained by summing these df values.

$$df_{\text{within}} = \Sigma(n - 1) = N - k \tag{14.10}$$

For the data in Table 14.1,

$$df_{\text{within}} = 12 - 3$$
$$= 9$$

This completes the first stage of the analysis of degrees of freedom (see Figure 14.3). As always, you should check that the two components (between and within) add up to the total.

Stage 2 In the second stage of the analysis, the variability within treatments is partitioned into two components: between subjects and error. The between-subjects SS measures the variability among the person totals, the P values. Because the number of P values is n, the between-subjects df is given by

$$df_{\text{between subjects}} = n - 1 \tag{14.11}$$

Using the data from Table 14.1,

$$df_{\text{between subjects}} = 4 - 1$$
$$= 3$$

The final step in the analysis is to find df for the error variance. Remember, the variability due to error is not computed directly, but rather is defined as the residual that is left when you subtract between-subject variability (individual differences) from the within-treatments variability. We obtain df_{error} in exactly the same manner.

$$df_{\text{error}} = df_{\text{within}} - df_{\text{between subjects}} \tag{14.12}$$
$$= (N - k) - (n - 1)$$

For the data in Table 14.1,

$$df_{\text{error}} = 9 - 3$$
$$= 6$$

CALCULATION OF THE VARIANCES (MS) AND THE F-RATIO

The F-ratio is a ratio of two variances. These variances, called mean squares (MS), are obtained by dividing a sum of squares by degrees of freedom. The MS in the numerator of the F-ratio, in part, is influenced by the amount of treatment effect that is present. This is the between-treatments MS, and it is calculated by dividing the between-treatments SS by the between-treatments df:

$$MS_{\text{between treatments}} = \frac{SS_{\text{between treatments}}}{df_{\text{between treatments}}} \tag{14.13}$$

The error term of the F-ratio consists of MS_{error} for a repeated-measures ANOVA. This MS is computed by dividing the error SS by the error df:

$$MS_{\text{error}} = \frac{SS_{\text{error}}}{df_{\text{error}}} \tag{14.14}$$

The F-ratio, therefore, consists of

$$F = \frac{MS_{\text{between treatments}}}{MS_{\text{error}}} \tag{14.15}$$

Once again, notice that the repeated-measures F-ratio uses MS_{error} as an error term in place of MS_{within}. The new error term is used because it maintains the expected F-ratio of 1.00 if the null hypothesis is true. This is confirmed when the structure of the repeated-measures F-ratio is examined:

$$F = \frac{\text{treatment effect} + \text{experimental error}}{\text{experimental error}}$$

When H_0 is true, the treatment effect will be zero, and the expected value of the F-ratio is 1.00. Alternatively, when H_0 is false, the presence of a treatment effect in the numerator of the F-ratio should give us a large value that falls in the critical region.

For the data in Table 14.1, we obtain the following MS values:

$$MS_{\text{between treatments}} = \frac{SS_{\text{between treatments}}}{df_{\text{between treatments}}}$$

$$= \frac{14}{2}$$

$$= 7$$

$$MS_{\text{error}} = \frac{SS_{\text{error}}}{df_{\text{error}}}$$

$$= \frac{6}{6}$$

$$= 1$$

The F-ratio for the example is obtained by dividing the between-treatments MS by the error MS:

$$F = \frac{MS_{\text{between treatments}}}{MS_{\text{error}}}$$

$$= \frac{7}{1}$$

$$= 7$$

The degrees of freedom for the F-ratio are determined by the two variances that form the numerator and denominator. For the repeated-measures ANOVA, the numerator and denominator are between treatments and error, respectively. The df values for the F-ratio are reported as

$$df = df_{\text{between treatments}}, df_{\text{error}}$$

Therefore, the df values associated with the repeated-measures F-ratio in our example are

$$df = 2, 6$$

Caution! A very common mistake is to use the value of within-treatments df instead of error df. Remember, the error term for a repeated-measures ANOVA is not the same as that of an independent-measures ANOVA.

The obtained F-ratio is evaluated by the same general procedure used for the independent-measures ANOVA. The experimenter must consult the F distribution table (p. A-29) to find the critical value of F. The df values printed across the top of the table are values for the df associated with the numerator of the F-ratio (between-treatments df). The column on the left-hand side of the table contains df values associated with the denominator of the F-ratio. For a repeated-measures ANOVA, this value is the error df.

LEARNING CHECK

1. $SS_{\text{within treatments}} - SS_{\text{between subjects}} = $ _____

2. What two df components are associated with the repeated-measures F-ratio? How are they computed?

3. For the following set of data, compute all of the SS components for a repeated-measures ANOVA:

SUBJECT	TREATMENT 1	2	3	4	
A	2	2	2	2	$G = 32$
B	4	0	0	4	$\Sigma X^2 = 96$
C	2	0	2	0	
D	4	2	2	4	

4. Which two MS components are used to form the F-ratio of the repeated-measures ANOVA? How are they computed?

ANSWERS

1. SS_{error}

2. Between-treatments df and error df; $df_{\text{between treatments}} = k - 1$; $df_{\text{error}} = (N - k) - (n - 1)$

3. $SS_{\text{total}} = 32$, $SS_{\text{between treatments}} = 10$, $SS_{\text{within treatments}} = 22$, $SS_{\text{between subjects}} = 8$, $SS_{\text{error}} = 14$

4. Between-treatments MS and error MS;

$$MS_{\text{between treatments}} = \frac{SS_{\text{between treatments}}}{df_{\text{between treatments}}}$$

$$MS_{\text{error}} = \frac{SS_{\text{error}}}{df_{\text{error}}}$$

14.4 TESTING HYPOTHESES WITH THE REPEATED-MEASURES ANOVA

Let us consider a complete example of hypothesis testing with a repeated-measures study. This task will be accomplished in the four steps that should be familiar by now: (1) State the hypotheses, and set the alpha level; (2) compute *df,* and locate the critical region; (3) compute the test statistic; and (4) evaluate the hypotheses.

EXAMPLE 14.1

Software manuals:
Minitab (Section 7)
SPSS (Section 6)

A school psychologist would like to test the effectiveness of a behavior-modification technique in controlling classroom outbursts of unruly children. A teacher is instructed to use the response-cost technique. Every time a child disrupts the class, he or she is told that the behavior has cost him or her 10 minutes of free time. That is, the free-time period is shortened for each unruly act. For a sample of $n = 4$ children, the number of outbursts is measured for a day before the treatment is initiated and again one week, one month, and six months after the response-cost technique began. Note that the measurements taken after the response-cost technique is administered serve as a long-term follow-up on the effectiveness of the treatment. This underscores the usefulness of the repeated-measures design in evaluating the effectiveness of clinical treatments. The data are summarized in Table 14.2.

STEP 1 State the hypotheses, and select an alpha level. According to the null hypothesis, the response-cost technique will be ineffective in producing a change in the number of classroom disruptions. In symbols, the null hypothesis states that

$$H_0: \quad \mu_{\text{before}} = \mu_{1 \text{ week}} = \mu_{1 \text{ month}} = \mu_{6 \text{ months}}$$

TABLE 14.2

The effect of response-cost treatment on the number of outbursts in class after different periods of time

SUBJECT	BEFORE TREATMENT	ONE WEEK LATER	ONE MONTH LATER	SIX MONTHS LATER	P
A	8	2	1	1	12
B	4	1	1	0	6
C	6	2	0	2	10
D	8	3	4	1	16
	$T_1 = 26$	$T_2 = 8$	$T_3 = 6$	$T_4 = 4$	
	$SS_1 = 11$	$SS_2 = 2$	$SS_3 = 9$	$SS_4 = 2$	
	$n = 4$	$k = 4 \quad N = 16$	$G = 44$	$\Sigma X^2 = 222$	

FIGURE 14.4

The critical region in the F distribution for $\alpha = .05$ and $df = 3, 9$.

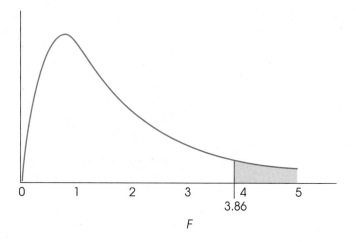

The alternative hypothesis may take on many forms. Somewhere among the four levels of the treatment there will be a difference. Because there are a number of possibilities, the alternative hypothesis states that

H_1:   At least one mean is different from the others.

For the level of significance, the experimenter selects $\alpha = .05$. In other words, the researcher is willing to take only a 5% chance of committing a Type I error.

STEP 2   Find df, and locate the critical region. For a repeated-measures study, the degrees of freedom associated with the F-ratio are between-treatments df and error df. In this example,

We have computed only those df values that are needed to evaluate the F-ratio. However, it is useful to compute all df components of ANOVA in order to check the computations (see Figure 14.3).

$$df_{\text{between treatments}} = k - 1$$
$$= 4 - 1$$
$$= 3$$
$$df_{\text{error}} = (N - k) - (n - 1)$$
$$= (16 - 4) - (4 - 1)$$
$$= 12 - 3$$
$$= 9$$

Therefore, for this F-ratio, $df = 3, 9$. Consulting the F distribution table for $\alpha = .05$, we observe that the critical region begins with $F = 3.86$. Figure 14.4 illustrates the distribution. An obtained F-ratio that exceeds this critical value justifies rejecting H_0.

STEP 3   Compute the test statistic. To compute the F-ratio, we must first calculate the values for SS, df, and MS. This analysis begins by finding the value for total SS.

$$SS_{total} = \Sigma X^2 - \frac{G^2}{N}$$

$$= 222 - \frac{44^2}{16}$$

$$= 222 - 121$$

$$= 101$$

Total variability is partitioned into between-treatments SS and within-treatments SS. For between-treatments variability, we get

$$SS_{between\ treatments} = \Sigma\frac{T^2}{n} - \frac{G^2}{N}$$

$$= \frac{26^2}{4} + \frac{8^2}{4} + \frac{6^2}{4} + \frac{4^2}{4} - \frac{44^2}{16}$$

$$= 169 + 16 + 9 + 4 - 121$$

$$= 77$$

The first stage of the partitioning of variability is completed by computing within-treatment SS:

$$SS_{within\ treatments} = \Sigma SS_{inside\ each\ treatment}$$

$$= 11 + 2 + 9 + 2$$

$$= 24$$

At this point of the analysis, the work may be checked to see if total SS equals between-treatments SS plus within-treatments SS.

In the second stage of the analysis, within-treatments SS is partitioned into between-subjects SS and error SS. This analysis is accomplished by first calculating between-subjects SS and then subtracting it from within-treatments SS. The residual will be error SS:

$$SS_{between\ subjects} = \Sigma\frac{P^2}{k} - \frac{G^2}{N}$$

$$= \frac{12^2}{4} + \frac{6^2}{4} + \frac{10^2}{4} + \frac{16^2}{4} - \frac{44^2}{16}$$

$$= 36 + 9 + 25 + 64 - 121$$

$$= 13$$

$$SS_{error} = SS_{within\ treatments} - SS_{between\ subjects}$$

$$= 24 - 13$$

$$= 11$$

Finally, we can compute the MS values and then the F-ratio. The repeated-measures F-ratio uses between-treatments MS in the numerator and error MS

TABLE 14.3

Analysis of variance summary for Example 14.1

SOURCE	SS	df	MS	F
Between treatments	77	3	25.67	21.04
Within treatments	24	12		
Between subjects	13	3		
Error	11	9	1.22	
Total	101	15		

in the denominator. These are readily obtained by dividing *SS* by the appropriate number of degrees of freedom:

$$MS_{\text{between treatments}} = \frac{SS_{\text{between treatments}}}{df_{\text{between treatments}}}$$

$$= \frac{77}{3}$$

$$= 25.67$$

$$MS_{\text{error}} = \frac{SS_{\text{error}}}{df_{\text{error}}}$$

$$= \frac{11}{9}$$

$$= 1.22$$

$$F = \frac{MS_{\text{between treatments}}}{MS_{\text{error}}}$$

$$= \frac{25.67}{1.22}$$

$$= 21.04$$

STEP 4 Evaluate the hypotheses. The obtained *F*-ratio is 21.04. This value falls in the critical region that begins at 3.86. The statistical decision is to reject the null hypothesis. The school psychologist may conclude that the response-cost technique had an effect on the number of disruptions. A report might state:

> There was a significant effect of response-cost training on the number of outbursts exhibited by the children, $F(3, 9) = 21.04$, $p < .05$.

The analysis of variance summary table is shown in Table 14.3.

IN THE LITERATURE:
REPORTING THE RESULTS OF A REPEATED-MEASURES ANOVA

As described in Chapter 13 (p. 395), the format for reporting ANOVA results in journal articles consists of

1. A summary of descriptive statistics (at least treatment means and standard deviations, and tables or graphs as needed) and

2. A concise statement of the outcome of the analysis of variance.

For the study in Example 14.1, the report could state:

The means and standard deviations for the sample of children are shown in Table 1. A repeated-measures analysis of variance revealed that the response-cost technique produced a significant decrease in classroom disruptions over the course of the study, $F(3, 9) = 21.04$, $p < .05$.

TABLE 1

Number of outbursts over course of treatment

	BEFORE TREATMENT	ONE WEEK LATER	ONE MONTH LATER	SIX MONTHS LATER
M	6.5	2.0	1.5	1.0
SD	1.91	0.82	1.73	0.82

For the descriptive statistics, the APA format use M, rather that $\overline{X}$, for the sample mean. Likewise, SD is used in place of s for the sample standard deviation. The report of the ANOVA results indicates a *significant* change. That is, the null hypothesis was rejected. Finally, the F-ratio specifies the degrees of freedom values (between-treatments $df = 3$, error $df = 9$), as well as the probability of committing a Type I error ($p < \alpha$ or $p < .05$).

POST HOC TESTS WITH REPEATED MEASURES

Recall that ANOVA provides an overall test of significance for the treatment. When the null hypothesis is rejected, it only indicates that there is a difference between at least two of the treatment means. If $k = 2$, it is obvious where the difference lies in the experiment. However, when k is greater than 2, the situation becomes more complex. To determine exactly where significant differences exist, the researcher must follow the ANOVA with post hoc tests. In Chapter 13, we used Tukey's HSD and the Scheffé test to make these multiple comparisons among treatment means. These two procedures attempt to control the overall alpha level by making adjustments for the number of potential comparisons.

For a repeated-measures ANOVA, Tukey's HSD and the Scheffé test can be used in the exact same manner as was done for the independent-measures ANOVA, *provided* that you substitute MS_{error} in place of MS_{within} in the formulas and use df_{error} in place of df_{within} when locating the critical value in a statistical table. It should be noted that statisticians are not in complete agreement about the appropriate error term in post hoc tests for repeated-measures designs (for a discussion, see Keppel, 1973, or Keppel and Zedeck, 1989).

14.5 ADVANTAGES OF THE REPEATED-MEASURES DESIGN

When we first encountered the repeated-measures design (Chapter 11), it was noted that this type of research study has certain advantages and disadvantages (pp. 324–329). On the bright side, a repeated-measures study may be desirable if the supply of subjects is limited. A repeated-measures study is economical in that the experimenter can get by using fewer subjects. However, the disadvantages may be very great. These take the form of carry-over effects or progressive error, such as fatigue, that can make the interpretation of the data very difficult.

Now that we have introduced the repeated-measures ANOVA, we can examine another advantage, namely, the elimination of the role of variability due to individual differences. Consider the structure of the F-ratio for both the independent- and the repeated-measures designs. For the independent-measures design, the F-ratio takes the following form:

$$F = \frac{\text{treatment effect} + \text{individual differences} + \text{experimental error}}{\text{individual differences} + \text{experimental error}}$$

The structure of the repeated-measures F-ratio reveals that the influence of individual differences has been eliminated altogether:

$$F = \frac{\text{treatment effect} + \text{experimental error}}{\text{experimental error}}$$

The removal of individual differences from the analysis becomes an advantage in situations where very large individual differences exist among the subjects being studied. When individual differences are extraordinarily large, the presence of a treatment effect may be masked if an independent-measures study is performed. In this case, a repeated-measures design would be more sensitive in detecting a treatment effect because individual differences do not influence the value of the F-ratio.

This point will become evident in the following example. Suppose that an experiment is performed in two ways, with an independent-measures design and a repeated-measures experiment. Also, let's suppose that we know how much variability is accounted for by the different sources of variance. For example,

$$\text{treatment effect} = 10 \text{ units of variance}$$

$$\text{individual differences} = 1000 \text{ units of variance}$$

$$\text{experimental error} = 1 \text{ unit of variance}$$

Notice that a very large amount of the variability in the experiment is due to individual differences. By comparing the F-ratios of both types of experiments, we will be able to see a fundamental difference between the two types of experimental designs. For the independent-measures experiment, we obtain

$$F = \frac{\text{treatment effect} + \text{individual differences} + \text{experimental error}}{\text{individual differences} + \text{experimental error}}$$

$$= \frac{10 + 1000 + 1}{1000 + 1}$$

$$= \frac{1011}{1001}$$

$$= 1.01$$

However, the repeated-measures F-ratio provides a different outcome:

$$F = \frac{\text{treatment effect} + \text{experimental error}}{\text{experimental error}}$$

$$= \frac{10 + 1}{1}$$

$$= \frac{11}{1}$$

$$= 11$$

All things (sources of variability) being equal, the repeated-measures F-ratio is larger. In this example, the F-ratio is much larger for the repeated-measures study because the individual differences, which are extremely large, have been removed (see Box 14.2). In the independent-measures ANOVA, the presence of a treatment effect is obscured by the influence of individual differences. This problem is remedied by the repeated-measures design in which variability due to individual differences has been partitioned out of the analysis. When the amount of individual differences is great, a repeated-measures experiment may provide a more sensitive test for a treatment effect. In statistical terms, a repeated-measures test has more *power* than an independent-measures test; that is, it is more likely to reject a false H_0.

14.6 ASSUMPTIONS OF THE REPEATED-MEASURES ANOVA

The basic assumptions for the repeated-measures ANOVA are identical to those required for the independent-measures ANOVA.

1. The observations within each treatment condition must be independent (see p. 244).
2. The population distribution within each treatment must be normal. (As before, the assumption of normality is important only with small samples.)
3. The variances of the population distributions for each treatment should be equivalent.

14.2 DATA THAT PRODUCE A LARGE MS_{ERROR}

TO GET some idea of a situation that results in a large MS_{error}, it is useful to examine hypothetical data in the form of a graph. Suppose that an experimenter examines the effect of amount of reward on maze performance in rats. A sample of $n = 4$ rats that have learned to solve a maze is subsequently tested in all four reward conditions: 2, 4, 6, and 8 grams of food reward. The experimenter measures the speed with which they solve the maze after experiencing the new amount of reward. The broken line in Figure 14.5 represents a graph of the means of each treatment. The speed of maze running seems to increase with amount of reward.

Figure 14.5 also shows a set of hypothetical data for each individual (solid lines) that would produce the treatment means (broken line). Notice that there are individual differences in these data. The subject totals (P values) differ, indicating that some subjects generally run faster than others. Also note that the individual differences are consistent from one treatment to the next. For example, in all four treatment conditions, subject 1 is fastest, and subject 2 is slowest. This means that much of the variability within treatments is due to consistent, predictable individual differences. When the individual differences are subtracted out of the analysis, the result will be a very small value for MS_{error}. Remember that a small value for MS_{error} will tend to produce a large value for the F-ratio, indicating a significant difference between treatments. The consistency in these data can be described in another way that may help you to understand the F-ratio. For the data in figure 14.5, the effect of the treatment is consistent for all subjects: Every rat shows an increase in speed when the amount of reward is increased. Because the treatment effect is very consistent, you should expect to find a significant difference between treatments.

Figure 14.6 depicts another possibility for individual subjects. Although these data will produce the same treatment means as the previous example (Figure 14.5), the treatment effect is no longer consistent across subjects. Now when the amount of reward is increased, some subjects run faster, and some run slower. Because the treatment effect is not consistent, you should not expect to find significant differences between treatments. Also note that the data in Figure 14.6 do not show consistent individual differences from one treatment to another. For example,

subject 2 is the slowest rat in the first treatment, but is the fastest in the second treatment. Because there are no consistent individual differences, most of the variability within treatments is due to experimental error. As a result, MS_{error} will be large and will tend to produce a relatively small F-ratio.

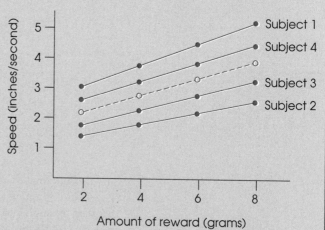

FIGURE 14.5

The effect of amount of reward on running speed. Treatment means are depicted by the broken line. Individual scores for each subject at each level of reward are shown by solid lines.

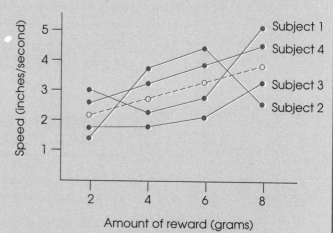

FIGURE 14.6

The effect of amount of reward on running speed. The treatment means are depicted by the broken line. Individual scores for each subject at each level of reward are shown by solid lines.

For the repeated-measures ANOVA, there is an additional assumption, called homogeneity of covariance. Basically, it refers to the requirement that the relative standing of each subject be maintained in each treatment condition. This assumption will be violated if the effect of the treatment is not consistent for all of the subjects or if carry-over effects exist for some, but not other, subjects. This issue is a very complex one and beyond the scope of this book. However, methods do exist for dealing with violations of this assumption (for a discussion, see Keppel, 1973).

LEARNING CHECK

1. It has been suggested that pupil size increases during emotional arousal. A researcher would, therefore, like to see if the increase in pupil size is a function of the type of arousal (pleasant versus aversive). A random sample of five subjects is selected for the study. Each subject views *all* three stimuli: neutral, pleasant, and aversive photographs. The neutral photograph portrays a plain brick building. The pleasant photograph consists of a young man and woman sharing a large ice cream cone. Finally, the aversive stimulus is a graphic photograph of an automobile accident. Upon viewing each stimulus, the pupil size is measured (in millimeters) with sophisticated equipment. The data are as follows. Perform an ANOVA, and state a conclusion about the findings.

	STIMULUS		
SUBJECT	NEUTRAL	PLEASANT	AVERSIVE
A	4	8	3
B	3	6	3
C	2	5	2
D	3	3	6
E	3	8	1

ANSWER

SOURCE	SS	df	MS	F
Between treatments	30	2	15	4.29
Within treatments	34	12		
Between subjects	6	4		
Error	28	8	3.5	
Total	64	14		

$F(2, 8) = 4.29$. For an alpha level of .05, the obtained F-ratio fails to reach statistical significance. The null hypothesis cannot be rejected. There is not sufficient evidence for an effect of stimulus type on pupil size.

SUMMARY

1. ANOVA for a repeated-measures design initially partitions total variability into between-treatments SS and within-treatments SS.

2. Between-treatments SS is influenced by the treatment effect and experimental error. Individual differences do not play a role in this source of variability because the same sample of subjects serves in all treatments.

3. Within-treatments SS is affected by individual differences and experimental error.

4. The structure of the repeated-measures F is

$$F = \frac{\text{treatment effect} + \text{experimental error}}{\text{experimental error}}$$

5. To obtain the error term for the F-ratio, within-treatment SS is partitioned into between-subjects SS and error SS.

6. Degrees of freedom are partitioned in a similar fashion. That is, there is a df value for each SS value in the analysis.

7. The estimated variances, or MS values, are computed by dividing each SS used in the F-ratio by the appropriate df value. For the repeated-measures ANOVA,

$$MS_{\text{between treatments}} = \frac{SS_{\text{between treatments}}}{df_{\text{between treatments}}}$$

$$MS_{\text{error}} = \frac{SS_{\text{error}}}{df_{\text{error}}}$$

8. The F-ratio for the repeated-measures ANOVA is computed by

$$F = \frac{MS_{\text{between treatments}}}{MS_{\text{error}}}$$

9. When the obtained F-ratio is significant (that is, H_0 is rejected), it indicates that a significant difference lies between at least two of the treatment conditions. To determine exactly where the difference lies, post hoc comparisons may be made. Post hoc tests, such as Tukey's HSD, use MS_{error} rather than $MS_{\text{within treatments}}$ and df_{error} instead of $df_{\text{within treatments}}$.

10. A repeated-measures ANOVA eliminates the influence of individual differences from the analysis. If individual differences are extremely large, a treatment effect might be masked in an independent-measures experiment. In this case, a repeated-measures design might be a more sensitive test for a treatment effect.

KEY TERMS

between-treatments variability

within-treatments variability

between-subjects variability

error variability

treatment effect

individual differences

experimental error

mean squares

F-ratio

——— FOCUS ON PROBLEM SOLVING ———

1. Before you begin a repeated-measures ANOVA, complete all the preliminary calculations needed for the ANOVA formulas. This requires that you find the total for each treatment (Ts), the total for each person (Ps), the grand total (G), the SS for each treatment condition, and ΣX^2 for the entire set of N scores. As a partial check on these calculations, be sure that the T values add up to G and that the P values have a sum of G.

2. To help remember the structure of repeated-measures ANOVA, keep in mind that a repeated-measures experiment eliminates the contribution of individual differences. There are no individual differences contributing to the numerator of the F-ratio ($MS_{\text{between treatments}}$) because the same individuals are used for all treatments. Therefore, you must also eliminate individual differences in the denominator. This is accomplished by partitioning within-treatments variability into two components: between-subjects variability and error variability. It is the MS value for error variability that is used in the denominator of the F-ratio.

3. As with any ANOVA, it helps to organize your work so you do not get lost. Compute the SS values first, followed by the df values. You can then calculate the MS

values and the F-ratio. Filling in the columns on an ANOVA summary table (for example, p. 434) as you do the computations will help guide your way through the problem.

4. Be careful when using df values to find the critical F value. Remember, df_{error} (*not* df_{within}) is used for the denominator.

DEMONSTRATION 14.1

REPEATED-MEASURES ANOVA

The following data were obtained from an experiment examining the effect of sleep deprivation on motor-skills performance. A sample of five subjects was tested on a motor-skills task after 24 hours of sleep deprivation, tested again after 36 hours, and tested once more after 48 hours. The dependent variable is the number of errors made on the motor skills task.

SUBJECT	24 HOURS	36 HOURS	48 HOURS
A	0	0	6
B	1	3	5
C	0	1	5
D	4	5	9
E	0	1	5

Do these data indicate that the number of hours of sleep deprivation has a significant effect on motor skill performance?

STEP 1 *State the hypotheses, and specify alpha.* The null hypothesis states that there are no differences among the three deprivation conditions. In symbols,

$$H_0: \quad \mu_1 = \mu_2 = \mu_3$$

The general form of the alternative hypothesis states that there are differences among the conditions.

$$H_1: \quad \text{At least one of the treatment means is different.}$$

We will set alpha at $\alpha = .05$.

STEP 2 *Locate the critical region.* To locate the critical region, we must obtain the df values for the F-ratio, specifically, $df_{between\ treatments}$ for the numerator and df_{error} for the denominator. (Often it is easier to postpone this step until the analysis of the df values in step 3.)

$$df_{between\ treatments} = k - 1 = 3 - 1 = 2$$

$$df_{error} = (N - k) - (n - 1)$$
$$= (15 - 3) - (5 - 1)$$
$$= 12 - 4$$
$$= 8$$

Thus, the final F-ratio will have $df = 2, 8$. With $\alpha = .05$, the critical value for the F-ratio is $F = 4.46$. The obtained F-ratio must exceed this critical value to reject H_0.

S T E P 3 *Perform the analysis.* The complete repeated-measures ANOVA can be divided into a series of stages:

1. Compute the summary statistics for the data. This involves calculating T and SS for each treatment condition, obtaining G and ΣX^2 for the entire set of scores, and finding the P totals for each person.
2. Perform the first stage of the analysis: Separate the total variability (SS and df) into the between- and within-treatment components.
3. Perform the second stage of the analysis: Separate the within-treatment variability (SS and df) into the between-subjects and error components.
4. Calculate the mean squares for the F-ratio.
5. Calculate the F-ratio.

Compute summary statistics. We will use the computational formula to obtain SS for each treatment condition. These calculations will also provide numerical values for the treatment totals (T), G, and ΣX^2.

24 HOURS		36 HOURS		48 HOURS	
X	X^2	X	X^2	X	X^2
0	0	0	0	6	36
1	1	3	9	5	25
0	0	1	1	5	25
4	16	5	25	9	81
0	0	1	1	5	25
$\Sigma X = 5$	$\Sigma X^2 = 17$	$\Sigma X = 10$	$\Sigma X^2 = 36$	$\Sigma X = 30$	$\Sigma X^2 = 192$

For the 24-hour condition,

$$T = \Sigma X = 5$$

$$SS = \Sigma X^2 - \frac{(\Sigma X)^2}{n} = 17 - \frac{5^2}{5} = 17 - 5 = 12$$

For the 36-hour condition,

$$T = \Sigma X = 10$$

$$SS = \Sigma X^2 - \frac{(\Sigma X)^2}{n} = 36 - \frac{10^2}{5} = 36 - 20 = 16$$

For the 48-hour condition,

$$T = \Sigma X = 30$$

$$SS = \Sigma X^2 - \frac{(\Sigma X)^2}{n} = 192 - \frac{30^2}{5} = 192 - 180 = 12$$

The grand total is obtained by summing the three treatment totals.

$$G = \Sigma T = 5 + 10 + 30 = 45$$

The value of ΣX^2 for the entire set of scores is obtained by summing the ΣX^2 values from each of the treatment conditions.

$$\Sigma X^2 = 17 + 36 + 192 = 245$$

The person totals, P values, are obtained by summing the three scores for each individual.

$$P_1 = 0 + 0 + 6 = 6$$

$$P_2 = 1 + 3 + 5 = 9$$

$$P_3 = 0 + 1 + 5 = 6$$

$$P_4 = 4 + 5 + 9 = 18$$

$$P_5 = 0 + 1 + 5 = 6$$

Stage 1 of the analysis. We begin by analyzing SS:

$$SS_{\text{total}} = \Sigma X^2 - \frac{G^2}{N} = 245 - \frac{45^2}{15} = 245 - 135 = 110$$

$$SS_{\text{between}} = \Sigma \frac{T^2}{n} - \frac{G^2}{N} = \frac{5^2}{5} + \frac{10^2}{5} + \frac{30^2}{5} - \frac{45^2}{15}$$

$$= 5 + 20 + 180 - 135$$

$$= 205 - 135$$

$$= 70$$

$$SS_{\text{within}} = \Sigma SS_{\text{each treatment}} = 12 + 16 + 12 = 40$$

For this stage, the *df* values are

$$df_{\text{total}} = N - 1 = 15 - 1 = 14$$

$$df_{\text{between}} = k - 1 = 3 - 1 = 2$$

$$df_{\text{within}} = N - k = 15 - 3 = 12$$

Stage 2 of the analysis. We begin by analyzing SS_{within}:

$$SS_{\text{between subjects}} = \Sigma \frac{P^2}{k} - \frac{G^2}{N}$$

$$= \frac{6^2}{3} + \frac{9^2}{3} + \frac{6^2}{3} + \frac{18^2}{3} + \frac{6^2}{3} - \frac{45^2}{15}$$

$$= 171 - 135$$

$$= 36$$

$$SS_{\text{error}} = SS_{\text{within}} - SS_{\text{between subjects}}$$

$$= 40 - 36$$

$$= 4$$

For stage 2, the *df* values are

$$df_{\text{between subjects}} = n - 1 = 5 - 1 = 4$$

$$df_{\text{error}} = (N - k) - (n - 1)$$

$$= 12 - 4 = 8$$

Calculate the two MS values.

$$MS_{\text{between}} = \frac{SS_{\text{between}}}{df_{\text{between}}} = \frac{70}{2} = 35$$

$$MS_{\text{error}} = \frac{SS_{\text{error}}}{df_{\text{error}}} = \frac{4}{8} = 0.50$$

Calculate the F-ratio.

$$F = \frac{MS_{\text{between}}}{MS_{\text{error}}} = \frac{35}{0.50} = 70.00$$

STEP 4 *Make a decision about H_0, and state a conclusion.* The obtained *F*-ratio, $F = 70.00$, exceeds the critical value of 4.46. Therefore, we reject the null hypothesis. We conclude that the number of hours of sleep deprivation has a significant effect on the number of errors committed, $F(2, 8) = 70.00$, $p < .05$. The following table summarizes the results of the analysis:

SOURCE	SS	df	MS	
Between treatments	70	2	35	$F = 70.00$
Within treatments	40	12		
Between subjects	36	4		
Error	4	8	0.50	
Total	110	14		

PROBLEMS

1. What advantages does a repeated-measures design have over an independent-measures design?

2. How does the error term differ for repeated-versus independent-measures ANOVA?

3. The following data represent idealized results from an experiment comparing two treatments. Notice that the mean for treatment II is four points higher than the mean for treatment I. Also notice that this four-point treatment effect is perfectly consistent for all subjects.

PERSON	TREATMENTS	
	I	II
A	1	5
B	4	8
C	7	11
D	4	8
E	6	10
F	2	6
	$T = 24$	$T = 48$
	$\bar{X} = 4$	$\bar{X} = 8$

a. Calculate the within-treatments SS for these data.

b. Calculate the between-subjects SS for these data. You should find that all of the within-treatments variability is accounted for by variability between subjects; that is, $SS_{within} = SS_{between\ subjects}$. For these data, the treatment effect is perfectly consistent across subjects, and there is no error variability ($SS_{error} = 0$).

4. A researcher reports an F-ratio with $df = 3, 36$ for a repeated-measures ANOVA.

   a. How many treatment conditions were evaluated in this experiment?

   b. How many subjects participated in this experiment?

5. A researcher conducts a repeated-measures experiment using a sample of $n = 12$ subjects to evaluate the differences among three treatment conditions. If the results are examined with an ANOVA, what would be the df values for the F-ratio?

6. A psychologist studies the effect of practice on maze learning for rats. Rats are tested in the maze in one daily session for four days. The psychologist records the number of errors made in each daily session. The data are as follows:

RAT	SESSION			
	1	2	3	4
1	3	1	0	0
2	3	2	2	1
3	6	3	1	2

Is there evidence for a practice effect? use the .05 level of significance.

7. One of the main advantages of a repeated-measures design is that the variability caused by individual differences is removed before the test statistic is computed. To demonstrate this fact, we have taken the data from Problem 6 and exaggerated the individual differences by adding six points to each of the scores for rat 3. As the following data show, this rat now has scores substantially different from those of the other two rats.

   a. How will increasing the individual differences affect the between-treatments variance? Compare the mean differences for these data versus the data in Problem 6. Compare the $MS_{between}$ for these data with the corresponding value from Problem 6.

   b. How will the increased individual differences affect the error term for the F-ratio? Calculate MS_{error} for these data, and compare the result with MS_{error} from Problem 6.

c. Compute the F-ratio for the following data, and compare the result with the F-ratio from Problem 6. What happened to the individual differences that were added to the data?

RAT	SESSION			
	1	2	3	4
1	3	1	0	0
2	3	2	2	1
3	12	9	7	8

8. The following data were obtained to compare three experimental treatments:

TREATMENTS		
1	2	3
2	4	6
5	5	5
1	2	3
0	1	2

   a. If these data were obtained from an *independent-measures design,* then could you conclude that there is a significant difference among the treatment conditions? Test with alpha set at .05.

   b. If these data were obtained from a *repeated-measures design* so that each row of scores represents data from a single subject, then could you conclude that there is a significant difference among the treatments? Test at the .05 level of significance.

   c. Explain the difference in the results of part a and part b.

9. The following data are from an experiment comparing three different treatment conditions:

A	B	C
0	1	2
2	5	5
1	2	6
5	4	9
2	8	8

   a. If the experiment uses an *independent-measures design,* then can the researcher conclude that the treatments are significantly different? Test at the .05 level of significance.

b. If the experiment were done with a *repeated-measures design,* should the researcher conclude that the treatments are significantly different? Set alpha at .05 again.

c. Explain why the results are different in the analyses of parts a and b.

10. It has been demonstrated that when subjects must memorize a list of words serially (in the order of presentation), words at the beginning and end of the list are remembered better than words in the middle. This observation has been called the *serial-position effect.* The following data represent the number of errors made in recall of the first eight, second eight, and last eight words in the list:

| | SERIAL POSITION | | |
PERSON	FIRST	MIDDLE	LAST
A	1	5	0
B	3	7	2
C	5	6	1
D	3	2	1

a. Compute the mean number of errors for each position, and draw a graph of the data.

b. Is there evidence for a significant effect of serial position? Test at the .05 level of significance. Based on the ANOVA, explain the results of the study.

11. A psychologist is asked by a dog food manufacturer to determine if animals will show a preference among three new food mixes recently developed. The psychologist takes a sample of $n = 6$ dogs. They are deprived of food overnight and presented simultaneously with three bowls of the mixes on the next morning. After 10 minutes, the bowls are removed, and the amount of food (in ounces) consumed is determined for each type of mix. The data are as follows:

| | MIX | | |
SUBJECT	1	2	3
1	3	2	1
2	0	5	1
3	2	7	3
4	1	6	5
5	1	2	3
6	3	0	3

Is there evidence for a significant preference? Test at the .05 level of significance.

12. A repeated-measures experiment comparing only two treatments can be evaluated with either a *t* statistic or an ANOVA. As we found with the independent-measures design, the *t* test and the ANOVA will produce equivalent conclusions, and the two test statistics are related by the equation $F = t^2$.

The following data are from a repeated-measures study:

SUBJECT	TREATMENT 1	TREATMENT 2	DIFFERENCE
1	2	4	+2
2	1	3	+2
3	0	10	+10
4	1	3	+2

a. Use a repeated-measures *t* statistic with $\alpha = .05$ to determine whether or not the data provide evidence of a significant difference between the two treatments.

b. Use a repeated-measures ANOVA with $\alpha = .05$ to evaluate the data. (You should find $F = t^2$.) (*Caution:* ANOVA calculations are done with the X values, but for *t* you use the difference scores.)

13. A researcher reports an *F*-ratio with $df = 2, 40$ from a repeated-measures experiment.

a. How many treatment conditions were compared in this experiment?

b. How many subjects participated in the experiment?

14. A researcher used an analysis of variance to evaluate the results from a single-factor repeated-measures experiment. The reported *F*-ratio was $F(2, 28) = 6.35$.

a. How many different treatments were compared in this experiment?

b. How many subjects participated in the experiment?

15. To determine the long-term effectiveness of relaxation training on anxiety, a researcher uses a repeated-measures study. A random sample of $n = 10$ subjects is first tested for the severity of anxiety with a standardized test. In addition to this pretest, subjects are tested again one week, one month, six months, and one year after treatment. The investigator used ANOVA to evaluate these data, and portions of the results are presented in the following summary table. Fill in the missing values. (*Hint:* Start with the *df* values.)

SOURCE	SS	df	MS	
Between treatments	——	——	——	F = 5
Within treatments	500	——		
Between subjects	——	——		
Error	——	——	10	
Total	——	——		

16. A teacher studies the effectiveness of a reading skills course on comprehension. A sample of $n = 15$ students is studied. The instructor assesses their comprehension with a standardized reading test. The test is administered at the beginning of the course, at midterm, and at the end of the course. The instructor uses analysis of variance to determine whether or not a significant change has occurred in the students' reading performance. The following summary table presents a portion of the ANOVA results. Provide the missing values in the table. (Start with the df values.)

SOURCE	SS	df	MS	
Between treatments	——	——	24	F = 8
Within treatments	120	——		
Between subjects	——	——		
Error	——	——	——	
Total	——	——		

17. The following summary table presents the results of an ANOVA from a repeated-measures experiment comparing four treatment conditions with a sample of $n = 10$ subjects. Fill in all missing values in the table.

SOURCE	SS	df	MS	
Between treatments	——	——	20	F = ——
Within treatments	——	——		
Between subjects	36	——		
Error	——	——	——	
Total	150	——		

18. A manufacturer of business machines would like to compare the four most popular brands of electric typewriters. A sample of eight typists is selected, and each typist spends 15 minutes testing each of the four typewriters and then rates its performance. The manufacturer would like to know if there are any significant differences among the four brands. The data from this study were

examined using an analysis of variance. The results are shown in the following summary table. Fill in all missing values.

SOURCE	SS	df	MS	
Between treatments	270	——	——	F = 9
Within treatments	——	——		
Between subjects	——	——		
Error	——	——	——	
Total	680	——		

19. An educational psychologist is studying student motivation in elementary school. A sample of $n = 5$ students is followed over three years from fourth grade to sixth grade. Each year the students complete a questionnaire measuring their motivation and enthusiasm for school. The psychologist would like to know whether there are significant changes in motivation across the three grade levels. The data from this study are as follows:

STUDENT	FOURTH GRADE	FIFTH GRADE	SIXTH GRADE
A	4	3	1
B	8	6	4
C	5	3	3
D	7	4	2
E	6	4	0

a. Compute the mean motivation score for each grade level.
b. Use an ANOVA to determine whether there are any significant differences in motivation among the three grade levels. Use the .05 level of significance.

20. The following data represent a second sample of $n = 5$ students from the motivation study described in Problem 19.

STUDENT	FOURTH GRADE	FIFTH GRADE	SIXTH GRADE
A	10	0	4
B	0	10	0
C	4	6	0
D	14	0	6
E	2	4	0

a. Compute the mean motivation score for each grade level.

b. Use an ANOVA to determine whether there are any significant differences in motivation among the three grade levels. Use the .05 level of significance.

c. You should find that the means for these data are identical to the means obtained in Problem 19. How do you explain the fact that the two ANOVAs produce different results?

21. A habituation task is often used to test memory for infants. In the habituation procedure, a stimulus is shown to the infant for a brief period, and the researcher records how much time the infant spends looking at the stimulus. This same process is repeated again and again. If the infant begins to lose interest in the stimulus (decreases the time looking at it), the researcher can conclude that the infant "remembers" the earlier presentations and is demonstrating habituation to an old familiar stimulus. Hypothetical data from a habituation experiment are as follows:

| | AMOUNT OF TIME (IN SEC.) ATTENTING TO THE STIMULUS | | |
INFANT	FIRST PRESENTATION	SECOND PRESENTATION	THIRD PRESENTATION
A	112	81	20
B	97	35	42
C	82	58	27
D	104	70	39
E	78	51	46

Do these data indicate a significant change in the amount of time looking at the stimulus for successive presentations? Test with $\alpha = .01$.

22. When a stimulus is presented continuously and it does not vary in intensity, the individual will eventually perceive the stimulus as less intense or not perceive it at all. This phenomenon is known as sensory adaptation. Years ago, Zigler (1932) studied adaptation for skin (cutaneous) sensation by placing a small weight on part of the body and measuring how much time lapsed until subjects reported they felt nothing at all. Suppose that a researcher does a similar study, comparing adaptation for four regions of the body for a sample of $n = 7$ subjects. A 500-milligram weight is gently placed on the region, and the latency (in seconds) for a report that it is no longer felt is recorded for each subject. The data are as follows:

| | AREA OF STIMULATION | | | |
SUBJECT	BACK OF HAND	LOWER BACK	MIDDLE OF PALM	CHIN BELOW LOWER LIP
1	6.5	4.6	10.2	12.1
2	5.8	3.5	9.7	11.8
3	6.0	4.2	9.9	11.5
4	6.7	4.7	8.1	10.7
5	5.2	3.6	7.9	9.9
6	4.3	3.5	9.0	11.3
7	7.4	4.8	10.8	12.6

Does the area of stimulation have a significant effect on the latency of adaptation? Set the alpha level to .01.

23. A researcher is examining the effect of sleep deprivation on basic mental processes. A sample of eight subjects is obtained. These subjects agree to stay awake for a total of 48 hours. Every 12 hours the researcher gives each subject a series of arithmetic problems as a test of mental alertness. The number of problems worked correctly in 10 minutes is recorded for each subject. The data are as follows:

| | HOURS AWAKE | | | |
SUBJECT	12	24	36	48
1	8	7	8	6
2	10	12	9	11
3	9	9	8	10
4	7	8	6	6
5	12	10	10	8
6	10	9	12	8
7	7	7	6	8
8	9	10	11	11

On the basis of these data, can the researcher conclude that sleep deprivation has a significant effect on basic mental processing? Test with $\alpha = .05$.

CHAPTER 15

TWO-FACTOR ANALYSIS OF VARIANCE (INDEPENDENT MEASURES)

TOOLS YOU WILL NEED

The following items are considered essential background material for this chapter. If you doubt your knowledge of any of these items, you should review the appropriate chapter or section before proceeding.

- Introduction to analysis of variance (Chapter 13)
- The logic of analysis of variance
- ANOVA notation and formulas
- Distribution of F-ratios

CONTENTS

PREVIEW

Imagine that you are seated at your desk, ready to take the final exam in statistics. Just before the exams are handed out, a television crew appears and sets up a camera and lights aimed directly at you. They explain that they are filming students during exams for a television special. You are told to ignore the camera and go ahead with your exam.

Would the presence of a TV camera affect your performance on an exam? For some of you, the answer to this question is "definitely yes" and for others, "probably not." In fact, both answers are right; whether or not the TV camera affects performance depends on your personality. Some of you would become terribly distressed and self-conscious, while others really could ignore the camera and go on as if everything were normal.

In an experiment that duplicates the situation we have described, Shrauger (1972) tested subjects on a concept formation task. Half the subjects worked alone (no audience), and half the subjects worked with an audience of people who claimed to be interested in observing the experiment. Shrauger also divided the subjects into two groups on the basis of personality: those high in self-esteem and those low in self-esteem. The dependent variable for this experiment was the number of errors on the concept formation task. Data similar to those obtained by Shrauger are shown in Figure 15.1 Notice that the audience had no effect on the high-self-esteem subjects. However, the low-self-esteem subjects made nearly twice as many errors with an audience as when working alone.

We have presented Shrauger's study as an introduction to research studies that have two independent variables. In this study, the independent variables are

1. Audience (present or absent)
2. Self-esteem (high or low)

The results of this study indicate that the effect of one variable (audience) *depends on* another variable (self-esteem).

You should realize that it is quite common to have experimental variables that interact in this way. For example, a par-

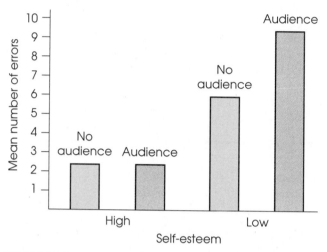

FIGURE 15.1

Results of an experiment examining the effect of an audience on the number of errors made on a concept formation task for subjects who are rated either high or low in self-esteem. Notice that the effect of the audience depends on the self-esteem of the subjects.

Shrauger, J.S. (1972). Self-esteem and reactions to being observed by others. *Journal of Personality and Social Psychology, 23,* 192-200. Copyright (1972) by the American Psychological Association. Adapted by permission of the author.

ticular drug may have a profound effect on some patients and have no effect whatsoever on others. Some children develop normally in a single-parent home, while others show serious difficulties. In general, the effects of a particular treatment often depend on other factors. To determine whether two variables are interdependent, it is necessary to examine both variables together in a single study. In this chapter, we will introduce the experimental techniques that are used for studies with two independent variables.

15.1   OVERVIEW

In the preceding two chapters, we examined analysis of variance for research designs using a single independent variable. In this chapter, we consider research situations involving two independent variables—that is, two-factor experiments.

FIGURE 15.2

The structure of a two-factor experiment presented as a matrix. The factors are teaching program and class size. There are two levels for the program factor (program I and program II), and there are three levels for the class-size factor (18 students, 24 students, and 30 students).

	FACTOR B (CLASS SIZE)		
	18-STUDENT CLASS	24-STUDENT CLASS	30-STUDENT CLASS
FACTOR A (program) Program I	Scores for $n = 15$ subjects taught by program I in a class of 18	Scores for $n = 15$ subjects taught by program I in a class of 24	Scores for $n = 15$ subjects taught by program I in a class of 30
Program II	Scores for $n = 15$ subjects taught by program II in a class of 18	Scores for $n = 15$ subjects taught by program II in a class of 24	Scores for $n = 15$ subjects taught by program II in a class of 30

An example of a two-factor design is shown in Figure 15.2. This experiment compares two different programs for teaching third-grade mathematics and three different class sizes. Thus, the independent variables are teaching program and class size. The dependent variable is the mathematics achievement test score obtained for each child at the end of the school year. You should recall that the different values for each factor are called the *levels* of the factor. For this example, the program factor has two levels (program I and program II), and the class-size factor has three levels (18 students, 24 students, and 30 students). An experiment with this structure is often called a *two-by-three factorial design.*

Notice that the structure of a two-factor design can be represented by a matrix listing the values of one factor across the top and the values of the second factor down the left-hand side. Each box, or *cell,* in the matrix represents a specific treatment condition. For example, the lower left-hand cell in Figure 15.2 contains scores for those students who were taught by program II in a class containing 18 students. For the research design in Figure 15.2, there are $2 \times 3 = 6$ different treatment conditions. You should also notice that each of the six treatments has its own *separate sample.* Hence, this study is an *independent-measures design.* In this chapter, we will examine only independent-measures designs, that is, two-factor research studies that use a separate sample for each of the different treatment conditions. In addition, we only look at situations where the sample size is the same for all treatments; that is, studies where we have equal *n*s.

The two-factor analysis of variance will allow the researcher to test for mean differences in this experiment. Specifically, the ANOVA will test for

1. Mean difference between the two teaching programs

2. Mean differences between the three class sizes

3. Any other mean differences that may result from unique combinations of a specific teaching program and a specific class size (For example, program I may be especially effective with a small class of only 18 students.)

Thus, the two-factor ANOVA combines three separate hypothesis tests in one analysis. Each of these three tests will be based on its own *F*-ratio computed from the data. The three *F*-ratios will all have the same basic structure.

$$F = \frac{\text{variance (differences) between sample means}}{\text{variance (differences) expected from sampling error}}$$

TABLE 15.1

These are hypothetical data from an experiment examining two different teaching programs (factor A) and three different class sizes (factor B). Assume that the same number of students were selected for testing from each cell.

	18-STUDENT CLASS	24-STUDENT CLASS	30-STUDENT CLASS	
PROGRAM I	$\overline{X} = 85$	$\overline{X} = 80$	$\overline{X} = 75$	$\overline{X} = 80$
PROGRAM II	$\overline{X} = 75$	$\overline{X} = 70$	$\overline{X} = 65$	$\overline{X} = 70$
	$\overline{X} = 80$	$\overline{X} = 75$	$\overline{X} = 70$	

As always in ANOVA, a large value for the F-ratio indicates that the sample mean differences are greater than chance. To determine whether the obtained F-ratios are *significantly* greater than chance, we will need to compare each F-ratio with the critical values found in the F distribution table in Appendix B.

15.2 MAIN EFFECTS AND INTERACTIONS

As noted in the previous section, a two-factor ANOVA actually involves three distinct hypothesis tests. In this section, we will examine these three tests in more detail.

Traditionally, the two independent variables in a two-factor study are identified as *factor A* and *factor B*. For the experiment presented in Figure 15.2, teaching program would be factor A, and class size would be factor B. The goal of the experiment is to evaluate the mean differences that may be produced by either of these factors independently or by the two factors acting together.

MAIN EFFECTS One purpose of the experiment is to determine whether differences in teaching program (factor A) result in differences in student performance. To answer this question, we will compare the mean score for all students taught in program I versus the mean score for students taught in program II. Notice that this process evaluates mean differences between the rows in Figure 15.2.

To make this process more concrete, we have presented a set of hypothetical data in Table 15.1. This table shows the mean score for each of the treatment conditions (cells) as well as the mean for each column (each class size) and for each row (teaching program). These data indicate that the students in program I obtained an overall mean score of $\overline{X} = 80$. This mean was computed by averaging the three means for the three groups of students in program I. In contrast, program II resulted in an overall mean of $\overline{X} = 70$. The difference between these means constitutes what is called the *main effect* for programs, or the *main effect for factor A*.

Assume that the same number (n) of students are actually tested from each class, making sample size equal for all cells. (For example, $n = 15$ students per class are tested.)

Similarly, the main effect for factor B (class size) is defined by the mean differences between columns of the matrix. For the data in Table 15.1, students taught in a class of 18 obtained an average test score of $\overline{X} = 80$. Students in a class of 24 averaged only $\overline{X} = 75$, and students in a class of 30 achieved a mean score of $\overline{X} = 70$. The differences among these means constitute the *main effect* for class size, or the *main effect for factor B*.

DEFINITION The mean differences among the levels of one factor are referred to as the *main effect* of that factor. If the design of the research study is represented as a matrix with one factor determining the rows and the second factor determining the columns, then the mean differences among the rows would describe the main effect of one factor, and the mean differences among the columns would describe the main effect for the second factor.

You should realize that the mean differences between columns or rows simply *describe* the main effects for a two-factor study. As we have observed in earlier chapters, the existence of sample mean differences does not necessarily imply that the differences are *statistically significant*. In the case of a two-factor study, any main effects that are observed in the data must be evaluated with a hypothesis test to determine whether or not they are statistically significant effects. Unless the hypothesis test demonstrates that the main effects are significant, you must conclude that the observed mean differences are simply the result of sampling error.

The evaluation of main effects will make up two or the three hypothesis tests contained in a two-factor ANOVA. We will state hypotheses concerning the main effect of factor A and the main effect of factor B and then calculate two separate F-ratios to evaluate the hypotheses.

For the example we are considering, factor A involves the comparison of two different teaching programs. The null hypothesis would state that there is no difference between the two programs—that is, teaching program has no effect on test performance. In symbols,

$$H_0: \mu_{A1} = \mu_{A2}$$

The alternative hypothesis is that the two programs do produce different test scores:

$$H_1: \mu_{A1} \neq \mu_{A2}$$

To evaluate these hypotheses, we will compute an F-ratio that compares the actual mean difference between the two programs versus the amount of difference that would be expected by chance (sampling error).

$$F = \frac{\text{variance (differences) between the means for factor } A}{\text{variance (differences) expected from sampling error}}$$

$$= \frac{\text{variance (differences) between row means}}{\text{variance (differences) expected by sampling error}}$$

Similarly, factor B involves the comparison of three different class sizes. The null hypothesis states that, overall, there are no differences among the three class sizes. In symbols,

$$H_0: \mu_{B1} = \mu_{B2} = \mu_{B3}$$

As always, the alternative hypothesis states that there are differences:

$$H_1: \quad \text{At least one mean is different from the others.}$$

Again, the F-ratio will compare the obtained mean differences among the three class sizes versus the difference that would be expected by chance.

TABLE 15.2

Hypothetical data from an experiment examining two different teaching programs (factor A) and three different class sizes (factor B) (These data show the same main effects as the data in Table 15.1, but the individual treatment means have been modified to produce an interaction. Assume that an equal number of students are tested in each cell.)

	18-STUDENT CLASS	24-STUDENT CLASS	30-STUDENT CLASS	
PROGRAM I	$\overline{X} = 80$	$\overline{X} = 80$	$\overline{X} = 80$	$\overline{X} = 80$
PROGRAM II	$\overline{X} = 80$	$\overline{X} = 70$	$\overline{X} = 60$	$\overline{X} = 70$
	$\overline{X} = 80$	$\overline{X} = 75$	$\overline{X} = 70$	

$$F = \frac{\text{variance (differences) between the means for factor } B}{\text{variance (differences) expected from sampling error}}$$

$$= \frac{\text{variance (differences) between column means}}{\text{variance (differences) expected by sampling error}}$$

INTERACTIONS

In addition to evaluating the main effects for each of the two independent variables, the two-factor ANOVA allows you to evaluate other mean differences that may result from unique combinations of the two factors. For example, it is possible for the effects of a treatment to depend on the specific circumstances under which it is administered. Or it is possible that a treatment affects one group differently than it does another. When the effects of one treatment (factor) depend on a second treatment (factor), you have an *interaction*.

DEFINITION

There is an *interaction* between two factors if the effect of one factor depends on the levels of the second factor. When the two factors are identified as A and B, the interaction is identified as the $A \times B$ interaction.

To make the concept of an interaction more concrete, we will reexamine the data shown in Table 15.1. For these data, there is no interaction. Specifically, the effect of the program variable (factor A) does not depend on class size (factor B). Overall, these data show a 10-point difference between the two programs, $\overline{X} = 80$ versus $\overline{X} = 70$. This 10-point difference is the main effect for program. Notice that this 10-point effect is *constant* for each of the three class sizes. That is, within each column of the matrix, you find exactly the same 10-point difference between the two programs. Thus, the program effect does not depend on class size, and there is no interaction.

Now consider the data shown in Table 15.2. These new data show exactly the same main effects that existed in Table 15.1 (the column means and the row means have not been changed). But now there is an interaction between the two factors. Specifically, the 10-point main effect for the program ($\overline{X} = 80$ versus $\overline{X} = 70$) is *not constant* across the three class sizes: For classes of 18 students, there is zero difference between programs; with 24 students, there is a 10-point difference; and for classes of 30 students, the program difference is 20 points. For these data, the effect of factor A (program difference) does depend on class size (the levels of factor B), so there is an interaction.

Graphing results from a two-factor experiment is discussed in Box 15.1.

Finally, consider the two graphs shown in Figure 15.3. The graph in Figure 15.3(a) shows the data from Table 15.1 (no interaction), and the graph in Figure

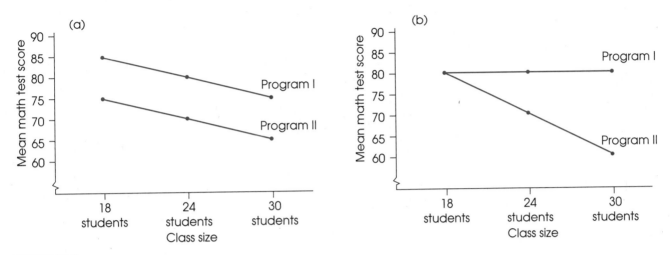

FIGURE 15.3

(a) Graph showing the data from Table 15.1 where there is no interaction. (b) Graph showing the data from Table 15.2 showing where there is an interaction between program and class size.

15.3(b) shows the data from Table 15.2 (interaction). Notice that when there is no interaction in a set of data, the lines in the graph are parallel. In Figure 15.3(a), the effect of programs (10-point difference) is constant across the three class sizes, which results in a constant distance between the two lines. On the other hand, when there is an interaction, the lines in the graph will not be parallel. In Figure 15.3(b), the program effect (distance between the lines) varies from one class size to the next, and the resulting lines are not parallel. In general, an easy way to spot an interaction is to look for lines that are not parallel—that is, look for lines that converge or cross.

To evaluate the interaction, the two-factor ANOVA first identifies mean differences between the treatment conditions that cannot be explained by the main effects. For the data in Table 15.1 [or Figure 15.3(a)], for example, the mean difference between the two cells in each column can be explained by the 10-point main effect for program. In this case, the overall 10-point difference between the two programs completely explains the difference between treatments for all of the three class sizes considered. By contrast, the data in Table 15.2 [or Figure 15.3(b)] shows mean differences between treatment conditions that cannot be explained by the main effects. For example, the data show a 20-point difference between program I and program II when classes contain 30 students. This 20-point difference cannot be explained by the 10-point main effect for programs. After these "extra" mean differences are identified, they are evaluated by an F-ratio with the following structure:

> The mean differences that make up an interaction must be evaluated with a hypothesis test to demonstrate statistical significance.

$$F = \frac{\text{variance (mean differences) not explained by main effects}}{\text{variance (differences) expected from sampling error}}$$

The null hypothesis for this F-ratio simply states that there is no interaction:

H_0: There is no interaction between factors A and B. The effect of factor A does not depend on the levels of factor B (and B does not depend on A).

GRAPHING RESULTS FROM A TWO-FACTOR DESIGN

ONE OF the best ways to get a quick overview of the results from a two-factor study is to present the data in a graph. Because the graph must display the means obtained for *two* independent variables (two factors), constructing the graph can be a bit more complicated than the single-factor graphs we presented in Chapter 3 (pp. 94–96). The following step-by-step procedure should help you construct graphs and interpret graphs showing results from a two-factor study.

1. The easiest way to begin is with a matrix showing the set of means for all the individual treatment combinations. For this demonstration, we will use the following data, representing the results from a two-factor study with two levels of factor A and three levels of factor B. The subscripts indicate the levels for both factors. The numerical values inside the matrix are the means for the different treatment combinations. Notice that with a 2×3 design we have a total of $2 \times 3 = 6$ separate means.

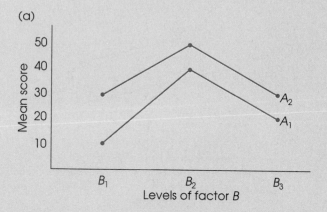

		FACTOR B		
		B_1	B_2	B_3
FACTOR A	A_1	10	40	20
	A_2	30	50	30

2. The values for the dependent variable (the treatment means) are always shown on the vertical axis. For these data, the means range from 10 to 50, and this range of values is displayed on the vertical axis in Figure 15.4.

3. Next, you select one of the factors and display the different values (levels) for that factor on the horizontal axis. Although you may choose either one of the two factors, the best advice is to select a factor for which the different levels are measured on an interval or ratio scale. The reason for this suggestion is that an interval or ratio scale will permit you to construct a *line graph*, which usually provides a better picture of the results. If neither of the factors is measured on an interval or a ratio scale, then you should use a *bar graph* to display the results. (You should recall from Chapters 2 and 3 that line graphs (polygons) are used for interval or ratio scales and bar graphs are used for nominal or ordinal scales.)

4. *Line graphs:* In Figure 15.4(a), we have assumed that factor B is an interval or a ratio variable, and the three levels for this factor are listed on the horizontal axis. Directly above the B_1 value on the horizontal axis, we have placed two dots corresponding to the

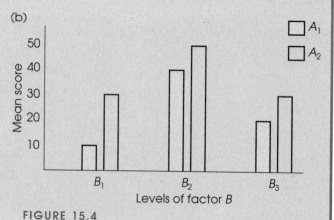

FIGURE 15.4

(a) A line graph and (b) a bar graph showing the results from a two-factor experiment.

two means in the B_1 column of the data matrix. Similarly, we have placed two dots above B_2 and another two dots above B_3. Finally, we have drawn a line connecting the three dots corresponding to level 1 of factor A (the three means in the top row of the data matrix). We have also drawn a second line that connects the three dots corresponding to level 2 of factor A. These lines are labeled A_1 and A_2 in the figure.

Bar graphs: Figure 15.4(b) also shows the three levels of factor B displayed on the horizontal axis. This time, however, we assume that factor B is measured on a nominal or ordinal scale, and the result is a bar graph. Directly above the B_1 value, we have drawn two bars so that the height of the bars correspond to the two means in the B_1 column of the data matrix. Similarly, we have drawn two bars above B_2 and two more bars above B_3. Finally, the three bars corresponding to level 1 of factor A (the top row of the data matrix) are all colored (or shaded) to differentiate them from the three bars for level 2 of factor A.

The alternative hypothesis is that there is an interaction between the two factors:

H_1: The effect of one factor does depend on the levels of the other factor.

Thus, the two-factor ANOVA is composed of three distinct hypothesis tests:

1. The main effect of factor A (called the A-effect)
2. The main effect of factor B (called the B-effect)
3. The interaction (called $A \times B$ interaction)

In each case, we are looking for mean differences between treatments that are larger than would be expected by chance, and in each case, the magnitude of the treatment effect will be evaluated by an F-ratio. Each of the three F-ratios will have the same basic structure:

$$F = \frac{\text{variance between treatments}}{\text{variance within treatments}}$$

The between-treatments variance is assumed to be caused by three things:

1. Treatment effect (factor A, or factor B, or $A \times B$ interaction)
2. Individual differences (there are different subjects for each treatment condition)
3. Experimental error (there always is a margin of error in measurements)

The variance within treatments will provide a measure of the variability expected by chance. differences within treatments are assumed to be caused by

1. Individual differences
2. Experimental error

With these components of variability in mind, the three F-ratios will all have this basic form:

$$F = \frac{\text{variance (mean differences) between treatments}}{\text{variance (differences) within treatments}}$$

$$F = \frac{\text{treatment effect} + \text{individual differences} + \text{experimental error}}{\text{individual differences} + \text{experimental error}}$$

The level of significance helps us decide if the value for the F-ratio is sufficiently larger than 1.00.

As always, a value of F near 1.00 indicates that there is no treatment effect (the numerator and denominator of F are nearly the same). A value of F much greater than 1.00 indicates that the treatment effect is real.

MORE ON MAIN EFFECTS AND INTERACTIONS

The two-factor ANOVA consists of three hypothesis tests, each evaluating specific mean differences: the A-effect, the B-effect, and the $A \times B$ interaction. As we have noted, these are three *separate* tests, but you should also realize that the three tests are *independent*. That is, the outcome for any one of the three tests is totally unrelated to the outcome for either of the other two. Thus, it is possible for data from a two-factor study to display any possible combination of significant and/or nonsignificant main effects and interactions. The data sets in Table 15.3 show several possibilities.

TABLE 15.3

Three sets of data showing different combinations of main effects and interaction for a two-factor study (the numerical value in each cell of the matrices represents the mean value obtained for the sample in that treatment condition.)

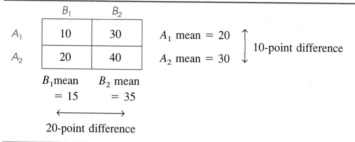

(a) Data showing a main effect for factor A, but no B-effect and no interaction

	B_1	B_2
A_1	20	20
A_2	10	10

A_1 mean $= 20$

A_2 mean $= 10$

10-point difference

B_1 mean $= 15$ B_2 mean $= 15$

No difference

(b) Data showing main effects for both factor A and factor B, but no interaction

	B_1	B_2
A_1	10	30
A_2	20	40

A_1 mean $= 20$

A_2 mean $= 30$

10-point difference

B_1 mean $= 15$ B_2 mean $= 35$

20-point difference

(c) Data showing no main effect for either factor, but an interaction

	B_1	B_2
A_1	10	20
A_2	20	10

A_1 mean $= 15$

A_2 mean $= 15$

No difference

B_1 mean $= 15$ B_2 mean $= 15$

No difference

The subscripts 1 and 2 refer to the level of that factor.

Table 15.3(a) shows data with mean differences between levels of factor A (an A-effect), but no mean differences for factor B or for an interaction. To identify the A-effect, notice that the overall mean for A_1 (the top row) is 10 points higher than the overall mean for A_2 (the bottom row). This 10-point difference is the main effect for factor A. To evaluate the B-effect, notice that both columns have exactly the same overall mean, indicating no difference between levels of factor B; hence, no B-effect. Finally, the absence of an interaction is indicated by the fact that the overall A-effect (the 10-point difference) is constant within each column; that is, the A-effect *does not depend* on the levels of factor B. (Alternatively, the data indicate that the overall B-effect is constant within each row.)

Table 15.3(b) shows data with an A-effect and a B-effect, but no interaction. For these data, the A-effect is indicated by the 10-point mean difference between rows, and the B-effect is indicated by the 20-point mean difference between columns. The fact that the 10-point A-effect is constant within each column indicates no interaction.

Finally, Table 15.3(c) shows data that display an interaction, but no main effect for factor A or for factor B. For these data, note that there is no mean difference between rows (no *A*-effect) and no mean difference between columns (no *B*-effect). However, within each row (or within each column) there are mean differences. The "extra" mean differences within the rows and columns cannot be explained by the overall main effects and, therefore, indicate an interaction.

LEARNING CHECK

1. A research assesses verbal ability in children, both male and female, at 5 or 9 years of age. The mean test scores for the groups are as follows:

5-year-old males	$\bar{X} = 20$
5-year-old females	$\bar{X} = 22$
9-year-old males	$\bar{X} = 30$
9-year-old females	$\bar{X} = 45$

   a. Draw a graph of the data. (*Hint:* Put age on the *X*-axis and test score on the *Y*-axis. Use separate lines for males and females.)

   b. Judging from the graph, does there appear to be an interaction between age and sex? Explain your answer.

2. A two-factor ANOVA makes *three* hypothesis tests. What are they?

3. It is impossible to have an interaction unless main effects are also present. (True or false?)

ANSWERS   1. a.

   b. The graph indicates an interaction because the lines are not parallel. The difference between males and females depends on age.

2. The three separate hypothesis tests in the two-factor ANOVA are the main effect for the first factor, the main effect for the second factor, and the interaction between the two factors.

3. False

FIGURE 15.5

Matrix showing the general design of a two-factor study. The factors are identified by the letters A and B. The levels of each factor are identified by adding numerals to the factor letters; for example, the third level of factor B is identified by B_3.

FACTOR B

		LEVEL B_1	LEVEL B_2	LEVEL B_3
FACTOR A	Level A_1	Treatment (cell) A_1B_1	Treatment (cell) A_1B_2	Treatment (cell) A_1B_3
	Level A_2	Treatment (cell) A_2B_1	Treatment (cell) A_2B_2	Treatment (cell) A_2B_3

15.3 NOTATION AND FORMULAS

The general format for any two-factor experiment is shown in Figure 15.5. Notice that we have identified the factors by using the letters A and B. By convention, the number of levels of factor A is specified by the symbol a, and the number of levels of factor B is specified by b. The $A \times B$ matrix gives a picture of the total experiment, with each cell corresponding to a specific treatment condition. In the example shown in Figure 15.5, $a = 2$ and $b = 3$, so we have a total of $ab = 2 \times 3 = 6$ different treatment conditions.

It is possible to use either an independent or a repeated-measures design with a two-factor research study. In this chapter, we will only look at independent-measures designs. By definition, independent measures means that there is a separate group of subjects for each treatment condition, that is, a separate sample for each cell in the design. For the study shown in Figure 15.5, there are six treatment conditions, so we would need six different groups of subjects.

To develop the formulas for the two-factor analysis of variance, we must be able to study all the totals, numbers, and SS values in the data. The notation system for the two-factor design is as follows:

1. G = the grand total of all the scores in the experiment
2. N = the total number of scores in the entire experiment
3. a = the number of levels of factor A
4. b = the number of levels of factor B
5. n = the number of scores in each treatment condition (in each cell of the $A \times B$ matrix)
6. The totals for each treatment condition will be specified by using the capital letters (A and B) that represent that condition. For example, A_1B_2 would represent the total of the scores in the cell where the level of A is 1 and the level of B is 2. When we want to talk in general about the cell totals, we will refer to the AB totals (without specifying a particular cell). Notice that there are n scores in each AB total.

In addition, A_1 will refer to the total of all the scores for subjects in the first level of factor A (all the scores in the first row of the $A \times B$ matrix). A_2 refers to the total for the second row, and so on. When speaking in general about the row totals, we will refer to the A totals. Notice that there are bn scores in each A total.

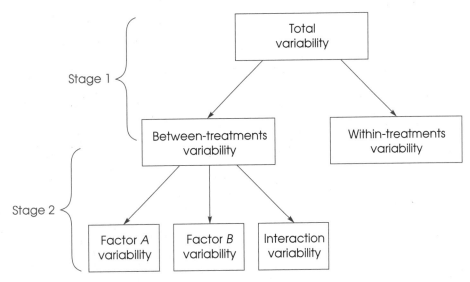

FIGURE 15.6

Structure of the analysis for a two-factor analysis of variance.

In a similar way, B_1 will refer to the total of all the scores in the first column. In general, the column totals will be called B totals. Note that you add an scores to obtain each B total.

FORMULAS   The general structure for the analysis of a two-factor experiment is shown in Figure 15.6. Notice that the overall analysis can be divided into two stages. At the first stage of the analysis, the total variability is separated into two components: between-treatments variability and within-treatments variability. You should notice that this first stage is identical to the structure used for the single-factor analysis of variance in Chapters 13 and 14 (see Figures 13.4 and 14.1). The second stage of the analysis partitions the between-treatments variability into separate components. With a two-factor experiment, the differences between treatment conditions (cells) could be caused by either of the two factors (A or B) or by the interaction. These three components are examined individually in the second stage of the analysis.

The goal of this analysis is to compute the variance values needed for the three F-ratios. We will need three between-treatments variances (one for factor A, one for factor B, and one for the interaction), and we will need a within-treatments variance. Each of these variances (or means squares) will be determined by a sum of squares value (SS) and a degrees of freedom value (df):

Remember, in ANOVA a variance is called a mean square, or MS.

$$\text{mean square} = MS = \frac{SS}{df}$$

The actual formulas for the two-factor analysis of variance are almost identical to the formulas for the single-factor analysis (Chapters 13 and 14). You may find it useful to refer to these chapters for a more detailed explanation of the formulas. To help demonstrate the use of the formulas, we will use the data in Table 15.4. You

TABLE 15.4

Hypothetical data for a two-factor experiment with two levels of factor A and three levels of factor B[a]

		FACTOR B			
		B_1	B_2	B_3	
	A_1	5	9	3	$A_1 = 90$
		3	9	8	
		3	13	3	
		8	6	3	
		6	8	3	
		$AB = 25$	$AB = 45$	$AB = 20$	
FACTOR A		$SS = 18$	$SS = 26$	$SS = 20$	
	A_2	0	0	0	$A_2 = 30$
		2	0	3	
		0	0	7	
		0	5	5	
		3	0	5	
		$AB = 5$	$AB = 5$	$AB = 20$	
		$SS = 8$	$SS = 20$	$SS = 28$	
		$B_1 = 30$	$B_2 = 50$	$B_3 = 40$	$N = 30$
					$G = 120$
					$\Sigma X^2 = 820$

[a]The individual scores are given for each treatment cell (n = 5), along with the cell totals (AB values) and the SS for each cell.

should notice that the analysis consists of two parts: We must analyze the SS values as well as the df values. We will begin with the analysis of the sum of squares (SS).

The first stage of the analysis separates the total SS into two components: between treatments and within treatments. Remember that in a two-factor design each cell is considered to be a separate treatment condition.

ANALYSIS OF SUM OF SQUARES: **Total sum of squares, SS_{total}** SS_{total} computes the sum of squares for the total
STAGE 1 set of N scores:

$$SS_{total} = \Sigma X^2 - \frac{G^2}{N} \tag{15.1}$$

You should notice that this formula is identical to the SS formula that was used for single-factor ANOVA in Chapters 13 and 14 [see equations (13.3) and (14.3)]. For the data in Table 15.4, this total sum of squares would be

$$SS_{total} = 820 - \frac{120^2}{30}$$

$$= 820 - 480$$

$$= 340$$

Within-treatments sum of squares, SS_{within}   The variability within, or "inside," the treatments is found by simply calculating SS for each individual cell and then adding up these SS values. The formula is

$$SS_{within} = \Sigma SS_{inside\ each\ treatment\ cell} \qquad (15.2)$$

For the data in Table 15.4, SS_{within} is

$$SS_{within} = 18 + 26 + 20 + 8 + 20 + 28$$

$$= 120$$

Between-treatments sum of squares, $SS_{between}$ In the single-factor analysis of variance, the formula for computing sum of squares between treatments focused on the treatment totals (T values) and computed SS for these totals:

$$SS_{between} = \Sigma \frac{T^2}{n} - \frac{G^2}{N}$$

In the two-factor design, each treatment corresponds to a particular cell, and the cell totals are identified by AB rather than T, so the between-treatments formula becomes

$$SS_{between} = \Sigma \frac{AB^2}{n} - \frac{G^2}{N} \qquad (15.3)$$

This SS is also called $SS_{between\ cells}$. It measures between-cell variability.

Applying this formula to the data in Table 15.4 gives

$$SS_{between} = \frac{25^2}{5} + \frac{45^2}{5} + \frac{20^2}{5} + \frac{5^2}{5} + \frac{5^2}{5} + \frac{20^2}{5} - \frac{120^2}{30}$$

$$= 125 + 405 + 80 + 5 + 5 + 80 - 480$$

$$= 700 - 480$$

$$= 220$$

This completes the first level of the analysis. When you are performing the calculations for a two-factor analysis of variance, you should stop at this stage and be sure that the two components add up to the total:

$$SS_{total} = SS_{between} + SS_{within}$$

$$340 = 220 + 120$$

ANALYSIS OF SUM OF SQUARES: STAGE 2

We now move to the second stage of the analysis. Remember, we are still measuring treatment effects or differences between treatments. But now we want to determine how much of the overall treatment effect can be attributed to factor A, how much is due to factor B, and how much is due to the interaction between these two factors. To compute the SS for each of the two separate factors, we will continue to use the same basic formula for sum of squares between treatments. The first part of this formula uses the total for each treatment condition and the number of scores in each condition (see equation 15.3). For factor A, the totals are identified by As, and the number of scores in each level of A is given by bn. Thus, the formula for SS between the levels of factor A would be

$$SS_A = \Sigma \frac{A^2}{bn} - \frac{G^2}{N} \qquad (15.4)$$

To get an A total, we must sum scores across the levels of factor B. Therefore, bn (or 15) scores are added to obtain an A total.

The A totals for the data in Table 15.4 are $A_1 = 90$ and $A_2 = 30$. Each of these totals is obtained by adding up a set of $3(5) = 15$ scores. Therefore, the sum of squares for factor A would be

$$SS_A = \frac{90^2}{15} + \frac{30^2}{15} - \frac{120^2}{30}$$

$$= 540 + 60 - 480$$

$$= 120$$

For factor B, the totals are identified by Bs, and the number of scores in each total is determined by an. The formula for sum of squares for factor B is

$$SS_B = \Sigma\frac{B^2}{an} - \frac{G^2}{N} \tag{15.5}$$

To get a B total, we must sum across levels of factor A. Therefore, an (or 10) scores are added to find the B total.

For the data in Table 15.4, this SS would be

$$SS_B = \frac{30^2}{10} + \frac{50^2}{10} + \frac{40^2}{10} - \frac{120^2}{30}$$

$$= 90 + 250 + 160 - 480$$

$$= 20$$

Finally, the SS for the interaction is found by subtraction. According to Figure 15.6, the between-treatments variability is partitioned into three parts: factor A, factor B, and the interaction. Therefore, if you start with $SS_{between}$ and subtract out SS_A and SS_B, the amount that is left will be the SS for the interaction. Thus, the "formula" for the interaction is

$$SS_{A \times B} = SS_{between} - SS_A - SS_B \tag{15.6}$$

Using this formula on the data from Table 15.4 gives

$$SS_{A \times B} = 220 - 120 - 20$$

$$= 80$$

The complete analysis of SS for the data in Table 15.4 is presented in Figure 15.7. Notice that the separate parts at each level of the analysis add up to the total amount of variability at the level above. For example, the SS for factor A, factor B, and the $A \times B$ interaction add up to the $SS_{between}$.

ANALYSIS OF DEGREES OF FREEDOM

Each SS value in the analysis of variance has a corresponding degrees of freedom. Normally, SS measures the amount of variability (or differences) among a number of "things." The corresponding df value is found by counting the number of things and subtracting 1. For a set of n scores, for example, $df = n - 1$. Using this general principle, we will define the df value associated with each of the SSs in the analysis.

Stage 1   In the first stage of the analysis, the total degrees of freedom is partitioned into two components: between treatments and within treatments.

FIGURE 15.7

Analysis of the sum of squares *(SS)* for a two-factor experiment. The values are those obtained from the data in Table 15.4.

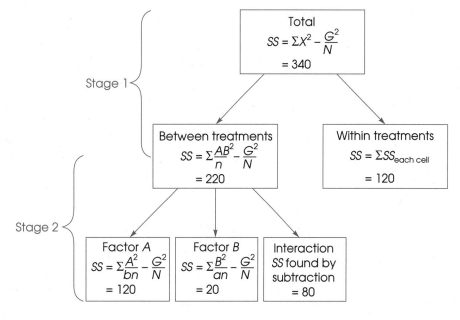

Total degrees of freedom, *df*_{total}. The df_{total} is simply the degrees of freedom associated with the SS_{total}. When we computed this *SS,* we used all *N* scores. Therefore,

$$df_{total} = N - 1 \qquad (15.7)$$

For the data in Table 15.4, there is a total of $N = 30$ scores, so $df_{total} = 29$.

Degrees of freedom within treatments, *df*_{within}. To compute SS_{within}, we added up the *SS* values inside each of the treatment conditions. Because there are *n* scores inside each treatment, each *SS* value has $df = n - 1$. When these are added up, you get

$$df_{within} = \Sigma(n - 1) \qquad (15.8)$$
$$= N - ab$$

For the data in Table 15.4, there are $n = 5$ scores in each treatment condition. Therefore, $df = 4$ inside each treatment. Summing over the six treatments gives an overall within-treatments *df* of 24. This same value is obtained if we start with $N = 30$ scores and subtract $ab = 6$ treatments.

Degrees of freedom between treatments, *df*_{between}. $SS_{between}$ was computed using the *AB* totals from each of the treatment cells. Because there are *ab* separate cells,

$$df_{between} = ab - 1 \qquad (15.9)$$

The example we are considering has a total of six treatment conditions (two levels of factor *A* and three levels of factor *B*). Therefore, the between-treatments $df = 3 \times 2 - 1 = 6 - 1 = 5$.

Notice that the analysis of the df values follows the same pattern shown in Figure 15.6. Specifically, the $df_{between}$ and the df_{within} will combine to equal the df_{total}:

$$df_{total} = df_{between} + df_{within}$$

$$29 = 5 + 24$$

Stage 2   In the second stage of the analysis, the between-treatments df is separated into df for factor A, df for factor B, and df for the A $\times$ B interaction.

Degrees of freedom for factor A, df_A.   The SS for factor A measures the variability among the A totals. Because the number of levels of factor A is identified by a,

$$df_A = a - 1 \tag{15.10}$$

Because there are two levels of factor A ($a = 2$) in Table 15.4, this factor has $df = 1$.

Degrees of freedom for factor B, df_B.   There are b different levels for factor B, and the SS for factor B is computed by using these totals. Therefore,

$$df_B = b - 1 \tag{15.11}$$

For the data we are considering, factor B has three levels ($b = 3$), so factor B has $df = 2$.

Degrees of freedom for the interaction, $df_{A \times B}$ The df for the A $\times$ B interaction can be computed two different ways. First, you can use the structure of the analysis shown in Figure 15.6 to find $df_{A \times B}$ by subtraction. If you start with $df_{between}$ and subtract the df values for factors A and B, the value that is left is df for the interaction:

$$df_{A \times B} = df_{between} - df_A - df_B \tag{15.12}$$

The data in Table 15.4 have $df_{between}$ equal to 5, df_A equal to 1, and df_B equal to 2. Therefore, the df for the interaction is

$$df_{A \times B} = 5 - 1 - 2$$

$$= 2$$

An easy shortcut for finding df for the interaction is to notice that

$$df_{A \times B} = df_A \times df_B \tag{15.13}$$

Using this shortcut formula for the data in Table 15.4, the A $\times$ B interaction has $df = 1 \times 2 = 2$. An intuitive explanation of this formula for df is presented in Box 15.2.

The complete analysis of df values is shown in Figure 15.10. Again, notice that the separate components always add up to the total. For example, the $df_{between}$ (5) and the df_{within} (24) add up to the df_{total} (29).

IMPORTANT

15.2 ADDITIVE AND MULTIPLICATIVE RELATIONSHIPS BETWEEN FACTORS

ONE WAY to think about interactions is to consider the difference between factors that multiply together and factors that add together.

When there is no interaction, the effect of one factor simply adds to the effect of the other factor. This situation is shown in Figure 15.8. Notice that the effect of factor A is to add three points to each mean (the means in A_2 are each three points greater than the corresponding means in A_1). When these means are placed in a graph, the lines for A_1 and A_2 are parallel. There is no interaction. When an additive relationship exists between the two factors, there is no interaction.

An interaction means that there is a non-additive relationship. A multiplicative relationship is one example of a non-additive relationship. Consider the data shown in Figure 15.9. In this case, the effect of factor A is to multiply each mean by three points (each mean in A_2 is three times greater than the corresponding mean in A_1). When these means are placed in a graph, the lines for A_1

Treatment means

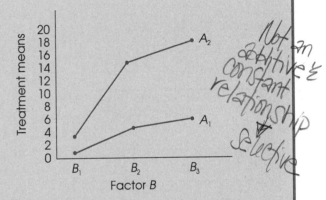

		Factor B		
		B_1	B_2	B_3
Factor A	A_1	1	5	6
	A_2	3	15	18

Factor A multiplies by 3 points

FIGURE 15.9

Treatment means for a two-factor experiment showing a multiplicative relationship between the two factors. Notice that there is a large $A \times B$ interaction.

Not an additive & constant relationship & selective

and A_2 are not parallel. This time there is an interaction.

The notation used to represent an interaction is consistent with this idea of a multiplicative relationship between two factors. For example, an interaction is identified as $A \times B$. Also, you can find the degrees of freedom for an interaction by multiplication:

$$df \text{ for } A \times B = df \text{ for } A \times df \text{ for } B$$

The notion that a multiplicative relationship can be described as an interaction is common in areas other than statistics. For example, pharmacists often speak of "drug interactions." This term is used when the effects of one drug multiply the effects of another. You should note that in some cases the multiplication produces a much greater effect than would be expected by simply "adding" the two drugs together. In other cases, two drugs can cancel each other, so that the combination is less effective than would be expected by simple addition.

Treatment means

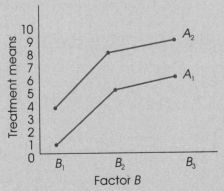

		Factor B		
		B_1	B_2	B_3
Factor A	A_1	1	5	6
	A_2	4	8	9

Factor A adds 3 points

FIGURE 15.8

Treatment means for a two-factor experiment showing an additive relationship between the two factors. Notice that there is no $A \times B$ interaction.

FIGURE 15.10

Analysis of the degrees of freedom for a two-factor analysis of variance. The values are those obtained from the data in Table 15.4.

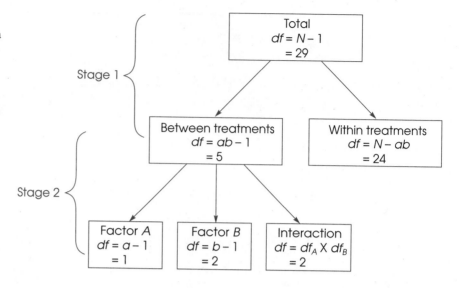

MEAN SQUARES (MSs) AND F-RATIOS

The final step in the analysis is to compute the mean square values and the F-ratios. Recall that each mean square (MS) is actually a sample variance and is computed from the SS and df values:

$$MS = \frac{SS}{df}$$

For the example we are considering,

$$MS \text{ for } A = MS_A = \frac{SS_A}{df_A} = \frac{120}{1} = 120$$

$$MS \text{ for } B = MS_B = \frac{SS_B}{df_B} = \frac{20}{2} = 10$$

$$MS \text{ for } A \times B = MS_{A \times B} = \frac{SS_{A \times B}}{df_{A \times B}} = \frac{80}{2} = 40$$

The denominator of each F-ratio is MS_{within}:

$$MS_{\text{within}} = \frac{SS_{\text{within}}}{df_{\text{within}}} = \frac{120}{24} = 5$$

For factor A, the F-ratio is

$$F = \frac{MS_A}{MS_{\text{within}}} = \frac{120}{5} = 24.00$$

This F-ratio has $df = 1, 24$ ($df = 1$ for the numerator of the ratio and $df = 24$ for the denominator). Commonly, this would be written as

$$F(1, 24) = 24.00$$

FIGURE 15.11

Distribution of *F* for *df* = 1, 24 for evaluating the *F*-ratio for factor *A* and the distribution with *df* = 2, 24 for evaluating factor *B* and the *A* × *B* interaction. In each case, the critical value for α = .05 is shown.

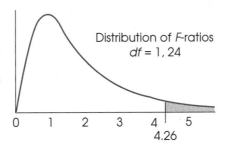

Distribution of *F*-ratios
df = 1, 24

0   1   2   3   4   5
4.26

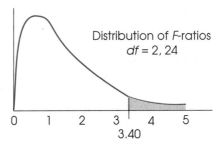

Distribution of *F*-ratios
df = 2, 24

0   1   2   3   4   5
3.40

For factor *B*,

$$F(2, 24) = \frac{MS_B}{MS_{within}}$$

$$= \frac{10}{5}$$

$$= 2.00$$

Software manuals:
Minitab (Section 7)
Mystat (Section 3)
SPSS (Section 6)

And for the *A* × *B* interaction,

$$F(2, 24) = \frac{MS_{A \times B}}{MS_{within}}$$

$$= \frac{40}{5}$$

$$= 8.00$$

To determine whether or not these values fall in the critical region and thereby indicate a significant treatment effect, it is necessary to look at the distribution of *F*-ratios. The *F* distributions for *df* = 1, 24 and for *df* = 2, 24 are shown in Figure 15.11. The critical values are shown for the .05 level of significance (check the table on p. A-29).

Note that for factor *A* our obtained *F*-ratio of *F*(1, 24) = 24.00 is in the critical region. This indicates that the obtained difference between treatments (the numerator of the ratio) is significantly greater than what would be expected by chance (the denominator of the ratio). We conclude that factor *A* does have a significant effect.

On the other hand, the obtained *F*-ratio for factor *B*, *F*(2, 24) = 2.00, is not in the critical region. According to these data, factor *B* does not have a significant effect; that is, the difference we obtained is not larger than would be expected by chance.

Caution: Be sure to check the appropriate critical region. Factors *A* and *B* have different critical values because these factors have different values for degrees of freedom in this example.

Finally, the *F*-ratio for the *A* × *B* interaction, *F*(2, 24) = 8.00, is in the critical region. This indicates that there is a significant interaction. There are several equivalent ways of expressing this result. You could say that the specific combinations of factors *A* and *B* produce significant differences. Or you could say that the effect of factor *A* depends on the different levels of factor *B*. Or you could say that the effect of factor *B* depends on the different levels of factor *A*.

FIGURE 15.12

The data from Table 15.4 are summarized in a table and a graph showing the means for each of the six treatment conditions (cells) in the experiment.

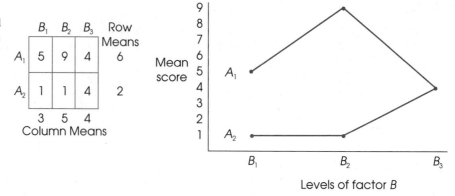

OBSERVING AND DESCRIBING MAIN EFFECTS AND INTERACTIONS

The preceding example demonstrated a complete two-factor ANOVA using the data from Table 15.4. The outcome of the analysis indicates

1. A significant main effect for factor A
2. No significant main effect for factor B
3. A significant interaction

To help make these conclusions more concrete, the original data have been reproduced in a table and a graph in Figure 15.12. Both the table and the graph show the mean value obtained for each of the six treatment conditions.

The main effect for factor A is seen most clearly in the table by comparing the overall mean for the first row (A_1) and the overall mean for the second row (A_2). These means show a four-point difference between A_1 and A_2, and this four-point difference accounts for the significant main effect for factor A. In the graph, the main effect for factor A can be seen by observing that the line for A_1 is generally higher than the line for A_2. The average distance between the two lines is the A-effect.

The non-significant main effect for factor B can be seen by comparing the three column means in the table. The B_1 column shows a mean of 3, B_2 shows a mean of 5, and B_3 shows a mean of 4. As you compare the means from column to column, you find that they differ by only one or two points. The ANOVA indicates that these small differences are not significant. In the graph, the B-effect can be visualized by first imaging a dot located midway between the two data points above each level of B. These imagined dots represent the average score for B_1, B_2, and B_3. Then imagine a line connecting the three dots. For this example, you should find that your imagined line is nearly horizontal, indicating very little difference as you move from B_1 to B_2 to B_3, that is, no significant differences for factor B.

Finally, the interaction is easy to see in the graph. The fact that the two lines are not parallel should immediately notify you that an interaction exists. In this example, the distance between the lines (the A-effect) clearly changes depending on which level of B you select.

A concise summary of the formulas and structure for the two-factor analysis of variance is presented in Figure 15.13. This figure contains nearly all of the information you need to conduct the analysis and should help you to understand the relationships among all the parts.

FIGURE 15.13

The complete analysis of variance for an independent-measures two-factor design.

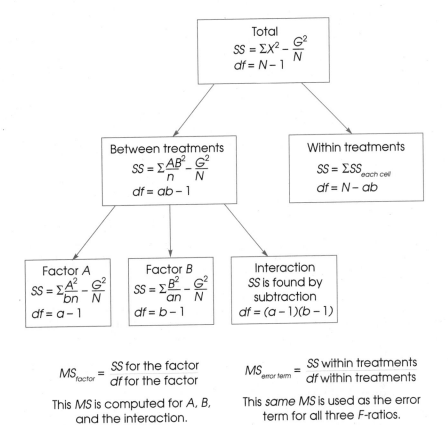

$$\text{Total}$$
$$SS = \Sigma X^2 - \frac{G^2}{N}$$
$$df = N - 1$$

$$\text{Between treatments}$$
$$SS = \Sigma \frac{AB^2}{n} - \frac{G^2}{N}$$
$$df = ab - 1$$

$$\text{Within treatments}$$
$$SS = \Sigma SS_{each\ cell}$$
$$df = N - ab$$

$$\text{Factor } A$$
$$SS = \Sigma \frac{A^2}{bn} - \frac{G^2}{N}$$
$$df = a - 1$$

$$\text{Factor } B$$
$$SS = \Sigma \frac{B^2}{an} - \frac{G^2}{N}$$
$$df = b - 1$$

$$\text{Interaction}$$
$$SS \text{ is found by subtraction}$$
$$df = (a - 1)(b - 1)$$

$$MS_{factor} = \frac{SS \text{ for the factor}}{df \text{ for the factor}}$$

This *MS* is computed for *A, B,* and the interaction.

$$MS_{error\ term} = \frac{SS \text{ within treatments}}{df \text{ within treatments}}$$

This *same MS* is used as the error term for all three *F*-ratios.

LEARNING CHECK   1. The following data summarize the results from a two-factor, independent-measures experiment:

		FACTOR B		
		B_1	B_2	B_3
	A_1	$n = 10$ $AB = 0$ $\overline{X} = 0$ $SS = 30$	$n = 10$ $AB = 10$ $\overline{X} = 1$ $SS = 40$	$n = 10$ $AB = 20$ $\overline{X} = 2$ $SS = 50$
FACTOR A	A_2	$n = 10$ $AB = 40$ $\overline{X} = 4$ $SS = 60$	$n = 10$ $AB = 30$ $\overline{X} = 3$ $SS = 50$	$n = 10$ $AB = 20$ $\overline{X} = 2$ $SS = 40$

$\Sigma X^2 = 610$

a. Sketch a graph similar to those in Figures 15.3 and 15.4a to show the results of this experiment.

b. Looking at your graph, does there appear to be a main effect for factor A? Does factor B have an effect? Is there an interaction?

c. Use an analysis of variance with $\alpha = .05$ to evaluate the effects of factor A, factor B, and the $A \times B$ interaction for these data.

ANSWERS **1. a.** Your graph should show two converging lines.

b. In a graph, the points for level 1 of factor A are much lower than the means for level 2. This mean difference indicates a main effect for factor A. There is no main effect for factor B. The fact that the lines are not parallel indicates an interaction.

c. The results of the ANOVA are summarized in the following table:

SOURCE	SS	df	MS	
Between treatments	100	5		
Factor A	60	1	60	$F = 12.00$
Factor B	0	2	0	$F = 0$
$A \times B$ interaction	40	2	20	$F = 4.00$
Within treatments	270	54	5	
Total	370	59		

(*Note:* The fact that $SS_B = 0$ should be clear from looking at the data. The B totals are all the same; they are not variable.)

15.4 EXAMPLES OF THE TWO-FACTOR ANOVA

Example 15.1 presents the complete hypothesis-testing procedure for a two-factor independent-measures study.

EXAMPLE 15.1 In 1968, Schachter published an article in *Science* reporting a series of experiments on obesity and eating behavior. One of these studies examined the hypothesis that obese individuals do not respond to internal, biological signals of hunger. In simple terms, this hypothesis says that obese individuals tend to eat whether or not their bodies are actually hungry.

In Schachter's study, subjects were led to believe that they were taking part in a "taste test." All subjects were told to come to the experiment without eating for several hours beforehand. The study used two independent variables or factors:

1. Weight (obese versus normal subjects)

2. Full stomach versus empty stomach (half the subjects were given a full meal, as much as they wanted, after arriving at the experiment, and half were left hungry)

All subjects were then invited to taste and rate five different types of crackers. The dependent variable was the number of crackers eaten by each subject.

TABLE 15.5

Results from an experiment examining the eating behavior of normal and obese individuals who have either a full or an empty stomach[a]

		FACTOR B (FULLNESS)		
		EMPTY STOMACH	FULL STOMACH	
FACTOR A (WEIGHT)	NORMAL	$n = 20$ $\overline{X} = 22$ $AB = 440$ $SS = 1540$	$n = 20$ $\overline{X} = 15$ $AB = 300$ $SS = 1270$	$A_1 = 740$
	OBESE	$n = 20$ $\overline{X} = 17$ $AB = 340$ $SS = 1320$	$n = 20$ $\overline{X} = 18$ $AB = 360$ $SS = 1266$	$A_1 = 700$
		$B_1 = 780$	$B_2 = 660$	$G = 1440$ $\Sigma X^2 = 31{,}836$ $N = 80$

[a]The dependent variable is the number of crackers eaten in a taste test (hypothetical data).

The prediction for this study was that the obese subjects would eat the same amount of crackers whether or not they were full. The normal subjects were expected to eat more with empty stomachs and less with full stomachs. Notice that the primary prediction of this study is that there will be an interaction between weight and fullness.

Hypothetical data similar to those obtained by Schachter are presented in Table 15.5.

For this analysis, we will identify weight as factor A and fullness as factor B.

STEP 1 State the hypotheses, and select α. For factor A, the null hypothesis states that there is no difference in the amount eaten for normal versus obese subjects. In symbols,

$$H_0: \mu_{A_1} = \mu_{A_2}$$

$$H_1: \mu_{A_1} \neq \mu_{A_2}$$

For factor B, the null hypothesis states that the amount eaten will be the same for full-stomach subjects as for empty-stomach subjects. In symbols,

$$H_0: \mu_{B_1} = \mu_{B_2}$$

$$H_1: \mu_{B_1} \neq \mu_{B_2}$$

For the $A \times B$ interaction, the null hypothesis can be stated two different ways. First, if there is a difference in eating between the full-stomach and empty-stomach conditions, it will be the same for normal and obese subjects. Second, if there is a difference in eating between the normal and obese subjects, it will be the same for the full-stomach and empty-stomach conditions. In more general terms,

H_0: The effect of factor A does not depend on the levels of factor B (and B does not depend on A).

H_1: The effect of one factor does depend on the levels of the other factor.

We will use $\alpha = .05$ for all tests.

STEP 2 Locate the critical region. To locate the critical values for each of the three F-ratios, we first must determine the df values. For these data (Table 15.5),

Notice that the F distribution table has no entry for $df = 1, 76$. A close and conservative estimate of this critical value may be obtained by using $df = 1, 70$ (critical $F = 3.98$). Whenever there is no entry for the df value of the error term, use the nearest smaller df value in the table.

$$df_{total} = N - 1 = 79$$

$$df_{between} = ab - 1 = 3$$

$$df_{within} = N - ab = 76$$

$$df_A = a - 1 = 1$$

$$df_B = b - 1 = 1$$

$$df_{A \times B} = df_A df_B = 1$$

Thus, all three F-ratios will have $df = 1, 76$. With $\alpha = .05$, the critical F value is 3.98 for all three tests.

STEP 3 Use the data to compute the F-ratios. First, we will analyze the SS values:

$$SS_{total} = \Sigma X^2 - \frac{G^2}{N} = 31,836 - \frac{1440^2}{80}$$

$$= 31,836 - 25,920$$

$$= 5916$$

$$SS_{between} = \Sigma \frac{AB^2}{n} - \frac{G^2}{N}$$

$$= \frac{440^2}{20} + \frac{300^2}{20} + \frac{340^2}{20} + \frac{360^2}{20} - \frac{1440^2}{80}$$

$$= 26,440 - 25,920$$

$$= 520$$

$$SS_{within} = \Sigma SS_{inside\ each\ cell}$$

$$= 1540 + 1270 + 1320 + 1266$$

$$= 5396$$

$$SS_A = \Sigma \frac{A^2}{bn} - \frac{G^2}{N}$$

$$= \frac{740^2}{40} + \frac{700^2}{40} - \frac{1440^2}{80}$$

$$= 25,940 - 25,920$$

$$= 20$$

$$SS_B = \Sigma \frac{B^2}{an} - \frac{G^2}{N}$$

$$= \frac{780^2}{40} + \frac{660^2}{40} - \frac{1440^2}{80}$$

$$= 26{,}100 - 25{,}920$$

$$= 180$$

$$SS_{A \times B} = SS_{between} - SS_A - SS_B$$

$$= 520 - 20 - 180$$

$$= 320$$

The *MS* values needed for the *F*-ratios are

$$MS_A = \frac{SS_A}{df_A} = \frac{20}{1} = 20$$

$$MS_B = \frac{SS_B}{df_B} = \frac{180}{1} = 180$$

$$MS_{A \times B} = \frac{SS_{A \times B}}{df_{A \times B}} = \frac{320}{1} = 320$$

$$MS_{within} = \frac{SS_{within}}{df_{within}} = \frac{5396}{76} = 71$$

Finally, the *F*-ratios are

$$F_A = \frac{MS_A}{MS_{within}} = \frac{20}{71} = 0.28$$

$$F_B = \frac{MS_B}{MS_{within}} = \frac{180}{71} = 2.54$$

$$F_{A \times B} = \frac{MS_{A \times B}}{MS_{within}} = \frac{320}{71} = 4.51$$

STEP 4　Make decisions. For these data, factor *A* (weight) has no significant effect; $F(1, 76) = 0.28$. Statistically, there is no difference in the number of crackers eaten by normal versus obese subjects.

Similarly, factor *B* (fullness) has no significant effect; $F(1, 76) = 2.54$. Statistically, the number of crackers eaten by full subjects is no different from the number eaten by hungry subjects. (*Note:* This conclusion concerns the combined group of normal and obese subjects. The interaction concerns these two groups separately. See page 477 for information concerning the interpretation of results when there is a significant interaction.)

These data produce a significant interaction; $F(1, 76) = 4.51, p < .05$. This means that the effect of fullness does depend on weight. Specifically, the degree of fullness did affect the normal subjects, but it has no effect on the obese subjects.

As we saw in Chapters 13 and 14, the results from an ANOVA can be organized in a summary table, which shows all the components of the analysis (*SS, df,* etc.) as well as the final *F*-ratios. For this example, the summary table would be as follows:

SOURCE	SS	df	MS	F
Between treatments	520	3		
Factor *A* (weight)	20	1	20	0.28
Factor *B* (fullness)	180	1	180	2.54
A × *B* interaction	320	1	320	4.51
Within treatments	5396	76	71	
Total	5916	79		

IN THE LITERATURE
REPORTING THE RESULTS OF A TWO-FACTOR ANOVA

The APA format for reporting the results of a two-factor analysis of variance follows the same basic guidelines as the single-factor report. First, the means and standard deviations are reported. Because a two-factor design typically involves several treatment conditions, these descriptive statistics usually are presented in a table or a graph. Next, the results of all three hypothesis tests (*F*-ratios) are reported. For the research study in Example 15.1, the report would have the following form:

> The means and standard deviations are presented in Table 1. The two-factor analysis of variance showed no significant main effect for the weight factor, $F(1, 76) = 0.28$, $p > .05$; no significant main effect for the fullness factor, $F(1, 76) = 2.54$, $p > .05$; but the interaction between weight and fullness was significant, $F(1, 76) = 4.51$, $p < .05$.
>
> **TABLE 1**
>
> Mean number of crackers eaten in each treatment condition
>
> | | | FULLNESS | |
> |---|---|---|---|
> | | | EMPTY STOMACH | FULL STOMACH |
> | WEIGHT | NORMAL | $M = 22.0$ $SD = 9.00$ | $M = 15.0$ $SD = 8.18$ |
> | | OBESE | $M = 17.0$ $SD = 8.34$ | $M = 18.0$ $SD = 8.16$ |

You should recognize the elements of this report as being identical to other examples reporting the results from an analysis of variance. Each of the obtained F-ratios is reported with its *df* values in parentheses. The term *significant* is used to indicate that the null hypothesis was rejected (the mean differences are greater than what would be expected by chance), and the term *not significant* indicates that the test failed to reject the null hypothesis. Finally, the *p* value reported with each F-ratio reflects the alpha level used for the test. For example, $p < .05$ indicates that the probability is less than .05 that the obtained mean difference is simply due to chance or sampling error.

INTERPRETING INTERACTIONS AND MAIN EFFECTS: SIMPLE MAIN EFFECTS

When a two-factor ANOVA produces a significant interaction, you should be very cautious about accepting the main effects (whether significant or not significant) at face value. In particular, a significant interaction can distort, conceal, or exaggerate the main effects. Therefore, the best advice is to start with the interaction, not the main effects, as the basis for interpreting the results of the study.

The data from Example 15.1 provide a good demonstration of how a significant interaction can influence the interpretation of main effects. The data have been summarized in a table and a graph in Figure 15.14. For these data, the ANOVA resulted in a significant interaction, but no significant main effect for factor *A* (normal/obese) or for factor *B* (full/empty stomach). If you ignore the interaction and focus on the main effects, you might be tempted to conclude that there is no significant difference in eating behavior between normal and obese subjects and that being full versus being hungry has no effect on eating behavior. Looking more closely at the data, however, it is immediately apparent that the main effects do not tell the whole story. Although the obese subjects seem to eat the same amount whether they are full or hungry, the normal subjects show that hunger has a large effect on eating behavior. You should realize that this discrepancy between normal and obese subjects is exactly what Schachter predicted, and it is the source of the significant interaction.

Again, whenever a two-factor ANOVA produces a significant interaction, you should use the interaction, not the main effects, as the basis for interpreting the results. Often (as in the Schachter experiment), an interaction is the primary research prediction. In this case, the existence of a significant interaction and the *pattern* of the interaction may be sufficient for interpreting the results. In Schachter's study, for example, the data show the predicted pattern in the form of a significant interaction. In this case, there may not be any need for additional statistical analysis.

On the other hand, a researcher may want more than a simple description of an interaction. Specifically, a researcher may want to use a statistical analysis to evaluate the separate components of the interaction. For example, the data in Figure 15.14 appear to show that normal subjects eat more when they are hungry than when they are full; but do they eat *significantly* more? Also, the data indicate that with full stomachs the obese subjects tend to eat more than the normal subjects; but is this difference *significant?* In each case, we are asking questions about specific mean differences within the interaction. Because the questions are phrased in terms of statistical significance, you should realize that additional hypothesis tests will be needed to obtain answers. These additional statistical tests are discussed in the following section.

FIGURE 15.14

A table and a graph showing the mean number of crackers eaten for each of the four groups in Example 15.1.

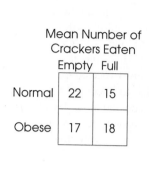

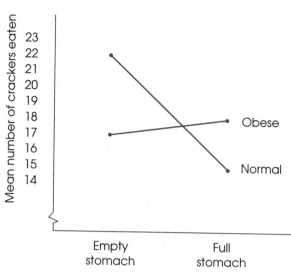

Testing simple main effects   The existence of a significant interaction indicates that the effect (mean differences) for one factor depends on the levels of the second factor. When the data are presented in a matrix showing treatment means, a significant interaction indicates that the mean differences within one column (or row) show a different pattern than the mean differences within another column (or row). In this case, a researcher may want to perform a separate analysis for each of the individual columns (or rows). In effect, the researcher is separating the two-factor experiment into a series of separate single-factor experiments. The process of testing the significance of mean differences within one column (or one row) of a two-factor design is called testing *simple main effects*. To demonstrate this process, we will once again use the data from the Schachter study (Example 15.1), which are summarized in Figure 15.14.

EXAMPLE 15.2   For this demonstration, we will test for significant mean differences within each row of the two-factor data matrix. That is, we will test for significant mean differences between full stomach versus empty stomach for the normal subjects and then repeat the test for the obese subjects. In terms of the two-factor notational system, we will test the simple main effects of factor B for each level of factor A.

For the normal subjects   We will begin by considering only the normal subjects. Because we are restricting the data to the top row of the data matrix, the data effectively have been reduced to a single-factor study comparing only two treatment conditions. Therefore, the analysis is essentially a single-factor ANOVA duplicating the procedure presented in Chapter 13. To facilitate the change from a two-factor to a single-factor analysis, the data for the normal subjects (top row of the matrix) are reproduced as follows, using the notation for a single-factor study:

EMPTY STOMACH	FULL STOMACH	
$n = 20$	$n = 20$	$N = 40$
$T = 440$	$T = 300$	$G = 740$

STEP 1   State the hypothesis. For this restricted set of the data, the null hypothesis would state that there is no difference between the mean for the empty stomach condition and the mean for the full stomach condition. In symbols,

$$H_0:\ \mu_{empty} = \mu_{full} \text{ for the normal subjects}$$

STEP 2   To evaluate this hypothesis, we will use an F-ratio where the numerator, $MS_{between}$, is determined by the mean differences between these two groups, and the denominator consists of MS_{within} from the original analysis of variance. Thus, the F-ratio will have the structure

$$F = \frac{\text{variance (differences) for the means in row 1}}{\text{variance (differences) expected by chance}}$$

$$= \frac{MS_{between} \text{ for the two treatments in row 1}}{MS_{within} \text{ from the original ANOVA}}$$

To compute $MS_{between}$, we begin with the two treatment totals $T = 440$ and $T = 300$. Each of these totals is based on $n = 20$ scores, and the two totals sum to a grand total of $G = 740$. $SS_{between}$ for the two treatments is

$$SS_{between} = \Sigma\frac{T^2}{n} - \frac{G^2}{N}$$

$$= \frac{440^2}{20} + \frac{300^2}{20} - \frac{740^2}{40}$$

$$= 9680 + 4500 - 13690$$

$$= 490$$

Because this SS value is based on only two treatments, it has $df = 1$. Therefore, $MS_{between}$ is

$$MS_{between} = \frac{SS_{between}}{df_{between}} = \frac{490}{1} = 490$$

Remember that the F-ratio uses MS_{within} from the original ANOVA. This $MS = 71$ with $df = 76$.

Using $MS_{within} = 71$ from the original two-factor analysis, the final F-ratio is

$$F = \frac{MS_{between}}{MS_{within}} = \frac{490}{71} = 6.90$$

Note that this F-ratio has the same df values (1, 76) as the test for factor B main effects (empty versus full) in the original ANOVA. Therefore, the critical value for the F-ratio will be the same as the one we used in the original ANOVA. With $df = 1, 76$, the critical value is 3.98. In this case, our F-ratio far exceeds the critical value, so we conclude that the two treatments, empty versus full, are significantly different for the normal subjects.

For the obese subjects   The test for the obese subjects follows exactly the same pattern. First, the data for the obese subjects are as follows:

EMPTY STOMACH	FULL STOMACH	
$n = 20$	$n = 20$	$N = 40$
$T = 340$	$T = 360$	$G = 700$

For these data,

$$SS_{\text{between}} = \Sigma \frac{T^2}{n} - \frac{G^2}{N} = \frac{340^2}{20} + \frac{360^2}{20} - \frac{700^2}{40}$$

$$= 5780 + 6480 - 12250$$

$$= 10$$

Again, we are comparing only two treatment conditions, so $df = 1$ and

$$MS_{\text{between}} = \frac{SS_{\text{between}}}{df_{\text{between}}} = \frac{10}{1} = 10$$

Thus, for the obese subjects, the final F-ratio is

$$F = \frac{MS_{\text{between}}}{MS_{\text{within}}} = \frac{10}{71} = 0.14$$

As before, this F-ratio has $df = 1, 76$ and is compared with the critical value, $F = 3.98$. This time the data indicate that there is no significant difference between empty stomach versus full stomach for the obese subjects.

As a final note, we should point out that the evaluation of simple main effects is used to account for the interaction as well as the overall main effect for one factor. In Example 15.1, the significant interaction indicates that the effect of fullness (factor B) depends on the subjects' weights (factor A). The evaluation of the simple main effects demonstrates this dependency. Specifically, fullness has a significant effect on eating behavior for the normal subjects, but has no significant effect for the obese subjects. Thus, the analysis of simple main effects provides a detailed evaluation of the effects of one factor *including its interaction with a second factor.*

The fact that the simple main effects for one factor encompass both the interaction and the overall main effect of the factor can be seen if you consider the SS values. For this demonstration,

	Simple Main Effects	Overall ANOVA
	$SS_{\text{fullness for normal}} = 490$	$SS_{A \times B} = 320$
	$SS_{\text{fullness for obese}} = 10$	$SS_B = 180$
	Total $SS = 500$	Total $SS = 500$

Notice that the total variability from the simple main effects of fullness (factor B) completely accounts for the total variability of factor B and the $A \times B$ interaction.

REDUCTION OF UNCONTROLLED VARIANCE BY A TWO-FACTOR DESIGN

One advantage of a two factor design is that it allows you to "control" some of the variability within a study. The following example demonstrates how you can "add" a second factor to a single-factor study in order to reduce the error variability and thereby increase the chances of obtaining a significant treatment effect. The rationale for this technique comes from the fact that the independent-measures analysis of variance uses the variability within treatments (MS_{within}) as the denominator of the F-ratio. This variance inside the treatments provides a measure of how much variability is expected just by chance, that is, how much variability is due to individual differences and experimental error.

Often the variability within treatments is not all unexplained and uncontrolled variance. For example, a researcher may notice that a particular treatment seems to have a large effect on the young animals in the sample, but not much effect on the older animals. In this case, much of the variability within the treatment condition is caused by the age of the animals. Whenever variability can be explained or predicted in this way, it is possible to measure it and remove it from the F-ratio. The following example demonstrates this process.

EXAMPLE 15.3

The data in Table 15.6 represent the outcome of a single-factor experiment comparing two treatment conditions. Each treatment condition contains $n = 10$ subjects, 5 males and 5 females.

TABLE 15.6

Hypothetical data from a single-factor experiment comparing two treatment conditions[a]

TREATMENT 1		TREATMENT 2
3		5
3		4
1		3
2		5
1	Males	3
7	Females	7
7		7
5		8
6		9
5		9
$T_1 = 40$		$T_2 = 60$
$SS_1 = 48$		$SS_2 = 48$

[a]Each treatment contains a sample of $n = 10$ subjects, 5 males and 5 females.

Using a single-factor ANOVA on these data, the researcher obtains

$$SS_{between} = \Sigma \frac{T^2}{n} - \frac{G^2}{N}$$

$$= \frac{40^2}{10} + \frac{60^2}{10} - \frac{100^2}{20}$$

$$= 520 - 500$$

$$= 20$$

The within-treatments SS for these data is

$$SS_{within} = \Sigma SS_{inside\ each\ treatment}$$

$$= 48 + 48$$

$$= 96$$

The MS values are

$$MS_{between} = \frac{SS}{df} = \frac{20}{1}$$

$$= 20$$

$$MS_{within} = \frac{SS}{df} = \frac{96}{18}$$

$$= 5.33$$

The resulting F-ratio is $F(1, 18) = 3.75$, which is not in the critical region. Therefore, the researcher must conclude that these data do not demonstrate a significant treatment effect.

The researcher noticed, however, that much of the variability inside the treatments appears to come from the fact that the females tend to have higher scores than the males. If this is true, then much of the within-treatments variability (the denominator of the F-ratio) can be explained. Table 15.7 reproduces the data, but this time the scores for males and females are separated by using sex as a second factor. If we call the original treatments factor A and use sex as factor B, the two-factor ANOVA gives the following results:

$$SS_A = \Sigma \frac{A^2}{bn} - \frac{G^2}{N}$$

$$= \frac{40^2}{10} + \frac{60^2}{10} - \frac{100^2}{20}$$

$$= 20$$

(Notice that the treatment effect is the same whether you use a one- or a two-factor analysis.)

$$SS_B = \Sigma \frac{B^2}{an} - \frac{G^2}{N}$$

$$= \frac{30^2}{10} + \frac{70^2}{10} - \frac{100^2}{20}$$

$$= 80$$

(This is the variability due to sex differences.) The SS for the $A \times B$ interaction is zero for these data. (Check it for yourself.)

With the data arranged in a two-factor design, SS_{within} is

$$SS_{within} = SS_{inside\ each\ cell}$$

$$= 4 + 4 + 4 + 4$$

$$= 16$$

Finally, the mean square values are

$$MS_A = \frac{SS_A}{df_A} = \frac{20}{1}$$

$$= 20$$

$$MS_B = \frac{SS_B}{df_B} = \frac{80}{1}$$

$$= 80$$

$$MS_{within} = \frac{SS_{within}}{df_{within}} = \frac{16}{16}$$

$$= 1$$

TABLE 15.7

The same hypothetical data shown in Table 15.6 with a second factor (sex) added to create a two-factor experiment

		FACTOR A (TREATMENT)		
		TREATMENT 1	TREATMENT 2	
	MALES	3	5	
		3	4	
		1	3	
		2	5	$B_1 = 30$
		1	3	
		$AB = 10$	$AB = 20$	
		$SS = 4$	$SS = 4$	
FACTOR B (SEX)	FEMALES	7	7	
		7	7	
		5	8	
		6	9	$B_2 = 70$
		5	9	
		$AB = 30$	$AB = 40$	
		$SS = 4$	$SS = 4$	
		$A_1 = 40$	$A_2 = 60$	

The F-ratios are as follows:

$$\text{For factor } A: \quad F(1, 16) = \frac{20}{1} = 20$$

$$\text{For factor } B: \quad F(1, 16) = \frac{80}{1} = 80$$

Now the treatment effect (factor A) gives an F-ratio of 20, which is in the critical region. The researcher can conclude that there is a significant treatment effect.

The difference between the two analyses is entirely in the denominator of the F-ratios. In the two-factor analysis, much of the "error" variability is accounted for and removed from the denominator of the F-ratio. This makes it much more likely to obtain a significant result. You also should notice that the two-factor analysis provides additional information about the second factor and the interaction between the two factors.

15.5 ASSUMPTIONS FOR THE TWO-FACTOR ANOVA

The validity of the analysis of variance presented in this chapter depends on the same three assumptions we have encountered with other hypothesis tests for independent-measures designs (the t test in Chapter 10 and the single-factor ANOVA in Chapter 13):

1. The observations within each sample must be independent (see p. 244).
2. The populations from which the samples are selected must be normal.
3. The populations from which the samples are selected must have equal variances (homogeneity of variance).

As before, the assumption of normality generally is not a cause for concern, especially when the sample size is relatively large. The homogeneity of variance assumption is more important, and if it appears that your data fail to satisfy this requirement, you should conduct a test for homogeneity before you attempt the ANOVA. Hartley's F-max test (see p. 304) allows you to use the sample variances from your data to determine whether there is evidence for any differences among the population variances.

HIGHER-ORDER FACTORIAL DESIGNS The basic concepts of the two-factor ANOVA can be extended to more complex designs involving three or more factors. A three-factor design, for example, might look at academic performance scores for two different teaching methods (factor A), for boys versus girls (factor B), and for first-grade versus second-grade classes (factor C). The logic of the analysis and many of the formulas from the two-factor ANOVA are simply extended to the situation with three (or more) factors. In a three-factor experiment, for example, you would evaluate the main effects for each of the three factors, and you would evaluate a set of two-way interactions: $A \times B$,

$B \times C$, and $A \times C$. In addition, however, the extra factor introduces the potential for a three-way interaction: $A \times B \times C$.

The general logic for defining and interpreting higher-order interactions follows the pattern set by two-way interactions. For example, a two-way interaction, $A \times B$, means that the effect of factor A depends on the levels of factor B. Extending this definition, a three-way interaction, $A \times B \times C$, indicates that the two-way interaction between A and B depends on the levels of factor C. Although you may have a good understanding of two-way interactions and you may grasp the general idea of a three-way interaction, most people have great difficulty comprehending or interpreting a four-way (or more) interaction. For this reason, factorial experiments involving three or more factors can produce very complex results that are difficult to understand and thus often have limited practical value.

SUMMARY

1. A research study with two independent variables is called a two-factor design. Such a design can be diagrammed as a matrix by listing the levels of one factor across the top and the levels of the other factor down the side. Each *cell* in the matrix corresponds to a specific combination of the two factors.

2. Traditionally, the two factors are identified as factor A and factor B. The purpose of the analysis of variance is to determine whether there are any significant mean differences among the treatment conditions or cells in the experimental matrix. These treatment effects are classified as follows:
   a. The A-effect: Differential effects produced by the different levels of factor A.
   b. The B-effect: Differential effects produced by the different level of factor B.

   c. The $A \times B$ interaction: Differences that are produced by unique combinations of A and B. An interaction exists when the effect of one factor depends on the levels of the other factor.

3. The two-factor analysis of variance produces three F-ratios: one for factor A, one for factor B, and one for the $A \times B$ interaction. Each F-ratio has the same basic structure:

$$F = \frac{MS_{\text{treatment effect}}(\text{either } A \text{ or } B \text{ or } A \times B)}{MS_{\text{within}}}$$

The formulas for the SS, df, and MS values for the two-factor ANOVA are presented in Figure 15.13.

KEY TERMS

two-factor experiment   matrix   cells   main effect   interaction

FOCUS ON PROBLEM SOLVING

1. Before you begin a two-factor ANOVA, you should take time to organize and summarize the data. It is best if you summarize the data in a matrix with rows corresponding to the levels of one factor and columns corresponding to the levels of the other factor. In each cell of the matrix, show the number of scores (n), the total and mean for the cell, and the SS within the cell. Also compute the row totals and column totals that will be needed to calculate main effects.

2. To draw a graph of the result from a two-factor experiment, first prepare a matrix with each cell containing the mean for that treatment condition.

Next, list the levels of factor B on the X-axis (B_1, B_2, etc.), and put the scores (dependent variable) on the Y-axis. Starting with the first row of the matrix, place a dot above each B level so that the height of the dot corresponds to the cell mean. Connect the dots with a line, and label the line A_1. In the same way, construct a separate line for each level of factor A (that is, a separate line for each row of the matrix). In general, your graph will be easier to draw and easier to understand if the factor with the larger number of levels is placed on the X-axis (factor B in this example).

3. The concept of an interaction is easier to grasp if you sketch a graph showing the means for each treatment. Remember, parallel lines indicate no interaction. Crossing or converging lines indicate that the effect of one treatment depends on the levels of the other treatment you are examining. This indicates that an interaction exists between the two treatments.

4. For a two-factor ANOVA, there are three separate F-ratios. These three F-ratios use the same error term in the denominator (MS_{within}). On the other hand, these F-ratios will have different numerators and may have different df values associated with each of these numerators. Therefore, you must be careful when you look up the critical F values in the table. The two factors and the interaction may have different critical F values.

5. As we have mentioned in previous ANOVA chapters, it helps tremendously to organize your computations; start with SS and df values, and then compute MS values and F-ratios. Once again, using an ANOVA summary table (see p. 476) can be of great assistance.

DEMONSTRATION 15.1

TWO-FACTOR ANOVA

The following data are from an experiment examining the phenomenon of encoding specificity. According to this psychological principle, recall of information will be best if the testing conditions are the same as the conditions that existed at the time of learning.

The experiment involves presenting a group of students with a lecture on an unfamiliar topic. One week later, the students are given a test on the lecture material. To manipulate the conditions at the time of learning, some students receive the lecture in a large classroom, and some hear the lecture in a small classroom. For those students who were lectured in the large room, one-half are tested in the same large room, and the others are changed to the small room for testing. Similarly, one-half of the students who were lectured in the small room are tested in the same small room, and the other half are tested in the large room. Thus, the experiment involves four groups of subjects in a two-factor design, as shown in the following table. The score for each subject is the number of correct answers on the test.

	TESTING CONDITION	
	LARGE TESTING ROOM	SMALL TESTING ROOM
LARGE LECTURE ROOM	15	5
	20	8
	11	1
	18	1
	16	5
SMALL LECTURE ROOM	1	22
	4	15
	2	20
	5	17
	8	16

LECTURE CONDITION (row label, at left of the two lecture-room groups)

Do these data indicate that the size of the lecture room and/or testing room has a significant effect on test performance?

STEP 1   *State the hypotheses, and specify α.* The two-factor ANOVA evaluates three separate sets of hypotheses:

1. The main effect of lecture room size: Is there a significant difference in test performance for students who received the lecture in a large room versus students who received the lecture in a small room? With lecture room size identified as factor A, the null hypothesis states that there is no difference between the two room sizes. In symbols,

    H_0: $\mu_{A_1} = \mu_{A_2}$

    The alternative hypothesis states that there is a difference between the two lecture room sizes.

    H_1: $\mu_{A_1} \neq \mu_{A_2}$

2. The main effect of testing room size: Is there a significant difference in test performance for students who were tested in a large room versus students who were tested in a small room? With testing room size identified as factor B, the null hypothesis states that there is no difference between the two room sizes. In symbols,

    H_0: $\mu_{B_1} = \mu_{B_2}$

    The alternative hypothesis states that there is a difference between the two testing room sizes.

    H_1: $\mu_{B_1} \neq \mu_{B_2}$

3. The interaction between lecture room size and testing room size: The null hypothesis states that there is no interaction:

H_0: The effect of testing room size does not depend on the size of the lecture room.

The alternative hypothesis states that there is an interaction:

H_1: The effect of testing room size does depend on the size of the lecture room.

Notice that the researcher is not predicting any main effects for this study: There is no prediction that one room size is better than another for either learning or testing. However, the researcher is predicting that there will be an interaction. Specifically, the small testing room should be better for students who learned in the small room, and the large testing room should be better for students who learned in the large room. Remember, the principle of encoding specificity states that the better the match between testing and learning conditions, the better the recall. We will set alpha at $\alpha = .05$.

S T E P 2   *Locate the critical region.* To locate the critical region, we must obtain the *df* values for each of the three *F*-ratios. Specifically, we will need df_A, df_B, and $df_{A \times B}$ for the numerators and df_{within} for the denominator. (Often it is easier to postpone this step until the analysis of the *df* values in step 3.)

$$df_A = a - 1 = 2 - 1 = 1$$
$$df_B = b - 1 = 2 - 1 = 1$$
$$df_{A \times B} = (a - 1)(b - 1) = (1)(1) = 1$$
$$df_{within} = N - ab = 20 - (2)(2) = 20 - 4 = 16$$

Thus, all three *F*-ratios will have $df = 1, 16$. With $\alpha = .05$, the critical value for each *F*-ratio is $F = 4.49$. For each test, the obtained *F*-ratio must exceed this critical value to reject H_0.

S T E P 3   *Perform the analysis.* The complete two-factor ANOVA can be divided into a series of stages:

1. Compute the summary statistics for the data. This involves calculating the *AB* total and *SS* for each treatment condition, finding the *A* totals and *B* totals for the rows and columns, respectively, and obtaining *G* and ΣX^2 for the entire set of scores.

2. Perform the first stage of the analysis: Separate the total variability (*SS* and *df*) into the between- and within-treatment components.

3. Perform the second stage of the analysis: Separate the between-treatment variability (*SS* and *df*) into the *A*-effect, *B*-effect, and interaction components.

4. Calculate the mean squares for the *F*-ratios.

5. Calculate the *F*-ratios.

Compute summary statistics. We will use the computational formula to obtain *SS* for each treatment condition. These calculations will also provide numerical values for the row and column totals *(A and B)* as well as *G* and ΣX^2.

LARGE TESTING LARGE LECTURE	
X	X^2
15	225
20	400
11	121
18	324
16	256

$\Sigma X = 80 \qquad \Sigma X^2 = 1326$

$$SS = \Sigma X^2 - \frac{(\Sigma X)^2}{n}$$
$$= 1326 - \frac{80^2}{5}$$
$$= 1326 - 1280$$
$$= 46$$
$$AB = \Sigma X = 80$$

SMALL TESTING LARGE LECTURE	
X	X^2
5	25
8	64
1	1
1	1
5	25

$\Sigma X = 20 \qquad \Sigma X^2 = 116$

$$SS = \Sigma X^2 - \frac{(\Sigma X)^2}{n}$$
$$= 116 - \frac{20^2}{5}$$
$$= 116 - 80$$
$$= 36$$
$$AB = \Sigma X = 20$$

LARGE TESTING SMALL LECTURE	
X	X^2
1	1
4	16
2	4
5	25
8	64

$\Sigma X = 20 \qquad \Sigma X^2 = 110$

$$SS = \Sigma X^2 - \frac{(\Sigma X)^2}{n}$$
$$= 110 - \frac{20^2}{5}$$
$$= 110 - 80$$
$$= 30$$
$$AB = \Sigma X = 20$$

SMALL TESTING SMALL LECTURE	
X	X^2
22	484
15	225
20	400
17	289
16	256

$\Sigma X = 90 \qquad \Sigma X^2 = 1654$

$$SS = \Sigma X^2 - \frac{(\Sigma X)^2}{n}$$
$$= 1654 - \frac{90^2}{5}$$
$$= 1654 - 1620$$
$$= 34$$
$$AB = \Sigma X = 90$$

The column totals (factor *B*) are $B_1 = 100$ and $B_2 = 110$. The row totals (factor *A*) are $A_1 = 100$ and $A_2 = 110$. The grand total for these data is $G = 210$, and ΣX^2 for the entire set can be obtained by summing the ΣX^2 values for the four treatment conditions.

$$\Sigma X^2 = 1326 + 116 + 110 + 1654 = 3206$$

For this study, there are two levels for factor *A* and for factor *B*, so $a = b = 2$, and there are $n = 5$ scores in each of the four conditions, so $N = 20$.

Stage 1 of the analysis. We begin by analyzing SS into two basic components:

$$SS_{total} = \Sigma X^2 - \frac{G^2}{N} = 3206 - \frac{210^2}{20} = 3206 - 2205 = 1001$$

$$SS_{between\ cells} = \Sigma \frac{AB^2}{n} - \frac{G^2}{N} = \frac{80^2}{5} + \frac{20^2}{5} + \frac{20^2}{5} + \frac{90^2}{5} - \frac{210^2}{20}$$

$$= 1280 + 80 + 80 + 1620 - 2205$$

$$= 3060 - 2205$$

$$= 855$$

$$SS_{within} = \Sigma SS_{each\ cell} = 46 + 36 + 30 + 34 = 146$$

For this stage, the *df* values are

$$df_{total} = N - 1 = 20 - 1 = 19$$

$$df_{between\ cells} = ab - 1 = 4 - 1 = 3$$

$$df_{within} = N - ab = 20 - 4 = 16$$

Stage 2 of the analysis. We begin by analyzing $SS_{between}$.

$$SS_A = \Sigma \frac{A^2}{bn} - \frac{G^2}{N}$$

$$= \frac{100^2}{10} + \frac{110^2}{10} - \frac{210^2}{20}$$

$$= 1000 + 1210 - 2205$$

$$= 5$$

$$SS_B = \Sigma \frac{B^2}{an} - \frac{G^2}{N}$$

$$= \frac{100^2}{10} + \frac{110^2}{10} - \frac{210^2}{20}$$

$$= 1000 + 1210 - 2205$$

$$= 5$$

$$SS_{A \times B} = SS_{between\ cells} - SS_A - SS_B$$

$$= 855 - 5 - 5$$

$$= 845$$

For stage 2, the *df* values are

$$df_A = a - 1 = 2 - 1 = 1$$

$$df_B = b - 1 = 2 - 1 = 1$$

$$df_{A \times B} = (a - 1)(b - 1) = (1)(1) = 1$$

Calculate the MS values.

$$MS_A = \frac{SS_A}{df_A} = \frac{5}{1} = 5$$

$$MS_B = \frac{SS_B}{df_B} = \frac{5}{1} = 5$$

$$MS_{A \times B} = \frac{SS_{A \times B}}{df_{A \times B}} = \frac{845}{1} = 845$$

$$MS_{\text{within}} = \frac{SS_{\text{within}}}{df_{\text{within}}} = \frac{146}{16} = 9.125$$

Calculate the F-ratios. For factor A (lecture-room size),

$$F = \frac{MS_A}{MS_{\text{within}}} = \frac{5}{9.125} = 0.55$$

For factor B (testing-room size),

$$F = \frac{MS_B}{MS_{\text{within}}} = \frac{5}{9.125} = 0.55$$

For the A × B interaction,

$$F = \frac{MS_{A \times B}}{MS_{\text{within}}} = \frac{845}{9.125} = 92.60$$

STEP 4 *Make a decision about each H_0, and state conclusions.* For factor A, lecture-room size, the obtained F-ratio, $F = 0.55$, is not in the critical region. Therefore, we fail to reject the null hypothesis. We conclude that the size of the lecture room does not have a significant effect on test performance, $F(1, 16) = 0.55$, $p > .05$.

For factor B, testing-room size, the obtained F-ratio, $F = 0.55$, is not in the critical region. Therefore, we fail to reject the null hypothesis. We conclude that the size of the testing room does not have a significant effect on test performance, $F(1, 16) = 0.55$, $p > .05$.

For the A × B interaction, the obtained F-ratio, $F = 92.60$, exceeds the critical value of $F = 4.46$. Therefore, we reject the null hypothesis. We conclude that there is a significant interaction between lecture-room size and testing-room size, $F(1, 16) = 92.60$, $p < .05$.

Notice that the significant interaction means that you must be cautious interpreting the main effects (see p. 477). In this experiment, for example, the size of the testing room (factor B) does have an effect on performance, depending on which room was used for the lecture. Specifically, performance is higher when the testing room and lecture room match, and performance is lower when the lecture and testing occur in different rooms.

The following table summarizes the results of the analysis:

SOURCE	SS	df	MS	
Between cells	855	3		
A (lecture room)	5	1	5	$F = 0.55$
B (testing room)	5	1	5	$F = 0.55$
A × B interaction	845	1	845	$F = 92.60$
Within cells	146	16	9.125	
Total	1001	19		

PROBLEMS

1. Define each of the following terms:
   a. Factor
   b. Level
   c. Two-factor study

2. The structure of a two-factor study can be presented as a matrix with one factor determining the rows and the second factor determining the columns. With this structure in mind, identify the three separate hypothesis tests that make up a two-factor ANOVA, and explain the purpose of each test.

3. Sketch a graph showing each of the following sets of data. Use line graphs with the levels of factor B on the X-axis. In each case, state whether or not the data indicate the presence of a main effect for factor A, a main effect for factor B, and an interaction between A and B. (*Hint:* Main effects are easier to determine by comparing column or row mean differences in the matrix. Interactions are easier to determine by looking at the pattern in the graph.)

a.

		FACTOR B	
		B_1	B_2
FACTOR A	A_1	$\bar{X} = 40$	$\bar{X} = 10$
	A_2	$\bar{X} = 60$	$\bar{X} = 30$

b.

		FACTOR B	
		B_1	B_2
FACTOR A	A_1	$\bar{X} = 20$	$\bar{X} = 20$
	A_2	$\bar{X} = 10$	$\bar{X} = 50$

c.

		FACTOR B	
		B_1	B_2
FACTOR A	A_1	$\bar{X} = 20$	$\bar{X} = 20$
	A_2	$\bar{X} = 10$	$\bar{X} = 10$

4. Sketch a line graph with the levels of factor B on the X-axis, showing the pattern of results for a 2 × 2 factorial experiment for each of the following descriptions:
   a. There is an A-effect but no B-effect and no interaction.
   b. There is an A-effect and a B-effect, but no interaction.
   c. There is an interaction, but no A-effect and no B-effect.

5. The results of a two-factor experiment are examined using an ANOVA, and the researcher reports an F-ratio for factor A with $df = 1, 54$ and an F-ratio for factor B with $df = 2, 108$. Explain why this report cannot be correct.

6. A psychologist conducts a two-factor study comparing the effectiveness of two different therapy techniques (factor A) for treating mild and severe phobias (factor B). The dependent variable is a measure of fear for each subject. If the study uses $n = 10$ subjects in each of the four conditions, then identify the df values for each of the three F-ratios.
   a. What are the df values for the F-ratio for factor A?
   b. What are the df values for the F-ratio for factor B?
   c. What are the df values for the F-ratio for the A × B interaction?

7. The following matrix presents the results of a two-factor experiment with two levels of factor A, two levels of fac-

tor B, and $n = 10$ subjects in each treatment condition. Each value in the matrix is the mean score for the subjects in that treatment condition. Notice that one of the mean values is missing.

	FACTOR B	
	B_1	B_2
A_1	10	40
A_2	30	?

FACTOR A

a. What value should be assigned to the missing mean so that the resulting data would show no main effect for factor *A?*
b. What value should be assigned to the missing mean so that the data would show no main effect for factor *B?*
c. What value should be assigned to the missing mean so that the data would show no interaction?

8. Occasionally, a researcher will read about a significant treatment effect and wonder if the same effect would be found with a different population or under different conditions. In this case, the researcher often creates a two-factor study where the primary prediction is that the data will produce a significant interaction. For each of the following examples, describe a two-factor study that would replicate the original report, and test the researcher's prediction. Identify the two factors (independent variables), and explain why the researcher is expecting a significant interaction.
   a. A research report indicates that memory performance is significantly better for subjects who study material for several brief periods spaced over time (distributed practice) than for subjects who cram all of their study into one long session (massed practice). However, this result was obtained when memory was tested two weeks after the material was studied. After reading this report, a researcher predicts that if memory is tested immediately after study (instead of waiting two weeks), the data will show exactly the opposite results; that is, the subjects who cram will show better performance because the material is still fresh in their minds.
   b. A research report concludes that children who watch violent shows on television tend to be more aggressive than children who watch non-violent programs. In this study, however, the violent television shows all involved human characters. One explanation for the result is that the children are modeling their own behavior based on what they see on television. A psy-

chologist predicts that the modeling behavior will only occur when the television characters are real (human). Specifically, the psychologist predicts that there will be no difference in aggressive behavior between children who watch violent versus non-violent programs if the program characters are non-human (cartoons).

9. The following data are from a two-factor experiment with $n = 10$ subjects in each treatment condition (each cell):

	FACTOR B	
	B_1	B_2
A_1	$AB = 40$ $SS = 70$	$AB = 10$ $SS = 80$
A_2	$AB = 30$ $SS = 73$	$AB = 20$ $SS = 65$

FACTOR A

$$\Sigma X^2 = 588$$

Test for a significant A-effect, B-effect, and $A \times B$ interaction using $\alpha = .05$ for all tests.

10. The following data are from a study examining the extent to which different personality types are affected by distraction. Individuals were selected to represent two different personality types: introverts and extroverts. Half the individuals in each group were tested on a monotonous task in a relatively quiet, calm room. The individuals in the other half of each group were tested in a noisy room filled with distractions. The dependent variable was the number of errors committed by each individual. The results of this study are as follows:

		FACTOR B (PERSONALITY)	
		INTROVERT	EXTROVERT
FACTOR A (DISTRACTION)	QUIET	$n = 5$ $AB = 10$ $SS = 15$	$n = 5$ $AB = 10$ $SS = 25$
	NOISY	$n = 5$ $AB = 20$ $SS = 10$	$n = 5$ $AB = 40$ $SS = 30$

$$\Sigma X^2 = 520$$

a. Use a two-factor ANOVA with $\alpha = .05$ to evaluate these results.
b. Does distraction (quiet versus noisy) have a significant effect on the performance of the introverted subjects? Test the simple main effect using $\alpha = .05$.
c. Does distraction (quiet versus noisy) have a significant effect on the performance of the extroverted subjects? Test the simple main effect using $\alpha = .05$.

11. The following data were obtained from an independent-measures experiment using $n = 5$ subjects in each treatment condition:

FACTOR A

	FACTOR B	
	B_1	B_2
A_1	$AB = 15$ $SS = 80$	$AB = 25$ $SS = 90$
A_2	$AB = 5$ $SS = 70$	$AB = 55$ $SS = 80$

$$\Sigma X^2 = 1100$$

a. Compute the means for each cell, and draw a graph showing the results of this experiment. Your graph should be similar to those shown in Figure 15.3 and Box 5.1.
b. Just from looking at your graph, does there appear to be a main effect for factor A? What about factor B? Does there appear to be an interaction?
c. Use an analysis of variance with $\alpha = .05$ to evaluate these data.

12. Many species of animals communicate using odors. A researcher suspects that specific chemicals contained in the urine of male rats can influence the behavior of other males in the colony. The researcher predicts that male rats will become anxious and more active if they think they are in territory that has been marked by another male. Also, it is predicted that these chemicals will have no effect on female rats. To test this theory, the researcher obtains samples of 15 male and 15 female rats. One-third of each group is tested in a sterile cage. Another one-third of each group is tested in a cage that has been painted with a small amount of the chemicals. The rest of the rats are tested in a cage that has been painted with a large amount of the chemicals. The dependent variable is the activity level of each rat. The data from this experiment are as follows:

	FACTOR B (AMOUNT OF CHEMICAL)		
	NONE	SMALL	LARGE
FACTOR A (SEX) MALE	$n = 5$ $AB = 10$ $SS = 15$	$n = 5$ $AB = 20$ $SS = 19$	$n = 5$ $AB = 30$ $SS = 31$
FEMALE	$n = 5$ $AB = 10$ $SS = 19$	$n = 5$ $AB = 10$ $SS = 21$	$n = 5$ $AB = 10$ $SS = 15$

$$\Sigma X^2 = 460$$

Use an ANOVA with $\alpha = .05$ to test the researcher's predictions. Explain the results.

13. It has been demonstrated in a variety of experiments that memory is best when the conditions at the time of testing are identical to the condition at the time of learning. This phenomenon is called *encoding specificity* because the specific cues that you use to learn (or encode) new information are the best possible cues to help you recall the information at a later time. In an experimental demonstration of encoding specificity, Tulving and Osler (1968) prepared a list of words to be memorized. For each word on the list, they selected an associated word to serve as a cue. For example, if the word *queen* were on the list, the word *lady* could be a cue. Four groups of subjects participated in the experiment. One group was given the cues during learning and during the recall test. Another group received the cues only during recall. A third group received the cues only during learning, and the final group was not given any cues at all. The dependent variable was the number of words correctly recalled. Data similar to Tulving and Osler's results are as follows:

		CUES AT LEARNING	
		YES	NO
CUES AT RECALL	YES	$n = 10$ $\bar{X} = 3$ $SS = 22$	$n = 10$ $\bar{X} = 1$ $SS = 15$
	NO	$n = 10$ $\bar{X} = 1$ $SS = 16$	$n = 10$ $\bar{X} = 1$ $SS = 19$

$$\Sigma X^2 = 192$$

Use an ANOVA with $\alpha = .05$ to evaluate the data. Describe the results.

14. The following data show the results of a two-factor experiment with $n = 10$ in each treatment condition (cell):

		FACTOR B	
		B_1	B_2
FACTOR A	A_1	$\bar{X} = 4$ $SS = 40$	$\bar{X} = 2$ $SS = 50$
	A_2	$\bar{X} = 3$ $SS = 50$	$\bar{X} = 1$ $SS = 40$
		$\Sigma X^2 = 480$	

a. Sketch a graph showing the results of this experiment. (See Box 15.1 for examples.)
b. Looking at your graph, does there appear to be an $A \times B$ interaction? Does factor A appear to have any effect? Does factor B appear to have any effect?
c. Evaluate these data using an ANOVA with $\alpha = .05$.

15. When subjects are presented with a list of items to be remembered, there are two common methods for testing memory. A *recall* test simply asks each subject to report as many items as he/she can remember. In a *recognition* test, subjects are shown a second list of items (including some items from the original list as well as some new items) and asked to identify which items they remember having seen on the first list. Typically, recall performance is very poor for young children, but improves gradually with age. Recognition performance, on the other hand, is relatively good for all ages. The following data are intended to demonstrate this phenomenon. There are $n = 10$ children in each of the six samples, and the dependent variable is a measure of the number of items correctly remembered for each child. Use an ANOVA with $\alpha = .05$ to evaluate these data.

	AGE 2	AGE 6	AGE 10
RECALL TEST	$\bar{X} = 3$ $SS = 16$	$\bar{X} = 7$ $SS = 19$	$\bar{X} = 12$ $SS = 14$
RECOGNITION TEST	$\bar{X} = 15$ $SS = 21$	$\bar{X} = 16$ $SS = 20$	$\bar{X} = 17$ $SS = 18$

16. Hyperactivity in children usually is treated by counseling, or by drugs, or by both. The following data are from an experiment designed to evaluate the effectiveness of these different treatments. The dependent variable is a measure of attention span (how long each child was able to concentrate on a specific task).

	DRUG	NO DRUG
COUNSELING	$n = 10$ $AB = 140$ $SS = 40$	$n = 10$ $AB = 80$ $SS = 36$
NO COUNSELING	$n = 10$ $AB = 120$ $SS = 45$	$n = 10$ $AB = 100$ $SS = 59$
	$\Sigma X^2 = 5220$	

a. Use an ANOVA with $\alpha = .05$ to evaluate these data.
b. Do the data indicate that the drug has a significant effect? Does the counseling have an effect? Describe these results in terms of the effectiveness of the drug and counseling and their interaction.

17. Often two-factor studies occur when researchers want to extend the results of a single-factor study by adding a new population or treatment condition. For example, Problem 21 in Chapter 10 demonstrated significant differences in language development among single children, twins, and triplets. However, the significant differences were found when the children were three years old. A researcher would like to determine whether the differences continue into adolescence. The researcher repeats the original experiment with 3-year-olds, but adds a second factor (age) by including samples of 14-year-olds in the study. The dependent variable is a measure of language skill. The resulting data, with $n = 5$ children in each group, are as follows:

	SINGLE CHILD	TWIN	TRIPLET
AGE 3	$\bar{X} = 10$ $SS = 10$	$\bar{X} = 6$ $SS = 9$	$\bar{X} = 5$ $SS = 10$
AGE 14	$\bar{X} = 15$ $SS = 11$	$\bar{X} = 14$ $SS = 11$	$\bar{X} = 15$ $SS = 10$

a. Sketch a graph showing the mean scores for the six groups in this study. Does it appear that language skill is related to the number of siblings for three-year-old children? Are there still differences at age 14?

b. Evaluate the mean differences with a two-factor ANOVA, using $\alpha = .05$ for all tests.

c. Using $\alpha = .05$, test the simple main effect of number of siblings for each of the two ages. Do the results confirm your description of the graph in part a?

18. The general relationship between performance and arousal level is described by the Yerkes-Dodson law. This law states that performance is best at a moderate level of arousal. When arousal is too low, people do not care about what they are doing, and performance is poor. At the other extreme, when arousal is too high, people become overly anxious, and performance suffers. In addition, the exact form of the relationship between arousal and performance depends on the difficulty of the task. The following data demonstrate the Yerkes-Dodson law. The dependent variable is a measure of performance.

	AROUSAL LEVEL		
	LOW	MEDIUM	HIGH
EASY TASK	$n = 10$ $AB = 80$ $SS = 30$	$n = 10$ $AB = 100$ $SS = 36$	$n = 10$ $AB = 120$ $SS = 45$
HARD TASK	$n = 10$ $AB = 60$ $SS = 42$	$n = 10$ $AB = 100$ $SS = 27$	$n = 10$ $AB = 80$ $SS = 36$

$$\Sigma X^2 = 5296$$

a. Sketch a graph showing the mean level of performance for each treatment condition.

b. Use a two-factor ANOVA to evaluate these data.

c. Describe and explain the main effect for task difficulty.

d. Describe and explain the interaction between difficulty and arousal.

19. The following data are from a study examining the influence of a specific hormone on eating behavior. Three different drug doses were used, including a control condition (no drug), and the study measured eating behavior for males and females. The dependent variable was the amount of food consumed over a 48-hour period.

	NO DRUG	SMALL DOSE	LARGE DOSE
MALES	1 6 1 1 1	7 7 11 4 6	3 1 1 6 4
FEMALES	0 3 7 5 5	0 0 0 5 0	0 2 0 0 3

Use an ANOVA with $\alpha = .05$ to evaluate these data, and describe the results (i.e., the drug effect, the sex difference, and the interaction).

20. In the Preview section of this chapter, we presented an experiment that examined the effect of an audience on the performance of two different personality types. Data from this experiment are as follows. The dependent variable is the number of errors made by each subject.

		ALONE	AUDIENCE
SELF-ESTEEM	HIGH	3 6 2 2 4 7	9 4 5 8 4 6
	LOW	7 7 2 6 8 6	10 14 11 15 11 11

Use an ANOVA with $\alpha = .05$ to evaluate these data. Describe the effect of the audience and the effect of personality on performance.

21. Individuals who are identified as having an antisocial personality disorder also tend to have reduced physiological responses to painful or anxiety-producing stimuli. In everyday terms, these individuals show a limited physical response to fear, guilt, or anxiety. One way of measuring this response is with the galvanic skin response (GSR). Normally, when a person is aroused, there is an increase in perspiration, which causes a measurable reduction in the electrical resistance on the skin. The following data represent the results of a study measuring GSR for normal and antisocial individuals in regular and stress-provoking situations:

	AROUSAL LEVEL			
	BASELINE		STRESS	
NORMAL PERSONALITY	27	25	15	21
	26	23	20	18
	19	24	14	21
	27	26	19	24
	21	19	13	17
ANTISOCIAL PERSONALITY	24	26	29	22
	28	29	27	25
	23	27	22	20
	25	22	20	29
	21	25	28	21

a. Compute the cell means, and sketch a graph of the results.
b. Use an ANOVA with $\alpha = .05$ to evaluate these data.
c. Explain the findings of this study.

22. The process of interference is assumed to be responsible for much of forgetting in human memory. New information going into memory interferes with the information that already is there. One demonstration of interference examines the process of forgetting while people are asleep versus while they are awake. Because there should be less interference during sleep, there also should be less forgetting. The following data are the results from an experiment examining four groups of subjects. All subjects were given a list of words to remember. Then half of the subjects went to sleep, and the others stayed awake. Within both the asleep and the awake groups, half of the subjects were tested after 2 hours, and the rest were tested after 8 hours. The dependent variable is the number of words correctly recalled.

	DELAY OF MEMORY TEST			
	2 HOURS		8 HOURS	
ASLEEP	5	7	6	4
	6	10	8	4
	4	5	5	7
	3	8	10	8
	6	5	7	6
AWAKE	3	2	1	2
	4	3	0	1
	5	4	0	2
	3	2	1	0
	2	4	1	1

a. Use a two-factor ANOVA to examine these data.
b. Describe and explain the interaction.

23. A researcher studies the effects of need for achievement and task difficulty on problem solving. A two-factor design is used, in which there are two levels of amount of achievement motivation (high versus low need for achievement) and four levels of task difficulty, yielding eight treatment cells. Each cell consists of $n = 6$ subjects. The number of errors each subject made was recorded, and the data were analyzed. The following table summarizes the results of the ANOVA, but it is not complete. Fill in the missing values. (Start with df values).

SOURCE	SS	df	MS	
Between treatments	280	——		
Main effect for achievement motivation	——	——	——	$F =$ ——
Main effect for task difficulty	——	——	48	$F =$ ——
Interaction	120	——	——	$F =$ ——
Within treatments	——	——	——	
Total	600	——		

ONCE AGAIN it is time to pause and consider the material that has been presented thus far before we move on to new topics. In this final "Time Out," we will look all the way back to Chapter 1 and consider the general themes that tie together the preceding 15 chapters.

LOOKING BACK

Early in Chapter 1, we stated that the primary goal of science is to establish relationships between variables. Until this point, the statistics we have presented all attempt to accomplish this goal by comparing *groups of scores,* using *means* and *variances* as the basic statistical measures. Although we have considered a variety of statistical techniques, they all share some common elements. Specifically,

1. One variable is used to create the groups that will be compared. Commonly, this is the independent variable. For example, if a researcher wants to examine the relationship between temperature and problem-solving ability, the temperature variable is used to create different treatment conditions (such as 50°, 70°, and 90°), with a group of subjects measured in each treatment. Or if a researcher wants to examine the relationship between gender and attitude, the gender variable is used to create two groups of subjects: males and females.

2. A second variable, the dependent variable, is measured for each individual to obtain a set of scores, X values. For each group, we calculate the mean and the variance. The mean score is used to describe each group and to make comparisons between groups. The variance also serves to describe each group, but, more important, the variance is used to calculate a measure of error for each sample mean. In order to calculate means and variances, the dependent variable (the X values) must be measured on an interval or a ratio scale. These scales allow you to measure distances, which is essential for calculating and comparing means.

3. The sample means are used to test hypotheses about population means. If the test indicates a sig-

nificant difference, we conclude that there is a relationship between the two variables. For example, if the mean attitude score for men is significantly different from the mean attitude score for women, we have demonstrated that attitude is related to gender.

In summary, the statistics we have seen thus far use means and variances to compare groups of scores that have been measured on interval or ratio scales. Although these statistics are appropriate for many research situations, there are occasions where a research study does not meet the criteria that these statistical techniques demand. In the following chapters, we will introduce alternative statistical methods that are available for situations where a researcher does not have groups of scores, or does not have interval/ratio data, or does not compute means and variances.

LOOKING AHEAD

In the remaining chapters, we will still examine relationships between variables, and we will still use sample data to make inferences about populations. However, there will be some differences:

1. The research study might not involve a comparison between groups. For example, a researcher might investigate the relationship between two variables by measuring both variables (e.g., IQ and self-esteem) for a single group of individuals.

2. The measurement for each subject may involve nominal or ordinal scales. For example, subjects might indicate their preferences among different soft drinks by selecting a favorite brand or by rank ordering several brands.

3. A research study may not involve means (or mean differences) for either the data or the hypotheses, but rather population proportions or frequencies. For example, a researcher may want to investigate what proportion of attorneys are women and whether this proportion has changed significantly over the past 10 years.

CHAPTER 16

CORRELATION AND REGRESSION

TOOLS YOU WILL NEED

The following items are considered essential background material for this chapter. If you doubt your knowledge of any of these items, you should review the appropriate chapter or section before proceeding.

- Sum of squares (*SS*) (Chapter 4)
  - Computational formula
  - Definitional formula
- *z*-scores (Chapter 5)
- Hypothesis testing (Chapter 8)

CONTENTS

PREVIEW

Having been a student and taken exams for much of your life, you probably have noticed a curious phenomenon. In every class, there are some students who zip through exams and turn in their papers while everyone else is still on page 1. Other students cling to their exams and are still working frantically when the instructor announces that time is up and demands that all papers be turned in. Have you wondered what grades these students receive? Are the students who finish first the best in the class, or are they completely unprepared and simply accepting their failure? Are the *A* students the last to finish because they are compulsively checking and rechecking their answers? To help answer these questions, we carefully observed a recent exam and recorded the amount of time each student spent and the grade each student received. These data are shown in Figure 16.1. Note that we have listed time along the *X*-axis and grade on the *Y*-axis. Each student is identified by a point on the graph that is located directly above the student's time and directly across from the student's grade. Also note that we have drawn a line through the middle of the data points in Figure 16.1. The line helps make the relationship between time and grade more obvious. The graph shows that the highest grades tend to go to the students who finished their exams early. Students who held their papers to the bitter end tended to have low grades.

In statistical terms, these data show a correlation between time and grade. In this chapter, we will see how correlations are used to measure and describe relationships. Just as a sample mean provides a concise description of an entire sample, a correlation will provide a description of a relationship. We also will look at how correlations are used and in-

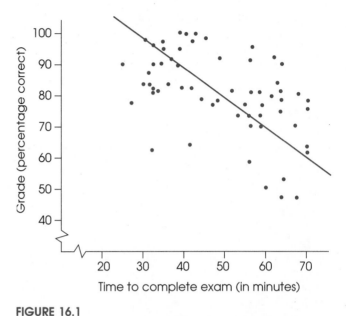

FIGURE 16.1

The relationship between exam grade and time needed to complete the exam. Notice the general trend in these data: Students who finish the exam early tend to have better grades.

terpreted. For example, now that you have seen the relationship between time and grades, don't you think it might be a good idea to start turning in your exam papers a little sooner? Wait and see.

16.1 OVERVIEW

Correlation is a statistical technique that is used to measure and describe a relationship between two variables. Usually the two variables are simply observed as they exist naturally in the environment—there is no attempt to control or manipulate the variables. For example, a researcher interested in the relationship between nutrition and IQ could observe (and record) the dietary patterns for a group of preschool children and then measure IQ scores for the same group. Notice that the researcher is not trying to manipulate the children's diet or IQ, but is simply observing what occurs naturally. You also should notice that a correlation requires two scores for each individual (one score from each of the two variables). These scores normally are identified as *X* and *Y*. The pairs of scores can be listed in a table, or they can be presented graphically in a scatterplot (see Figure 16.2). In the

FIGURE 16.2

The same set of $n = 6$ pairs of scores (X and Y values) is shown in a table and in a scatterplot. Notice that the scatterplot allows you to see the relationship between X and Y.

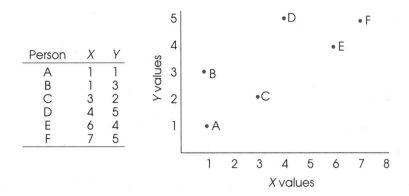

Person	X	Y
A	1	1
B	1	3
C	3	2
D	4	5
E	6	4
F	7	5

scatterplot, the X values are placed on the horizontal axis of a graph, and the Y values are placed on the vertical axis. Each individual is then identified by a single point on the graph so that the coordinates of the point (the X and Y values) match the individual's X score and Y score. The value of the scatterplot is that it allows you to see the nature of the relationship (see Figure 16.2).

THE CHARACTERISTICS OF A RELATIONSHIP

A correlation measures three characteristics of the relationship between X and Y. These three characteristics are as follows:

1. The Direction of the Relationship. Correlations can be classified into two basic categories: positive and negative.

DEFINITIONS

In a *positive correlation,* the two variables tend to move in the same direction: When the X variable increases, the Y variable also increases; if the X variable decreases, the Y variable also decreases.

In a *negative correlation,* the two variables tend to go in opposite directions. As the X variable increases, the Y variable decreases. That is, it is an inverse relationship.

The direction of a relationship is identified by the sign of the correlation. A positive value ($+$) indicates a positive relationship; a negative value ($-$) indicates a negative relationship. The following example provides a description of positive and negative relationships.

EXAMPLE 16.1

Remember that the actual data appear as *points* in the figures. The dashed lines have been added as visual aids to help make the direction of the relationship easier to see.

Suppose that you run the drink concession at the football stadium. After several seasons, you begin to notice a relationship between the temperature at game time and the beverages you sell. Specifically, you have noted that when the temperature is high, you tend to sell a lot of beer. When the temperature is low, you sell relatively little beer [see Figure 16.3(a)]. This is an example of a positive correlation. At the same time, you have noted a relationship between temperature and coffee sales: On cold days, you sell much more coffee than on hot days [see Figure 16.3(b)]. This an example of a negative relationship.

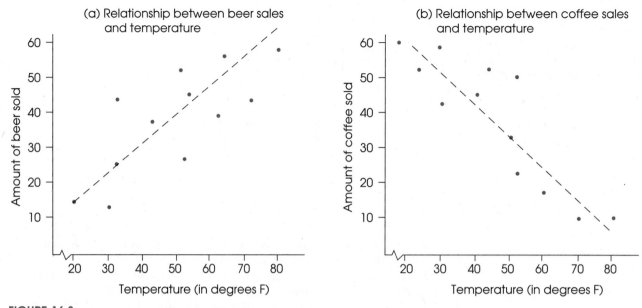

FIGURE 16.3

Examples of positive and negative relationship. (a) Beer sales are positively related to temperature. (b) Coffee sales are negatively related to temperature.

2. The Form of the Relationship. In the preceding coffee and beer examples, the relationships tend to have a linear form; that is, the points in the scatterplot tend to form a straight line. Notice that we have drawn a line through the middle of the data points in each figure to help show the relationship. The most common use of correlation is to measure straight-line relationships. However, you should note that other forms of relationship do exist and that there are special correlations used to measure them. Figure 16.4(a) shows the typical relationship between practice and performance. This is not a straight-line relationship. In the early stages of practice, performance increases rapidly. But with a great deal of practice, the improvement in performance becomes less noticeable. (Ask anyone who has taken piano lessons for 10 years.) Figure 16.4(b) shows the relationship between vocabulary scores and gender for five-year-old children. Again, this is not a straight-line relationship. These data show a tendency for females to have higher scores than males. Many different types of correlations exist. In general, each type is designed to evaluate a specific form of relationship. In this text, we will concentrate on the correlation that measures linear relations.

3. The Degree of the Relationship. Finally, a correlation measures how well the data fit the specific form being considered. For example, a linear correlation measures how well the data points fit on a straight line. A *perfect correlation* always is identified by a correlation of 1.00 and indicates a perfect fit, whereas a correlation of 0 indicates no fit at all. Intermediate values represent the degree to which the data points approximate the perfect fit. The numerical value of the correlation also reflects the degree to which there is a consistent, predictable relationship between the two variables. Again, a correlation of 1.00 (or −1.00) indicates a perfectly consistent relationship.

A correlation of −1.00 also indicates a perfect fit. The direction of the relationship (positive or negative) should be considered separately from the degree of the relationship.

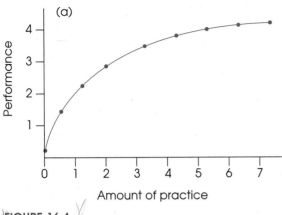

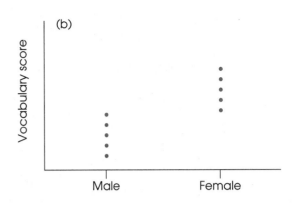

FIGURE 16.4

Examples of relationships that are not linear. (a) Relationship between performance and amount of practice. (b) Relationship between vocabulary score and gender.

Examples of different values for linear correlations are shown in Figure 16.5. Notice that in each example we have sketched a line around the data points. This line, called an *envelope* because it encloses the data, often helps you to see the overall trend in the data.

WHERE AND WHY CORRELATIONS ARE USED

Although correlations have a number of different applications, a few specific examples are presented next to give an indication of the value of this statistical measure.

1. Prediction. If two variables are known to be related in some systematic way, it is possible to use one of the variables to make accurate predictions about the other. For example, when you applied for admission to college, you were required to submit a great deal of personal information, including your scores on the Scholastic Achievement Test (SAT). College officials want this information so they can predict your chances of success in college. It has been demonstrated over several years that SAT scores and college grade point averages are correlated. Students who do well on the SAT tend to do well in college; students who have difficulty with the SAT tend to have difficulty in college. Based on this relationship, the college admissions office can make a prediction about the potential success of each applicant. You should note that this prediction is not perfectly accurate. Not everyone who does poorly on the SAT will have trouble in college. That is why you also submit letters of recommendation, high school grades, and other information with your application.

2. Validity. Suppose that a psychologist develops a new test for measuring intelligence. How could you show that this test truly is measuring what it claims; that is, how could you demonstrate the validity of the test? One common technique for demonstrating validity is to use a correlation. If the test actually is measuring intelligence, then the scores on the test should be related to other measures of intelligence, for example, standardized IQ tests, performance on learning tasks, problem-solving ability, etc. The psychologist could measure the correlation between the new test and each of these other measures of intelligence in order to demonstrate that the new test is valid.

FIGURE 16.5

Examples of different values for linear correlations: (a) shows a strong positive relationship, approximately +0.90; (b) shows a relatively weak negative correlation, approximately −0.40; (c) shows a perfect negative correlation, −1.00; (d) shows no linear trend, 0.00.

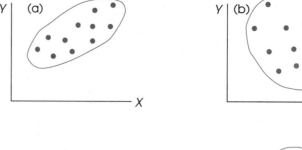

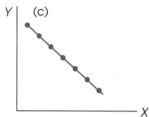

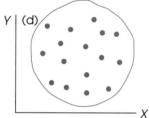

✓ **3. Reliability.** In addition to evaluating the validity of a measurement procedure, correlations are used to determine reliability. A measurement procedure is considered reliable to the extent that it produces stable, consistent measurements. That is, a reliable measurement procedure will produce the same (or nearly the same) scores when the same individuals are measured under the same conditions. For example, if your IQ were measured as 113 last week, you would expect to obtain nearly the same score if your IQ were measured again this week. One way to evaluate reliability is to use correlations to determine the relationship between two sets of measurements. When reliability is high, the correlation between two measurements should be strong and positive.

✓ **4. Theory Verification.** Many psychological theories make specific predictions about the relationship between two variables. For example, a theory may predict a relationship between brain size and learning ability; a developmental theory may predict a relationship between the parents' IQs and the child's IQ; a social psychologist may have a theory predicting a relationship between personality type and behavior in a social situation. In each case, the prediction of the theory could be tested by determining the correlation between the two variables.

LEARNING CHECK

1. If the world were fair, would you expect a positive or negative relationship between grade point average (X) and weekly studying hours (Y) for college students?

2. Data suggest that, on the average, children from large families have lower IQs than children from small families. Do these data indicate a positive or a negative relationship between family size and average IQ?

3. If you are measuring linear relationship, correlations of +0.50 and −0.50 are equally good in terms of how well the data fit on a straight line. (True or false?)

4. It is impossible to have a correlation greater than $+1.00$ or less than -1.00. (True or false?)

ANSWERS **1.** Positive. More hours studying should be associated with higher grade point averages.

2. Negative

3. True. The degree of fit is measured by the magnitude of the correlation independent of sign.

4. True. Correlations are always from $+1.00$ to -1.00

16.2 THE PEARSON CORRELATION

By far the most common correlation is the Pearson correlation (or the Pearson product-moment correlation).

DEFINITION   The *Pearson correlation* measures the degree and direction of linear relationship between two variables.

The Pearson correlation is identified by the letter r. Conceptually, this correlation is computed by

$$r = \frac{\text{degree to which } X \text{ and } Y \text{ vary together}}{\text{degree to which } X \text{ and } Y \text{ vary separately}}$$

$$= \frac{\text{covariability of } X \text{ and } Y}{\text{variability of } X \text{ and } Y \text{ separately}}$$

When there is a perfect linear relationship, every change in the X variable is accompanied by a corresponding change in the Y variable. In Figure 16.5(c), for example, every time the value of X increases, there is a perfectly predictable decrease in Y. The result is a perfect linear relationship, with X and Y always varying together. In this case, the covariability (X and Y together) is identical to the variability of X and Y separately, and the formula produces a correlation of -1.00. At the other extreme, when there is no linear relationship, a change in the X variable does not correspond to any predictable change in Y. In this case, there is no covariability, and the resulting correlation is zero.

THE SUM OF PRODUCTS OF DEVIATIONS   To calculate the Pearson correlation, it is necessary to introduce one new concept: the sum of products of deviations. In the past, we have used a similar concept, SS (the sum of squared deviations), to measure the amount of variability for a single variable. The *sum of products,* or SP, provides a parallel procedure for measuring the amount of covariability between two variables. The value for SP can be calculated with either a definitional formula or a computational formula.

16.1 **COMPARING THE *SP*
AND *SS* FORMULAS**

IT WILL help you to learn the formulas for *SP* if you note the similarity between the two *SP* formulas and the corresponding formulas for *SS* that were presented in Chapter 4. The definitional formula for *SS* is

$$SS = \Sigma(X - \overline{X})^2$$

In this formula, you must square each deviation, which is equivalent to multiplying it by itself. With this in mind, the formula can be rewritten as

$$SS = \Sigma(X - \overline{X})(X - \overline{X})$$

The similarity between the *SS* formula and the *SP* formula should be obvious—the *SS* formula uses squares and the *SP* formula uses products. This same relationship exists for the computational formulas. For *SS*, the computational formula is

$$SS = \Sigma X^2 - \frac{(\Sigma X)^2}{n}$$

As before, each squared value can be rewritten so that the formula becomes

$$SS = \Sigma XX - \frac{\Sigma X \Sigma X}{n}$$

Again, you should note the similarity in structure between the *SS* formula and the *SP* formula. If you remember that *SS* uses squares and *SP* uses products, the two new formulas for the sum of products should be easy to learn.

The *definitional formula* for the sum of products is

$$SP = \Sigma(X - \overline{X})(Y - \overline{Y}) \tag{16.1}$$

This formula instructs you to first find the product of each *X* deviation and *Y* deviation and then add up these products. Notice that the terms in the formula define the value being calculated: the sum of the products of the deviations.

The *computational formula* for the sum of products is

Caution: The *n* in this formula refers to the number of pairs of scores.

$$SP = \Sigma XY - \frac{\Sigma X \Sigma Y}{n} \tag{16.2}$$

Because the computational formula uses the original scores (*X* and *Y* values), it usually results in easier calculations than those required with the definitional formula. However, both formulas will always produce the same value for *SP*.

You may have noted that the formulas for *SP* are similar to the formulas you have learned for *SS* (sum of squares). The relationship between the two sets of formulas is described in Box 16.1. The following example demonstrates the calculation of *SP* with both formulas.

EXAMPLE 16.2   The same set of *n* = 4 pairs of scores will be used to calculate *SP*, first using the definitional formula and then using the computational formula.

For the definitional formula, you need deviation scores for each of the *X* values and each of the *Y* values. Note that the mean for the *X*s is $\overline{X} = 3$ and that the mean for the Ys is $\overline{Y} = 5$. The deviations and the products of deviations are shown in the following table:

Caution: The signs ($+$ and $-$) are critical in determining the sum of products, *SP*.

SCORES		DEVIATIONS		PRODUCTS
X	Y	$X - \overline{X}$	$Y - \overline{Y}$	$(X - \overline{X})(Y - \overline{Y})$
1	3	-2	-2	$+4$
2	6	-1	$+1$	-1
4	4	$+1$	-1	-1
5	7	$+2$	$+2$	$+4$
				$+6 = SP$

For these scores, the sum of the products of the deviations is $SP = +6$.

For the computational formula, you need the sum of the X values, the sum of the Y values, and the sum of the XY products for each pair. These values are as follows:

X	Y	XY	
1	3	3	
2	6	12	
4	4	16	
5	7	35	
12	20	66	Totals

Substituting the sums in the formula gives

$$SP = \Sigma XY - \frac{\Sigma X \Sigma Y}{n}$$

$$= 66 - \frac{12(20)}{4}$$

$$= 66 - 60$$

$$= 6$$

Note that both formulas produce the same result, $SP = 6$.

CALCULATION OF THE PEARSON CORRELATION

As noted earlier, the Pearson correlation consists of a ratio comparing the covariability of X and Y (the numerator) with the variability of X and Y separately (the denominator). In the formula for the Pearson r, we will use SP to measure the co-variability of X and Y. The variability of X and Y will be measured by computing SS for the X scores and SS for the Y scores separately. With these definitions, the formula for the Pearson correlation becomes

Note that you *multiply SS* for X and SS for Y in the denominator of the Pearson formula.

$$r = \frac{SP}{\sqrt{SS_X SS_Y}} \tag{16.3}$$

FIGURE 16.6

Scatterplot of the data from Example 16.3.

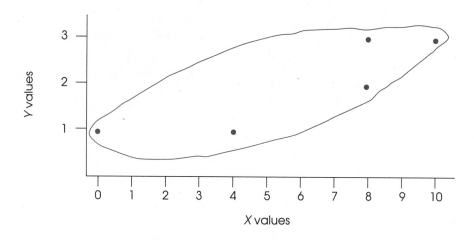

The following example demonstrates the use of this formula with a simple set of scores.

E X A M P L E   1 6 . 3

X	Y
0	1
10	3
4	1
8	2
8	3

The Pearson correlation is computed for the set of $n = 5$ pairs of scores shown in the margin.

Before starting any calculations, it is useful to put the data in a scatterplot and make a preliminary estimate of the correlation. These data have been graphed in Figure 16.6. Looking at the scatterplot, it appears that there is a very good (but not perfect) positive correlation. You should expect an approximate value of $r = +.8$ or $+.9$. To find the Pearson correlation, we will need SP, SS for X, and SS for Y. Each of these values is calculated using the definitional formula.

SCORES		DEVIATIONS		SQUARED DEVIATIONS		PRODUCTS
X	Y	$X - \bar{X}$	$Y - \bar{Y}$	$(X - \bar{X})^2$	$(Y - \bar{Y})^2$	$(X - \bar{X})(Y - \bar{Y})$
0	1	−6	−1	36	1	+6
10	3	+4	+1	16	1	+4
4	1	−2	−1	4	1	+2
8	2	+2	0	4	0	0
8	3	+2	+1	4	1	+2
				64 = SS for X	4 = SS for Y	+14 = SP

Software manuals:
Minitab (Section 8)
Mystat (Section 3)
SPSS (Section 6)

By using these values, the Pearson correlation is

$$r = \frac{SP}{\sqrt{SS_X SS_Y}} = \frac{14}{\sqrt{64(4)}}$$

$$= \frac{14}{16} = +0.875$$

Note that the value we obtained is in agreement with the prediction based on the scatterplot.

THE PEARSON CORRELATION AND z-SCORES

The Pearson correlation measures the relationship between an individual's location in the X distribution and his or her location in the Y distribution. For example, a positive correlation means that individuals who score high on X also tend to score high on Y. Similarly, a negative correlation indicates that individuals with high X scores tend to have low Y scores.

You should recall from Chapter 5 that z-scores provide a precise way to identify the location of an individual score within a distribution. Because the Pearson correlation measures the relationship between locations and because z-scores are used to specify locations, the formula for the Pearson correlation can be expressed entirely in terms of z-scores:

$$r = \frac{\Sigma z_X z_Y}{n} \qquad (16.4)$$

In this formula, z_X identifies each individual's position within the X distribution, and z_Y identifies the position within the Y distribution. The product of the z-scores (like the product of the deviation scores) determines the strength and direction of the correlation.

Because z-scores are considered to be the best way to describe a location within a distribution, equation 16.4 often is considered to be the best way to define the Pearson correlation. However, you should realize that this formula requires a lot of tedious calculations (changing each score to a z-score), so it rarely is used to calculate a correlation.

LEARNING CHECK

1. Describe what is measured by a Pearson correlation.

2. Can SP ever have a value less than zero?

3. Calculate the sum of products of deviations (SP) for the following set of scores. Use the definitional formula and then the computational formula. Verify that you get the same answer with both formulas.

X	Y
1	0
3	1
7	6
5	2
4	1

Remember, it is useful to sketch a scatterplot and make an estimate of the correlation before you begin calculations.

4. Compute the Pearson correlation for the following data:

X	Y
2	9
1	10
3	6
0	8
4	2

ANSWERS

1. The Pearson correlation measures the degree and direction of linear relationship between two variables.

2. Yes. *SP* can be positive, negative, or zero depending on the relationship between *X* and *Y*.

3. *SP* = 19   4. $r = -\dfrac{16}{20} = -0.80$

16.3 UNDERSTANDING AND INTERPRETING THE PEARSON CORRELATION

When you encounter correlations, there are four additional considerations that you should bear in mind:

1. Correlation simply describes a relationship between two variables. It does not explain why the two variables are related. Specifically, a correlation should not and cannot be interpreted as proof of a cause-and-effect relationship between the two variables.

2. The value of a correlation can be affected greatly by the range of scores represented in the data.

3. One or two extreme data points, often called *outriders,* can have a dramatic effect on the value of a correlation.

4. When judging "how good" a relationship is, it is tempting to focus on the numerical value of the correlation. For example, a correlation of +0.5 is halfway between 0 and 1.00 and, therefore, appears to represent a moderate degree of relationship. However, a correlation should not be interpreted as a proportion. Although a correlation of 1.00 does mean that there is a 100% perfectly predictable relationship between *X* and *Y,* a correlation of 0.5 does not mean that you can make predictions with 50% accuracy. To describe how accurately one variable predicts the other, you must square the correlation. Thus, a correlation of $r = 0.5$ provides only $r^2 = 0.5^2 = 0.25$, or 25% accuracy.

Each of these four points will now be discussed in detail.

CORRELATION AND CAUSATION

One of the most common errors in interpreting correlations is to assume that a correlation necessarily implies a cause-and-effect relationship between the two variables. (Even Pearson blundered by asserting causation from correlational data [Blum, 1978]). We constantly are bombarded with reports of relationships: Cigarette smoking is related to heart disease; alcohol consumption is related to birth defects; carrot consumption is related to good eyesight. Do these relationships mean that cigarettes cause heart disease or carrots cause good eyesight? The answer is *no.* Although there may be a causal relationship, the simple existence of a correlation does not prove it. This point should become clear in the following hypothetical example.

FIGURE 16.7

Hypothetical data showing the logical relationship between the number of churches and the number of serious crimes for a sample of U.S. cities.

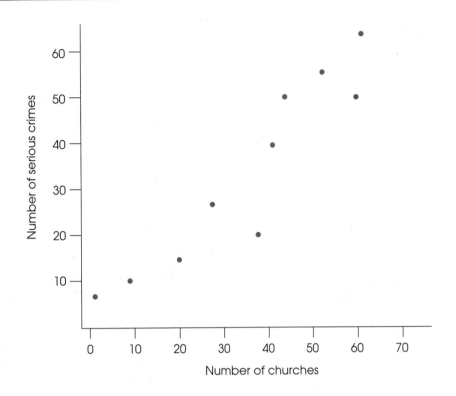

EXAMPLE 16.4

serious crime d churches have a strong correlation but not caused cause effect

Suppose that we select a variety of different cities and towns throughout the United States and measure the number of serious crimes (*Y* variable) and the number of churches (*X* variable) for each. A scatterplot showing hypothetical data for this study is presented in Figure 16.7 Notice that this scatterplot shows a strong, positive correlation between churches and crime. You also should note that these are realistic data. It is reasonable that the smaller towns would have less crime and fewer churches and that the large cities would have large values for both variables. Does this relationship mean that churches cause crime? Does it mean the crime causes churches? It should be clear that the answer is no. Although a strong correlation exists between churches and crime, the real cause of the relationship is the size of the population.

CORRELATION AND RESTRICTED RANGE

Whenever a correlation is computed from scores that do not represent the full range of possible values, you should be cautious in interpreting the correlation. Suppose, for example, that you are interested in the relationship between IQ and creativity. If you select a sample of your fellow college students, your data probably will represent only a limited range of IQ scores (most likely from 110 to 130). The correlation within this restricted range could be completely different from the correlation that would be obtained from a full range of IQ scores. Two extreme examples are shown in Figure 16.8.

Figure 16.8(a) shows an example where there is strong positive relationship between *X* and *Y* when the entire range of scores is considered. However, this rela-

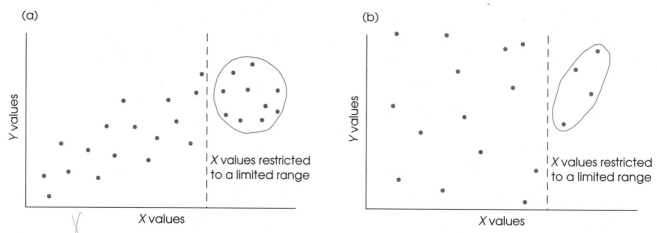

FIGURE 16.8

(a) An example where the full range of X and Y values shows a strong, positive correlation, but the restricted range of scores produces a correlation near zero. (b) An example where the full range of X and Y values shows a correlation near zero, but the scores in the restricted range produce a strong, positive correlation.

tionship is obscured when the data are limited to a *restricted range*. In Figure 16.8(b), there is no consistent relationship between X and Y for the full range of scores. However, when the range of X values is restricted, the data show a strong positive relationship.

To be safe, you should not generalize any correlation beyond the range of data represented in the sample. For a correlation to provide an accurate description for the general population, there should be a wide range of X and Y values in the data.

OUTRIDERS   An outrider is an individual with X and/or Y values that are substantially greater (or smaller) than the values obtained for the other individuals in a data set. A single outrider can have a dramatic effect on the value obtained for a correlation. This phenomenon is shown in Figure 16.9. Figure 16.9(a) shows a set of $n = 5$ data points where the correlation between X and Y is near zero (the actual value is $r = -0.08$). In Figure 16.9(b), one extreme data point has been added to the original set. When this outrider is included, a strong, positive correlation emerges (the correlation is now $r = 0.85$). Notice that the single outrider drastically alters the correlation and, thereby, can change the interpretation of the relationship between X and Y.

CORRELATION AND THE STRENGTH OF THE RELATIONSHIP   A correlation measures the degree of relationship between two variables on a scale from 0 to 1.00. Although this number provides a measure of the degree of relationship, many researchers prefer to square the correlation and use the resulting value to measure the strength of the relationship.

One of the common uses of correlation is for prediction. If two variables are correlated, you can use the value of one variable to predict the other. For example, college admissions officers do not just guess which applicants are likely to do well; they use other variables (SAT scores, high school grades, etc.) to predict which

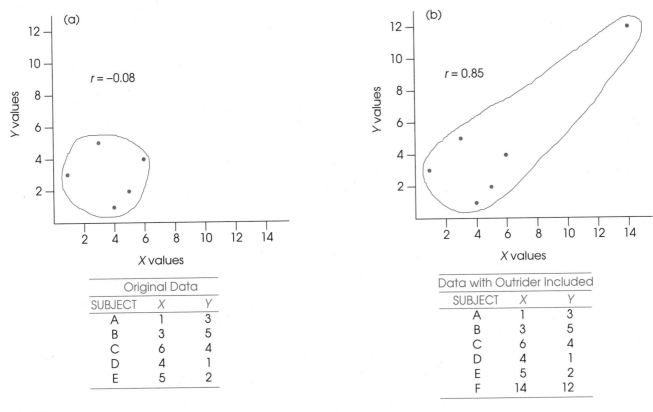

FIGURE 16.9

A demonstration of how one extreme data point (an outrider) can influence the value of a correlation.

students are most likely to be successful. These predictions are based on correlations. By using correlations, the admissions officers expect to make more-accurate predictions than would be obtained by chance. In general, the squared correlation (r^2) measures the gain in accuracy that is obtained from using the correlation for prediction. The squared correlation measures the proportion of variability in the data that is explained by the relationship between X and Y. It is sometimes called the *coefficient of determination*.

DEFINITION   The value r^2 is called the *coefficient of determination* because it measures the proportion of variability in one variable that can be determined from the relationship with the other variable. A correlation of $r = 0.80$ (or -0.80), for example, means that $r^2 = 0.64$ (or 64%) of the variability in the Y scores can be predicted from the relationship with X.

A more detailed discussion of the coefficient of determination is presented in Section 16.6. For now, you simply should realize that whenever two variables are consistently related, it is possible to use one variable to predict the values of the second variable. For example, when $r = 0$, none of the variability (or changes) in Y can be predicted by variation (or changes) in X. When $r = 0.80$, r^2 will equal

(a) With $r = 0$, X and Y are independent. None of the Y variability can be predicted from X; $r^2 = 0$.

(b) With $r = 0.8$, the Y variability is partially predicted from the relationship with X; $r^2 = 0.64$ or 64%.

(c) With $r = 1$, all the Y variability is predicted from the relationship with X; $r^2 = 1.00$ or 100%.

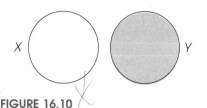 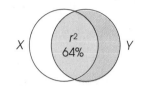 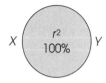

FIGURE 16.10

A graphic representation of the coefficient of determination, r^2. Each circle represents the amount of variability for each variable. Overlapping areas (gray) represent variability explained by the relationship between X and Y.

0.64. Thus, 64% of the variability (changes) in Y can be predicted by changes in X. Finally, when $r = 1.00$, r^2 also will equal 1.00. Thus, knowing the value of X will allow you to make accurate predictions of Y 100% of the time. This is illustrated in Figure 16.10. Each circle represents the amount of variability for a variable, X or Y. Shared variance, that is, variability explained by the relationship between X and Y, is represented by regions of overlap. When $r^2 = 0$, there is no covariation between X and Y, and thus no overlap in the diagram [Figure 16.10(a)]. When $r^2 = 0.64$, the overlapping area is 64% of the variability. This area represents the portion of variability explained by the relationship between X and Y [Figure 16.10(b)]. Finally, with $r^2 = 1.00$, X and Y show complete overlap [Figure 16.10(c)]. That is, 100% of the variability can be explained by the relationship between X and Y.

One final consideration concerning the interpretation of correlations is presented in Box 16.2.

16.4 HYPOTHESIS TESTS WITH THE PEARSON CORRELATION

The Pearson correlation is generally computed for sample data. As with most sample statistics, however, a sample correlation often is used to answer questions about the general population. That is, the sample correlation is used as the basis for drawing inferences about the corresponding population correlation. For example, a psychologist would like to know whether there is a relationship between IQ and creativity. This is a general question concerning a population. To answer the question, a sample would be selected, and the sample data would be used to compute the correlation value. You should recognize this process as an example of inferential statistics: using samples to draw inferences about populations. In the past, we have been concerned primarily with using sample means as the basis for answering questions about population means. In this section, we will examine the procedures for using a sample correlation as the basis for testing hypotheses about the corresponding population correlation.

The basic question for this hypothesis test is whether or not a correlation exists in the population. The null hypothesis is "No, there is no correlation in the popu-

16.2 REGRESSION TOWARD THE MEAN

good example

CONSIDER THE following problem.

Explain why the rookie of the year in major-league baseball usually does not perform as well in his second season.

Notice that this question does not appear to be statistical or mathematical in nature. However, the answer to the question is directly related to the statistical concepts of correlation and regression. Specifically, there is a simple observation about correlations known as *regression toward the mean*.

DEFINITION   When there is a less-than-perfect correlation between two variables, extreme scores (high or low) on one variable tend to be paired with the less extreme scores (more toward the mean) on the second variable. This fact is called *regression toward the mean*.

Figure 16.11 shows a scatterplot with a less-than-perfect correlation between two variables. The data points in this figure might represent batting averages for baseball rookies in 1990 (variable 1) and batting averages for the same players in 1991 (variable 2). Because the correlation is less than perfect, the highest scores on variable 1 are generally *not* the highest scores on variable 2. In baseball terms, the rookies with the highest averages in 1990 do not have the highest averages in 1991.

Remember that a correlation does not explain *why* one variable is related to the other; it simply says that there is a relationship. The correlation cannot explain why the best rookie does not perform as well in his second year. But, because the correlation is not perfect, it is a statistical fact that extremely high scores in one year generally will *not* be paired with extremely high scores in the next year.

Regression toward the mean often poses a problem for interpreting experimental results. Suppose, for example, that you want to evaluate the effects of a special pre-school program for disadvantaged children. You select a sample of children who score extremely low on an aca-

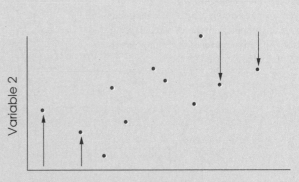

FIGURE 16.11

A demonstration of regression toward the mean. The figure shows a scatterplot for a set of data with a less-than-perfect correlation. Notice that the highest scores on variable 1 (extreme right-hand points) are not the highest scores on variable 2, but are displaced downward toward the mean. Also, the lowest scores on variable 1 (extreme left-hand points) are not the lowest scores on variable 2, but are displaced upward toward the mean.

demic performance test. After participating in your preschool program, these children score significantly higher on the test. Why did their scores improve? One answer is that the special program helped. But an alternative answer is regression toward the mean. If there is a less-than-perfect correlation between scores on the first test and scores on the second test (which is usually the case), individuals with extremely low scores on test 1 will tend to have higher scores on test 2. It is a statistical fact of life, not necessarily the result of any special program.

Now try using the concept of regression toward the mean to explain the following phenomena:

1. You have a truly outstanding meal at a restaurant. However, when you go back with a group of friends, you find that the food is disappointing.

2. You have the highest score on exam I in your statistics class, but score only a little above average on exam II.

lation" or "The population correlation is zero." The alternative hypothesis is "Yes, there is a real, non-zero correlation in the population." Because the population correlation is traditionally represented by ρ (the Greek letter rho), these hypotheses would be stated in symbols as

FIGURE 16.12

Scatterplot of a population of X and Y values with a near-zero correlation. However, a small sample of $n = 3$ data points from this population shows a relatively strong, positive correlation. Data points in the sample are circled.

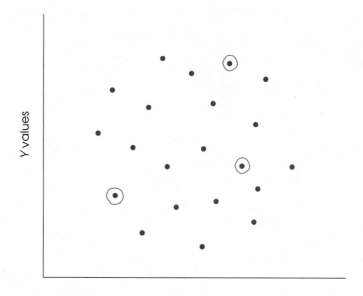

Directional hypotheses for a "one-tailed" test would specify either a positive correlation ($\rho > 0$) or a negative correlation ($\rho < 0$).

H_0: $\rho = 0$ (no population correlation)

H_1: $\rho \neq 0$ (there is a real correlation)

The correlation from the sample data (r) will be used to evaluate these hypotheses. As always, samples are not expected to be identical to the populations from which they come; there will be some discrepancy (sampling error) between a sample statistic and the corresponding population parameter. Specifically, you should always expect some error between a sample correlation and the population correlation it represents. One implication of this fact is that even when there is no correlation in the population ($\rho = 0$), you are still likely to obtain a non-zero value for the sample correlation. This is particularly true for small samples (see Figure 16.12). The purpose of the hypothesis test is to decide between the following two alternatives:

1. The non-zero sample correlation is simply due to chance. That is, there is no correlation in the population, and the sample value is simply the result of sampling error. This is the situation specified by H_0.

2. The non-zero sample correlation accurately represents a real, non-zero correlation in the population. This is the alternative stated in H_1.

The table lists critical values in terms of degrees of freedom: $df = n - 2$. Remember to subtract 2 when using this table.

Although it is possible to conduct the hypothesis test by computing either a t statistic or an F-ratio, the computations have been completed and are summarized in Table B.6 in Appendix B. To use this table, you must know the sample size (n), the magnitude of the sample correlation (independent of sign), and the alpha level. Table B.6 has df values listed in the left margin. For the Pearson correlation, $df = n - 2$, where n is the sample size. Because each individual provides two scores (X and Y), n is also the number of pairs of scores. Alpha levels are listed across the top of the table. The body of the table contains critical r values. To be significant, the magnitude of the sample correlation (r) must equal or exceed the value in the table. The following examples demonstrate the use of the table.

EXAMPLE 16.5

A researcher is using a regular, two-tailed test with $\alpha = .05$ to determine whether or not a non-zero correlation exists in the population. A sample of $n = 30$ individuals is obtained. With $\alpha = .05$ and $n = 30$, the table lists a value of 0.361. Thus, the sample correlation (independent of sign) must have a value greater than or equal to 0.361 to reject H_0 and conclude that there is a significant correlation in the population. Any sample correlation between 0.361 and -0.361 is considered within the realm of sampling error and, therefore, not significant.

EXAMPLE 16.6

This time the researcher is using a directional, one-tailed test to determine whether or not there is a positive correlation in the population.

H_0: $\rho \leq 0$ (not positive)

H_1: $\rho > 0$ (positive)

With $\alpha = .05$ and a sample of $n = 30$, the table lists a value of 0.306 for a one-tailed test. Thus, the researcher must obtain a sample correlation that is positive (as predicted) and has a value greater than or equal to 0.306 to reject H_0 and conclude that there is a significant positive correlation in the population.

IN THE LITERATURE
REPORTING CORRELATIONS

When correlations are computed, the results are reported using APA format. The statement should include the sample size, the calculated value for the correlation, whether or not it is a statistically significant relationship, the probability level, and the type of test used (one- or two-tailed). For example, a correlation might be reported as follows:

> A correlation for the data revealed that amount of education and annual income were significantly related, $r = +.65$, $n = 30$, $p < .01$, two tails.

Sometimes a study might look at several variables, and correlations between all possible variable pairings are computed. Suppose, for example, that a study measured people's annual income, amount of education, age, and intelligence. With four variables, there are six possible pairings. Correlations were computed for every pair of variables. These results are most easily reported in a table called a *correlation matrix,* using footnotes to indicate which correlations are significant. For example, the report might state:

The analysis examined the relationships between income, amount of education, age, and intelligence for $n = 30$ subjects. The correlations between pairs of variables are reported in Table 1. Significant correlations are noted in the table.

TABLE 1

Correlation matrix for income, amount of education, age, and intelligence

	EDUCATION	AGE	IQ
Income	+.65*	+.41**	+.27
Education		+.11	+.38**
Age			−.02

$n = 30$
*$p < .01$, two tails
**$p < .05$, two tails

LEARNING CHECK

1. A researcher obtains a correlation of $r = -.41$ for a sample of $n = 25$ individuals. Does this sample provide sufficient evidence to conclude that there is a significant, non-zero correlation in the population? Assume a non-directional test with $\alpha = .05$.

2. For a sample of $n = 20$, how large a correlation is needed to conclude at the .05 level that there is a non-zero correlation in the population? Assume a non-directional test.

3. As sample size gets smaller, what happens to the magnitude of the correlation necessary for significance? Explain why this occurs.

ANSWERS

1. Yes. For $n = 25$, the critical value is $r = .396$. The sample value is in the critical region.

2. For $n = 20$, the critical value is $r = .444$.

3. As the sample size gets smaller, the magnitude of the correlation needed for significance gets larger. With a small sample, it is easy to get a relatively good correlation just by chance (see Figure 16.12). Therefore, a small sample requires a very large correlation before you can be confident that there is a real (non-zero) relationship in the population.

16.5 OTHER MEASURES OF RELATIONSHIP

Although the Pearson correlation is the most commonly used method for evaluating the relationship between two variables, there are many other measures of relationship that exist. Many of these alternative correlations are simply special applications of the Pearson formula. In this section, we examine three alternative correlations. Notice that each alternative simply applies the Pearson formula to data with special characteristics.

THE SPEARMAN CORRELATION   The Spearman correlation is intended to measure the degree and direction of relationship between two variables where both variables are measured on ordinal scales; that is, both X and Y consist of ranks. The Spearman correlation is identified by the symbol r_s and is computed using the regular Pearson equation (equation 16.3) with the ranked data.

The Spearman correlation generally is used in one of the following two situations.

1. The original data for both X and Y are ranks. For example, a first-grade teacher may rank order the students in a class in terms of leadership ability (X variable) and then rank order the same students in terms of social development (Y variable). Thus, each student would have a rank for X (first, second, third, and so on for leadership) and a rank for Y. The Spearman correlation would measure the relationship between leadership ability and social development.

2. The original data consist of interval-scale or ratio-scale scores, but the researcher chooses to rank order the scores before computing the correlation. For example, a set of data may have one or two extreme scores that would distort the Pearson correlation (see p. 512). The process of ranking will eliminate a huge difference between one extreme score and the rest of the data points. This process is demonstrated in the following example.

EXAMPLE 16.7   A researcher obtains two measurements (X and Y values for each individual in a sample of $n = 5$). One of these individuals has extremely high scores relative to the rest of the sample. However, when the scores are ranked, the extreme individual no longer appears as an extreme outrider in the group.

ORIGINAL SCORES			RANKED SCORES		
SUBJECT	X	Y	SUBJECT	X RANK	Y RANK
A	3	8	A	1 (1st)	2 (2nd)
B	7	6	B	3 (3rd)	1 (1st)
C	4	9	C	2 (2nd)	3 (3rd)
D	8	10	D	4 (4th)	4 (4th)
E	19	24	E	5 (5th)	5 (5th)

The Spearman correlation is examined in greater detail in Chapter 19.

THE POINT-BISERIAL CORRELATION

The point-biserial correlation is used to measure the relationship between two variables in situations where one variable is measured on an interval or ratio scale ("regular" scores), but the *second variable has only two different values.* Variables with only two values are called *dichotomous variables.* Some examples of dichotomous variables are

1. Male versus female
2. College graduate versus not a college graduate
3. First-born child versus later-born child
4. Success versus failure on a particular task
5. Over 30 years old versus under 30 years old

It is customary to use the numerical values 0 and 1, but any two different numbers would work equally well and would not affect the value of the correlation.

To compute the point-biserial correlation, the dichotomous variable is first converted to numerical values by assigning a value of zero (0) to one category and a value of one (1) to the other category. Then the regular Pearson correlation formula is used with the converted data. This process is demonstrated in the following example.

EXAMPLE 16.8

The following data represent measurements of attitude (X) and gender (Y) for each individual in a sample of $n = 8$. In the original data, one variable consists of two categories: male and female. In the converted data, the categories are assigned numerical values: male = 0 and female = 1. The point-biserial correlation is obtained by using the Pearson formula for the converted data.

Because the assignment of numerical values 0 and 1 to male and female is arbitrary, the sign (+ or −) of the point-biserial correlation is unimportant.

ORIGINAL DATA		CONVERTED DATA	
ATTITUDE SCORE X	GENDER Y	ATTITUDE SCORE X	GENDER Y
5	MALE	5	0
0	FEMALE	0	1
4	MALE	4	0
1	MALE	1	0
1	FEMALE	1	1
2	MALE	2	0
3	FEMALE	3	1
0	FEMALE	0	1

THE RELATIONSHIP BETWEEN THE POINT-BISERIAL CORRELATION AND THE INDEPENDENT-MEASURES t HYPOTHESIS TEST

You may have noticed that the data for a point-biserial correlation are identical to the data that are used for an independent-measures t hypothesis test (Chapter 10). The dichotomous variable can be used to separate the sample into two independent groups. For example, the data from Example 16.8 could be reorganized and presented as follows:

MALES	FEMALES
5	0
4	1
1	3
2	0

With the data in this form, the independent-measures t (or ANOVA) would be used to evaluate the mean difference between the two groups.

In many respects, the point-biserial correlation and the hypothesis tests (t or ANOVA) are evaluating the same thing. Both statistical techniques are examining the relationship between two variables—for this example, the relationship between sex and attitude. Specifically,

1. The correlation is measuring the degree of relationship between the two variables. A large correlation (near 1.00) would indicate that there is a consistent, predictable relationship between sex and attitude. The correlation measures the *strength* of the relationship. The value of r^2, the coefficient of determination, describes how much of the variability in the attitude scores can be predicted on the basis of sex (see Box 16.3).

2. On the other hand, the independent-measures hypothesis test is evaluating the mean difference between groups. A large value for t would indicate that there is a consistent, predictable tendency for one sex to have attitudes different from the other. The hypothesis test determines whether the mean difference in attitude between males and females is more than can be explained by chance.

In fact, the point-biserial correlation and the independent-measures t are directly related by the following equation:

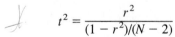

$$t^2 = \frac{r^2}{(1 - r^2)/(N - 2)}$$

In general, a large value for t (indicating a significant difference) will be accompanied by a large value for r (indicating a strong relationship).

THE PHI-COEFFICIENT

When both variables (X and Y) measured for each individual are dichotomous, the correlation between the two variables is called the phi-coefficient. To compute phi (ϕ), you follow a two-step procedure:

1. Convert each of the dichotomous variables to numerical values by assigning a 0 to category 1 and a 1 to category 2 for each of the variables.

2. Use the regular Pearson formula with the converted scores.

This process is demonstrated in the following example.

EXAMPLE 16.9

A researcher is interested in examining the relationship between birth-order position and personality. A random sample of $n = 8$ individuals is obtained, and each individual is classified in terms of birth-order position as first-born

16.3 ANALYSIS OF VARIANCE, THE POINT-BISERIAL CORRELATION, AND r^2

EARLIER IN this chapter, we introduced the *coefficient of determination*, r^2, as a measure of the amount of variability in one variable that can be determined by the relationship with a second variable. The point-biserial correlation provides an excellent opportunity to demonstrate this concept. The data used to introduce the point-biserial correlation in Example 16.8 will be used to show the relationship between r^2 and variability.

First, when the data are organized as follows, you can use the Pearson correlation formula to calculate the point-biserial correlation. For these data, the point-biserial correlation is $r = 0.5773$. (Check it for yourself.)

ATTITUDE X	GENDER Y
5	0
0	1
4	0
1	0
1	1
2	0
3	1
0	1

$SS_X = 24$
$SS_Y = 2$
$SP = 4$

$$r = \frac{4}{\sqrt{(24)(2)}} = 0.5773$$

Second, when the data are organized as two separate groups, you can use ANOVA to test for a mean difference. For this demonstration, we have computed only the SS part of the analysis of variance. (Again, you should check our calculations.)

MALES	FEMALES
5	0
4	1
1	3
2	0
$T = 12$	$T = 4$
$SS = 10$	$SS = 6$

$N = 8$ $SS_{total} = 24$
$G = 16$ $SS_{between} = 8$
$\Sigma X^2 = 56$ $SS_{within} = 16$

Although the two statistical analyses we have just completed may appear to be very different, they are directly connected. Specifically, the coefficient of determination, r^2, serves as the link between the two methods.

Starting with the point-biserial correlation, we obtained a value of $r = 0.5773$. The squared value, $r^2 = 0.3333$ describes how much of the variability in attitude scores is explained by gender. In this example, gender differences account for 33.33% of the variability in attitude.

Now shift your attention to the ANOVA. In this analysis, we computed the variability for the entire set of attitude scores and obtained $SS_{total} = 24$. According to the coefficient of determination, $r^2 = 0.3333$, we should find that 33.33% of the total variability is explained by gender differences. Performing the arithmetic, we obtain

$$33.33\% \text{ of } 24 = 0.3333(24) = 8 \text{ points}$$

Notice that this is exactly the value we obtained for $SS_{between}$. In the ANOVA, the total variability, $SS_{total} = 24$, is partitioned into $SS_{between} = 8$ and $SS_{within} = 16$. In particular, $SS_{between} = 8$ measures how much of the total variability is accounted for by differences between groups (male versus female). For these data, gender differences account for 8 out of 24 points of variability, which is $8/24 = 33.33\%$, exactly the value specified by the coefficient of determination.

or only child versus later-born. Then each individual's personality is classified as either introvert or extrovert.

The original measurements are then converted to numerical values by the following assignments:

BIRTH ORDER	PERSONALITY
1st or only child = 0	Introvert = 0
Later-born child = 1	Extrovert = 1

The original data and the converted scores are as follows:

ORIGINAL DATA		CONVERTED SCORES	
BIRTH ORDER X	PERSONALITY Y	BIRTH ORDER X	PERSONALITY Y
1st	Introvert	0	0
3rd	Extrovert	1	1
Only	Extrovert	0	1
2nd	Extrovert	1	1
4th	Extrovert	1	1
2nd	Introvert	1	0
Only	Introvert	0	0
3rd	Extrovert	1	1

The Pearson correlation formula would then be used with the converted data to compute the phi-coefficient.

Because the assignment of numerical values is arbitrary (either category could be designated 0 or 1), the sign of the resulting correlation is meaningless. As with most correlations, the *strength* of the relationship is best described by the value of r^2, the coefficient of determination, which measures how much of the variability in one variable is predicted or determined by the association with the second variable.

We also should note that although the phi-coefficient can be used to assess the relationship between two dichotomous variables, the more common statistical procedure is a chi-square statistic, which is examined in Chapter 17.

LEARNING CHECK

1. Define a *dichotomous* variable.

2. The following data represent job-related stress scores for a sample of $n = 8$ individuals. These people also are classified by salary level.

   a. Convert the data into a form suitable for the point-biserial correlation.

   b. Compute the point-biserial correlation for these data.

SALARY OVER $40,000	SALARY UNDER $40,000
8	4
7	2
5	1
3	3

ANSWERS

1. A dichotomous variable has only two possible values.

2. Salary level is a dichotomous variable and can be coded as 0 = over $40,000, 1 = under $40,000 for each subject. The resulting point-biserial correlation is −0.719.

FIGURE 16.13

Hypothetical data showing the relationship between SAT scores and GPA with a regression line drawn through the data points. The regression line defines a precise, one-to-one relationship between each *X* value (SAT score) and its corresponding *Y* value (GPA).

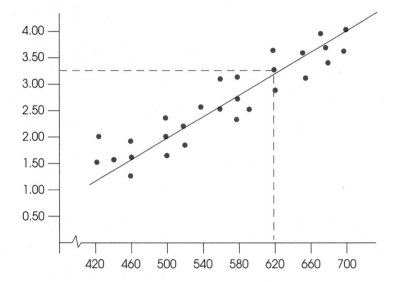

16.6 INTRODUCTION TO REGRESSION

Earlier in this chapter, we introduced the Pearson correlation as a technique for describing and measuring the linear relationship between two variables. Figure 16.13 presents hypothetical data showing the relationship between SAT scores and college grade-point average (GPA). Note that the figure shows a good, but not perfect, positive relationship. Also note that we have drawn a line through the middle of the data points. This line serves several purposes:

a. The line makes the relationship between SAT and GPA easier to see.

b. The line identifies the center, or "central tendency," of the relationship, just as the mean describes central tendency for a set of scores. Thus, the line provides a simplified description of the relationship. For example, if the data points were removed, the straight line would still give a general picture of the relationship between SAT and GPA.

c. Finally, the line can be used for prediction. The line establishes a precise relationship between each *X* value (SAT score) and a corresponding *Y* value (GPA). For example, an SAT score of 620 corresponds to a GPA of 3.25 (see Figure 16.13). Thus, the college admissions office could use the straight-line relationship to predict that a student entering college with an SAT score of 620 should achieve a college GPA of approximately 3.25.

Our goal in this section is to develop a procedure that identifies and defines the straight line that provides the best fit for any specific set of data. You should realize that this straight line does not have to be drawn on a graph; it can be presented in a simple equation. Thus, our goal is to find the equation for the line that best describes the relationship for a set of *X* and *Y* data.

FIGURE 16.14

Relationship between total cost and number of hours playing tennis. The tennis club charges a $25 membership fee plus $5 per hour. The relationship is described by a linear equation:

total cost = $5(number of hours) + $25

$$Y = bX + a$$

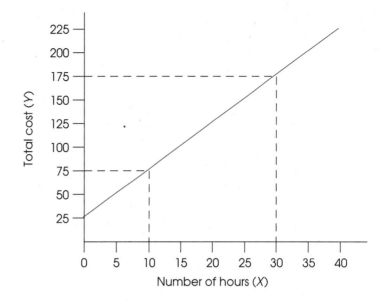

LINEAR EQUATIONS

In general, a *linear relationship* between two variables X and Y can be expressed by the equation $Y = bX + a$, where b and a are fixed constants.

For example, a local tennis club charges for a fee of $5 per hour plus an annual membership fee of $25. With this information, the total cost of playing tennis can be computed using a *linear equation* that describes the relationship between the total cost (Y) and the number of hours (X).

$$Y = 5X + 25$$

Note that a positive slope means that Y increases when X increases, and a negative slope indicates that Y decreases when X increases.

In the general linear equation, the value of b is called the *slope*. The slope determines how much the Y variable will change when X is increased by one point. For the tennis club example, the slope is b = $5 and indicates that your total cost will increase by $5 for each hour you play. The value of a in the general equation is called the *Y-intercept* because it determines the value of Y when X = 0. (On a graph, the a value identifies the point where the line intercepts the Y-axis.) For the tennis club example, a = $25; there is a $25 charge even if you never play tennis.

Figure 16.14 shows the general relationship between cost and number of hours for the tennis club example. Notice that the relationship results in a straight line. To obtain this graph, we picked any two values of X and then used the equation to compute the corresponding values for Y. For example,

when X = 10:	when X = 30:
$Y = bX + a$	$Y = bX + a$
$= \$5(10) + \$25$	$= \$5(30) + \$25$
$= \$50 + \$25$	$= \$150 + \$25$
$= \$75$	$= \$175$

When drawing a graph of a linear equation, it is wise to compute and plot at least three points to be certain you have not made a mistake.

Next, these two points are plotted on the graph: one point at $X = 10$ and $Y = 75$, the other point at $X = 30$ and $Y = 175$. Because two points completely determine a straight line, we simply drew the line so that it passed through these two points.

Because a straight line can be extremely useful for describing a relationship between two variables, a statistical technique has been developed that provides a standardized method for determining the best-fitting straight line for any set of data. The statistical procedure is regression, and the resulting straight line is called the regression line.

DEFINITION

The statistical technique for finding the best-fitting straight line for a set of data is called *regression,* and the resulting straight line is called the *regression line.*

The goal for regression is to find the best-fitting straight line for a set of data. To accomplish this goal, however, it is first necessary to define precisely what is meant by "best fit." For any particular set of data, it is possible to draw lots of different straight lines that all appear to pass through the center of the data points. Each of these lines can be defined by a linear equation of the form

$$Y = bX + a$$

where b and a are constants that determine the slope and Y-intercept of the line, respectively. Each individual line has its own unique values for b and a. The problem is to find the specific line that provides the best fit to the actual data points.

LEARNING CHECK

1. Identify the slope and Y-intercept for the following linear equation:

$$Y = -3X + 7$$

2. Use the linear equation $Y = 2X - 7$ to determine the value of Y for each of the following values of X: 1, 3, 5, 10.

3. If the slope constant (b) in a linear equation is positive, then a graph of the equation will be a line tilted from lower left to upper right. (True or false?)

ANSWERS

1. Slope $= -3$ and Y-intercept $= +7$.

2.

X	Y
1	−5
3	−1
5	3
10	13

3. True. A positive slope indicates that Y increases (goes up in the graph) when X increases (goes to the right in the graph).

THE LEAST-SQUARES SOLUTION

To determine how well a line fits the data points, the first step is to define mathematically the distance between the line and each data point. For every X value in the data, the linear equation will determine a Y value on the line. This value is the

FIGURE 16.15

The distance between the actual data point (Y) and the predicted point on the line ($\hat{Y}$) is defined as $Y - \hat{Y}$. The goal of regression is to find the equation for the line that minimizes these distances.

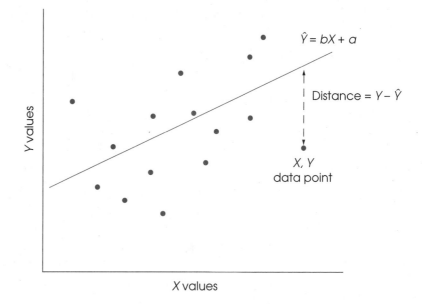

predicted Y and is called $\hat{Y}$ ("Y hat"). The distance between this predicted value and the actual Y value in the data is determined by

$$\text{distance} = Y - \hat{Y}$$

Notice that we simply are measuring the vertical distance between the actual data point (Y) and the predicted point on the line. This distance measures the error between the line and the actual data (see Figure 16.15).

Because some of these distances will be positive and some will be negative, the next step is to square each distance in order to obtain a uniformly positive measure of error. Finally, to determine the total error between the line and the data, we sum the squared errors for all of the data points. The result is a measure of overall squared error between the line and the data:

$$\text{total squared error} = \Sigma(Y - \hat{Y})^2$$

Now we can define the *best-fitting* line as the one that has the smallest total squared error. For obvious reasons, the resulting line is commonly called the *least-squared-error* solution.

In symbols, we are looking for a linear equation of the form

$$\hat{Y} = bX + a$$

For each value of X in the data, this equation will determine the point on the line ($\hat{Y}$) *that gives the best prediction of Y.* The problem is to find the specific values for a and b that will make this the best-fitting line.

The calculations that are needed to find this equation require calculus and some sophisticated algebra, so we will not present the details of the solution. The results,

A commonly used alternative formula for the slope is

$$b = r\frac{s_Y}{s_X}$$

where s_X and s_Y are the standard deviations for X and Y, respectively.

however, are relatively straightforward, and the solutions for b and a are as follows:

$$b = \frac{SP}{SS_X} \tag{16.5}$$

where SP is the sum of products and SS_X is the sum of squares for the X scores.

$$a = \overline{Y} - b\overline{X} \tag{16.6}$$

Note that these two formulas determine the linear equation that provides the best prediction of Y values. This equation is called the regression equation for Y.

DEFINITION

The regression equation for Y is the linear equation

$$\hat{Y} = bX + a$$

where the constants b and a are determined by equations 16.5 and 16.6, respectively. This equation results in the least squared error between the data points and the line.

You should notice that the values of SS and SP are needed in the formulas for b and a just as they are needed to compute the Pearson correlation. An example demonstrating the calculation and use of this best-fitting line is presented now.

EXAMPLE 16.10 The following table presents X and Y scores for a sample of $n = 5$ individuals. These data will be used to demonstrate the procedure for determining the linear regression equation for predicting Y values.

X	Y	$X - \overline{X}$	$Y - \overline{Y}$	$(X - \overline{X})(Y - \overline{Y})$	$(X - \overline{X})^2$
7	11	2	5	10	4
4	3	−1	−3	3	1
6	5	1	−1	−1	1
3	4	−2	−2	4	4
5	7	0	1	0	0
				16 = SP	10 = SS_X

Software Manuals:
Minitab (Section 8)
Mystat (Section 3)
SPSS (Section 6)

For these data, $\Sigma X = 25$, so $\overline{X} = 5$. Also, $\Sigma Y = 30$, so $\overline{Y} = 6$. These means have been used to compute the deviation scores for each X and Y value. The final two columns show the products of the deviation scores and the squared deviations for X. Based on these values,

$$SP = \Sigma(X - \overline{X})(Y - \overline{Y}) = 16$$

$$SS_X = \Sigma(X - \overline{X})^2 = 10$$

Our goal is to find the values for b and a in the linear equation so that we obtain the best-fitting straight line for these data.

FIGURE 16.16

The scatterplot for the data in Example 16.10 is shown with the best-fitting straight line. The predicted Y values ($\hat{Y}$) are on the regression line. Unless the correlation is perfect ($+1.00$ or -1.00), there will be some error between the actual Y values and the predicted Y values. The larger the correlation is, the less the error will be.

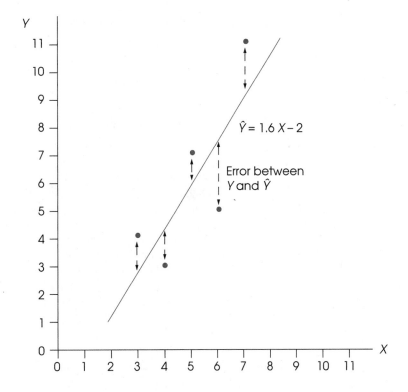

By using equations 16.5 and 16.6, the solutions for b and a are

$$b = \frac{SP}{SS_X} = \frac{16}{10} = 1.6$$
$$a = \overline{Y} - b\overline{X}$$
$$= 6 - 1.6(5)$$
$$= 6 - 8$$
$$= -2$$

The resulting regression equation is

$$\hat{Y} = 1.6X - 2$$

The original data and the regression line are shown in Figure 16.16.

As we noted at the beginning of this section, one common use of regression equations is for prediction. For any given value of X, we can use the equation to compute a predicted value for Y. For the equation from Example 16.10, an individual with an X score of $X = 5$ would be predicted to have a Y score of

$$\hat{Y} = 1.6X - 2$$
$$= 1.6(5) - 2$$
$$= 8 - 2$$
$$= 6$$

Although regression equations can be used for prediction, there are a few cautions that should be considered whenever you are interpreting the predicted values:

1. The predicted value is not perfect (unless $r = +1.00$ or -1.00). If you examine Figure 16.16, it should be clear that the data points do not fit perfectly on the line. In general, there will be some error between the predicted Y values (on the line) and the actual data. Although the amount of error will vary from point to point, on the average the errors will be directly related to the magnitude of the correlation. With a correlation near 1.00 (or -1.00), the data points will generally be close to the line (small error), but as the correlation gets nearer to zero, the magnitude of the error will increase. The statistical procedure for measuring this error is described in the following section.

2. The regression equation should not be used to make predictions for X values that fall outside the range of values covered by the original data. For example 16.10, the X values ranged from $X = 3$ to $X = 7$, and the regression equation was calculated as the best-fitting line within this range. Because you have no information about the X-Y relationship outside this range, the equation should not be used to predict Y for any X value lower than 3 or greater than 7.

LEARNING CHECK

1. Sketch a scatterplot for the following data, that is, a graph showing the X, Y data points:

X	Y
1	4
3	9
5	8

a. Find the regression equation for predicting Y and X. Draw this line on your graph. Does it look like the best-fitting line?

b. Use the regression equation to find the predicted Y value corresponding to each X in the data.

ANSWERS **1. a.** $SS_X = 8$, $SP = 8$, $b = 1$, $a = 4$.
The equation is

$$\hat{Y} = X + 4$$

b. The predicted Y values are 5, 7, and 9.

THE STANDARD ERROR
OF ESTIMATE

It is possible to determine a best-fitting regression equation for any set of data by simply using the formulas already presented. The linear equation you obtain is then used to generate predicted Y values for any known value of X. However, it should be clear that the accuracy of this prediction depends on how well the points on the line correspond to the actual data points, that is, the amount of error between the predicted values, $\hat{Y}$, and the actual scores, Y values. Figure 16.17 shows two different sets of data that have exactly the same regression equation. In one case, there is a perfect correlation ($r = +1$) between X and Y, so the linear equation fits the data perfectly. For the second set of data, the predicted Y values on the line only approximate the real data points.

A regression equation, by itself, allows you to make predictions, but it does not provide any information about the accuracy of the predictions. To measure the precision of the regression, it is customary to compute a standard error of estimate.

DEFINITION

The *standard error of estimate* gives a measure of the standard distance between a regression line and the actual data points.

Conceptually, the standard error of estimate is very much like a standard deviation: Both provide a measure of standard distance. You also should note that the calculation of the standard error of estimate is very similar to the calculation of standard deviation.

To calculate the standard error of estimate, we first will find a sum of squared deviations (SS). Each deviation will measure the distance between the actual Y value (from the data) and the predicted Y value (from the regression line). This sum of squares is commonly called SS_{error} because it measures the sum of squared distances, or errors, between the actual data and the predicted values:

$$SS_{error} = \Sigma(Y - \hat{Y})^2 \tag{16.7}$$

The obtained SS value is then divided by its degrees of freedom to obtain a measure of variance. This procedure should be very familiar:

$$\text{variance} = \frac{SS}{df}$$

The degrees of freedom for the standard error of estimate are $df = n - 2$. The reason for having $n - 2$ degrees of freedom, rather than the customary $n - 1$, is that we now are measuring deviations from a line rather than deviations from a mean. You should recall that it is necessary to know SP to find the slope of the regression line (the value of b in the equation). To calculate SP, you must know the means for both the X and the Y scores. Specifying these two means places two

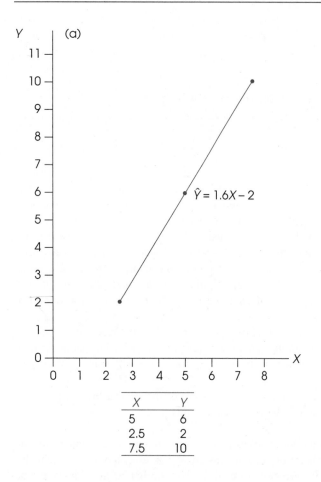

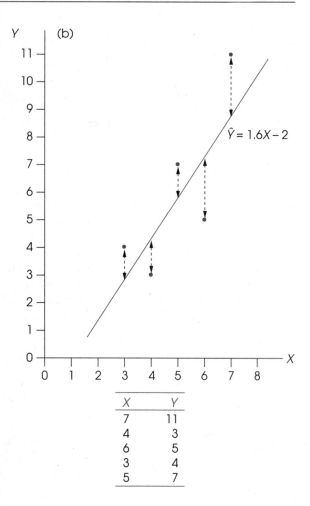

X	Y
5	6
2.5	2
7.5	10

X	Y
7	11
4	3
6	5
3	4
5	7

FIGURE 16.17

(a) Scatterplot showing data points that perfectly fit the regression equation $\hat{Y} = 1.6X - 2$. Note that the correlation is $r = 1.00$. (b) Scatterplot for the data from Example16.10. Notice there is error between the actual data points and the predicted Y values of the regression line.

restrictions on the variability of the data, with the result that the scores have only $n - 2$ degrees of freedom. (A more intuitive explanation for the fact that the SS_{error} has $df = n - 2$ comes from the simple observation that it takes exactly two points to determine a straight line. If there are only two data points, they always fit perfectly on a straight line, so there will be no error. It is only when you have more than two points that there is some freedom in determining the best-fitting line.)

The final step in the calculation of the standard error of estimate is to take the square root of the variance in order to obtain a measure of standard distance. The final equation is

$$\text{standard error of estimate} = \sqrt{\frac{SS_{\text{error}}}{df}} = \sqrt{\frac{\Sigma(Y - \hat{Y})^2}{n - 2}}$$

The following example demonstrates the calculation of this standard error.

EXAMPLE 16.11 The data in Example 16.10 will be used to demonstrate the calculation of the standard error of estimate. These data have the regression equation:

$$\hat{Y} = 1.6X - 2$$

Using this regression equation, we have computed the predicted Y value, the error, and the squared error for each individual in the data.

DATA		PREDICTED Y VALUES $\hat{Y} = 1.6X - 2$	ERROR $Y - \hat{Y}$	SQUARED ERROR $(Y - \hat{Y})^2$
X	Y			
7	11	9.2	1.8	3.24
4	3	4.4	−1.4	1.96
6	5	7.6	−2.6	6.76
3	4	2.8	1.2	1.44
5	7	6.0	1.0	1.00
				$14.40 = SS_{error}$

For these data, the sum of the squared errors is $SS_{error} = 14.40$. With $n = 5$, the data have $df = n - 2 = 3$, so the standard error of estimate is

$$\text{standard error of estimate} = \sqrt{\frac{SS_{error}}{df}} = \sqrt{\frac{14.40}{3}} = 2.19$$

Remember, the standard error of estimate provides a measure of how accurately the regression equation predicts the Y values. In this case, the standard distance between the actual data points and the regression line is measured by standard error of estimate = 2.19.

RELATIONSHIP BETWEEN THE STANDARD ERROR AND THE CORRELATION

It should be clear from Example 16.11 that the standard error of estimate is directly related to the magnitude of the correlation between X and Y. If the correlation is near 1.00 (or −1.00), the data points will be clustered close to the line, and the standard error of estimate will be small. As the correlation gets nearer to zero, the line will provide less accurate predictions, and the standard error of estimate will grow larger. Earlier (p. 513) we observed that squaring the correlation provides a measure of the accuracy of prediction: r^2 is called the coefficient of determination because it determines what proportion of the variability in Y is predicted by the relationship with X. Figure 16.18 should help make this concept more concrete. In the figure, we show three sets of data: one with a correlation of $r = 0$, one with $r = 0.8$, and one with a perfect correlation of $r = 1.00$. For each set of data, the variability in the Y scores is represented by the black vertical lines showing the deviation from the mean for each value of Y. In addition, we have drawn colored vertical lines to show the unpredicted (error) variability in Y by measuring the deviation from the regression line for each value of Y.

In Figure 16.18(a), there is no correlation between X and Y, so all the variability in Y is unpredicted error variability. In this case, the coefficient of determination is

—— Variability of Y scores (deviation from mean)
—— Error variability (deviation from regression line)

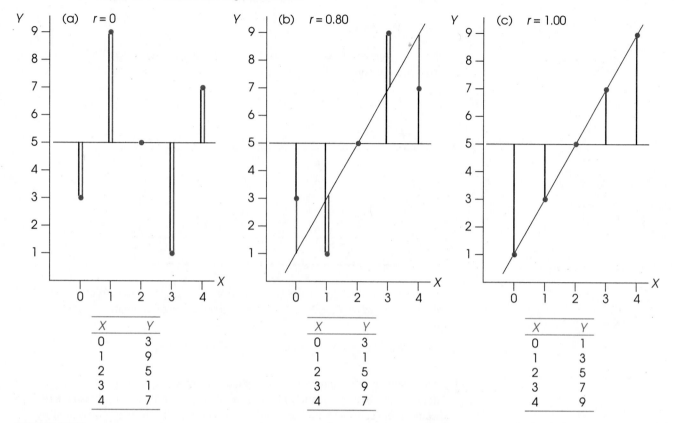

FIGURE 16.18

Error variability as a function of the magnitude of the correlation. (a) Data where the correlation is zero and all the variability in the Y scores is unpredicted error variability. (b) The correlation is $r = 0.80$, and the error variability is reduced. (c) A perfect correlation, where there is no unpredicted error variability.

zero, which means that none of the Y variability can be predicted from the association with X.

Figure 16.18(b), however, shows that the error variability (colored lines) is substantially less than the original variability in the Y scores (black lines). In this case, the coefficient of determination is $r^2 = 0.64$, which means that 64% of the Y variability can be predicted from the association with X.

Finally, Figure 16.18(c) shows that the unpredicted variability is completely eliminated with a correlation of 1.00. Now the coefficient of determination is $r^2 = 1.00$, which means that 100% of the Y variability is predictable from the association with X.

Because r^2 measures the predicted portion of the variability in Y, we can use the expression $1 - r^2$ to measure the unpredicted, or error, portion. With a correlation of $r = 0.80$, for example, the predicted portion of the Y variability is

$$r^2 = 0.64 \quad \text{(or 64%)}$$

The remaining, unpredicted portion is

$$1 - r^2 = 1 - 0.64 = 0.36 \quad \text{(or 36\%)}$$

The unpredicted variability is exactly what we have defined as error variability in the standard error of estimate. Because the total variability in Y is measured by SS_Y, the error portion can be calculated as

$$SS_{error} = (1 - r^2)SS_Y \tag{16.8}$$

Notice that when $r = 1.00$, there is no error (perfect prediction) and that as the correlation approaches zero, the error will grow larger. By using this formula for SS_{error}, the standard error of estimate can be computed as

$$\text{standard error of estimate} = \sqrt{\frac{SS_{error}}{df}} = \sqrt{\frac{(1 - r^2)SS_Y}{n - 2}}$$

The following example demonstrates this new formula.

EXAMPLE 16.12   The same data used in Examples 16.10 and 16.11 are reproduced in the following table:

X	Y	$X - \bar{X}$	$Y - \bar{Y}$	$(X - \bar{X})^2$	$(Y - \bar{Y})^2$	$(X - \bar{X})(Y - \bar{Y})$
7	11	2	5	4	25	10
4	3	−1	−3	1	9	3
6	5	1	−1	1	1	−1
3	4	−2	−2	4	4	4
5	7	0	1	0	1	0
				$SS_X = 10$	$SS_Y = 40$	$SP = 16$

For these data, the Pearson correlation is

$$r = \frac{SP}{\sqrt{SS_X SS_Y}} = \frac{16}{\sqrt{10(40)}} = \frac{16}{20} = 0.80$$

With $SS_Y = 40$ and a correlation of 0.80, the error portion of the Y variability is

$$SS_{error} = (1 - r^2)SS_Y = (1 - 0.64)(40)$$

$$= 0.36(40)$$

$$= 14.40$$

Notice that the new formula for SS_{error} produces exactly the same value that we obtained by summing the squared errors in Example 16.11. Also note that this new formula is generally much easier to use because it requires only the correlation value (r) and the SS for Y. The primary point of this example, however, is that the standard error of estimate is closely related to the value of the correlation. With a large correlation (near $+1.00$ or -1.00), the data points will be close to the regression line, and the standard error of estimate will be small. As a correlation gets smaller (near zero), the data points move away from the regression line, and the standard error of estimate gets larger.

Because it is possible to have the same regression line for sets of data that have different correlations [compare the regression lines in Figure 16.18(b) and (c)], it is important to examine r^2 and the standard error of estimate. The regression equation simply describes the best-fitting line and is used for making predictions. However, r^2 and the standard error of estimate indicate how accurate these predictions will be.

LEARNING CHECK 1. Use the following set of data:

X	Y	
1	4	$SS_X = 10$
2	1	
3	7	$SS_Y = 90$
4	13	
5	10	$SP = 24$

a. Find the regression equation for predicting Y from X.

b. Use the regression equation to find the predicted Y value for each X in the data.

c. Find the error $(Y - \hat{Y})$ for each data point. Square each error value, and sum the results to find SS_{error}.

d. Calculate the Pearson correlation for these data.

e. Use the correlation and SS_Y to compute S_{error}.

2. Assuming that all other factors are held constant, what happens to the standard error of estimate as the correlation between X and Y moves toward zero?

ANSWERS 1. a. $\hat{Y} = 2.4X - 0.2$

b. c.

Y	$\hat{Y}$	ERROR	ERROR^2
4	2.2	1.8	3.24
1	4.6	−3.6	12.96
7	7.0	0	0
13	9.4	3.6	12.96
10	11.8	−1.8	3.24
			$32.40 = SS_{error}$

d. $r = 0.80$

e. $(1 - r^2)SS_Y = 0.36(90) = 32.40 = SS_{error}$

2. The standard error of estimate would get larger.

SUMMARY

1. A correlation measures the relationship between two variables, X and Y. The relationship is described by three characteristics:

   a. *Direction.* A relationship can be either positive or negative. A positive relationship means that X or Y vary in the same direction. A negative relationship means that X and Y vary in opposite directions. The sign of the correlation ($+$ or $-$) specifies the direction.

   b. *Form.* The most common form for a relationship is a straight line. However, special correlations exist for measuring other forms. The form is specified by the type of correlation used. For example, the Pearson correlation measures linear form.

   c. *Degree.* The magnitude of the correlation measures the degree to which the data points fit the specified form. A correlation of 1.00 indicates a perfect fit, and a correlation of 0 indicates no degree of fit.

2. The most commonly used correlation is the Pearson correlation, which measures the degree of linear relationship. The Pearson correlation is identified by the letter r and is computed by

$$r = \frac{SP}{\sqrt{SS_X SS_Y}}$$

In this formula, SP is the sum of products of deviations and can be calculated with either a definitional formula or a computational formula:

definitional formula: $\quad SP = \Sigma(X - \overline{X})(Y - \overline{Y})$

computational formula: $\quad SP = \Sigma XY - \dfrac{\Sigma X \Sigma Y}{n}$

3. The Pearson correlation and z-scores are closely related because both are concerned with the location of individuals within a distribution. When X and Y scores are transformed into z-scores, the Pearson correlation can be computed by

$$r = \frac{\Sigma z_X z_Y}{n}$$

4. A correlation between two variables should not be interpreted as implying a causal relationship. Simply because X and Y are related does not mean that X causes Y or that Y causes X.

5. When the X or Y values used to compute a correlation are limited to a relatively small portion of the potential range, you should exercise caution in generalizing the value of the correlation. Specifically, a limited range of values can either obscure a strong relationship or exaggerate a poor relationship.

6. To evaluate the strength of a relationship, you should square the value of the correlation. The resulting value, r^2, is called the *coefficient of determination* because it measures the portion of the variability in one variable that can be predicted using the relationship with the second variable.

7. Special correlations exist to measure relationships between variables with specific characteristics. The Spearman correlation is used when both variables are measured on ordinal scales. The point-biserial correlation is used when one of the two variables is dichotomous, and the phi-coefficient is used when both variables are dichotomous.

8. When there is a general linear relationship between two variables, X and Y, it is possible to construct a linear equation that allows you to predict the Y value corresponding to any known value of X:

$$\text{predicted } Y \text{ value} = \hat{Y} = bX + a$$

The technique for determining this equation is called regression. By using a *least-squares* method to minimize the error between the predicted Y values and the actual Y values, the best-fitting line is achieved when the linear equation has

$$b = \frac{SP}{SS_X} \quad \text{and} \quad a = \overline{Y} - b\overline{X}$$

9. The linear equation generated by regression (called the *regression equation*) can be used to compute a predicted Y value for any value of X. The accuracy of the prediction is measured by the standard error of estimate, which provides a measure of the standard distance (or error) between the predicted Y value on the line and the actual data point. The standard error of estimate is computed by

$$\text{standard error of estimate} = \sqrt{\frac{SS_{\text{error}}}{n - 2}}$$

where SS_{error} may be computed directly from the error scores,

$$SS_{\text{error}} = \Sigma(Y - \hat{Y})^2$$

or as a proportion of the original Y variability,

$$SS_{\text{error}} = (1 - r^2)SS_Y$$

KEY TERMS

correlation	sum of products (SP)	phi-coefficient	least squares solution
positive correlation	restricted range	linear relationship	regression equation for Y
negative correlation	coefficient of determination	linear equation	regression
perfect correlation	Spearman correlation	slope	regression line
Pearson correlation	point-biserial correlation	Y-intercept	standard error of estimate

———— FOCUS ON PROBLEM SOLVING ————

1. A correlation always has a value from $+1.00$ to -1.00. If you obtain a correlation outside this range, then you have made a computational error.

2. When interpreting a correlation, do not confuse the sign ($+$ or $-$) with its numerical value. The sign and numerical value must be considered separately. Remember, the sign indicates the direction of the relationship between X and Y. On the other hand, the numerical value reflects the strength of the relationship or how well the points approximate a linear (straight-line) relationship. Therefore, a correlation of -0.90 is just as strong as a correlation of $+0.90$. The signs tell us that the first correlation is an inverse relationship.

3. Before you begin to calculate a correlation, you should sketch a scatterplot of the data and make an estimate of the correlation. (Is it positive or negative? Is it near 1 or near 0?) After computing the correlation, compare your final answer with your original estimate.

4. The definitional formula for the sum of products (SP) should be used only when you have a small set (n) of scores and the means for X and Y are both whole numbers. Otherwise, the computational formula will produce quicker, easier, and more accurate results.

5. For computing a correlation, n is number of individuals (and, therefore, the number of *pairs* of X and Y values).

6. To draw a graph from a linear equation, choose any three values for X, put each value in the equation, and calculate the corresponding values for Y. Then plot the three X, Y points on the graph. It is a good idea to use $X = 0$ for one of the three values because this will give you the Y-intercept. You can get a quick idea of what the graph should look like if you know the Y-intercept and the slope. Remember, the Y-intercept is the point where the line crosses the Y-axis, and the slope identifies the tilt of the line. For example, suppose that the Y-intercept is 5 and the slope is -3. The line would pass through the point 0, 5, and its slope indicates that the Y value goes down 3 points each time X increases by 1.

7. Rather than memorizing the formula for the Y-intercept in the regression equation, simply remember that the graphed line of the regression equation always goes through the point $\overline{X}, \overline{Y}$. Therefore, if you plug the mean value for X ($\overline{X}$) into the regression equation, the result equals the mean value for Y ($\overline{Y}$).

$$\overline{Y} = b\overline{X} + a$$

FIGURE 16.19

The scatterplot for the data of Demonstration 16.1. An envelope is drawn around the points to estimate the magnitude of the correlation. A line is drawn through the middle of the envelope to roughly estimate the Y-intercept for the regression equation.

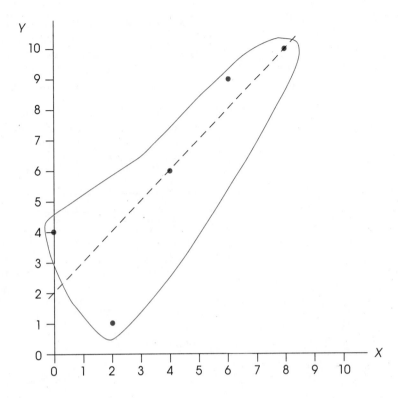

If you simply solve this equation for a, you get the formula for the Y-intercept.

$$a = \bar{Y} - b\bar{X}$$

DEMONSTRATION 16.1

CORRELATION AND REGRESSION

For the following data, calculate the Pearson correlation, and find the regression equation:

PERSON	X	Y
A	0	4
B	2	1
C	8	10
D	6	9
E	4	6

STEP 1   *Sketch a scatterplot.* We have constructed a scatterplot for the data (Figure 16.19) and placed an envelope around the data points to make a preliminary estimate of the correlation. Note that the envelope is narrow and elongated. This indicates that the correlation is large—perhaps 0.80 to 0.90. Also, the correlation is positive because increases in X are generally accompanied by increases in Y.

We can sketch a straight line through the middle of the envelope and data points. Now we can roughly approximate the slope and Y-intercept of the best-fitting line. This is only an educated guess, but it will tell us what values are reasonable when we actually compute the regression line. The line has a positive slope (as X increases, Y increases), and it intersects the Y-axis in the vicinity of $+2$.

S T E P   2   *Obtain the values for SS and SP.* To compute the Pearson correlation, we must find the values for SS_X, SS_Y, and SP. These values are needed for the regression equation as well. The following table illustrates these calculations with the computational formulas for SS and SP:

X	Y	X^2	Y^2	XY
0	4	0	16	0
2	1	4	1	2
8	10	64	100	80
6	9	36	81	54
4	6	16	36	24
$\Sigma X = 20$	$\Sigma Y = 30$	$\Sigma X^2 = 120$	$\Sigma Y^2 = 234$	$\Sigma XY = 160$

For SS_X, we obtain

$$SS_X = \Sigma X^2 - \frac{(\Sigma X)^2}{n} = 120 - \frac{20^2}{5} = 120 - \frac{400}{5} = 120 - 80$$

$$= 40$$

For Y, the sum of squares is

$$SS_Y = \Sigma Y^2 - \frac{(\Sigma Y)^2}{n} = 234 - \frac{30^2}{5} = 234 - \frac{900}{5} = 234 - 180$$

$$= 54$$

The sum of products equals

$$SP = \Sigma XY - \frac{\Sigma X \Sigma Y}{n} = 160 - \frac{20(30)}{5} = 160 - \frac{600}{5} = 160 - 120$$

$$= 40$$

S T E P   3   *Compute the Pearson correlation.* For these data, the Pearson correlation is

$$r = \frac{SP}{\sqrt{SS_X SS_Y}} = \frac{40}{\sqrt{40(54)}} = \frac{40}{\sqrt{2160}} = \frac{40}{46.48}$$

$$= 0.861$$

In step 1, our preliminary estimate for the correlation was between $+0.80$ and $+0.90$. The calculated correlation is consistent with this estimate.

S T E P   4   *Compute the values for the regression equation.* The general form of the regression equation is

$$\hat{Y} = bX + a$$

We will need to compute the values for the slope (b) of the line and the Y-intercept (a). For slope, we obtain

$$b = \frac{SP}{SS_X} = \frac{40}{40} = +1$$

The formula for the Y-intercept is

$$a = \overline{Y} - b\overline{X}$$

Thus, we will need the values for the sample means. For these data, the sample means are

$$\overline{X} = \frac{\Sigma X}{n} = \frac{20}{5} = 4$$

$$\overline{Y} = \frac{\Sigma Y}{n} = \frac{30}{5} = 6$$

Now we can compute the Y-intercept

$$a = 6 - 1(4) = 6 - 4 = 2$$

Finally, the regression equation is

$$\hat{Y} = bX + a$$
$$= 1X + 2$$

or

$$\hat{Y} = X + 2$$

PROBLEMS

1. What information is provided by the sign ($+$ or $-$) of the Pearson correlation?

2. What information is provided by the numerical value of the Pearson correlation?

3. For each of the following sets of scores,

SET 1		SET 2		SET 3	
X	Y	X	Y	X	Y
1	1	1	9	1	3
2	3	2	7	2	9
3	5	3	5	3	5
4	7	4	3	4	1
5	9	5	1	5	7

a. Sketch a scatterplot showing the data, and describe the relationship between X and Y.

b. Calculate the Pearson correlation. Does the obtained value correspond with your description?

4. A single individual can have a large influence on the value of the Pearson correlation, especially with a small sample. Starting with the following data,

X	Y
1	4
2	1
3	2
4	3

a. Sketch a scatterplot showing the data, and calculate the Pearson correlation.

b. Suppose that a new individual with scores of $X = 10$ and $Y = 10$ is added to the sample. Sketch the scatterplot for the new data, and calculate the new value of the Pearson correlation.

5. When the Pearson correlation is computed for a restricted range of X values (or Y values), the obtained correlation can be very different from the correlation for the full range. Use the following data to demonstrate this fact:

X	Y
1	2
2	4
3	1
4	5
5	3
6	9
7	10
8	7
9	8
10	6

a. Sketch a graph showing the X, Y points.
b. Compute the Pearson correlation for the full set of data.
c. Compute the Pearson correlation using only the first five individuals in the sample (the five smallest X values).
d. Compute the Pearson correlation for the final five individuals in the sample (the five largest X values).
e. Explain why the results from parts c and d are so different from the overall correlation obtained in part b.

6. Use the following set of data:

X	Y
5	2
6	4
0	2
8	4
6	3

a. Sketch a scatterplot showing the X and Y values. Just by looking at your graph, estimate the Pearson correlation for these data.
b. Compute the Pearson correlation.
c. Add 3 points to each Y value, and sketch a new scatterplot showing the new X and Y values. Just by looking at your graph, estimate what happens to the Pearson correlation when a constant is added to each score.

d. Compute the Pearson correlation for the data from part c.

7. Use the following set of data:

X	Y
1	2
2	8
3	0
1	3
3	2

a. Sketch a scatterplot showing the X and Y values. Just by looking at your graph, estimate the Pearson correlation for these data.
b. Compute the Pearson correlation.
c. Multiply each Y value by 3, and sketch a new scatterplot showing the new X and Y values. Just by looking at your graph, estimate what happens to the Pearson correlation when each score is multiplied by a constant.
d. Compute the Pearson correlation for the data from part c.

8. A health psychologist is interested in the relationship between regular exercise and general health. A sample of six individuals is obtained. Each person is interviewed to determine how much exercise the person gets in an average week, and each person undergoes a physical exam to determine general health. A 10-point scale is used to rate both health and exercise, with higher scores indicating better health and more exercise. The data are as follows:

PERSON	EXERCISE RATING	HEALTH RATING
A	9	10
B	1	3
C	10	6
D	3	3
E	5	4
F	8	4

a. Compute the Pearson correlation between exercise and health for these data.
b. Can the psychologist conclude that regular exercise causes better health? Explain your answer.

9. To measure the relationship between anxiety level and test performance, a psychologist obtains a sample of $n = 6$ college students from an introductory statistics course.

The students are asked to come to the laboratory 15 minutes before the final exam. In the lab, the psychologist records physiological measures of anxiety (heart rate, GSR, blood pressure, etc.) for each subject. In addition, the psychologist obtains the exam score for each subject. Compute the Pearson correlation for the following data:

STUDENT	ANXIETY RATING	EXAM SCORE
A	5	80
B	2	88
C	7	80
D	7	79
E	4	86
F	5	85

10. If you obtain a random sample of $n = 2$ people and measure each person's annual salary and shoe size, what would you expect to obtain for the Pearson correlation? (Be careful. Try making up some data points to see what happens.) How would you interpret a correlation of $r = +1.00$ obtained for a sample of $n = 2$? Should you generalize this sample correlation and conclude that a strong relationship between X and Y exists in the population?

11. A psychologist would like to determine whether there is any consistent relationship between intelligence and creativity. A random sample of $n = 18$ people is obtained, and the psychologist administers a standardized IQ test and a creativity test to each individual. Using these data, the psychologist obtains a Pearson correlation of $r = +0.20$ between IQ and creativity.
    a. Do the sample data provide sufficient evidence to conclude that a real (non-zero) correlation exists in the population? Test at the .05 level of significance.
    b. If the same correlation, $r = 0.20$, was obtained for a sample of $n = 102$ people, what decision would be made about the population correlation?

12. A researcher obtains a sample correlation of $r = 0.25$, which is sufficient (with $\alpha = .05$) to conclude that there is a significant correlation in the population. Based on this information, how large was the researcher's sample? Find the smallest possible n that would justify the conclusion.

13. For a sample of $n = 15$ students, a researcher obtains a correlation of $r = -.53$ between college grade-point average and number of errors committed on a learning task.
    a. Is this result sufficient to conclude that a real (non-zero relationship exists in the population.) Use $\alpha = .05$.

b. What decision would be made about the population correlation if the researcher had used a sample of $n = 12$ students?

14. Hunt and his colleagues (1975) have conducted several studies examining the relationship between intelligence and the speed of basic mental processes. In a typical experiment, Hunt measured reaction time for a simple mental task (e.g., determining whether two letters are the same or different) and then computed the correlation between the subjects' reaction times and their IQ scores. Hypothetical data representing the results of one experiment are as follows:

SUBJECT	IQ	REACTION TIME
A	118	238
B	124	198
C	105	220
D	98	216
E	115	223
F	128	206

a. Compute the Pearson correlation between IQ and reaction time.
b. Is the sample correlation significant at the .05 level?

15. A psychology instructor asked each student to report the number of hours he or she had spent preparing for the final exam. In addition, the instructor recorded the number of incorrect answers on each student's exam. These data are as follows:

HOURS	NUMBER WRONG
4	5
0	12
2	3
3	1
6	4

a. Compute the Pearson correlation between study hours and number wrong.
b. Convert the original scores to ranks, and compute the Spearman correlation for these data.
c. Sketch a scatterplot for the original X and Y values and a scatterplot for the ranks. Notice that the extreme data point (0 hours and 12 wrong) has less influence after the data are ranked.

16. To test the effectiveness of a new studying strategy, a

psychologist randomly divides a sample of 8 students into two groups, with $n = 4$ in each group. The students in one group receive training in the new studying strategy. Then all students are given 30 minutes to study a chapter from a history textbook before they take a quiz on the chapter. The quiz scores for the two groups are as follows:

TRAINING	NO TRAINING
9	4
7	7
6	3
10	6

a. Convert these data into a form suitable for the point-biserial correlation. (Use $X = 1$ for training, $X = 0$ for no training, and the quiz score for Y.)
b. Calculate the point-biserial correlation for these data.

17. The data in Problem 16 showed a mean difference of 3 points between the training group and the no-training group ($\overline{X} = 8$ versus $\overline{X} = 5$). Because there is a 3-point difference, you would expect to find that quiz scores are related to training (there is a non-zero correlation). Now consider the following data, where there is no mean difference between the two groups:

TRAINING	NO TRAINING
2	4
5	7
6	3
7	6

a. Without doing any calculations, estimate the point-biserial correlation for these data.
b. Convert the data to a form suitable for the point-biserial, and compute the correlation.

18. A researcher would like to evaluate the relationship between a person's age and his or her preference between two leading brands of cola. In a sample of 12 people, the researcher found that 5 out of 8 people over 30 years old preferred brand A and only 1 out of 4 people under 30 years old preferred brand A.
a. Convert the data to a form suitable for computing the phi-coefficient. (Code the two age categories as 0 and 1 for the X variable, and code the preferred brand of soft drink as 0 and 1 for the Y variable.)
b. Compute the phi-coefficient for the data.

19. Sketch a graph showing the linear equation $Y = 3X - 2$.

20. Two major companies supply laboratory animals for psychologists. Company A sells laboratory rats for $6 each and charges a $10 fee for delivery. Company B sells rats for only $5 each, but has a $20 delivery charge. In each case, the delivery fee is a one-time charge and does not depend on the number of rats in the order.
a. For each company, what is the linear equation that defines the total cost (Y) as a function of the number of rats (X)? Each equation should be of the form

$$Y = bX + a$$

b. What would the total cost be for an order of 10 rats from company A? From company B?
c. If you were buying 20 rats, which company gives you the better deal?

21. a. Find the regression equation for the following data:

X	Y
1	2
4	7
3	5
2	1
5	14
3	7

b. Compute the predicted Y value for each X in the data.
c. Compute the error ($Y - \hat{Y}$) for each individual, and find SS_{error} for these data.

22. A set of $n = 6$ pairs of X and Y values has a Pearson correlation of $r = +0.60$ and $SS_Y = 100$. If you are using these data as the basis for a regression equation,
a. On the average, how much error would you expect if the regression equation were used to predict the Y score for a specific individual? That is, find the standard error of estimate.
b. How much error would you expect if the sample size were $n = 102$ instead of $n = 6$?
c. How much error would you expect if the sample correlation were $r = +0.80$ instead of 0.60?

23. Many research studies have found a negative relationship between average IQ and family size. Zajonc and Markus (1975) have developed a mathematical model for predicting the intellectual climate of a family based on the number of family members and their ages. For this exercise, we are asking you to develop your own linear model (much simpler than the one Zajonc and Markus proposed) for predicting intellectual climate (Y) from the

number of children in a family (X). Use the following data to calculate the appropriate regression equation:

NUMBER OF CHILDREN (X)	INTELLECTUAL CLIMATE (Y)
3	8
0	18
4	8
2	14
1	12

24. A college professor claims that the scores on the first exam provide an excellent indication of how students will perform throughout the term. To test this claim, first-exam scores and final grades were recorded for a sample of $n = 12$ students in an introductory psychology class. The data are as follows:

FIRST EXAM	FINAL GRADE
62	74
73	93
88	68
82	79
85	91
77	72
94	96
65	61
91	92
74	82
85	93
98	95

a. Is the professor right? Is there a significant correlation between scores on the first exam and final grades? Test with $\alpha = .01$.

b. How accurately do the exam scores predict final grades? Compute the standard error of estimate.

CHAPTER 17

THE CHI-SQUARE STATISTIC: TESTS FOR GOODNESS OF FIT AND INDEPENDENCE

CONTENTS

Imagine that you are walking into an amusement park and someone gives you a handbill advertising an entertainment program scheduled for that evening: DON'T MISS TO-NIGHT'S SHOW. Assuming that you are not an avid collector of handbills, you are now stuck with a piece of paper that you don't want. As you continue to walk down the path, you realize that there are no trash cans in sight. What do you do with the handbill?

In a study examining littering in public places, Cialdini, Reno, and Kallgren (1990) looked at people's behavior in the situation we have just described. One specific factor the researchers considered was the amount of litter already on the ground. After receiving the handbill, the subjects entered a path that had been prepared with either 0, 1, 2, 4, 8, or 16 handbills scattered around, apparently discarded by other visitors. Did the amount of existing litter influence littering by the subjects?

The data from this study are shown in Table 17.1 and seem to indicate that littering behavior is directly related to the amount of preexisting litter. When the path had 0 or 1 pieces of litter, only 14% of the subjects (17 out of 119) dropped their handbills. When the amount of litter was increased to 2 or 4 pieces, the rate of littering increased to 23% (28 out of 119 subjects). And, when the path was heavily littered with 8 or 16 handbills, the data show that 41% of the subjects (49 out of 120 people) dropped their own handbills and contributed to the mess.

Although the Cialdini study involves a dependent variable (littering behavior) and an independent variable (the amount of preexisting litter), you should realize that this experiment is different from any we have considered in the past. Specifically, the Cialdini study does not produce a numerical score for each subject. Instead, each individual is simply classified

TABLE 17.1

The number of people littering or not littering depending on the amount of litter already on the ground.

	AMOUNT OF EXISTING LITTER		
	0 OR 1 PIECES	2 OR 4 PIECES	8 OR 16 PIECES
LITTERING	17	28	49
NOT LITTERING	102	91	71

Cialdini, R.B., Reno, R.R., and Kallgren, C.A. (1990). A focus theory of normative conduct: Recycling the concept of norms to reduce littering in public places. *Journal of Personality and Social Psychology, 58,* 1015-1020. Copyright © 1990 by the American Psychological Association. Adapted with permission.

into one of two categories (littering or not littering) and the data consist of *frequencies* showing how many individuals are in each category. Because there are no numerical scores, it is impossible to calculate a mean or a variance or a standard deviation for the sample data. Therefore, it is impossible to use any of the familiar hypothesis tests (such as a *t* statistic or ANOVA) to determine whether or not there are *significant* differences between the treatment conditions.

Fortunately, statistical techniques have been developed specifically to analyze and interpret frequency data. In this chapter we will introduce a statistic called *chi-square* and two hypothesis tests based on the chi-square statistic. Unlike earlier tests that require numerical scores (X values), the chi-square tests use frequencies and proportions from a sample to test hypotheses about the corresponding population.

17.1 OVERVIEW: PARAMETRIC AND NON-PARAMETRIC STATISTICAL TESTS

All the statistical tests we have examined thus far are designed to test hypotheses about specific population parameters. For example, we used *t* tests to assess hypotheses about about μ and later about $\mu_1 - \mu_2$. In addition, these tests typically make assumptions about the shape of the population distribution and about other population parameters. Recall that for analysis of variance the population distributions are assumed to be normal and homogeneity of variance is required. Because these tests all concern parameters and require assumptions about parameters, they are called *parametric tests*.

Another general characteristic of parametric tests is that they require a numerical score for each individual in the sample. The scores then are added, squared, averaged, and otherwise manipulated using basic arithmetic. In terms of measurement scales, parametric tests require data from an interval or a ratio scale (see Chapter 1).

Often researchers are confronted with experimental situations that do not conform to the requirements of parametric tests. In these situations, it may not be appropriate to use a parametric test. Remember, when the assumptions of a test are violated, the test may lead to an erroneous interpretation of the data. Fortunately, there are several hypothesis-testing techniques that provide alternatives to parametric tests. These alternatives are called *non-parametric tests*.

In this chapter, we introduce some commonly used non-parametric tests. You should notice that these non-parametric tests usually do not state hypotheses in terms of a specific parameter, and they make few (if any) assumptions about the population distribution. For the latter reason, non-parametric tests sometimes are called *distribution-free tests*. Another distinction is that non-parametric tests are well suited for data that are measured on nominal or ordinal scales. Finally, you should be warned that non-parametric tests generally are not as sensitive as parametric tests; non-parametric tests are more likely to fail in detecting a real difference between two treatments. Therefore, whenever the experimental data give you a choice between a parametric and a non-parametric test, you always should choose the parametric alternative.

17.2   THE CHI-SQUARE TEST FOR GOODNESS OF FIT

Parameters such as the mean and standard deviation are the most common way to describe a population, but there are situations where a researcher has questions about the proportions or relative frequencies for a distribution. For example,

How does the number of women lawyers compare with the number of men in the profession?

Of the three leading brands of soft drinks, which is preferred by most Americans? Which brands are second and third, and how big are the differences in popularity among the three?

To what extent are different ethnic groups represented in the population of your city?

The name of the test comes from the Greek letter χ (chi, pronounced "kye"), which is used to identify the test statistic.

Notice that each of the preceding examples asks a question about *how many*—in other words, these are all questions about frequencies. The chi-square test for goodness of fit is specifically designed to answer these type of questions. In general terms, this chi-square test is a hypothesis-testing procedure that uses the proportions obtained for a sample distribution to test a hypothesis about the corresponding proportions in the population distribution.

DEFINITION

The *chi-square test for goodness of fit* uses sample data to test hypotheses about the shape or proportions of a population distribution. The test determines how well the obtained sample proportions fit the population proportions specified by the null hypothesis.

FIGURE 17.1

Distribution of eye colors for a sample of $n = 40$ individuals. The same frequency distribution is shown as a bar graph, as a table, and with the frequencies written in a series of boxes.

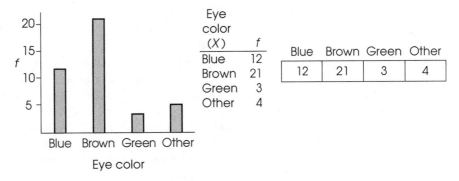

You should recall from Chapter 2 that a frequency distribution is defined as a record of the number of individuals located in each category of the scale of measurement. In a frequency distribution graph, the categories that make up the scale of measurement are listed on the X-axis. In a frequency distribution table, the categories are listed in the first column. With chi-square tests, however, it is customary to present the scale of measurement as a series of boxes, with each box corresponding to a separate category on the scale. The frequency corresponding to each category is simply presented as a number written inside the box. Figure 17.1 shows how a distribution of eye colors for a set of $n = 40$ students can be presented as a graph, a table, or a series of boxes. Notice that the scale of measurement for this example consists of four categories of eye color (brown, blue, green, other).

THE NULL HYPOTHESIS FOR THE GOODNESS-OF-FIT TEST

For the chi-square test of goodness of fit, the null hypothesis specifies the proportion (or percentage) of the population in each category. For example, a hypothesis might state that 90% of all lawyers are men and only 10% are women. The simplest way of presenting this hypothesis, is to put the hypothesized proportions in the series of boxes representing the scale of measurement:

	MEN	WOMEN
H_0:	90%	10%

Although it is conceivable that a researcher could choose any proportions for the null hypothesis, there usually is some well-defined rationale for stating a null hypothesis. Generally, H_0 will fall into one of the following categories:

1. No Preference. The null hypothesis often states that there is no preference among the different categories. In this case, H_0 states that the population is divided equally among the categories. For example, a hypothesis stating that there is no preference among the three leading brands of soft drinks would specify a population distribution as follows:

	BRAND X	BRAND Y	BRAND Z
H_0:	$\frac{1}{3}$	$\frac{1}{3}$	$\frac{1}{3}$

(Preferences in the population are equally divided among the three soft drinks.)

The no-preference hypothesis is used in situations where a researcher wants to determine whether there are any preferences among categories or any variation from one category to another.

2. No Difference from a Comparison Population. The null hypothesis can state that the frequency distribution for one population is not different from the distribution that is known to exist for another population. For example, suppose that it is known that 60% of U.S. residents favor the president's foreign policy and 40% are in opposition. A researcher might wonder if this same pattern of attitudes exists among Europeans. The null hypothesis would state that there is no difference between the two populations and specify that the Europeans would be distributed as follows:

	FAVOR	OPPOSE
H_0:	60%	40%

(Proportions for the European population are not different from the American proportions.)

The no-difference hypothesis is used in situations where a specific population frequency distribution is already known. You may have a known frequency distribution from an earlier time, and the question is whether there has been any change in the distribution. Or you may have a known distribution for one population, and the question is whether a second population has the same distribution.

Because the null hypothesis for the goodness-of-fit test specifies an exact distribution for the population, the alternative hypothesis (H_1) simply states that the population distribution has a different shape from that specified in H_0. If the null hypothesis stated that the population is equally divided among three categories, the alternative hypothesis would say that the population is not divided equally.

THE DATA FOR THE GOODNESS-OF-FIT TEST

The data for a chi-square test are remarkably simple. There is no need to calculate a sample mean or *SS;* you just select a sample of *n* individuals and count how many are in each category. The resulting values are called *observed frequencies.* The symbol for observed frequency is f_o. For example, the following data represent observed frequencies for a sample of $n = 40$ subjects. Each person was given a personality questionnaire and classified into one of three personality categories: A, B, or C.

CATEGORY A	CATEGORY B	CATEGORY C	
15	19	6	$n = 40$

Notice that each individual in the sample is classified into one and only one of the categories. Thus, the frequencies in this example represent three completely separate groups of individuals: 15 who were classified as category A, 19 classified as B, and 6 classified as C. Also note that the observed frequencies add up to the total sample size: $\Sigma f_o = n$.

DEFINITION

The *observed frequency* is the number of individuals from the sample who are classified in a particular category. Each individual is counted in one and only one category.

EXPECTED FREQUENCIES The general goal of the chi-square test for goodness of fit is to compare the data (the observed frequencies) with the null hypothesis. The problem is to determine how well the data fit the distribution specified in H_0—hence the name *goodness of fit*.

The first step in the chi-square test is to determine how the sample distribution would look if the sample provided a perfect image of the population according to the null hypothesis. Suppose, for example, that the null hypothesis states that the population is distributed in three categories with the following proportions:

CATEGORY A	CATEGORY B	CATEGORY C
25%	50%	25%

If this hypothesis is correct, how would you expect a random sample of $n = 40$ individuals to be distributed among the three categories? It should be clear that your best strategy is to predict that 25% of the sample would be in category A, 50% would be in category B, and 25% would be in category C. To find the exact frequency expected for each category, multiply the sample size (n) by the proportion (or percentage) from the null hypothesis. For this example, you would expect

$$25\% \text{ of } 40 = 0.25(40) = 10 \text{ individuals in category A}$$

$$50\% \text{ of } 40 = 0.50(40) = 20 \text{ individuals in category B}$$

$$25\% \text{ of } 40 = 0.25(40) = 10 \text{ individuals in category C}$$

The frequency values predicted from the null hypothesis are called *expected frequencies*. The symbol for expected frequency is f_e, and the expected frequency for each category is computed by

$$\text{expected frequency} = f_e = pn \tag{17.1}$$

where p is the proportion stated in the null hypothesis and n is the sample size. Note that the no-preference null hypothesis will always produce equal f_e values for all categories because the proportions (p values) are the same for all categories. On the other hand, the no-difference null hypothesis typically will not produce equal values for the expected frequencies.

DEFINITION The *expected frequency* for each category is the frequency value that is predicted from the null hypothesis and the sample size (n). The expected frequencies define an ideal, *hypothetical* sample distribution that would be obtained if the sample proportions were in perfect agreement with the proportions specified in the null hypothesis.

THE CHI-SQUARE STATISTIC The general purpose of any hypothesis test is to determine whether the sample data support or refute a hypothesis about the population. In the chi-square test for goodness of fit, the sample is expressed as a set of observed frequencies (f_o values), and the null hypothesis has been used to generate a set of expected frequencies (f_e values). The *chi-square statistic* simply measures how well the data (f_o) fit the

17.1 THE CHI-SQUARE FORMULA

WE HAVE seen that the chi-square formula compares observed frequencies to expect frequencies in order to assess how well the sample data match the hypothesized data. This function of the chi-square statistic is easy to spot in the numerator of the equation, $(f_o - f_e)^2$. The difference between the observed and the expected frequencies is found first. The greater this difference is, the more discrepancy there is between what is observed and what is expected. The difference is then squared to remove the negative signs (large discrepancies may have negative signs as well as positive signs). The summation sign in front of the equation indicates that we must examine the amount of discrepancy for every category. Why, then, must we divide the squared differences by f_e for each category before we sum the category values? The answer to this question is that the obtained discrepancy between f_o and f_e is viewed as *relatively* large or *relatively* small, depending on the size of the expected

frequency. This point is demonstrated in the following analogy.

Suppose that you were going to throw a party and you *expected* 1000 people to show up. However, at the party you count the number of guests and *observed* that 1040 actually showed up. Forty more guests than expected are no major problem when all along you were planning for 1000. There will still probably be enough beer and potato chips for everyone. On the other hand, suppose that you had a party and you expected 10 people to attend, but instead 50 actually showed up. Forty more guests in this case spell big trouble. How "significant" the discrepancy is depends in part on what you were originally expecting. With very large expected frequencies, allowances are made for more error between f_o and f_e. This is accomplished in the chi-square formula by dividing the squared discrepancy for each category, $(f_o - f_e)^2$, by its expected frequency.

hypothesis (f_e). The symbol for the chi-square statistic is χ^2. The formula for the chi-square statistic is

$$\text{chi-square} = \chi^2 = \Sigma \frac{(f_o - f_e)^2}{f_e} \tag{17.2}$$

As the formula indicates, the value of chi-square is computed by the following steps:

1. Find the difference between f_o (the data) and f_e (the hypothesis) for each category.

2. Square the difference. This ensures that all values are positive.

3. Next, divide the squared difference by f_e. A justification for this step is given in Box 17.1.

4. Finally, sum the values from all categories.

THE CHI-SQUARE DISTRIBUTION AND DEGREES OF FREEDOM

It should be clear from the chi-square formula that the value of chi-square is measuring the discrepancy between the observed frequencies (data) and the expected frequencies (H_0). When there are large differences between f_o and f_e, the value of chi-square will be large, and we will conclude that the data do not fit the hypothesis. Thus, a large value for chi-square will lead us to reject H_0. On the other hand, when the observed frequencies are very close to the expected frequencies, chi-square will be small, and we will conclude that there is a very good fit between the data and the hypothesis. Thus, a small chi-square value indicates that we should

FIGURE 17.2

Chi-square distributions are positively skewed. the critical region is placed in the extreme tail, which reflects large chi-square values.

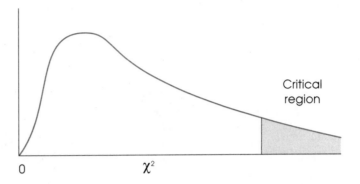

fail to reject H_0. To decide whether a particular chi-square value is "large" or "small," we must refer to a *chi-square distribution*. This distribution is the set of chi-square values for all the possible random samples when H_0 is true. Much like other distributions we have examined (*t* distribution, *F* distribution), the chi-square distribution is a theoretical distribution with well-defined characteristics. Some of these characteristics are easy to infer from the chi-square formula.

1. The formula for chi-square involves adding squared values, so you can never obtain a negative value. Thus, all chi-square values are zero or larger.

2. When H_0 is true, you expect the data (f_o values) to be close to the hypothesis (f_e values). Thus, we expect chi-square values to be small when H_0 is true.

These two factors suggest that the typical chi-square distribution will be positively skewed (see Figure 17.2). Note that small values, near zero, are expected when H_0 is true, and large values (in the right-hand tail) are very unlikely. Thus, unusually large values of chi-square will form the critical region for the hypothesis test.

Although the typical chi-square distribution is positively skewed, there is one other factor that plays a role in the exact shape of the chi-square distribution—the number of categories. You should recall that the chi-square formula requires that you sum values from every category. The more categories you have, the more likely it is that you will obtain a large sum for the chi-square value. On the average, chi-square will be larger when you are summing over 10 categories than when you are summing over only 3 categories. As a result, there is a whole family of chi-square distributions, with the exact shape of each distribution determined by the number of categories used in the study. Technically, each specific chi-square distribution is identified by degrees of freedom (*df*) rather than the number of categories. For the goodness-of-fit test, the degrees of freedom are determined by

Caution: The *df* for a chi-square test is *not* related to sample size (*n*) as it is in most other tests.

$$df = C - 1 \qquad\qquad (17.3)$$

where *C* is the number of categories. A brief discussion of this *df* formula is presented in Box 17.2. Figure 17.3 shows the general relationship between *df* and the shape of the chi-square distribution. Note that the typical chi-square value (the mode) gets larger as the number of categories is increased.

17.2   A CLOSER LOOK AT DEGREES OF FREEDOM

DEGREES OF freedom for the chi-square test literally measure the number of free choices that exist when you are determining the null hypothesis or the expected frequencies. For example, when you are classifying individuals into three categories, you have exactly two free choices in stating the null hypothesis. You may select any two proportions for the first two categories, but then the third proportion is determined. If you hypothesize 25% in the first category and 50% in the second category, then the third category must be 25% in order to account for 100% of the population. In general, you are free to select proportions for all but one of the categories, but then the final proportion is determined by the fact that the entire set must total 100%. Thus, you have $C - 1$ free choices, where C is the number of categories: degrees of freedom, df, equals $C - 1$.

The same restriction holds when you are determining the expected frequencies. Again, suppose that you have three categories and a sample of $n = 40$ individuals. If you specify expected frequencies of $f_e = 10$ for the first category and $f_e = 20$ for the second category, then you must use $f_e = 10$ for the final category.

CATEGORY A	CATEGORY B	CATEGORY C	
10	20	???	$n = 40$

As before, you may distribute the sample freely among the first $C - 1$ categories, but then the final category is determined by the total number of individuals in the sample.

LOCATING THE CRITICAL REGION FOR A CHI-SQUARE TEST

To evaluate the results of a chi-square test, we must determine whether the chi-square statistic is large or small. Remember, an unusually large value indicates a big discrepancy between the data and the hypothesis and suggests that we reject H_0. To determine whether or not a particular chi-square value is significantly large, you first select an alpha level, typically .05 or .01. Then you consult the table entitled The Chi-Square distribution (Appendix B). A portion of the chi-square dis-

---

FIGURE 17.3

The shape of the chi-square distribution for different values of df. As the number of categories increases the peak (mode) of the distribution has a larger chi-square value.

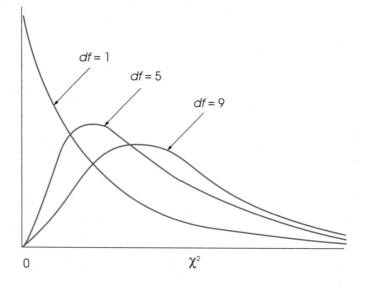

TABLE 17.2

A portion of the table of critical values for the chi-square distribution

| | | PROPORTION IN CRITICAL REGION | | | |
df	0.10	0.05	0.025	0.01	0.005
1	2.71	3.84	5.02	6.63	7.88
2	4.61	5.99	7.38	9.21	10.60
3	6.25	7.81	9.35	11.34	12.84
4	7.78	9.49	11.14	13.28	14.86
5	9.24	11.07	12.83	15.09	16.75
6	10.64	12.59	14.45	16.81	18.55
7	12.02	14.07	16.01	18.48	20.28
8	13.36	15.51	17.53	20.09	21.96
9	14.68	16.92	19.02	21.67	23.59

tribution table is shown in Table 17.2. The first column in the table lists df values for chi-square. The top row of the table lists proportions of area in the extreme right-hand tail of the distribution. The numbers in the body of the table are the critical values of chi-square. The table shows, for example, that in a chi-square distribution with $df = 3$, only 5% (0.05) of the values are larger than 7.81, and only 1% (0.01) are larger than 11.34.

EXAMPLE OF THE CHI-SQUARE TEST FOR GOODNESS OF FIT

We will use the same step-by-step process for testing hypotheses with chi-square as we used for other hypothesis tests. In general, the steps consists of stating the hypotheses, locating the critical region, computing the test statistic, and making a decision about H_0. The following example demonstrates the complete process of hypothesis testing with the goodness-of-fit test.

EXAMPLE 17.1 A researcher is interested in the factors that are involved in course selection. A sample of 50 students is asked, "Which of the following factors is most important to you when selecting a course?" Students must choose one and only one of the following alternatives:

1. Interest in course topic
2. Ease of passing the course
3. Instructor for the course
4. Time of day course is offered

The frequency distribution of responses for this sample (the set of observed frequencies) is as follows:

INTEREST IN TOPIC	EASE OF PASSING	COURSE INSTRUCTOR	TIME OF DAY
18	17	7	8

The question for the hypothesis test is whether any of the factors plays a greater role than others for course selection.

FIGURE 17.4

For Example 17.1, the critical region begins at a chi-square value of 7.81.

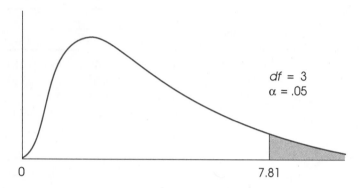

STEP 1 We must state the hypotheses and select a level of significance. The hypotheses may be stated as follows:

H_0: The population of students shows no preference in selecting any one of the four factors over the others. Thus, the four factors are named equally often, and the population distribution has the following proportions:

INTEREST IN TOPIC	EASE OF PASSING	COURSE INSTRUCTOR	TIME OF DAY
¼	¼	¼	¼

H_1: In the population of students, one or more of these factors plays a greater role in course selection (the factor is named more frequently by students).

The level of significance is set at a standard value, $\alpha = .05$.

STEP 2 The value for degrees of freedom is determined, and then the critical region is located. For this example, the value for degrees of freedom is

$$df = C - 1 = 4 - 1 = 3$$

For $df = 3$ and $\alpha = .05$, the table for critical values of chi-square indicates that the critical χ^2 has a value of 7.81. The critical region is sketched in Figure 17.4.

STEP 3 The expected frequencies for all categories must be determined, and then the chi-square statistic can be calculated. If H_0 were true and the students display no response preference for the four alternatives, then the proportion of the population responding to each category would be ¼. Because the sample size (n) is 50, the null hypothesis predicts expected frequencies of 12.5 for all categories (Table 17.3):

It is acceptable for expected frequencies to have fractional or decimal values.

$$f_e = pn = \frac{1}{4}(50) = 12.5$$

TABLE 17.3

Observed and expected frequencies for Example 17.1

(a) The most important factor in course selection (observed frequencies)

INTEREST IN TOPIC	EASE OF PASSING	COURSE INSTRUCTOR	TIME OF DAY
18	17	7	8

(b) The most important factor in course selection (expected frequencies computed from the no-preference null hypothesis)

INTEREST IN TOPIC	EASE OF PASSING	COURSE INSTRUCTOR	TIME OF DAY
12.5	12.5	12.5	12.5

The observed frequencies and the expected frequencies are presented in Table 17.3. Using these values, the chi-square statistic may now be calculated.

$$\chi^2 = \Sigma \frac{(f_o - f_e)^2}{f_e}$$

$$= \frac{(18 - 12.5)^2}{12.5} + \frac{(17 - 12.5)^2}{12.5} + \frac{(7 - 12.5)^2}{12.5} + \frac{(8 - 12.5)^2}{12.5}$$

$$= \frac{30.25}{12.5} + \frac{20.25}{12.5} + \frac{30.25}{12.5} + \frac{20.25}{12.5}$$

$$= 2.42 + 1.62 + 2.42 + 1.62$$

$$= 8.08$$

STEP 4 The obtained chi-square value is in the critical region. Therefore, H_0 is rejected, and the researcher may conclude that some of the factors are more important than others in course selection.

IN THE LITERATURE:
REPORTING THE RESULTS FOR CHI-SQUARE

The APA style specifies the format for reporting the chi-square statistic in scientific journals. For the results of Example 17.1, the report might state:

> The students showed a significant preference on the question concerning factors involved in course selection, $\chi^2(3, n = 50) = 8.08, p < .05$.

Note that the form of the report is similar to that of other statistical tests we have examined. Degrees of freedom are indicated in parentheses following the chi-square symbol. Also contained in the parentheses is the sample size (n). This additional information is important because the degrees of freedom value is based on the number of categories (C), not sample size. Next, the calculated value of chi-square is presented, followed by the probability that a Type I error has been committed. Because the null hypothesis was rejected, the probability is *less than* the alpha level.

Additionally, the report should provide the observed frequencies (f_o) for each category. This information may be presented in a simple sentence or in a table [see, for example, Table 17.3(a)]. ❑

GOODNESS OF FIT AND THE SINGLE-SAMPLE *t* TEST

We began this chapter with a general discussion of the difference between parametric tests and non-parametric tests. In this context, the chi-square test for goodness of fit is an example of a non-parametric test; that is, it makes no assumptions about the parameters of the population distribution, and it does not require data from an interval or ratio scale. In contrast, the single-sample *t* test introduced in Chapter 9 is an example of a parametric test: It assumes a normal population, it tests hypotheses about the population mean (a parameter), and it requires numerical scores that can be summed, squared, divided, and so on.

Although the chi-square test and the single-sample *t* are clearly distinct, they are also very similar. In particular, both tests are intended to use the data from a single sample to test hypotheses about a single population. Thus, the chi-square test for goodness of fit can be viewed as an alternative procedure that may be used when the sample data do not satisfy the assumptions or requirements of the single-sample *t* test. To demonstrate this notion, consider the following example.

EXAMPLE 17.2

Suppose that a major soft-drink company has developed a new formula for its top-selling cola. To test public response to the new formula, the company would like to conduct a research study comparing the original formula with the new version.

One researcher obtains a sample of individuals and asks each person to taste the two colas and then rate their reactions using the following five-point scale.

OLD IS MUCH BETTER	OLD IS A LITTLE BETTER	NO DIFF	NEW IS A LITTLE BETTER	NEW IS MUCH BETTER
1	2	3	4	5

This researcher will obtain a numerical score for each subject and will be able to compute a sample mean and *SS* for the data. In this case, the researcher can use a single-sample *t* test to evaluate the difference between the two formulas. The null hypothesis would state that there is no difference; that is, $\mu = 3.00$.

A second researcher also obtains a sample, but simply asks each person to taste the two colas and then identify which one is preferred. This researcher will obtain frequency data. For example, a sample of $n = 50$ people may show that 22 prefer the new formula and 28 pick the old formula. With frequency data, the researcher would use a chi-square test to evaluate the difference between the two formulas. In this case, the null hypothesis would state that there is no preference.

Notice that the two researchers are addressing exactly the same question: Is there any difference in the public response to the two cola formulas? Also, notice that both researchers are using one sample of subjects to obtain information about one population. The primary difference between the two research studies is the method used to measure the subject's responses or preferences. One researcher obtains numerical scores suitable for a t test, and the other researcher obtains frequency data suitable for a chi-square test.

LEARNING CHECK

1. A researcher for an insurance company would like to know if high-performance, overpowered automobiles are more likely to be involved in accidents than other types of cars. For a sample of 50 insurance claims, the investigator classifies the automobiles as high-performance, subcompact, midsize, or full-size. The observed frequencies are as follows:

Observed Frequencies of Insurance Claims

HIGH-PERFORMANCE	SUBCOMPACT	MIDSIZE	FULL-SIZE	TOTAL
20	14	7	9	50

In determining the f_e values, assume that only 10% of the cars in the population are the high-performance variety. However, subcompacts, midsize cars, and full-size cars make up 40%, 30%, and 20%, respectively. Can the researcher conclude that the observed pattern of accidents does not fit the predicted (f_e) values? Test with $\alpha = .05$.

   a. In a few sentences, state the hypotheses.
   b. Determine the value for df, and locate the critical region.
   c. Determine f_e values, and compute chi-square.
   d. Make a decision regarding H_0.

ANSWERS

1. a. H_0: In the population, no particular type of car shows a disproportionate number of accidents. H_1: In the population, a disproportionate number of the accidents occur with certain types of cars.

   b. $df = 3$; the critical χ^2 value is 7.81.

   c. The f_e values for high-performance, subcompact, midsize, and full-size cars are 5, 20, 15, and 10, respectively. The obtained chi-square is 51.17.

   d. Reject H_0.

17.3 THE CHI-SQUARE TEST FOR INDEPENDENCE

The chi-square statistic may also be used to test whether or not there is a relationship between two variables. In this situation, each individual in the sample is measured or classified on two separate variables. For example, a group of students could be classified in terms of personality (introvert, extrovert) and in terms of color preference (red, yellow, green, or blue). Usually the data from this classification are

TABLE 17.4

Color preferences according to personality types

	RED	YELLOW	GREEN	BLUE	
INTROVERT	20	6	30	44	100
EXTROVERT	180	34	50	36	300
	200	40	80	80	$n = 400$

presented in the form of a matrix, where the rows correspond to the categories of one variable and the columns correspond to the categories of the second variable. Table 17.4 presents some hypothetical data for a sample of $n = 400$ students who have been classified by personality and color preference. The number in each box, or cell, of the matrix depicts the frequency of that particular group. In Table 17.4, for example, there are 20 introverted students who selected red as their preferred color and 180 extroverted students who preferred red. To obtain these data, the researcher first selects a random sample of $n = 400$ students. Each student is then given a personality test, and each student is asked to select a preferred color from among the four choices. Notice that the classification is based on the measurements for each student; the researcher does not assign students to categories. Also notice that the data consist of frequencies, not scores, from a sample. These sample data will be used to test a hypothesis about the corresponding population frequency distribution. Once again, we will be using the chi-square statistic for the test, but in this case the test is called the chi-square *test for independence*.

THE NULL HYPOTHESIS

The null hypothesis for the chi-square test for independence states that the two variables being measured are independent; that is, for each individual, the value obtained for one variable is not related to (or influenced by) the value for the second variable. This general hypothesis can be expressed in two different conceptual forms, each viewing the data and the test from slightly different perspectives. The data in Table 17.4 describing color preference and personality will be used to present both versions of the null hypothesis.

H_0 **version 1**   The first version of H_0 focuses on the two variables in the study and simply states that there is no relationship between them. For the color preference and personality study, the null hypothesis would state

> H_0:   For the general population of students, there is no relationship between color preference and personality.

This version of H_0 demonstrates the similarity between the chi-square test and a correlation. Specifically, the data are viewed as a single sample with each individual measured on two variables. For this example, the data in Table 17.4 would be viewed as a single sample of $n = 400$ individuals, with measurements of each person's personality and color preference. The goal of the correlation or the chi-square test is to evaluate the relationship between the two variables. For a correlation, the data consist of numerical scores, and you compute means, *SS, SP,* and so on to measure the correlation between variables. For the chi-square test, on the other hand, the data consist of frequencies, and the test uses the frequency data to determine whether or not there is a relationship between the two variables (H_0 says there is no relationship).

For this version of H_0, the alternative hypothesis, H_1, states that there is a relationship between the two variables. For this example, H_1 states that color preference does depend on personality.

H_0 **version 2**   The second version of the null hypothesis demonstrates the similarity between the chi-square test and an independent-measures t test (or ANOVA); that is, a hypothesis test that is intended to compare two (or more) separate samples. For this version of H_0, the data in Table 17.4 are viewed as consisting of two separate samples: a sample of $n = 100$ introverts (the top row) and a sample of $n = 300$ extroverts (the bottom row). The goal of the chi-square test is now to determine whether the distribution of color preferences for the introverts (sample 1) is significantly different from the distribution of color preferences for the extroverts (sample 2). The null hypothesis now states that there is no difference between the two distributions; that is, the distribution of color preferences has the same shape (same proportions) for introverts as it does for extroverts. Using this alternative perspective, the null hypothesis is restated as follows:

> H_0:   In the general population, the distribution of color preferences has the same shape (same proportions) for both categories of personality.

Stated in this new form, the null hypothesis focuses on the difference between two samples, much the same as an independent-measures t test (or ANOVA). However, the t test (or ANOVA) requires numerical scores (you must compute $\overline{X}$, SS, and so on for each sample), and the test evaluates a hypothesis about the population means. For the chi-square test, on the other hand, the data consist of frequencies, and the test uses the sample proportions to evaluate a hypothesis about the corresponding population proportions (H_0 states that there is no difference between population proportions).

For this second version of H_0, the alternative hypothesis, H_1, would state that there is a difference between the populations. For the example we are considering, H_1 would state that the distribution of color preferences for introverts has a different shape (different proportions) than the distribution for extroverts.

Equivalence of H_0 version 1 and H_0 version 2   Although we have presented two different statements of the null hypothesis, you should realize that these two versions are equivalent. The first version of H_0 states that color preference is not related to personality. If this hypothesis is correct, then the distribution of color preferences should not depend on personality. In other words, the distribution of color preferences should be the same for introverts and extroverts, which is the second version of H_0.

For example, if we found that 60% of the introverts preferred red, then H_0 would predict that we also should find that 60% of the extroverts prefer red. In this case, knowing that an individual prefers red does not help you predict his/her personality. Notice that finding the *same proportions* indicates *no relationship*.

On the other hand, if the proportions were different, it would suggest that there is a relationship. For example, if red were preferred by 60% of the extroverts, but only 10% of the introverts, then there is a clear, predictable relationship between personality and color preference. (If I know your personality, I can predict your color preference.) Thus, finding *different proportions* means that there *is a relationship*.

In general, when two variables are independent, the distribution for one variable will not depend on the categories of the second variable. In other words, the frequency distribution for one variable will have the *same shape* (same proportions) for all categories of the second variable.

DEFINITION

Two variables are *independent* when the frequency distribution for one variable is not related to (or dependent on) the categories of the second variable. As a result, the frequency distribution for one variable will have the same shape for all categories of the second variable. Thus, stating that the two variables are not related (version 1 of H_0) is equivalent to stating that the distributions have equal proportions (version 2 of H_0).

OBSERVED AND EXPECTED FREQUENCIES

The chi-square test for independence uses the same basic logic that was used for the goodness-of-fit test. First, a sample is selected, and each individual is classified or categorized. Because the test for independence considers two variables, every individual is classified on both variables, and the resulting frequency distribution is presented as a two-dimensional matrix (see Table 17.4). As before, the frequencies in the sample distribution are called observed frequencies and are identified by the symbol f_o.

The next step is to find the expected frequencies, or f_e values, for this chi-square test. As before, the expected frequencies define an ideal, hypothetical distribution that is in perfect agreement with the null hypothesis. Once the expected frequencies are obtained, we will compute a chi-square statistic to determine how well the data (observed frequencies) fit the null hypothesis (expected frequencies).

Although you can use either version of the null hypothesis to find the expected frequencies, the logic of the process is much easier when you use H_0 stated in terms of equal proportions. For the example we are considering, the null hypothesis states

H_0:   The frequency distribution of color preference has the same shape (same proportions) for both categories of personality.

Now we must determine how the sample *should* be distributed according to this hypothesis. The first step is to look at the general characteristics of the original sample. The data in Table 17.4 show an overall sample of $n = 400$ individuals. However, the total sample is divided into a set of subgroups. For example, the sample contains 100 introverts and 300 extroverts. Similarly, the sample consists of 200 people who selected red as their favorite color, 40 people who picked yellow, 80 people who chose green, and 80 who preferred blue. These pre-existing subgroups are defined by the row totals and the column totals in the original data and will be crucial to the calculation of the expected frequencies. Table 17.5(a) presents an empty frequency distribution table showing only the row and column totals for the sample. To compute the expected frequencies, we will use the null hypothesis to create an ideal distribution for the sample. In other words, we will use H_0 to fill in the empty spaces in Table 17.5(a).

Once again, the null hypothesis states that the distribution of color preferences should have the same shape for introverts as for extroverts. But what is the "distribution of color preferences"? The best information we have about this distribu-

TABLE 17.5

Expected frequencies for color preferences and personality types

(a) An empty frequency distribution matrix showing only the row totals and column totals (These numbers describe the basic characteristics of the sample from Table 17.4.)

	RED	YELLOW	GREEN	BLUE	
INTROVERT					100
EXTROVERT					300
	200	40	80	80	

(b) Expected frequencies (This is the distribution that is predicted by the null hypothesis.)

	RED	YELLOW	GREEN	BLUE	
INTROVERT	50	10	20	20	100
EXTROVERT	150	30	60	60	300
	200	40	80	80	

tion comes from the sample data. The column totals from the sample show the following distribution [see Table 17.5(a)]:

$$200 \text{ out of } 400 \text{ choose red: } \frac{200}{400} = 50\% \text{ red}$$

$$40 \text{ out of } 400 \text{ choose yellow: } \frac{40}{400} = 10\% \text{ yellow}$$

$$80 \text{ out of } 400 \text{ choose green: } \frac{80}{400} = 20\% \text{ green}$$

$$80 \text{ out of } 400 \text{ choose blue: } \frac{80}{400} = 20\% \text{ blue}$$

If H_0 is true, we would expect to obtain this same distribution of color preferences for both introverts and extroverts. Therefore, expected frequencies can be obtained by applying the color-preference distribution equally to the set of 100 introverts and to the set of 300 extroverts. The resulting f_e values are as follows.

For the 100 introverts, we expect

$$50\% \text{ choose red: } f_e = 0.50(100) = 50$$
$$10\% \text{ choose yellow: } f_e = 0.10(100) = 10$$
$$20\% \text{ choose green: } f_e = 0.20(100) = 20$$
$$20\% \text{ choose blue: } f_e = 0.20(100) = 20$$

For the 300 extroverts, we expect

$$50\% \text{ choose red: } f_e = 0.50(300) = 150$$
$$10\% \text{ choose yellow: } f_e = 0.10(300) = 30$$
$$20\% \text{ choose green: } f_e = 0.20(300) = 60$$
$$20\% \text{ choose blue: } f_e = 0.20(300) = 60$$

These expected frequencies are shown in Table 17.5(b). Notice that the row totals and column totals for the expected frequencies are the same as those for the original data in Table 17.4.

A SIMPLE FORMULA FOR DETERMINING EXPECTED FREQUENCIES

Although you should understand that expected frequencies are derived directly from the null hypothesis and the sample characteristics, it is not necessary to go through extensive calculations in order to find f_e values. In fact, there is a simple formula that determines f_e for any cell in the frequency distribution table.

$$f_e = \frac{f_c f_r}{n}$$

(17.4)

where f_c is the frequency total for the column (column total), f_r is the frequency total for the row (row total), and n is the number of individuals in the entire sample. To demonstrate this formula, we will compute the expected frequency for introverts selecting red in Table 17.5(a). First, note that this cell is located in the top row and first column in the table. The column total is $f_c = 200$, the row total is $f_r = 100$, and the sample size is $n = 400$. Using these values in equation 17.4, we obtain

$$f_e = \frac{f_c f_r}{n} = \frac{200(100)}{400} = 50$$

Notice that this is identical to the expected frequency we obtained using percentages from the overall distribution.

THE CHI-SQUARE STATISTIC AND DEGREES OF FREEDOM

The chi-square test of independence uses exactly the same chi-square formula as the test for goodness of fit:

$$\chi^2 = \Sigma \frac{(f_o - f_e)^2}{f_e}$$

As before, the formula measures the discrepancy between the data (f_o values) and the hypothesis (f_e values). A large discrepancy will produce a large value for chi-square and will indicate that H_0 should be rejected. To determine whether a particular chi-square statistic is significantly large, you must first determine degrees of freedom (df) for the statistic and then consult the chi-square distribution in the appendix. For the chi-square test of independence, degrees of freedom are based on the number of cells for which you can freely choose expected frequencies. You should recall that the f_e values are partially determined by the sample size (n) and by the row totals and column totals from the original data. These various totals restrict your freedom in selecting expected frequencies. This point is illustrated in Table 17.6. Once three of the f_e values have been selected, all the other f_e values in the table are also determined. In general, the row totals and column totals restrict the final choices in each row and column. Thus, we may freely choose all but one expected frequency in each row and all but one f_e in each column. The total num-

TABLE 17.6

Degrees of freedom and expected frequencies (Once three values have been selected, all the remaining expected frequencies are determined by the row totals and the column totals. This example has only three free choices, so $df = 3$.)

RED	YELLOW	GREEN	BLUE	
50	10	20	?	100
?	?	?	?	300
200	40	80	80	

ber of f_e values that you can freely choose is $(R - 1)(C - 1)$, where R is the number of rows and C is the number of columns. The degrees of freedom for the chi-square test of independence are given by the formula

$$df = (R - 1)(C - 1) \tag{17.5}$$

Further discussion of the relationships among chi-square and other statistical procedures is presented in Section 17.5.

Before we begin a step-by-step example of the chi-square test for independence, we ask you to consider a general research situation that demonstrates the similarities among the chi-square test for independence, the Pearson correlation, and the independent-measures t hypothesis test. For this demonstration, we will assume that a researcher is investigating the relationship between academic performance and self-esteem for 10-year-old children. Notice that the researcher has identified two variables, and the general research question concerns the relationship between them. Depending on how the researcher decides to measure the two variables, a correlation, an independent-measures t statistic, or a chi-square test for independence will be the appropriate statistical procedure for evaluating the relationship.

For example, if the researcher obtained a numerical score for both variables, the resulting data would permit the calculation of a Pearson correlation (see Chapter 16). In this case, the data would appear as follows:

SUBJECT	ACADEMIC PERFORMANCE SCORE	SELF-ESTEEM SCORE
A	94	31
B	78	26
C	81	27
D	65	23
.	.	.
.	.	.

The researcher would compute means, SS values, and SP for the data, and the Pearson correlation would describe the degree and direction of the relationship between academic performance and self-esteem.

On the other hand, if the researcher measured academic performance by simply classifying individuals into two categories, high and low, and then obtained a numerical score for each individual's self-esteem, the resulting data would be appro-

TABLE 17.7

A frequency distribution showing the level of self-esteem according to the level of academic performance for a sample of $n = 150$ 10-year-old children

		LEVEL OF SELF-ESTEEM			
		HIGH	MEDIUM	LOW	
ACADEMIC PERFORMANCE	HIGH	17	32	11	60
	LOW	13	43	34	90
		30	75	45	$n = 150$

priate for an independent-measures t test (see Chapter 11). In this case, the data would appear as follows:

ACADEMIC PERFORMANCE		
HIGH (SAMPLE 1)	LOW (SAMPLE 2)	
31	26	
29	23	Self-esteem
33	25	scores
.	.	
.	.	

Now the researcher has two separate samples and would proceed by computing the mean and *SS* for each sample. The independent-measures t statistic would be used to determine whether or not there is a significant difference in self-esteem between high academic achievers and low academic achievers. A significant difference would indicate that self-esteem does depend on academic performance; that is, there is a relationship between the two variables.

Finally, the researcher may choose simply to classify individuals into categories for both variables. For example, each student could be classified as either high or low for academic performance and classified as high, medium, or low for self-esteem. The resulting data would produce a frequency distribution that could be displayed in a matrix such as the data shown in Table 17.7. Notice that these data do not involve any numerical scores, but rather consist of a set of frequencies appropriate for a chi-square test.

The following example will use the data in Table 17.7 to demonstrate the chi-square test for independence. Before we begin the chi-square test, however, please note once again that the Pearson correlation, the independent-measures t, and the chi-square test for independence all serve the same general purpose; that is, they all are intended to evaluate the relationship between two variables. Thus, the chi-square test for independence can be viewed as an alternative to the other statistical procedures, specifically, an alternative that is available when research data consist of frequencies instead of numerical scores.

EXAMPLE 17.3

Software manuals:
Minitab (Section 9)
Mystat (Section 3)
SPSS (Section 6)

Once again, our researcher is investigating the relationship between academic performance and self-esteem. A sample of $n = 150$ 10-year-old children is obtained, and each child is classified by level of academic performance and level of self-esteem. The frequency distribution for this sample, the set of observed frequencies, is shown in Table 17.7.

STEP 1 State the hypotheses, and select a level of significance. According to the null hypothesis, the two variables are independent. This general hypothesis can be stated in two different ways:

Version 1

H_0: In the general population, there is no relationship between academic performance and self-esteem.

This version of H_0 emphasizes the similarity between the chi-square test and a correlation. The corresponding alternative hypothesis would state

H_1: There is a consistent, predictable relationship between academic performance and self-esteem.

Version 2

H_0: In the general population, the distribution of self-esteem is the same for high and low academic performers.

The corresponding alternative hypothesis would state

H_1: The distribution for self-esteem for high academic performers is different from the distribution for low academic performers.

The second version of H_0 emphasizes the similarity between the chi-square test and the independent-measures t test.
Remember, the two versions for the hypotheses are equivalent. The choice between them is largely determined by how the researcher wants to describe the outcome. For example, a researcher may want to emphasize the *relationship* between variables or may want to emphasis the *difference* between groups.
For this test, we will use $\alpha = .05$.

STEP 2 Determine the degrees of freedom, and locate the critical region. For the chi-square test for independence,

$$df = (R - 1)(C - 1)$$

Therefore, for this study,

$$df = (2 - 1)(3 - 1) = 2$$

With $df = 2$ and $\alpha = .05$, the critical value for chi-square is 5.99 (see Table B7, p. A-34).

STEP 3 Determine the expected frequencies, and compute the chi-square statistic. The following table shows an empty matrix with the same row totals and column totals as the original data. The calculation of expected frequencies requires that this table be filled in so that the resulting values provide an ideal frequency distribution that perfectly represents the null hypothesis.

LEVEL OF SELF-ESTEEM

		HIGH	MEDIUM	LOW	
ACADEMIC PERFORMANCE	HIGH				60
	LOW				90
		30	75	45	$n = 150$

The column totals indicate that 30 out of 150 subjects are classified as high self-esteem. This value represents a proportion of $30/150$ or 20% of the subjects. Similarly, $75/150 = 50\%$ are medium self-esteem, and $45/150 = 30\%$ are low self-esteem. The null hypothesis (version 2) states that this distribution of self-esteem is the same for high and low performers. Therefore, we simply apply the same proportions to each group to obtain the expected frequencies. For the 60 students classified as high academic performers, it is expected that

20% of 60 = 12 students would have high self-esteem

50% of 60 = 30 students would have medium self-esteem

30% of 60 = 18 students would have low self-esteem

For the low academic performers, it is expected that

20% of 90 = 18 students would have high self-esteem

50% of 90 = 45 students would have medium self-esteem

30% of 90 = 27 students would have low self-esteem

These expected frequencies are summarized in Table 17.8.

The chi-square statistic is now used to measure the discrepancy between the data (the observed frequencies in Table 17.7) and the null hypothesis that was used to generate the expected frequencies in Table 17.8.

$$\chi^2 = \frac{(17 - 12)^2}{12} + \frac{(32 - 30)^2}{30} + \frac{(11 - 18)^2}{18}$$

$$+ \frac{(13 - 18)^2}{18} + \frac{(43 - 45)^2}{45} + \frac{(34 - 27)^2}{27}$$

$$= 2.08 + 0.13 + 2.72 + 1.39 + 0.09 + 1.81$$

$$= 8.22$$

STEP 4   Make a decision regarding the null hypothesis and the outcome of the study. The obtained chi-square value exceeds the critical value (5.99). Therefore, the deci-

TABLE 17.8

The expected frequencies (f_e values) that would be predicted if academic performance and self-esteem were completely independent

LEVEL OF SELF-ESTEEM

		HIGH	MEDIUM	LOW	
ACADEMIC PERFORMANCE	HIGH	12	30	18	60
	LOW	18	45	27	90
		30	75	45	$n = 150$

sion is to reject the null hypothesis. In the literature, this would be reported as a significant result with $\chi^2(2, n = 150) = 8.22, p < .05$. According to version 1 of H_0, this means that we have decided that there is a significant relationship between academic performance and self-esteem. Expressed in terms of version 2 of H_0, the data show a significant difference between the distribution of self-esteem for high academic performers versus low academic performers. To describe the details of the significant result, you must compare the original data (Table 17.7) with the expected frequencies from the null hypothesis (Table 17.8). Looking at the two tables, it should be clear that the high performers had higher self-esteem than would be expected if the two variables were independent and the low performers had lower self-esteem than would be expected.

LEARNING CHECK   1. A researcher suspects that color blindness is inherited by a sex-linked gene. This possibility is examined by looking for a relationship between gender and color vision. A sample of 1000 people is tested for color blindness, and then they are classified according to their sex and color vision status (normal, red-green blind, other color blindness). Is color blindness related to gender? The data are as follows:

Observed Frequencies of Color
Vision Status According to Sex

	NORMAL COLOR VISION	RED-GREEN COLOR BLINDNESS	OTHER COLOR BLINDNESS	TOTALS
MALE	320	70	10	400
FEMALE	580	10	10	600
TOTALS	900	80	20	

a. State the hypotheses.
b. Determine the value for df, and locate the critical region.
c. Compute the f_e values and then chi-square.
d. Make a decision regarding H_0.

ANSWERS   1. a. H_0:   In the population, there is no relationship between gender and color vision.
   H_1:   In the population, gender and color vision are related.

b. $df = 2$; critical $\chi^2 = 5.99$ for $\alpha = .05$.

c. f_e values are as follows:

EXPECTED FREQUENCIES

	NORMAL	RED-GREEN	OTHER
MALE	360	32	8
FEMALE	540	48	12

Obtained $\chi^2 = 83.44$

d. Reject H_0.

17.4 ASSUMPTIONS AND RESTRICTIONS FOR CHI-SQUARE TESTS

To use a chi-square test for goodness of fit or a test of independence, several conditions must be satisfied. For any statistical test, violation of assumptions and restrictions will cast doubt on the results. For example, the probability of committing a Type I error may be distorted when assumptions of statistical tests are not satisfied. Some important assumptions and restrictions for using chi-square tests are the following:

1. Independence of Observations. This is *not* to be confused with the concept of independence between *variables* as seen in the test of independence (Section 17.3). One consequence of independent observations is that each observed frequency is generated by a different subject. A chi-square test would be inappropriate if a person could produce responses that can be classified in more than one category or contribute more than one frequency count to a single category. (See p. 244 for more information on independence.)

2. Size of Expected Frequencies. A chi-square test should not be performed when the expected frequency of any cell is less than 5. The chi-square statistic can be distorted when f_e is very small. Consider the chi-square computations for a single cell. Suppose that the cell has values of $f_e = 1$ and $f_o = 5$. The contribution of this cell to the total chi-square value is

$$\text{cell} = \frac{(f_o - f_e)^2}{f_e} = \frac{(5 - 1)^2}{1} = \frac{4^2}{1} = 16$$

Now consider another instance, where $f_e = 10$ and $f_o = 14$. The difference between the observed and the expected frequencies is still 4, but the contribution of this cell to the total chi-square value differs from that of the first case:

$$\text{cell} = \frac{(f_o - f_e)^2}{f_e} = \frac{(14 - 10)^2}{10} = \frac{4^2}{10} = 1.6$$

It should be clear that a small f_e value can have a great influence on the chi-square value. This problem becomes serious when f_e values are less than 5. When f_e is very small, what would otherwise be a minor discrepancy between f_o and f_e will now result in large chi-square values. The test is too sensitive when f_e vales are extremely small. One way to avoid small expected frequencies is to use large samples.

17.5 SPECIAL APPLICATIONS OF THE CHI-SQUARE TESTS

At the beginning of this chapter, we introduced the chi-square tests as examples of non-parametric tests. Although non-parametric tests serve a function that is uniquely their own, they also can be viewed as alternatives to the common parametric techniques that were examined in earlier chapters. In general, non-parametric tests are used as substitutes for parametric techniques in situations where one of the following occurs:

1. The data do not meet the assumptions needed for a standard parametric test.
2. The data consist of nominal or ordinal measurements, so that it is impossible to compute standard descriptive statistics such as the mean and standard deviation.

In this section, we will examine some of the relationships between chi-square tests and the parametric procedures for which they may substitute.

CHI-SQUARE AND THE PEARSON CORRELATION

The chi-square test of independence and the Pearson correlation are both statistical techniques intended to evaluate the relationship between two variables. The type of data obtained in a research study determines which of these two statistical procedures is appropriate.

The Pearson correlation is used to evaluate a relationship in situations where both variables consist of numerical values; that is, X and Y are numbers obtained from measurement on interval or ratio scales. The chi-square test for independence, on the other hand, is used in situations where the data are obtained by classifying individuals into categories, usually determined by a nominal or ordinal scale of measurement. Although both statistical techniques are used to measure the relationship between two variables, the distinction between them is determined by the type of data that a researcher has obtained. For the chi-square test, the numbers in the data are frequencies, not scores. For the Pearson correlation, the scores are numerical values.

THE PHI-COEFFICIENT

In Chapter 16 (p. 521), we introduced the phi-coefficient as a correlational statistic for measuring the degree of association between two dichotomous variables. A dichotomous variable is one for which there are exactly two categories of measurement; for example, gender can be classified as male or female; people's opinions concerning a new law can be classified as "for" or "against." The phi-coefficient allows you to compute a correlation measuring the degree of relationship between two such variables.

The same data that are used to compute the phi-coefficient can be reorganized into a matrix of frequencies that is suitable for the chi-square test for independence. This process is shown in Figure 17.5. In the figure, the original data show that each individual is classified according to gender (male, female) and according to opinion concerning a proposal to ban smoking in all college buildings (for, against). To compute the phi-coefficient, the original data are transformed into numerical values by substituting values of 0 and 1 for the two categories of each variable, and the Pearson formula is used. The transformed data are shown in the lower left-hand side of Figure 17.5. On the other hand, the original two variables can be used to create a 2×2 matrix, with the categories of one variable determining the two columns and the categories of the second variable determining the two rows of the matrix. This process is demonstrated in the lower right-hand side of Figure 17.5. The number in each cell of the matrix is the frequency, or number of individuals classified in that cell. The chi-square statistic is computed from the frequency data

FIGURE 17.5

Hypothetical data showing the first four individuals in a sample where each person is classified on two dichotomous variables. The original data (top of figure) can be reorganized into a form suitable for computing the phi-coefficient (lower left) or into a form suitable for computing a chi-square test for independence (lower right).

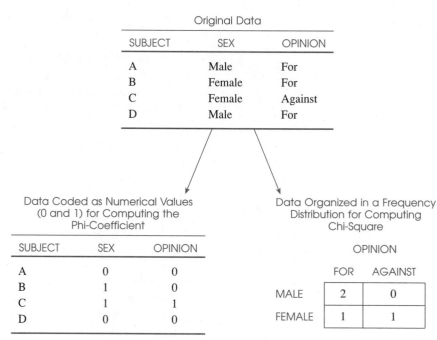

using the procedures described in Section 17.3. The value for the phi-coefficient (φ) may be computed directly from chi-square by the following formula:

$$\phi = \sqrt{\frac{\chi^2}{n}}$$

(17.6)

A strong relationship between the two variables will produce a large value (near 1.00) for the phi-coefficient.

INDEPENDENT-MEASURES
t **AND ANOVA**

The independent-measures *t* test and ANOVA are statistical procedures used to examine the relationship between an independent variable and a dependent variable. Both tests require that the scores for the dependent variable consist of numerical values measured on an interval or a ratio scale. The chi-square test for independence often can be used as a substitute for *t* or ANOVA, particularly in the following situations:

1. The independent variable is actually a quasi-independent variable (Chapter 1) consisting of distinct subject groups (men versus women; 8-year-olds versus 10-year-olds)

2. The dependent variable involves classifying individuals into nominal or ordinal categories.

For example, suppose that a researcher is interested in examining the difference in vocabulary skills between four-year-old boys and girls. The data for this study would require two independent samples (boys versus girls). If each child's vocabulary skill were measured by a numerical score, the mean difference between boys

TABLE 17.9

Two possible sets of data from a study comparing vocabulary skills for 4-year-old boys versus girls (In data set A, vocabulary skill is measured by numerical scores suitable for an independent-measures t [or ANOVA] hypothesis test. In data set B, each child's vocabulary skill is classified into one of three categories [high, medium, low], and the numbers represent the frequency, or number of children in each category.)

DATA SET A VOCABULARY SCORES	
BOYS	GIRLS
18	20
4	9
21	24
17	18
10	5
3	11
.	.
.	.
.	.

DATA SET B
FREQUENCY DISTRIBUTION
OF VOCABULARY SKILL

	BOYS	GIRLS
HIGH	6	11
MEDIUM	12	14
LOW	8	7

and girls could be evaluated using either an independent-measures t test or an ANOVA. On the other hand, if each child were simply classified as being either high, medium, or low with respect to vocabulary skill, the data would be suitable for a chi-square test. Examples of both types of data are shown in Table 17.9.

THE MEDIAN TEST FOR INDEPENDENT SAMPLES

The median test provides a non-parametric alternative to the independent-measures t hypothesis test (or ANOVA) in situations where the data do not meet the assumptions for the t statistic (or F-ratio). The median test is used to determine whether there is a significant difference in the distribution of scores from two or more independent samples.

The null hypothesis for the median test states that the populations from which the samples were obtained are all distributed evenly around a common median. The alternative hypothesis is that the population distributions are significantly different and do not share a common median.

The first step in conducting the median test is to combine all the scores from the separate samples into one group and then find the median for the combined group (see Chapter 3, p. 82, for instructions for finding the median). Next, a matrix is constructed with a column for each of the separate samples and two rows: one row for individuals scoring above the combined median and one row for individuals scoring below the combined median. Finally, frequencies are entered in the cells of the matrix, with each frequency corresponding to the number of individuals in the specific sample (column) who scored above the combined median (top row) and who scored below the combined median (bottom row).

The frequency distribution matrix is evaluated using a chi-square test for independence. The expected frequencies and a value for chi-square are computed exactly as described in Section 17.3. A significant value for chi-square indicates that the discrepancy between the individual sample distributions is greater than would be expected by chance.

The median test is demonstrated in the following example.

EXAMPLE 17.4 The following data represent self-esteem scores obtained from a sample of $n = 40$ children. The children are then separated into three groups based on their level of academic performance (high, medium, low). The median test will evaluate whether there is a significant relationship between self-esteem and level of academic performance.

SELF-ESTEEM SCORES FOR CHILDREN AT THREE LEVELS OF ACADEMIC PERFORMANCE							
HIGH		**MEDIUM**				**LOW**	
22	14	22	13	24	20	11	19
19	18	18	22	10	16	13	15
12	21	19	15	14	19	20	16
20	18	11	18	11	10	10	18
23	20	12	19	15	12	15	11

The median for the combined group of $n = 40$ scores is $X = 17$ (exactly 20 scores are above this value and 20 are below). For the first sample, 8 out of 10 scores are above the combined median. For the second sample, 9 out of 20 are above the median, and for the third sample, only 3 out of 10 are above the median. These observed frequencies are shown in the following matrix:

ACADEMIC PERFORMANCE

	HIGH	MEDIUM	LOW
ABOVE MEDIAN	8	9	3
BELOW MEDIAN	2	11	7

The expected frequencies for this test are as follows:

ACADEMIC PERFORMANCE

	HIGH	MEDIUM	LOW
ABOVE MEDIAN	5	10	5
BELOW MEDIAN	5	10	5

The chi-square statistic is

$$\chi^2 = \frac{9}{5} + \frac{9}{5} + \frac{1}{10} + \frac{1}{10} + \frac{4}{5} + \frac{4}{5} = 5.40$$

With $df = 2$ and $\alpha = .05$, the critical value for chi-square is 5.99. The obtained chi-square of 5.40 does not fall in the critical region, so we would fail to reject the null hypothesis. These data do not provide sufficient evidence to conclude that there are significant differences among the self-esteem distributions for these three groups of students.

A few words of caution are in order concerning the interpretation of the median test. First, the median test is *not* a test for mean differences. Remember, the mean for a distribution can be strongly affected by a few extreme scores. Therefore, the mean and the median for a distribution are not necessarily the same, and they may not even be related. The results from a median test *cannot* be interpreted as indicating that there is (or is not) a difference between means.

Second, you may have noted that the median test does not directly compare the median from one sample with the median from another. Thus, the median test is not a test for significant differences between medians. Instead, this test compares the distribution of scores for one sample versus the distribution for another sample. If the samples are distributed evenly around a common point (the group median), the test will conclude that there is no significant difference. On the other hand, finding a significant difference simply indicates that the samples are not distributed evenly around the common median. Thus, the best interpretation of a significant result is that there is a *difference in the distributions* of the samples.

TESTING DIFFERENCES IN PROPORTIONS FOR INDEPENDENT SAMPLES

Although the chi-square test of independence is typically viewed as a method for testing the relationship between two variables, it also serves the purpose of testing for differences in proportions between two (or more) independent samples. When the individuals in each sample are classified into categories, the chi-square test can be used to determine whether the proportions (shape of the distribution) for one sample are significantly different from the proportions obtained for another sample. Consider the following example.

EXAMPLE 17.5

Suppose that the city is considering a budget proposal that would allocate extra funding toward the renovation of city parks. A survey is conducted to measure pubic opinion concerning this proposal. A total of 300 individuals responds to the survey: 100 who live within the city limits and 200 from the surrounding suburbs. Of the city respondents, 68% (68 our of 100) favor the proposal. But only 43% (86 out of 200) of the suburban respondents favor using tax money for city parks. Is there a significant difference in opinion between these two groups?

This question can be answered using the chi-square test for independence. The data from the survey are the observed frequencies and can be summarized in a matrix as follows:

	FAVOR	OPPOSE	
CITY	68	32	100
SUBURB	86	114	200
	154	146	

The expected frequencies and the value for chi-square would be computed exactly as described in Section 17.3. A significant value for chi-square would indicate a significant difference in the distribution of preference for city dwellers versus the distribution for suburbanites.

SUMMARY

1. Chi-square tests are a type of non-parametric technique that tests hypotheses about the form of the entire frequency distribution. Two types of chi-square tests are the test for goodness of fit and the test for independence. The data for these tests consist of the frequency of observations that fall into various categories of a variable.

2. The test for goodness of fit compares the frequency distribution for a sample to the frequency distribution that is predicted by H_0. The test determines how well the observed frequencies (sample data) fit the expected frequencies (data predicted by H_0).

3. The expected frequencies for the goodness-of-fit test are determined by

$$\text{expected frequency} = f_e = pn$$

where p is the hypothesized proportion (according to H_0) of observations falling into a category and n is the size of the sample.

4. The chi-square statistic is computed by

$$\text{chi-square} = \chi^2 = \Sigma \frac{(f_o - f_e)^2}{f_e}$$

where f_o is the observed frequency for a particular category and f_e is the expected frequency for that category. Large values for χ^2 indicate that there is a large discrepancy between the observed (f_o) and the expected (f_e) frequencies and may warrant rejection of the null hypothesis.

5. Degrees of freedom for the test for goodness of fit are

$$df = C - 1$$

where C is the number of categories in the variable. Degrees of freedom measure the number of categories for which f_e values can be freely chosen. As can be seen from the formula, all but the last f_e value to be determined are free to vary.

6. The chi-square distribution is positively skewed and begins at the value of zero. Its exact shape is determined by degrees of freedom.

7. The test for independence is used to assess the relationship between two variables. The null hypothesis states

that the two variables in question are independent of each other. That is, the frequency distribution for one variable does not depend on the categories of the second variable. On the other hand, if a relationship does exist, then the form of the distribution for one variable will depend on the categories of the other variable.

8. For the test for independence, the expected frequencies for H_0 can be directly calculated from the marginal frequency totals,

$$f_e = \frac{f_c f_r}{n}$$

where f_c is the total column frequency and f_r is the total row frequency for the cell in question.

9. Degrees of freedom for the test for independence are computed by

$$df = (R - 1)(C - 1)$$

where R is the number of row categories and C is the number of column categories.

10. For the test of independence, a large chi-square value means there is a large discrepancy between the f_o and f_e values. Rejecting H_0 in this test provides support for a relationship between the two variables.

11. Both chi-square tests (for goodness of fit and independence) are based on the assumption that each observation is independent of the others. That is, each observed frequency reflects a different individual, and no individual can produce a response that would be classified in more than one category or more than one frequency in a single category.

12. The chi-square statistic is distorted when f_e values are small. Chi-square tests, therefore, are restricted to situations where f_e values are 5 or greater. The test should not be performed when the expected frequency of any cell is less than 5.

13. The test for independence also can be used to test whether two sample distributions share a common median. Observed frequencies are obtained by classifying each individual as above or below the median value for the combined samples. A significant value for chi-square indicates a difference between the two sample distributions.

KEY TERMS

goodness-of-fit test   expected frequencies   distribution of chi-square   test for independence

observed frequencies   chi-square statistic   median test

--- FOCUS ON PROBLEM SOLVING ---

1. The expected frequencies that you calculate must satisfy the constraints of the sample. For the goodness-of-fit test, $\Sigma f_e = \Sigma f_o = n$. For the test of independence, the row totals and column totals for the expected frequencies should be identical to the corresponding totals for the observed frequencies.

2. It is entirely possible to have fractional (decimal) values for expected frequencies. Observed frequencies, however, are always whole numbers.

3. Whenever $df = 1$, the difference between observed and expected frequencies $(f_o - f_e)$ will be identical (the same value) for all cells. This makes the calculation of chi-square easier.

4. Although you are advised to compute expected frequencies for all categories (or cells), you should realize that it is not essential to calculate all f_e values separately. Remember, df for chi-square identifies the number of f_e values that are free to vary. Once you have calculated that number of f_e values, the remaining f_e values are determined. You can get these remaining values by subtracting the calculated f_e values from their corresponding row or column totals.

5. Remember, unlike previous statistical tests, the degrees of freedom (df) for a chi-square test are *not* determined by the sample size (n). Be careful!

--- DEMONSTRATION 17.1 ---

TEST FOR INDEPENDENCE

A manufacturer of watches would like to examine preferences for digital versus analog watches. A sample of $n = 200$ people is selected, and these individuals are classified by age and preference. The manufacturer would like to know if there is a relationship between age and watch preference. The observed frequencies (f_o) are as follows:

		PREFERENCE		
		DIGITAL	ANALOG	UNDECIDED
AGE	UNDER 30	90	40	10
	OVER 30	10	40	10

STEP 1   *State the hypotheses, and select an alpha level.* The null hypothesis states that there is no relationship between the two variables.

H_0: Preference is independent of age. That is, the frequency distribution of preference has the same form for people under 30 as for people over 30.

The alternative hypothesis states that there is a relationship between the two variables.

H_1: Preference is related to age. That is, the type of watch preferred depends on a person's age.

We will set alpha to $\alpha = .05$.

STEP 2 *Locate the critical region.* Degrees of freedom for the chi-square test for independence are determined by

$$df = (C - 1)(R - 1)$$

For these data,

$$df = (3 - 1)(2 - 1) = 2(1) = 2$$

For $df = 2$ with $\alpha = .05$, the critical chi-square value is 5.99. Thus, our obtained chi-square must exceed 5.99 to be in the critical region and to reject H_0.

STEP 3 *Compute the test statistic.* Computing the chi-square statistic requires the following preliminary calculations:

1. Obtain the row and column totals.
2. Calculate expected frequencies.

Row and column totals. We start by determining the row and column totals from the original observed frequencies, f_o.

	DIGITAL	ANALOG	UNDECIDED	TOTALS
UNDER 30	90	40	10	140
OVER 30	10	40	10	60
COLUMN TOTALS	100	80	20	$n = 200$

Expected frequencies, f_e. For the test for independence, the following formula is used to obtain expected frequencies:

$$f_e = \frac{f_c f_r}{n}$$

For people under 30, we obtain the following expected frequencies:

$$f_e = \frac{100(140)}{200} = \frac{14000}{200} = 70 \text{ for digital}$$

$$f_e = \frac{80(140)}{200} = \frac{11200}{200} = 56 \text{ for analog}$$

$$f_e = \frac{20(140)}{200} = \frac{2800}{200} = 14 \text{ for undecided}$$

For individuals over 30, the expected frequencies are as follows:

$$f_e = \frac{100(60)}{200} = \frac{6000}{200} = 30 \text{ for digital}$$

$$f_e = \frac{80(60)}{200} = \frac{4800}{200} = 24 \text{ for analog}$$

$$f_e = \frac{20(60)}{200} = \frac{1200}{200} = 6 \text{ for undecided}$$

The following table summarizes the expected frequencies:

	DIGITAL	ANALOG	UNDECIDED
UNDER 30	70	56	14
OVER 30	30	24	6

The chi-square statistic. The chi-square statistic is computed from the formula

$$\chi^2 = \Sigma \frac{(f_o - f_e)^2}{f_e}$$

That is, we must

1. Find the $f_o - f_e$ difference for each cell.
2. Square these differences.
3. Divide the squared differences by f_e.
4. Sum the results of 3.

The following table summarizes these calculations:

CELL	f_o	f_e	$(f_o - f_e)$	$(f_o - f_e)^2$	$(f_o - f_e)^2/f_e$
Under 30—digital	90	70	20	400	5.71
Under 30—analog	40	56	−16	256	4.57
Under 30—undecided	10	14	−4	16	1.14
Over 30—digital	10	30	−20	400	13.33
Over 30—analog	40	24	16	256	10.67
Over 30—undecided	10	6	4	16	2.67

Finally, we can sum the last column to get the chi-square value.

$$\chi^2 = 5.71 + 4.57 + 1.14 + 13.33 + 10.67 + 2.67$$

$$= 38.09$$

STEP 4 *Make a decision about H_0, and state the conclusion.* The chi-square value is in the critical region. Therefore, we can reject the null hypothesis. There is a relationship between watch preference and age, $\chi^2(2, n = 200) = 38.09$, $p < .05$.

PROBLEMS

1. Parametric tests (such as t or ANOVA) differ from non-parametric tests (such as chi-square) primarily in terms of the assumptions they require and the data they use. Explain these differences.

2. A psychology professor is trying to decide which textbook to use for next year's introductory class. To help make the decision, the professor asks the current students to review three texts and identify which one is preferred. The distribution of preferences for the current class is as follows:

BOOK 1	BOOK 2	BOOK 3
52	41	27

Do these data indicate any significant preferences among the three books? Test with $\alpha = .05$.

3. Automobile insurance is much more expensive for teenage drivers than for older drivers. To justify this cost difference, insurance companies claim that the younger drivers are much more likely to be involved in costly accidents. To test this claim, a researcher obtains information about registered drivers from the department of motor vehicles and selects a sample of $n = 300$ accident reports from the police department. The motor vehicle department reports the percentage of registered drivers in each age category as follows: 16% are under age 20; 28% are 20 to 29 years old, and 56% are age 30 or older. The number of accident reports for each age group is as follows:

UNDER AGE 20	AGE 20 TO 29	AGE 30 OR OLDER
68	92	140

Do these data demonstrate a significantly disproportionate number of accidents among the younger drivers? Test with $\alpha = .05$.

4. The college is planning to build a fast-food restaurant in the student union. To determine what kind of food should be offered, a sample of $n = 100$ students was surveyed. Each student was asked to identify his/her preference from a list of food categories. The resulting data are summarized in the following frequency distribution:

HAMBURGERS	MEXICAN	CHINESE	CHICKEN	PIZZA
28	15	11	13	33

Do the data indicate significant differences in the students' preference for different types of food? Test with $\alpha = .05$.

5. A researcher would like to determine if any particular age group has a greater risk of influenza-related death. A sample of 50 such cases is categorized according to the victim's age. The observed frequencies are as follows:

NUMBER OF FLU-RELATED DEATHS

UNDER 30	30 TO 60	OVER 60
5	5	40

It should be noted that in the city from which the sample was selected, 30% of the population is in the "under 30" bracket, 40% in "30 to 60," and 30% in "over 60." (This information should help in determining f_e values.) Can the investigator conclude the risk differs with age? Test with the .05 level of significance.

6. A reseacher noticed that one of the laboratory rats seemed to have a strong preference for taking the right-hand branch in a T-maze. During a series of 20 trials, this rat took the right-hand branch 17 times and went left only 3 times. Explain why you should not use a chi-square goodness-of-fit test to evaluate these data.

7. A questionnaire given to last year's freshman class indicated that 30% intended to be science majors, 50% intended to major in the social sciences or humanities, and 20% were interested in professional programs. A random sample of 100 students from the current freshman class yielded the following frequency distribution:

INTENDED MAJOR

SCIENCES	SOCIAL SCIENCES OR HUMANITIES	PROFESSIONAL
35	40	25

a. On the basis of these data, should the university officials conclude that there has been a significant change in student interests? Test at the .05 level of significance.

b. If twice as many students had been sampled, with the result that the observed frequencies were doubled in each of the three categories, would there be evidence for a significant change? Again, test with $\alpha = .05$.

c. How do you explain the different conclusions for parts a and b?

8. A researcher is investigating the physical characteristics that influence whether or not a person's face is judged as beautiful. The researcher selects a photograph of a woman and then creates two modifications of the photo by (1) moving the eyes slightly farther apart and (2) moving the eyes slightly closer together. The original photograph and the two modifications are then shown to a sample of $n = 150$ college students, and each student is asked to select the "most beautiful" of the three faces. The distribution of responses is as follows:

ORIGINAL PHOTO	EYES MOVED APART	EYES MOVED TOGETHER
51	72	27

Do these data indicate any significant preferences among the three versions of the photograph? Test at the .05 level of significance.

9. A researcher is interested in the relationship between IQ and vocabulary for five-year-old children.
   a. Explain how the relationship might be examined using a Pearson correlation. Specifically, describe the data that the researcher would need to collect.
   b. Explain how the relationship might be examined using a chi-square test for independence. Again, describe the data that the researcher would need to collect.

10. Gender differences in dream content are well documented (see Winget & Kramer, 1979). Suppose that a researcher studies aggression content in the dreams of men and women. Each subject reports his or her most recent dream. Then each dream is judged by a panel of experts to have low, medium, or high aggression content. The observed frequencies are shown in the following matrix:

		AGGRESSION CONTENT		
		LOW	MEDIUM	HIGH
GENDER	FEMALE	18	4	2
	MALE	4	17	15

Is there a relationship between gender and the aggression content of dreams? Test with = = 0.1.

11. Recent studies have demonstrated that naltrexone, a drug that reduces the craving for heroin, can prevent relapse of drinking in alcoholics (Volpicelli et al., 1992). Suppose that you studied a group of alcoholics who were receiving counseling and were currently abstaining from drinking. One-third of the people also received a small dose of naltrexone, one-third received a larger dose, and the remainder got a placebo. You obtained the following data, which show the number of people in each group that re-

lapsed (began drinking heavily again). Does naltrexone have an effect on relapse? Set alpha at .05.

	PLACEBO	SMALL DOSE	LARGE DOSE
RELAPSE	20	10	6
NO RELAPSE	10	20	24

12. In Problem 2, a professor asked students to rate three textbooks to determine whether there were any preferences among them. Although the data appear to indicate an overall preference for book 1, the professor would like to know whether this opinion is shared by students with different levels of academic ability. To answer this question, the median grade was used to separate the students into two groups: the upper half and the lower half of the class. The distribution of preferences for these two groups is as follows:

	BOOK 1	BOOK 2	BOOK 3	
UPPER HALF	17	31	12	60
LOWER HALF	35	10	15	60
	52	41	27	

Do these data indicate that the distribution of preferences for students in the upper half of the class is significantly different from the distribution for students in the lower half? Test at the .05 level of significance.

13. Sociologists often point to negative childhood experiences as possible causal factors in the criminal behavior of adults. A sample of 25 individuals convicted of violent crimes and a matching sample of 25 college students are obtained. A sociologist interviews each individual to determine whether there is any history of childhood abuse (physical or sexual). The resulting frequency distribution is as follows:

	NO ABUSE	HISTORY OF ABUSE
CRIMINALS	9	16
STUDENTS	19	6

Do the data indicate that a history of abuse is significantly more common for violent criminals than it is for non-criminal college students? Test with $\alpha = .05$.

14. McClelland (1961) suggested that the strength of a person's need for achievement can predict behavior in a number of situations, including risk-taking situations.

This experiment is patterned after his work. A random sample of college students is given a standardized test that measures the need for achievement. On the basis of their test scores, they are classified into high achievers and low achievers. They are then confronted with a task for which they can select the level of difficulty. Their selections are classified as "cautious" (low risk of failure), "moderate" risk of failure, or "high" risk of failure. The observed frequencies for this study are as follows:

RISK TAKEN BY SUBJECT

	CAUTIOUS	MODERATE	HIGH
HIGH ACHIEVER	8	24	6
LOW ACHIEVER	17	7	16

Can you conclude there is a relationship between the need for achievement and risk-taking behavior? Set alpha to .05. Describe the outcome of the study.

15. Friedman and Rosenman (1974) have suggested that personality type is related to heart disease. Specifically, type A people, who are competitive, driven, pressured, and impatient, are more prone to heart disease. On the other hand, type B individuals, who are less competitive and more relaxed, are less likely to have heart disease. Suppose that an investigator would like to examine the relationship between personality type and disease. For a random sample of individuals, personality type is assessed with a standardized test. These individuals are then examined and categorized according to the type of disorder they have. The observed frequencies are as follows:

TYPE OF DISORDER

	HEART	VASCULAR	HYPERTENSION	NONE
TYPE A PERSONALITY	38	29	43	60
TYPE B PERSONALITY	18	22	14	126

Is there a relationship between personality and disorder? Test at the .05 level of significance.

16. A psychologist would like to examine the factors that are involved in the development of romantic relationships. The psychologist suspects that people at different ages will place emphasis on different factors when looking for a romantic partner. A sample of 30 adolescent males (ages 13–15) and a sample of 30 male college students

(ages 19–32) are obtained. Each subject is asked to identify the single most important factor determining whether or not he is likely to pursue a romantic relationship with a new female acquaintance. The frequency data for this study are as follows:

	PHYSICAL APPEARANCE	POPULARITY	PERSONALITY
ADOLESCENTS	15	10	5
COLLEGE STUDENTS	12	8	10

Do these data indicate a significant difference in the relative importance of different factors for adolescents versus college students? Test with $\alpha = .05$.

17. In the Preview section of this chapter, we presented a study by Cialdini, Reno, and Kallgren (1990) examining how people conform to norms concerning littering. The researchers wanted to determine whether a person's tendency to litter depended on the amount of litter already in the area. People were handed a handbill as they entered an amusement park that already had either 0, 1, 2, 4, 8, or 16 handbills lying on the ground. Then the people were observed to determine whether or not they dropped the handbill on the ground. The frequency data are as follows:

AMOUNT OF EXISTING LITTER

	0 OR 1 PIECE	2 OR 4 PIECES	8 OR 16 PIECES
LITTERING	17	28	49
NOT LITTERING	102	91	71

Do these data indicate a significant tendency for people to litter when there already is litter in the area? That is, does the proportion of litterers depend on the amount of litter? Test at the .05 level of significance.

18. Numerous studies have shown that a person's decision whether or not to respond to a survey depends on *who* presents the survey. To examine this phenomenon, 100 surveys were mailed to students at a local college. Half of the surveys were distributed with a cover letter signed by the president of the student body. The other half of the surveys included a cover letter signed by a fictitious administrator (the "Vice President for Student Information"). Of the surveys signed by the student president, 28 were returned, and 22 were discarded. For the surveys signed by the unknown administrator, only 11 were returned, and 39 were discarded. Do these data indicate

that the individual requesting a survey can have a significant effect on the proportion of surveys returned? Test at the .01 level of significance.

19. A scientist would like to see if there is a relationship between handedness and eye preference. A random sample of $n = 150$ subjects is selected. For each subject, the researcher determines two things: (1) whether the person is left-handed or right-handed and (2) which eye the person prefers to use when looking through a camera viewfinder. The observed frequencies are as follows:

		HAND PREFERENCE	
		LEFT	RIGHT
EYE PREFERENCE	LEFT	20	40
	RIGHT	10	80

Is there a relationship between the two variables? Test at the .01 level of significance.

20. As part of a campaign to prove sex discrimination in salary within the county government, a sample of $n = 200$ county employees was selected, and each individual was classified according to gender and salary. The obtained frequency distribution was as follows:

	UNDER $20,000	$20,001–$40,000	OVER $40,000
MALES	14	38	28
FEMALES	45	63	12

Do these data indicate a significant difference in the salary distribution for men versus women? Test at the .05 level of significance.

CHAPTER 18

THE BINOMIAL TEST

TOOLS YOU WILL NEED

The following items are considered essential background material for this chapter. If you doubt your knowledge of any of these items, you should review the appropriate chapter or section before proceeding.

- Binomial distribution (Chapter 6)
- z-score hypothesis tests (Chapter 8)
- Chi-square test for goodness of fit (Chapter 17)

CONTENTS

In 1960, Gibson and Walk designed a classic piece of apparatus to test depth perception (Gibson and Walk, 1960). Their device, called a *visual cliff,* consisted of a wide board with a deep drop (the cliff) to one side and a shallow drop on the other side. An infant was placed on the board and then observed to see whether he or she crawled off the shallow side or crawled off the cliff. (*Note:* Infants who moved to the deep side actually crawled onto a sheet of heavy glass, which prevented them from falling. Thus, the deep side only appeared to be a cliff—hence the name *visual cliff.*)

Gibson and Walk reasoned that if infants are born with the ability to perceive depth, they would recognize the deep side and not crawl off the cliff. On the other hand, if depth perception is a skill that develops over time through learning and experience, then infants should not be able to perceive any difference between the shallow and the deep sides.

Out of 27 infants who moved off the board, only 3 ventured onto the deep side at any time during the experiment. Gibson and Walk interpreted these data as convincing evidence that depth perception is innate. The infants showed a systematic preference for the shallow side.

You should notice immediately that the data from this experiment are different from any we have encountered before. There are no scores. Gibson and Walk simply counted the number of infants who went off the deep side and the number who went to the shallow side. Still, we would like to use these data to make statistical decisions. Do these sample data provide sufficient evidence to make a confident conclusion about depth perception in the population? Suppose that 8 of the 27 infants had crawled to the deep side. Would you still be convinced that there is a significant preference for the shallow side? What about 12 out of 27?

Notice that we are asking questions about probability and statistical significance. In this chapter, we will examine the statistical techniques designed for use with data similar to those obtained in the visual cliff experiments. Each individual in the sample is classified into one of two possible categories (for example, deep or shallow), and we simply count the number in each category. These frequency data are then used to draw inferences about the general population.

18.1 OVERVIEW

In Chapter 6, we introduced the concept of binomial data. You should recall that binomial data exist whenever a measurement procedure classifies individuals into exactly two distinct categories. For example, the outcomes from tossing a coin can be classified as heads and tails; people can be classified as male or female, plastic products can be classified as recyclable or non-recyclable. In general, binomial data exist when

1. The measurement scale consists of exactly two categories.

2. Each individual observation in a sample is classified in only one of the two categories.

3. The sample data consist of the frequency or number of individuals in each category.

The traditional notation system for binomial data identifies the two categories as A and B and identifies the probability (or proportion) associated with each category as p and q, respectively, For example, a coin toss results in either heads (A) or tails (B), with probabilities $p = \frac{1}{2}$ and $q = \frac{1}{2}$.

In this chapter, we will examine the statistical process of using binomial data for testing hypotheses about the values of p and q for the population. This type of hypothesis test is called a *binomial test.*

DEFINITION A *binomial test* uses sample data to evaluate hypotheses about the values of p and q for a population consisting of binomial data.

Consider the following two situations:

1. In a sample of $n = 34$ color-blind students, 30 are male, and only 4 are female. Does this sample indicate that color blindness is significantly more common for males in the general population?

2. In 1980, only 10% of American families had incomes below the poverty level. This year, in a sample of 100 families, 19 were below the poverty level. Does this sample indicate that there has been a significant change in the population proportions?

Notice that both of these examples have binomial data (exactly two categories). Although the data are relatively simple, we are asking the same statistical question about significance that is appropriate for a hypothesis test: Do the sample data provide sufficient evidence to make a conclusion about the population?

18.2 LOGIC AND FORMULAS FOR THE BINOMIAL TEST

As noted earlier, the data for a binomial situation consist of frequencies: the number of individuals classified in category A and the number classified in category B. We focus attention on the number of individuals classified in category A and identify this variable with the symbol X. For a sample of $n = 20$ coin tosses, for example, the variable X would be the number of heads.

You should recall from Chapter 6 that X can have any value from 0 to n and that each value of X has an associated probability. In a sample of $n = 20$ coin tosses, you could obtain any value from 0 heads up to 20 heads, and each of the possible outcomes has a specific probability. The distribution of probabilities for each value of X is called the binomial distribution.

As we noted in Chapter 6, when the values pn and qn are both equal to or greater than 10, the binomial distribution approximates a normal distribution. This fact is important because it allows us to compute z-scores and use the unit normal table to answer probability questions about binomial events. In particular, when pn and qn are both at least 10, the binomial distribution will have the following properties:

1. The shape of the distribution is approximately normal.
2. The mean of the distribution is $\mu = pn$.
3. The standard deviation of the distribution is

$$\sigma = \sqrt{npq}$$

With these parameters in mind, it is possible to compute a z-score corresponding to each value of X in the binomial distribution.

$$z = \frac{X - \mu}{\sigma} = \frac{X - pn}{\sqrt{npq}} \quad \text{(See equation 6.4.)} \tag{18.1}$$

This is the basic z-score formula that will be used for the binomial test. However, we will modify the formula slightly to make it more compatible with the logic of the binomial hypothesis test. The modification consists of dividing both the numerator and the denominator of the z-score by n. (You should realize that dividing both the numerator and the denominator by the same value does not change the value of the z-score.) The resulting equation is

$$z = \frac{X/n - p}{\sqrt{pq/n}}$$

(18.2)

For the binomial test, the values in this formula are defined as follows:

1. X/n is the proportion of individuals in the sample data who are classified in category A.

2. p is the hypothesized value (from H_0) for the proportion of individuals in the population who are classified in category A.

3. $\sqrt{pq/n}$ is the standard error for the sampling distribution of X/n and provides a measure of the standard distance between the sample statistic (X/n) and the population parameter (p).

Thus, the structure of the binomial z-score (equation 18.2) can be expressed as

$$z = \frac{X/n - p}{\sqrt{pq/n}} = \frac{\begin{array}{c}\text{sample} \\ \text{proportion} \\ \text{(data)}\end{array} - \begin{array}{c}\text{hypothesized} \\ \text{population} \\ \text{proportion}\end{array}}{\text{standard error}}$$

The logic underlying the binomial test is exactly the same as we encountered with the original z-score hypothesis test in Chapter 8. The hypothesis test involves comparing the sample data with the hypothesis. If the data are consistent with the hypothesis, we will conclude that the hypothesis is reasonable. But if there is a big discrepancy between the data and the hypothesis, we will reject the hypothesis. The value of the standard error will provide a benchmark for determining whether the discrepancy between the data and the hypothesis is more than would be expected by chance. The alpha level for the test will provide a criterion for deciding whether or not the discrepancy is significant. The hypothesis-testing procedure is demonstrated in the following section.

18.3 THE BINOMIAL TEST

The binomial test will follow the same four-step procedure presented earlier with other examples for hypothesis testing. The four steps are summarized as follows.

STEP 1   *State the hypotheses.* In the binomial test, the null hypothesis specifies values for the population proportions p and q. For example, a null hypothesis might state that for particular coin, $p(\text{heads}) = \frac{1}{2}$ and $p(\text{tails}) = \frac{1}{2}$. Note that the null hypothesis often states that there is "nothing wrong or unusual" about the population probabilities or proportions. For example, this hypothesis states that the coin is balanced, so that heads and tails are equally likely. Also notice that the null hypothesis requires that you specify a value only for p, the proportion associated with category A. The value of q is directly determined from p by the relationship

$q = 1 - p$. Finally, you should realize that the hypothesis, as always, addresses the probabilities or proportions for the *population*. Although we will use a sample to test the hypothesis, the hypothesis itself always concerns a population.

STEP 2   *Locate the critical region.* When both values for *pn* and *qn* are greater than or equal to 10, the *z*-score defined by equation 18.1 or 18.2 will form an approximately normal distribution. Thus, the unit normal table can be used to find the boundaries for the critical region. With $\alpha = .05$, for example, you may recall that the critical region is defined as *z*-score values greater than $+1.96$ or less than -1.96.

STEP 3   *Compute the test statistic (z-score).* At this time, you obtain a sample of *n* individuals (or events) and count the number of times category *A* occurs in the sample. The number of occurrences of *A* in the sample is the *X* value for equation 18.1 or 18.2. Because the two *z*-score equations are equivalent, you may use either one for the hypothesis test. usually equation 18.1 is easier to use because it involves larger numbers (fewer decimals) and it is less likely to be affected by rounding error.

STEP 4   *Make a decision.* If the *z*-score for the sample data is in the critical region, you reject H_0 and conclude that the discrepancy between the sample proportions and the hypothesized population proportions is significantly greater than chance. That is, the data are not consistent with the null hypothesis, so H_0 must be wrong. On the other hand, if the *z*-score is not in the critical region, you fail to reject H_0.

The following example demonstrates a complete binomial test.

EXAMPLE 18.1   In the Preview section, we described the *visual cliff* experiment designed to examine depth perception in infants. To summarize briefly, an infant is placed on a wide board that has an apparently deep drop on one side and a relatively shallow drop on the other. An infant who is able to perceive depth should avoid the deep side and move toward the shallow side. Without depth perception, the infant should show no preference between the two sides. In the experiment, only 3 out of 27 infants moved onto the deep side. The purpose of the hypothesis test is to determine whether these data demonstrate that infants have a significant preference for the shallow side.

This is a binomial hypothesis-testing situation. The two categories are

A = move onto the deep side

B = move onto the shallow side

STEP 1   The null hypothesis states that for the general population of infants, there is no preference between the deep and the shallow sides; the direction of movement is determined by chance. In symbols,

H_0: $p = p(\text{deep side}) = \frac{1}{2}$ (and $q = \frac{1}{2}$)

H_1: $p \neq \frac{1}{2}$ (There is a preference.)

We will use $\alpha = .05$.

S T E P 2   With a sample of $n = 27$, $pn = 13.5$ and $qn = 13.5$. Both values are greater than 10, so the distribution of z-scores will be approximately normal. With $\alpha = .05$, the critical region is determined by boundaries of $z = \pm 1.96$.

S T E P 3   For this experiment, the data consist of $X = 3$ out of $n = 27$. Using equation 18.1, these data produce a z-score value of

$$z = \frac{X - pn}{\sqrt{npq}} = \frac{3 - 13.5}{\sqrt{27(\frac{1}{2})(\frac{1}{2})}} = \frac{-10.5}{2.60} = -4.04$$

To use equation 18.2, you first compute the sample proportion, $X/n = 3/27 = 0.111$. The z-score is then

$$z = \frac{X/n - p}{\sqrt{pq/n}} = \frac{0.111 - 0.5}{\sqrt{\frac{1}{2}(\frac{1}{2})/27}} = \frac{-0.389}{0.096} = -4.05$$

Within rounding error, the two equations produce the same result.

S T E P 4   Because the data are in the critical region, our decision is to reject H_0. These data do provide sufficient evidence to conclude that there is a significant preference for the shallow side. Gibson and Walk (1960) interpreted these data as convincing evidence that depth perception is innate.

IN THE LITERATURE
REPORTING THE RESULTS OF A BINOMIAL TEST

Reporting the results of the binomial test typically consists of describing the data and reporting the z-score value and the probability that the results are due to chance. It is also helpful to note that a binomial test was used because z-scores are used in other hypothesis-testing situations (see, for example, Chapter 8). For Example 18.1, the report might state:

> Three out of 27 infants moved to the deep side of the visual cliff. A binomial test revealed that there is a significant preference for the shallow side of the cliff, $z = -4.04$, $p < .05$.

Once more, p is *less than* alpha (.05), indicating the null hypothesis has been rejected. The probability that these results are simply due to chance is less than 5%. ❏

ASSUMPTIONS FOR
THE BINOMIAL TEST

The binomial test requires two very simple assumptions:

1. The sample must consist of *independent* observations (see Chapter 8, p. 244).

2. The values for pn and qn must both be greater than or equal to 10 to justify using the unit normal table for determining the critical region.

LEARNING CHECK 1. The makers of brand X beer claim that people like their beer more than the leading brand. The basis for this claim is an experiment in which 64 beer drinkers compared the two brands in a side-by-side taste test. In this sample, 38 preferred brand X, and 26 preferred the leading brand. Do these data support the claim that there is a significant preference? Test at the .05 level.

ANSWER 1. H_0: $p = \frac{1}{2} = q$, $X = 38$, $\mu = 32$, $\sigma = 4$, $z = +1.50$, fail to reject H_0. Conclude that there is no evidence for a significant preference.

18.4 THE RELATIONSHIP BETWEEN CHI-SQUARE AND THE BINOMIAL TEST

You may have noticed that the binomial test evaluates the same basic hypotheses as the chi-square test for goodness of fit; that is, both tests evaluate how well the sample proportions fit a hypothesis about the population proportions. When an experiment produces binomial data, these two tests are equivalent, and either one may be used. The relationship between the two tests can be expressed by the equation.

$$\chi^2 = z^2$$

where χ^2 is the statistic from the chi-square test for goodness of fit and z is the z-score from the binomial test.

To demonstrate the relationship between the goodness-of-fit test and the binomial test, we will reexamine the data from Example 18.1.

STEP 1 *Hypotheses.* In the visual cliff experiment from Example 18.1, the null hypothesis states that there is no preference between the shallow side and the deep side. For the binomial test, the null hypothesis states

H_0: $p = p(\text{deep side}) = q = p(\text{shallow side}) = \frac{1}{2}$

The chi-square test for goodness of fit would state the same hypothesis, specifying the population proportions as

	SHALLOW SIDE	DEEP SIDE
H_0:	½	½

STEP 2 *Critical region.* For the binomial test, the critical region is located by using the unit normal table. With $\alpha = .05$, the critical region consists of any z-score value beyond ± 1.96. The chi-square test would have $df = 1$, and with $\alpha = .05$, the critical region consists of chi-square values greater than 3.84. Notice that the basic relationship, $\chi^2 = z^2$, holds:

$$3.84 = (1.96)^2$$

STEP 3 *Test statistic.* For the binomial test (Example 18.1), we obtained a z-score of $z = -4.04$. For the chi-square test, the expected frequencies would be

	SHALLOW SIDE	DEEP SIDE
f_e	13.5	13.5

With observed frequencies of 24 and 3, respectively, the chi-square statistic is

$$\chi^2 = \frac{(24 - 13.5)^2}{13.5} + \frac{(3 - 13.5)^2}{13.5}$$

$$= \frac{(10.5)^2}{13.5} + \frac{(10.5)^2}{13.5}$$

$$= 8.167 + 8.167$$

$$= 16.33$$

With a little rounding error, the values obtained for the z-score and chi-square are related by the equation

$$\chi^2 = z^2$$

$$16.33 = (-4.04)^2$$

STEP 4 *Decision.* Because the critical values for both tests are related by the equation $\chi^2 = z^2$ and the test statistics are related in the same way, these two tests *always* will result in the same statistical conclusion.

18.5 THE SIGN TEST

Although hypothesis tests with the binomial distribution are used in many situations, there is one specific case that merits special attention. Throughout this book, we have observed that one of the basic experimental designs is repeated measures. You should recall that in a repeated-measures experiment each subject is measured in several different experimental conditions; that is, you "repeat measurements" on the same subjects. The binomial test can use the data from a repeated-measures experiment to test hypotheses about the difference between two treatment conditions. In this situation, the binomial test commonly is called a *sign test*.

The data for the sign test require that each individual be measured in two experimental conditions. The researcher then records the *direction of the difference* between the treatments. An example is as follows:

SUBJECT	TREATMENT 1	TREATMENT 2	DIRECTION OF DIFFERENCE
1	18	14	− (decrease)
2	23	10	− (decrease)
3	17	12	− (decrease)
4	31	33	+ (increase)
5	27	24	− (decrease)

Notice that the magnitude of the treatment effect is not important; the researcher records only the direction of the effect. Traditionally, increases and decreases in scores are noted by plus and minus signs in the data—hence the name *sign test*.

The null hypothesis for the sign test states that there is no difference between the two treatments. Therefore, any change in a subject's score is due to chance. In terms of probabilities, this means that increases and decreases are equally likely, so

$$p = p(\text{increase}) = \tfrac{1}{2}$$

$$q = p(\text{decrease}) = \tfrac{1}{2}$$

Because the data from the repeated measures experiment have been transformed into two categories (increases and decreases), we now have dichotomous data appropriate for a binomial test. The null hypothesis specifies probabilities for these two categories ($p = \tfrac{1}{2} = q$). A complete example of a sign test follows.

EXAMPLE 18.2   A researcher tests the effect of a diet plan on body weight. A sample of 36 people is selected. Weights are measured at the start of the diet and one month later. The observations revealed that 23 people lost weight and 13 people gained weight.

STEP 1   State the hypothesis. The null hypothesis states that the diet has no effect. Any change in weight is due to chance, so increases and decreases are equally likely. Expressed as probabilities, the hypotheses are

$$H_0: \quad p = p(\text{lose weight}) = \tfrac{1}{2}$$

$$q = p(\text{gain weight}) = \tfrac{1}{2}$$

$$H_1: \quad p \neq q \qquad \text{(Changes are consistently in one direction or the other.)}$$

Set $\alpha = .05$.

STEP 2   Locate the critical region. With $p = q = \tfrac{1}{2}$ and $n = 36$, the normal approximation to the binomial distribution is appropriate:

$$pn = qn = 18 \quad \text{(both greater than 10)}$$

With $\alpha = .05$, the critical region is defined as the most extreme 5% of the distribution. This portion is bounded by z-scores of $z = +1.96$ at one extreme and $z = -1.96$ at the other.

STEP 3   Compute the test statistic. For this sample, we have $X = 23$ people who lost weight. This score corresponds to a z-score of

$$z = \frac{X - pn}{\sqrt{npq}} = \frac{23 - 18}{\sqrt{36(\tfrac{1}{2})(\tfrac{1}{2})}} = \frac{5}{3} = 1.67$$

STEP 4   Make a decision. Because the data are not in the critical region, we fail to reject H_0. These data do not provide sufficient evidence to conclude that the diet plan has any consistent effect on weight, $z = 1.67$, $p > .05$.

ZERO DIFFERENCES IN THE SIGN TEST

You should notice that the null hypothesis in the sign test refers only to those individuals who show some difference between treatment 1 versus treatment 2. The null hypothesis states that if there is any change in an individual's score, then the probability of an increase is equal to the probability of a decrease. Stated in this form, the null hypothesis does not consider individuals who show zero difference between the two treatments. As a result, the usual recommendation is that these individuals be discarded from the data and the value of n be reduced accordingly. However, if the null hypothesis is interpreted more generally, it states that there is no difference between the two treatments. Phrased this way, it should be clear that individuals who show no difference actually are supporting the null hypothesis and should not be discarded. Therefore, an alternative approach to the sign test is to divide individuals who show zero differences equally between the positive and negative categories. (With an odd number of zero differences, discard one, and divide the rest evenly.) This alternative results in a more conservative test; that is, the test is more likely to fail to reject the null hypothesis.

EXAMPLE 18.3

It has been demonstrated that stress or exercise causes an increase in the concentration of certain chemicals called endorphins in the brain. Endorphins are similar to morphine and produce a generally relaxed feeling and a sense of well-being. The endorphins may explain the "high" experienced by long-distance runners. To demonstrate this phenomenon, a researcher tested pain tolerance for 40 athletes before and after they completed a mile run. Immediately after running, the ability to tolerate pain increased for 21 of the athletes, decreased for 12, and showed no change for the remaining 7.

Following the standard recommendation for handling zero differences, you would use $n = 33$ for the sign test because only 33 subjects showed any difference between the two treatments. The other 7 athletes are eliminated from the sample. With the more conservative approach, only 1 of the 7 athletes who showed no difference would be discarded, and the other 6 would be divided equally between the two categories. This would result in a total of $n = 39$ in the sample data with 24 (21 + 3) in one category and 15 (12 + 3) in the other.

WHEN TO USE THE SIGN TEST

In many cases, data from a repeated-measures experiment can be evaluated using either a sign test or a repeated-measures t test. In general, you should use the t test whenever possible. Because the t test uses the actual difference scores (not just the signs), it makes maximum use of the available information and results in a more powerful test. However, there are some cases where a t test cannot or should not be used, and in these situations, the sign test can be valuable. Three specific cases where a t test is inappropriate or inconvenient will now be described.

BEFORE	AFTER	DIFFERENCE
20	23	+3
14	39	+25
27	Failed	+??
.	.	.
.	.	.
.	.	.

1. When you have infinite or undetermined scores, a t test is impossible, and the sign test is appropriate. Suppose, for example, that you are evaluating the effects of a sedative drug on problem-solving ability. A sample of rats is obtained, and each animal's performance is measured before and after receiving the drug. Hypothetical data are shown in the left margin. Note that the third rat in this sample failed to solve the problem after receiving the drug. Because there is no score for this animal, it is impossible to compute

a sample mean, an *SS*, or a *t* statistic. But you could do a sign test because you know that the animal made more errors (an increase) after receiving the drug.

2. Often it is possible to describe the difference between two treatment conditions without precisely measuring a score in either condition. In a clinical setting, for example, a doctor can say whether a patient is improving, growing worse, or showing no change even though the patient's condition is not precisely measured by a score. In this situation, the data are sufficient for a sign test, but you could not compute a *t* statistic without individual scores.

3. Often a sign test is done as a preliminary check on an experiment before serious statistical analysis begins. For example, a researcher may predict that scores in treatment 2 should be consistently greater than scores in treatment 1. However, examination of the data after one week indicates that only 8 of 15 subjects showed the predicted increase. On the basis of these preliminary results, the researcher may choose to reevaluate the experiment before investing additional time.

LEARNING CHECK 1. A developmental psychologist is using a behavior-modification program to help control the disruptive behavior of 40 children in a local school. After one month, 26 of these children have improved, 10 are worse, and 4 show no change in behavior. On the basis of these data, can the psychologist conclude that the program is working? Test at the .05 level.

ANSWER 1. Discarding the 4 subjects who showed zero difference, $X = 26$ increases out of $n = 36$; $z = 2.67$; reject H_0; the program is working.

SUMMARY

1. The binomial test is used with dichotomous data, that is, when each individual in the sample is classified in one of two categories. The two categories are identified as A and B, with probabilities of

$$p(A) = p \quad \text{and} \quad p(B) = q$$

2. The binomial distribution gives the probability for each value of X, where X equals the number of occurrences of category A in a sample of n events. For example, X equals the number of heads in $n = 10$ tosses of a coin.

3. When pn and qn are both at least 10, the binomial distribution is closely approximated by a normal distribution with

$$\mu = pn$$

$$\sigma = \sqrt{npq}$$

By using this normal approximation, each value of X has a corresponding z-score:

$$z = \frac{X - \mu}{\sigma} = \frac{X - pn}{\sqrt{npq}} \quad \text{or} \quad z = \frac{X/n - p}{\sqrt{pq/n}}$$

4. The binomial test uses sample data to test hypotheses about the binomial proportions, p and q, for a population. The null hypothesis specifies p and q, and the binomial distribution (or the normal approximation) is used to determine the critical region.

5. One common use of the binomial distribution is for the sign test. This test evaluates the difference between two treatments using the data from a repeated measures design. The difference scores are coded as being either increases ($+$) or decreases ($-$). Without a consistent treatment effect, the increases and decreases should be mixed randomly, so the null hypothesis states that

$$p(\text{increase}) = \tfrac{1}{2} = p(\text{decrease})$$

With dichotomous data and hypothesized values for p and q, this is a binomial test.

KEY TERMS

dichotomous data   binomial distribution   binomial test   sign test

—— FOCUS ON PROBLEM SOLVING ——

1. For all binomial tests, the values of p and q must sum to 1.00 (or 100%).

2. Remember that both pn and qn must be at least 10 before you can use the normal distribution to determine critical values for a binomial test.

3. Although the binomial test usually specifies the critical region in terms of z-scores, it is possible to identify the X values that determine the critical region. With $\alpha = .05$, the critical region is determined by z-scores greater than 1.96 or less than -1.96. That is, to be significantly different from chance, the individual score must be above (or below) the mean by at least 1.96 standard deviations. For example, in an ESP experiment where an individual is trying to predict the suit of a playing card for a sequence of $n = 64$ trials, chance probabilities would be

$$p = p(\text{right}) = \tfrac{1}{4} \quad q = p(\text{wrong}) = \tfrac{3}{4}$$

For this example, the binomial distribution would have a mean of $pn = (\tfrac{1}{4})(64) = 16$ right and a standard deviation of $\sqrt{npq} = \sqrt{64(\tfrac{1}{4})(\tfrac{3}{4})} = \sqrt{12} = 3.46$. To be significantly different from chance, a score must be above (or below) the mean by at least $1.96(3.46) = 6.78$. Thus, with a mean of 16, an individual would need to score above 22.78 ($16 + 6.78$) or below 9.22 ($16 - 6.78$) to be significantly different from chance.

—— DEMONSTRATION 18.1 ——

THE BINOMIAL TEST

The population of students in the psychology department at the State College consists of 60% females and 40% males. Last semester, the psychology of gender course had a total of 36 students, of which 26 were female and only 10 were male. Can you conclude from these data that the gender course attracts more females than would be expected by chance? Test at the .05 level of significance.

STEP 1   *State the hypotheses, and specify alpha.* The null hypothesis states that the male/female proportions for the gender class are not different from the population proportions. In symbols,

$$H_0: \quad p = p(\text{female}) = 0.60 \quad \text{and} \quad q = p(\text{male}) = 0.40$$

The alternative hypothesis is that the proportions for this class are different from the population proportions.

$$H_1: \quad p \neq 0.60 \quad (\text{and } q \neq 0.40)$$

We will set alpha at $\alpha = .05$.

STEP 2   *Locate the critical region.* Because pn and qn are both greater than 10, we can use the normal approximation to the binomial distribution. With $\alpha = .05$, the critical region is defined as any z-score value greater than $+1.96$ or less than -1.96.

STEP 3   *Calculate the test statistic.* The sample has 26 females out of 36 students, so the sample proportion is

$$\frac{X}{n} = \frac{26}{36} = 0.72$$

The corresponding z-score (using equation 18.2) is

$$z = \frac{X/n - p}{\sqrt{pq/n}} = \frac{0.72 - 0.60}{\sqrt{\dfrac{0.60(0.40)}{36}}} = \frac{0.12}{0.0816} = 1.47$$

STEP 4   *Make a decision about H_0, and state a conclusion.* The obtained z-score is not in the critical region. Therefore, we fail to reject the null hypothesis. On the basis of these data, you cannot conclude that the male/female proportions in the gender class are significantly different from the proportions in the psychology department as a whole.

PROBLEMS

1. An extensive survey two years ago indicated that 80% of the population of New York State favored income tax over sales tax as a means of increasing state revenue. In a recent sample of 100 people, 72 preferred income tax, and 28 preferred sales tax. Do these data indicate a significant change in opinion? Test at the .05 level of significance. (*Caution:* Be careful in setting the values of p and q for H_0. They are not equal.)

2. In a recent study examining color preferences in infants, 30 babies were offered a choice between a red rattle and a green rattle. Twenty-five of the 30 selected the red rattle. Do these data provide evidence for a significant color preference? Test at the .01 level of significance.

3. A college dormitory recently sponsored a taste comparison between two major soft drinks. Of the 64 students who participated, 39 selected brand A, and only 25 selected brand B. Do these data indicate a significant preference? Test at the .05 level of significance.

4. Nationwide, only 4% of the population develops ulcers each year. In a sample of 200 executive vice presidents, 40 had developed ulcers during the previous 12 months. Do these data indicate that vice presidents have an incidence of ulcers different from the general population? Test at the .05 level of significance.

5. Use $\alpha = .05$ to answer each of the following questions. Use the normal approximation to the binomial distribution.

a. For a true-false test with 20 questions, how many would you have to get right to do significantly better than chance?

b. How many would you need to get right on a 40-question test?

c. How many would you need to get right on a 100-question test?

6. A multiple-choice exam has 48 questions, each with four possible answers. What score (X = number correct) is needed on this exam to do significantly better than chance? Assume a one-tailed test with $\alpha = .05$.

7. Research at the Monell Institute for Chemical Senses examined the type of food cravings commonly experienced. It revealed that women between the ages of 18 and 35 crave sweets (especially in chocolates) 2 to 1 over other alternatives (steak, lasagna, and so on). That is, 67% would have cravings for sweets and 33% for other foods. Now researchers want to determine if there are any gender differences in food cravings. A sample of $n = 50$ men in the same age group is selected, and the types of cravings they have are determined. Fifteen out of 50 men indicated having cravings for chocolate. Is there evidence for a gender difference in specific food cravings? Set alpha to .01.

8. For the previous problem, it was stated that there is a 2-to-1 preference for chocolates among women between 18 and 35. Next, the researchers focused on women over age 65. In this study, 18 out of 30 participants reported having had cravings for chocolates and other sweets. Does food craving change with age? Use the .01 level of significance.

9. Eyewitness identification of a criminal suspect is far from error-free. One type of error is a false positive, that is, "recognizing" someone as a suspect who actually did not commit any crime. When photographs (none of whom is the actual suspect) are presented by arranging them on a flat surface so that they could be viewed simultaneously, 65% of the individuals select a photograph (false positives). A forensic psychologist presents the same photographs, only one at a time, to a sample of $n = 60$ witnesses. Eighteen of these individuals had false positives. Does the method of presentation have an effect of the number of false positives? Set α at .05.

10. The habituation technique is one method that is used to examine memory for infants. The procedure involves presenting a stimulus to an infant (usually projected on the ceiling above the crib) for a fixed time period and recording how long the infant spends looking at the stimulus. After a brief delay, the stimulus is presented again. If the infant spends less time looking at the stimulus during the second presentation, it is interpreted as indicating that the stimulus is remembered and, therefore, is less novel and less interesting than it was on the first presentation. This procedure is used with a sample of $n = 30$ two-week-old infants. For this sample, 22 infants spent less time looking at the stimulus during the second presentation than during the first. Do these data indicate a significant difference? Test at the .01 level of significance.

11. Thirty percent of the students in the local elementary school are classified as only children (no siblings). However, in the special program for talented and gifted children, 43 out of 90 students are only children. Is the proportion of only children in the special program significantly different from the proportion for the school? Test at the .05 level of significance.

12. Last year the college counseling center offered a workshop for students who claimed to suffer from extreme exam anxiety. Of the 45 students who attended the workshop, 31 had higher grade point averages this semester than they did last year. Do these data indicate a significant difference from what would be expected by chance? Test at the .01 level of significance.

13. A social psychologist is examining the transition from elementary school to a middle school. One aspect of this transition is that elementary students spend all day with a single teacher and the same group of classmates. In the middle school, the students move from teacher to teacher with a different set of classmates each class period. The psychologist believes that the lack of social stability in the middle school will cause the students to place more importance on belonging to a well-defined peer group. To test this hypothesis, the psychologist gave a questionnaire to the elementary students and found that only 35% rated peer-group membership as being important or very important. When the same questionnaire was given to a sample of $n = 50$ middle school students, 38 rated peer-group membership as important or very important. Do these data indicate a significant difference between the two school groups? Test at the .05 level of significance.

14. In an attempt to increase productivity, $n = 24$ workers are placed on piecework. For piecework, a person gets paid a certain amount for each unit produced (for example, for each ballpoint pen assembled) rather than receiving an hourly wage. After one week, 18 workers showed an increase in units produced. Did the piecework schedule increase productivity? Test with $\alpha = .01$, one tail.

15. In Problem 14, the amount paid to the workers for each unit was not much. Although productivity was increased for the first week, 17 out of the 24 workers actually showed a decrease in earnings that week. They complain that the earnings per unit are set too low. Do they have a case? Were there significantly lower earnings for the group? Use the .01 level of significance for a one-tailed test.

16. In the general population, 8 out of 10 people can be hypnotized. A researcher suspects that the ability to be hypnotized is partially determined by an individual's personality. A sample of $n = 80$ subjects is obtained. All these subjects are known to be *field independent*, which means that they tend to rely on internal cues rather than external cues for making judgments. The researcher finds that 51 of these 80 subjects can be hypnotized. Do these data indicate that field-independent people are different from the general population in terms of their ability to be hypnotized? Use an alpha of .05.

17. In a study of human memory, Sachs (1967) demonstrated that people recall the meaning of verbal material, but tend to forget the exact word-for word details. In this study, people read a passage of text. Then the people were shown a test sentence and asked whether or not the identical sentence had appeared in the text. In one condition, the test sentence was phrased differently, but had the same meaning as a sentence that was in the text. For example, the sentence in the text might be "The boy hit the ball," and the test sentence might be "The ball was hit by the boy." If only 27 out of 45 people correctly notice that change in the sentence, can you conclude that their performance is significantly better than chance? Test at the .05 level of significance.

18. A psychologist examining the psychology of art appreciation selected an abstract painting that had no obvious top or bottom. Hangers were placed on the painting so that it could be hung with any one of the four sides at the top. This painting was shown to a sample of $n = 50$ undergraduates, and each was asked to hang the painting in whatever orientation "looked best." Twenty-five of the subjects in this sample placed the painting so that the correct side was up. Is this significantly better than would be expected by chance? Test with $\alpha = .05$.

19. We expect the weather to be "average." Some days it is a little warmer than the mean temperature for that day of the year. Some days it is a little colder. But, overall, the temperature should "balance out" around the expected values. A local meteorologist reports that out of 30 days in June, 22 days had above-average temperatures. Is this a significant departure from the norm? Set α at .05.

20. Trying to fight a drug-resistant bacteria, a researcher tries an experimental drug on infected subjects. Out of 70 monkeys, 42 showed improvement, 22 got worse, and 6 showed no change. Is this researcher working in the right direction? Is there a significant effect of the drug on the infection? Use the .05 level of significance.

21. A sample of 40 children is selected for an experiment to evaluate the effect of teacher's sex on classroom performance. Each child is given a task while being observed by a male teacher and then a similar task while being observed by a female teacher. Of these 40 children, 20 were judged to work better for the female teacher, 8 worked better for the male teacher, and 12 worked equally well in the two situations. Do these results indicate that the teacher's sex has a significant influence on performance? Test with $\alpha = .05$.

22. An English professor conducts a special one-week course in writing skills for freshmen who are poorly prepared for college-level writing. To test the effectiveness of this course, each student in a recent class of $n = 36$ was required to write a short paragraph describing a painting before the course started. At the end of the course, the students were once again required to write a paragraph describing the same painting. The students' paragraphs were then given to another instructor to be evaluated. For 25 students, the writing was judged to be better after the course. For the rest of the class, the first paragraph was judged to be better. Do these results indicate a significant change in performance? Test at the .05 level of significance.

23. Biofeedback training is often used to help people who suffer migraine headaches. A recent study found that 29 out of 50 subjects reported a decrease in the frequency and severity of their headaches after receiving biofeedback training. Of the remaining subjects in this study, 10 reported that their headaches were worse, and 11 reported no change.
    a. Discard the zero-difference subjects, and use a sign test with $\alpha = .05$ to determine whether or not the biofeedback produced a significant different.
    b. Divide the zero-difference subjects between the two groups, and use a sign test to evaluate the effect of biofeedback training.

24. The sense of smell plays an important role in the taste of food. A favorite demonstration of this fact involves having people hold their noses while tasting slices of apple and onion. Without smell, these two taste much the same. In a sample of 25 people who tried this demonstration, only 15 were able to identify the onion correctly. Is this significantly better than chance? Test at the .05 level of significance.

CHAPTER 19

STATISTICAL TECHNIQUES FOR ORDINAL DATA: MANN-WHITNEY AND WILCOXON TESTS AND SPEARMAN CORRELATION

TOOLS YOU WILL NEED

The following items are considered essential background material for this chapter. If you doubt your knowledge of any of these items, you should review the appropriate chapter or section before proceeding.

- Ordinal scales (Chapter 1)
- Probability (Chapter 6)
  - The unit normal table
- Introduction to hypothesis testing (Chapter 8)
- Correlation (Chapter 16)

CONTENTS

PREVIEW

People have a passion for ranking things. Everyone wants to know who is number one, and we all tend to describe things in terms of their relationship to others. For example, the Nile is the longest river in the world, the Labrador retriever is the number one registered dog in the United States, the state with the highest average SAT math score is Iowa, *Reader's Digest* is the most popular magazine in the United States, English is the fourth most common native language in the world (after Chinese, Hindi, and Spanish), and Lake Superior is the largest lake in North America and the second largest in the world.

Part of the fascination with ranks is that they are easy to obtain and they are easy to understand. For example, what is your favorite ice-cream flavor? Notice that you do not need to conduct any sophisticated measurement to arrive at an answer. There is no need to rate 31 different flavors on a 100-point scale, and you do not need to worry about how much difference there is between your first and second choices.

You should recall from Chapter 1 that ranking is an example of measurement on an ordinal scale. In general, ordinal scales are less demanding and less sophisticated than the interval or ratio scales that are most commonly used to measure variables. Because ordinal scales are less demanding, they are often easier to use. On the other hand, because they are less sophisticated, they can cause some problems for statistical analysis. Consider the data presented in Table 19.1. The table shows the top-ranked television shows for the past four decades. Because the ranks in the table are numbers, it is tempting to perform some routine statistical calculations with them. For example, you may want to compare the three major networks by computing the mean rank for CBS, NBC, and ABC. Or you may want to look at trends across the years. For example, shows named after a celebrity star were highly ranked in the 60s, but gradually declined. What about the ranking of 30-minute shows versus one-hour shows? Are Americans' attention spans decreasing? Although these are statistical questions about means and trends, the data are different from any we have encountered before, and they will require different statistical procedures. The "scores" in Table 19.1 are all ranks, measured on an ordinal scale, and the statistical analysis of these data will require special techniques developed specifically for ordinal data. In this chapter, we will introduce some statistical methods that exist for evaluating and interpreting ordinal data.

TABLE 19.1

Most popular TV shows by decade as reported in *The Universal Almanac, 1995.*

1960–69		1970–79	
1. Bonanza	NBC	1. All in the Family	CBS
2. The Red Skeleton Show	CBS	2. M*A*S*H	CBS
3. The Andy Griffith Show	CBS	3. Hawaii Five-O	CBS
4. The Beverly Hillbillies	CBS	4. Happy Days	ABC
5. The Ed Sullivan Show	CBS	5. The Waltons	CBS
6. The Lucy Show/Here's Lucy	CBS	6. The Mary Tyler Moore Show	CBS
7. The Jackie Gleason Show	CBS	7. Sanford & Son	NBC
8. Bewitched	ABC	8. One Day at a Time	CBS
9. Gomer Pyle	CBS	9. Three's Company	ABC
10. Candid Camera	CBS	10. 60 Minutes	CBS

1980–89		1990–93	
1. 60 Minutes	CBS	1. 60 Minutes	CBS
2. Dallas	CBS	2. Roseanne	ABC
3. The Cosby Show	NBC	3. Cheers	NBC
4. Dynasty	ABC	4. Murphy Brown	CBS
5. Knots Landing	CBS	5. Murder, She Wrote	CBS
6. Cheers	NBC	6. Monday Night Football	ABC
7. Magnum, P.I.	CBS	7. Coach	ABC
8. Murder, She Wrote	CBS	8. Full House	ABC
9. Who's the Boss?	ABC	9. Unsolved Mysteries	NBC
10. Family Ties	NBC	10. CBS Sunday Night Movies	CBS

19.1 DATA FROM AN ORDINAL SCALE

Occasionally, a research study will generate data that consist of measurements on an ordinal scale. You should recall from Chapter 1 that an ordinal scale simply produces a *rank ordering* for the individuals being measured. For example, a kindergarten teacher may rank children in terms of their maturity, or a business manager may rank employee suggestions in terms of creativity. Whenever a set of data consists of ranks, you should be very cautious about choosing a statistical procedure to describe or to interpret the data. Specifically, most of the commonly used statistical methods such as the mean, the standard deviation, hypothesis tests with the *t* statistic, and the Pearson correlation are generally considered to be inappropriate for ordinal data.

The concern about using traditional statistical methods with ranked data stems from the fact that most statistical procedures begin by calculating a sample mean and computing deviations from the mean. When scores are measured on an interval or a ratio scale, the concepts of the *mean* and *distance* are very well defined. On a ruler, for example, a measurement of 2 inches is exactly halfway between a measurement of 1 inch and a measurement of 3 inches. In this case, the mean $\overline{X} = 2$ provides a precise central location that defines a balance point that is equidistant from the two scores, $X = 1$ and $X = 3$. However, ordinal measurements do not provide this same degree of precision. Specifically, ordinal values (ranks) tell you only the direction from one score to another, but provide no information about the distance between scores. Thus, you know that first place is better than second or third, but you do not know how much better. In a horse race, for example, you know that the second-place horse is somewhere between the first- and third-place horses, but you do not know exactly where. In particular, a rank of second is not necessarily halfway between first and third.

Because the concepts of *mean* and *distance* are not well defined with ordinal data and because most of the traditional statistical methods are based on these concepts, it generally is considered unwise to use traditional statistics with ordinal data. Therefore, statisticians have developed special techniques that are intended and designed specifically for use with ordinal data. In the remainder of this chapter, we will introduce several of these special statistical methods.

OBTAINING ORDINAL MEASUREMENTS

The process of ranking can be based directly on observations of individuals. For example, you could arrange a group of people in order of height by simply comparing them side by side to see who is tallest, who is next tallest, and so on. This kind of direct ordinal measurement is fairly common because it is easy to do. Notice that you do not need any absolute measurement to complete the ranking; that is, you never need to know anyone's exact height. It is necessary only to make relative judgments—given any two individuals, you must decide who is taller. Because ordinal scales do not require any absolute measurements, they can be used with variables that are not routinely measured. Variables such as beauty or talent can be observed, judged, and ranked, although they may be difficult to define and measure with more-sophisticated scales.

In addition to obtaining ranks by direct observation, a researcher may begin with a set of numerical measurements and convert these scores into ranks. For example, if you had a listing of the actual heights for a group of individuals, you could arrange the numbers in order from greatest to least. This process converts data from an interval or a ratio scale into ordinal measurements. There are a number of reasons for converting scores into ranks, but the following list should give you some indication of why this might be done.

1. Ranks are simpler. If someone asks you how tall your sister is, you could reply with a specific numerical value, such as 5 feet 7¾ inches tall. Or you could answer, "She is a little taller than I am." For many situations, the relative answer would be better.

2. The original scores may violate some of the basic assumptions that underly certain statistical procedures. For example, the *t* tests and analysis of variance assume that the data come from normal distributions. Also, the independent-measures tests assume that the different populations all have the same variance (the homogeneity of variance assumption). If a researcher suspects that the data do not satisfy these assumptions, it may be safer to convert the scores to ranks and use a statistical technique designed for ranks.

3. Occasionally, an experiment will produce an undetermined, or infinite, score. For example, a rat may show no sign of solving a particular maze after hundreds of trials. This animal has an infinite, or undetermined, score. Although there is no absolute score that can be assigned, you can say that this rat has the highest score for the sample and then rank the rest of the scores by their numerical values.

RANKING TIED SCORES

When you are converting scores into ranks, you may encounter two (or more) identical scores. Whenever two scores have exactly the same value, their ranks should also be the same. This is accomplished by the following procedure:

1. List the scores in order from smallest to largest. Include tied values in this list.

2. Assign a rank (first, second, etc.) to each position in the ordered list.

3. When two (or more) scores are tied, compute the mean of their ranked positions, and assign this mean value as the final rank for each score.

The process of finding ranks for tied scores is demonstrated here. These scores have been listed in order from smallest to largest.

SCORES	RANK POSITION	FINAL RANK	
3	1	1.5	Mean of 1 and 2
3	2	1.5	
5	3	3	
6	4	5	
6	5	5	Mean of 4, 5, and 6
6	6	5	
12	7	7	

Note that this example has seven scores and uses all seven ranks. For $X = 12$, the largest score, the appropriate rank is 7. It cannot be given a rank of 6 because that rank has been used for the tied scores.

FIGURE 19.1

In part (a), the scores from the two samples are clustered at opposite ends of the rank ordering. In this case, the data suggest a systematic difference between the two treatments. Part (b) shows the two samples intermixed evenly along the scale, indicating no consistent difference between treatments.

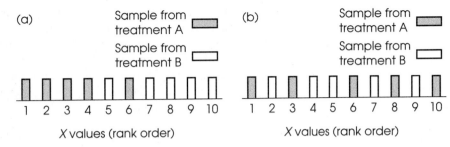

HYPOTHESIS TESTS AND CORRELATION WITH ORDINAL DATA

The remainder of this chapter examines three statistical procedures that are used with ordinal data. The first two procedures we consider are hypothesis tests. Both tests use sample data to evaluate the difference between two treatments or populations. The Mann-Whitney *U*-test works with data from an independent-measures research design (two separate samples), and the Wilcoxon test is intended for data from a repeated-measures design. The third procedure we consider is a correlation measuring the degree and direction of relationship between two variables measured on ordinal scales.

19.2 THE MANN-WHITNEY *U*-TEST

You should recall that an independent-measures study requires a separate sample for each of the treatments or populations being compared.

The Mann-Whitney test is designed to evaluate the difference between two treatments (or two populations), using data from an independent-measures study. The calculations for this test require that the individual scores in the two samples be rank ordered. The mathematics of the Mann-Whitney test are based on the following simple observation:

> A real difference between the two treatments should cause the scores in one sample to be generally larger than the scores in the other sample. If the two samples are combined and all the scores placed in rank order on a line, then the scores from one sample should be concentrated at one end of the line, and the scores from the other sample should concentrate at the other end.
>
> On the other hand, if there is no treatment difference, then large and small scores will be mixed evenly in the two samples because there is no reason for one set of scores to be systematically larger or smaller than the other.

This observation is demonstrated in Figure 19.1.

CALCULATION OF THE MANN-WHITNEY *U*

The first steps in the calculations for the Mann-Whitney test have already been discussed. To summarize,

1. A separate sample is obtained from each of the two treatments. We will use n_A to refer to the number of subjects in sample A and n_B to refer to the number in sample B.

2. These two samples are combined, and the total group of $n_A + n_B$ subjects is rank ordered.

The remaining problem is to decide whether the scores from the two samples are mixed randomly in the rank ordering or whether they are systematically clustered at opposite ends of the scale. This is the familiar question of statistical significance: Are the data simply the result of chance, or has some systematic effect produced these results? We will answer this question exactly as we always have answered it. First, look at all the possible results that could have been obtained. Next, separate these outcomes into two groups:

1. Those results that are reasonably likely to occur by chance
2. Those results that are very unlikely to occur by chance (this is the critical region)

For the Mann-Whitney test, the first step is to identify each of the possible outcomes. This is done by assigning a numerical value to every possible set of sample data. This number is called the Mann-Whitney U. The value of U is computed as if the two samples were two teams of athletes competing in a sports event. Each individual in sample A (the A team) gets one point whenever he or she is ranked ahead of an individual from sample B. The total number of points accumulated for sample A is called U_A. In the same way, a U value, or team total, is computed for sample B. The final Mann-Whitney U is the smaller of these two values. This process is demonstrated in the following example.

EXAMPLE 19.1   We begin with two separate samples with $n = 6$ scores in each.

sample A (treatment 1): 27   2   9   48   6   15

sample B (treatment 2): 71   63   18   68   94   8

Next, the two samples are combined, and all 12 scores are placed in rank order.* Each individual in sample A is assigned 1 point for every score in sample B that has a higher rank.

RANK	ORDERED SCORES SCORE	SAMPLE	POINTS FOR SAMPLE A
1	2	(A)	6 points
2	6	(A)	6 points
3	8	(B)	
4	9	(A)	5 points
5	15	(A)	5 points
6	18	(B)	
7	27	(A)	4 points
8	48	(A)	4 points
9	63	(B)	
10	68	(B)	
11	71	(B)	
12	94	(B)	

Finally, the points from all the individuals in sample A are combined, and the total number of points is computed for the sample. In this example, the total points or the U value for sample A is $U_A = 30$. In the same say, you can compute the U value for sample B. You should obtain $U_B = 6$. As a simple check on your arithmetic, note that

$$U_A + U_B = n_A n_B \qquad (19.1)$$

To avoid errors, it is wise to compute both U values and verify that the sum is equal to $n_A n_B$.

For these data,

$$30 + 6 = 6(6)$$

FORMULAS FOR THE MANN-WHITNEY *U*

Because the process of counting points to determine the Mann-Whitney U can be tedious, especially with large samples, there is a formula that will generate the U value for each sample. To use this formula, you combine the samples and rank order all the scores as before. Then you must find ΣR_A, which is the sum of the ranks for individuals in sample A, and the corresponding ΣR_B for sample B. The U value for each sample is then computed as follows: For sample A,

$$U_A = n_A n_B + \frac{n_A(n_A + 1)}{2} - \Sigma R_A \qquad (19.2)$$

and for sample B,

$$U_B = n_A n_B + \frac{n_B(n_B + 1)}{2} - \Sigma R_B \qquad (19.3)$$

These formulas are demonstrated using the data from Example 19.1. For sample A, the sum of the ranks is

$$\Sigma R_A = 1 + 2 + 4 + 5 + 7 + 8$$
$$= 27$$

For sample B, the sum of the ranks is

$$\Sigma R_B = 3 + 6 + 9 + 10 + 11 + 12$$
$$= 51$$

---

*For this example, we are assuming that the researcher has obtained a score (X value) for each individual. You should realize, however, that it is not necessary to have a set of previously obtained scores. The researcher could have started with the group of 12 individuals (two samples of $n = 6$) and then have rank ordered the subjects from 1st to 12th with respect to the variable being measured. The end result, in either case, is that the two samples are combined into one group and all the individuals are then ranked.

By using the special formula, for sample A,

$$U_A = n_A n_B + \frac{n_A(n_A + 1)}{2} - \Sigma R_A$$

$$= 6(6) + \frac{6(7)}{2} - 27$$

$$= 36 + 21 - 27$$

$$= 30$$

For sample B,

$$U_B = n_A n_B + \frac{n_B(n_B + 1)}{2} - \Sigma R_B$$

$$= 6(6) + \frac{6(7)}{2} - 51$$

$$= 36 + 21 - 51$$

$$= 6$$

Notice that these are the same U values we obtained in Example 19.1 using the counting method. The Mann-Whitney U value is the smaller of these two,

$$U = 6$$

HYPOTHESIS TESTS WITH THE MANN-WHITNEY U

Now that we have developed a method for identifying each rank order with a numerical value, the remaining problem is to decide whether the U value provides evidence for a real difference between the two treatment conditions. We will look at each possibility separately.

A large difference between the two treatments will cause all the ranks from sample A to cluster at one end of the scale and all the ranks from sample B to cluster at the other (see Figure 19.1). At the extreme, there will be no overlap between the two samples. In this case, the Mann-Whitney U will be zero because one of the samples will get no points at all. In general, a Mann-Whitney U of zero indicates the greatest possible difference between the two samples. As the two samples become more alike, their ranks begin to intermix, and the U becomes larger. If there is no consistent tendency for one treatment to produce larger scores than the other, then the ranks from the two samples should be intermixed evenly. In terms of a competition between the two samples (the A team versus the B team), a final score of 49 to 51 indicates that the two teams were nearly equal; a final score of 100 to 0 indicates a real difference between the two teams.

Notice that the null hypothesis does not specify any population parameter.

The null hypothesis for the Mann-Whitney test states that there is no systematic difference between the two treatments being compared; that is, there is no real difference between the two populations from which the samples are selected. In this case, the most likely outcome is that the two samples would be similar and that the U value would be relatively large. On the other hand, a very small value of U, near zero, is evidence that the two samples are very different. Therefore, a U value near zero would tend to refute the null hypothesis. The distribution of all the possible U values has been constructed, and the critical values for $\alpha = .05$ and $\alpha = .01$ are presented in Table B.8 of Appendix B. When sample data produce a U that is *less than or equal to* the table value, we reject H_0.

A complete example of a hypothesis test using the Mann-Whitney U follows.

EXAMPLE 19.2

Software manual:
Minitab (Section 9)

A psychologist interested in the development of manual dexterity prepared a block-manipulation task for three-year-old children. A sample of 13 children was obtained, 5 boys and 8 girls. The psychologist recorded the amount of time (in seconds) required by each child to arrange the blocks in a specified pattern. The data are as follows:

boys: 23 18 29 42 21

girls: 37 56 39 34 26 104 48 25

STEP 1   The null hypothesis states that there is no consistent difference between the two populations. For this example,

H_0:   There is no systematic difference between the solution times for boys versus the times for girls.

H_1:   There is a systematic difference.

STEP 2   For a non-directional test with $\alpha = .05$ and with $n_A = 5$ and $n_B = 8$, the Mann-Whitney table gives a critical value of $U = 6$. If the data produce a U less than or equal to 6, we will reject the null hypothesis.

STEP 3   We will designate the boys as sample A and the girls as sample B. Combining the two samples and arranging the scores in order produce the following result:

Rank	1	2	3	4	5	6	7	8	9	10	11	12	13
Score	18	21	23	25	26	29	34	37	39	42	48	56	104
Sample	A	A	A	B	B	A	B	B	B	A	B	B	B
Points for				:	:		:	:	:		:	:	:
the girls (B)				2	2		1	1	1		0	0	0

Because the girls (sample B) tend to cluster at the bottom of the rankings, they should have the smaller U. Therefore, we have identified the points for this sample. The girls' point total is $U_B = 7$.

It is not necessary to compute U for the boys, but we will continue with this calculation to demonstrate the formula for U. The boys (sample A) have ranks of 1, 2, 3, 6, and 10. The sum is $\Sigma R_A = 22$, so the U_A value is

$$U_A = n_A n_B + \frac{n_A(n_A + 1)}{2} - \Sigma R_A$$

$$= 5(8) + \frac{5(6)}{2} - 22$$

$$= 40 + 15 - 22$$

$$= 33$$

Notice that the larger sample does not always have the larger point total.

To check our calculations,

$$U_A + U_B = n_A n_B$$

$$33 + 7 = 5(8)$$

$$40 = 40$$

The final U is the smaller of the two values, so the Mann-Whitney U statistic is $U = 7$.

STEP 4 Because $U = 7$ is greater than the critical value of $U = 6$, we fail to reject the null hypothesis. At the .05 level of significance, these data do not provide sufficient evidence to conclude that there is a significant difference in manual dexterity between boys and girls at three years of age.

IN THE LITERATURE
REPORTING THE RESULTS OF A MANN-WHITNEY U-TEST

Unlike many other statistical results, there are no strict rules for reporting the outcome of a Mann-Whitney U-test. APA guidelines, however, do suggest that the report include a summary of the data (including such information as the sample size and the sum of the ranks) and the obtained statistic and p value. For the study presented in Example 19.2, the results could be reported as follows:

> The original scores, measured in seconds, were rank ordered and a Mann-Whitney U-test was used to compare the ranks for the $n = 5$ boys versus the $n = 8$ girls. The results indicate no significant difference between genders, $U = 7$, $p > .05$, with the sum of the ranks equal to 22 for the boys and 69 for the girls.

NORMAL APPROXIMATION FOR THE MANN-WHITNEY U

When samples are large (about $n = 20$), the distribution of the Mann-Whitney U statistic tends to approximate a normal shape. In this case, the Mann-Whitney hypotheses can be evaluated using a z-score statistic and the unit normal distribution. You may have noticed that the table of critical values for the Mann-Whitney test does not list values for samples larger than $n = 20$. This is because the normal approximation typically is used with larger samples. The procedure for this normal approximation is as follows:

1. Find the U values for sample A and sample B as before. The Mann-Whitney U is the smaller of these two values.

2. When both samples are relatively large (around $n = 20$ or more), the distribution of the Mann-Whitney U statistic tends to form a normal distribution with

$$\mu = \frac{n_A n_B}{2}$$

and

$$\sigma = \sqrt{\frac{n_A n_B (n_A + n_B + 1)}{12}}$$

The Mann-Whitney U obtained from the sample data can be located in this distribution using a z-score:

This approximation is intended for data without tied scores or with very few ties. A special formula has been developed for data with many ties and can be found in most advanced statistics texts such as Hays (1981).

$$z = \frac{X - \mu}{\sigma} = \frac{U - \frac{n_A n_B}{2}}{\sqrt{\frac{n_A n_B (n_A + n_B + 1)}{12}}} \tag{19.4}$$

3. Use the unit normal table to establish the critical region for this z-score. For example, with $\alpha = .05$ the critical values would be ± 1.96.

An example of this normal approximation for the Mann-Whitney U follows.

EXAMPLE 19.3 To demonstrate the normal approximation, we will use the same data that were used in Example 19.2. This experiment tested manual dexterity for three-year-olds, using a sample of $n = 5$ boys and a sample of $n = 8$ girls. The data produced a value of $U = 7$. (You should realize that when samples are this small, you would normally use the Mann-Whitney table rather than the normal approximation. However, we will use the normal approximation so that we can compare the outcome to the result from the regular Mann-Whitney test.)

STEP 1 The normal approximation does not affect the statement of the hypotheses.

H_0: There is no systematic difference between the manual dexterity scores for boys versus the scores for girls.

H_1: There is a systematic difference.

We will use $\alpha = .05$.

STEP 2 The critical region for this test is defined in terms of z-scores and the normal distribution. The unit normal table states that the extreme 5% of this distribution is located beyond z-scores of ± 1.96 (see Figure 19.2).

STEP 3 The sample value of $U = 7$ is used to compute a z-score from the normal approximation formula.

$$z = \frac{U - \frac{n_A n_B}{2}}{\sqrt{\frac{n_A n_B (n_A + n_B + 1)}{12}}}$$

$$= \frac{7 - \frac{5(8)}{2}}{\sqrt{\frac{5(8)(5 + 8 + 1)}{12}}}$$

$$= \frac{-13}{\sqrt{\frac{560}{12}}}$$

$$= -1.90$$

FIGURE 19.2

The normal distribution of *z*-scores used with the normal approximation to the Mann-Whitney *U*-test. The critical region for $\alpha = .05$ has been shaded.

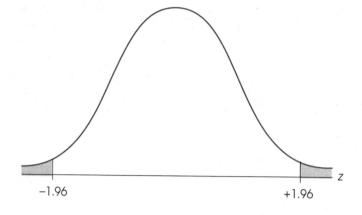

-1.96 $+1.96$

STEP 4

Notice that we reached the same conclusion with the original Mann-Whitney test in Example 19.2

Because this *z*-score is not in the critical region, our decision is to fail to reject the null hypothesis. These data do not provide sufficient evidence to conclude that there is a significant difference in manual dexterity between boys and girls at age three.

ASSUMPTIONS AND CAUTIONS FOR THE MANN-WHITNEY *U*

The Mann-Whitney *U*-test is a very useful alternative to the independent-measures *t* test. Because the Mann-Whitney test does not require homogeneity of variance or normal distributions, it can be used in situations where the *t* test would be inappropriate. However, the *U*-test does require independent observations, and it assumes that the dependent variable is continuous. You should recall from Chapter 1 that a continuous scale has an infinite number of distinct points. One consequence of this fact is that it is very unlikely for two individuals to have exactly the same score. This means that there should be few, if any, tied scores in the data. When sample data do have several tied scores, you should suspect that a basic assumption underlying the Mann-Whitney *U*-test has been violated. In this situation, you should be cautious about using the Mann-Whitney *U*.

When there are relatively few tied scores in the data, the Mann-Whitney test may be used, but you must follow the standard procedure for ranking tied scores.

LEARNING CHECK

1. Rank the following scores, using tied ranks where necessary: 14, 3, 4, 0, 3, 5, 14, 3.

2. An experiment using $n = 25$ in one sample and $n = 10$ in the other produced a Mann-Whitney *U* of $U = 50$. Assuming that this is the smaller of the two *U* values, what was the value of *U* for the other sample?

3. A developmental psychologist is examining social assertiveness for preschool children. Three- and four-year-old children are observed for 10 hours in a day-care center. The psychologist records the number of times each child initiates a social interaction with another child. The scores for the sample of four boys and nine girls are as follows:

   boys' scores: 8 17 14 21

   girls' scores: 18 25 23 21 34 28 32 30 13

Use a Mann-Whitney test to determine whether these data provide evidence for a significant difference in social assertiveness between preschool boys and girls. Test at the .05 level.

4. According to the Mann-Whitney table, a value of $U = 30$ is significant (in the critical region) with $\alpha = .05$ when both samples have $n = 11$. If this value is used in the normal approximation, does it produce a z-score in the critical region?

ANSWERS 1. Scores: 0   3   3   3   4   5   14   14
            Ranks: 1   3   3   3   5   6   7.5   7.5

2. With $n_A = 25$ and $n_B = 10$, the two U values must total $n_A n_B = 25(10) = 250$. If the smaller value is 50, then the larger value must be 200.

3. For the boys, $U = 31.5$. For the girls, $U = 4.5$. The critical value in the table is 4, so fail to reject H_0.

4. $U = 30$ produces a z-score of $z = -2.00$. This is in the critical region.

19.3 THE WILCOXON SIGNED-RANKS TEST

The Wilcoxon test is designed to evaluate the difference between two treatments, using the data from a repeated-measures experiment. You should recall that a repeated-measures study involves only one sample, with each individual in the sample being measured twice: once in the first treatment and once in the second treatment. The difference between the two scores for each individual is computed, resulting in a sample of *difference scores*. The data for the Wilcoxon test consist of the difference scores from the repeated-measures design. The test requires that these differences be ranked from smallest to largest in terms of their *absolute values* (without regard to the sign). This process is demonstrated in the following example.

EXAMPLE 19.4   The following data are from a repeated-measures experiment using a sample of $n = 6$ subjects to compare two treatment conditions:

SUBJECT	TREATMENTS 1	2	DIFFERENCE	RANK	
1	18	43	+25	6	(Largest)
2	9	14	+5	2	
3	21	20	-1	1	(Smallest)
4	30	48	+18	5	
5	14	21	+7	3	
6	12	4	-8	4	

The null hypothesis for this test states that there is no difference between the two treatments. If this hypothesis is true, any differences that exist in the sample data must be due to chance. Therefore, we would expect positive and negative differences to be intermixed evenly. On the other hand, a consistent difference between the two treatments should cause the scores in one treatment to be consistently larger than the scores in the other. This should produce difference scores that tend to be consistently positive or consistently negative. The Wilcoxon test uses the signs and the ranks of the difference scores to decide whether or not there is a significant difference between the two treatments.

CALCULATION AND INTERPRETATION OF THE WILCOXON T

As with most non-parametric tests, the calculations for the Wilcoxon are quite simple. After ranking the absolute values of the difference scores as in Example 19.4, you separate the ranks into two groups: those associated with positive differences and those associated with negative differences. Next, find the sum of the ranks for each group. The smaller of these two sums is the test statistic for the Wilcoxon test and is identified by the letter T. For the data in Example 19.4, the ranks for positive differences are 6, 2, 3, and 5. These ranks sum to $\Sigma R = 16$. The ranks for negative differences are 1 and 4, which sum to $\Sigma R = 5$. The smaller of these two sums is 5, so the Wilcoxon T for these data is $T = 5$.

We noted earlier that a strong treatment effect should cause the difference scores to be consistently positive or consistently negative. In the extreme case, all of the differences will be in the same direction. This will produce a Wilcoxon T of zero. For example, when all of the differences are positive, the sum of the negative ranks will be zero. On the other hand, when there is no treatment effect, the signs of the difference scores should be intermixed evenly. In this case, the Wilcoxon T will be relatively large. In general, a small T value (near zero) provides evidence for a real difference between the two treatment conditions. The distribution of all the possible T values has been constructed, and the critical values for $\alpha = .05$ and $\alpha = .01$ are given in Table B.9 of appendix B. Whenever sample data produce a T that is *less than or equal to* this critical value, we will reject H_0.

See Box 19.1 for information concerning how the distribution of Wilcoxon T values is constructed.

TIED SCORES AND ZERO SCORES

Although the Wilcoxon test does not require normal distributions, it does assume that the dependent variable is continuous. As noted with the Mann-Whitney test, this assumption implies that tied scores should be very unlikely. When ties do appear in sample data, you should be concerned that the basic assumption of continuity has been violated, and the Wilcoxon test may not be appropriate. If there are relatively few ties in the data, most researchers assume that the data actually are continuous, but have been crudely measured. In this case, the Wilcoxon test may be used, but the tied values must receive special attention in the calculations.

With the Wilcoxon test, there are two different types of tied scores:

1. A subject may have the same score in treatment 1 and in treatment 2, resulting in a difference score of zero.

2. Two (or more) subjects may have identical difference scores (ignoring the sign of the difference).

19.1 A CLOSER LOOK AT THE WILCOXON T DISTRIBUTION

YOU MAY have wondered how statisticians develop all the tables you find in the back of statistics books. The Wilcoxon test provides a good opportunity to demonstrate how one of these tables is constructed.

To determine the critical values for a statistical test, you must first look at the distribution of all the possible results that could be obtained. Next, you determine the probability values for each portion of the distribution and identify the results that are very unlikely, that is, the results with probability less than .01 or less than .05 (for $\alpha = .01$ or .05, respectively). Usually the calculation of these probabilities requires sophisticated mathematics, but for the Wilcoxon test the computations are relatively simple. For example, suppose that you are using a sample of $n = 6$ in a repeated-measures experiment. The data would consist of a set of $n = 6$ difference scores. The first step in computing the Wilcoxon T is to rank order the difference scores (ignoring the signs) from smallest to largest. Each position in the rank ordering is then classified as either a *positive* difference or a *negative* difference. With exactly two possibilities (positive or negative) for the first position, two for the second, two for the third, and so on, there is a total of

$$2 \times 2 \times 2 \times 2 \times 2 \times 2 = 64$$

different sequences of positives and negatives. When H_0 is true and there is no systematic treatment effect, all 64 sequences are equally likely, and each has a probability of $p = \frac{1}{64}$.

Rather than list all 64 possible outcomes, we will focus on results that produce small values for T. For example, there are only two outcomes that result in $T = 0$: Either all six difference scores are negative, so that the positive ranks sum to zero, or all six are positive and the negative ranks sum to zero. Thus, only 2 out of 64 possible results will give $T = 0$. In terms of probabilities,

$$p(T = 0) = \frac{2}{64} = 0.031$$

Because an outcome with $T = 0$ has a probability less than .05, we can conclude that data producing this outcome are significant at the $\alpha = .05$ level of significance.

Similarly, there are only two outcomes that produce $T = 1$: Either there is exactly one positive difference with a rank of 1, or there is one negative difference with a rank of 1. Thus,

$$p(T = 1) = \frac{2}{64} = 0.031$$

By combining the two probabilities obtained so far, we can find the probability of obtaining a T value less than or equal to 1.

$$p(T \leq 1) = p(T = 0 \text{ or } 1) = \frac{4}{64} = 0.062$$

Notice that the probability of T being less than or equal to 1 is greater than .05. Thus, experimental results that produce $T = 1$ would not be significant at the .05 level of significance. These probabilities are reflected in the critical values listed in the Wilcoxon table. Checking the table, you will find that the critical value for $n = 6$ and $\alpha = .05$ is $T = 0$. Thus, an outcome of $T = 0$ is significant ($p < .05$), but an outcome of $T = 1$ is not significant ($p > .05$).

Remember, the null hypothesis says there is no difference between the two treatments. Subjects with difference scores of zero tend to support this hypothesis.

When the data include individuals with difference scores of zero, some texts recommend that these subjects be discarded from the analysis and the sample size (n) reduced. However, this procedure ignores the fact that a difference score of zero is evidence for retaining the null hypothesis. A better procedure is to divide the zero differences evenly between the positives and negatives. (If you have an odd number of zero differences, one should be discarded and the rest divided evenly.) This second procedure will tend to increase ΣR for both the positive and the negative ranks, which increases the final value of T and makes it more likely that H_0 will be retained.

When you have ties among the difference scores, each of the tied scores should be assigned the average of the tied ranks. This procedure was presented in detail in an earlier section of this chapter (see p. 602).

HYPOTHESIS TESTS WITH THE WILCOXON *T*

A complete example of the Wilcoxon test showing both types of tied scores will now be presented.

EXAMPLE 19.5

Software manual:
Minitab (Section 9)

The local Red Cross has conducted an intensive campaign to increase blood donations. This campaign has been concentrated in 10 local businesses. In each company, the goal was to increase the percentage of employees who participate in the blood donation program. Figures showing the percentages of participation from last year (before the campaign) and from this year are as follows. We will use the Wilcoxon test to decide whether these data provide evidence that the campaign had a significant impact on blood donations. Note that the 10 companies are listed in rank order according to the absolute value of the difference scores.

COMPANY	PERCENTAGE OF PARTICIPATION			RANK DISCARDING ZEROS	RANK INCLUDING ZEROS
	BEFORE	AFTER	DIFFERENCE		
A	18	18	0	—	1.5
B	24	24	0	—	1.5
C	31	30	−1	1	3
D	28	24	−4	2	4
E	17	24	+7	3	5
F	16	24	+8	4	6
G	15	26	+11	5.5	7.5
H	18	29	+11	5.5	7.5
I	20	36	+16	7	9
J	9	28	+19	8	10

Note: We will conduct the Wilcoxon test using the recommendation that difference scores of zero be discarded. Following this test, we will examine what would happen if the difference scores of zero were included.

STEP 1 The null hypothesis states that the campaign had no effect. Therefore, any differences are due to chance, and there should be no consistent pattern.

STEP 2 The two companies with difference scores of zero are discarded, and n is reduced to 8. With $n = 8$ and $\alpha = .05$, the critical value for the Wilcoxon test is $T = 3$. A sample value that is less than or equal to 3 will lead us to reject H_0.

STEP 3 For these data, the positive differences have ranks of 3, 4, 5.5, 5.5, 7, and 8:

$$\Sigma R_+ = 33$$

The negative differences have ranks of 1 and 2:

$$\Sigma R_- = 3$$

The Wilcoxon T is the smaller of these sums, so $T = 3$.

STEP 4   The T value from the data is in the critical region. This value is very unlikely to occur by chance ($p < .05$); therefore, we reject H_0 and conclude that there is a significant change in participation after the Red Cross campaign.

Note: If we include the difference scores of zero in this test, then $n = 10$, and with $\alpha = .05$, the critical value for the Wilcoxon T is 8. Because the difference scores of zero are tied for first and second in the ordering, each is given a rank of 1.5. One of these ranks is assigned to the positive group and one to the negative group. As a result, the sums are

$$\Sigma R_+ = 1.5 + 5 + 6 + 7.5 + 7.5 + 9 + 10$$
$$= 46.5$$

and

$$\Sigma R_- = 1.5 + 3 + 4$$
$$= 8.5$$

The Wilcoxon T is the smaller of these two sums, $T = 8.5$. Because this T value is larger than the critical value, we fail to reject H_0 and conclude that these data do not indicate a significant change in blood donor participation.

By including the difference scores of zero in the test, we have changed the statistical conclusion. Remember, the difference scores of zero are an indication that the null hypothesis is correct. When these scores are considered, the test is more likely to retain H_0.

IN THE LITERATURE
REPORTING THE RESULTS OF A WILCOXON *T*-TEST

As with the Mann-Whitney U-test, there is no specified format for reporting the results of a Wilcoxon T-test. It is suggested, however, that the report include a summary of the data and the value obtained for the test statistic as well as the p value. It also is suggested that the report describe the treatment of zero-difference scores in the analysis. For the study presented in Example 19.5, the report could be as follows:

> Two companies showing no change in participation were discarded prior to analysis. The remaining eight companies were rank ordered by the magnitude of the change in level of participation, and a Wilcoxon T was used to evaluate the data. The results show a significant increase in participation following the campaign, $T = 3, p < .05$, with the ranks for increases totaling 33 and the ranks for decreases totaling 3.

LEARNING CHECK   1. A physician is testing the effectiveness of a new arthritis drug by measuring patients' grip strength before and after they receive the drug. The difference scores for 10 patients are as follows: $+3, +46, +16, -2, +38, +14, 0$ (no change), $-8, +25,$ and $+41$. Each score is the difference in strength, with a positive value indicating a stronger grip after receiving the drug. Use a Wil-

FIGURE 19.3

Hypothetical data showing the relationship between practice and performance. Although this relationship is not linear, there is a consistent positive relationship. An increase in performance tends to accompany an increase in practice.

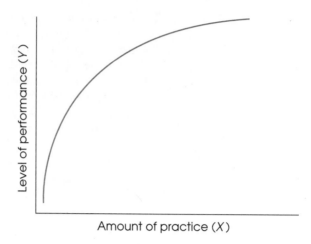

coxon test to determine whether these data provide sufficient evidence to conclude that the drug has a significant effect. Test at the .05 level.

ANSWER   **1.** The Wilcoxon $T = 4$. Because one patient showed no change, n is reduced to 9, and the critical value is $T = 5$. Therefore, we reject H_0 and conclude that there is a significant effect.

19.4   THE SPEARMAN CORRELATION

In Chapter 16, we introduced the concept of correlation as a statistical method for measuring and describing the relationship between two variables. As we noted in Chapter 16, the Pearson correlation, which measures linear relationship, is by far the most commonly used measure of relationship. However, other correlations have been developed for special purposes or for special types of data. One of these other correlations is called the *Spearman correlation.*

The Spearman correlation measures the relationship between two variables that are both measured on ordinal scales. As we have noted, ordinal data are fairly common because they often are easier to obtain than interval or ratio data. If only one of the variables is measured on an ordinal scale, it usually is easy to convert the other variable to ranks so that a Spearman correlation can be computed.

In addition to measuring relationships for ordinal data, the Spearman correlation can be used as a valuable alternative to the Pearson correlation with data from interval or ratio scales. As we have noted, the Pearson correlation measures the degree of linear relationship between the two variables—that is, how well the data points fit on a straight line. However, a researcher often expects the data to show a *consistent* relationship, but not necessarily a *linear* relationship. For example, a researcher may be investigating the relationship between amount of practice (X) and level of performance (Y). For these data, the researcher expects a good positive relationship: More practice leads to better performance. However, the relationship probably does not fit a linear form, so a Pearson correlation would not be appropriate (see Figure 19.3). In this situation, the Spearman correlation can be

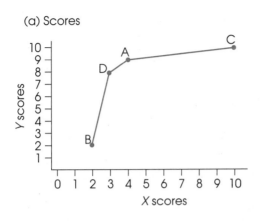
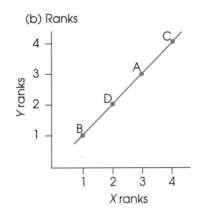

FIGURE 19.4

Scatterplots showing (a) the scores and (b) the ranks for the data in Example 19.6. Notice that there is a consistent, positive relation between the X and Y scores, although it is not a linear relationship. Also notice that the scatterplot of the ranks shows a perfect linear relationship.

used to obtain a measure of the consistency of relationship, independent of its specific form.

The reason that the Spearman correlation measures consistency, rather than form, comes from a simple observation: When two variables are consistently related, their ranks will be linearly related. For example, a perfectly consistent positive relationship means that every time the X variable increases, the Y variable also increases. Thus, the smallest value of X is paired with the smallest value of Y, the second-smallest value of X is paired with the second-smallest value of Y, and so on. This phenomenon is demonstrated in the following example.

EXAMPLE 19.6

TABLE 19.2

Scores for example 19.6

PERSON	X	Y
A	4	9
B	2	2
C	10	10
D	3	8

TABLE 19.3

Ranks for example 19.6

PERSON	X RANK	Y RANK
A	3	3
B	1	1
C	4	4
D	2	2

The data in Table 19.2 represent X and Y scores for a sample of n = 4 people. Note that person B has the lowest X score and the lowest Y score. Similarly, person D has the second-lowest score for both X and Y, person A has the third-lowest scores, and person C has the highest scores. These data show a perfectly consistent relationship: Each increase in X is accompanied by an increase in Y. However, the relationship is not linear, as can be seen in the graph of the data in Figure 19.4.

Now observe what happens when the X and Y scores are converted to ranks. Again, person B has the lowest X and Y scores, so this individual is ranked first on both variables. Similarly, person D is ranked second on both variables, person A is ranked third, and person C is ranked fourth (Table 19.3). When the ranks are plotted on a graph (see Figure 19.4), the result is a perfect linear relationship.

The preceding example has demonstrated that a consistent relationship among scores produces a linear relationship when the scores are converted to ranks. Thus, if you want to measure the consistency of a relationship for a set of scores, you can simply convert the scores to ranks and then use the Spearman correlation to measure the correlation for the ranked data. The degree of relationship for the ranks (the Spearman correlation) provides a measure of the degree of consistency for the original scores.

To summarize, the Spearman correlation measures the relationship between two variables when both are measured on ordinal scales (ranks). There are two general situations where the Spearman correlation is used:

1. Spearman is used when the original data are ordinal, that is, when the X and Y values are ranks.

2. Spearman is used when a researcher wants to measure the consistency of a relationship between X and Y, independent of the specific form of the relationship. In this case, the original scores are first converted to ranks; then the Spearman correlation is used to measure the relationship for the ranks. Incidentally, when there is a consistently one-directional relationship between two variables, the relationship is said to be *monotonic*. Thus, the Spearman correlation can be used to measure the degree of monotonic relationship between two variables.

The word *monotonic* describes a sequence that is consistently increasing (or decreasing). Like the word *monotonous*, it means constant and unchanging.

CALCULATION OF THE SPEARMAN CORRELATION

The calculation of the Spearman correlation is remarkably simple, provided you know how to compute a Pearson correlation. First, be sure that you have ordinal data (ranks) for the X scores and the Y scores. (If necessary, convert the original data into ranks. The smallest X value is called 1, the next smallest is 2, and so on. Note that the X and Y scores are ranked separately.) Then, compute a Pearson correlation using the ranks.

That's all there is to it. When you use the Pearson correlation formula for ordinal data, the result is called a Spearman correlation. The Spearman correlation is identified by the symbol r_S to differentiate it from the Pearson correlation. The complete process of computing the Spearman correlation, including ranking scores, is demonstrated in Example 19.7.

EXAMPLE 19.7

The following data show a nearly perfect monotonic relationship between X and Y. When X increases, Y tends to decrease, and there is only one reversal in this general trend. To compute the Spearman correlation, we first rank the X and Y values, and we then compute the Pearson correlation for the ranks.

We have listed the X values in order so that the trend is easier to recognize.

ORIGINAL DATA		RANKS		
X	Y	X	Y	XY
3	12	1	5	5
4	5	2	3	6
5	6	3	4	12
10	4	4	2	8
13	3	5	1	5
				$36 = \Sigma XY$

The scatterplots for the original data and the ranks are shown in Figure 19.5. To compute the correlation, we will need SS for X, SS for Y, and SP. Remember, all these values are computed with the ranks, not the original scores.

FIGURE 19.5

Scatterplots showing (a) the scores and (b) the ranks for the data in Example 19.7.

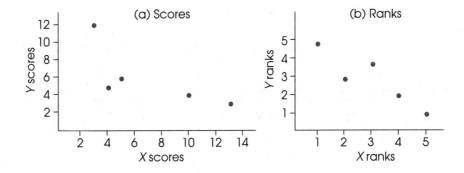

The X ranks are simply the integers 1, 2, 3, 4, 5. These values have $\Sigma X = 15$ and $\Sigma X^2 = 55$. The SS for the X ranks is

$$SS_X = \Sigma X^2 - \frac{(\Sigma X)^2}{n}$$

$$= 55 - \frac{(15)^2}{5}$$

$$= 55 - 45$$

$$= 10$$

You should note that the ranks for Y are identical to the ranks for X; that is, they are the integers 1, 2, 3, 4, and 5. Therefore, the SS for Y will be identical to the SS for X:

$$SS_Y = 10$$

To compute the SP value, we need ΣX, ΣY, and ΣXY for the ranks. The XY values are listed in the table with the ranks, and we already have found that both the Xs and the Ys have a sum of 15. Using these values, we obtain

$$SP = \Sigma XY - \frac{(\Sigma X)(\Sigma Y)}{n}$$

$$= 36 - \frac{(15)(15)}{5}$$

$$= 36 - 45$$

$$= -9$$

The final Spearman correlation is

$$r_S = \frac{SP}{\sqrt{(SS_X)(SS_Y)}}$$

$$= \frac{-9}{\sqrt{10(10)}}$$

$$= -0.9$$

The Spearman correlation indicates that the data show a strong (nearly perfect) negative trend.

SPECIAL FORMULA FOR THE SPEARMAN CORRELATION

After the original X values and Y values have been ranked, the calculations necessary for SS and SP can be greatly simplified. First, you should note that the X ranks and the Y ranks are really just a set of integers 1, 2, 3, 4, . . ., n. To compute the mean for these integers, you can locate the midpoint of the series by $\overline{X} = (n + 1)/2$. Similarly, the SS for this series of integers can be computed by

$$SS = \frac{n(n^2 - 1)}{12} \quad \text{(Try it out.)}$$

Also, because the X ranks and the Y ranks are the same values, the SS for X will be identical to the SS for Y.

Because calculations with ranks can be simplified and because the Spearman correlation uses ranked data, these simplifications can be incorporated into the final calculations for the Spearman correlation. Instead of using the Pearson formula after ranking the data, you can put the ranks directly into a simplified formula:

Caution: In this formula, you compute the value of the fraction and then subtract from 1. The 1 is not part of the fraction.

$$r_S = 1 - \frac{6\Sigma D^2}{n(n^2 - 1)} \tag{19.5}$$

where D is the difference between the X rank and the Y rank for each individual. This special formula will produce the same result that would be obtained from the Pearson formula. However, you should note that this special formula can be used only after the scores have been converted to ranks and only when there are no ties among the ranks. If there are relatively few tied ranks, the formula still may be used, but it loses accuracy as the number of ties increases. The application of this formula is demonstrated in the following example.

EXAMPLE 19.8

To demonstrate the special formula for the Spearman correlation, we will use the same data that were presented in Example 19.7. The ranks for these data are shown again here:

RANKS		DIFFERENCE	
X	Y	D	D^2
1	5	4	16
2	3	1	1
3	4	1	1
4	2	−2	4
5	1	−4	16
			$\overline{38} = \Sigma D^2$

Using the special formula for the Spearman correlation, we obtain

$$r_S = 1 - \frac{6\Sigma D^2}{n(n^2 - 1)}$$

$$= 1 - \frac{6(38)}{5(25 - 1)}$$

$$= 1 - \frac{228}{120}$$

$$= 1 - 1.90$$

$$= -0.90$$

Notice that this is exactly the same answer that we obtained in Example 19.7, using the Pearson formula on the ranks.

LEARNING CHECK

1. Describe what is measured by a Spearman correlation, and explain how this correlation is different from the Pearson correlation.

2. Identify the two procedures that can be used to compute the Spearman correlation.

3. Compute the Spearman correlation for the following set of scores:

X	Y
2	7
12	38
9	6
10	19

ANSWERS

1. The Spearman correlation measures the consistency of the direction of the relationship between two variables. The Spearman correlation does not depend on the form of the relationship, whereas the Pearson correlation measures how well the data fit a linear form.

2. After the X and Y values have been ranked, you can compute the Spearman correlation by using either the special formula or the Pearson formula.

3. $r_S = 0.80$

SUMMARY

1. The Mann-Whitney and Wilcoxon tests are non-parametric alternatives to the independent-measures t and repeated-measures t tests, respectively. These tests do not require normal distributions or homogeneity of variance. Both tests require that the data be rank ordered, and they as-

sume that the dependent variable is continuously distributed. For both tests, the null hypothesis states that there is no difference between the two treatments being compared.

2. The Mann-Whitney U can be computed either by a count-

ing process or by a formula. A small value of U (near zero) is evidence of a difference between the two treatments. With the counting procedure, U is determined by the following:

a. The scores from the two samples are combined and ranked from smallest to largest.

b. Each individual in sample A is awarded one point for every member of sample B with a larger rank.

c. U_A equals the total points for sample A. U_B is the total for sample B. The Mann-Whitney U is the smaller of these two values.

In formula form,

$$U_A = n_A n_B + \frac{n_A(n_A + 1)}{2} - \Sigma R_A$$

$$U_B = n_A n_B + \frac{n_B(n_B + 1)}{2} - \Sigma R_B$$

3. For large samples, larger than those normally presented in the Mann-Whitney table, the normal distribution can be used to evaluate the difference between the two treatments. This normal approximation to the Mann-Whitney is used as follows:

a. Find the value of U as before.

b. The Mann-Whitney U is converted to a z-score by the formula

$$z = \frac{U - \frac{n_A n_B}{2}}{\sqrt{\frac{n_A n_B (n_A + n_B + 1)}{12}}}$$

c. If this z-score is in the critical region of the unit normal distribution, the null hypothesis is rejected.

4. The test statistic for the Wilcoxon test is called a T score. A small value of T (near zero) provides evidence of a difference between the two treatments. T is computed as follows:

a. Compute a difference score (treatment 1 versus treatment 2) for each individual in the sample.

b. Rank these difference scores from smallest to largest without regard to the signs.

c. Sum the ranks for the positive differences, and sum the ranks for the negative differences. T is the smaller of these two sums.

5. The Spearman correlation (r_S) measures the consistency of direction in the relationship between X and Y, that is, the degree to which the relationship is one-directional, or monotonic. The Spearman correlation is computed by a two-stage process:

a. Rank the X scores and the Y scores.

b. Compute the Pearson correlation using the ranks.

Note: After the X and Y values are ranked, you may use a special formula to determine the Spearman correlation:

$$r_S = 1 - \frac{6\Sigma D^2}{n(n^2 - 1)}$$

where D is the difference between the X rank and the Y rank for each individual. The formula is accurate only when there are no tied scores in the data.

KEY TERMS

Mann-Whitney U	Spearman correlation	normal approximation for the Mann-Whitney U	monotonic relationship
Wilcoxon T			

FOCUS ON PROBLEM SOLVING

1. In computing the Mann-Whitney U, it will sometimes be obvious from the data which sample has the smaller U value. Even if this is the case, you should still compute both U values so that your computations can be checked using the formula

$$U_A + U_B = n_A n_B$$

2. Contrary to the previous statistical tests, the Mann-Whitney U and the Wilcoxon T are significant when the obtained value is *equal to or less than* the critical value in the table.

3. For the Wilcoxon T, remember to ignore the signs of the differences scores when assigning ranks to them.

4. When using the special formula for the Spearman correlation, remember that the fraction is computed separately and then subtracted from 1. Students often include the 1 as a part of the numerator, or they get so absorbed in computing the fractional part of the equation that they forget to subtract it from 1. Be careful using this formula.

5. When computing a Spearman correlation, be sure that both X and Y values have been ranked. Sometimes the data will consist of one variable already ranked with the other variable on an interval or a ratio scale. If one variable is ranked, do not forget to rank the other.

DEMONSTRATION 19.1

THE MANN-WHITNEY U-TEST

A local police expert claims to be able to judge an individual's personality on the basis of his or her handwriting. To test this claim, 10 samples of handwriting are obtained: 5 from prisoners convicted of violent crimes and 5 from psychology majors at the college. The expert ranks the handwriting samples from 1st to 10th, with 1 representing the most antisocial personality. The rankings are as follows:

RANKING	SOURCE
1	Prisoner
2	Prisoner
3	Student . . . 3 points
4	Prisoner
5	Prisoner
6	Student . . . 1 point
7	Prisoner
8	Student . . . 0 points
9	Student . . . 0 points
10	Student . . . 0 points

STEP 1 The null hypothesis states that there is no difference between the two populations. For this example, H_0 states that the police expert cannot differentiate the handwriting for prisoners from the handwriting for students.

The alternative hypothesis says there is a discernible difference.

STEP 2 For $\alpha = .05$ and with $n_A = n_B = 5$, the Mann-Whitney table gives a critical value of $U = 2$. If our data produce a U less than or equal to 2, we will reject the null hypothesis.

STEP 3   We designate the students as sample A and the prisoners as sample B. Because the students tended to cluster at the bottom of the rankings, they should have the smaller U. Therefore, we have identified the points for this sample. The students' point total is $U_A = 4$.

Because we have found the smaller of the two U values, it is not necessary to compute U for the sample of prisoners. However, we will continue with this calculation to demonstrate the formula for U. The sample of prisoners has ranks 1, 2, 4, 5, and 7. The sum is $\Sigma R_B = 19$, so the U_B value is

$$U_B = n_A n_B + \frac{n_B(n_B + 1)}{2} - \Sigma R_B$$

$$= 5(5) + \frac{5(6)}{2} - 19$$

$$= 25 + 15 - 19$$

$$= 21$$

To check our calculations,

$$U_A + U_B = n_A n_B$$

$$4 + 21 = 5(5)$$

$$25 = 25$$

The final U is the smaller of the two values, so the Mann-Whitney U statistic is $U = 4$.

STEP 4   Because $U = 4$ is not in the critical region, we fail to reject the null hypothesis. With $\alpha = .05$, these data do not provide sufficient evidence to conclude that there is a discernible difference in handwriting between the two populations.

DEMONSTRATION 19.2

THE WILCOXON SIGNED-RANKS TEST

A researcher obtains a random sample of $n = 7$ individuals and tests each person in two different treatment conditions. The data for this sample are as follows:

SUBJECT	TREATMENT 1	TREATMENT 2	DIFFERENCE
1	8	24	+16
2	12	10	−2
3	15	19	+4
4	31	52	+21
5	26	20	−6
6	32	40	+8
7	19	29	+10

STEP 1 *State the hypotheses, and select alpha.* The hypotheses for the Wilcoxon test do not refer to any specific population parameter.

H_0: There is no systematic difference between the two treatments.

H_1: There is a consistent difference between the treatments that causes the scores in one treatment to be generally higher than the scores in the other treatment.

We will use $\alpha = .05$.

STEP 2 *Locate the critical region.* A small value for the Wilcoxon T indicates that the difference scores were consistently positive or consistently negative, which indicates a systematic treatment difference. Thus, small values will tend to refute H_0. With $n = 7$ and $\alpha = .05$, the Wilcoxon table shows that a T value of 2 or smaller is needed to reject H_0.

STEP 3 *Compute the test statistic.* The calculation of the Wilcoxon T is very simple, but requires several stages:

a. Ignoring the signs (+ or −), rank the difference scores from smallest to largest.

b. Compute the sum of the ranks for the positive differences and the sum for the negative differences.

c. The Wilcoxon T is the smaller of the two sums.

For these data, we have the following:

DIFFERENCE	RANK	
(+) 16	6	$\Sigma R_+ = 6 + 2 + 7 + 4 + 5 = 24$
(−) 2	1	
(+) 4	2	
(+) 21	7	$\Sigma R_- = 1 + 3 = 4$
(−) 6	3	
(+) 8	4	
(+) 10	5	

The Wilcoxon T is $T = 4$.

STEP 4 *Make a decision.* The obtained T value is not in the critical region. These data are not significantly different from chance. Therefore, we fail to reject H_0 and conclude that there is not sufficient evidence to suggest a systematic difference between the two treatment conditions.

DEMONSTRATION 19.3

THE SPEARMAN CORRELATION

The following data will be used to demonstrate the calculation of the Spearman correlation. Both X and Y values are measurements on interval scales.

X	Y
5	12
7	18
2	9
15	14
10	13

STEP 1 *Rank the X and Y values.* Remember, the X values and Y values are ranked separately.

X SCORE	Y SCORE	X RANK	Y RANK
5	12	2	2
7	18	3	5
2	9	1	1
15	14	5	4
10	13	4	3

STEP 2 *Use the special Spearman formula to compute the correlation.* The special Spearman formula requires that you first find the difference (D) between the X rank and the Y rank for each individual and then square the differences and find the sum of the squared differences.

X RANK	Y RANK	D	D^2
2	2	0	0
3	5	2	4
1	1	0	0
5	4	1	1
4	3	1	1
			$6 = \Sigma D^2$

Using this value in the Spearman formula, we obtain

$$r_S = 1 - \frac{6\Sigma D^2}{n(n^2 - 1)}$$

$$= 1 - \frac{6(6)}{5(24)}$$

$$= 1 - \frac{36}{120}$$

$$= 1 - 0.30$$

$$= 0.70$$

There is a positive relationship between X and Y for these data. The Spearman correlation is fairly high, which indicates a very consistent positive relationship.

PROBLEMS

1. Under what circumstances is it necessary or advisable to convert interval or ratio scale measurements into ranked data before attempting a hypothesis test?

2. One of the advantages of using ranks (ordinal data) instead of interval or ratio scores is that ranks can reduce the impact of one extreme individual score. The following data represent results from an independent-measures study comparing two treatments. Notice that most subjects in treatment 1 have scores around 40, and most subjects in treatment 2 have scores around 15. However, there is one odd individual in treatment 2 with a score of $X = 104$. This extreme value distorts the mean for treatment 2 and greatly increases the variability of the scores in this treatment. As a result, an independent-measures t test indicates no significant difference between treatments, $t(10) = 0.868$, $p > .05$. (In addition, the extreme score increases the variability in treatment 2 so much that the data violate the homogeneity of variance assumption.) When the scores are converted to ranks, however, the extreme value is no longer as extreme, and the difference between treatments becomes more apparent. Transform the scores into ranks, and use a Mann-Whitney U-test to evaluate the difference between treatments. Use $\alpha = .05$.

TREATMENT 1	TREATMENT 2
41	10
39	14
37	9
44	17
40	12
45	104
$\bar{X} = 41.00$	$\bar{X} = 37.51$
$s = 3.03$	$s = 27.67$

3. Several publications like to present an annual report on the best places to live in the United States. Typically, the report lists the top 50 or 100 cities in rank order from best to worst. Using the data from a recent report, a psychologist noted that many of the best cities seemed to be located in the Sun Belt. To determine whether or not this is a significant trend, the psychologist classified the top 20 cities as having either a northern or a southern location. The ranks for these two categories are as follows:

ranks for northern cities: 5 8 9 14 17 19 20

ranks for southern cities: 1 2 3 4 6 7 10 11
12 13 15 16 18

Do these data indicate a significant difference between the two parts of the country? Test with $\alpha = .05$.

4. A researcher is trying to determine which of two species of laboratory rats should be housed in the psychology department. A sample of $n = 10$ rats is obtained for each species, and the researcher records the amount of food each rat consumes during a one-week period. The data are as follows:

species A: 7 9 14 20 16 18 10 22 25 13

species B: 24 19 21 26 21 29 13 28 32 17

Do these data indicate that one species eats significantly more than the other? Use a Mann-Whitney test with $\alpha = .05$.

5. A doctor has been collecting data on the birthweight of newborn children for smoking and non-smoking mothers:

smoking mothers: 92 oz   111 oz   108 oz
120 oz   101 oz

non-smoking mothers: 127 oz   118 oz   134 oz
136 oz   109 oz   122 oz
115 oz   129 oz   113 oz

Do these data indicate a significant difference in birthweight between these two groups? Use a Mann-Whitney U-test at the .05 level of significance.

6. An instructor teaches two sections of the same statistics course. All students take a common final exam, and the instructor receives a printout of the grades in rank order (lowest to highest). For the morning section with $n = 14$ students, the sum of the ranks is $\Sigma R = 192$. The afternoon section with $n = 10$ students has $\Sigma R = 108$. Do these data indicate a significant difference between the two sections: Test at the .05 level.

7. Hyperactive children often are treated with a stimulant such as Ritalin to improve their attention spans. In one test of this drug treatment, hyperactive children were given a boring task to work on. A psychologist recorded the amount of time (in seconds) each child spent on the task before becoming distracted. Each child's performance was measured before he or she received the drug and again after the drug was administered. Because the scores on this task are extremely variable, the psychologist decided to convert the data to ranks. Use a Wilcoxon test with $\alpha = .05$

to determine whether the following data provide evidence that the drug has a significant effect:

CHILD	TREATMENT 1 (WITHOUT THE DRUG)	TREATMENT 2 (WITH THE DRUG)
1	28	135
2	15	309
3	183	150
4	48	224
5	30	25
6	233	345
7	21	43
8	110	188
9	12	15

8. Psychosis such as schizophrenia often is expressed in the artistic work produced by patients. To test the reliability of this phenomenon, a psychologist collected 10 paintings done by schizophrenic patients and another 10 paintings done by normal college students. A professor in the art department was asked to rank order all 20 paintings in terms of bizarreness. These ranks are as follows:

ranks for schizophrenics: 1   3   4   5   6   8   9
11   12   14

ranks for students: 2   7   10   13   15
16   17   18   19
20

On the basis of these data, can the psychologist conclude that there is a significant difference between the paintings for these two populations? Test at the .05 level of significance.

9. As part of a product-testing program, a paint manufacturer painted 12 houses in a suburban community. Six of the houses were painted with the company's own product, and the other six were painted with a competitor's paint. After five years, a panel of homeowners inspected the 12 houses and ranked them according to how well the paint was holding up. The rankings are as follows:

ranks for company's paint: 1   3   4   5   7   8

ranks for competitor's paint: 2   6   9   10   11   12

Do these data indicate a significant difference between the two brands of paint? Test with $\alpha = .05$.

10. One assumption for parametric tests with independent-measures data is that the different treatment conditions have the same variance (homogeneity of variance assumption). However, a treatment effect that increases the mean often will also increase the variability. In this situation, the parametric t test or ANOVA is not justified, and a Mann-Whitney test should be used. The following data represent an example of this situation:

TREATMENT 1 (SAMPLE A)	TREATMENT 2 (SAMPLE B)
1	8
5	20
0	14
2	27
4	6
2	10
3	19

a. Compute the mean and variance for each sample. Note the difference between the two sample variances.
b. Use a Mann-Whitney test, with $\alpha = .05$, to test for a significant difference between the two treatments.

11. One situation where ranking can be very useful is when research results produce undetermined scores. Undetermined scores occur when a subject fails to complete a task. The following data represent the time (in seconds) required for subjects to unscramble the letters in an anagram. The researcher is comparing the difficulty of four-letter anagrams and eight-letter anagrams, using a repeated-measures design where each subject is tested on both types of anagrams. Notice that subject F failed to solve the eight-letter anagram during the course of the experiment. Without a score for this subject, it is impossible to compute a mean or use a repeated-measures t test to evaluate the data. However, you can rank the scores and use a Wilcoxon T to compare the two treatment conditions. Perform the test with $\alpha = .05$.

SUBJECT	4-LETTER ANAGRAM	8-LETTER ANAGRAM
A	17	48
B	15	31
C	9	52
D	21	20
E	12	18
F	23	(Failed)

12. The school psychologist at an elementary school is conducting a counseling program for disruptive students. To evaluate the program, the students' teacher is asked to rate the change in behavior for each student using a scale from $+10$ (maximum positive change) to -10 (maximum negative change). A rating of 0 indicates no change in behavior. Because the teacher's ratings are subjective evaluations, the psychologist feels more comfortable treating the scores as ordinal values instead of interval or ratio scores. Convert the following data to ranks, and use a Wilcoxon T to evaluate the effectiveness of the counseling:

STUDENT	CHANGE IN BEHAVIOR AS RATED BY TEACHER
A	$+1$
B	$+6$
C	0
D	$+8$
E	-3
F	$+10$
G	$+4$
H	$+3$

13. A new cold remedy contains a chemical that causes drowsiness and disorientation. Part of the testing for this drug involved measuring maze-learning performance for rats. Individual rats were tested with and without the drug. The dependent variable is the number of errors before the rat solves the maze. In the drug condition, two rats failed to solve the maze after 200 errors and were simply marked as "failed."

SUBJECT	NO DRUG	DRUG
1	28	125
2	43	90
3	37	(Failed)
4	16	108
5	47	40
6	51	75
7	23	91
8	31	23
9	26	115
10	53	55
11	26	(Failed)
12	32	87

Do these data indicate that the drug has a significant effect on maze-learning performance? Test at the .05 level of significance.

14. For the vast majority of right-handed people, language is controlled in the left hemisphere of the brain. The left hemisphere also manages motor control for the right side of the body. Because language and fine motor control with the right hand are dependent on the same general area of the brain, these two activities can interfere with each other if an individual tries both at the same time. To demonstrate this fact, a psychologist asked subjects to balance a ruler on the index finger of their right hand. The psychologist recorded the amount of time the ruler was balanced under two conditions. In one condition, the subject was allowed to concentrate on balancing the ruler. In the second condition, the subject was required to recite a nursery rhyme while balancing the ruler. The data for this experiment are as follows:

SUBJECT	JUST BALANCING	BALANCING AND RECITING
1	43 seconds	15 seconds
2	127 seconds	21 seconds
3	18 seconds	25 seconds
4	28 seconds	6 seconds
5	21 seconds	10 seconds
6	47 seconds	9 seconds
7	12 seconds	14 seconds
8	25 seconds	6 seconds
9	53 seconds	24 seconds
10	17 seconds	11 seconds

On the basis of these data, can the psychologist conclude that the language task (nursery rhyme) significantly interferes with right-hand motor skill? Use a Wilcoxon test with $\alpha = .05$.

15. Rank the following scores and compute the Spearman correlation between X and Y:

X	Y
7	19
2	4
11	34
15	28
32	104

16. While grading essay exams, a professor noticed huge differences in the writing skills of the students. To investigate a possible cause for the differences, the professor asked the students how many English courses they had completed. The number of courses completed and the professor's ranking of the essay are reported for each student in the following table. Compute the correlation between writing ability and English background. (*Note:* You must convert the data before computing the correlation.)

QUALITY OF ESSAY (PROFESSOR'S RANKING)	NUMBER OF ENGLISH COURSES
1 (best)	7
2	4
3	1
4	3
5	1
6	1
7	0
8	2

17. A common concern for students (and teachers) is the assignment of grades for essays or term papers. Because there are no absolute right or wrong answers, these grades must be based on a judgment of quality. To demonstrate that these judgments actually are reliable, an English instructor asked a colleague to rank order a set of term papers. The ranks and the instructor's grades for these papers are as follows:

RANK	GRADE
1	A
2	B
3	A
4	B
5	B
6	C
7	D
8	C
9	C
10	D
11	E

a. Calculate the Spearman correlation for these data. (*Note:* You must convert the letter grades to ranks.)

b. Based on this correlation, does it appear that there is reasonable agreement between these two instructors in their judgment of the papers?

18. In the following data, X and Y are related by the equation $Y = X^2$:

X	Y
0	0
1	1
2	4
3	9
4	16
5	25

a. Sketch a graph showing the relationship between X and Y. Describe the relationship shown in your graph.

b. Compute the Spearman correlation for these data.

19. A physiological psychologist is interested in the relationship between brain weight and learning ability. It is expected that there should be a consistent relationship, but the psychologist has no prediction concerning the form (linear or non-linear) of the relationship. The data for a sample of $n = 10$ animals are as follows:

BRAIN WEIGHT	LEARNING SCORE
1.04	1.5
2.75	1.8
4.14	1.9
7.81	1.6
8.11	2.1
8.35	4.5
8.50	4.2
8.73	6.2
8.81	10.3
8.97	14.7

a. Explain why the Spearman correlation is appropriate for these data.

b. Calculate the Spearman correlation.

20. The local supermarket sells a variety of foods under its own brand name. To evaluate the quality of these foods, a panel of students purchases 10 of the store-brand items and the national brand-name versions of the same items. The students taste and compare each food, using a subjective scale consisting of the following categories: not much difference, somewhat better, much better, and incredibly better. The ratings for the 10 items are as follows:

FOOD ITEM	STUDENTS' RATING
Potato chips	National brand is much better
Cola	National brand is somewhat better
White bread	Store brand is somewhat better
Frozen pizza	National brand is incredibly better
Chocolate chip cookies	Store brand is much better
Canned corn	Not much difference
Vanilla ice cream	National brand is somewhat better
Peanut butter	National brand is much better
Ketchup	Not much difference
Frozen orange juice	National brand is somewhat better

Do these data indicate a significant difference between the store brand and the national brands? Test at the .05 level.

APPENDIX A BASIC MATHEMATICS REVIEW

PREVIEW

This appendix reviews some of the basic math skills that are necessary for the statistical calculations presented in this book. Many students already will know some or all of this material. Others will need to do extensive work and review. To help you assess your own skills, we are including a skills assessment exam here. You should allow approximately 30 minutes to complete the test. When you finish, grade your test using the answer key on page A-22.

Notice that the test is divided into five sections. If you miss more than three questions in any section of the test, you probably need help in that area. Turn to the section of this appendix that corresponds to your problem area. In each sec-

tion, you will find a general review, some examples, and some additional practice problems. After reviewing the appropriate section and doing the practice problems, turn to the end of the appendix. You will find another version of the skills assessment exam. If you still miss more than three questions in any section of the exam, continue studying. Get assistance from an instructor or tutor if necessary. At the end of this appendix is a list of recommended books for individuals who need a more extensive review than can be provided here. We must stress that mastering this material now will make the rest of the course much easier.

SKILLS ASSESSMENT PREVIEW EXAM

SECTION 1

(corresponding to Section A.1 of this appendix)

1. $3 + 2 \times 7 = ?$
2. $(3 + 2) \times 7 = ?$
3. $3 + 2^2 - 1 = ?$
4. $(3 + 2)^2 - 1 = ?$
5. $12/4 + 2 = ?$
6. $12/(4 + 2) = ?$
7. $12/(4 + 2)^2 = ?$
8. $2 \times (8 - 2^2) = ?$
9. $2 \times (8 - 2)^2 = ?$
10. $3 \times 2 + 8 - 1 \times 6 = ?$
11. $3 \times (2 + 8) - 1 \times 6 = ?$
12. $3 \times 2 + (8 - 1) \times 6 = ?$

SECTION 2

(corresponding to Section A.2 of this appendix)

1. The fraction ¾ corresponds to a percentage of _____.
2. Express 30% as a fraction.
3. Convert ¹²⁄₄₀ to a decimal.
4. $\frac{2}{13} + \frac{8}{13} = ?$
5. $1.375 + 0.25 = ?$
6. $\frac{2}{5} \times \frac{1}{4} = ?$
7. $\frac{1}{8} + \frac{2}{3} = ?$

8. $3.5 \times 0.4 = ?$

9. $\frac{1}{5} \div \frac{3}{4} = ?$

10. $3.75/0.5 = ?$

11. In a group of 80 students, 20% are psychology majors. How many psychology majors are in this group?

12. A company reports that two-fifths of its employees are women. If there are 90 employees, how many are women?

SECTION 3

(corresponding to Section A.3 of this appendix)

1. $3 + (-2) + (-1) + 4 = ?$

2. $6 - (-2) = ?$

3. $-2 - (-4) = ?$

4. $6 + (-1) - 3 - (-2) - (-5) = ?$

5. $4 \times (-3) = ?$

6. $-2 \times (-6) = ?$

7. $3 \times 5 = ?$

8. $-2 \times (-4) \times (-3) = ?$

9. $12 \div (-3) = ?$

10. $-18 \div (-6) = ?$

11. $-16 \div 8 = ?$

12. $-100 \div (-4) = ?$

SECTION 4

(corresponding to Section A.4 of this appendix)

For each equation, find the value of X.

1. $X + 6 = 13$

2. $X - 14 = 15$

3. $5 = X - 4$

4. $3X = 12$

5. $72 = 3X$

6. $X/5 = 3$

7. $10 = X/8$

8. $3X + 5 = -4$

9. $24 = 2X + 2$

10. $(X + 3)/2 = 14$

11. $(X - 5)/3 = 2$

12. $17 = 4X - 11$

SECTION 5

(corresponding to Section A.5 of this appendix)

1. $4^3 = ?$

2. $\sqrt{25 - 9} = ?$

3. If $X = 2$ and $Y = 3$, then $XY^3 = ?$

4. If $X = 2$ and $Y = 3$, then $(X + Y)^2 = ?$

5. If $a = 3$ and $b = 2$, then $a^2 + b^2 = ?$

6. $-3^3 = ?$

7. $-4^4 = ?$

8. $\sqrt{4} \times 4 = ?$

9. $36/\sqrt{9} = ?$

10. $(9 + 2)^2 = ?$

11. $5^2 + 2^3 = ?$

12. If $a = 3$ and $b = -1$, then $a^2 b^3 = ?$

The answers to the skills assessment exam are at the end of the appendix (p. A-22).

A.1 SYMBOLS AND NOTATION

Table A.1 presents the basic mathematical symbols that you should know, and it provides examples of their use. Statistical symbols and notation will be introduced and explained throughout this book as they are needed. Notation for exponents and square roots is covered separately at the end of this appendix.

Parentheses are a useful notation because they specify and control the order of computations. Everything inside the parentheses is calculated first. For example,

$$(5 + 3) \times 2 = 8 \times 2 = 16$$

Changing the placement of the parentheses also changes the order of calculations. For example,

$$5 + (3 \times 2) = 5 + 6 = 11$$

TABLE A.1

SYMBOL	MEANING	EXAMPLE
$+$	Addition	$5 + 7 = 12$
$-$	Subtraction	$8 - 3 = 5$
$\times$, ( )	Multiplication	$3 \times 9 = 27$, $3(9) = 27$
$\div$, /	Division	$15 \div 3 = 5$, $15/3 = 5$, $\frac{15}{3} = 5$
$>$	Greater than	$20 > 10$
$<$	Less than	$7 < 11$
$\neq$	Not equal to	$5 \neq 6$

ORDER OF OPERATIONS

Often a formula or a mathematical expression will involve several different arithmetic operations, such as adding, multiplying, squaring, and so on. When you encounter these situations, you must perform the different operations in the correct sequence. Following is a list of mathematical operations, showing the order in which they are to be performed.

1. Any calculation contained within parentheses is done first.
2. Squaring (or raising to other exponents) is done second.
3. Multiplying and/or dividing is done third. A series of multiplication and/or division operations should be done in order from left to right.
4. Adding and/or subtracting is done fourth.

The following examples demonstrate how this sequence of operations is applied in different situations.

To evaluate the expression

$$(3 + 1)^2 - 4 \times 7/2$$

first, perform the calculation within parentheses,

$$(4)^2 - 4 \times 7/2$$

Next, square the value as indicated,

$$16 - 4 \times 7/2$$

Then perform the multiplication and division,

$$16 - 14$$

Finally, do the subtraction

$$16 - 14 = 2$$

A sequence of operations involving multiplication and division should be performed in order from left to right. For example, to compute $12/2 \times 3$, you divide 12 by 2 and then multiply the result by 3:

$$12/2 \times 3 = 6 \times 3 = 18$$

Notice that violating the left-to-right sequence can change the result. For this example, if you multiply before dividing, you will obtain

$$12/2 \times 3 = 12/6 = 2 \qquad \text{(This is wrong.)}$$

A sequence of operations involving only addition and subtraction can be performed in any order. For example, to compute $3 + 8 - 5$, you can add 3 and 8 and then subtract 5,

$$(3 + 8) - 5 = 11 - 5 = 6$$

Or you can subtract 5 from 8 and then add the result to 3,

$$3 + (8 - 5) = 3 + 3 = 6$$

A mathematical expression or formula is simple a concise way to write a set of instructions. When you evaluate an expression by performing the calculation, you simply follow the instructions. For example, assume that you are given the instructions that follow:

1. First add 3 and 8.
2. Next, square the result.
3. Next, multiply the resulting value by 6.
4. Finally, subtract 50 from the value you have obtained.

You can write these instructions as a mathematical expression.

1. The first step involved addition. Because addition is normally done last, use parentheses to give this operation priority in the sequence of calculations.

$$(3 + 8)$$

2. The instruction to square a value is noted by using the exponent 2 beside the value to be squared.

$$(3 + 8)^2$$

3. Because squaring has priority over multiplication, you can simply introduce the multiplication into the expression.

$$6 \times (3 + 8)^2$$

4. Addition and subtraction are done last, so simply write in the requested subtraction.

$$6 \times (3 + 8)^2 - 50$$

To calculate the value of the expression, you work through the sequence of operations in the proper order:

$$6 \times (3 + 8)^2 - 50 = 6 \times (11)^2 - 50$$
$$= 6 \times (121) - 50$$
$$= 726 - 50$$
$$= 676$$

As a final note, you should realize that the operation of squaring (or raising to any exponent) applies only to the value that immediately precedes the exponent. For example,

$$2 \times 3^2 = 2 \times 9 = 18 \qquad \text{(only the 3 is squared)}$$

If the instructions require multiplying values and then squaring the product, you must use parentheses to give the multiplication priority over squaring. For example, to multiply 2 times 3 and then square the product, you would write

$$(2 \times 3)^2 = (6)^2 = 36$$

LEARNING CHECK

1. Evaluate each of the following expressions:
   a. $4 \times 8/2^2$
   b. $4 \times (8/2)^2$
   c. $100 - 3 \times 12/(6 - 4)^2$
   d. $(4 + 6) \times (3 - 1)^2$
   e. $(8 - 2)/(8 - 9)^2$
   f. $6 + (4 - 1)^2 - 3 \times 4^2$
   g. $4 \times (8 - 3) + 8 - 3$

ANSWERS

1. a. 8 b. 64 c. 91 d. 40 e. 6 f. −33 g. 25

A.2 PROPORTIONS: FRACTIONS, DECIMALS, AND PERCENTAGES

A proportion is a part of a whole and can be expressed as a fraction, or a decimal, or a percentage. For example, in a class of 40 students, only 3 failed the final exam. The proportion of the class that failed can be expressed as a fraction,

$$\text{fraction} = \frac{3}{40}$$

or as a decimal value,

$$\text{decimal} = 0.075$$

or as a percentage,

$$\text{percentage} = 7.5\%$$

In a fraction, such as ¾, the bottom value (the denominator) indicates the number of equal pieces into which the whole is split. Here the "pie" is split into four equal pieces:

If the denominator has a larger value—say, 8—then each piece of the whole pie is smaller:

A larger denominator indicates a smaller fraction of the whole.

The value on top of the fraction (the numerator) indicates how many pieces of the whole are being considered. Thus, the fraction ¾ indicates that the whole is split evenly into four pieces and that three of them are being used:

A fraction is simply a concise way of stating a proportion: "Three out of four" is equivalent to ¾. To convert the fraction to a decimal, you divide the numerator by the denominator:

$$\tfrac{3}{4} = 3 \div 4 = 0.75$$

To convert the decimal to a percentage, simply multiply by 100 and place a percent sign (%) after the answer:

$$0.75 \times 100 = 75\%$$

The U.S. money system is a convenient way of illustrating the relationship between fractions and decimals. "One quarter," for example, is one-fourth (¼) of a dollar, and its decimal equivalent is 0.25. Other familiar equivalencies are as follows:

	DIME	QUARTER	50 CENTS	75 CENTS
Fraction	$\frac{1}{10}$	$\frac{1}{4}$	$\frac{1}{2}$	$\frac{3}{4}$
Decimal	0.10	0.25	0.50	0.75
Percentage	10%	25%	50%	75%

FRACTIONS   **1. Finding Equivalent Fractions.** The same proportional value can be expressed by many equivalent fractions. For example,

$$\tfrac{1}{2} = \tfrac{2}{4} = \tfrac{10}{20} = \tfrac{50}{100}$$

To create equivalent fractions, you can multiply the numerator and denominator by the same value. As long as both the numerator and the denominator of the fraction are multiplied by the same value, the new fraction will be equivalent to the original. For example,

$$\tfrac{3}{10} = \tfrac{9}{30}$$

because both the numerator and the denominator of the original fraction have been multiplied by 3. Dividing the numerator and denominator of a fraction by the same value will also result in an equivalent fraction. By using division, you can reduce a fraction to a simpler form. For example,

$$\frac{40}{100} = \frac{2}{5}$$

because both the numerator and the denominator of the original fraction have been divided by 20.

You can use these rules to find specific equivalent fractions. For example, find the fraction that has a denominator of 100 and is equivalent to ¾. That is,

$$\frac{3}{4} = \frac{?}{100}$$

Notice that the denominator of the original fraction must be multiplied by 25 to produce the denominator of the desired fraction. For the two fractions to be equal, both the numerator and the denominator must be multiplied by the same number. Therefore, we also multiply the top of the original fraction by 25 and obtain

$$\frac{3 \times 25}{4 \times 25} = \frac{75}{100}$$

2. Multiplying Fractions. To multiply two fractions, you first multiply the numerators and then multiply the denominators. For example,

$$\frac{3}{4} \times \frac{5}{7} = \frac{3 \times 5}{4 \times 6} = \frac{15}{28}$$

3. Dividing Fractions. To divide one fraction by another, you invert the second fraction and then multiply. For example,

$$\frac{1}{2} \div \frac{1}{4} = \frac{1}{2} \times \frac{4}{1} = \frac{1 \times 4}{2 \times 1} = \frac{4}{2}$$

4. Adding and Subtracting Fractions. Fractions must have the same denominator before you can add or subtract them. If the two fractions already have a common denominator, you simply add (or subtract as the case may be) *only* the values in the numerators. For example,

$$\frac{2}{5} + \frac{1}{5} = \frac{3}{5}$$

Suppose that you divided a pie into five equal pieces (fifths). If you first ate two-fifths of the pie and then another one-fifth, the total amount eaten would be three-fifths of the pie:

If the two fractions do not have the same denominator, you must first find equivalent fractions with a common denominator before you can add or subtract. The product of the two denominators will always work as a common denominator for equivalent fractions (although it may not be the lowest common denominator). For example,

$$\frac{2}{3} + \frac{1}{10} = ?$$

Because these two fractions have different denominators, it is necessary to convert each into an equivalent fraction and find a common denominator. We will use $3 \times 10 = 30$ as the common denominator. Thus, the equivalent fraction of each is

$$\frac{2}{3} = \frac{20}{30} \quad \text{and} \quad \frac{1}{10} = \frac{3}{30}$$

Now the two fractions can be added:

$$\frac{20}{30} + \frac{3}{30} = \frac{23}{30}$$

5. Comparing the Size of Fractions. When comparing the size of two fractions with the same denominator, the larger fraction will have the larger numerator. For example,

$$\frac{5}{8} > \frac{3}{8}$$

The denominators are the same, so the whole is partitioned into pieces of the same size. Five of these pieces are more than three of them:

When two fractions have different denominators, you must first convert them to fractions with a common denominator to determine which is larger. Consider the following fractions:

$$\frac{3}{8} \quad \text{and} \quad \frac{7}{16}$$

If the numerator and denominator of ⅜ are multiplied by 2, the resulting equivalent fraction will have a denominator of 16:

$$\frac{3}{8} = \frac{3 \times 2}{8 \times 2} = \frac{6}{16}$$

Now a comparison can be made between the two fractions:

$$\frac{6}{16} < \frac{7}{16}$$

Therefore,

$$\frac{3}{8} < \frac{7}{16}$$

DECIMALS

1. Converting Decimals to Fractions. Like a fraction, a decimal represents part of the whole. The first decimal place to the right of the decimal point indicates how many tenths are used. For example,

$$0.1 = \frac{1}{10} \qquad 0.7 = \frac{7}{10}$$

The next decimal place represents $\frac{1}{100}$, the next $\frac{1}{1000}$, the next $\frac{1}{10,000}$, and so on. To change a decimal to a fraction, just use the number without the decimal point for the numerator. Use the denominator that the last (on the right) decimal place represents. For example,

$$0.32 = \frac{32}{100} \qquad 0.5333 = \frac{5333}{10,000} \qquad 0.05 = \frac{5}{100} \qquad 0.001 = \frac{1}{1000}$$

2. Adding and Subtracting Decimals. To add and subtract decimals, the only rule is that you must keep the decimal points in a straight vertical line. For example,

$$
\begin{array}{r}
0.27 \\
+1.326 \\
\hline
1.596
\end{array}
\qquad
\begin{array}{r}
3.595 \\
-0.67 \\
\hline
2.925
\end{array}
$$

3. Multiplying Decimals. To multiply two decimal values, you first multiply the two numbers, ignoring the decimal points. Then you position the decimal point in the answer so that the number of digits to the right of the decimal point is equal to the total number of decimal places in the two numbers being multiplied. For example,

$$
\begin{array}{r}
1.73 \\
\times 0.251 \\
\hline
173 \\
865 \\
346 \\
\hline
0.43423
\end{array}
\begin{array}{l}
\text{(two decimal places)} \\
\text{(three decimal places)} \\
\\
\\
\\
\text{(five decimal places)}
\end{array}
\qquad
\begin{array}{r}
0.25 \\
\times 0.005 \\
\hline
125 \\
00 \\
00 \\
\hline
0.00125
\end{array}
\begin{array}{l}
\text{(two decimal places)} \\
\text{(three decimal places)} \\
\\
\\
\\
\text{(five decimal places)}
\end{array}
$$

4. Dividing Decimals. The simplest procedure for dividing decimals is based on the fact that dividing two numbers is identical to expressing them as a fraction:

$$0.25 \div 1.6 \text{ is identical to } \frac{0.25}{1.6}$$

You now can multiply both the numerator and the denominator of the fraction by 10, 100, 1000, or whatever number is necessary to remove the decimal places. Remember, multiplying both the numerator and the denominator of a fraction by the *same* value will create an equivalent fraction. Therefore,

$$\frac{0.25}{1.6} = \frac{0.25 \times 100}{1.6 \times 100} = \frac{25}{160}$$

The result is a division problem without any decimal places in the two numbers.

PERCENTAGES

1. Converting a Percentage to a Fraction or a Decimal. To convert a percentage to a fraction, remove the percent sign, place the number in the numerator, and use 100 for the denominator. For example,

$$52\% = \frac{52}{100} \qquad 5\% = \frac{5}{100}$$

To convert a percentage to a decimal, remove the percent sign, and divide by 100, or simply move the decimal point two places to the left. For example,

$$83\% = \underset{\smile}{83.} = 0.83$$

$$14.5\% = \underset{\smile}{14.5} = 0.145$$

$$5\% = \underset{\smile}{5.} = 0.05$$

2. Arithmetic Operations with Percentages. There are situations when it is best to express percent values as decimals in order to perform certain arithmetic operations. For example, what is 45% of 60? This question may be stated as

$$45\% \times 60 = ?$$

The 45% should be converted to decimal form to find the solution to this question. Therefore,

$$0.45 \times 60 = 27$$

LEARNING CHECK

1. Convert ³⁄₂₅ to a decimal.
2. Convert ³⁄₈ to a percentage.
3. Next to each set of fractions, write "true" if they are equivalent and "false" if they are not:

   a. $\frac{3}{8} = \frac{9}{24}$ _____   **b.** $\frac{7}{9} = \frac{17}{19}$ _____

   c. $\frac{2}{7} = \frac{4}{14}$ _____

4. Compute the following:

   a. $\frac{1}{6} \times \frac{7}{10}$ **b.** $\frac{7}{8} - \frac{1}{2}$ **c.** $\frac{9}{10} \div \frac{2}{3}$ **d.** $\frac{7}{22} + \frac{2}{3}$

5. Identify the larger fraction of each pair:

   a. $\frac{7}{10}, \frac{21}{100}$ **b.** $\frac{3}{4}, \frac{7}{12}$ **c.** $\frac{22}{3}, \frac{19}{3}$

6. Convert the following decimals into fractions:
   a. 0.012   **b.** 0.77   **c.** 0.005
7. $2.59 \times 0.015 = ?$
8. $1.8 \div 0.02 = ?$
9. What is 28% of 45?

ANSWERS   **1.** 0.12   **2.** 37.5%   **3. a.** True   **b.** False   **c.** True

4. a. $\frac{7}{60}$ **b.** $\frac{3}{8}$ **c.** $\frac{27}{20}$ **d.** $\frac{65}{66}$ **5. a.** $\frac{7}{10}$ **b.** $\frac{3}{4}$ **c.** $\frac{22}{3}$

6. a. $\frac{12}{1000}$ **b.** $\frac{77}{100}$ **c.** $\frac{5}{1000}$ **7.** 0.03885   **8.** 90   **9.** 12.6

A.3 NEGATIVE NUMBERS

Negative numbers are used to represent values less than zero. Negative numbers may occur when you are measuring the difference between two scores. For example, a researcher may want to evaluate the effectiveness of a propaganda film by measuring people's attitude with a test both before and after viewing the film:

	BEFORE	AFTER	AMOUNT OF CHANGE
Person A	23	27	+4
Person B	18	15	−3
Percent C	21	16	−5

Notice that the negative sign provides information about the direction of the difference: A plus sign indicates an increase in value, and a minus sign indicates a decrease.

Because negative numbers are frequently encountered, you should be comfortable working with these values. This section reviews basic arithmetic operations using negative numbers. You should also note that any number without a sign (+ or −) is assumed to be positive.

1. Adding Negative Numbers. When adding numbers that include negative values, simply interpret the negative sign as subtraction. For example,

$$3 + (-2) + 5 = 3 - 2 + 5 = 6$$

When adding a long string of numbers, it often is easier to add all the positive values to obtain the positive sum and then to add all of the negative values to obtain the negative sum. Finally, you subtract the negative sum from the positive sum. For example,

$$-1 + 3 + (-4) + 3 + (-6) + (-2)$$

positive sum = 6   negative sum = 13

Answer: $6 - 13 = -7$

2. Subtracting Negative Numbers. To subtract a negative number, change it to a positive number, and add. For example,

$$4 - (-3) = 4 + 3 = 7$$

This rule is easier to understand if you think of positive numbers as financial gains and negative numbers as financial losses. In this context, taking away a debt is equivalent to a financial gain. In mathematical terms, taking away a negative number is equivalent to adding a positive number. For example, suppose that you are meeting a friend for lunch. You have $7 but you owe your friend $3. Thus, you really have only $4 to spend for lunch. But your friend forgives (takes away) the $3 debt. The result is that you now have $7 to spend. Expressed as an equation

$$\$4 \text{ minus a } \$3 \text{ debt} = \$7$$

$$4 - (-3) = 4 + 3 = 7$$

3. Multiplying and Dividing Negative Numbers. When the two numbers being multiplied (or divided) have the same sign, the result is a positive number. When the two numbers have different signs, the result is negative. For example,

$$3 \times (-2) = -6$$

$$-4 \times (-2) = +8$$

The first example is easy to explain by thinking of multiplication as repeated addition. In this case,

$$3 \times (-2) = (-2) + (-2) + (-2) = -6$$

You take three negative 2s, which result in a total of negative 6. In the second example, we are multiplying by a negative number. This amounts to repeated subtraction. That is,

$$-4 \times (-2) = -(-2) - (-2) - (-2) - (-2)$$

$$= 2 + 2 + 2 + 2 = 8$$

By using the same rule for both multiplication and division, we ensure that these two operations are compatible. For example,

$$-6 \div 3 = -2$$

which is compatible with

$$3 \times (-2) = -6$$

Also,

$$8 \div (-4) = -2$$

which is compatible with

$$-4 \times (-2) = +8$$

LEARNING CHECK **1.** Complete the following calculations:
   a. $3 + (-8) + 5 + 7 + (-1) + (-3)$
   b. $5 - (-9) + 2 - (-3) - (-1)$
   c. $3 - 7 - (-21) + (-5) - (-9)$
   d. $4 - (-6) - 3 + 11 - 14$
   e. $9 + 8 - 2 - 1 - (-6)$
   f. $9 \times (-3)$
   g. $-7 \times (-4)$

h. $-6 \times (-2) \times (-3)$
i. $-12 \div (-3)$
j. $18 \div (-6)$

ANSWERS   **1. a.** 3   **b.** 20   **c.** 21   **d.** 4   **e.** 20
          f. -27 **g.** 28   **h.** -36 **i.** 4   **j.** -3

A.4 BASIC ALGEBRA: SOLVING EQUATIONS

An equation is a mathematical statement that indicates two quantities are identical. For example,

$$12 = 8 + 4$$

Often an equation will contain an unknown (or variable) quantity that is identified with a letter or symbol rather than a number. For example,

$$12 = 8 + X$$

In this event, your task is to find the value of X that makes the equation "true," or balanced. For this example, an X value of 4 will make a true equation. Finding the value of X is usually called *solving the equation*.

To solve an equation, there are two points to be kept in mind:

1. Your goal is to have the unknown value (X) isolated on one side of the equation. This means that you need to remove all of the other numbers and symbols that appear on the same side of the equation as the X.

2. The equation will remain balanced provided you treat both sides exactly the same. For example, you could add 10 points to *both* sides, and the solution (the X value) for the equation would be unchanged.

FINDING THE SOLUTION FOR AN EQUATION   We will consider four basic types of equations and the operations needed to solve them.

1. When X Has a Value Added to It. An example of this type of equation is

$$X + 3 = 7$$

Your goal is to isolate X on one side of the equation. Thus, you must remove the $+3$ on the left-hand side. The solution is obtained by subtracting 3 from *both* sides of the equation:

$$X + 3 - 3 = 7 - 3$$
$$X = 4$$

The solution is $X = 4$. You should always check your solution by returning to the original equation and replacing X with the value you obtained for the solution. For this example,

$$X + 3 = 7$$
$$4 + 3 = 7$$
$$7 = 7$$

2. When X Has a Value Subtracted from It. An example of this type of equation is

$$X - 8 = 12$$

In this example, you must remove the -8 from the left-hand side. Thus, the solution is obtained by adding 8 to *both* sides of the equation:

$$X - 8 + 8 = 12 + 8$$
$$X = 20$$

Check the solution:

$$X - 8 = 12$$
$$20 - 8 = 12$$
$$12 = 12$$

3. When X Is Multiplied by a Value. An example of this type of equation is

$$4X = 24$$

In this instance, it is necessary to remove the 4 that is multiplied by X. This may be accomplished by dividing both sides of the equation by 4:

$$\frac{4X}{4} = \frac{24}{4}$$
$$X = 6$$

Check the solution:

$$4X = 24$$
$$4(6) = 24$$
$$24 = 24$$

4. When X Is Divided by a Value. An example of this type of equation is

$$\frac{X}{3} = 9$$

Now the X is divided by 3, so the solution is obtained by multiplying by 3. Multiplying both sides yields

$$3\left(\frac{X}{3}\right) = 9(3)$$

$$X = 27$$

For the check,

$$\frac{X}{3} = 9$$

$$\frac{27}{3} = 9$$

$$9 = 9$$

SOLUTIONS FOR MORE-COMPLEX EQUATIONS

More-complex equations can be solved by using a combination of the preceding simple operations. Remember, at each stage you are trying to isolate X on one side of the equation. For example,

$$3X + 7 = 22$$

$$3X + 7 - 7 = 22 - 7 \qquad \text{(remove } +7 \text{ by subtracting 7 from both sides)}$$

$$3X = 15$$

$$\frac{3X}{3} = \frac{15}{3} \qquad \text{(remove 3 by dividing both sides by 3)}$$

$$X = 5$$

To check this solution, return to the original equation, and substitute 5 in place of X:

$$3X + 7 = 22$$

$$3(5) + 7 = 22$$

$$15 + 7 = 22$$

$$22 = 22$$

Following is another type of complex equation that is frequently encountered in statistics:

$$\frac{X + 3}{4} = 2$$

First, remove the 4 by multiplying both sides by 4:

$$4\left(\frac{X + 3}{4}\right) = 2(4)$$

$$X + 3 = 8$$

Now remove the $+3$ by subtracting 3 from both sides:

$$X + 3 - 3 = 8 - 3$$
$$X = 5$$

To check this solution, return to the original equation, and substitute 5 in place of X:

$$\frac{X + 3}{4} = 2$$

$$\frac{5 + 3}{4} = 2$$

$$\frac{8}{4} = 2$$

$$2 = 2$$

LEARNING CHECK **1.** Solve for X and check the solutions:

a. $3X = 18$ **b.** $X + 7 = 9$ **c.** $X - 4 = 18$ **d.** $5X - 8 = 12$

e. $\frac{X}{9} = 5$ **f.** $\frac{X + 1}{6} = 4$ **g.** $X + 2 = -5$ **h.** $\frac{X}{5} = -5$

i. $\frac{2X}{3} = 12$ **j.** $\frac{X}{3} + 1 = 3$

ANSWERS **1. a.** $X = 6$ **b.** $X = 2$ **c.** $X = 22$ **d.** $X = 4$ **e.** $X = 45$
f. $X = 23$ **g.** $X = -7$ **h.** $X = -25$ **i.** $X = 18$ **j.** $X = 6$

A.5 EXPONENTS AND SQUARE ROOTS

EXPONENTIAL NOTATION A simplified notation is used whenever a number is being multiplied by itself. The notation consists of placing a value, called an exponent, on the right-hand side of and raised above another number, called a base. For example,

$7^3 \leftarrow$ exponent
↑
base

The exponent indicates how many times the base is multiplied by itself. Following are some examples:

$7^3 = 7(7)(7)$ (read "7 cubed," or "7 raised to the third power")

$5^2 = 5(5)$ (read "5 squared")

$2^5 = 2(2)(2)(2)(2)$ (read "2 raised to the fifth power")

There are a few basic rules about exponents that you will need to know for this course. They are outlined here.

1. Numbers Raised to One or Zero. Any number raised to the first power equals itself. For example,

$$6^1 = 6$$

Any number (except zero) raises to the zero power equals 1. For example,

$$9^0 = 1$$

2. Exponents for Multiple Terms. The exponent applies only to the base that is just in front of it. For example,

$$XY^2 = XYY$$
$$a^2b^3 = aabbb$$

3. Negative Bases Raised to an Exponent. If a negative number is raised to a power, then the result will be positive for exponents that are even and negative for exponents that are odd. For example,

$$-4^3 = -4(-4)(-4)$$
$$= 16(-4)$$
$$= -64$$

and

$$-3^4 = -3(-3)(-3)(-3)$$
$$= 9(-3)(-3)$$
$$= 9(9)$$
$$= 81$$

4. Exponents and Parentheses. If an exponent is present outside of parentheses, then the computations within the parentheses are done first, and the exponential computation is done last:

$$(3 + 5)^2 = 8^2 = 64$$

Notice that the meaning of the expression is changed when each term in the parentheses is raised to the exponent individually:

$$3^2 + 5^2 = 9 + 25 = 34$$

Therefore,

$$X^2 + Y^2 \neq (X + Y)^2$$

5. Fractions Raised to a Power. If the numerator and denominator of a fraction are each raised to the same exponent, then the entire fraction can be raised to that exponent. That is,

$$\frac{a^2}{b^2} = \left(\frac{a}{b}\right)^2$$

For example,

$$\frac{3^2}{4^2} = \left(\frac{3}{4}\right)^2$$

$$\frac{9}{16} = \frac{3}{4}\left(\frac{3}{4}\right)$$

$$\frac{9}{16} = \frac{9}{16}$$

SQUARE ROOTS   The square root of a value equals a number that when multiplied by itself yields the original value. For example, the square root of 16 equals 4 because 4 times 4 equals 16. The symbol for the square root is called a radical, $\sqrt{}$. The square root is taken for a number under the radical. For example,

$$\sqrt{16} = 4$$

The square root is the inverse of raising a number to the second power (squaring). Thus,

$$\sqrt{a^2} = a$$

For example,

$$\sqrt{3^2} = \sqrt{9} = 3$$

Also,

$$(\sqrt{b})^2 = b$$

For example,

$$(\sqrt{64})^2 = 8^2 = 64$$

Computations under the same radical are performed *before* the square root is taken. For example,

$$\sqrt{9 + 16} = \sqrt{25} = 5$$

Note that with addition (or subtraction) separate radicals yield a different result:

$$\sqrt{9} + \sqrt{16} = 3 + 4 = 7$$

Therefore,

$$\sqrt{X} + \sqrt{Y} \neq \sqrt{X + Y}$$
$$\sqrt{X} - \sqrt{Y} \neq \sqrt{X - Y}$$

If the numerator and denominator of a fraction each have a radical, then the entire fraction can be placed under a single radical:

$$\frac{\sqrt{16}}{\sqrt{4}} = \sqrt{\frac{16}{4}}$$

$$\frac{4}{2} = \sqrt{4}$$

$$2 = 2$$

Therefore,

$$\frac{\sqrt{X}}{\sqrt{Y}} = \sqrt{\frac{X}{Y}}$$

Also, if the square root of one number is multiplied by the square root of another number, then the same result would be obtained by taking the square root of the product of both numbers. For example,

$$\sqrt{9} \times \sqrt{16} = \sqrt{9 \times 16}$$

$$3 \times 4 = \sqrt{144}$$

$$12 = 12$$

Therefore,

$$\sqrt{a} \times \sqrt{b} = \sqrt{ab}$$

LEARNING CHECK
1. Perform the following computations:
   a. $(-6)^3$
   b. $(3 + 7)^2$
   c. $a^3 b^2$ when $a = 2$ and $b = -5$
   d. $a^4 b^3$ when $a = 2$ and $b = 3$
   e. $(XY)^2$ when $X = 3$ and $Y = 5$
   f. $X^2 + Y^2$ when $X = 3$ and $Y = 5$
   g. $(X + Y)^2$ when $X = 3$ and $Y = 5$
   h. $\sqrt{5 + 4}$
   i. $(\sqrt{9})^2$
   j. $\dfrac{\sqrt{16}}{\sqrt{4}}$

ANSWERS
1. a. -216 b. 100   c. 200   d. 432   e. 225
   f. 34   g. 64   h. 3   i. 9   j. 2

PROBLEMS FOR APPENDIX A   Basic Mathematics Review

1. $50/(10 - 8) = ?$
2. $(2 + 3)^2 = ?$
3. $20/10 \times 3 = ?$
4. $12 - 4 \times 2 + 6/3 = ?$
5. $24/(12 - 4) + 2 \times (6 + 3) = ?$
6. Convert $7/20$ to a decimal.
7. Express $9/25$ as a percentage.
8. Convert 0.91 to a fraction.
9. Express 0.0031 as a fraction.
10. Next to each set of fractions, write "true" if they are equivalent and "false" if they are not:

    a. $\dfrac{4}{1000} = \dfrac{2}{100}$ _____

    b. $\dfrac{5}{6} = \dfrac{52}{62}$ _____

    c. $\dfrac{1}{8} = \dfrac{7}{56}$ _____

11. Perform the following calculations:

    a. $\dfrac{4}{5} \times \dfrac{2}{3} = ?$

    b. $\dfrac{7}{9} \div \dfrac{2}{3} = ?$

    c. $\dfrac{3}{8} + \dfrac{1}{5} = ?$

    d. $\dfrac{5}{18} - \dfrac{1}{6} = ?$

12. $2.51 \times 0.017 = ?$
13. $3.88 \times 0.0002 = ?$
14. $3.17 + 17.0132 = ?$
15. $5.55 + 10.7 + 0.711 + 3.33 + 0.031 = ?$
16. $2.04 \div 0.2 = ?$
17. $0.36 \div 0.4 = ?$

18. $5 + 3 - 6 - 4 + 3 = ?$
19. $9 - (-1) - 17 + 3 - (-4) + 5 = ?$
20. $5 + 3 - (-8) - (-1) + (-3) - 4 + 10 = ?$
21. $8 \times (-3) = ?$
22. $-22 \div (-2) = ?$
23. $-2(-4) \times (-3) = ?$
24. $84 \div (-4) = ?$

Solve the equations in Problems 25–32 for X.

25. $X - 7 = -2$
26. $9 = X + 3$
27. $\dfrac{X}{4} = 11$
28. $-3 = \dfrac{X}{3}$
29. $\dfrac{X + 3}{5} = 2$
30. $\dfrac{X + 1}{3} = -8$
31. $6X - 1 = 11$
32. $2X + 3 = -11$
33. $-5^2 = ?$
34. $-5^3 = ?$
35. If $a = 4$ and $b = 3$, then $a^2 + b^4 = ?$
36. If $a = -1$ and $b = 4$, then $(a + b)^2 = ?$
37. If $a = -1$ and $b = 5$, then $ab^2 = ?$
38. $\dfrac{18}{\sqrt{4}} = ?$
39. $\sqrt{\dfrac{20}{5}} = ?$

SKILLS ASSESSMENT FINAL EXAM

SECTION 1

1. $4 + 8/4 = ?$
2. $(4 + 8)/4 = ?$
3. $4 \times 3^2 = ?$
4. $(4 \times 3)^2 = ?$
5. $10/5 \times 2 = ?$
6. $10/(5 \times 2) = ?$
7. $40 - 10 \times 4/2 = ?$

8. $(5 - 1)^2/2 = ?$

9. $2 \times 6 - 3^2 = ?$

10. $2 \times (6 - 3)^2 = ?$

11. $4 \times 3 - 1 + 8 \times 2 = ?$

12. $4 \times (3 - 1 + 8) \times 2 = ?$

SECTION 2

1. Express $^{14}\!/_{80}$ as a decimal.

2. Convert $^6\!/_{25}$ to a percentage.

3. Convert 18% to a fraction.

4. $\frac{3}{5} \times \frac{2}{3} = ?$

5. $\frac{5}{24} + \frac{5}{6} = ?$

6. $\frac{7}{12} \div \frac{5}{6} = ?$

7. $\frac{5}{9} - \frac{1}{3} = ?$

8. $6.11 \times 0.22 = ?$

9. $0.18 \div 0.9 = ?$

10. $8.742 + 0.76 = ?$

11. In a statistics class of 72 students, three-eighths of the students received a B on the first test. How many Bs were earned?

12. What is 15% of 64?

SECTION 3

1. $3 - 1 - 3 + 5 - 2 + 6 = ?$

2. $-8 - (-6) = ?$

3. $2 - (-7) - 3 + (-11) - 20 = ?$

4. $-8 - 3 - (-1) - 2 - 1 = ?$

5. $8(-2) = ?$

6. $-7(-7) = ?$

7. $-3(-2)(-5) = ?$

8. $-3(5)(-3) = ?$

9. $-24 \div (-4) = ?$

10. $36 \div (-6) = ?$

11. $-56/7 = ?$

12. $-7/(-1) = ?$

SECTION 4

Solve for X.

1. $X + 5 = 12$

2. $X - 11 = 3$

3. $10 = X + 4$

4. $4X = 20$

5. $\frac{X}{2} = 15$

6. $18 = 9X$

7. $\frac{X}{5} = 35$

8. $2X + 8 = 4$

9. $\frac{X + 1}{3} = 6$

10. $4X + 3 = -13$

11. $\frac{X + 3}{3} = -7$

12. $23 = 2X - 5$

SECTION 5

1. $5^3 = ?$

2. $-4^3 = ?$

3. $-2^5 = ?$

4. $-2^6 = ?$

5. If $a = 4$ and $b = 2$, then $ab^2 = ?$

6. If $a = 4$ and $b = 2$, then $(a + b)^3 = ?$

7. If $a = 4$ and $b = 2$, then $a^2 + b^2 = ?$

8. $(11 + 4)^2 = ?$

9. $\sqrt{7^2} = ?$

10. If $a = 36$ and $b = 64$, the $\sqrt{a + b} = ?$

11. $\frac{25}{\sqrt{25}} = ?$

12. If $a = -1$ and $b = 2$, then $a^3 b^4 = ?$

ANSWER KEY   Skills Assessment Exams

PREVIEW EXAM

SECTION 1

1. 17
2. 35
3. 6
4. 24
5. 5
6. 2
7. $\frac{1}{3}$
8. 8
9. 72
10. 8
11. 24
12. 48

SECTION 2

1. 75%
2. $\frac{30}{100}$, or $\frac{3}{10}$
3. 0.3
4. $\frac{10}{13}$
5. 1.625
6. $\frac{2}{20}$
7. $\frac{19}{24}$
8. 1.4
9. $\frac{4}{15}$
10. 7.5
11. 16
12. 36

SECTION 3

1. 4
2. 8
3. 2
4. 9
5. -12
6. 12
7. -15
8. -24
9. -4
10. 3
11. -2
12. 25

SECTION 4

1. $X = 7$
2. $X = 29$
3. $X = 9$
4. $X = 4$
5. $X = 24$
6. $X = 15$
7. $X = 80$
8. $X = -3$
9. $X = 11$
10. $X = 25$
11. $X = 11$
12. $X = 7$

FINAL EXAM

SECTION 1

1. 6
2. 3
3. 36
4. 144
5. 4
6. 1
7. 20
8. 8
9. 9
10. 18
11. 27
12. 80

SECTION 2

1. 0.175
2. 24%
3. $\frac{18}{100}$, or $\frac{9}{50}$
4. $\frac{6}{15}$
5. $\frac{25}{24}$
6. $\frac{42}{60}$, or $\frac{7}{10}$
7. $\frac{2}{9}$
8. 1.3442
9. 0.2
10. 9.502
11. 27
12. 9.6

SECTION 3

1. 8
2. -2
3. -25
4. -13
5. -16
6. 49
7. -30
8. 45
9. 6
10. -6
11. -8
12. 7

SECTION 4

1. $X = 7$
2. $X = 14$
3. $X = 6$
4. $X = 5$
5. $X = 30$
6. $X = 2$
7. $X = 175$
8. $X = -2$
9. $X = 17$
10. $X = -4$
11. $X = -24$
12. $X = 14$

SECTION 5

1. 64
2. 4
3. 54
4. 25
5. 13
6. −27

7. 256
8. 8
9. 12
10. 121
11. 33
12. −9

SECTION 5

1. 125
2. −64
3. −32
4. 64
5. 16
6. 216

7. 20
8. 225
9. 7
10. 10
11. 5
12. −16

SOLUTIONS TO SELECTED PROBLEMS FOR APPENDIX A   Basic Mathematics Review

1. 25
3. 6
5. 21
6. 0.35
7. 36%

9. $\dfrac{31}{10,000}$
10. b. False
11. a. $\dfrac{8}{15}$ b. $\dfrac{21}{18}$ c. $\dfrac{23}{40}$
12. 0.04267

14. 20.1832
17. 0.9
19. 5
21. −24
22. 11

25. $X = 5$
28. $X = -9$
30. $X = -25$
31. $X = 2$

34. −125
36. 9
37. −25
39. 2

SUGGESTED REVIEW BOOKS

There are many basic mathematics review books available if you need a more extensive review than this appendix can provide. The following books are but a few of the many that you may find helpful:

Barker, V. C., and Aufmann, R. N. (1982). *Essential Mathematics*. Boston: Houghton Mifflin.

Bloomfield, D. I. (1994). *Introductory Algebra*. St. Paul: West Publishing.

Falstein, L. D. (1986). *Basic Mathematics,* 2d ed. Reading, Mass.: Addison-Wesley.

Goodman, A., and Hirsch, L. (1994). *Understanding Elementary Algebra*. St. Paul: West Publishing.

Washington, A.J. (1984). *Arithmetic and Beginning Algebra*. Menlo Park, Calif.: Benjamin/Cummings.

APPENDIX B STATISTICAL TABLES

TABLE B.1   THE UNIT NORMAL TABLE*

*Column A lists z-score values. A vertical line drawn through a normal distribution at a
z-score location divides the distribution into two sections.
Column B identifies the proportion in the larger section, called the *body*.
Column C identifies the proportion in the smaller section, called the *tail*.

Note: Because the normal distribution is symmetrical, the proportions for negative
z-scores are the same as those for positive z-scores.

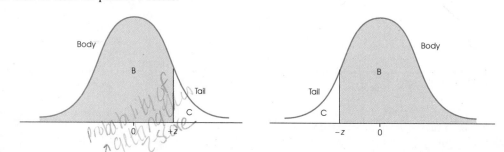

(A) z	(B) PROPORTION IN BODY	(C) PROPORTION IN TAIL	(A) z	(B) PROPORTION IN BODY	(C) PROPORTION IN TAIL	(A) z	(B) PROPORTION IN BODY	(C) PROPORTION IN TAIL
0.00	.5000	.5000	0.20	.5793	.4207	0.40	.6554	.3446
0.01	.5040	.4960	0.21	.5832	.4168	0.41	.6591	.3409
0.02	.5080	.4920	0.22	.5871	.4129	0.42	.6628	.3372
0.03	.5120	.4880	0.23	.5910	.4090	0.43	.6664	.3336
0.04	.5160	.4840	0.24	.5948	.4052	0.44	.6700	.3300
0.05	.5199	.4801	0.25	.5987	.4013	0.45	.6736	.3264
0.06	.5239	.4761	0.26	.6026	.3974	0.46	.6772	.3228
0.07	.5279	.4721	0.27	.6064	.3936	0.47	.6808	.3192
0.08	.5319	.4681	0.28	.6103	.3897	0.48	.6844	.3156
0.09	.5359	.4641	0.29	.6141	.3859	0.49	.6879	.3121
0.10	.5398	.4602	0.30	.6179	.3821	0.50	.6915	.3085
0.11	.5438	.4562	0.31	.6217	.3783	0.51	.6950	.3050
0.12	.5478	.4522	0.32	.6255	.3745	0.52	.6985	.3015
0.13	.5517	.4483	0.33	.6293	.3707	0.53	.7019	.2981
0.14	.5557	.4443	0.34	.6331	.3669	0.54	.7054	.2946
0.15	.5596	.4404	0.35	.6368	.3632	0.55	.7088	.2912
0.16	.5636	.4364	0.36	.6406	.3594	0.56	.7123	.2877
0.17	.5675	.4325	0.37	.6443	.3557	0.57	.7157	.2843
0.18	.5714	.4286	0.38	.6480	.3520	0.58	.7190	.2810
0.19	.5753	.4247	0.39	.6517	.3483	0.59	.7224	.2776

TABLE B.1 continued

(A) z	(B) PROPORTION IN BODY	(C) PROPORTION IN TAIL	(A) z	(B) PROPORTION IN BODY	(C) PROPORTION IN TAIL	(A) z	(B) PROPORTION IN BODY	(C) PROPORTION IN TAIL
0.60	.7257	.2743	1.05	.8531	.1469	1.50	.9332	.0668
0.61	.7291	.2709	1.06	.8554	.1446	1.51	.9345	.0655
0.62	.7324	.2676	1.07	.8577	.1423	1.52	.9357	.0643
0.63	.7357	.2643	1.08	.8599	.1401	1.53	.9370	.0630
0.64	.7389	.2611	1.09	.8621	.1379	1.54	.9382	.0618
0.65	.7422	.2578	1.10	.8643	.1357	1.55	.9394	.0606
0.66	.7454	.2546	1.11	.8665	.1335	1.56	.9406	.0594
0.67	.7486	.2514	1.12	.8686	.1314	1.57	.9418	.0582
0.68	.7517	.2483	1.13	.8708	.1292	1.58	.9429	.0571
0.69	.7549	.2451	1.14	.8729	.1271	1.59	.9441	.0559
0.70	.7580	.2420	1.15	.8749	.1251	1.60	.9452	.0548
0.71	.7611	.2389	1.16	.8770	.1230	1.61	.9463	.0537
0.72	.7642	.2358	1.17	.8790	.1210	1.62	.9474	.0526
0.73	.7673	.2327	1.18	.8810	.1190	1.63	.9484	.0516
0.74	.7704	.2296	1.19	.8830	.1170	1.64	.9495	.0505
0.75	.7734	.2266	1.20	.8849	.1151	1.65	.9505	.0495
0.76	.7764	.2236	1.21	.8869	.1131	1.66	.9515	.0485
0.77	.7794	.2206	1.22	.8888	.1112	1.67	.9525	.0475
0.78	.7823	.2177	1.23	.8907	.1093	1.68	.9535	.0465
0.79	.7852	.2148	1.24	.8925	.1075	1.69	.9545	.0455
0.80	.7881	.2119	1.25	.8944	.1056	1.70	.9554	.0446
0.81	.7910	.2090	1.26	.8962	.1038	1.71	.9564	.0436
0.82	.7939	.2061	1.27	.8980	.1020	1.72	.9573	.0427
0.83	.7967	.2033	1.28	.8997	.1003	1.73	.9582	.0418
0.84	.7995	.2005	1.29	.9015	.0985	1.74	.9591	.0409
0.85	.8023	.1977	1.30	.9032	.0968	1.75	.9599	.0401
0.86	.8051	.1949	1.31	.9049	.0951	1.76	.9608	.0392
0.87	.8078	.1922	1.32	.9066	.0934	1.77	.9616	.0384
0.88	.8106	.1894	1.33	.9082	.0918	1.78	.9625	.0375
0.89	.8133	.1867	1.34	.9099	.0901	1.79	.9633	.0367
0.90	.8159	.1841	1.35	.9115	.0885	1.80	.9641	.0359
0.91	.8186	.1814	1.36	.9131	.0869	1.81	.9649	.0351
0.92	.8212	.1788	1.37	.9147	.0853	1.82	.9656	.0344
0.93	.8238	.1762	1.38	.9162	.0838	1.83	.9664	.0336
0.94	.8264	.1736	1.39	.9177	.0823	1.84	.9671	.0329
0.95	.8289	.1711	1.40	.9192	.0808	1.85	.9678	.0322
0.96	.8315	.1685	1.41	.9207	.0793	1.86	.9686	.0314
0.97	.8340	.1660	1.42	.9222	.0778	1.87	.9693	.0307
0.98	.8365	.1635	1.43	.9236	.0764	1.88	.9699	.0301
0.99	.8389	.1611	1.44	.9251	.0749	1.89	.9706	.0294
1.00	.8413	.1587	1.45	.9265	.0735	1.90	.9713	.0287
1.01	.8438	.1562	1.46	.9279	.0721	1.91	.9719	.0281
1.02	.8461	.1539	1.47	.9292	.0708	1.92	.9726	.0274
1.03	.8485	.1515	1.48	.9306	.0694	1.93	.9732	.0268
1.04	.8508	.1492	1.49	.9319	.0681	1.94	.9738	.0262

B / STATISTICAL TABLES

TABLE B.1   continued

(A) z	(B) PROPORTION IN BODY	(C) PROPORTION IN TAIL	(A) z	(B) PROPORTION IN BODY	(C) PROPORTION IN TAIL	(A) z	(B) PROPORTION IN BODY	(C) PROPORTION IN TAIL
1.95	.9744	.0256	2.42	.9922	.0078	2.88	.9980	.0020
1.96	.9750	.0250	2.43	.9925	.0075	2.89	.9981	.0019
1.97	.9756	.0244	2.44	.9927	.0073	2.90	.9981	.0019
1.98	.9761	.0239	2.45	.9929	.0071	2.91	.9982	.0018
1.99	.9767	.0233	2.46	.9931	.0069	2.92	.9982	.0018
2.00	.9772	.0228	2.47	.9932	.0068	2.93	.9983	.0017
2.01	.9778	.0222	2.48	.9934	.0066	2.94	.9984	.0016
2.02	.9783	.0217	2.49	.9936	.0064	2.95	.9984	.0016
2.03	.9788	.0212	2.50	.9938	.0062	2.96	.9985	.0015
2.04	.9793	.0207	2.51	.9940	.0060	2.97	.9985	.0015
2.05	.9798	.0202	2.52	.9941	.0059	2.98	.9986	.0014
2.06	.9803	.0197	2.53	.9943	.0057	2.99	.9986	.0014
2.07	.9808	.0192	2.54	.9945	.0055	3.00	.9987	.0013
2.08	.9812	.0188	2.55	.9946	.0054	3.01	.9987	.0013
2.09	.9817	.0183	2.56	.9948	.0052	3.02	.9987	.0013
2.10	.9821	.0179	2.57	.9949	.0051	3.03	.9988	.0012
2.11	.9826	.0174	2.58	.9951	.0049	3.04	.9988	.0012
2.12	.9830	.0170	2.59	.9952	.0048	3.05	.9989	.0011
2.13	.9834	.0166	2.60	.9953	.0047	3.06	.9989	.0011
2.14	.9838	.0162	2.61	.9955	.0045	3.07	.9989	.0011
2.15	.9842	.0158	2.62	.9956	.0044	3.08	.9990	.0010
2.16	.9846	.0154	2.63	.9957	.0043	3.09	.9990	.0010
2.17	.9850	.0150	2.64	.9959	.0041	3.10	.9990	.0010
2.18	.9854	.0146	2.65	.9960	.0040	3.11	.9991	.0009
2.19	.9857	.0143	2.66	.9961	.0039	3.12	.9991	.0009
2.20	.9861	.0139	2.67	.9962	.0038	3.13	.9991	.0009
2.21	.9864	.0136	2.68	.9963	.0037	3.14	.9992	.0008
2.22	.9868	.0132	2.69	.9964	.0036	3.15	.9992	.0008
2.23	.9871	.0129	2.70	.9965	.0035	3.16	.9992	.0008
2.24	.9875	.0125	2.71	.9966	.0034	3.17	.9992	.0008
2.25	.9878	.0122	2.72	.9967	.0033	3.18	.9993	.0007
2.26	.9881	.0119	2.73	.9968	.0032	3.19	.9993	.0007
2.27	.9884	.0116	2.74	.9969	.0031	3.20	.9993	.0007
2.28	.9887	.0113	2.75	.9970	.0030	3.21	.9993	.0007
2.29	.9890	.0110	2.76	.9971	.0029	3.22	.9994	.0006
2.30	.9893	.0107	2.77	.9972	.0028	3.23	.9994	.0006
2.31	.9896	.0104	2.78	.9973	.0027	3.24	.9994	.0006
2.32	.9898	.0102	2.79	.9974	.0026	3.30	.9995	.0005
2.33	.9901	.0099	2.80	.9974	.0026	3.40	.9997	.0003
2.34	.9904	.0096	2.81	.9975	.0025	3.50	.9998	.0002
2.35	.9906	.0094	2.82	.9976	.0024	3.60	.9998	.0002
2.36	.9909	.0091	2.83	.9977	.0023	3.70	.9999	.0001
2.37	.9911	.0089	2.84	.9977	.0023	3.80	.99993	.00007
2.38	.9913	.0087	2.85	.9978	.0022	3.90	.99995	.00005
2.39	.9916	.0084	2.86	.9979	.0021	4.00	.99997	.00003
2.40	.9918	.0082	2.87	.9979	.0021			
2.41	.9920	.0080						

Generated by the Minitab statistical program using the CDL command.

TABLE B.2   THE *t* DISTRIBUTION

	PROPORTION IN ONE TAIL					
	0.25	0.10	0.05	0.025	0.01	0.005
	PROPORTION IN TWO TAILS					
df	0.50	0.20	0.10	0.05	0.02	0.01
1	1.000	3.078	6.314	12.706	31.821	63.657
2	0.816	1.886	2.920	4.303	6.965	9.925
3	0.765	1.638	2.353	3.182	4.541	5.841
4	0.741	1.533	2.132	2.776	3.747	4.604
5	0.727	1.476	2.015	2.571	3.365	4.032
6	0.718	1.440	1.943	2.447	3.143	3.707
7	0.711	1.415	1.895	2.365	2.998	3.499
8	0.706	1.397	1.860	2.306	2.896	3.355
9	0.703	1.383	1.833	2.262	2.821	3.250
10	0.700	1.372	1.812	2.228	2.764	3.169
11	0.697	1.363	1.796	2.201	2.718	3.106
12	0.695	1.356	1.782	2.179	2.681	3.055
13	0.694	1.350	1.771	2.160	2.650	3.012
14	0.692	1.345	1.761	2.145	2.624	2.977
15	0.691	1.341	1.753	2.131	2.602	2.947
16	0.690	1.337	1.746	2.120	2.583	2.921
17	0.689	1.333	1.740	2.110	2.567	2.898
18	0.688	1.330	1.734	2.101	2.552	2.878
19	0.688	1.328	1.729	2.093	2.539	2.861
20	0.687	1.325	1.725	2.086	2.528	2.845
21	0.686	1.323	1.721	2.080	2.518	2.831
22	0.686	1.321	1.717	2.074	2.508	2.819
23	0.685	1.319	1.714	2.069	2.500	2.807
24	0.685	1.318	1.711	2.064	2.492	2.797
25	0.684	1.316	1.708	2.060	2.485	2.787
26	0.684	1.315	1.706	2.056	2.479	2.779
27	0.684	1.314	1.703	2.052	2.473	2.771
28	0.683	1.313	1.701	2.048	2.467	2.763
29	0.683	1.311	1.699	2.045	2.462	2.756
30	0.683	1.310	1.697	2.042	2.457	2.750
40	0.681	1.303	1.684	2.021	2.423	2.704
60	0.679	1.296	1.671	2.000	2.390	2.660
120	0.677	1.289	1.658	1.980	2.358	2.617
∞	0.674	1.282	1.645	1.960	2.326	2.576

Table III of R. A. Fisher and F. Yates, *Statistical Tables for Biological, Agricultural and Medical Research*, 6th ed. London: Longman Group Ltd., 1974 (previously published by Oliver and Boyd Ltd., Edinburgh). Adapted and reprinted with permission of the Longman Group Ltd.

Handwritten notes:

Type I error: rejecting Ho when it is true
Type II error: fail to reject Ho that is false

$$z = \frac{\bar{x} - \mu}{\sigma}$$

$$SS = \Sigma x^2 - \frac{(\Sigma x)^2}{n}$$

formulas for practice probs. on t-tests

$$t = \frac{\bar{x} - \mu}{s/\sqrt{n}}$$

$$df = n - 1$$

tcrit - look at df & prop. in tails

α = prob. of rejecting Ho when it is correct

power = prob. of rejecting Ho when it is false

if sample size ↑es, tcrit ↓es

eq. #3, practice exam. Did course help?

$$n = 25, \bar{x} = 68, SS = 48600$$

$$s = \sqrt{\frac{SS}{n-1}} = \sqrt{\frac{48600}{24}} = \sqrt{2025} = 45$$

$$s/\sqrt{n} = 45/\sqrt{25} = 45/5 = 9$$

standard dev.

$$s^2 = \frac{SS}{n-1}$$ or

$$s = \sqrt{\frac{SS}{n-1}}$$

$$t = \frac{\bar{x} - \mu}{s/\sqrt{n}} = \frac{68-0}{9} = \frac{68}{9} = 7.56$$

Reject Ho

TABLE B.3 CRITICAL VALUES FOR THE *F*-MAX STATISTIC*

*The critical values for $\alpha = .05$ are in lightface type, and for $\alpha = .01$, they are in bold-face type.

$n-1$	\multicolumn{11}{c}{k = NUMBER OF SAMPLES}										
	2	3	4	5	6	7	8	9	10	11	12
4	9.60	15.5	20.6	25.2	29.5	33.6	37.5	41.4	44.6	48.0	51.4
	23.2	**37.**	**49.**	**59.**	**69.**	**79.**	**89.**	**97.**	**106.**	**113.**	**120.**
5	7.15	10.8	13.7	16.3	18.7	20.8	22.9	24.7	26.5	28.2	29.9
	14.9	**22.**	**28.**	**33.**	**38.**	**42.**	**46.**	**50.**	**54.**	**57.**	**60.**
6	5.82	8.38	10.4	12.1	13.7	15.0	16.3	17.5	18.6	19.7	20.7
	11.1	**15.5**	**19.1**	**22.**	**25.**	**27.**	**30.**	**32.**	**34.**	**36.**	**37.**
7	4.99	6.94	8.44	9.70	10.8	11.8	12.7	13.5	14.3	15.1	15.8
	8.89	**12.1**	**14.5**	**16.5**	**18.4**	**20.**	**22.**	**23.**	**24.**	**26.**	**27.**
8	4.43	6.00	7.18	8.12	9.03	9.78	10.5	11.1	11.7	12.2	12.7
	7.50	**9.9**	**11.7**	**13.2**	**14.5**	**15.8**	**16.9**	**17.9**	**18.9**	**19.8**	**21.**
9	4.03	5.34	6.31	7.11	7.80	8.41	8.95	9.45	9.91	10.3	10.7
	6.54	**8.5**	**9.9**	**11.1**	**12.1**	**13.1**	**13.9**	**14.7**	**15.3**	**16.0**	**16.6**
10	3.72	4.85	5.67	6.34	6.92	7.42	7.87	8.28	8.66	9.01	9.34
	5.85	**7.4**	**8.6**	**9.6**	**10.4**	**11.1**	**11.8**	**12.4**	**12.9**	**13.4**	**13.9**
12	3.28	4.16	4.79	5.30	5.72	6.09	6.42	6.72	7.00	7.25	7.48
	4.91	**6.1**	**6.9**	**7.6**	**8.2**	**8.7**	**9.1**	**9.5**	**9.9**	**10.2**	**10.6**
15	2.86	3.54	4.01	4.37	4.68	4.95	5.19	5.40	5.59	5.77	5.93
	4.07	**4.9**	**5.5**	**6.9**	**6.4**	**6.7**	**7.1**	**7.3**	**7.5**	**7.8**	**8.0**
20	2.46	2.95	3.29	3.54	3.76	3.94	4.10	4.24	4.37	4.49	4.59
	3.32	**3.8**	**4.3**	**4.6**	**4.9**	**5.1**	**5.3**	**5.5**	**5.6**	**5.8**	**5.9**
30	2.07	2.40	2.61	2.78	2.91	3.02	3.12	3.21	3.29	3.36	3.39
	2.63	**3.0**	**3.3**	**3.5**	**3.6**	**3.7**	**3.8**	**3.9**	**4.0**	**4.1**	**4.2**
60	1.67	1.85	1.96	2.04	2.11	2.17	2.22	2.26	2.30	2.33	2.36
	1.96	**2.2**	**2.3**	**2.4**	**2.4**	**2.5**	**2.5**	**2.6**	**2.6**	**2.7**	**2.7**

TABLE B.4   THE *F* DISTRIBUTION*

*Table entries in lightface type are critical values for the .05 level of significance. Bold-face type values are for the .01 level of significance.

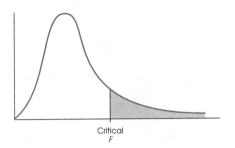

Critical
F

DEGREES OF FREEDOM: DENOMINATOR	DEGREES OF FREEDOM: NUMERATOR														
	1	2	3	4	5	6	7	8	9	10	11	12	14	16	20
1	161	200	216	225	230	234	237	239	241	242	243	244	245	246	248
	4052	**4999**	**5403**	**5625**	**5764**	**5859**	**5928**	**5981**	**6022**	**6056**	**6082**	**6106**	**6142**	**6169**	**6208**
2	18.51	19.00	19.16	19.25	19.30	19.33	19.36	19.37	19.38	19.39	19.40	19.41	19.42	19.43	19.44
	98.49	**99.00**	**99.17**	**99.25**	**99.30**	**99.33**	**99.34**	**99.36**	**99.38**	**99.40**	**99.41**	**99.42**	**99.43**	**99.44**	**99.45**
3	10.13	9.55	9.28	9.12	9.01	8.94	8.88	8.84	8.81	8.78	8.76	8.74	8.71	8.69	8.66
	34.12	**30.92**	**29.46**	**28.71**	**28.24**	**27.91**	**27.67**	**27.49**	**27.34**	**27.23**	**27.13**	**27.05**	**26.92**	**26.83**	**26.69**
4	7.71	6.94	6.59	6.39	6.26	6.16	6.09	6.04	6.00	5.96	5.93	5.91	5.87	5.84	5.80
	21.20	**18.00**	**16.69**	**15.98**	**15.52**	**15.21**	**14.98**	**14.80**	**14.66**	**14.54**	**14.45**	**14.37**	**14.24**	**14.15**	**14.02**
5	6.61	5.79	5.41	5.19	5.05	4.95	4.88	4.82	4.78	4.74	4.70	4.68	4.64	4.60	4.56
	16.26	**13.27**	**12.06**	**11.39**	**10.97**	**10.67**	**10.45**	**10.27**	**10.15**	**10.05**	**9.96**	**9.89**	**9.77**	**9.68**	**9.55**
6	5.99	5.14	4.76	4.53	4.39	4.28	4.21	4.15	4.10	4.06	4.03	4.00	3.96	3.92	3.87
	13.74	**10.92**	**9.78**	**9.15**	**8.75**	**8.47**	**8.26**	**8.10**	**7.98**	**7.87**	**7.79**	**7.72**	**7.60**	**7.52**	**7.39**
7	5.59	4.47	4.35	4.12	3.97	3.87	3.79	3.73	3.68	3.63	3.60	3.57	3.52	3.49	3.44
	12.25	**9.55**	**8.45**	**7.85**	**7.46**	**7.19**	**7.00**	**6.84**	**6.71**	**6.62**	**6.54**	**6.47**	**6.35**	**6.27**	**6.15**
8	5.32	4.46	4.07	3.84	3.69	3.58	3.50	3.44	3.39	3.34	3.31	3.28	3.23	3.20	3.15
	11.26	**8.65**	**7.59**	**7.01**	**6.63**	**6.37**	**6.19**	**6.03**	**5.91**	**5.82**	**5.74**	**5.67**	**5.56**	**5.48**	**5.36**
9	5.12	4.26	3.86	3.63	3.48	3.37	3.29	3.23	3.18	3.13	3.10	3.07	3.02	2.98	2.93
	10.56	**8.02**	**6.99**	**6.42**	**6.06**	**5.80**	**5.62**	**5.47**	**5.35**	**5.26**	**5.18**	**5.11**	**5.00**	**4.92**	**4.80**
10	4.96	4.10	3.71	3.48	3.33	3.22	3.14	3.07	3.02	2.97	2.94	2.91	2.86	2.82	2.77
	10.04	**7.56**	**6.55**	**5.99**	**5.64**	**5.39**	**5.21**	**5.06**	**4.95**	**4.85**	**4.78**	**4.71**	**4.60**	**4.52**	**4.41**
11	4.84	3.98	3.59	3.36	3.20	3.09	3.01	2.95	2.90	2.86	2.82	2.79	2.74	2.70	2.65
	9.65	**7.20**	**6.22**	**5.67**	**5.32**	**5.07**	**4.88**	**4.74**	**4.63**	**4.54**	**4.46**	**4.40**	**4.29**	**4.21**	**4.10**
12	4.75	3.88	3.49	3.26	3.11	3.00	2.92	2.85	2.80	2.76	2.72	2.69	2.64	2.60	2.54
	9.33	**6.93**	**5.95**	**5.41**	**5.06**	**4.82**	**4.65**	**4.50**	**4.39**	**4.30**	**4.22**	**4.16**	**4.05**	**3.98**	**3.86**
13	4.67	3.80	3.41	3.18	3.02	2.92	2.84	2.77	2.72	2.67	2.63	2.60	2.55	2.51	2.46
	9.07	**6.70**	**5.74**	**5.20**	**4.86**	**4.62**	**4.44**	**4.30**	**4.19**	**4.10**	**4.02**	**3.96**	**3.85**	**3.78**	**3.67**
14	4.60	3.74	3.34	3.11	2.96	2.85	2.77	2.70	2.65	2.60	2.56	2.53	2.48	2.44	2.39
	8.86	**6.51**	**5.56**	**5.03**	**4.69**	**4.46**	**4.28**	**4.14**	**4.03**	**3.94**	**3.86**	**3.80**	**3.70**	**3.62**	**3.51**
15	4.54	3.68	3.29	3.06	2.90	2.79	2.70	2.64	2.59	2.55	2.51	2.48	2.43	2.39	2.33
	8.68	**6.36**	**5.42**	**4.89**	**4.56**	**4.32**	**4.14**	**4.00**	**3.89**	**3.80**	**3.73**	**3.67**	**3.56**	**3.48**	**3.36**
16	4.49	3.63	3.24	3.01	2.85	2.74	2.66	2.59	2.54	2.49	2.45	2.42	2.37	2.33	2.28
	8.53	**6.23**	**5.29**	**4.77**	**4.44**	**4.20**	**4.03**	**3.89**	**3.78**	**3.69**	**3.61**	**3.55**	**3.45**	**3.37**	**3.25**

TABLE B.4   continued

DEGREES OF FREEDOM: DENOMINATOR	DEGREES OF FREEDOM: NUMERATOR														
	1	2	3	4	5	6	7	8	9	10	11	12	14	16	20
17	4.45	3.59	3.20	2.96	2.81	2.70	2.62	2.55	2.50	2.45	2.41	2.38	2.33	2.29	2.23
	8.40	**6.11**	**5.18**	**4.67**	**4.34**	**4.10**	**3.93**	**3.79**	**3.68**	**3.59**	**3.52**	**3.45**	**3.35**	**3.27**	**3.16**
18	4.41	3.55	3.16	2.93	2.77	2.66	2.58	2.51	2.46	2.41	2.37	2.34	2.29	2.25	2.19
	8.28	**6.01**	**5.09**	**4.58**	**4.25**	**4.01**	**3.85**	**3.71**	**3.60**	**3.51**	**3.44**	**3.37**	**3.27**	**3.19**	**3.07**
19	4.38	3.52	3.13	2.90	2.74	2.63	2.55	2.48	2.43	2.38	2.34	2.31	2.26	2.21	2.15
	8.18	**5.93**	**5.01**	**4.50**	**4.17**	**3.94**	**3.77**	**3.63**	**3.52**	**3.43**	**3.36**	**3.30**	**3.19**	**3.12**	**3.00**
20	4.35	3.49	3.10	2.87	2.71	2.60	2.52	2.45	2.40	2.35	2.31	2.28	2.23	2.18	2.12
	8.10	**5.85**	**4.94**	**4.43**	**4.10**	**3.87**	**3.71**	**3.56**	**3.45**	**3.37**	**3.30**	**3.23**	**3.13**	**3.05**	**2.94**
21	4.32	3.47	3.07	2.84	2.68	2.57	2.49	2.42	2.37	2.32	2.28	2.25	2.20	2.15	2.09
	8.02	**5.78**	**4.87**	**4.37**	**4.04**	**3.81**	**3.65**	**3.51**	**3.40**	**3.31**	**3.24**	**3.17**	**3.07**	**2.99**	**2.88**
22	4.30	3.44	3.05	2.82	2.66	2.55	2.47	2.40	2.35	2.30	2.26	2.23	2.18	2.13	2.07
	7.94	**5.72**	**4.82**	**4.31**	**3.99**	**3.76**	**3.59**	**3.45**	**3.35**	**3.26**	**3.18**	**3.12**	**3.02**	**2.94**	**2.83**
23	4.28	3.42	3.03	2.80	2.64	2.53	2.45	2.38	2.32	2.28	2.24	2.20	2.14	2.10	2.04
	7.88	**5.66**	**4.76**	**4.26**	**3.94**	**3.71**	**3.54**	**3.41**	**3.30**	**3.21**	**3.14**	**3.07**	**2.97**	**2.89**	**2.78**
24	4.26	3.40	3.01	2.78	2.62	2.51	2.43	2.36	2.30	2.26	2.22	2.18	2.13	2.09	2.02
	7.82	**5.61**	**4.72**	**4.22**	**3.90**	**3.67**	**3.50**	**3.36**	**3.25**	**3.17**	**3.09**	**3.03**	**2.93**	**2.85**	**2.74**
25	4.24	3.38	2.99	2.76	2.60	2.49	2.41	2.34	2.28	2.24	2.20	2.16	2.11	2.06	2.00
	7.77	**5.57**	**4.68**	**4.18**	**3.86**	**3.63**	**3.46**	**3.32**	**3.21**	**3.13**	**3.05**	**2.99**	**2.89**	**2.81**	**2.70**
26	4.22	3.37	2.98	2.74	2.59	2.47	2.39	2.32	2.27	2.22	2.18	2.15	2.10	2.05	1.99
	7.72	**5.53**	**4.64**	**4.14**	**3.82**	**3.59**	**3.42**	**3.29**	**3.17**	**3.09**	**3.02**	**2.96**	**2.86**	**2.77**	**2.66**
27	4.21	3.35	2.96	2.73	2.57	2.46	2.37	2.30	2.25	2.20	2.16	2.13	2.08	2.03	1.97
	7.68	**5.49**	**4.60**	**4.11**	**3.79**	**3.56**	**3.39**	**3.26**	**3.14**	**3.06**	**2.98**	**2.93**	**2.83**	**2.74**	**2.63**
28	4.20	3.34	2.95	2.71	2.56	2.44	2.36	2.29	2.24	2.19	2.15	2.12	2.06	2.02	1.96
	7.64	**5.45**	**4.57**	**4.07**	**3.76**	**3.53**	**3.36**	**3.23**	**3.11**	**3.03**	**2.95**	**2.90**	**2.80**	**2.71**	**2.60**
29	4.18	3.33	2.93	2.70	2.54	2.43	2.35	2.28	2.22	2.18	2.14	2.10	2.05	2.00	1.94
	7.60	**5.42**	**4.54**	**4.04**	**3.73**	**3.50**	**3.33**	**3.20**	**3.08**	**3.00**	**2.92**	**2.87**	**2.77**	**2.68**	**2.57**
30	4.17	3.32	2.92	2.69	2.53	2.42	2.34	2.27	2.21	2.16	2.12	2.09	2.04	1.99	1.93
	7.56	**5.39**	**4.51**	**4.02**	**3.70**	**3.47**	**3.30**	**3.17**	**3.06**	**2.98**	**2.90**	**2.84**	**2.74**	**2.66**	**2.55**
32	4.15	3.30	2.90	2.67	2.51	2.40	2.32	2.25	2.19	2.14	2.10	2.07	2.02	1.97	1.91
	7.50	**5.34**	**4.46**	**3.97**	**3.66**	**3.42**	**3.25**	**3.12**	**3.01**	**2.94**	**2.86**	**2.80**	**2.70**	**2.62**	**2.51**
34	4.13	3.28	2.88	2.65	2.49	2.38	2.30	2.23	2.17	2.12	2.08	2.05	2.00	1.95	1.89
	7.44	**5.29**	**4.42**	**3.93**	**3.61**	**3.38**	**3.21**	**3.08**	**2.97**	**2.89**	**2.82**	**2.76**	**2.66**	**2.58**	**2.47**
36	4.11	3.26	2.86	2.63	2.48	2.36	2.28	2.21	2.15	2.10	2.06	2.03	1.98	1.93	1.87
	7.39	**5.25**	**4.38**	**3.89**	**3.58**	**3.35**	**3.18**	**3.04**	**2.94**	**2.86**	**2.78**	**2.72**	**2.62**	**2.54**	**2.43**
38	4.10	3.25	2.85	2.62	2.46	2.35	2.26	2.19	2.14	2.09	2.05	2.02	1.96	1.92	1.85
	7.35	**5.21**	**4.34**	**3.86**	**3.54**	**3.32**	**3.15**	**3.02**	**2.91**	**2.82**	**2.75**	**2.69**	**2.59**	**2.51**	**2.40**
40	4.08	3.23	2.84	2.61	2.45	2.34	2.25	2.18	2.12	2.07	2.04	2.00	1.95	1.90	1.84
	7.31	**5.18**	**4.31**	**3.83**	**3.51**	**3.29**	**3.12**	**2.99**	**2.88**	**2.80**	**2.73**	**2.66**	**2.56**	**2.49**	**2.37**
42	4.07	3.22	2.83	2.59	2.44	2.32	2.24	2.17	2.11	2.06	2.02	1.99	1.94	1.89	1.82
	7.27	**5.15**	**4.29**	**3.80**	**3.49**	**3.26**	**3.10**	**2.96**	**2.86**	**2.77**	**2.70**	**2.64**	**2.54**	**2.46**	**2.35**
44	4.06	3.21	2.82	2.58	2.43	2.31	2.23	2.16	2.10	2.05	2.01	1.98	1.92	1.88	1.81
	7.24	**5.12**	**4.26**	**3.78**	**3.46**	**3.24**	**3.07**	**2.94**	**2.84**	**2.75**	**2.68**	**2.62**	**2.52**	**2.44**	**2.32**
46	4.05	3.20	2.81	2.57	2.42	2.30	2.22	2.14	2.09	2.04	2.00	1.97	1.91	1.87	1.80
	7.21	**5.10**	**4.24**	**3.76**	**3.44**	**3.22**	**3.05**	**2.92**	**2.82**	**2.73**	**2.66**	**2.60**	**2.50**	**2.42**	**2.30**
48	4.04	3.19	2.80	2.56	2.41	2.30	2.21	2.14	2.08	2.03	1.99	1.96	1.90	1.86	1.79
	7.19	**5.08**	**4.22**	**3.74**	**3.42**	**3.20**	**3.04**	**2.90**	**2.80**	**2.71**	**2.64**	**2.58**	**2.48**	**2.40**	**2.28**

TABLE B.4   continued

DEGREES OF FREEDOM: DENOMINATOR	DEGREES OF FREEDOM: NUMERATOR														
	1	2	3	4	5	6	7	8	9	10	11	12	14	16	20
50	4.03	3.18	2.79	2.56	2.40	2.29	2.20	2.13	2.07	2.02	1.98	1.95	1.90	1.85	1.78
	7.17	**5.06**	**4.20**	**3.72**	**3.41**	**3.18**	**3.02**	**2.88**	**2.78**	**2.70**	**2.62**	**2.56**	**2.46**	**2.39**	**2.26**
55	4.02	3.17	2.78	2.54	2.38	2.27	2.18	2.11	2.05	2.00	1.97	1.93	1.88	1.83	1.76
	7.12	**5.01**	**4.16**	**3.68**	**3.37**	**3.15**	**2.98**	**2.85**	**2.75**	**2.66**	**2.59**	**2.53**	**2.43**	**2.35**	**2.23**
60	4.00	3.15	2.76	2.52	2.37	2.25	2.17	2.10	2.04	1.99	1.95	1.92	1.86	1.81	1.75
	7.08	**4.98**	**4.13**	**3.65**	**3.34**	**3.12**	**2.95**	**2.82**	**2.72**	**2.63**	**2.56**	**2.50**	**2.40**	**2.32**	**2.20**
65	3.99	3.14	2.75	2.51	2.36	2.24	2.15	2.08	2.02	1.98	1.94	1.90	1.85	1.80	1.73
	7.04	**4.95**	**4.10**	**3.62**	**3.31**	**3.09**	**2.93**	**2.79**	**2.70**	**2.61**	**2.54**	**2.47**	**2.37**	**2.30**	**2.18**
70	3.98	3.13	2.74	2.50	2.35	2.23	2.14	2.07	2.01	1.97	1.93	1.89	1.84	1.79	1.72
	7.01	**4.92**	**4.08**	**3.60**	**3.29**	**3.07**	**2.91**	**2.77**	**2.67**	**2.59**	**2.51**	**2.45**	**2.35**	**2.28**	**2.15**
80	3.96	3.11	2.72	2.48	2.33	2.21	2.12	2.05	1.99	1.95	1.91	1.88	1.82	1.77	1.70
	6.96	**4.88**	**4.04**	**3.56**	**3.25**	**3.04**	**2.87**	**2.74**	**2.64**	**2.55**	**2.48**	**2.41**	**2.32**	**2.24**	**2.11**
100	3.94	3.09	2.70	2.46	2.30	2.19	2.10	2.03	1.97	1.92	1.88	1.85	1.79	1.75	1.68
	6.90	**4.92**	**3.98**	**3.51**	**3.20**	**2.99**	**2.82**	**2.69**	**2.59**	**2.51**	**2.43**	**2.36**	**2.26**	**2.19**	**2.06**
125	3.92	3.07	2.68	2.44	2.29	2.17	2.08	2.01	1.95	1.90	1.86	1.83	1.77	1.72	1.65
	6.84	**4.78**	**3.94**	**3.47**	**3.17**	**2.95**	**2.79**	**2.65**	**2.56**	**2.47**	**2.40**	**2.33**	**2.23**	**2.15**	**2.03**
150	3.91	3.06	2.67	2.43	2.27	2.16	2.07	2.00	1.94	1.89	1.85	1.82	1.76	1.71	1.64
	6.81	**4.75**	**3.91**	**3.44**	**3.14**	**2.92**	**2.76**	**2.62**	**2.53**	**2.44**	**2.37**	**2.30**	**2.20**	**2.12**	**2.00**
200	3.89	3.04	2.65	2.41	2.26	2.14	2.05	1.98	1.92	1.87	1.83	1.80	1.74	1.69	1.62
	6.76	**4.71**	**3.88**	**3.41**	**3.11**	**2.90**	**2.73**	**2.60**	**2.50**	**2.41**	**2.34**	**2.28**	**2.17**	**2.09**	**1.97**
400	3.86	3.02	2.62	2.39	2.23	2.12	2.03	1.96	1.90	1.85	1.81	1.78	1.72	1.67	1.60
	6.70	**4.66**	**3.83**	**3.36**	**3.06**	**2.85**	**2.69**	**2.55**	**2.46**	**2.37**	**2.29**	**2.23**	**2.12**	**2.04**	**1.92**
1000	3.85	3.00	2.61	2.38	2.22	2.10	2.02	1.95	1.89	1.84	1.80	1.76	1.70	1.65	1.58
	6.66	**4.62**	**3.80**	**3.34**	**3.04**	**2.82**	**2.66**	**2.53**	**2.43**	**2.34**	**2.26**	**2.20**	**2.09**	**2.01**	**1.89**
∞	3.84	2.99	2.60	2.37	2.21	2.09	2.01	1.94	1.88	1.83	1.79	1.75	1.69	1.64	1.57
	6.64	**4.60**	**3.78**	**3.32**	**3.02**	**2.80**	**2.64**	**2.51**	**2.41**	**2.32**	**2.24**	**2.18**	**2.07**	**1.99**	**1.87**

TABLE B.5   THE STUDENTIZED RANGE STATISTIC (q)*

*The critical values for q corresponding to $\alpha = .05$ (lightface type) and $\alpha = .01$ (bold-face type).

df FOR ERROR TERM	k = NUMBER OF TREATMENTS										
	2	3	4	5	6	7	8	9	10	11	12
5	3.64	4.60	5.22	5.67	6.03	6.33	6.58	6.80	6.99	7.17	7.32
	5.70	**6.98**	**7.80**	**8.42**	**8.91**	**9.32**	**9.67**	**9.97**	**10.24**	**10.48**	**10.70**
6	3.46	4.34	4.90	5.30	5.63	5.90	6.12	6.32	6.49	6.65	6.79
	5.24	**6.33**	**7.03**	**7.56**	**7.97**	**8.32**	**8.61**	**8.87**	**9.10**	**9.30**	**9.48**
7	3.34	4.16	4.68	5.06	5.36	5.61	5.82	6.00	6.16	6.30	6.43
	4.95	**5.92**	**6.54**	**7.01**	**7.37**	**7.68**	**7.94**	**8.17**	**8.37**	**8.55**	**8.71**
8	3.26	4.04	4.53	4.89	5.17	5.40	5.60	5.77	5.92	6.05	6.18
	4.75	**5.64**	**6.20**	**6.62**	**6.96**	**7.24**	**7.47**	**7.68**	**7.86**	**8.03**	**8.18**
9	3.20	3.95	4.41	4.76	5.02	5.24	5.43	5.59	5.74	5.87	5.98
	4.60	**5.43**	**5.96**	**6.35**	**6.66**	**6.91**	**7.13**	**7.33**	**7.49**	**7.65**	**7.78**
10	3.15	3.88	4.33	4.65	4.91	5.12	5.30	5.46	5.60	5.72	5.83
	4.48	**5.27**	**5.77**	**6.14**	**6.43**	**6.67**	**6.87**	**7.05**	**7.21**	**7.36**	**7.49**
11	3.11	3.82	4.26	4.57	4.82	5.03	5.20	5.35	5.49	5.61	5.71
	4.39	**5.15**	**5.62**	**5.97**	**6.25**	**6.48**	**6.67**	**6.84**	**6.99**	**7.13**	**7.25**
12	3.08	3.77	4.20	4.51	4.75	4.95	5.12	5.27	5.39	5.51	5.61
	4.32	**5.05**	**5.50**	**5.84**	**6.10**	**6.32**	**6.51**	**6.67**	**6.81**	**6.94**	**7.06**
13	3.06	3.73	4.15	4.45	4.69	4.88	5.05	5.19	5.32	5.43	5.53
	4.26	**4.96**	**5.40**	**5.73**	**5.98**	**6.19**	**6.37**	**6.53**	**6.67**	**6.79**	**6.90**
14	3.03	3.70	4.11	4.41	4.64	4.83	4.99	5.13	5.25	5.36	5.46
	4.21	**4.89**	**5.32**	**5.63**	**5.88**	**6.08**	**6.26**	**6.41**	**6.54**	**6.66**	**6.77**
15	3.01	3.67	4.08	4.37	4.59	4.78	4.94	5.08	5.20	5.31	5.40
	4.17	**4.84**	**5.25**	**5.56**	**5.80**	**5.99**	**6.16**	**6.31**	**6.44**	**6.55**	**6.66**
16	3.00	3.65	4.05	4.33	4.56	4.74	4.90	5.03	5.15	5.26	5.35
	4.13	**4.79**	**5.19**	**5.49**	**5.72**	**5.92**	**6.08**	**6.22**	**6.35**	**6.46**	**6.56**
17	2.98	3.63	4.02	4.30	4.52	4.70	4.86	4.99	5.11	5.21	5.31
	4.10	**4.74**	**5.14**	**5.43**	**5.66**	**5.85**	**6.01**	**6.15**	**6.27**	**6.38**	**6.48**
18	2.97	3.61	4.00	4.28	4.49	4.67	4.82	4.96	5.07	5.17	5.27
	4.07	**4.70**	**5.09**	**5.38**	**5.60**	**5.79**	**5.94**	**6.08**	**6.20**	**6.31**	**6.41**
19	2.96	3.59	3.98	4.25	4.47	4.65	4.79	4.92	5.04	5.14	5.23
	4.05	**4.67**	**5.05**	**5.33**	**5.55**	**5.73**	**5.89**	**6.02**	**6.14**	**6.25**	**6.34**
20	2.95	3.58	3.96	4.23	4.45	4.62	4.77	4.90	5.01	5.11	5.20
	4.02	**4.64**	**5.02**	**5.29**	**5.51**	**5.69**	**5.84**	**5.97**	**6.09**	**6.19**	**6.28**
24	2.92	3.53	3.90	4.17	4.37	4.54	4.68	4.81	4.92	5.01	5.10
	3.96	**4.55**	**4.91**	**5.17**	**5.37**	**5.54**	**5.69**	**5.81**	**5.92**	**6.02**	**6.11**
30	2.89	3.49	3.85	4.10	4.30	4.46	4.60	4.72	4.82	4.92	5.00
	3.89	**4.45**	**4.80**	**5.05**	**5.24**	**5.40**	**5.54**	**5.65**	**5.76**	**5.85**	**5.93**
40	2.86	3.44	3.79	4.04	4.23	4.39	4.52	4.63	4.73	4.82	4.90
	3.82	**4.37**	**4.70**	**4.93**	**5.11**	**5.26**	**5.39**	**5.50**	**5.60**	**5.69**	**5.76**
60	2.83	3.40	3.74	3.98	4.16	4.31	4.44	4.55	4.65	4.73	4.81
	3.76	**4.28**	**4.59**	**4.82**	**4.99**	**5.13**	**5.25**	**5.36**	**5.45**	**5.53**	**5.60**
120	2.80	3.36	3.68	3.92	4.10	4.24	4.36	4.47	4.56	4.64	4.71
	3.70	**4.20**	**4.50**	**4.71**	**4.87**	**5.01**	**5.12**	**5.21**	**5.30**	**5.37**	**5.44**
∞	2.77	3.31	3.63	3.86	4.03	4.17	4.28	4.39	4.47	4.55	4.62
	3.64	**4.12**	**4.40**	**4.60**	**4.76**	**4.88**	**4.99**	**5.08**	**5.16**	**5.23**	**5.29**

TABLE B.6   CRITICAL VALUES FOR THE PEARSON CORRELATION*

*To be significant, the sample correlation, r, must be greater than or equal to the critical value in the table.

df = n − 2	LEVEL OF SIGNIFICANCE FOR ONE-TAILED TEST			
	.05	0.25	.01	.005
	LEVEL OF SIGNIFICANCE FOR TWO-TAILED TEST			
	.10	.05	.02	.01
1	.988	.997	.9995	.9999
2	.900	.950	.980	.990
3	.805	.878	.934	.959
4	.729	.811	.882	.917
5	.669	.754	.833	.874
6	.622	.707	.789	.834
7	.582	.666	.750	.798
8	.549	.632	.716	.765
9	.521	.602	.685	.735
10	.497	.576	.658	.708
11	.476	.553	.634	.684
12	.458	.532	.612	.661
13	.441	.514	.592	.641
14	.426	.497	.574	.623
15	.412	.482	.558	.606
16	.400	.468	.542	.590
17	.389	.456	.528	.575
18	.378	.444	.516	.561
19	.369	.433	.503	.549
20	.360	.423	.492	.537
21	.352	.413	.482	.526
22	.344	.404	.472	.515
23	.337	.396	.462	.505
24	.330	.388	.453	.496
25	.323	.381	.445	.487
26	.317	.374	.437	.479
27	.311	.367	.430	.471
28	.306	.361	.423	.463
29	.301	.355	.416	.456
30	.296	.349	.409	.449
35	.275	.325	.381	.418
40	.257	.304	.358	.393
45	.243	.288	.338	.372
50	.231	.273	.322	.354
60	.211	.250	.295	.325
70	.195	.232	.274	.302
80	.183	.217	.256	.283
90	.173	.205	.242	.267
100	.164	.195	.230	.254

Table VI of R. A. Fisher and F. Yates, *Statistical Tables for Biological, Agricultural and Medical Research,* 6th ed. London: Longman Group Ltd., 1974 (previously published by Oliver and Boyd Ltd., Edinburgh). Adapted and reprinted with permission of the Longman Group Ltd.

TABLE B.7   THE CHI-SQUARE DISTRIBUTION*

*The table entries are critical values of χ^2.

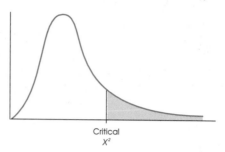

Critical
X^2

df	PROPORTION IN CRITICAL REGION				
	0.10	0.05	0.025	0.01	0.005
1	2.71	3.84	5.02	6.63	7.88
2	4.61	5.99	7.38	9.21	10.60
3	6.25	7.81	9.35	11.34	12.84
4	7.78	9.49	11.14	13.28	14.86
5	9.24	11.07	12.83	15.09	16.75
6	10.64	12.59	14.45	16.81	18.55
7	12.02	14.07	16.01	18.48	20.28
8	13.36	15.51	17.53	20.09	21.96
9	14.68	16.92	19.02	21.67	23.59
10	15.99	18.31	20.48	23.21	25.19
11	17.28	19.68	21.92	24.72	26.76
12	18.55	21.03	23.34	26.22	28.30
13	19.81	22.36	24.74	27.69	29.82
14	21.06	23.68	26.12	29.14	31.32
15	22.31	25.00	27.49	30.58	32.80
16	23.54	26.30	28.85	32.00	34.27
17	24.77	27.59	30.19	33.41	35.72
18	25.99	28.87	31.53	34.81	37.16
19	27.20	30.14	32.85	36.19	38.58
20	28.41	31.41	34.17	37.57	40.00
21	29.62	32.67	35.48	38.93	41.40
22	30.81	33.92	36.78	40.29	42.80
23	32.01	35.17	38.08	41.64	44.18
24	33.20	36.42	39.36	42.98	45.56
25	34.38	37.65	40.65	44.31	46.93
26	35.56	38.89	41.92	45.64	48.29
27	36.74	40.11	43.19	46.96	49.64
28	37.92	41.34	44.46	48.28	50.99
29	39.09	42.56	45.72	49.59	52.34
30	40.26	43.77	46.98	50.89	53.67
40	51.81	55.76	59.34	63.69	66.77
50	63.17	67.50	71.42	76.15	79.49
60	74.40	79.08	83.30	88.38	91.95
70	85.53	90.53	95.02	100.42	104.22
80	96.58	101.88	106.63	112.33	116.32
90	107.56	113.14	118.14	124.12	128.30
100	118.50	124.34	129.56	135.81	140.17

TABLE B.8A CRITICAL VALUES OF THE MANN-WHITNEY U FOR $\alpha = .05$*

*Critical values are provided for a *one-tailed* test at $\alpha = .05$ (lightface type) and for a *two-tailed* test at $\alpha = .05$ (boldface type). To be significant for any given n_A and n_B, the obtained U must be *equal to* or *less than* the critical value in the table. Dashes (—) in the body of the table indicate that no decision is possible at the stated level of significance and values of n_A and n_B.

n_B \ n_A	1	2	3	4	5	6	7	8	9	10	11	12	13	14	15	16	17	18	19	20
1	—	—	—	—	—	—	—	—	—	—	—	—	—	—	—	—	—	—	0	0
	—	—	—	—	—	—	—	—	—	—	—	—	—	—	—	—	—	—	—	—
2	—	—	—	—	0	0	0	1	1	1	1	2	2	2	3	3	3	4	4	4
	—	—	—	—	—	—	—	**0**	**0**	**0**	**0**	**1**	**1**	**1**	**1**	**1**	**2**	**2**	**2**	**2**
3	—	—	0	0	1	2	2	3	3	4	5	5	6	7	7	8	9	9	10	11
	—	—	—	—	**0**	**1**	**1**	**2**	**2**	**3**	**3**	**4**	**4**	**5**	**5**	**6**	**6**	**7**	**7**	**8**
4	—	—	0	1	2	3	4	5	6	7	8	9	10	11	12	14	15	16	17	18
	—	—	—	**0**	**1**	**2**	**3**	**4**	**4**	**5**	**6**	**7**	**8**	**9**	**10**	**11**	**11**	**12**	**13**	**13**
5	—	0	1	2	4	5	6	8	9	11	12	13	15	16	18	19	20	22	23	25
	—	—	**0**	**1**	**2**	**3**	**5**	**6**	**7**	**8**	**9**	**11**	**12**	**13**	**14**	**15**	**17**	**18**	**19**	**20**
6	—	0	2	3	5	7	8	10	12	14	16	17	19	21	23	25	26	28	30	32
	—	—	**1**	**2**	**3**	**5**	**6**	**8**	**10**	**11**	**13**	**14**	**16**	**17**	**19**	**21**	**22**	**24**	**25**	**27**
7	—	0	2	4	6	8	11	13	15	17	19	21	24	26	28	30	33	35	37	39
	—	—	**1**	**3**	**5**	**6**	**8**	**10**	**12**	**14**	**16**	**18**	**20**	**22**	**24**	**26**	**28**	**30**	**32**	**34**
8	—	1	3	5	8	10	13	15	18	20	23	26	28	31	33	36	39	41	44	47
	—	**0**	**2**	**4**	**6**	**8**	**10**	**13**	**15**	**17**	**19**	**22**	**24**	**26**	**29**	**31**	**34**	**36**	**38**	**41**
9	—	1	3	6	9	12	15	18	21	24	27	30	33	36	39	42	45	48	51	54
	—	**0**	**2**	**4**	**7**	**10**	**12**	**15**	**17**	**20**	**23**	**26**	**28**	**31**	**34**	**37**	**39**	**42**	**45**	**48**
10	—	1	4	7	11	14	17	20	24	27	31	34	37	41	44	48	51	55	58	62
	—	**0**	**3**	**5**	**8**	**11**	**14**	**17**	**20**	**23**	**26**	**29**	**33**	**36**	**39**	**42**	**45**	**48**	**52**	**55**
11	—	1	5	8	12	16	19	23	27	31	34	38	42	46	50	54	57	61	65	69
	—	**0**	**3**	**6**	**9**	**13**	**16**	**19**	**23**	**26**	**30**	**33**	**37**	**40**	**44**	**47**	**51**	**55**	**58**	**62**
12	—	2	5	9	13	17	21	26	30	34	38	42	47	51	55	60	64	68	72	77
	—	**1**	**4**	**7**	**11**	**14**	**18**	**22**	**26**	**29**	**33**	**37**	**41**	**45**	**49**	**53**	**57**	**61**	**65**	**69**
13	—	2	6	10	15	19	24	28	33	37	42	47	51	56	61	65	70	75	80	84
	—	**1**	**4**	**8**	**12**	**16**	**20**	**24**	**28**	**33**	**37**	**41**	**45**	**50**	**54**	**59**	**63**	**67**	**72**	**76**
14	—	2	7	11	16	21	26	31	36	41	46	51	56	61	66	71	77	82	87	92
	—	**1**	**5**	**9**	**13**	**17**	**22**	**26**	**31**	**36**	**40**	**45**	**50**	**55**	**59**	**64**	**67**	**74**	**78**	**83**
15	—	3	7	12	18	23	28	33	39	44	50	55	61	66	72	77	83	88	94	100
	—	**1**	**5**	**10**	**14**	**19**	**24**	**29**	**34**	**39**	**44**	**49**	**54**	**59**	**64**	**70**	**75**	**80**	**85**	**90**
16	—	3	8	14	19	25	30	36	42	48	54	60	65	71	77	83	89	95	101	107
	—	**1**	**6**	**11**	**15**	**21**	**26**	**31**	**37**	**42**	**47**	**53**	**59**	**64**	**70**	**75**	**81**	**86**	**92**	**98**
17	—	3	9	15	20	26	33	39	45	51	57	64	70	77	83	89	96	102	109	115
	—	**2**	**6**	**11**	**17**	**22**	**28**	**34**	**39**	**45**	**51**	**57**	**63**	**67**	**75**	**81**	**87**	**93**	**99**	**105**
18	—	4	9	16	22	28	35	41	48	55	61	68	75	82	88	95	102	109	116	123
	—	**2**	**7**	**12**	**18**	**24**	**30**	**36**	**42**	**48**	**55**	**61**	**67**	**74**	**80**	**86**	**93**	**99**	**106**	**112**
19	0	4	10	17	23	30	37	44	51	58	65	72	80	87	94	101	109	116	123	130
	—	**2**	**7**	**13**	**19**	**25**	**32**	**38**	**45**	**52**	**58**	**65**	**72**	**78**	**85**	**92**	**99**	**106**	**113**	**119**
20	0	4	11	18	25	32	39	47	54	62	69	77	84	92	100	107	115	123	130	138
	—	**2**	**8**	**13**	**20**	**27**	**34**	**41**	**48**	**55**	**62**	**69**	**76**	**83**	**90**	**98**	**105**	**112**	**119**	**127**

TABLE B.8B   CRITICAL VALUES OF THE MANN-WHITNEY *U* FOR α = .05*

*Critical values are provided for a *one-tailed* test at α = .01 (lightface type) and for a *two-tailed* test at α = .01 (boldface type). To be significant for any given n_A and n_B, the obtained *U* must be *equal to* or *less than* the critical value in the table. Dashes (—) in the body of the table indicate that no decision is possible at the stated level of significance and values of n_A and n_B.

n_B \ n_A	1	2	3	4	5	6	7	8	9	10	11	12	13	14	15	16	17	18	19	20
1	—	—	—	—	—	—	—	—	—	—	—	—	—	—	—	—	—	—	—	—
2	—	—	—	—	—	—	—	—	—	—	—	—	0	0	0	0	0	0	1	1
	—	—	—	—	—	—	—	—	—	—	—	—	—	—	—	—	—	—	**0**	**0**
3	—	—	—	—	—	—	0	0	1	1	1	2	2	2	3	3	4	4	4	5
	—	—	—	—	—	—	—	—	**0**	**0**	**0**	**1**	**1**	**1**	**2**	**2**	**2**	**2**	**3**	**3**
4	—	—	—	—	0	1	1	2	3	3	4	5	5	6	7	7	8	9	9	10
	—	—	—	—	—	**0**	**0**	**1**	**1**	**2**	**2**	**3**	**3**	**4**	**5**	**5**	**6**	**6**	**7**	**8**
5	—	—	—	0	1	2	3	4	5	6	7	8	9	10	11	12	13	14	15	16
	—	—	—	—	**0**	**1**	**1**	**2**	**3**	**4**	**5**	**6**	**7**	**7**	**8**	**9**	**10**	**11**	**12**	**13**
6	—	—	—	1	2	3	4	6	7	8	9	11	12	13	15	16	18	19	20	22
	—	—	—	**0**	**1**	**2**	**3**	**4**	**5**	**6**	**7**	**9**	**10**	**11**	**12**	**13**	**15**	**16**	**17**	**18**
7	—	—	0	1	3	4	6	7	9	11	12	14	16	17	19	21	23	24	26	28
	—	—	—	**0**	**1**	**3**	**4**	**6**	**7**	**9**	**10**	**12**	**13**	**15**	**16**	**18**	**19**	**21**	**22**	**24**
8	—	—	0	2	4	6	7	9	11	13	15	17	20	22	24	26	28	30	32	34
	—	—	—	**1**	**2**	**4**	**6**	**7**	**9**	**11**	**13**	**15**	**17**	**18**	**20**	**22**	**24**	**26**	**28**	**30**
9	—	—	1	3	5	7	9	11	14	16	18	21	23	26	28	31	33	36	38	40
	—	—	**0**	**1**	**3**	**5**	**7**	**9**	**11**	**13**	**16**	**18**	**20**	**22**	**24**	**27**	**29**	**31**	**33**	**36**
10	—	—	1	3	6	8	11	13	16	19	22	24	27	30	33	36	38	41	44	47
	—	—	**0**	**2**	**4**	**6**	**9**	**11**	**13**	**16**	**18**	**21**	**24**	**26**	**29**	**31**	**34**	**37**	**39**	**42**
11	—	—	1	4	7	9	12	15	18	22	25	28	31	34	37	41	44	47	50	53
	—	—	**0**	**2**	**5**	**7**	**10**	**13**	**16**	**18**	**21**	**24**	**27**	**30**	**33**	**36**	**39**	**42**	**45**	**48**
12	—	—	2	5	8	11	14	17	21	24	28	31	35	38	42	46	49	53	56	60
	—	—	**1**	**3**	**6**	**9**	**12**	**15**	**18**	**21**	**24**	**27**	**31**	**34**	**37**	**41**	**44**	**47**	**51**	**54**
13	—	0	2	5	9	12	16	20	23	27	31	35	39	43	47	51	55	59	63	67
	—	—	**1**	**3**	**7**	**10**	**13**	**17**	**20**	**24**	**27**	**31**	**34**	**38**	**42**	**45**	**49**	**53**	**56**	**60**
14	—	0	2	6	10	13	17	22	26	30	34	38	43	47	51	56	60	65	69	73
	—	—	**1**	**4**	**7**	**11**	**15**	**18**	**22**	**26**	**30**	**34**	**38**	**42**	**46**	**50**	**54**	**58**	**63**	**67**
15	—	0	3	7	11	15	19	24	28	33	37	42	47	51	56	61	66	70	75	80
	—	—	**2**	**5**	**8**	**12**	**16**	**20**	**24**	**29**	**33**	**37**	**42**	**46**	**51**	**55**	**60**	**64**	**69**	**73**
16	—	0	3	7	12	16	21	26	31	36	41	46	51	56	61	66	71	76	82	87
	—	—	**2**	**5**	**9**	**13**	**18**	**22**	**27**	**31**	**36**	**41**	**45**	**50**	**55**	**60**	**65**	**70**	**74**	**79**
17	—	0	4	8	13	18	23	28	33	38	44	49	55	60	66	71	77	82	88	93
	—	—	**2**	**6**	**10**	**15**	**19**	**24**	**29**	**34**	**39**	**44**	**49**	**54**	**60**	**65**	**70**	**75**	**81**	**86**
18	—	0	4	9	14	19	24	30	36	41	47	53	59	65	70	76	82	88	94	100
	—	—	**2**	**6**	**11**	**16**	**21**	**26**	**31**	**37**	**42**	**47**	**53**	**58**	**64**	**70**	**75**	**81**	**87**	**92**
19	—	1	4	9	15	20	26	32	38	44	50	56	63	69	75	82	88	94	101	107
	—	**0**	**3**	**7**	**12**	**17**	**22**	**28**	**33**	**39**	**45**	**51**	**56**	**63**	**69**	**74**	**81**	**87**	**93**	**99**
20	—	1	5	10	16	22	28	34	40	47	53	60	67	73	80	87	93	100	107	114
	—	**0**	**3**	**8**	**13**	**18**	**24**	**30**	**36**	**42**	**48**	**54**	**60**	**67**	**73**	**79**	**86**	**92**	**99**	**105**

TABLE B.9   CRITICAL VALUES OF *T* FOR THE WILCOXON SIGNED-RANKS TEST*

*To be significant, the obtained *T* must be *equal to* or *less than* the critical value. Dashes (—) in the columns indicate that no decision is possible for the stated α and *n*.

	LEVEL OF SIGNIFICANCE FOR ONE-TAILED TEST					LEVEL OF SIGNIFICANCE FOR ONE-TAILED TEST			
	.05	0.25	.01	.005		.05	.025	.01	.005
	LEVEL OF SIGNIFICANCE FOR TWO-TAILED TEST					LEVEL OF SIGNIFICANCE FOR TWO-TAILED TEST			
n	.10	.05	.02	.01	*n*	.10	.05	.02	.01
5	0	—	—	—	28	130	116	101	91
6	2	0	—	—	29	140	126	110	100
7	3	2	0	—	30	151	137	120	109
8	5	3	1	0	31	163	147	130	118
9	8	5	3	1	32	175	159	140	128
10	10	8	5	3	33	187	170	151	138
11	13	10	7	5	34	200	182	162	148
12	17	13	9	7	35	213	195	173	159
13	21	17	12	9	36	227	208	185	171
14	25	21	15	12	37	241	221	198	182
15	30	25	19	15	38	256	235	211	194
16	35	29	23	19	39	271	249	224	207
17	41	34	27	23	40	286	264	238	220
18	47	40	32	27	41	302	279	252	233
19	53	46	37	32	42	319	294	266	247
20	60	52	43	37	43	336	310	281	261
21	67	58	49	42	44	353	327	296	276
22	75	65	55	48	45	371	343	312	291
23	83	73	62	54	46	389	361	328	307
24	91	81	69	61	47	407	378	345	322
25	100	89	76	68	48	426	396	362	339
26	110	98	84	75	49	446	415	379	355
27	119	107	92	83	50	466	434	397	373

Adapted from F. Wilcoxon, S. K. Katti, and R. A. Wilcox, *Critical Values and Probability Levels of the Wilcoxon Rank-Sum Test and the Wilcoxon Signed-Ranks Test*. Wayne, N.J.: American Cyanamid Company, 1963. Also adapted from R. P. Runyon and A. Haber, *Fundamentals of Behavioral Statistics*, 5th ed. Copyright © 1984 by McGraw-Hill (originally by Addison-Wesley), p. 435, Table J. Adapted and reprinted with permission of the American Cyanamid Company and McGraw-Hill, Inc.

APPENDIX C SOLUTIONS FOR ODD-NUMBERED PROBLEMS IN THE TEXT

Note: Many of the problems in the text require several stages of computation. At each stage, there is an opportunity for rounding answers. Depending on the exact sequence of operations used to solve a problem, different individuals will round their answers at different times and in different ways.

As a result, you may obtain answers that are slightly different from those presented here. As long as these differences are small, they probably can be attributed to rounding error and should not be a matter for concern.

CHAPTER 1 INTRODUCTION TO STATISTICS

1. Descriptive statistics simplify and summarize data. Inferential statistics use sample data to make general conclusions about populations.

3. The distinguishing characteristics of the experimental method are *manipulation* and *control*. In the experimental method, the researcher manipulates one variable and observes a second variable. All other variables are controlled to prevent them from affecting the outcome.

5. In an experiment, the researcher manipulates one variable and observes a second variable for changes. The manipulated variable is called the *independent variable,* and the observed variable is the *dependent variable.*

7. **a.** quasi-experimental, comparing pre-existing groups
   b. The dependent variable is vocabulary skill.

9. **a.** The dependent variable is whether or not each subject has a cold.
   b. discrete
   c. nominal scale
   d. experimental (amount of vitamin C is manipulated)

11. **a.** nominal scale
    b. interval scale
    c. ordinal scale
    d. ratio scale

13. **a.** The independent variable is the color of the room, and the dependent variable is the score on the mood questionnaire.

   b. Room color is measured on a nominal scale.

15. **a.** discrete
    b. ratio scale (zero means no errors)

17. **a.** $\Sigma X = 13$
    b. $\Sigma X^2 = 57$
    c. $(\Sigma X)^2 = (13)^2 = 169$
    d. $\Sigma(X - 1) = 9$

19. **a.** $\Sigma X + 3$
    b. $\Sigma(X - 2)^2$
    c. $\Sigma X^2 - 10$

21. **a.** $\Sigma X = 9$
    b. $\Sigma X^2 = 35$
    c. $\Sigma(X + 1) = 13$
    d. $\Sigma(X + 1)^2 = 57$

23. **a.** $\Sigma X = -3$
    b. $\Sigma Y = 14$
    c. $\Sigma XY = -14$

25. **a.** $\dfrac{\Sigma X}{n} = 4$
    b. $\Sigma(X - 4) = 0$
    c. $\Sigma(X - 4)^2 = 14$
    d. $\Sigma X^2 - \dfrac{(\Sigma X)^2}{n} = 14$

CHAPTER 2 **FREQUENCY DISTRIBUTIONS**

1.

X	f	p	%
5	3	.15	15%
4	4	.20	20%
3	8	.40	40%
2	3	.15	15%
1	2	.10	10%

3.

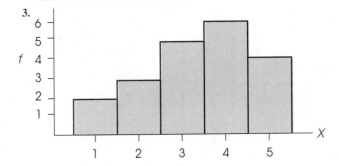

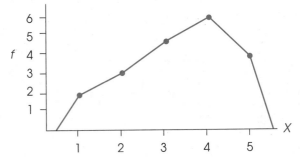

5. a.

X	f
10	2
9	7
8	2
7	1
6	0
5	2
4	0
3	2
2	8
1	2

b.

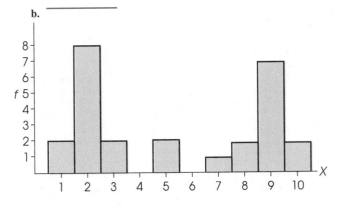

c. (1) The distribution is symmetrical, with half the class scoring high and half scoring low.
(2) The class is sharply divided into two distinct groups. For some, the quiz was easy, and for some, the quiz was hard.

7. a. $N = 12$
b. $\Sigma X = 43$

9. $N = \Sigma f = 13$, $\Sigma X = 38$, $\Sigma X^2 = 128$

11. a.

SET I		SET II	
X	f	X	f
5	1	14–15	1
4	2	12–13	0
3	4	10–11	1
2	2	8–9	2
1	1	6–7	1
		4–5	2
		2–3	1
		0–1	1

b.

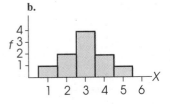

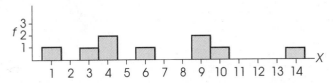

c. Set I forms a symmetrical distribution, centered at $X = 3$, with most of the scores clustered close to the center. Set II forms a flat distribution with a center near $X = 7$ or $X = 8$, but the scores are spread evenly across the entire scale.

13. a.

X	f
10	1
9	3
8	2
7	1
6	1
5	2
4	3
3	2
2	1

b.

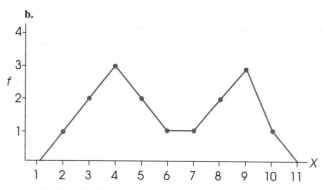

c. (1) The distribution is roughly symmetrical, with scores piled at each end of the scale.
   (2) The center is near $X = 6$.
   (3) The scores are spread across the entire scale.

15. a. width = 2   **b.** width = 5   **c.** width = 50

X	X	X
18–19	95–99	650–699
16–17	90–94	600–649
14–15	85–89	550–599
12–13	80–84	500–549
10–11	75–79	450–499
8–9	70–74	400–449
6–7	65–69	350–399
4–5	60–64	300–349
2–3	55–59	250–299
	50–54	

17. a.

X	f
10	1
9	0
8	1
7	3
6	1
5	2
4	5
3	4
2	2
1	1

b.

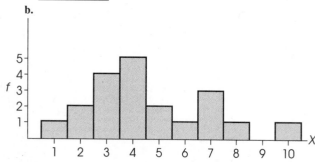

c.

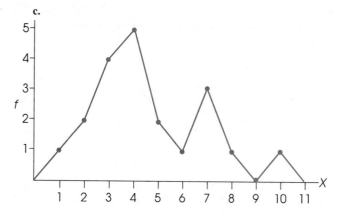

19. a. $X = 7.5$
   b. 72%
   c. $X = 10.5$
   d. 8%

21.

X	f	cf	c%
10	2	20	100%
9	3	18	90%
8	5	15	75%
7	6	10	50%
6	2	4	20%
5	2	2	10%

   a. 20%
   b. 90%
   c. $X = 7.5$
   d. $X = 9.5$ or greater

23. a. 20%
   b. $X = 18.25$
   c. 82%

25.

6	61
5	62750
4	37863790
3	599

27.

X	f
65–69	1
60–64	1
55–59	3
50–54	2
45–49	5
40–44	3
35–39	3

CHAPTER 3 CENTRAL TENDENCY

1. The purpose of central tendency is to identify the single score that serves as the best representative for an entire distribution, usually a score from the center of the distribution.

3. **a.** The mean is the *balance point* of a distribution because the total of the distances above the mean are exactly equal to the total of the distances below the mean.
   b. The median is the *midpoint* of a distribution because exactly 50% of the scores are greater than the median and 50% are less than the median.

5. The mean, median, and mode are identical for a symmetrical distribution with one mode.

7. mean $= 22/8 = 2.75$, median $= 2.5$, mode $= 2$

9. **a.** $120/3 = 40$ cards each
   b. $\overline{X} = 120/3 = 40$
   c. $6(8) = 48$ pieces of candy
   d. $\Sigma X = 48$

11. **a.** mean $= 83/20 = 4.15$, median $= 4.5$, mode $= 5$
    b. The distribution is negatively skewed (the mean is displaced toward the tail).

13. $n = 64$

15. **a.** For the original sample, $\Sigma X = 96$.
    b. For the new sample, $\Sigma X = 100$.
    c. For the new sample, $n = 9$.
    d. For the new sample, $\overline{X} = 100/9 = 11.11$.

17. **a.** The new mean is $\overline{X} = 54/6 = 9$.
    b. The new mean is $\overline{X} = 32/4 = 8$.
    c. The new mean is $\overline{X} = 65/5 = 13$.

19. For the original sample, $\Sigma X = 10(23) = 230$. After the score is removed, $\Sigma X = 9(25) = 225$. The score that was removed is $X = 5$.

21. **a.** the mode (TV shows form a nominal scale)
    b. the mean
    c. the median (the distribution is positively skewed)

23. Negatively skewed (the mean is displaced toward the lower tail of the distribution)

25. **a.** mean $= 115/16 = 7.1875$, median $= 6.5$
    b. Using the mean as the definition of average, the class is above the national norm.
    c. Using the median as the definition of average, the class is below the national norm.

27. **a.** The independent variable is the number of training sessions. The dependent variable is the amount of time needed to fall asleep.
    b. ratio scale
    c. line graph
    d.

(graph: Mean Time (in min.) on the y-axis ranging 10 to 70, Number of Training Sessions on the x-axis ranging 0 to 8; a decreasing line)

CHAPTER 4 VARIABILITY

1. **a.** *SS* is the sum of squared deviation scores.
   b. Variance is the mean squared deviation.
   c. Standard deviation is the square root of the variance. It provides a measure of the standard distance from the mean.

3. $SS = 20$, $s^2 = 5$, $s = 2.24$

5. **a.** The definitional formula is easier to use when the mean is a whole number and there is a relatively small set of scores.
   b. The computational formula is easier to use when the mean is a decimal value and/or there are a large number of scores.

7. $SS = 8$, $s^2 = 8/8 = 1$, $s = 1$

9. **a.** $\sigma = 0$ (all deviations from the mean are zero)
   b. $\sigma = 1$ (all scores are 1 point from the mean)

11. **a.**

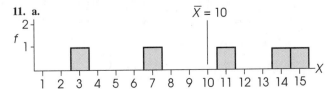

b. The mean is $\overline{X} = 50/5 = 10$, and the standard deviation appears to be about 4 or 5.
c. $SS = 100$; $s^2 = 25$; $s = 5$

13. **a.**

(histogram: frequency f on y-axis, X values 1–14 on x-axis, with $\mu = 8$ marked)

b. The mean is $48/6 = 8$, and the standard deviation appears to be about 3 or 4.
c. $SS = 54$, $\sigma^2 = 9$, $\sigma = 3$

15. a.

THE NUMBER OF PROBLEMS SOLVED UNDER
DIFFERENT LEVELS OF AROUSAL

AROUSAL LEVEL		
Low	$M = 5.1$	$SD = 1.52$
Moderate	$M = 17.0$	$SD = 2.16$
High	$M = 7.7$	$SD = 1.25$

b. Performance is best with a moderate level of arousal. If arousal is either too high or too low, performance suffers.

17. The total of the deviation scores must be zero, so the "mystery person" has a deviation of -6. Therefore, the score for this person is $X = 14$.

19. A standard deviation of zero means that there is no variability. All the scores have exactly the same value.

21. a.

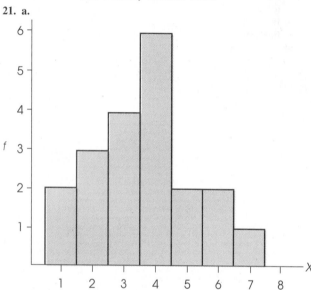

b. range $= 7$
c. interquartile range $= (4.5 - 2.5) = 2$
d. semi-interquartile range $= 1$

23. $\sigma^2 = (3.5)^2 = 12.25$

25. a.

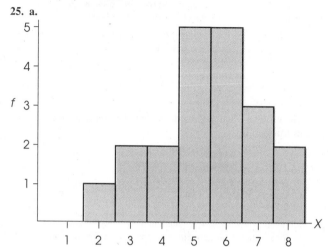

b. Estimate $\mu = 5.5$ and $\sigma = 1.5$.
c. $\mu = 5.4$ and $\sigma = 1.59$

27. a. Sample B covers a wider range.
b. For sample A, $\overline{X} = 9.17$ and $s = 1.72$.
For sample B, $\overline{X} = 9.00$ and $s = 5.66$.
c. Sample A

29. $\overline{X} = 433$, $SS = 24$, $s^2 = 4$, $s = 2$

CHAPTER 5 *z*-SCORES

---

1. A *z*-score describes a precise location within a distribution. The sign of the *z*-score tells whether the location is above ($+$) or below ($-$) the mean, and the magnitude tells the distance from the mean in terms of the number of standard deviations.

3. a. With $\sigma = 25$, $X = 250$ corresponds to $z = +2.00$.
b. With $\sigma = 100$, $X = 250$ corresponds to $z = +0.50$.

5. a.

X	z	X	z
58	0.50	46	-0.25
34	-1.00	62	0.75
82	2.00	74	1.50

b.

X	z	X	z
90	2.50	54	0.25
42	-0.50	34	-1.00
26	-1.50	62	0.75

7.

X	z	X	z
40	1.00	29	-1.20
42	1.40	47	2.40
34	-0.20	26	-1.80

9. $\sigma = 6$

11. $\mu = 45$

13. The distance between scores is 12 points, which corresponds to 3 standard deviations. Therefore, $\sigma = 4$, and $\mu = 58$.

15. $\sigma = 8$ gives $z = -1.00$.
$\sigma = 16$ gives $z = -0.50$ (better score).

17. Tom's CPE score corresponds to $z = 35/50 = 0.70$. Bill's CBT score corresponds to $z = 40/100 = 0.40$. Tom's z-score places him higher in the distribution, so he is more likely to be admitted.

19.

RAW SCORE	STANDARDIZED SCORE
41	13.0
32	8.5
38	11.5
44	14.5
45	15.0
36	10.5
27	6.0

21.

ORIGINAL SCORE	STANDARDIZED SCORE
84	125
78	110
80	115
66	80
62	70
72	95

23. a. $\mu = 5$ and $\sigma = 2$

b.

X	z
8	1.50
6	0.50
2	-1.50
4	-0.50
5	0

c.

ORIGINAL X	NEW X
8	130
6	110
2	70
4	90
5	100

CHAPTER 6 **PROBABILITY**

1. a. $p = 45/60 = 0.75$
b. $p = 25/60 = 0.42$
c. $p = 5/60 = 0.08$

3. a. left = .8413, right = .1587
b. left = .0668, right = .9332
c. left = .5987, right = .4013
d. left = .3085, right = .6915

5. a. 0.3336
b. 0.0465
c. 0.0885
d. 0.3859

7. a. $z = 0.25$
b. $z = 1.28$
c. $z = -0.84$

9. a. $z = 0.52$, $X = 552$
b. $z = 0.67$, $X = 567$
c. $z = -1.28$, $X = 372$

11. a. 0.1747
b. 0.6826
c. 0.4332
d. 0.7506

13. The portion of the distribution consisting of scores greater than 50 is more than one-half of the whole distribution. The answer must be greater than 0.50.

15. a. $p(z < 1.22) = 0.8888$
b. $p(z > -1.67) = 0.9525$
c. $p(z > 0.56) = 0.2877$
d. $p(z > 2.11) = 0.0174$
e. $p(-1.33 < z < 1.44) = 0.8333$
f. $p(-0.33 < z < 0.33) = .2586$

17. Converted to z-scores, the correct order is
John $z = +0.75$ highest
Tom $z = +0.50$ middle
Mary $z = +0.25$ lowest

19. You cannot find the probability. You cannot use the unit normal table because the distribution is not normal.

21. a. $z = 1.28$, $X = 264$
b. $z = -0.52$, $X = 174$
c. $z = 0.67$, $X = 233.5$

23. a. $Q1: z = -0.67$, $X = 79.90$
$Q2: z = 0$, $X = 100$
$Q3: z = 0.67$, $X = 120.10$
b. interquartile range $= 120.10 - 79.90 = 40.20$
semi-interquartile range $= 20.10$

25. a. With four suits possible, the probability of guessing correctly is $p = 1/4$.

b. With $n = 48$, $p = 1/4$, and $q = 3/4$, it is possible to use the normal approximation to the binomial distribution with $\mu = 12$ and $\sigma = 3$. Using the real limit of 18.5, $p(X > 18.5) = p(z > 2.17) = 0.0150$.

27. a. $\mu = pn = 80$

b. Using the real limit of 95.5, $p(X > 95.5) = p(z > 3.88) = 0.00005$.

c. Using the real limit of 94.5, $p(X < 94.5) = p(z < 3.63) = 0.9998$.

d. Using the answers from parts b and c, $p(X = 95) = 1.00 - (0.00005 + 0.9998) = 0.00015$.

29. If you are just guessing, then $p = q = 1/2$, and with $n = 36$, the normal approximation has $\mu = 18$ and $\sigma = 3$. Using the lower real limit of 23.5, $p(X > 23.5) = p(z > 1.83) = 0.0336$.

CHAPTER 7 PROBABILITY AND SAMPLES: THE DISTRIBUTION OF SAMPLE MEANS

1. a. The distribution of sample means is the set of all possible sample means for random samples of a specific size (n) from a specific population.

b. The expected value of $\overline{X}$ is the mean of the distribution of sample means (μ).

c. The standard error of $\overline{X}$ is the standard deviation of the distribution of sample means ($\sigma_{\overline{X}} = \sigma/\sqrt{n}$).

3. A sample of $n = 25$ would be more accurate, with a standard error of 3 points. A sample of $n = 9$ would have a standard error of 5 points.

5. a. $z = -1.00$

b. $z = +2.00$

c. $z = +2.00$

7. a. The distribution is normal, with $\mu = 100$ and $\sigma_{\overline{X}} = 4$.

b. The z-score boundaries are ± 1.96. The X boundaries are 92.16 and 107.84.

c. $\overline{X} = 106$ corresponds to $z = 1.50$. This is not in the extreme 5%.

9. a. The distribution is normal, with $\mu = 55$ and $\sigma_{\overline{X}} = 2$.

b. $z = +2.00$, $p = 0.0228$

c. $z = +0.50$, $p = 0.6915$

d. $p(-1.00 < z < +1.00) = 0.6826$

11. a. The distribution is normal, with $\mu = 50$ and $\sigma = 10$. The z-score boundaries are ± 0.50, and $p = 0.3830$.

b. The distribution is normal, with $\mu = 50$ and $\sigma_{\overline{X}} = 2$. The z-score boundaries are ± 2.50, and $p = 0.9876$.

13. a. $\sigma_{\overline{X}} = 10$, $z = 0.50$, $p = .3085$

b. $\sigma_{\overline{X}} = 5$, $z = 1.00$, $p = .1587$

c. $\sigma_{\overline{X}} = 2$, $z = 2.50$, $p = .0062$

15. a. $\sigma_{\overline{X}} = 6$, $p(-0.83 < z < 0.83) = .5934$

b. $\sigma_{\overline{X}} = 3$, $p(-1.67 < z < 1.67) = .9050$

17. a. For $n = 25$, $\sigma_{\overline{X}} = 16$ points.

b. For $n = 100$, $\sigma_{\overline{X}} = 8$ points.

c. For $n = 400$, $\sigma_{\overline{X}} = 4$ points.

d. Increasing the sample size by a factor of 4 decreases the standard error by a factor of 2. The standard error changes with the square root of n.

19. With $n = 4$, $\sigma_{\overline{X}} = 5$, and $p(\overline{X} \geq 150) = p(z \geq 2.00) = 0.0228$.

21. With $n = 16$, $\sigma_{\overline{X}} = 0.50$, and $p(\overline{X} \leq 31) = p(z \leq -2.00) = .0228$. This is a very unlikely outcome by chance alone. The inspector should suspect some problem with the machinery.

23. a.

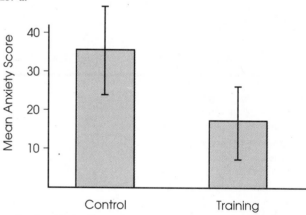

b. Considering the standard error for each group, the mean for the control group could be as low as 24, and the mean for the training group could be as high as 28. There is overlap between the two groups when the error is considered, so you cannot be certain that the training worked.

CHAPTER 8 INTRODUCTION TO HYPOTHESIS TESTING

1. a. A Type I error is rejecting a true H_0. This can occur if you obtain a very unusual sample with scores that are much different from those of the general population.

b. A Type II error is failing to reject a false H_0. This can happen when the treatment effect is very small. In this case, the treated sample is not noticeably different from the original population.

3. a. The dependent variable is the reaction time, and the independent variable is the position of the indicator light.

b. The position of the indicator light has no effect on reaction time.

c. $H_0:\mu = 200$
$H_1:\mu \neq 200$
where μ refers to the mean reaction time with the light at eye level.

d. When H_0 is true, the distribution of sample means is normal, with $\mu = 200$ and $\sigma_{\overline{X}} = 4$. The critical region corresponds to z-score values greater than $+1.96$ or less than -1.96.

e. $\overline{X} = 195$ corresponds to $z = -1.25$. Fail to reject H_0.

f. With $n = 100$, $\sigma_{\overline{X}} = 2$, and $\overline{X} = 195$ corresponds to $z = -2.50$. Reject H_0. With the larger sample, there is less error, so the 5-point difference is sufficient to reject the null hypothesis.

5. a. $\overline{X} - \mu$ measures the difference between the sample data and the hypothesized population mean.

b. A sample mean is not expected to be identical to the population mean. The standard error indicates how much difference between $\overline{X}$ and μ is expected by chance.

7. The null hypothesis states that the mean completion time for the MS population is not different from the mean time for the regular population; $H_0:\mu = 185$ seconds. With $\alpha = .01$, the critical value is $z = \pm2.58$. For this sample mean, the standard error is 3.77, and z is 7.16. Reject the null hypothesis, and conclude that the MS population is significantly different.

9. The null hypothesis states that the price change has no effect on weekly sales. The critical value is $z = \pm1.96$. For these data, $\overline{X} = 161.75$, the standard error is 8.13, and the z-score statistic is -2.86. Reject the null hypothesis, and conclude that there has been a significant change in weekly sales.

11. a. The null hypothesis states that there is no change and the population mean is still $\mu = 8.4$. The critical value is $z = \pm2.58$. The standard error is 0.23, and the sample mean corresponds to $z = -5.65$. This is a very unlikely value, so reject the null hypothesis and conclude that there has been a change in homework time.

b. With $n = 20$, the standard error would be 0.74, and the z-score for this sample would be $z = -1.76$. In this case, you would fail to reject the null hypothesis.

13. $H_0:\mu = 55$ (patients' scores are not different from those of the normal population). The critical region consists of z-scores greater than $+2.58$ or less than -2.58. For these data, $\overline{X} = 76.62$, the standard error is 2.62, and $z = 8.25$. Reject the null hypothesis. Scores for depressed patients are significantly different from scores for normal individuals on this test.

15. $H_0:\mu = 7$ feet (Middle Eastern social distance is no different from that in the United States). The critical region consists of z-scores greater than $+1.96$ or less than -1.96. For these data, the standard error is 0.53, and $z = -4.72$. Reject the null hypothesis. Social distance in the Middle East is significantly different from social distance in the United States.

17. a. The null hypothesis states that the training program has no effect on the problem-solving scores ($H_0:\mu = 80$). The critical region consists of z-score values beyond ±1.96. For these data, the standard error is 2.36, and $z = 1.88$. Fail to reject H_0. There is not sufficient evidence to conclude that the training program has any effect.

b. For a one-tailed test, the null hypothesis would state that training does not improve problem-solving ability; $H_0:\mu \leq 80$. The critical region consists of z-score values greater than $+1.65$. For the one-tailed test, the z-score is in the critical region, and the decision is to reject H_0.

19. The analyses are contradictory. The critical region for the two-tailed tests consists of the extreme 2.5% in each tail of the distribution. The two-tailed conclusion indicates that the data were not in this critical region. However, the one-tailed test indicates that the data were in the extreme 1% of one tail. Data cannot be in the extreme 1% and at the same time fail to be in the extreme 2.5%.

21. Increasing the alpha level results in increased power and an increased risk of a Type I error.

23. a. Increasing alpha would make the test more powerful, but it has the undesirable effect of increasing the risk of a Type I error.

b. Increasing sample size with a small alpha would increase power and keep the risk of a Type I error small.

c. Using a one-tailed test would increase power, but many researchers would argue that it also produces an indirect increase in the risk of a Type I error.

25. $H_0:\mu \geq 20$ (not reduced), and $H_1:\mu < 20$ (reduced). The critical region consists of z-score values less than -1.65. For these data, the standard error is 1, and the z-score is $z = -4.50$. Reject H_0.

27. $H_0:\mu \leq 80$ (not more depressed), and $H_1:\mu > 80$ (more depressed). The critical region consists of z-score values greater than 1.65. For these data, $\overline{X} = 87.7$, and $z = 2.03$. Reject H_0, and conclude that children from divorced families have higher scores on the depression questionnaire.

CHAPTER 9 INTRODUCTION TO THE t STATISTIC

1. The t statistic is used when the population standard deviation is unknown. You use the sample data to estimate the standard deviation and the standard error.

3. a. As variability increases, t becomes smaller (closer to zero.

b. As sample size increases, the standard error decreases, and the t value increases.

c. The larger the difference between $\overline{X}$ and μ, the larger the t value.

5. The t statistic assumes random sampling from a normal distribution and independent observations.

7. As df increase, the t distribution becomes less variable (less spread out) and more like a normal distribution. For $\alpha = .05$, the critical t values move toward ±1.96 as df increases.

9. The null hypothesis states that self-esteem for the athletes is not different from self-esteem for the general population. In symbols, $H_0:\mu = 70$. The critical boundaries are ±2.064. For these data, $s_{\overline{X}} = 2$, and $t(24) = 1.50$, which is not in the critical region. Fail to reject the null hypothesis.

11. $H_0:\mu = 10$ (no different from chance). Because $df = 35$ is not in the table, use $df = 30$ to obtain critical values of $t = \pm 2.042$. For these data, the standard error is 2, and $t(35) = 1.75$. Fail to reject H_0.

13. a. With $n = 25$, the critical boundaries are ± 2.064. For these data, the standard error is 2.00, and the t statistic is $t(24) = -2.00$. Fail to reject H_0.

    b. Because $df = 399$ is not in the table, use $df = 120$ to obtain critical boundaries of ± 1.98. With $n = 400$, the standard error is 0.50, and the t statistic is $t(399) = -8.00$. Reject H_0.

    c. The larger the sample, the smaller the standard error (denominator of the t statistic). If other factors are held constant, a smaller standard error will produce a larger t statistic, which is more likely to be significant.

15. a. $H_0:\mu = 5.00$. The two-tailed critical boundaries are $t = \pm 2.064$. With a standard error of 0.10, $t(24) = 2.00$. Fail to reject H_0, and conclude that the average weight is not significantly different from 5 pounds.

    b. $H_0:\mu \le 5.00$ (not more than 5 pounds). With a one-tailed test, the critical boundary is $t = 1.711$. The obtained statistic, $t(24) = 2.00$, is in the critical region. Reject H_0, and conclude that the average weight is significantly more than 5 pounds.

17. $H_0:\mu = 40$. Because $df = 35$ is not in the table, use $df = 30$ to obtain critical values of $t = \pm 2.042$. For these data, $s^2 = 144$, the standard error is 2.00, and $t(35) = 2.25$. Reject H_0, and conclude that depression for the elderly is significantly different from depression for the general population.

19. $H_0:\mu = 166$ (no change). Because $df = 99$ is not in the table, use $df = 60$ to obtain critical values of $t = \pm 2.660$. For these data, the standard error is 2.3, and $t(99) = 3.04$. Reject H_0, and conclude that there has been a significant change in weight.

21. $H_0:\mu \le 20$ (not more than chance). The critical region consists of t values greater than 1.860. For these data, $\overline{X} = 22.22$, $s^2 = 17.44$, the standard error is 1.39, and $t(8) = 1.60$. Fail to reject H_0. The performance for this sample is not significantly better than chance.

23. $H_0:\mu \ge 15$. The critical region consists of t values less than -1.943. For these data, $\overline{X} = 11.71$, $s^2 = 12.24$, and the standard error is 1.32. $t(6) = -2.49$. Reject H_0, and conclude right hemisphere brain damage does significantly reduce spatial skills.

25. $H_0:\mu = 27$. The critical region consists of values beyond $t = \pm 2.201$. For these data, $\overline{X} = 24.58$, $s^2 = 12.08$, the standard error is 1.00, and $t(11) = -2.41$. Reject H_0, and conclude that the data are significantly different (less time) from the therapist's claim.

CHAPTER 10   HYPOTHESIS TESTS WITH TWO INDEPENDENT SAMPLES

1. An independent-measures study requires a separate sample for each of the treatments or populations being compared. An independent-measures t statistic is appropriate when a researcher has two samples and wants to use the sample mean difference to test hypotheses about the population mean difference.

3. The homogeneity of variance assumption specifies that $\sigma_1^2 = \sigma_2^2$ for the two populations from which the samples are obtained. If this assumption is violated, the t statistic can cause misleading conclusions for a hypothesis test.

5. Both experiments show a 10-point difference between the two sample means. However, the variability in experiment II is substantially greater than that in experiment I. The smaller variability is experiment I will make the mean difference more apparent and is more likely to produce a significant t statistic.

7. The null hypothesis states that birth order has no effect on self-esteem and pride, $H_0:\mu_1 - \mu_2 = 0$. With $\alpha = .01$, the critical region consists of t values beyond ± 2.763. The pooled variance is 60, the standard error is 3, and $t(28) = 2.33$. Fail to reject H_0, and conclude that there is no significant difference in self-esteem between the two groups.

9. The null hypothesis states that college class has no effect on political attitude, $H_0:\mu_1 - \mu_2 = 0$. With $\alpha = .05$, the critical region consists of t values beyond ± 2.101. The pooled variance is 500, the standard error is 10, and $t(18) = 1.30$. Fail to reject H_0, and conclude that there is no significant difference in political attitudes for freshmen versus seniors.

11. The null hypothesis states that the type of presentation has no effect on learning, $H_0:\mu_1 - \mu_2 = 0$. With $\alpha = .05$, the critical region consists of t values beyond ± 2.101. The pooled variance is 20, the standard error is 2, and $t(18) = 1.50$. Fail to reject H_0, and conclude that there is no significant difference in test scores between the two groups.

13. The null hypothesis states that the form of the anagram has no effect on difficulty, $H_0:\mu_1 - \mu_2 = 0$. With $\alpha = .01$, the critical region consists of t values beyond ± 2.977. The pooled variance is 400, the standard error is 10, and $t(14) = 2.10$. Fail to reject H_0, and conclude that there is no significant difference between the two conditions.

15. The null hypothesis states that the amount paid has no effect on attitude, $H_0:\mu_1 - \mu_2 = 0$. Because $df = 38$ is not in the table, use $df = 30$ to obtain critical values of $t = \pm 2.750$. For the students paid \$1, $\overline{X} = 5.1$, with $SS = 49.80$. For the students paid \$20, $\overline{X} = 2.95$, with $SS = 38.95$. $t(38) = 4.45$. Reject H_0, and conclude that there is a significant difference in opinion concerning the experiment.

17. The null hypothesis states that owning a pet has no effect on health, $H_0:\mu_1 - \mu_2 = 0$. The critical boundaries are $t = \pm 2.228$. For the control group, $\overline{X} = 11.14$, and $SS = 56.86$. For the dog owners, $\overline{X} = 6.4$, and $SS = 17.2$. The pooled variance is 7.41, and $t(10) = 2.98$. Reject H_0. The data show a significant difference between the dog owners and the control group.

19. The null hypothesis states that there is no difference in personality between artists and pilots, $H_0: \mu_1 - \mu_2 = 0$. With $\alpha = .05$, the critical region consists of t values beyond ± 2.056. For the artists, $\overline{X} = 7.071$, and $SS = 36.91$. For the pilots, $\overline{X} = 3.143$, and $SS = 27.71$. The pooled variance is 2.485, the standard error is 0.595, and $t(26) = 6.60$. Reject H_0. The data indicate a significant difference between the two professions.

CHAPTER 11 STATISTICAL INFERENCE WITH RELATED SAMPLES

1. a. This is an independent-measures experiment with two separate samples.
  b. This is repeated measures. The same sample is measured twice.
  c. This is a matched-subjects design. The repeated-measures t statistic is appropriate.

3. For a repeated-measures design, the same subjects are used in both treatment conditions. In a matched-subjects design, two different sets of subjects are used. However, in a matched-subjects design, each subject in one condition is matched with respect to a specific variable with a subject in the second condition so that the two separate samples are equivalent with respect to the matching variable.

5. The null hypothesis says that there is no change, $H_0: \mu_D = 0$. The critical region consists of t values beyond ± 2.131. For these data, $s^2 = 25$, the standard error is 1.25, and $t(15) = 2.56$. Reject H_0, and conclude that there has been a significant change in the number of cigarettes.

7. The null hypothesis says that the medication has no effect, $H_0: \mu_D = 0$. Because $df = 35$ is not in the table, use $df = 30$ to obtain critical values of $t = \pm 2.042$. For these data, the standard error is 1.33, and $t(35) = 18.05$. Reject H_0, and conclude that the medication produces a significant change in reaction time.

9. a. The null hypothesis states that there is no difference between the two treatments, $H_0: \mu_1 - \mu_2 = 0$. With $\alpha = .05$, the critical region consists of t values beyond ± 2.306. The pooled variance is 35.5, the standard error is 3.77, and $t(8) = -0.53$. Fail to reject H_0. There is no significant difference between the two treatments.
  b. For the repeated-measures design, $H_0: \mu_D = 0$. With $\alpha = .05$, the critical region consists of t values beyond ± 2.776. For these data, $s = 1$, the standard error is 0.45, and $t(4) = 4.44$. Reject H_0, and conclude that there is a significant difference between treatments.

  c. The repeated-measures design has less variability and a smaller standard error. The smaller standard error results in a larger t statistic, which is big enough to be significant.

11. The null hypothesis says that there is no difference between the two food mixes, $H_0: \mu_D = 0$. With $\alpha = .05$, the critical region consists of t values beyond ± 2.306. For these data, $s^2 = 36$, the standard error is 2, and $t(8) = 3.00$. Reject H_0, and conclude that there is a significant difference between the two food mixes.

13. The null hypothesis says that there is no change in the number of dreams, $H_0: \mu_D = 0$. With $\alpha = .05$, the critical region consists of t values beyond ± 2.131. For these data, $s^2 = 4$, the standard error is 0.50, and $t(15) = 8.60$. Reject H_0, and conclude that there has been a significant change.

15. The null hypothesis says that the amount of exercise makes no difference in overall health, $H_0: \mu_D = 0$. With $\alpha = .05$, the critical region consists of t values beyond ± 2.447. For these data, $\overline{D} = 0.43$, with $SS = 33.71$. The standard error is 0.90, and $t(6) = 0.48$. Fail to reject H_0, and conclude that there is no difference between two hours and five hours of exercise.

17. The null hypothesis says that deprivation has no effect on hearing threshold, $H_0: \mu_D = 0$. With $\alpha = .05$, the critical region consists of t values beyond ± 2.447. For these data, $\overline{D} = -2.29$, $SS = 51.43$, $s^2 = 8.57$, the standard error is 1.11, and $t(6) = -2.06$. Fail to reject H_0, and conclude that the data show no significant change in hearing threshold.

19. The null hypothesis says that the type of sentence has no effect on memory, $H_0: \mu_D = 0$. With $\alpha = .01$, the critical region consists of t values beyond ± 4.032. For these data, $\overline{D} = 6.33$, $SS = 47.33$, $s^2 = 9.47$, the standard error is 1.26, and $t(5) = 5.02$. Reject H_0, and conclude that the data show a significant difference in memory performance.

CHAPTER 12 ESTIMATION

1. The general purpose of a hypothesis test is to determine whether or not a treatment effect exists. A hypothesis test always addresses a "yes/no" question. The purpose of estimation is to determine the size of the effect. Estimation addresses a "how much" question.

3. a. The larger the sample, the narrower the interval.
  b. The larger the sample standard deviation (s), the wider the interval.

  c. The higher the percentage of confidence, the wider the interval.

5. a. Use the sample mean, $\overline{X} = 5.1$ hours, as the best point estimate of μ.
  b. Decrease of 0.4 hours.
  c. With a standard error of 0.20 and z-scores ranging from -1.28 to $+1.28$ for 80% confidence, the interval extends from 4.844 hours to 5.356 hours.

7. a. Use $\overline{X} = 820$ for the point estimate.
   b. Using $z = \pm 1.28$, the 80% confidence interval extends from 817.44 to 822.56.
   c. Using $z = \pm 2.58$, the 99% confidence interval extends from 814.84 to 825.16.

9. a. $s = 2.91$
   b. Use $\overline{X} = 10.09$ for the point estimate. Using $t = \pm 2.228$ and a standard error of 0.88, the 95% confidence interval extends from 8.13 to 12.05.

11. a. Use $\overline{X} = 95$ for the boys. With a standard error of 3 and using a range of t values from -1.341 to 1.341, the interval extends from 90.977 to 99.023.
   b. Use $\overline{X} = 40$ for the girls. With a standard error of 4 and using a range of t values from -1.397 to 1.397, the interval extends from 34.412 to 45.588.
   c. Use the sample mean difference, 55 millimeters, for the point estimate. Using an independent-measures t statistic with $df = 23$, the pooled variance is 144, the standard error is 5, the t score boundaries for 80% confidence are ± 1.319, and the interval extends from 48.405 to 61.595.

13. Use the sample mean difference, 14 points, for the point estimate. Using an independent-measures t statistic with $df = 28$, the pooled variance is 120, the standard error is 4, the t score boundaries for 90% confidence are ± 1.701, and the interval extends from 7.196 to 20.804.

15. Use the sample mean difference, 8 minutes, for the point estimate. Using a repeated-measures t statistic with $df = 8$, the standard error is 2, the t score boundaries for 80% confidence are ± 1.397, and the interval extends from 5.206 to 10.794 minutes.

17. Use the sample mean difference, 4.2, for the point estimate. Using a repeated-measures t statistic with $df = 3$, the standard error is 1, the t score boundaries for 95% confidence are ± 3.182, and the interval extends from 1.018 to 7.382.

19. Use the sample mean difference, 2.83, for the point estimate. Using a repeated-measures t statistic with $df = 5$, the standard error is 1.08, the t score boundaries for 80% confidence are ± 1.476, and the interval extends from 1.236 to 4.424.

CHAPTER 13 INTRODUCTION TO ANALYSIS OF VARIANCE

1. When there is no treatment effect, the numerator and the denominator of the F-ratio are both measuring the same sources of variability (individual differences and experimental error). In this case, the F-ratio is balanced and should have a value near 1.00.

3. As the differences between sample means increase, $MS_{between}$ also increases, and the F-ratio increases. Increases in sample variability cause MS_{within} to increase and thereby decrease the F-ratio.

5. Post-tests are done after an ANOVA where you reject the null hypothesis with three or more treatments. Post-tests determine which treatments are significantly different.

7. Within each treatment, all the scores are the same. There is no variability within treatments. MS_{within} should be zero.

9. a. The null hypothesis states that there are no differences among the age groups, $H_0: \mu_1 = \mu_2 = \mu_3$. The critical value for $\alpha = .05$ is 5.14.

SOURCE	SS	df	MS
Between treatments	26	2	13
Within treatments	12	6	2
Total	38	8	

$F(2, 6) = 6.50$

Reject H_0, and conclude that there are significant differences among the three age groups.

   b. Beginning with the largest difference between samples, the Scheffé comparisons and F-ratios are as follows:
   5- versus 7-year-olds: $F(2, 6) = 6.00$ (significant)
   6- versus 7-year-olds: $F(2, 6) = 3.38$ (not significant)
   No other differences are significant.

11.

NUMBER OF DAYS TO ADJUST TO JETLAG		
Westbound	$M = 2.50$	$SD = 1.05$
Eastbound	$M = 6.00$	$SD = 1.41$
Same time zone	$M = 0.50$	$SD = 0.55$

The null hypothesis states that the direction of flight has no effect on jet lag, $H_0: \mu_1 = \mu_2 = \mu_3$. The critical value for $\alpha = .05$ is 3.68.

SOURCE	SS	df	MS
Between treatments	93	2	46.50
Within treatments	17	15	1.13
Total	110	17	

$F(2, 15) = 41.029$

With a critical value of $F = 3.68$, you should reject H_0.

13. a. For treatments I and II only, the null hypothesis is $H_0: \mu_1 = \mu_2$. The critical value for $\alpha = .05$ is 5.99.

SOURCE	SS	df	MS
Between treatments	32	1	32
Within treatments	24	6	4
Total	56	7	

$F(1, 6) = 8.00$

The obtained F-ratio is in the critical region, so we reject H_0, and conclude that there is a significant difference between the two treatments.

   b. When the analysis includes all three treatments, the null hypothesis is, $H_0: \mu_1 = \mu_2 = \mu_3$. The critical value for $\alpha = .05$ is 4.26.

SOURCE	SS	df	MS
Between treatments	32	2	16
Within treatments	36	9	4
Total	68	11	

$F(2, 9) = 4.00$

The obtained F-ratio is not in the critical region, so we fail to reject H_0, and conclude that there are no significant differences among the three treatments.

c. When comparing only treatments I and II, there is a 4-point difference between means, $\overline{X}_1 = 1$ and $\overline{X}_2 = 5$. However, when the third treatment, with $\overline{X}_3 = 3$, is added, the study contains mean differences that are only 2 points (for example, $\overline{X}_1$ versus $\overline{X}_3$). Thus, when the third treatment is included, the average difference between means decreases, and $MS_{between}$ also decreases. As a result, the mean differences are no longer significant.

15.

SOURCE	SS	df	MS
Between treatments	45	3	15
Within treatments	108	36	3
Total	153	39	

$F(3, 36) = 5.00$

17. Converting the summarized data into totals (T) and SS values produces

2-year-olds: $T = 42$ and $SS = 32.11$
6-year-olds: $T = 86$ and $SS = 42.75$
10-year-olds: $T = 138$ and $SS = 61.56$

The null hypothesis states that there are no differences among the age groups, $H_0: \mu_1 = \mu_2 = \mu_3$. The critical value for $\alpha = .05$ is 4.02 (using $df = 1, 55$). The analysis of variance produces

SOURCE	SS	df	MS
Between treatments	230.93	2	115.47
Within treatments	136.42	57	2.39
Total	367.35	59	

$F(2, 57) = 48.31$

Reject H_0.

19. a. The null hypothesis states that there is no difference between the two treatments, $H_0: \mu_1 = \mu_2$. The critical value for $\alpha = .05$ is 5.32.

SOURCE	SS	df	MS
Between treatments	10	1	10
Within treatments	16	8	2
Total	26	9	

$F(1, 8) = 5.00$

Fail to reject H_0.

b. For the t statistic, the critical value is ± 2.306. The pooled variance $= 2$, and $t(8) = -2.24$. Fail to reject H_0. Note that $F = t^2, 5 = (-2.24)^2$.

21. a. The means and SS values are

SINGLE	TWIN	TRIPLET
$\overline{X} = 8$	$\overline{X} = 6$	$\overline{X} = 4$
$SS = 10$	$SS = 18$	$SS = 14$

The null hypothesis states that there are no differences in language development among the three groups, $H_0: \mu_1 = \mu_2 = \mu_3$. The critical value for $\alpha = .05$ is 3.88. The analysis of variance produces

SOURCE	SS	df	MS
Between treatments	40	2	20
Within treatments	42	12	3.5
Total	82	14	

$F(2, 12) = 5.71$

Reject H_0, and conclude that there are significant differences in language development among the three groups.

23. a. The means and SS values for these data are

ATTRACTIVE	AVERAGE	UNATTRACTIVE
$\overline{X} = 4.50$	$\overline{X} = 5.92$	$\overline{X} = 2.33$
$SS = 23.00$	$SS = 24.92$	$SS = 12.67$

b. The null hypothesis states that there are no differences in ratings among the three photos, $H_0: \mu_1 = \mu_2 = \mu_3$. The critical value for $\alpha = .05$ is 3.30.

SOURCE	SS	df	MS
Between treatments	78.17	2	39.08
Within treatments	60.59	33	1.84
Total	138.76	35	

$F(2, 33) = 21.24$

Reject H_0.

CHAPTER 14 REPEATED-MEASURES ANOVA

1. A repeated-measures design generally uses fewer subjects and is more likely to detect a treatment effect because it eliminates variability due to individual differences.

3. a. $SS_{within} = 26 + 26 = 52$

b. $SS_{between\ subjects} = 52$

5. $df = 2, 22$

7. a. The means have all increased by 2 points compared to the values in Problem 6, but the mean differences have not changed at all. $MS_{between}$ is still equal to 6.00, unchanged.

b. MS_{error} is not changed from the value obtained in Problem 6. The extra variability within treatments is all accounted for as variability between subjects, which is subtracted out before MS_{error} is computed.

c. The null hypothesis states that the mean number of errors does not change across sessions, $H_0:\mu_1 = \mu_2 = \mu_3 = \mu_4$. The critical value is 4.76. The complete analysis for the new data is as follows:

SOURCE	SS	df	MS
Between treatments	18	3	6.00
Within treatments	156	8	
Between subjects	152	2	
Error	4	6	0.67
Total	174	11	

$F(3, 6) = 8.96$

Reject H_0, and conclude that there is a significant practice effect.

9. a. The null hypothesis states that there are no differences between treatments, $H_0:\mu_1 = \mu_2 = \mu_3$. For an independent-measures design, the critical value is 3.88.

SOURCE	SS	df	MS
Between treatments	40	2	20.00
Within treatments	74	12	6.17
Total	114	14	

$F(2, 12) = 3.24$

b. The null hypothesis states that there are no differences between treatments, $H_0:\mu_1 = \mu_2 = \mu_3$. For a repeated-measures design, the critical value is 4.46.

SOURCE	SS	df	MS
Between treatments	40	2	20.0
Within treatments	74	12	
Between subjects	54	4	
Error	20	8	2.5
Total	114	14	

$F(2, 8) = 8.00$

c. The independent-measures design includes all the individual differences in the error term (MS_{within}). As a result, the F-ratio, $F(2, 12) = 3.24$, is not significant. With a repeated-measures design, the individual differences are removed, and the result is a significant F-ratio: $F(2, 8) = 8.00$, $p < .05$.

11. The null hypothesis states that there are no differences among the three food mixes, $H_0:\mu_1 = \mu_2 = \mu_3$. The critical value is 4.10.

SOURCE	SS	df	MS
Between treatments	12	2	6
Within treatments	56	15	
Between subjects	16	5	
Error	40	10	4
Total	68	17	

$F(2, 10) = 1.50$

Fail to reject H_0. There are no significant differences among the three mixes.

13. a. $k = 3$

b. $n = 21$

15.

SOURCE	SS	df	MS
Between treatments	200	4	50
Within treatments	500	45	
Between subjects	140	9	
Error	360	36	10
Total	700	49	

$F(4, 36) = 5.00$

17.

SOURCE	SS	df	MS
Between treatments	60	3	20
Within treatments	90	36	
Between subjects	36	9	
Error	54	27	2
Total	150	39	

$F = 10.00$

19. a. The means are 6, 4, and 2.

b. The null hypothesis states that there is no change in motivation across the three grade levels, $H_0:\mu_1 = \mu_2 = \mu_3$. The critical value is 4.46.

SOURCE	SS	df	MS
Between treatments	40.00	2	20
Within treatments	26.00	12	
Between subjects	19.33	4	
Error	6.67	8	0.83
Total	66.00	14	

$F(2, 8) = 24.1$

Reject H_0. There are significant differences among the three grade levels.

21. The means and SS values are

FIRST	SECOND	THIRD
$\overline{X} = 94.6$	$\overline{X} = 59.0$	$\overline{X} = 34.8$
$SS = 831.2$	$SS = 1246.0$	$SS = 474.8$

The null hypothesis states that there is no change in looking behavior across the three presentations, $H_0:\mu_1 = \mu_2 = \mu_3$. The critical value is 8.65.

SOURCE	SS	df	MS
Between treatments	9048.4	2	4524.2
Within treatments	2552.0	12	
Between subjects	685.06	4	
Error	1866.94	8	233.37
Total	11600.4	14	

$F(2, 8) = 19.39$

The data indicate a significant change in the amount of time spent looking as the same stimulus is repeatedly presented.

23. The null hypothesis states that the number of hours without sleep has no effect on mental alertness, $H_0: \mu_1 = \mu_2 = \mu_3 = \mu_4$. The critical value is 3.07.

SOURCE	SS	df	MS
Between treatments	1.37	3	0.46
Within treatments	101.50	28	
Between subjects	68.87	7	
Error	32.63	21	1.55
Total	102.87	31	

$F(3, 21) = 0.30$

Fail to reject H_0. There is no evidence that sleep deprivation affects performance.

CHAPTER 15 TWO-FACTOR ANALYSIS OF VARIANCE (INDEPENDENT MEASURES)

1. **a.** In analysis of variance, an independent variable is called a *factor*.
   b. The values of a factor that are used to create the different groups or treatment conditions are called the *levels* of the factor.
   c. A research study with two independent variables is called a *two-factor study*.

3. **a.** The graph shows parallel lines with the mean for A_1 consistently below the means for A_2. There appear to be main effects for both factors, but no interaction.
   b. The graph shows crossing lines (the line for A_1 is horizontal, and the line for A_2 slopes sharply). There is a definite interaction and some indication of main effects for both factors.
   c. The graph shows parallel, horizontal lines, with A_1 consistently above A_2. There appears to be a main effect for factor A, but no effect for factor B and no interaction.

5. All F-ratios have the same error term, MS_{within}, and therefore have the same df value for the denominator.

7. **a.** 20
   b. 0
   c. 60

9. The null hypotheses state that there is no difference between levels of factor A ($H_0: \mu_{A1} = \mu_{A2}$), no difference between levels of factor B ($H_0: \mu_{B1} = \mu_{B2}$), and no interaction. All F-ratios have $df = 1,36$, and the critical value is $F = 4.11$.

SOURCE	SS	df	MS
Between treatments	50	3	
A	0	1	0
B	40	1	40
A × B	10	1	10
Within treatments	288	36	8
Total	338	39	

$F(1, 36) = 0$ for A
$F(1, 36) = 5.00$ for B
$F(1, 36) = 1.25$ for $A \times B$

There is no significant A effect or interaction, but the B effect is significant at the .05 level.

11. **a.**

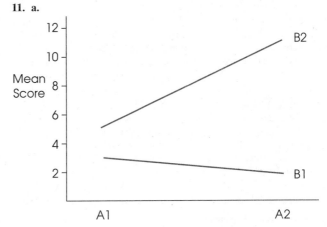

Levels of Factor A

b. Overall, the scores in A_1 are slightly lower than the scores in A_2. There may be a small main effect for factor A. There appears to be a large main effect for factor B, with scores in B_2 much larger than scores in B_1. The lines are not parallel, so there appears to be an interaction.

c. The null hypotheses state that there is no difference between levels of factor A ($H_0: \mu_{A1} = \mu_{A2}$), no difference between levels of factor B ($H_0: \mu_{B1} = \mu_{B2}$), and no interaction. All F-ratios have $df = 1, 16$, and the critical value is $F = 4.49$.

SOURCE	SS	df	MS
Between treatments	280	3	
A	20	1	20
B	180	1	180
A × B	80	1	80
Within treatments	320	16	20
Total	600	19	

$F(1, 16) = 1.00$ for A
$F(1, 16) = 9.00$ for B
$F(1, 16) = 4.00$ for $A \times B$

The A effect is not significant, but factor B does have a significant effect at the .05 level. The interaction does not reach significance at the .05 level.

13. The null hypotheses state that cues at learning have no effect ($H_0: \mu_{yes} = \mu_{no}$), that cues at recall have no effect ($H_0: \mu_{yes} = \mu_{no}$), and that there is no interaction. All F-ratios have $df = 1, 36$, and the critical value is $F = 4.11$.

SOURCE	SS	df	MS
Between treatments	30	3	
A (recall cues)	10	1	10
B (learning cues)	10	1	10
$A \times B$	10	1	10
Within treatments	72	36	2
Total	102	39	

$F(1, 36) = 5.00$ for A
$F(1, 36) = 5.00$ for B
$F(1, 36) = 5.00$ for $A \times B$

The significant interaction indicates that the effectiveness of cues given at recall (factor A) depends on whether or not the cues were also given during learning (factor B). Performance is best when cues are given both at learning and at recall. If cues are given only once, they are no more effective than giving no cues at all.

15. The null hypotheses state that there is no difference between the two memory tests ($H_0: \mu_{recall} = \mu_{recognition}$), that age has no effect ($H_0: \mu_{two} = \mu_{six} = \mu_{ten}$), and that there is no interaction. For $df = 1, 54$, the critical value is $F = 4.03$, and for $df = 2, 54$, the critical value is $F = 3.18$ (using $df = 50$ for the denominator because 54 is not in the table).

SOURCE	SS	df	MS
Between treatments	1553.33	5	
A (memory test)	1126.66	1	1126.66
B (age)	303.33	2	151.67
$A \times B$	123.34	2	61.67
Within treatments	108.00	54	2.00
Total	1661.33	59	

$F(1, 54) = 563.33$ for A
$F(2, 54) = 75.84$ for B
$F(2, 54) = 30.84$ for $A \times B$

The significant interaction indicates that age differences depend on the type of memory test. Examination of the treatment means indicates that age makes a big difference for the recall test, but has little or no effect for a recognition test.

17. a.

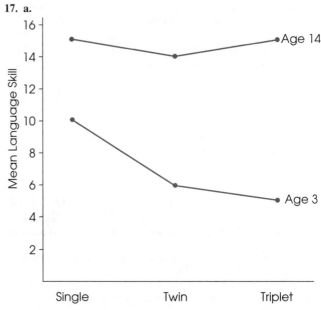

b. The null hypotheses state that age has no effect ($H_0: \mu_{three} = \mu_{fourteen}$), that the number of siblings has no effect ($H_0: \mu_{single} = \mu_{twin} = \mu_{triplet}$), and that there is no interaction. For $df = 1, 24$, the critical value is $F = 4.26$, and for $df = 2, 24$, the critical value is $F = 3.40$.

SOURCE	SS	df	MS
Between treatments	514.17	5	
A (age)	440.84	1	440.84
B (siblings)	41.67	2	20.84
$A \times B$	31.66	2	15.83
Within treatments	61.00	24	2.54
Total	575.17	29	

$F(1, 24) = 173.56$ for A
$F(2, 24) = 8.20$ for B
$F(2, 24) = 6.23$ for $A \times B$

c. For the 3-year-olds, $SS_{between} = 70$, $F(2, 24) = 13.78$. The number of siblings has a significant effect on language skill at age 3. For the 14-year-olds, $SS_{between} = 3.33$, $F(2, 24) = 0.66$. There is no significant difference between groups at age 14.

19. The null hypotheses state that gender has no effect ($H_0: \mu_{male} = \mu_{female}$), that the drug dosage has no effect ($H_0: \mu_{none} = \mu_{small} = \mu_{large}$), and that there is no interaction. For $df = 1, 24$, the critical value is $F = 4.26$, and for $df = 2, 24$, the critical value is $F = 3.40$.

SOURCE	SS	df	MS
Between treatments	130	5	
A (gender)	30	1	30
B (drug dose)	20	2	10
$A \times B$	80	2	40
Within treatments	120	24	5
Total	250	29	

$F(1, 24) = 6$ for A
$F(2, 24) = 2$ for B
$F(2, 24) = 8$ for $A \times B$

The significant interaction indicates that the hormone affects the eating behavior of males differently than females. For males, small doses appear to increase eating relative to no drug or a large dose. For females, the drug (in any dose) inhibits eating.

21. a. The means for normal subjects are baseline $\overline{X} = 23.7$ and stress $\overline{X} = 18.2$ The means for antisocial subjects are baseline $\overline{X} = 25.0$ and stress $\overline{X} = 24.3$.

b. The null hypotheses state that personality has no effect ($H_0: \mu_{normal} = \mu_{antisocial}$), that the arousal level has no effect ($H_0: \mu_{base} = \mu_{stress}$), and that there is no interaction. For $df = 1, 36$, the critical value is $F = 4.11$.

SOURCE	SS	df	MS
Between treatments	290.6	3	
A (personality)	136.9	1	136.9
B (arousal)	96.1	1	96.1
A × B	57.6	1	57.6
Within treatments	379.8	36	10.55
Total	670.4	39	

$F(1, 36) = 12.98$ for A
$F(1, 36) = 9.11$ for B
$F(1, 36) = 5.46$ for A × B

c. The significant interaction indicates that stress affects normal and antisocial people differently. Stress appears to have an effect on normal people, but no effect on antisocial individuals.

23.

SOURCE	SS	df	MS
Between treatments	280	7	
Achievement need	16	1	16
Task difficulty	144	3	48
Interaction	120	3	40
Within treatments	320	40	8
Total	600	47	

$F(1, 40) = 2.00$ for Achievement
$F(3, 40) = 6.00$ for Difficulty
$F(3, 40) = 5.00$ for Interaction

CHAPTER 16 CORRELATION AND REGRESSION

1. A positive correlation indicates that X and Y change in the same direction: As X increases, Y also increases. A negative correlation indicates that X and Y tend to change in opposite directions: As X increases, Y decreases.

3. a.

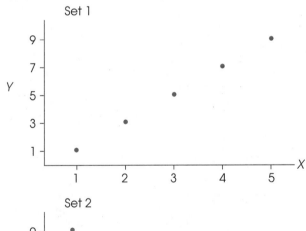

Set 1

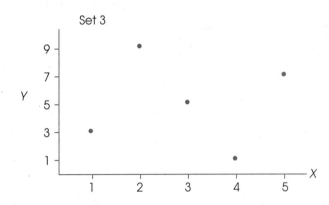

Set 3

b. For set 1, $SS_X = 10$, $SS_Y = 40$, $SP = 20$, and $r = 1.00$.
For set 2, $SS_X = 10$, $SS_Y = 40$, $SP = -20$, and $r = -1.00$.
For set 3, $SS_X = 10$, $SS_Y = 40$, $SP = 0$, and $r = 0$.

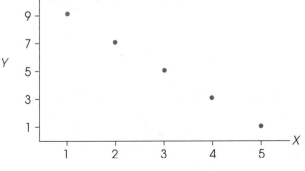

Set 2

5. a.

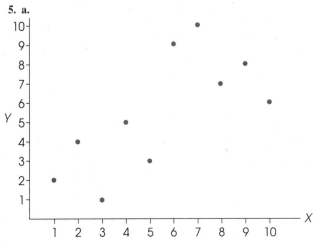

b. $r = 0.697$

c. $r = 0.30$

d. $r = -0.80$

e. The correlations for parts c and d were computed for a restricted range of scores and do not accurately represent the full range of X and Y values.

7. a. The graphs shows a very poor, negative correlation.

b. $r = -0.25$

c. The new graph is simply a magnified or an enlarged version of the original data. The relationship between X and Y is unchanged. Multiplying each score by a constant does not change the Pearson correlation.

d. $r = -0.25$

9. For these data, $SS_{anxiety} = 18$, $SS_{exam} = 72$, $SP = -32$, and the Pearson correlation is $r = -0.889$.

11. a. The null hypothesis states that there is no correlation in the population. With $n = 18$, the correlation must be greater than 0.468 to be significant at the .05 level. Fail to reject H_0. These data do not provide evidence for a significant correlation.

b. With $n = 102$, the critical value is 0.195. Reject H_0, and conclude that this sample provides enough evidence to conclude that a significant, non-zero correlation exists in the population.

13. a. The null hypothesis states that there is no correlation in the population. With $n = 15$, the correlation must be greater than 0.514 to be significant. Reject H_0, and conclude that there is a significant correlation in the population.

b. With $n = 12$, the critical value is 0.576, and the sample correlation would not be sufficient to reject H_0.

15. a. $r = -0.588$

b. $r = -0.200$

c.

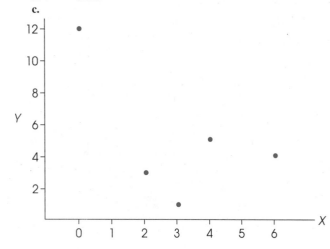

17. a. With no mean difference between the two groups, you would expect no relationship between training and performance, $r = 0$.

b.

X	Y	
1	2	$r = 0$
1	5	
1	6	
1	7	
0	4	
0	7	
0	3	
0	6	

19.

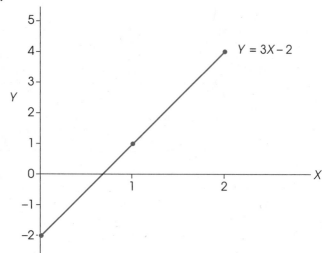

21. a. $\hat{Y} = 3X - 3$

b. and **c.** For each X, the predicted Y value, error, and squared error are

X	$\hat{Y}$	$(Y - \hat{Y})$	$(Y - \hat{Y})^2$
1	0	2	4
4	9	-2	4
3	6	-1	1
2	3	-2	4
5	12	2	4
3	6	1	$\dfrac{1}{18} = SS_{error}$

23. $SS_X = 10$, and $SP = -24$. The regression equation for predicting intellectual climate (Y) from the number of children (X) is $\hat{Y} = -2.4X + 16.8$.

CHAPTER 17 **CHI-SQUARE TESTS**

1. Non-parametric tests make few if any assumptions about the populations from which the data are obtained. For example, the populations do not need to form normal distributions, nor is it required that different populations in the same study have equal variances (homogeneity of variance assumption). Parametric tests require data measured on an interval or ratio scale. For non-parametric tests, any scale of measurement is acceptable.

3. H_0 states that the distribution of automobile accidents is the same as the distribution of registered drivers: 16% under age 20, 28% age 20 to 29, and 56% age 30 or older. With $df = 2$, the critical value is 5.99. The expected frequencies for these three categories are 48, 84, and 168. Chi-square = 13.76. Reject H_0, and conclude that the distribution of automobile accidents is not identical to the distribution of registered drivers.

5. H_0 states that the distribution of flu-related deaths is the same as the distribution of the population: 30% under 30, 40% for 30 to 60, and 30% for over 60. With $df = 2$, the critical value is 5.99. The expected frequencies for these three categories are 15, 20, and 15. Chi-square = 59.58. Reject H_0, and conclude that the distribution of flu-related deaths is not identical to the population distribution.

7. a. H_0:The population proportions have not changed and are still 30% science, 50% social science or humanities, and 20% professional. With $df = 2$, the critical value is 5.99. The expected frequencies for these three categories are 30, 50, and 20, respectively. Chi-square = 4.08. Fail to reject H_0, and conclude that there has been no significant change in freshman majors.

b. With $n = 200$, chi-square = 8.16. Reject H_0.

c. A larger sample should be more representative of the population. If the sample continues to be different from the hypothesis as n increases, the difference eventually will be significant.

9. a. The Pearson correlation would require an IQ score and a vocabulary score for each child. The correlation would measure the degree of linear relationship between the two variables.

b. The chi-square test would require that each child be classified in terms of IQ (for example, high, medium, or low) and classified in terms of vocabulary skill (good, medium, or poor). The chi-square test would determine whether the frequency distribution for vocabulary was dependent on IQ.

11. The null hypothesis states that alcohol relapse is independent of drug dosage. With $df = 2$ the critical value is 5.99. For the relapse subjects, the expected frequencies are $f_e = 12$ for all drug categories, and for the no-relapse subjects $f_e = 18$ for all drug categories. Chi-square = 14.44. You should reject H_o and con-

clude that there is a significant relation between relapse and drug dose.

13. The null hypothesis states that there is no relationship between a history of childhood abuse and criminal behavior. With $df = 1$, the critical value is 3.84. The expected frequencies are

	NO ABUSE	ABUSE
CRIMINALS	14	11
STUDENTS	14	11

Chi-square = 8.12. Reject H_0.

15. The null hypothesis states that there is no relationship between personality and heart disease. With $df = 3$, the critical value is 7.81. The expected frequencies are

	HEART	VASCULAR	HYPERTENSION	NONE
TYPE A	27.20	24.77	27.69	90.34
TYPE B	28.80	26.23	29.31	95.66

Chi-square = 46.02. Reject H_0.

17. The null hypothesis states that littering is independent of the amount of litter already on the ground. With $df = 2$, the critical value is 5.99. The expected frequencies are

	0 OR 1	2 OR 4	8 OR 16
LITTER	31.25	31.25	31.51
NOT LITTER	87.75	87.75	88.49

Chi-square = 22.41. Reject H_0.

19. The null hypothesis states that there is no relationship between handedness and eye preference. With $df = 1$ and $\alpha = .01$, the critical value is 6.63. The expected frequencies for left-handed subjects are 12 for left eye and 18 for right eye. For right-handed subjects, the expected frequencies are 48 for left eye and 72 for right eye. Chi-square = 11.11. There is a significant relationship between hand and eye preference.

CHAPTER 18 THE BINOMIAL TEST

1. $H_0:p = .80$ and $q = .20$ (no change). The critical boundaries are $z = \pm1.96$. With $X = 72$, $\mu = 80$, and $\sigma = 4$, we obtain $z = -2.00$. Reject H_0, and conclude that there has been a significant change in opinion.

3. $H_0:p = q = 1/2$ (no preference). The critical boundaries are $z = \pm1.96$. With $X = 39$, $\mu = 32$, and $\sigma = 4$, we obtain $z = 1.75$. Fail to reject H_0. There is no evidence of a significant preference between the two drinks.

5. a. With $n = 20$ and $p = q = 1/2$, you would need at least $X = 15$ to have a z-score above the critical boundary of $z = 1.96$ (for a two-tailed test).

b. With $n = 40$ and $p = q = 1/2$, you would need at least $X = 27$ to have a z-score above 1.96.

c. With $n = 100$ and $p = q = 1/2$, you would need at least $X = 60$ to have a z-score above 1.96.

7. $H_0:p = .67$ (craving for sweets) and $q = .33$ (no difference). The critical boundaries are $z = \pm2.58$. With $X = 15$, $\mu = 33.5$, and $\sigma = 3.32$, we obtain $z = -5.57$. Reject H_0, and conclude that there is a significant difference in food cravings.

9. $H_0:p = .65$ and $q = .35$ (no difference). The critical boundaries are $z = \pm1.96$. With $X = 18$, $\mu = 39$, and $\sigma = 3.69$, we obtain $z = -5.69$. Reject H_0, and conclude that there is a significant difference between the two methods of presentation.

11. $H_0:p = .30$ and $q = .70$ (proportions for the special program are the same as in the population). The critical boundaries are $z =$

± 1.96. The binomial distribution has $\mu = 27$ and $\sigma = 4.35$. With $X = 43$, we obtain $z = 3.68$. Reject H_0, and conclude that there is a significant difference between special program students and the general population.

13. H_0:$p = .35$ and $q = .65$ (no difference between the two school groups). The critical boundaries are $z = \pm 1.96$. The binomial distribution has $\mu = 17.5$ and $\sigma = 3.37$. With $X = 38$, we obtain $z = 6.08$. Reject H_0, and conclude that there is a significant difference between the two groups.

15. H_0:$p = q = 1/2$ (no difference in earnings). The critical boundary is $z = 2.33$. The binomial distribution has $\mu = 12$ and $\sigma = 2.45$. With $X = 17$, we obtain $z = 2.04$. Fail to reject H_0, and conclude that there is no significant difference between the wage schedules.

17. H_0:$p = q = 1/2$ (people are just guessing). The critical boundaries are $z = \pm 1.96$. (For a one-tailed test, the boundary is $z = -1.65$.) With $X = 27$, $\mu = 22.5$, and $\sigma = 3.35$, we obtain $z = 1.34$. Fail to reject H_0. Performance is not significantly better than chance.

19. H_0:$p = q = 1/2$ (no consistent departure from average). The critical boundaries are $z = \pm 1.96$. The binomial distribution has $\mu = 15$ and $\sigma = 2.74$. With $X = 22$, we obtain $z = 2.55$. Reject H_0, and conclude that the temperatures were significantly different from the average.

21. H_0:$p = q = 1/2$ (no difference between the two teachers). The critical boundaries are $z = \pm 1.96$. Discarding the 12 children who showed no difference, the binomial distribution has $\mu = 14$ and $\sigma = 2.65$. With $X = 20$, we obtain $z = 2.26$. Reject H_0, and conclude that the teacher's sex has a significant effect.

23. a. H_0:$p = q = 1/2$ (the training has no effect). The critical boundaries are $z = \pm 1.96$. Discarding the 11 people who showed no change, the binomial distribution has $\mu = 19.5$ and $\sigma = 3.12$. With $X = 29$, we obtain $z = 3.04$. Reject H_0, and conclude that biofeedback training has a significant effect.

   b. Discarding only 1 subject and dividing the others equally, the binomial distribution has $\mu = 24.5$ and $\sigma = 3.50$. With $X = 34$, we obtain $z = 2.71$. Reject H_0.

CHAPTER 19 STATISTICAL TECHNIQUES FOR ORDINAL DATA: MANN-WHITNEY AND WILCOXIN TESTS, AND SPEARMAN CORRELATION

1. If one or more sets of scores are extremely variable, it may violate the homogeneity of variance assumption and can create a very large error term for an F-ratio or a t statistic. Also, if the original scores include an undetermined value, it is impossible to compute a mean or variance. In these cases, ranking often can eliminate the problem.

3. The null hypothesis states that there is no consistent difference between the ranks for northern and southern cities. The critical value is 20. For the northern cities, $\Sigma R = 92$, and for the southern cities, $\Sigma R = 118$. $U = 27$. Fail to reject H_0, and conclude that there is no significant difference between the two parts of the country.

5. The null hypothesis states that there is no consistent difference in birth weight for children of smoking and non-smoking mothers. The critical value is $U = 7$. For the smoking mothers, $U = 40$, and for the non-smoking mothers, $U = 5$. Reject H_0, and conclude that there is a significant difference in birth weight for children of smoking versus non-smoking mothers.

7. The null hypothesis states that the drug has no effect. The critical value is $T = 5$. For the increases, $\Sigma R = 39$, and for the decreases, $\Sigma R = 6$. Wilcoxon $T = 6$. Fail to reject H_0. These data do not provide sufficient evidence to conclude that the drug works.

9. The null hypothesis states that there is no difference between the two paints. The critical value is $U = 5$. For the paint company, $\Sigma R = 28$, and for the competitor, $\Sigma R = 50$. Mann-Whitney $U = 7$. Fail to reject H_0. These data do not provide evidence for a significant difference between the two paints.

11. The null hypothesis states that the number of letters has no effect on solving anagrams. The critical value is 0. For the increases, $\Sigma R = 20$, and for the decreases, $\Sigma R = 1$. Wilcoxon $T = 1$. Fail to reject H_0, and conclude that the number of letters does not affect performance.

13. The null hypothesis states that the drug has no effect on maze-learning. The critical value is $T = 13$. For the increases, $\Sigma R = 73$, and for the decreases, $\Sigma R = 5$. Wilcoxon $T = 5$. Reject H_0, and conclude that the drug does affect maze-learning performance.

15. The ranked values are as follows:

X RANKS	Y RANKS	
2	2	
1	1	The Spearman correlation
3	4	is $r_S = +0.90$.
4	3	
5	5	

17. a. $r_S = +0.907$

   b. Yes, there is a strong positive relationship between the grades assigned by the two instructors.

19. a. The Spearman correlation is appropriate because the psychologist wants to measure the consistency of relationship and is not interested in whether or not it is a linear relationship.

   b. $r_S = +.952$

STATISTICS ORGANIZER

The following pages present an organized summary of the statistical procedures covered in this book. This organizer is divided into four sections, each of which groups together statistical techniques that serve a common purpose. You may notice that the four groups also correspond to major sections of the book. The four groups are

I. Descriptive Statistics

II. Parametric Tests for Means and Mean Differences

III. Non-parametric Tests

IV. Measures of Relationship Between Two Variables

Each of the four sections begins with a general overview that discusses the purpose for the statistical techniques that follow and points out some common characteristics of the different techniques. Next, there is a decision map that leads you, step by step, through the task of deciding which statistical technique is appropriate for the data you wish to analyze. Finally, there is a brief description of each technique and the necessary formulas.

I DESCRIPTIVE STATISTICS

The purpose of descriptive statistics is to simplify and organize a set of scores. Scores may be organized in a table or graph, or they may be summarized by computing one or two values that describe the entire set. The most commonly used descriptive techniques are as follows:

A. Frequency Distribution Tables and Graphs
A frequency distribution is an organized tabulation of the number of individuals in each category on the scale of measurement. A frequency distribution can be presented as either a table or a graph. The advantage of a frequency distribution is that it presents the entire set of scores rather than condensing the scores into a single descriptive value. The disadvantage of a frequency distribution is that it can be somewhat complex, especially with large sets of data.

CHOOSING DESCRIPTIVE STATISTICS: A DECISION MAP

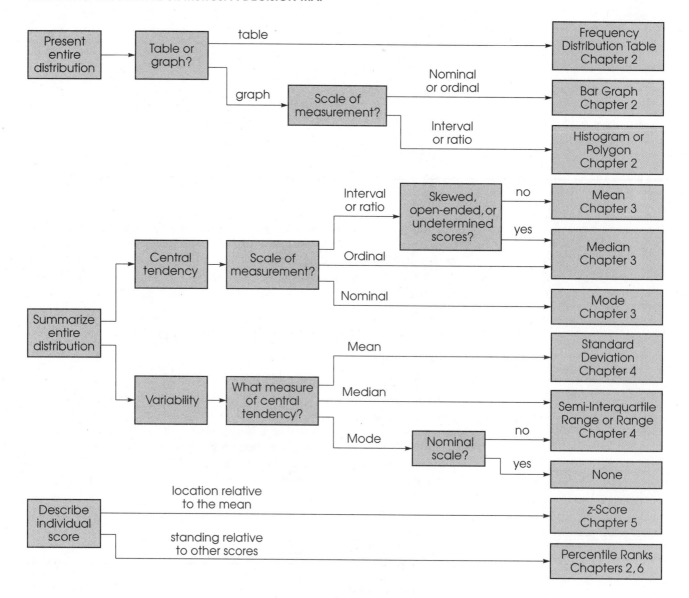

B. Measures of Central Tendency

The purpose of measuring central tendency is to identify a single score that represents an entire data set. The goal is to obtain a single value that is the best example of the average, or most typical, score from the entire set.

Measures of central tendency are used to describe a single data set, and they are the most commonly used measures for comparing two (or more) different sets of data.

C. Measures of Variability

Variability is used to provide a description of how spread out the scores are in a distribution. It also provides a measure of how accurately a single score selected from a distribution represents the entire set.

D. z-Scores

Most descriptive statistics are intended to provide a description of an entire set of scores. However, z-scores are used to describe individual scores within a distribution. The purpose of a z-score is to identify the precise location of an individual within a distribution by using a single number.

---

1. The Mean (Chapter 3)
The mean is the most commonly used measure of central tendency. It is computed by finding the total (ΣX) for the set of scores and then dividing the total by the number of individuals. Conceptually, the mean is the amount each individual will receive if the total is divided equally.

$$\text{Population: } \mu = \frac{\Sigma X}{N} \qquad \text{Sample: } \overline{X} = \frac{\Sigma X}{n}$$

---

2. The Median (Chapter 3)
Exactly 50% of the scores in a data set have values less than or equal to the median. The median is the 50th percentile. The median usually is computed for data sets in situations where the mean cannot be found (undetermined scores, open-ended distribution) or where the mean does not provide a good, representative value (ordinal scale, skewed distribution).

List the scores in order from smallest to largest.
a. With an odd number of scores, the median is the middle score.
b. With an even number of scores, the median is the average of the middle two scores.
c. With several scores tied at the median, use interpolation to find the 50th percentile.

---

3. The Mode (Chapter 3)
The mode is the score with the greatest frequency. The mode is used when the scores consist of measurements on a nominal scale.

No calculation. Simply count the frequency of occurrence for each different score.

---

4. The Range (Chapter 4)
The range is the distance from the lowest to the highest score in a data set. The range is considered to be a relatively crude measure of variability.

Find the upper real limit for the largest score and the lower real limit for the smallest score. The range is the difference between these two real limits.

---

5. The Semi-Interquartile Range (Chapter 4)
The semi-interquartile range is one-half of the range covered by the middle 50% of the distribution. The semi-interquartile range is often used to measure variability in situations where the median is used to report central tendency.

Find the first quartile (25th percentile) and the third quartile (75th percentile). The semi-interquartile range is one-half of the distance between the two quartiles.

6. Standard Deviation (Chapter 4) The standard deviation is a measure of the standard distance from the mean. Standard deviation is obtained by first computing SS (the sum of squared deviations) and variance (the mean squared deviation). Standard deviation is the square root of variance.	**Sum of Squares**	Definitional: $SS = \Sigma(X - \mu)^2$ Computational: $SS = \Sigma X^2 - \dfrac{(\Sigma X)^2}{N}$
	Variance	Population: $\sigma^2 = \dfrac{SS}{N}$ Sample: $s^2 = \dfrac{SS}{n-1}$
	Standard Deviation	Population: $\sigma = \sqrt{\dfrac{SS}{N}}$ Sample: $s = \sqrt{\dfrac{SS}{n-1}}$
7. z-Scores (Chapter 5) The sign of a z-score indicates whether an individual is above (+) or below (−) the mean. The numerical value of the z-score indicates how many standard deviations there are between the score and the mean.		$z = \dfrac{X - \mu}{\sigma}$

II PARAMETRIC TESTS: INFERENCES ABOUT POPULATION MEANS OR MEAN DIFFERENCES

All of the hypothesis tests covered in this section use the means obtained from sample data as the basis for testing hypotheses about population means. Although there are a variety of tests, used in a variety of research situations, all use the same basic logic, and all of the test statistics have the same basic structure. In each case, the test statistic (z, t, or F) involves computing a ratio with the following structure:

$$\text{test statistic} = \frac{\text{obtained difference between sample means}}{\text{mean difference expected by chance}}$$

The goal of each test is to determine whether the observed sample mean differences are larger than expected by chance. In general terms, a *significant result* means that the results obtained in a research study (sample differences) are more than would be expected by chance. In each case, a large value for the test statistic ratio indicates a significant result; that is, when the actual difference between sample means (numerator) is substantially larger than chance (denominator), you will obtain a large ratio, which indicates that the sample difference is significant.

The actual calculations differ slightly from one test statistic to the next, but all involve the same basic computations.

1. A set of scores (sample) is obtained for each population or each treatment condition.

2. The mean is computed for each set of scores, and some measure of variability (SS, standard deviation, or variance) is obtained for each individual set of scores.

CHOOSING A PARAMETRIC TEST: A DECISION MAP FOR MAKING INFERENCES ABOUT POPULATION MEANS OR MEAN DIFFERENCES

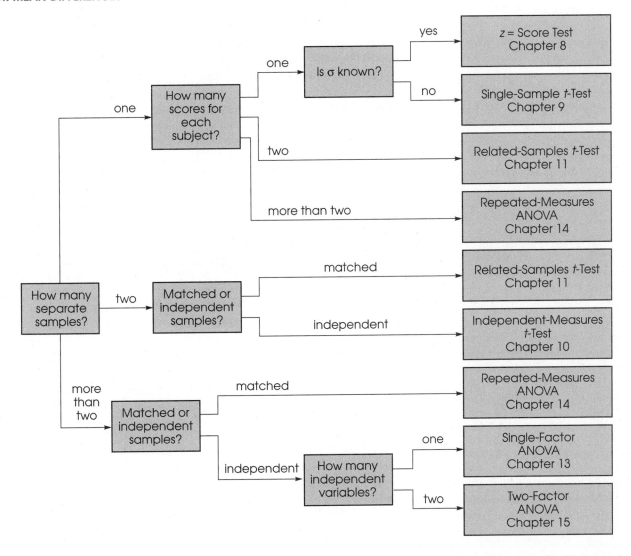

3. The differences between the sample means provide a measure of how much difference exists between treatment conditions. Because these mean differences may be caused by the treatment conditions, they are often called *systematic* or *predicted*. These differences are the numerator of the test statistic.

4. The variability within each set of scores provides a measure of unsystematic or unpredicted differences due to chance. Because the individuals within each treatment condition are treated exactly the same, there is nothing that should cause their scores to be different. Thus, any observed differences (variability) within treatments are assumed to be due to error or chance.

With these considerations in mind, each of the test statistic ratios can be described as follows:

$$\text{test statistic} = \frac{\text{differences (variability) between treatments}}{\text{differences (variability) within treatments}}$$

The hypothesis tests reviewed in this section apply to three basic research designs:

1. Single-Sample Designs. Data from a single sample are used to test a hypothesis about a single population.

2. Independent-Measures Designs. A separate sample is obtained to represent each individual population or treatment condition.

3. Related-Samples Designs. Related-sample designs include repeated-measures and matched-subjects designs. For a repeated-measures design, there is only one sample, with each individual subject being measured in all of the different treatment conditions. In a matched-subjects design, every individual in one sample is matched with a subject in each of the other samples.

Finally, you should be aware that all parametric tests place stringent restrictions on the sample data and the population distributions being considered. First, these tests all require measurements on an interval or a ratio scale (numerical values that allow you to compute means and differences). Second, each test makes assumptions about population distributions and sampling techniques. Consult the appropriate section of this book to verify that the specific assumptions are satisfied before proceeding with any parametric test.

---

1. The *z*-Score Test (Chapter 8)

The *z*-score test uses the data from a single sample to test a hypothesis about the population mean in situations where the population standard deviation (σ) is known. The null hypothesis states a specific value for the unknown population mean.

$$z = \frac{\overline{X} - \mu}{\sigma_{\overline{X}}} \quad \text{where } \sigma_{\overline{X}} = \frac{\sigma}{\sqrt{n}}$$

---

2. The Single-Sample *t* Test (Chapter 9)

This test uses the data from a single sample to test a hypothesis about a population mean in situations where the population standard deviation is unknown. The sample variance is used to estimate the unknown population variance. The null hypothesis states a specific value for the unknown population mean.

$$t = \frac{\overline{X} - \mu}{s_{\overline{X}}} \quad \text{where } s_{\overline{X}} = \sqrt{\frac{s^2}{n}}$$
$$df = n - 1$$

---

3. The Independent-Measures *t* Test (Chapter 10)

The independent-measures *t* test uses data from two separate samples to test a hypothesis about the difference between two population means. The variability within the two samples is combined to obtain a single (pooled) estimate of population variance. The null hypothesis states that there is no difference between the two population means.

$$t = \frac{(\overline{X}_1 - \overline{X}_2) - (\mu_1 - \mu_2)}{s_{\overline{X} - \overline{X}}} \quad \text{where } s_{\overline{X} - \overline{X}} = \sqrt{\frac{s_p^2}{n_1} + \frac{s_p^2}{n_2}}$$

$$\text{and } s_p^2 = \frac{SS_1 + SS_2}{df_1 + df_2}$$

$$df = df_1 + df_2 = (n_1 - 1) + (n_2 - 1)$$

4. **The Related-Samples *t* Test** (Chapter 11)
This test evaluates the mean difference between two treatment conditions using the data from a repeated-measures or a matched-subjects experiment. A difference score (*D*) is obtained for each subject (or each matched pair) by subtracting the score in treatment 1 from the score in treatment 2. The variability of the sample difference scores is used to estimate the population variability. The null hypothesis states that the population mean difference (μ_D) is zero.

$$t = \frac{\overline{D} - \mu_D}{s_{\overline{D}}} \quad \text{where } s_{\overline{D}} = \sqrt{\frac{s^2}{n}}$$

$$df = n - 1$$

5. **Single-Factor, Independent-Measures Analysis of Variance** (Chapter 13)
This test uses data from two or more separate samples to test for mean differences among two or more populations. The null hypothesis states that there are no differences among the population means. The test statistic is an *F*-ratio that uses the variability between treatment conditions (sample mean differences) in the numerator and the variability within treatment conditions (error variability) as the denominator. With only two samples, this test is equivalent to the independent-measures *t* test.

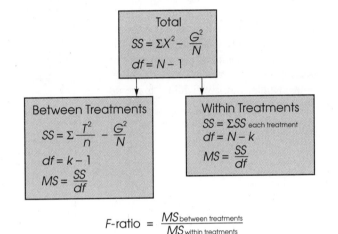

Total
$$SS = \Sigma X^2 - \frac{G^2}{N}$$
$$df = N - 1$$

Between Treatments
$$SS = \Sigma \frac{T^2}{n} - \frac{G^2}{N}$$
$$df = k - 1$$
$$MS = \frac{SS}{df}$$

Within Treatments
$$SS = \Sigma SS_{\text{each treatment}}$$
$$df = N - k$$
$$MS = \frac{SS}{df}$$

$$F\text{-ratio} = \frac{MS_{\text{between treatments}}}{MS_{\text{within treatments}}}$$

6. **Single-Factor, Repeated-Measures Analysis of Variance** (Chapter 14)
This test is used to evaluate mean differences among two or more treatment conditions using sample data from a repeated-measures (or matched-subjects) experiment. The null hypothesis states that there are no differences among the population means. The test statistic is an *F*-ratio using variability between treatment conditions (mean differences) in the numerator exactly like the independent-measures ANOVA. The denominator of the *F*-ratio (error term) is obtained by measuring variability within treatments and then subtracting out the variability between subjects. The research design and the test statistic remove variability due to individual differences and thereby provide a more sensitive test for treatment differences than is possible with an independent-measures design.

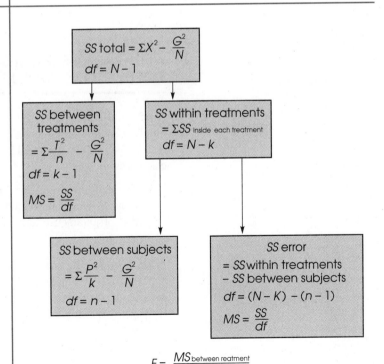

$$SS \text{ total} = \Sigma X^2 - \frac{G^2}{N}$$
$$df = N - 1$$

SS between treatments
$$= \Sigma \frac{T^2}{n} - \frac{G^2}{N}$$
$$df = k - 1$$
$$MS = \frac{SS}{df}$$

SS within treatments
$$= \Sigma SS_{\text{inside each treatment}}$$
$$df = N - k$$

SS between subjects
$$= \Sigma \frac{P^2}{k} - \frac{G^2}{N}$$
$$df = n - 1$$

SS error
$$= SS \text{ within treatments} - SS \text{ between subjects}$$
$$df = (N - K) - (n - 1)$$
$$MS = \frac{SS}{df}$$

$$F = \frac{MS_{\text{between reatment}}}{MS_{\text{error}}}$$

7. Two-Factor, Independent-Measures Analysis of Variance (Chapter 15)

This test is used to evaluate mean differences among populations or treatment conditions using sample data from research designs with two independent variables (factors). The two-factor ANOVA tests three separate hypotheses: mean differences among the levels of factor A (main effect for factor A), mean differences among the levels of factor B (main effect for factor B), and mean differences resulting from specific combinations of the two factors (interaction). Each of the three separate null hypotheses states that there are no population mean differences. Each of the three tests uses an F-ratio as the test statistic, with the variability between samples (sample mean differences) in the numerator and the variability within samples (error variability) in the denominator.

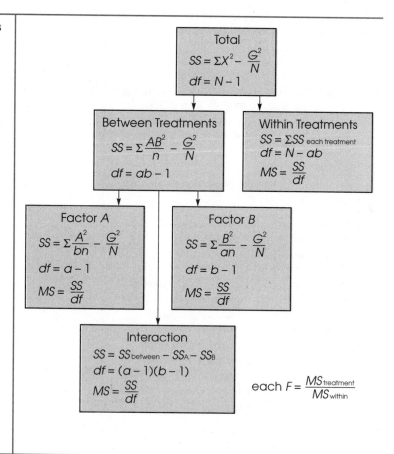

Total
$$SS = \Sigma X^2 - \frac{G^2}{N}$$
$$df = N - 1$$

Between Treatments
$$SS = \Sigma \frac{AB^2}{n} - \frac{G^2}{N}$$
$$df = ab - 1$$

Within Treatments
$$SS = \Sigma SS_{\text{each treatment}}$$
$$df = N - ab$$
$$MS = \frac{SS}{df}$$

Factor A
$$SS = \Sigma \frac{A^2}{bn} - \frac{G^2}{N}$$
$$df = a - 1$$
$$MS = \frac{SS}{df}$$

Factor B
$$SS = \Sigma \frac{B^2}{an} - \frac{G^2}{N}$$
$$df = b - 1$$
$$MS = \frac{SS}{df}$$

Interaction
$$SS = SS_{\text{between}} - SS_A - SS_B$$
$$df = (a - 1)(b - 1)$$
$$MS = \frac{SS}{df}$$

$$\text{each } F = \frac{MS_{\text{treatment}}}{MS_{\text{within}}}$$

III NON-PARAMETRIC TESTS: INFERENCES ABOUT POPULATIONS OR POPULATION DIFFERENCES

Although the parametric tests described in the previous section are the most commonly used inferential techniques, there are many research situations where parametric tests cannot or should not be used. These situations fall into two general categories:

1. The data involve measurements on nominal or ordinal scales. In these situations, you cannot compute the means and variances that are an essential part of parametric tests.

2. The data do not satisfy the assumptions underlying parametric tests.

When a parametric test cannot be used, there is usually a non-parametric alternative available. In general, parametric tests are more powerful than their non-parametric counterparts, and they are preferred over the non-parametric alternatives. However, when a parametric test is not appropriate, the non-parametric tests provide researchers with a backup statistical technique for conducting an analysis and statistical interpretation of research results.

CHOOSING A NON-PARAMETRIC TEST: A DECISION MAP FOR MAKING INFERENCES ABOUT POPULATIONS OR POPULATION DIFFERENCES

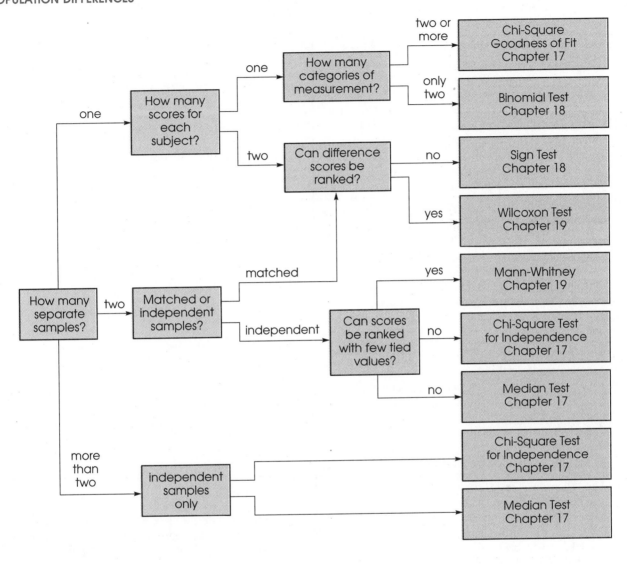

1. **The Chi-Square Test for Goodness of Fit** (Chapter 17)

   This chi-square test is used in situations where the measurement procedure results in classifying individuals into distinct categories. The test uses frequency data from a single sample to test a hypothesis about the population distribution. The null hypothesis specifies the proportion or percentage of the population for each category on the scale of measurement.

   $$\chi^2 = \Sigma\frac{(f_o - f_e)^2}{f_e}$$

   where $f_e = pn$

   $$df = C - 1$$

2. The Binomial Test (Chapter 18) When the individuals in a population can be classified into exactly two categories, the binomial test uses sample data to test a hypothesis about the proportion of the population in each category. The null hypothesis specifies the proportion of the population in each of the two categories.	$$z = \frac{X - pn}{\sqrt{npq}} \quad \text{or} \quad z = \frac{X/n - p}{\sqrt{\dfrac{pq}{n}}}$$
3. The Chi-Square Test for Independence (Chapter 17) This test serves as an alternative to the independent-measures t test (or ANOVA) in situations where the dependent variable involves classifying individuals into distinct categories. The sample data consist of frequency distributions (proportions across categories) for two or more separate samples. The null hypothesis states that the separate populations all have the same proportions (same shape). That is, the proportions across categories are independent of the different populations.	$$\chi^2 = \Sigma \frac{(f_o - f_e)^2}{f_e}$$ where $f_e = \dfrac{(\text{row total})(\text{column total})}{n}$ $$df = (R - 1)(C - 1)$$
4. The Median Test (Chapter 17) The median test is a special application of the chi-square test for independence. This test is used to determine whether two or more populations share a common median. The test uses data from two or more separate samples and requires that each individual be classified as being above or below the median. The null hypothesis states that all of the separate populations share a common median.	Use the chi-square formula and df from the chi-square test for independence.
5. The Mann-Whitney U Test (Chapter 19) This test uses ordinal data (rank orders) from two separate samples to test a hypothesis about the difference between two populations or two treatment conditions. The Mann-Whitney test is used as an alternative to the independent-measures t test in situations where the data can be rank ordered, but do not satisfy the more stringent requirements of the t test.	$$U_A = n_A n_B + \frac{n_A(n_A + 1)}{2} - \Sigma R_A$$ $$U_B = n_A n_B + \frac{n_B(n_B + 1)}{2} - \Sigma R_B$$
6. The Wilcoxon T Test (Chapter 19) The Wilcoxon test uses the data from a repeated-measures or matched-samples design to evaluate the difference between two treatment conditions. This test is used as an alternative to the related-samples t test in situations where the sample data (difference scores) can be rank ordered, but do not satisfy the more stringent requirements of the t test.	Rank order the difference scores, ignoring the signs ($+$ or $-$). Then compute the sum of the ranks for the positive differences and the negative differences. The Wilcoxon T is the smaller sum.
7. The Sign Test (Chapter 18) This test evaluates the difference between two treatment conditions using data from a repeated-measures or matched-subjects research design. The null hypothesis states that there is no difference between the two treatment conditions. The sign test is a special application of the binomial test and only requires that the difference between treatment 1 and treatment 2 for each subject be classified as an increase or a decrease. This test is used as an alternative to the related-samples t test or the Wilcoxon test in situations where the data do not satisfy the more stringent requirements of these two more powerful tests.	Count the number of positive differences (X) in the total sample (n). Then use the binomial test with $p = q = 1/2$.

IV MEASURES OF RELATIONSHIP BETWEEN TWO VARIABLES

As we noted in Chapter 1, a major purpose for scientific research is to investigate and establish orderly relationships between variables. The statistical techniques covered in this section all serve the purpose of measuring and describing relationships. The data for these statistics involve two observations for each individual—one observation for each of the two variables being examined. The goal is to determine whether or not a consistent, predictable relationship exists and to describe the nature of the relationship.

Each of the different statistical methods described in this section is intended to be used with a specific type of data. To determine which method is appropriate, you must first examine your data and identify what type of variable is involved and what scale of measurement was used for recording the observations.

CHOOSING A MEASURE OF RELATIONSHIP BETWEEN TWO VARIABLES: A DECISION MAP

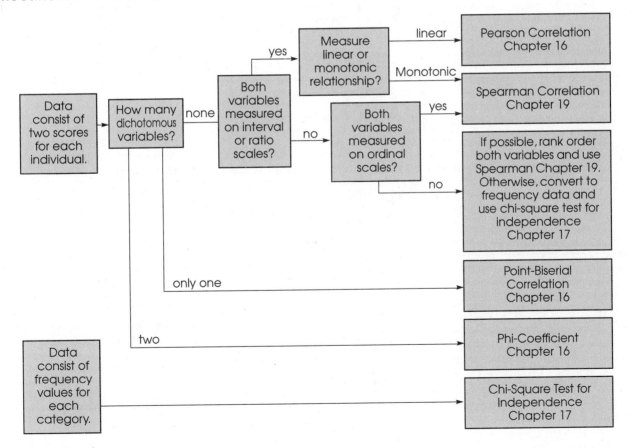

1. The Pearson Correlation (Chapter 16)
The Pearson correlation measures the degree of linear relationship between two variables. The sign (+ or −) of the correlation indicates the direction of the relationship. The magnitude of the correlation (from 0 to 1) indicates the degree to which the data points fit on a straight line.

$$r = \frac{SP}{\sqrt{SS_X SS_Y}}$$

where $SP = \Sigma(X - \overline{X})(Y - \overline{Y}) = \Sigma XY - \frac{(\Sigma X)(\Sigma Y)}{n}$

2. Linear Regression and Standard Error of Estimate (Chapter 16)
The purpose of linear regression is to find the equation for the best-fitting straight line for predicting Y scores from X scores. The regression process determines the linear equation with the least squared error between the actual Y values and the predicted Y values on the line. The standard error of estimate provides a measure of the standard distance (or error) between the actual Y values and the predicted Y values.

$$\hat{Y} = bX + a \quad \text{where } b = \frac{SP}{SS_X} \quad \text{and} \quad a = \overline{Y} - b\overline{X}$$

$$\text{Standard error of estimate} = \sqrt{\frac{\Sigma(Y - \hat{Y})^2}{n - 2}} = \sqrt{\frac{(1 - r^2)SS_Y}{n - 2}}$$

3. The Spearman Correlation (Chapter 19)
The Spearman correlation measures the degree to which the relationship between two variables is one-directional or monotonic. The Spearman correlation is used when both variables, X and Y, are ranks (measured on an ordinal scale).

Use the Pearson formula on the ranked data or the special Spearman formula:

$$r_S = 1 - \frac{6\Sigma D^2}{n(n^2 - 1)}$$

4. The Point-Biserial Correlation (Chapter 16)
The point-biserial correlation is a special application of the Pearson correlation that is used when one variable is dichotomous (only two values) and the second variable is measured on an interval or ratio scale. The value of the correlation measures the strength of the relationship between the two variables. The point-biserial correlation often is used as an alternative or a supplement to the independent-measures t hypothesis test.

Convert the two categories of the dichotomous variable to numerical values 0 and 1; then use the Pearson formula with the converted data.

5. The Phi-Coefficient (Chapter 16)
The phi-coefficient is a special application of the Pearson correlation that is used when both variables, X and Y, are dichotomous (only two values). The value of the correlation measures the strength of the relationship between the two variables. The phi-coefficient is often used as an alternative or a supplement to the chi-square test for independence.

For each variable, convert the two categories to numerical values 0 and 1; then use the Pearson formula with the converted data.

6. The Chi-Square Test for Independence
(Chapter 17)

This test uses frequency data to determine whether or not there is a significant relationship between two variables. The null hypothesis states that the two variables are independent. The chi-square test for independence is used when the scale of measurement consists of relatively few categories for both variables and can be used with nominal, ordinal, interval, or ratio scales.

$$\chi^2 = \Sigma \frac{(f_o - f_e)^2}{f_e}$$

$$\text{where } f_e = \frac{(\text{row total})(\text{column total})}{n}$$

$$df = (R - 1)(C - 1)$$

REFERENCES

American Psychological Association. (1994). *Publication manual of the American Psychological Association* (4th ed.) Washington, D.C.: Author.

Aronson, E., Turner, J. A., and Carlsmith, J. M. (1985). Communicator credibility and communication discrepancy as a determinant of opinion change. *Journal of Abnormal and Social Psychology, 67,* 31–36.

Betz, B. J., and Thomas, C. B. (1979). Individual temperament as a predictor of health or premature disease. *The Johns Hopkins Medical Journal, 144,* 81–89.

Blest, A. D. (1957). The functions of eyespot patterns in the Lepidoptera. *Behaviour, 11,* 209–255.

Blum, J. (1978). *Pseudoscience and mental ability.* New York: Monthly Review Press.

Boker, J. R. (1974). Immediate and delayed retention effects of interspersing questions in written instructional passages. *Journal of Educational Psychology, 66,* 96–98.

Bransford, J. D., and Johnson, M. K. (1972). Contextual prerequisites for understanding: Some investigations of comprehension and recall. *Journal of Verbal Learning and Verbal Behavior, 11,* 717–726.

Cattell, R. B. (1973). Personality pinned down. *Psychology Today,* July, 40–46.

Cervone, D. (1989). Effects of envisioning future activities on self-efficacy judgments and motivation: An availability heuristic interpretation. *Cognitive Therapy and Research, 13,* 247–261.

Ciadina, R. B., Reno, R. R., and Kallgren, C. A. (1990). A focus theory of normative conduct: Recycling the concept of norms to reduce littering in public places. *Journal of Personality and Social Psychology, 58(6),* 1015–1026.

Cook, M. (1977). Gaze and mutual gaze in social encounters. *American Scientist, 65,* 328–333.

Cowles, M., and Davis, C. (1982). On the origins of the .05 level of statistical significance. *American Psychologist, 37,* 553–558.

Craik, F. I. M., and Lockhart, R. S. (1972). Levels of processing: A framework for memory research. *Journal of Verbal Learning and Verbal Behavior, 11,* 671–684.

Craik, F. I. M., and Tulving, E. (1975). Depth of processing and the retention of words in episodic memory. *Journal of Experimental Psychology: General, 104,* 268–294.

Davis, E. A. (1937). *The development of linguistic skills in twins, single twins with siblings, and only children from age 5 to 10 years.* Institute of Child Welfare Series, No. 14. Minneapolis: University of Minnesota Press.

Duncker, K. (1945). On problem-solving. *Psychological Monographs, 58,* no. 270.

Festinger, L., and Carlsmith, J. M. (1959). Cognitive consequences of forced compliance. *Journal of Abnormal and Social Psychology, 58,* 203–210.

Friedman, M., and Rosenman, R. (1974). *Type A behavior and your heart.* New York: Knopf.

Gibson, E. J., and Walk, R. D. (1960). The "visual cliff." *Scientific American, 202,* 64–71.

Gintzler, A. R. (1980). Endorphin-mediated increases in pain threshold during pregnancy. *Science, 210,* 193–195.

Hays, W. L. (1981). *Statistics,* 3d ed. New York: Holt, Rinehart and Winston.

Horn, J. L. (1978). The nature and development of intellectual abilities. In R. T. Osborne, C. E. Noble, & N. Weyl (eds.), *Human variation.* New York: Academic Press.

Hunt, E., Lunneborg, C., and Lewis, J. (1975). What does it mean to be high verbal? *Cognitive Psychology, 7,* 194–227.

Hyman, A. (1993, August). *A suggestion for teaching two types of populations and samples.* Poster session presented at the annual meeting of the American Psychological Association. Toronto, Ontario, Canada.

Katona, G. (1940). *Organizing and memorizing.* New York: Columbia University Press.

Keppel, G. (1973). *Design and analysis. A researcher's handbook*. Englewood Cliffs, N.J.: Prentice-Hall.

Keppel, G., and Zedeck, S. (1989). *Data analysis for research designs*. New York: W. H. Freeman and Company.

Krech, D., Rosenzweig, M. R., and Bennett, E. L. (1962). Relations between brain chemistry and problem solving among rats raised in enriched and impoverished environments. *Journal of Comparative and Physiological Psychology, 55*, 801–807.

Levine, S. (1960). Stimulation in infancy. *Scientific American, 202*, 80–86.

McClelland, D. C. (1961). *The achieving society*. Princeton, N.J.: Van Nostrand.

Miller, N. E., and Dworkin, B. R. (1974). Visceral learning: Recent difficulties with curarized rats and significant problems for human research. In P. A. Obrist, A. H. Black, J. Brener, and L. V. DiCara (eds.), *Cardiovascular psychophysiology: Current issues in response mechanisms, biofeedback and methodology* (pp. 312–331). Chicago: Aldine.

Moore-Ede., M. C., Sulzman, F. M., and Fuller, C. A. (1982). *The clocks that time us*. Cambridge: Harvard University Press.

Pelton, T. (1983). The shootists. *Science83, 4*(4), 84–86.

Reifman, A. S., Larrick, R. P., and Fein, S. (1991). Temper and temperature on the diamond: The heat-aggression relationship in major league baseball. *Personality and Social Psychology Bulletin, 17*, 580–585.

Rogers, T. B., Kuiper, N. A., and Kirker, W. S. (1977). Self-reference and the encoding of personal information. *Journal of Personality and Social Psychology, 35*, 677–688.

Rosenthal, R. (1963). On the social psychology of the psychological experiment. The experimenter's hypothesis as unintended determinant of experimental results. *American Scientist, 51*, 268–283.

Rosenthal, R., and Fode, K. L. (1963). The effect of experimenter bias on the performance of the albino rat. *Behavioral Science, 8*, 183–189.

Sachs, J. (1967). Recognition memory for syntactic and semantic aspects of a connected discourse. *Perception and Psychophysics, 2*, 437–442.

Scaife, M. (1976). The response to eye-like shapes by birds. I. The effect of context: A predator and a strange bird. *Animal Behaviour, 24*, 195–199.

Schachter, S. (1968). Obesity and eating. *Science, 161*, 751–756.

Schleifer, S. J., Keller, S. E., Camerino, M., Thornton, J. C., and Stein, M. (1983). Suppression of lymphocyte stimulation following bereavement. *Journal of the American Medical Association, 250*, 374–377.

Sheldon, W. H. (1940). *The varieties of human physique: An introduction to constitutional psychology*. New York: Harper.

Shrauger, J. S. (1972). Self-esteem and reactions to being observed by others. *Journal of Personality and Social Psychology, 23*, 192–200.

Siegel, J. M. (1990). Stressful life events and use of physician services among the elderly: The moderating role of pet ownership. *Journal of Personality and Social Psychology, 58*, 1081–1086.

Snyder, S. H. (1977). Opiate receptors and internal opiates. *Scientific American, 236*, 44–56.

Tryon, R. C. (1940). Genetic differences in maze-learning ability in rats. *Yearbook of the National Society for the Study of Education, 39*, 111–119.

Tukey, J. W. (1977). *Exploratory data analysis*. Reading, Mass.: Addison-Wesley.

Tulving, E., and Osler, S. (1968). Effectiveness of retrieval cues in memory for words. *Journal of Experimental Psychology, 77*, 593–601.

Tversky, A., and Kahneman, D. (1973). Availability: A heuristic for judging frequency and probability. *Cognitive Psychology, 5*, 207–232.

Tversky, A., and Kahneman, D. (1974). Judgment under uncertainty: Heuristics and biases. *Science, 185*, 1124–1131.

Vopicelli, J. R., Alterman, A., Hayashida, M., and O'Brien, C. P. (1992). Naltrexone in the treatment of alcohol dependence. *Archives of General Psychiatry, 49*, 881–887.

Winget, C., and Kramer, M. (1979). *Dimensions of dreams*. Gainesville: University Press of Florida.

Wright, J. W. (ed.). *The universal almanac 1995*. Kansas City: Andrews and McMeel, Universal Press.

Zajonc, R. B., and Markus, G. B. (1975). Birth order and intellectual development. *Psychological Review, 82*, 74–88.

Zigler, M. J. (1932). Pressure adaptation time. A function of intensity and extensity. *American Journal of Psychology, 44*, 709–720.

INDEX